Regional Analysis and Development

In recent years there has been a tremendous growth of interest in the field of regional analysis. Geographers, economists and planners have all become involved in the process of recording and analysing economic disparities both between and within regions. They have striven to understand how these disparities have come about and to identify what effects they have on the trading and economic relations of regions within the nation state. The value and urgency of their enquiries has been augmented by the increasing efforts of governments of widely differing political complexions to control and plan their economies. In almost all cases this government action has included efforts to improve the lot of less-prosperous regions and to contain the growth of 'congested' ones. Naturally if government policies are to be effective they must be based on a sound understanding of how regional economic differences arise and how they perpetuate themselves.

This book is one reflection of that growing interest in regional analysis. It is a collection of papers and readings on regional economic variations and the patterns of trade between different parts of a nation. It has grown out of an Open University advanced course called Regional Analysis and Development. It reflects the convictions of the course writers that social science theory must be developed not only for its own sake but as a tool for analysing and changing the society in which we live. The introductions to each section of the reader attempt to set out the logical reasoning which we used in ordering the papers and to show the relationship between one paper and another. Thus we feel that the reader presents a coherent framework for the study of regional analysis of itself, although for our own students it will serve as a complement to the sixteen course units. We hope that it will play at least a small part in enhancing the knowledge of regional analysis and perhaps help to ensure that in future regional economic planning is at least informed, if not always enlightened.

Regional Analysis and Development

Edited by **John Blunden, Christopher Brook
Geoffrey Edge and Alan Hay**

at The Open University

John Blunden has been Senior Lecturer at the Open University since its inception. Previously he taught at the University of Sussex where he specialised in the problems of land use planning and was a tutor for the post graduate course in Regional Studies. He is at present based at Imperial College where he is Research Director of a Government project set up to examine the impact of the extractive industries on the environment.

Christopher Brook is Lecturer in Applied Regional Studies at The Open University. Most of his original training was as a geographer. In 1969 he gained an M.A. in Economic Geography at the University of Exeter. His main research interest is concerned with the spatial analysis of transport flows and their channels.

Geoff Edge is Lecturer in Geography at the Open University. Prior to moving to his present post he lectured on industrial location theory at Leicester University. His main research interest is the study of the causes of variations in employment growth rate in contiguous areas of conurbations.

Alan Hay is Lecturer in Geography at the University of Sheffield. He has also lectured at the Universities of Leicester and Washington. Among his research interests have been studies of interregional trends and regional planning in Nigeria.

Published for
The Open University Press
by Harper & Row, Publishers London   New York   Evanston   San Francisco

Published by Harper & Row Ltd
28 Tavistock Street, London WC2E 7PN

Standard Book Number 06-318012-X (cloth)
Standard Book Number 06-318013-8 (paper)

Typeset by Specialised Offset Services Limited, Liverpool
Printed by Fletcher & Son Limited, Norwich
Bound by Richard Clay (The Chaucer Press) Limited
Bungay, Suffolk

Preface

In recent years there has been a tremendous growth of interest in the field of regional analysis. Geographers, economists and planners have all become involved in the process of recording and analysing economic disparities both between and within regions. They have striven to understand how these disparities have come about and to identify what effects they have on the trading and economic relations of regions within the nation state. The value and urgency of their enquiries has been augmented by the increasing efforts of governments of widely differing political complexions to control and plan their economies. In almost all cases this government action has included efforts to improve the lot of less-prosperous regions and to contain the growth of 'congested' ones. Naturally if government policies are to be effective they must be based on a sound understanding of how regional economic differences arise and how they perpetuate themselves.

This book is one reflection of that growing interest in regional analysis. It is a collection of papers and readings on regional economic variations and the patterns of trade between different parts of a nation. It has grown out of an Open University advanced course called Regional Analysis and Development. It reflects the convictions of the course writers that social science theory must be developed not only for its sake but as a tool for analysing and changing the society in which we live. The introductions to each section of the Reader attempt to set out the logical reasoning which we used in ordering the papers and to show the relationships between one paper and another. Thus we hope that the Reader presents in itself a coherent framework for the study of regional analysis, although for our own students it will serve as a complement to the sixteen course units. We hope that it will play at least a small part in enhancing the knowledge of regional analysis and perhaps help to ensure that in future regional economic planning is at least informed, if not always enlightened.

G.E.

Editors' Acknowledgements
The editors are grateful to Jerry Millard and Roger Lubbock at The Open University for valuable assistance in the preparation of this volume.

Contents

Introduction

At the national scale, countries are often considered as 'developed' or, 'under-developed'. In addition to the problem of measurment standards, this concept can be criticised on the grounds that it is based on very generalised aggregates of areas of widely-varying economic and social prosperity. In countries which have developed as definable economic units over time, with a high degree of spatial interchange, variations in regional prosperity are less than in an undeveloped or developing nation. Yet even in the most developed countries variations in prosperity, though decreasing, are still considerable.

The object of this Reader is to highlight the existence of, and enquire into the reasons for, geographic variations in economic and social prosperity between regions within nations. The content and sequence of writings emphasise the causes and effects of spatial interaction, and its association with the economic and social conditions within a region.

The first two parts consider the nation's geographic area as a series of dimensionless regions, acting only as point locations in space. The categorisation of space as a number of 'homogeneous' areas can rightly be criticised on the grounds of its arbitrary geographic delineation, being as much aimed at planning efficiency as concerned with defining similarities in economic and social criteria. Such regional definition can however be considered on the grounds of expediency. The objectives here are to 'paint the picture' that interregional inequalities do exist, and to enquire into the interregional processes that effect this inequality. Regions are chosen for which indices of prosperity and interregional flow data are available.

The objective of the first part is to establish that, in addition to difference in the geographic content of regions (agriculture rather than industry or one type of industry rather than another), there are differences in the general prosperity and affluence of regions. Prosperity however has a number of differing aspects both economic and social, which only together give a complete picture. In the United Kingdom, as with many developed countries, undue emphasis for regional policy has been placed, until recently, on unemployment figures. There are serious dangers in using only one criterion to define regional prosperity. If unemployment is used as the indicator of regional health, there is a need for empirical investigation to understand the relationship between unemployment and economic indicators and between regional unemployment and cyclical fluctuations in the national labour market.

The explanation of spatial variations in prosperity in terms of interregional systems is introduced by a study of the bases of interregional trade and an example of an interregional trading system in which some of the regions are seen to have a favourable trading pattern for a wide range of commodities. The contribution of such favourable balances to a process of regional growth appears to be historically established. On the other hand a deficit region has to find ways of financing its deficits at least in the short to medium term. Such indebtedness cannot continue indefinitely but it is likely to continue as long as the terms of trade between regions remain unaltered. In the circumstances of prolonged deficits the region may undergo economic decline. This may in turn trigger off changes in the regional economy but these are slow to occur. Alternatively the decline in prosperity (increased unemployment or relatively declining wage rates for example) may stimulate out-migration. The net results of such an out-migration are not easily determined.

In the third part spatial differences are treated as differences between points on a continuously varying surface. Such surfaces will be determined by the location of natural resources and by the geographical distribution of population and wealth. Two types of process occur on such a surface; processes occurring at a point, or within a very small area, and processes which involve re-location or movement between points on the surface. The effects of such processes may be to accentuate or reduce the variability of the surface. On the one hand there is the idea that growth begets more growth (multiplier effects which are generally supposed to have the first result) but in addition differential growth effects may have the second result. Movement between locations on the surface can occur at local scales or regional scales. Such movement will only affect the nature of the surface when it shows particular types of spatial bias. Similarly the decisions of individuals or households to change their place of residence may be interpreted as a response to various socio-economic surfaces as seen by the migrant.

The first part established that regional differences occur, the second and third both indicate that these differences are not transient phenomena. If 'left to themselves' they may disappear, but they may become yet more marked. For this reason countries of widely different type and political system have found there is a need for regional planning. In most cases this planning has focussed upon the location of industrial plants and industrial complexes. It is frequently possible to identify broad policy objectives and the effect of particular measures. This is illustrated by the example of eastern Europe and particularly Polish industrial location policies; by the example of Nigeria and its industrial location policies, and by the example of the United Kingdom and its industrial location policies. The case studies characterise three distinct types of economy: a centrally planned economy, a partially planned developing economy and a partially planned developed economy.

C.R.P.B.
A.M.H.

Part I
Measures of Regional Inequality

Introduction

Part I introduces the fact that regional inequality does exist, looks briefly at some of the criteria which together measure regional inequality, and indicates research being undertaken to assess the relationships that exist within regional accounts.

Variations in an individual's inequality of opportunity exist in a number of forms, both economic (income and the cost of living) and social (education, health and recreation facilities). When considering the individual the boundary line between mainly economic and mainly social criteria is often difficult to define. Indeed, perhaps both issues are best thought of under the term 'welfare' (Perloff, 1957). This point is made plain when one considers unemployment which has both social and economic consequences to the individual. The differential opportunities of individuals can be aggregaged to give general regional variables. These indices can be mapped to show generalised variations in 'opportunity and affluence' (Rawstron and Coates, p. 13).

Rawstron and Coates' plea for a greater variety of regional accounts is taken up by McCrone (p. 22). McCrone stresses the need for a greater improvement in regional statistics in general, and in particular, with the United Kingdom in mind, the need for a move away from the sole use of one criterion — unemployment — to define problem regions. The main reason often given for the undue importance attributed to regional unemployment statistics is that unemployment has often been the problem that has focussed attention on regional differences in the more developed countries. Thus employment has often been termed 'the regional problem' (e.g. Hemming, 1963). The other common welfare criterion is personal income per capita. This varies relatively little within more developed exchange economies (Williamson, 1965). In many homogeneous industrialised states, like the United Kingdom, regional income statistics have not, until recently, been carefully investigated.

Paralleled by the need for greater variety of regional welfare statistics is the need for the inclusion of criteria defining other regional elements, for example efficiency and volume of productive sectors. Accounts on Regional Gross Domestic Product and Expenditure (such as those derived by Woodward (1970)) must be made available so that a fuller understanding can be made of a region's economic position. While comprehensive and continuous regional efficiency and production volume accounts would be extremely useful additions in the study of a region's general economic position it is probable that, for political reasons, unemployment and other welfare statistics will continue to define regional objectives.

A short but excellent review of some of the problems concerned with the assembly and use of most regional accounts is given in Brown (1969).

It has often been assumed that welfare criteria are highly correlated: for example that an increase in unemployment results in a decrease in income per capita and emigration. But this is not always so. Agricultural regions are renowned for their relatively low incomes, yet this does not always coincide with unemployment and emigration. Increases in minimum wages could possibly result in proportionately cheaper capital being substituted for labour, resulting in a higher income per capita, and an increase in unemployment.

Pullen (p. 28) makes an empirical analysis of the relationship between income (as expressed by wage rates for males) and unemployment in regions of the United Kingdom. Little general relationship was found to exist between wage rates and unemployment, and, when combined with the many weak correlations for individual regions over time, the indication was that predictions of regional income from unemployment accounts cannot be made with 'any degree of certainty'. Pullen draws attention to the inadequacy of the data available. Until data becomes more comprehensive and reliable such empirical work will always prove unsatisfactory.

The interpretation of unemployment figures is also the theme of Thirlwell's paper (p. 42). His interest lies in the relationship between regional and national unemployment over time. He finds that there is a 'cyclicality' of regional unemployment, a phenomenon often overlooked by economists; superimposed on a national trend of association between a region's unemployment and the national average for a given time period, there is a tendency for regions with unemployment rates above the national average to experience changes which are exaggerations of the national trend.

Thirlwell suggests that there are two major determinants of this phenomenon. Firstly some industries are more sensitive than others to fluctuations in demand. The distribution of sensitive industries between regions will be a determinant of a region's sensitivity. Secondly the sensitivity of an industry will vary between regions. The result of the correlation between a region's sensitivity to unemployment and its industrial structure showed that about 'one-half of the sensitivity of regions seemed to be accounted for by the uneven distribution of sensitive and insensitive industries'. Variance, not explained by this relationship, may be explained by the interregional differences in the sensitivity of individual industries.

It is important that empirical enquiry should be continued. Hopefully, this may contribute to the understanding of the complex relationships that exist within regional accounts. Until the paucity of suitable data is overcome the examination of interrelationships will continue to be indecisive.

Christopher Brook

References

Brown, A.J. (1969) 'Surveys of Applied Economics: Regional Economics with special reference to the United Kingdom', *The Economic Journal*, **LXXIX,** 316

Hemming, M.F.W. (1963) 'The regional problem', NIER, **25,** 40-57.

Perloff, H.S. (1957) 'Problems of Assessing Regional Economic Problems', *Studies in Income and Wealth*, NBER, **21.**

Williamson, J.G. (1965) 'Regional inequality and the Process of National development. A description of the patterns', *Economic Development and Cultural Change*, **13,** 3-45.

Woodward, V.H. (1970) *Regional Social Accounts for the United Kingdom*, Cambridge University Press.

1 Opportunity and Affluence

by E. M. Rawstron and B. E. Coates

Queen Mary College, University of London
University of Sheffield

I Prospects for Employment[1]

Just as a child's educational prospects vary from one district to another, so also do his prospects for type of employment and size of income when he leaves school. If he is willing to move and knows where to go, his opportunities increase. If he is reluctant to move, then they are circumscribed by the place in which he lives. Some places are good, some bad, and some indifferent, for there is in the United Kingdom a range from high incomes and high diversity of employment in some districts to low incomes and low diversity in others. But income is not always related to degree of diversity, and low earned incomes are not by any means a sure sight of local economic specialization. Nevertheless, places characterized by specialization are less secure and more restricted environments in which to begin working life than are diversified places.

In the United Kingdom about 7 per cent of the working population are employed by primary industries such as agriculture, mining, fishing and forestry; about 36 per cent are in secondary industries comprising the manufacturing and processing sector; 57 per cent are in tertiary industries including transport, the utilities, wholesale and retail distribution, construction, finance, the professions and public administration.

Opportunity for employment varies considerably over the country from a high degree of limited and narrow specialization in a declining group of industries in some places to highly diverse employment in flourishing manufacturing and service industries, notably in Southeast England. Lack of varied opportunity for employment restricts the local social environment, and it can also lead to the suppression of many talents, which may remain for ever latent and wasted.

If a school-leaver decides to stay and work in any of the following places — and there are many more like them — it means that he is severely limiting his employment opportunities: Bradford, where 11 per cent of employment is in textiles, mainly wool; Sheffield (30 per cent in metal trades); Stoke-on-Trent (34 per cent in ceramics); Kettering-Wellingborough-Rushden (36 per cent in clothing, mainly footwear); Luton and Dunstable (32 per cent in vehicles); Holland, Lincolnshire (32 per cent in agriculture); Dundee (21 per cent in textiles, mainly jute), or Barrow (40 per cent in shipbuilding and marine engineering).

These are not necessarily bad places in an absolute sense. Their restricted opportunities may provide reasonable security, tolerable prospects and adequate income. But they are bad in a comparative sense, and because they cater inefficiently for the wide range of potential talents of their inhabitants. As a class of town, they are likelier to lose population to areas with better opportunities and to attract population only on a selective basis. Thus Bradford would attract those seeking employment in wool if the industry were expanding, and Luton does attract workers to its motor industry which is a growing and prosperous trade.

In contrast, because opportunities are excellent, there is no general incentive on grounds of employment to leave Greater London, though other centrifugal forces do operate in a small way. London offers the best opportunities for many reasons. Employment in manufacturing approximates to the national average and is extremely diverse, and this diversity contains a higher proportion of expanding trades than elsewhere. The most rapidly expanding sector of all in the national economy is the service or tertiary sector, and of this London has more than its fair share. Moreover, a great deal of employment classed as manufacturing in London is office employment which in effect augments the expanding tertiary sector. Finally, security is high and incomes are above the national average in the Civil Service whose better-paid jobs are concentrated in London.

The employment structure makes people want to remain in London and induces others to seek work there. Thus people with a wide range of aptitudes and skills are drawn from the rest of the United Kingdom and from abroad. London's pre-eminence is bad for the country since it saps the strength of many other districts, causes the partial neglect of their resources, and lacks the benefit of the healthy competition of a rival within the United Kingdom. New York has several rivals within the United States of America; Tokyo does not dominate Japan: West Germany has no London at all;

Rome is not the only major centre in Italy; and Paris, which certainly dominates France, now faces competition from other centres in the Common Market.

Between the supposed good of London and the supposed bad of Londonderry or Dundee lie degrees of indifference. The West Midland Conurbation and the cities of Leicester and Nottingham present the best employment structures and opportunities outside London. They are diversified, though less so than London, and the major elements in their diversity flourish. They lack London's wealth of opportunity for service employment but provide an ample range of good jobs for those who wish to work on the shop-floor.

The national employment magnet thus has two poles, of which the south is the more powerful and concentrated. The weaker and more diffuse north pole functions between the Chilterns and the Trent, but more selectively with regard to employment and its ability strongly to attract population than does the south pole. Birmingham is a workshop, not a metropolis, more like a Pittsburgh or a Detroit than a Chicago or a Los Angeles.

Leeds is similar to Birmingham in its wide diversity and is better as a centre of service employment; but neighbouring towns in West Yorkshire fret under a blanket of wool. There is no rapid decline, but little advance. The industry is profitable for its owners and provides a reasonable living for its workers. There are few incentives to greater effort and the local range of opportunity is poor. But if London or the Midlands are out of reach, commuting to Leeds serves fairly well instead.

Glasgow and Clydeside have great diversity and yet the employment structure must be deemed very indifferent indeed; for, unlike Birmingham, their diversity has the appearance of a remnant sale, full of discontinued lines. New lines are introduced from time to time, but not at the required rate. This area is indifferent to bad in the opportunity it offers.

Manchester and its satellites are simply indifferent. Cotton has declined but is steadily and fairly adequately replaced. Diversity increases, and Manchester has more service employment (62 per cent) than Birmingham (43 per cent), but well-paid jobs are generally less plentiful in the Manchester region.

Other parts of the United Kingdom could be similarly classified according to the opportunities they offer for employment. But the main point must already stand out that the best area at present lies between London and the Trent, and that the quality of opportunity declines outwards from this 'magnetic' area. At least two hopeful

signs for improvement can be discerned. One is the success achieved during the past 15 years in replacing cotton by other enterprises in Lancashire. The other, which perhaps gives even more cause for optimism, is the quiet revolution that has occurred in South Wales, converting a very narrowly specialized economy in extraordinarily difficult natural and social conditions into one that is diverse beyond the hopes of the greatest optimist of 30 years ago.

2 Variations in Income[2]

Prospects for a good income vary from district to district as do those of employment. Although the available information from annual reports of the Commissioners for Inland Revenue is less detailed than for employment, the patterns of income are striking and correspond in large measure to many of the facts known about the distribution of employment.

The mean income of those who were subject to deduction of tax in the United Kingdom in 1959-60 – the latest detailed information shown on Figure 1.2 – was £732. This had risen by 1962-3 to £853, but no county data are available for that year.

The range was from £524 in Armagh, £645 in Argyll and Bute, £579 in Anglesey and £642 in Cornwall to £787 in Bedfordshire, £784 in Middlesex, £874 in the old County of London and £1158 in the City of London itself. Counties with a mean above that for the United Kingdom were concentrated, apart from Westmorland, in a belt from Surrey and Essex northwestwards to Staffordshire and Leicestershire. The anomaly of Westmoreland is explained by the unusually high proportion of Schedule 'D' (profits and professional earnings) and investment income returned there. Otherwise, incomes declined consistently away from the Southeast and Midlands except for Northumberland and Midlothian. When it is borne in mind that these county statistics exclude civil servants·and pensioners of the Crown, whose combined average income of £840 was well above the national mean, the dominance of the Southeast and London in particular is even stronger.

Between 1950 and 1960 Northern Ireland and much of Scotland showed a marked relative decline, whereas there were increases in several parts of Wales (compare Figure 1.2 with Figure 1.1). The striking change in England was the building up of the area of high average incomes between London and the Midlands. It is not surprising that, as incomes have grown in this area, few people have been induced to leave it, and many have moved in from less prosperous districts.

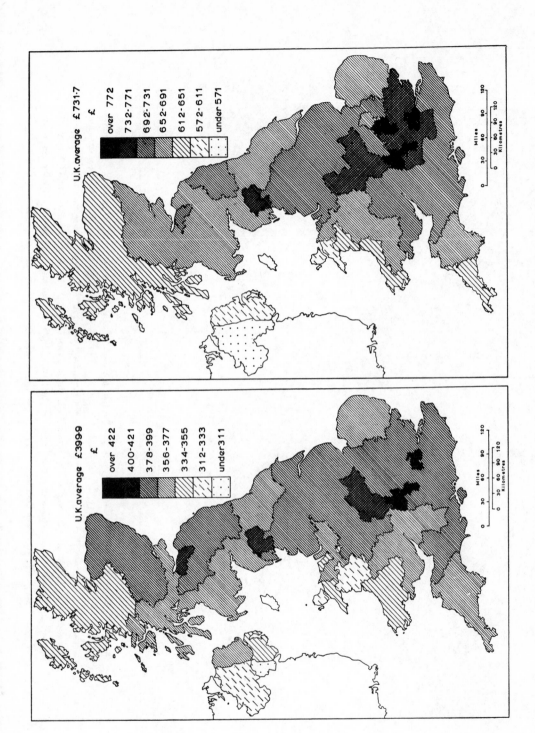

Figure 1.1 and 1.2 – *Affluence on the Move* – the distribution of total net incomes (before deduction of tax) – earned and unearned – in 1949-50 (1.1) compared with 1959-60 (1.2). On each map the two top categories represent incomes above the national average. The relative prosperity of Northern Ireland, most of Scotland, and Caernarvonshire and Cornwall, among other counties, declined. South Wales, Staffordshire and Southeast England were among the areas which improved their relative positions. (Data refer to place of work.)

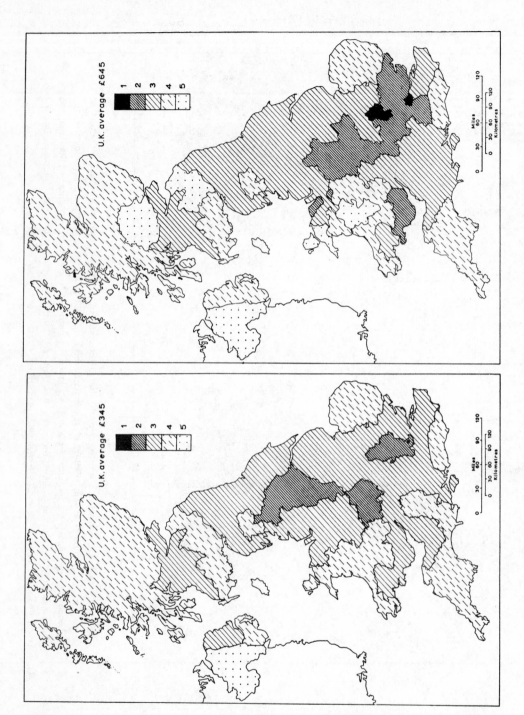

Figure 1.3 and 1.4 – *The Shifting Power to Earn* – the distribution of wages and salaries (Schedule 'E') incomes in 1949-50 (1.3) and in 1959-60 (1.4). Wage-earners in the West Riding, Worcester, Shropshire and Perth, for example, were relatively worse off in 1959-60; those in Flint, Glamorgan, Monmouth, Stafford, Leicester and the Southeast were relatively better off. National average schedule 'E' income was £345 in 1949-50 and £645 in 1959-60. Key: (1) more than 10 per cent above national average; (2) up to 10 per cent above national average; (3) 0-10 per cent below national average; (4) 10-20 per cent below national average; (5) more than 20 per cent below national average. (Data refer to place of work.)

Most people depend mainly upon Schedule 'E' earnings. They pay as they earn and have few investments or other income than a wage or a salary. The pattern of Schedule 'E' earnings (Figure 1.4) and the changes that have occurred since 1949 (compare Figure 1.3 with Figure 1.4) are of greater general and social interest than data for personal incomes from all sources. Categories 1 and 2 on both maps indicate areas where average wages and salaries exceeded the national averages of £645 in 1959-60 and £345 in 1949-50.

Once more it is clear that there has been a shift during the decade towards a concentration of high average earnings along the London-Birmingham axis. But the significance of the upgrading of South Wales should not be overlooked. As with employment, there is hope also in South Wales for incomes. What has been achieved there should be feasible elsewhere.

There is no doubt, however, that the best opportunities for high wages and salaries are now to be found in the large area extending from Derbyshire, Leicestershire and the West Midlands to Essex and Surrey.

Just over 15 per cent of taxable incomes exceeded £1000 in the United Kingdom in 1959-60; but London had 23 per cent while the City of London had 34 per cent. The City had more personal incomes over £1000 than the whole of Wales, and almost as many over £5000 as Wales and Scotland added together. Yet there were only 353,000 taxpayers in the City compared with 2,762,000 in Scotland and Wales. There were 56,000 personal incomes over £1500 in the City compared with 48,000 in the whole of the West Riding.

These are extreme examples which serve only to highlight the contrasts that exist over the United Kingdom. A more realistic index is the fact that the continuous area (marked 'very high' on Figure 1.5) of London, Middlesex, Surrey, Berkshire, Buckinghamshire and Oxfordshire exceeds the national proportion of incomes over £1000 according to place of work. The extra purchasing power thus created is spread over the more well-to-do residential areas of Southeast England.

Adjacent to the 'very high' area are two groups of counties – Essex, Hertfordshire, Bedfordshire; and Warwickshire, Staffordshire, Leicestershire and Worcestershire – with an excess of incomes between £800 and £1500. These seven counties are areas where manufacturing flourishes and work on the shop-floor brings a high return. Taken together with the 'very high' group of counties including London, they form the magnet for opportunities for both income and employment in Britain.

The remaining areas, apart from Flintshire, have an excess of 'medium', 'low' or 'very low' incomes. Particularly notable is the 'low' category for Central Scotland which does not match up to the industrial regions of England and Wales. The greatest excess of very low incomes occurs in Northern Ireland where Armagh, Fermanagh, Londonderry and Tyrone have more than 70 per cent of personal incomes under £600 compared with a national figure of 48 per cent. Indeed, Fermanagh has 77 per cent.

Among the poorer parts of the United Kingdom there were, however, some indications of wealth apart from that brought in by commuters who worked in neighbouring counties. Sussex, Cambridge, Gloucester, Hereford, Dorset and Somerset returned more than the national proportion of incomes over £1500, as did certain counties of mid-Wales. In Scotland the same could be said of Perthshire, the Border Counties and Midlothian. Westmorland was unique in having excessive numbers of incomes at the extremes, namely, over £1500 and under £400.

But there are no such redeeming features in Northern Ireland, North and Southwest Wales, Cornwall and Devon, the East and North Ridings, Norfolk, Suffolk and the parts of Scotland not mentioned in the preceding paragraph. Without doubt Northern Ireland as a whole has least of all to offer in opportunity for income and employment.

One final point must be made about affluence. Since 1961-2 relief has been given for the lower ranges of surtax on earned income. A far greater proportion of this bonus must have become available for spending in the London area than elsewhere. Thus has the effective affluence of Southeast England been appreciably increased by a stroke of a Chancellor's pen, even since the 1959-60 survey of personal incomes.

3. London against the Regions

Opportunities for a wide range of employment and high incomes largely coincide regionally within the United Kingdom. The magnet of employment, polarized between London and the Trent, is also the magnet of income. No kind of national plan can be socially or even economically sound unless adequate account is taken of these facts, especially when they are linked to the renewed upward trend in the rate of population increase, the persistence of inflation and the under-use of parts of the nation's resources.

The magnetism and internal problems of the area of greatest opportunity for employment and incomes in

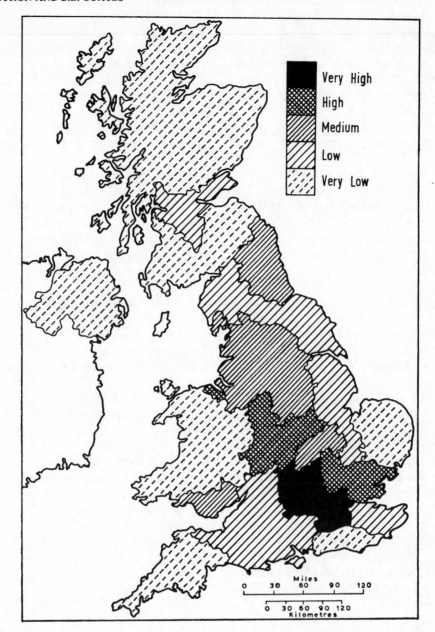

Figure 1.5 – *The Affluent Places*, 1959-60 – regional grades of affluence, ranging from a proportional excess of 'very high' incomes in one area to an excess of 'very low' incomes in seven areas. Northern Ireland has the largest proportion of 'very low' incomes. Lancashire and the West Riding, for example, have a slight excess of 'medium' incomes. London has a large excess of 'very high' incomes. (Data refer to place of work.)

Britain sap the strength of the country quite unnecessarily, and this adverse effect seems likely to intensify. The social injustice so clearly portrayed by the Schedule 'E' map for 1959-60 is in itself a sufficient case for policies aimed at a more even spread of wealth, and for action to resuscitate run-down environments in those districts where the legacies of nineteenth-century development and economic specialization dominate the social scene. But there are other, and perhaps stronger, arguments.

First, there is the suppression and draining-off of talents resulting from differential environmental influences. The alternative for potentially able people in poor environments is either to leave them for better, or to take jobs locally that do not give full scope to ability. The former is an inefficient selective process, but it is effective enough to skim off some of the cream. The latter alternative is simply wasteful.

Secondly, the magnetism of the affluent area imposes a harmful geographical distortion upon the national economy. The trend towards proportionately more and more people with higher and higher incomes in metropolitan England reinforces the accepted inflationary factors that do not so strikingly differentiate between areas. The harmful effects of the affluent area are twofold. There is a tendency to augment the forces that put up the price of labour, both throughout the country, for which London is the pace-setter for many basic wage and salary agreements, and locally through extra payments made necessary because of competition between employers for labour. There is also a tendency to raise the prices of those goods and services that are produced in London and that have high labour or high land components, because of the large geographical distortion that London creates in costs of labour and land. Furthermore, the comparative affluence of the huge market in the London area gives greater scope to pricing policies based on the ability and willingness of the customer to pay; in short, to careless expenditure. For 'postalized' items, for which the same price is charged throughout the country, this factor may well be relevant to general price increases in these commodities.

There are forces operating to mitigate these ill-effects and to justify higher wages and salaries in London. For example, the incentive to save labour is stronger and the feasibility of achieving economies of scale is greater. The cost of living is higher. But none of these is adequate to justify a *laissez-faire* attitude. And, in relation to the pattern of incomes, the cost-of-living argument is probably over-rated. Apart from obvious items such as

housing, land, commuting and second-hand cars, all of which cost more in London, there are many items in the ordinary weekly budget that are probably dearer outside London, and many are the same wherever they are purchased in Britain. Sound evidence on geographical variations in the prices of consumer goods is, however, lacking. Moreover, incomes are high between the Chilterns and the Trent where the cost-of-living argument could not be used in justification.

The strength of the foregoing argument depends on the quality and quantity of available data. More refined information not only on employment and incomes but on geographical variations in the cost of living, profits and costs of individual industries, productivity of labour, and the economy in general, is needed to permit sounder measurements and conclusions to be made about variations from place to place within the United Kingdom. Otherwise, regional and national economic planning will be undertaken blindly, and the prices and incomes policy, as well as the national plan, will miscarry. The authors are aware of a number of defects in the information that they have been obliged to use. It is the best that they and probably the Government have available; for in Britain, where planning has long been attempted, far fewer local and regional statistics are collected and published than in the free-enterprise United States of America.

4 Proposals

The metropolitan region has been turned into the inflation-leader for the country. Just as the supermarket runs loss-leaders to attract trade, so the United Kingdom is running a localized and powerful inflation-leader which raises prices, costs and incomes generally throughout the country. A prices, incomes, and productivity policy for the national economy is an alternative to periodic devaluation and balance-of-payments crises. It is an attempt to give us an edge over our overseas competitors and the ability to pay our way in the world. But as a broad-spectrum antibiotic to cure many ills throughout the national system, it will prove specifically ineffective against London as a primary source of infection for the general inflationary disease. One has also the feeling that many in London are beset by the apathy of affluence, and that London's monopoly of leadership infects the whole country with this disease.

Metropolitan Centres

Thus a national plan is needed not only to stabilize prices and incomes and to increase productivity, but also to diminish the inflationary and complacent ill-effects of the affluent area of metropolitan England and, at the same time, to cope with the expected increase in the population of the United Kingdom. The necessary cure is to make a start on two new and well-planned Londons elsewhere as quickly as possible. If, as seems likely, room for the equivalent for some 15 additional towns the size of Birmingham has to be found by the turn of the century, surely two new metropolitan centres could be created during this period to reduce the magnetism of London; to increase the spread of wealth and opportunity, and to restore the competition which existed at least between Manchester and London during the second half of the nineteenth century. Each of these metropolitan centres might aim at populations of at least 3 millions and each should have its own 'City', West End, theatre-land, etc.[3] Osaka was once called the Manchester of Japan; the converse is now required. We need at least one Osaka in Britain, more than 150 miles from London. By these means the pressure will also be removed from London, and the problems of planning the capital itself will be eased.

Several locations are feasible for new Londons, including a refurbished Manchester and Glasgow, a greatly expanded Edinburgh, Metropolitan Humberside or Tyneside. Even 'Rhubarb-land' in West Yorkshire would serve. Whatever the choice, it is certain that all the old nineteenth-century towns will have to be gutted and rebuilt before A.D. 2000. To choose two of the outlying conurbations for conversion to metropolitan status during this process would be quite feasible given a determined lead from the central Government.

The physical reconstruction is a small task in comparison with the social, economic and political difficulties that will arise in convincing those involved that a drastic rearrangement within the United Kingdom is necessary. But without such a rearrangement, inflation and apathy will continue until the ill-effects of present trends in the affluent area bring on a persistent depression, marking the transition to national senile decay.

New Londons will not be enough. The creation of new and expanded towns will also be needed, as far away from London as can reasonably be contrived. Plymouth and somewhere in Cornwall, Pembroke and Cardiganshire, the Welsh Marches and even Lleyn, Solway and Southwestern Scotland, Inverness and Northern Ireland could all receive a quota. *Rapprochement* and agreement with Southern Ireland would be of great mutual benefit, for there is no larger wastage of resources and potential amenities in the British Isles than has been contrived by history in Ireland.

Practical Difficulties

It may be argued that to set up new metropolitan centres and to enlarge many towns as growth points is all very well in theory, but it will not work in practice for three main reasons. First, most of us like to be left undisturbed. We prefer the routine, the devils we know and the security of the present to promises for the future. Secondly, most of the top decision-takers and top people prefer either to live in Southeast England, in or fairly near London, or to seek seclusion in some area like the Scottish Borders where they may remain undisturbed. Thirdly, management wishes to work no harder than it need and have ready access to what it deems are the good things of life.

The first preserves our 'Coronation Streets'. The second either augments the effect of the third, for top managers are top people, or indicates withdrawal from the unequal struggle. The third is crucial, for it is management which takes locational decisions for the rest of us to follow. Notwithstanding the restrictions of Industrial Development Certificates, the belated embargo on office building in Greater London and the normal planning procedures applicable to any economic enterprise, management has had a pretty clear run. Yet isolated locations are considered irksome. Distance from London is deemed a nuisance for both economic and social reasons, while distance from Birmingham is viewed as a nuisance simply from the supposed economic standpoint.

This inconvenience or nuisance factor makes for managerial errors, and thus diseconomies, and for harder work. It encourages the acceptance of the *status quo*; for moving to a location outside the magnet of employment and income involves changes in the work pattern, because more intricate forward planning of both supplies of materials and deliveries of product to market has to be arranged at a distant location than in a great commercial agglomeration like London. Personal contact, except by telephone, cannot be so easily maintained.

Swings and Roundabouts

Greater costs arising from a changed location would for most enterprises be offset by advantages accruing from the change, for what they might lose on the roundabout of transport they would more than gain on the swings of lower wages, reduced pressure for increases, cheaper land

and buildings, space, lack of congestion and readier access in many parts of the United Kingdom to open country that is far more plentiful and more attractive than almost anything in Southeast England or the Midlands.

Given new metropolitan centres within reach, pleasing architecture in the town chosen for the new location, and good transport and communications to other parts, there is no sizeable obstacle to a policy for redistributing secondary and much of tertiary industry, apart from the urgent need to convince managements of the benefits to be gained thereby.

The 'Coronation Street' mentality plays its part in the lives of management as well as labour, and only the Government can act effectively on the scale required and in the time available to dispel it before the damage is too great. The measure of the will of past Governments to act is seen in Lytham St. Annes, Newcastle, Cardiff, Chesterfield and other places to which Departments have been sent. Far better than remodelling Whitehall would be the total removal of the central Government to locations outside London – the core to Windsor, and routine departments right outside the present magnet.

Equality of opportunity has been a conventionally accepted goal towards which we have long been moving by degrees. Unless the pace is stepped up and the emphasis changed from individual equality to geographical equality, we shall be in sorrier straits long before the century is out. To achieve a more equitable spread of opportunity, it is necessary for the Government and all sections of industry to shift their emphasis from the individual as a person irrespective of where he lives and works to the individual in his geographical and, in the widest sense, environmental setting. Inequality of opportunity is a sufficient evil in itself to warrant vigorous action. When, additionally, it imperils the welfare of all sectors of the community, even of the sector that is more equal that others, it reflects not only the ineptitude of past Governments, but short-sighted selfishness among leaders of commerce and industry.

Notes

1 Data from *Ministry of Labour, Employment Record*, No. 2, June 1963.
2 Data from annual reports of the Commissioners of Her Majesty's Inland Revenue.
3 Care should be taken to avoid reproducing a great, continuous built-up area like London. The authors envisage the placing of two new metropolitan cores – one in the North and one in Scotland – each with catchment areas of at least 3 million people within comfortable distance of the core by public and private transport. Whether the cores themselves should be compact or linear or some other more novel shape is not the point at issue here.

Reprinted from *Geography*, 51 (1), January, 1966, G. Phillips and Sons, Ltd, London, with permission.

2 The Application of Regional Accounting in the United Kingdom

by G. McCrone

University of Glasgow

The purpose of this paper is to consider what improvements in regional statistics may be necessary to make regional policy more effective and in particular to show in what respects a system of regional accounting may be applicable to Britain. It will be argued that the lack of such statistics has been largely responsible for much of the confusion of thought over regional policy objectives to which attention has sometimes been drawn. Moreover, because of this, the economic implications of policy have often been hard to determine, with the result that social and political considerations have tended to take precedence in the framing of policy. Economic assertion has often taken the place of analysis and the imperfect understanding of the economic factors has led to policies being pursued which were either less effective or more costly than was desirable.

Existing Regional Accounting Studies

Regional statistics are far from adequate in most countries, although in most western European countries, where there is a regional problem, regional accounting systems are gradually being developed. Italy now has a very comprehensive set of official regional accounts for the Mezzogiorno showing regional product by industries since 1951, consumption, investments and even foreign trade (Istituto Centrale di Statistica). Estimates of the regional product by industries of the Belgian provinces from 1948-1959 were prepared by the Université Libre de Bruxelles and are now being extended (Chaput, 1962; Chaput and de Falleur, 1961; Glejser et al., 1966). In France the estimates are much less comprehensive though figures for income by départements do exist and work is in progress to provide more adequate data (Maillet, 1958). In Ireland some very detailed figures of income by counties have been published and no doubt examples may be found in other countries (Attwood and Geary, 1963). Regional economists in these countries lay stress on these developments as necessary to provide a sounder economic basis to regional policy; and there is therefore little doubt that the estimates will be built up and extended (see for instance Davin, 1964 and Lajugie, 1966). Considering that the United Kingdom was the

first country in western Europe to start a regional policy it is perhaps surprising that she is not also ahead in the development of regional statistics. The only *official* statistics for regional gross domestic product relate to Northern Ireland and were first published in the Wilson report (*Economic Development in Northern Ireland*, 1965) apart from this various University studies cover Northern Ireland, Wales and Scotland, but none of these is produced on a regular basis.[1] Official statistics by regions are limited mainly to employment or unemployment; income censuses by the Inland Revenue which are published at intervals of 5 years; output and investment which are given for certain industries in some of the censuses of Production, the latest figures being for 1958; and the regional figures of the Ministry of Labour Earnings Inquiries which have been published since 1960.

Towards an Analysis of the Regional Economy

The primary function of regional statistics must be to provide a better understanding of the state of the region's economy. The precise nature of the regional problem has to be clearly identified and the economic implications of alternative development policies considered. In the past these questions have often been far from clear because although there may be a good case for regional development on economic grounds, policy measures have more frequently been taken in response to social than economic considerations (McCrone, 1966, and Needleman, 1965). Yet ironically even where their primary purpose has been social, such measures rely for their effect on influencing the *economic* development of the region. Since lack of economic statistics has made the understanding of that economy minimal, it is not surprising that regional policy has often failed to be as effective as had been hoped.

One reason for this has been that unemployment has most often been the social problem which has brought a regional policy into existence in western Europe and unemployment statistics in Britain have been by far the most accurate and regularly published regional data. Policy measures have therefore been too often tied to unemployment percentages without adequate consideration of the geographical, industrial or cost aspects of a region's potential for growth. This approach reached its height in the Local Employment Act 1960 which replaced the old Development Areas with Development Districts, the latter being scheduled on strict unemployment criteria. The various forms of Government aid were thus available only in these areas even if there were other nearby areas within the regions with much greater growth potential which could have drawn upon the same labour resources. Since 1960 policy has fortunately been moving away from a strict unemployment criterion, especially in Scotland where some effort has been made to identify areas with growth prospects.[2] The same is happening abroad, especially in Italy and France where attempts are being made to put the 'growth pole' concept developed by Perroux (1955) into practice. It is therefore very discouraging from an economic point of view to find two economists, Mrs. Hemming and Mrs. Duffy (1965) asserting that all that is needed for a regional policy are statistics of employment and unemployment. This view is not only in contradiction to the trend of thought on this subject in most west European countries, but in arguing it the authors seem quite unaware of the past shortcomings in regional policy which sprang from adherence to it, nor do they explain how they would put regional policy on a sounder economic basis.

From an economic point of view unemployment means simply that unutilized labour resources are available in the region. It does not indicate the full extent of such resources, since this also depends on underemployment, participation rates and productivity levels within the region. Even from a social point of view unemployment is far from being the only criterion for a problem region: in many countries the level of income per head is considered to be of more importance. Economically the region's rate of economic growth compared with its potential is probably the most important criterion.

In many instances these different criteria coincide; but this is far from always being the case. Depressed agricultural regions tend to suffer from low incomes rather than high unemployment; while depressed industrial regions typically suffer from inadequate rates of growth which in turn give rise to unemployment and emigration. Thus, a ranking of British regions by level of income gives slightly different results than one by unemployment, and at the sub-regional level the differences are even greater. Thus, obsession with unemploy-

ment has meant that neither mid-Wales nor the Scottish Borders were included in regional policy legislation until 1966, although, as is now being realized, both had a certain growth potential which was not being properly utilized.[3] That these different criteria may well lead to differing views of the regional problem is well illustrated by Belgium where the Flemish provinces used to suffer serious unemployment and still have lower incomes than the rest of the country. Yet their rate of economic growth is for the most part most satisfactory and is enabling them to catch up, while the higher income Walloon provinces have now an industrial structure seriously in need of reconversion and a growth rate of only 1·4 per cent a year which is plainly well below their potential.

The economic criteria are obviously much more difficult to apply than a simple unemployment percentage, but regional accounting does enable a much more detailed appraisal to be made. Estimates of Gross Domestic Product, for example, show what the output and income of the region is in relation to the nation as a whole and whether important disparities in living standards exist as in Italy and Yugoslavia. When such estimates cover a period of years the regional rate of growth and trends in living standards may be compared with the nation. If the estimates are broken down by industries it becomes possible to see whether the differences between regional and national economic performance are accounted for (a) by differences in economic structure, (b) by the differing performance of a few key sectors and (c) by a tendency for the regional economy as a whole to perform in a different way than the nation as a whole.

Estimates of the composition of Gross Domestic Product by industries and sectors, with an analysis of the order group composition of manufacturing output, are essential if the economic structure of the region is to be properly analysed. It can then be established whether certain peculiarities in the weak economic performance of the region are due to the large part played by certain industries or whether the promotion of growth in the region will entail important changes in economic structure. Of course this is not the only way to analyse a region's economic structure; the breakdown of employment by industries provides an alternative method. But, since output per head varies substantially from one industry to another, the two methods may give a very different impression. In many cases such sectors as agriculture, distribution and construction have below-average productivity; and an analysis of structure based on output will therefore attach much less importance to these sectors than one based on employment.

A comparison of the two methods, the industrial composition of output and the composition of employment, may also be used to identify weak spots in the regional economy by showing how productivity compares industry by industry with the national average. Thus, in Scotland it was found that, as a percentage of the national average, output per head in manufacturing was 97, in agriculture, forestry and fishing 99, in gas, electricity and water 105; but in mining and quarrying it was only 80, in distribution 82 and in construction 86 (see McCrone, 1965). Such information is essential to a proper understanding of the state of the regional economy and in many cases it may indicate weaknesses which policy should tackle.

No assessment of the state of the regional economy and its performance would be complete without data on investment. At present this type of data is quite inadequate. Even for Scotland, which has a better provision of statistics than other regions, it is impossible to get an aggregate figure for investment which might be related to Gross Domestic Product. All that exist are data for some isolated parts of the public sector and some figures for manufacturing industry published in the Census of Production. These latter, however, vary tremendously in scope and definition with each Census so that numerous alterations and adjustments have to be made to get a comparable series for a number of years. The data for investment are, however, particularly interesting in relation to a region's growth performance. Incremental capital/output ratios may be used to show whether a given amount of investment is achieving as much in terms either of growth or of increased productivity in one region as in others. The sectoral breakdown of such data is also valuable: a clearer idea may be formed of the performance of individual industries by regions, and it may be possible to reach some conclusion about the way in which increased investment would best be spent if the region's rate of growth is to be improved. Ultimately, if such data were really well developed, it should be possible to discover which regions would give the best return in terms of growth for a given increase in investment. Regions with acute labour shortage would need capital intensive techniques to produce higher productivity; those suffering from congestion would need heavy expenditure on infrastructure; and those with sparse populations in remote areas would lack external economies and require heavy investments in transport. Such factors as these would all tend to give

investment a poorer return in terms of growth than would be the case in regions not suffering from these disadvantages. Perhaps it is unrealistic to suppose that the data could be developed in the near future to the point at which this type of analysis could be made, but such matters are undoubtedly essential to a proper formulation of an industrial location policy.

Regional Accounting and Regional Planning

Another major use of regional accounts is in the preparations of regional plans. This is not the place to argue the merits or demerits of regional planning. Suffice it to note that the Conservatives started regional planning and the present Government are even more firmly committed to it. Moreover the type of planning now adopted is not simply a survey of the regional economy and its basic needs, nor yet a programme of public investment expenditure as were the first regional plans the Conservatives introduced. The Labour conception of a plan is something which involves output targets for industries and a detailed picture of the region's probable economic growth which can be integrated into the objectives of the National Plan. This approach is exemplified by the Scottish Plan, the first regional plan of this type to be prepared (*The Scottish Economy 1965-70*, 1966).

This sort of exercise, however, is bound to be rather fatuous in the absence of regional accounting data. It is a pretty uncertain business to plan the future growth of an economy if one does not know the rates at which it has been or is growing. In the Scottish plan therefore no attempt is made to plan targets for Gross Domestic Product as a whole; instead the targets are limited to those sectors of the economy covered by the Scottish Index of Industrial Production. This accounts for some 50 per cent of total output. In most cases the Scottish target figures are set slightly above the corresponding figures in the U.K. National Plan and indeed this seems to be their main justification. The figures bear even less resemblance to past experience than the United Kingdom figures do. The fact is that one of the main purposes of this sort of plan should be to demonstrate that certain target objectives are attainable; thus, the necessary climate of confidence which helps in their attainment may be created. This can only be done if the various sectoral objectives of the economy can be matched to the resources which are likely to be available. But where only 50 per cent of the economy is covered and the behaviour of the remaining 50 per cent is uncharted the industrial targets cannot be adequately matched to the labour force let alone other resources.[4] For this reason it is impossible to regard such targets with confidence, and they are therefore deprived of a large part of their purpose.

If proper regional accounts for Gross Domestic Product were available, the exercise would be much more meaningful. Given certain alternative assumptions about the growth of productivity the effect of different target rates could be worked out. Too low a rate would either be unable to ensure full employment and keep emigration down to an acceptable level; too high a one would run up against shortages of certain types of labour and would therefore imply unreasonably rapid rates of increase in productivity; it might also imply an unrealistically large inflow of investment funds from outside the region. Within these extremes there will be a number of alternative target rates which are adequate to meet the minimum economic and social requirements of providing employment and keeping down emigration. The practicability of such rates may be judged according to three criteria: (i) The feasibility of individual objectives for industries when the target for Gross Domestic Product is broken down by industries and sectors. (ii) The difference between the target rate of growth for Gross Domestic Product and for individual industries and sectors compared with past trends. If there is an important difference, it must be possible to show that this is realistic. (iii) If the regional target rates of growth differ substantially from those of the nation, it must be possible to show that this is practicable within the requirements of national economic policy and that capital for the necessary regional investment in industry and infrastructure will be forthcoming.

The above exercise presupposes regional accounts which cover at least the following: (i) Gross Domestic Product at current and constant prices; (ii) Gross Domestic Product by sectors showing the order group composition of manufacturing industry; (ii) Output per head by main sectors and order group of manufacturing industry; (iv) Investment broken down by sectors and order groups; (v) Labour availability. This would not constitute a proper interlocking series of social accounts of the kind that is available at national level. Such a series would require estimates of regional consumption, savings, imports and exports which at the present time could scarcely be constructed and are in any event less necessary.

Most of the regional accounting data mentioned above has already been prepared for Scotland, Wales and Northern Ireland in the studies referred to above. These studies cover slightly different periods and none of them is now up to date. But the important thing is that the methods involved in preparing estimates of this type are now clearly established. The three studies referred to use broadly similar methods and these have been published in detail. There would therefore be no difficulty in continuing these estimates on a routine basis. For Scotland, Wales and Northern Ireland the task is no longer fearsomely complicated as some people have supposed. Indeed if the task were performed with more ready access to unpublished data collected for the Censuses of Production and for the Inland Revenue Returns than is available to a university research worker, it would be even more straightforward and could be brought more closely up to date. This could have been done to provide an adequate statistical basis for the Scottish Economic Plan; the targets would then have had far greater meaning and the plan itself would have been immeasurably improved. It is to be hoped that the effort to do this is yet made for the preparation of other regional plans. However, the regions of England would present more difficulty: not only are they uncharted by previous studies, but they are undoubtedly less well provided for with basic statistics. The feasibility of preparing similar estimates for these regions largely depends on the amount of unpublished regional data which could be obtained from the Inland Revenue and the Board of Trade Census of Production. The methods used would have to be broadly similar to those used for Northern Ireland, Scotland and Wales.

Data on Costs

There are of course many other statistics whose provision could immensely advance our handling of the regional problem. Here one thinks less of regional accounts and more of information on costs which would enable the location of economic activity to be more scientifically determined. This is an important aspect of the regional problem on which very little information is available at present; and because of it there is much disagreement, which might otherwise be resolved, about the merits of regional policy. Opponents of regional policy in Britain have traditionally argued that if entrepreneurs are unable to operate in locations of their choice, costs will be raised and efficiency lost. Those who advocate an active regional policy, on the other hand, quote various studies which appear to show that the majority of industrial enterprises can operate viably in the main industrial centres of most British regions, and that transport costs in particular are not a burdensome element of cost.[5] It is also argued that the high cost of providing social capital in congested regions coupled with other less tangible elements of social cost justify a policy of regional development on economic grounds. However sound this argument may be it would obviously be more convincing if it was backed up by the appropriate data on costs of congestion and on private industrial costs in different locations; indeed, until this is done much talent which might be better utilized in devising a satisfactory regional policy will be wasted in disputing the merits of having such a policy at all.

Related to this is the need to make regional policy as effective as possible at lowest cost. If the Government is to carry out a policy of intervention in the location of industry it should aim in the long run to have information on the cost characteristics of different locations so that a view might be formed on the sort of industry which could be attracted. Likewise for individual industries the main elements of cost need to be determined: in particular whether scale of output, the existence of external economies, the proximity of related suppliers and component manufacturers are important. This was just the sort of information which was lacking when the Government persuaded several of the motor-vehicle manufacturers to set up plants in Scotland and the North of England in the early 'sixties. In the case of the steel strip mills which were set up, one in Wales and one in Scotland, the consequences of ignoring these factors look as if they might be economically very serious.

It is thus clear that from many points of view the development of regional policy is hampered by inadequate regional statistics. Those who concern themselves with the regional question are sometimes accused of lack of rigour both in their application of the objectives and in their advocation of policy measures. But if regional economic policy is still insufficiently scientific this is in large measure because it is supported by inadequate statistical data.

Notes

1 See Carter and Robson (1954), Carter (1958), Nevin (1957) and McCrone (1965) which gives estimates of gross domestic products for Scotland and estimates of personal income for all the standard regions in the United Kingdom.
2 This view was emphasized in the *Report of the Committee of Inquiry on the Scottish Economy* (Toothill Committee) Scottish Council 1961 and followed up in *Central Scotland: A Programme for Development and Growth* (1963).
3 The problems of the Scottish Borders are clearly outlined in *The Scottish Economy 1965-70* (1966).
4 The way in which this sort of exercise ought to be done is admirably demonstrated in the Irish Plan *Second Programme for Economic Expansion* Pr. 7239 Dublin, see especially the Appendix to Vol. II by Professor W.J.L. Ryan, *The Methodology of the Second Programme for Economic Expansion.*
5 See for instance Luttrell (1962), and the Toothill Report (1961) where costs of firms operating in Scotland were examined. Similar conclusions were reached in France, cf. Lajugie (1966).

References

Attwood, E.A. and Geary, R.C. (1963) *Irish County Incomes in 1960*, No. 16. Economic Research Institute, Dublin.

Carter, C.F. and Robson, M. (1954) A comparison of the National Incomes and Social Accounts of Northern Ireland, *J. Statistical and Social Inquiry Society of Ireland*, 108th Session.

Carter, C.F. (1958) Estimates of the Gross Domestic Product of Northern Ireland 1950-56, *ibid.* 112th Session.

Central Scotland: A Programme for Development and Growth (1963) Cmnd. 2188 H.M.S.O.

Chaput, G. (1962) Les Produits Intérieurs Provinciaux 1948-59, *Cahiers Economiques de Bruxelles*, No. 13.

Chaput, G. and De Falleur, R. (1961) La Production et L'Investissement des Regions, *ibid*. Nos. 10 and 11.

Davin, L. (1964) La Politique Belge de Développement Régionale, *Revue d'Economie Politique*, 1964, No. 1.

Economic Development in Northern Ireland (1965) Cmnd. 479, Belfast.

Glejser *et al.* (1966) *Séries Statistiques de Bruxelles*, No. 11.

Hemming, M.F.W. and Duffy, H.M. (1965) Regional Statistics, *District Bank Review*.

Istituto Centrale di Statistica, *Annali di Statistica;*; also in *Relzione al Parlamento del Comitato dei Ministri per il Mezzogiorno* (*annual*). Independent estimates are published annually by G. Tagliacarne *I Conti Provinciali*, Banca Nazionale del Lavoro, Moneta e Credito 3rd Trimestre.

Lajugie, J. (1966) *Les Régions Sous-Développées en France*, paper delivered to a conference on Backward Regions in Industrialized Countries, Rome.

Luttrell, W.F. (1962) *Factory Location and Industrial Movement*, National Institute of Economic and Social Research, 2 vols.

Maillet, P. (1958) *La Structure Economique de la France*, P.U.F.

McCrone, G. (1965) *Scotland's Economic Progress* 1951-60, Allen & Unwin, London.

McCrone, G. (1966) The case for a Policy of Regional Development in Britain, Cahiers Economiques de Bruxelles, No. 29.

Needleman, L., (1965) What are we to do about the Regional Problem? *Lloyds Bank Review*.

Nevin, E.T. (Editor) (1957) *The Social Accounts of the Welsh Economy* 1948-56, University of Wales Press.

Nevin, E.T. *et al.* (1966) *The Structure of the Welsh Economy*, University of Wales Press.

Perroux, F. (1955) Note sur la Notion d'un pôle de Croissance, *Economie Appliquée.*

The Scottish Economy 1965-70 (1966) Cmnd. 2864, H.M.S.O.

Report of the Committee of Inquiry on the Scottish Economy (Toothill Committee) Scottish Council (1961).

Reprinted from *Regional Studies*, vol. 1, 1967, Pergamon Press, Oxford, with permission.

3 Unemployment and Regional Income Per Head

by M. J. Pullen

University of Manchester

This article, which seeks to examine the relationship between income and unemployment in the regions of Great Britain, has arisen from a consideration of the ancestry of regional economic planning in this country. The establishment of Regional Economic Councils by the Labour administration may be seen as a logical development of (a) the strengthening of national economic planning machinery and (b) the return to a regional emphasis on 'growth areas' in the first two regional plans for the North East and for Central Scotland[1] after what may be regarded as the temporary abandonment of the 'regional' view in the 1960 Local Employment Act. The importance of Government location of industry policy in the emerging regional planning machinery has inevitably meant that to some extent the objectives of the post-war location of industry policy, which were rooted in the desire to do something about the maldistribution of heavy unemployment in the inter-war years, have spilled over to the objectives of regional economic planning. Although the criticism is not so serious as when the 4.5% unemployment rule was being applied under the 1960 Local Employment Act, it is nevertheless true that undue emphasis is still placed upon the level of regional unemployment in assessing the economic well-being of a region.

The government in the post war location of industry legislation has used terminology[2] which has implied that the areas of Britain qualifying for government assistance in attracting industry are in some respect *underdeveloped*. The implication of relative underdevelopment compared with other regions of Britain is also evident in the necessity for the two white papers of 1963 – *Central Scotland – A Programme for Development and Growth* and *The North East – A Programme for Regional Development and Growth*. The worrying feature in the development of regional economic policy remains the emphasis on the level of unemployment in a region as an indicator of the relative level of economic development of the regions of Britain.

Important as the existence of full employment is in the concept of economic welfare, the more usual and more useful measure used to distinguish between the levels of development of nation states is real income per head. It is difficult to see why the term *development* on a national scale should denote means of achieving a growth in real income per head; and on a regional level denote means of reducing the level of unemployment *per se* – for this is what seems implied if unemployment levels are used as indicators of regional prosperity. It seems desirable on *a priori* grounds that regional economic policies should be aimed at removing regional differentials in income per head rather than removing regional differentials in unemployment rates *per se*. It is quite possible to remove unemployment in a region without tackling the fact that because of an obsolescent industrial structure with a predominance of declining low net output per head industries, a region has a relatively low level of income per head and will continue to do so unless some drastic surgery is done to the industrial structure. This last point can be illustrated by a simple example. In December 1963 in the North Region 57,014 persons were registered unemployed – 4.4 per cent of the working population. Of these 40,000 were men. The average weekly earnings for male manual workers in the North Region was 318.8 shillings compared with 334.9 shillings for Great Britain. If we assume that all the 40,000 unemployed males are found work in the chemicals industry which had the highest average weekly earnings, the effect on the average earnings of the North Region would be to raise average earnings to 320.0 shillings – hardly a major contribution to the equalization of regional income per head.

The need to make more use of estimates of real income per head in different regions as the basis for policy is stressed by Gavin McCrone in his study of regional accounting with special reference to Scotland:

The main objective of policy as seen in the White Papers[3] is the provision of employment in Scotland and the North East, sufficient to take account of national increase, reduce unemployment and migration and raise participation rates ... an equally important objective could be the promotion of economic growth to enable Scottish gross domestic product per head of the population to approach the U.K. level.[4]

If, however, there is a strong relationship between the level of regional income and the level of regional unemployment, the practice of using unemployment measures as indicators may not result in policy measures being adopted that prevent the objective of reducing differences in regional income from being achieved. It is the purpose of this article to show whether in fact such a relationship exists.

2. Unemployment and Low Income Per Head

If, in an unreal model of a national economy that is divided into a number of regions, the industrial structure (i.e. the pattern of employment) is identical in each region, and if all factors of production are equally productive in each region, and if the costs of laying off labour are zero, there would be a close relationship between the level of regional unemployment and the regional level of income per head. In such an improbable static situation it would be justifiable to infer that, to remove the difference in income per head between a region where there is unemployment and the other regions where there is full employment, it is necessary to stimulate activity in the low income per head region in these industries which have a proportion of their labour force unemployed.

Although obviously, the British Economy does not fit the above simple model, it is worth asking whether in fact there are any indications that the level of regional income per head is negatively correlated with the level of regional unemployment – or to put it more generally, whether the level of relative earnings in individual regions shows any relationship to the state of the regional labour market.

In comparing the pattern of unemployment between the regions with the level of income per head there are, however, a number of statistical difficulties. First, let us consider estimates of regional income per head.

One measure of regional income per head that is published is to be found in the Reports of the Board of Inland Revenue[5] where estimates are made on a regional basis of the average total net income per taxpayer. There are, however, a number of serious drawbacks to these estimates that will be mentioned briefly. First, the surveys are occasional so that it is not possible to get an adequate time series of income per head for the regions. Secondly, all incomes of below £180 per year are

excluded, as also from the regional figures are the incomes of civil servants, the armed forces and merchant seamen. Thirdly, the Inland Revenue returns are based upon place of business not the place of residence. This means that the place where the income is created and recorded for taxation purposes need not necessarily be in the same region where the income is finally spent. This difficulty is particularly acute in dealing with investment income as company profits are included in the income of the region where the company head-quarters is located, so that the regional figures of investment income do not indicate where the economic activity creating the investment income takes place, nor where the investment income is received when profits are distributed to shareholders. Fourthly, the average figure is *per tax case* and not per head of population, and for the Inland Revenue survey married couples are counted as one person (one tax case).

A second estimate regional income per head comes from the annual Family Expenditure Surveys and the Household Expenditure Enquiry of 1953-4.[6] The data from the Family Expenditure Survey is based on an annual sample of about 3,500 households and hence is liable to sampling errors especially in income ranges where the numbers of households was small. There is also a tendency for the response rate of high income groups to be lower than other income groups and for low income groups to understate their incomes. There is no evidence, however, that these characteristics vary from region to region.[7] The basis of the Family Expenditure Survey is the household rather than the individual, so that the immediate products of the survey are estimates of household income and head of house-hold income rather than income per head. These income estimates are in contrast with the Inland Revenue Estimates in being based on place of receipt of income not on the place where income was created. A difficulty again with these income estimates is to obtain an adequate comparable time series for each Standard Region.

A third estimate of regional increase per head may be gained from data on the average level of weekly earnings of male manual workers.[8] This information has been published on a regional basis using the Standard Regions of official statistics since April 1960 in the six monthly (April and October) summaries of the Ministry of Labour earnings enquiries. The average level of earnings of male manual workers is, of course, very incomplete as an estimate of income per head in each of the Standard Regions (it excludes all female earnings, much employ-

Table 3.1 Comparison of Estimates of Regional Prosperity

| Region | Inland Revenue Average Total Net Income 1959-60 £ per annum | Family Expenditure Survey | | Ministry of Labour Average Weekly Earnings of Male Manual Workers in Manf. Industry and Selected Service Industry Group October 1962 £ per week |
		Average Head of Household Income 1961-3 £ per week	Average Household Income 1961-3 £ per week	
London & South East	812 (1)	16.7 (1)	22.8 (1)	16.7 (1)
Midland & Yorkshire & Lincolnshire	731 (2)	15.5 (3)	21.3 (2)	16.1 (3)
Eastern & Southern	723 (3)	15.7 (2)	21.2 (3)	16.0 (4)
North West	709 (4)	14.7 (5)	20.4 (4)	15.4 (5)
South West	691 (5)	15.0 (4)	19.9 (5)	14.9 (7)
Northern	686 (6)	13.5 (8)	18.5 (8)	15.1 (6)
Wales	678 (7)	13.5 (7)	19.1 (7)	16.2 (2)
Scotland	674 (8)	14.1 (6)	19.5 (6)	14.7 (8)

(W = 0.79)

Sources: 105th *Report of Board of Inland Revenue. Ministry of Labour Gazette,* March 1965. *Statistics on Incomes, Prices, Employment and Production* (Ministry of Labour).

ment in the service industry sector, and all non-wage forms of income). As an estimate of regional income this series does have the advantage that a more adequate time series is provided from April 1960 on a six monthly basis, and hence is the one used later in this article.

A comparison of the various regional income estimates is presented in Table 3.1. The ranking of the regions by each measure is indicated by the figure in brackets. With minor exceptions, the ranking of the regions is broadly similar by each measure — the above average income regions being London and the South East, the Eastern and Southern regions, the Midlands and Yorkshire and Lincolnshire; and the North, Scotland and Wales having levels of income markedly below the national average. The broad similarity of ranking in Table 3.1 is indicated by the high coefficient of concordance (W) of 0.79 for the rank data.

The degree of correlation between the estimates would be even better if it were not for the positions of the South West and Wales in the average weekly earnings rank order. The average weekly earnings measure under-estimates the level of income per head in the South West because the low proportion of manual workers in the South West compared with the other regions[9] means that too great a weight is placed on the earnings of manual workers in the total income of the region. The South West region has a relatively large proportion of its

income from the service industry sector which is not fully covered by the Ministry of Labour Earnings data, and also has a relatively high investment income per head which again is excluded from the weekly earnings measure. Wales is ranked second by the weekly earnings measure, but is seventh by the other three measures. This is a result of a particularly low level of investment income per head in Wales and also of a low activity rate for females in the working population.[10] In using the earnings measure, therefore, it should be remembered that the prosperity of Wales will be over-estimated and the prosperity of the South West slightly under-estimated.

The pattern of regional income differentials as indicated by the Family Expenditure Survey estimates shows a marked stability if the rankings in 1953-4 and 1961-3 are compared. There is, however, in Table 3.2 a clear tendency shown for the prosperous regions in the top half of the table to increase the margin of income over the Great Britain average income, and for the less prosperous regions to continue to lose ground (indicated by the positive and negative signs respectively).

It must be remembered that all of these income estimates have been in terms of money income. Because of the impossibility of doing otherwise, it must be assumed that money income differences more or less correspond to real income differences. It is likely,

Table 3.2 Comparison of Household Income 1953-4 and 1961-3

Region	Head of Household Income Median Income as % of G.B. = 100			Household Income Median Income as % of G.B. = 100		
	1953-4	1961-3	Change 1953-4 to 1961-3	1953-4	1961-3	Change 1953-4 to 1961-3
London & South East	107	110	+	108	108	0
Midlands	107	114	+	108	115	+
North Midlands	102	104	+	103	99	-
Southern	99	109	+	97	105	+
E. & W. Ridings	96	98	+	96	99	+
Eastern	98	95	-	96	92	-
South West	95	93	-	95	91	-
North West	98	99	0	103	98	-
Northern	99	95	-	99	91	-
Wales	96	93	-	92	90	-
Scotland	91	92	0	93	92	0

Source: Notes on Regional Labour Statistics No. 4. *Ministry of Labour Gazette, March 1965.*
N.B.: The Regions used in this table are different from those used elsewhere in the article. For an explanation of the various changes that have been made to the Standard Regions of official statistics see 'Notes on Regional Labour Statistics No. 1.' *Ministry of Labour Gazette,* January 1965.

however, that, because of the higher cost of living, money income estimates are likely to overstate the real income of the London area compared with the remainder of the country. In other areas, the industrial structure may mean that a greater proportion of the reward for labour is in kind (e.g. in agricultural and mining districts with payment in the form of produce, tied housing, etc.). Money income estimates in these cases will tend to underestimate the real income per head of the region. The money income estimates will also exaggerate real income differences between the regions as a result of price variations – especially of housing and transport – between the 'congested' regions and the rest of Britain. It is probable, therefore, that the variation in real income per head between regions is not as great as that indicated in the data in Table 3.1.

There are also a number of difficulties with using the Ministry of Labour estimates of the percentage unemployed as a true measure of unemployment in the regions. The official unemployment figures do not for example, account for people who withdraw from the labour force and do not register as unemployed (e.g. women and persons nearing the retiring age). Neither do the figures account for hidden unemployment in the form of excess capacity in the employed labour force as a result

of the hoarding of labour when business is slack (this would be associated with a fall in output per man). Official figures of unfilled vacancies on the books of employment exchanges also are not an accurate guide to the demand for labour. Many firms, for example, do not notify the employment exchange of vacancies; while other firms make it a practice to always have vacancies notified at the employment exchange regardless of whether a true vacancy exists so that they may have the option of taking on any labour that appears on the market. The accuracy of official unemployment statistics however will not be considered here as they have been discussed elsewhere.[11]

As a first preliminary glance at the relationship between the level of unemployment and the average weekly earnings of male manual workers, the regions are ranked according to the two series in Table 3.3. For the earnings column the regional earnings are expressed as a ratio of the Great Britain average $\left(\dfrac{E_r}{E_n}\right)$, and for the unemployment column the regional unemployment rate is expressed as a ratio of Great Britain unemployed rate $\left(\dfrac{U_r}{U_n}\right)$.

Table 3.3 Comparison of Regional Unemployment and Regional Average Weekly Earnings

	Regional Unemployment Rate as % of G.B. Rate (Mean 1960-3)		Regional Average Weekly Earnings as % of G.B. Average Weekly Earning (Mean 1960-3)	
London & South East	0.6	(1)	105	(1)
Midlands & Yorkshire & Lincolnshire	0.7	(2)	105	(2)
Eastern & Southern	0.7	(3)	101	(4)
South West	0.8	(4)	93	(7)
North West	1.2	(5)	97	(5)
Wales	1.5	(6)	102	(3)
Northern	1.9	(7)	96	(6)
Scotland	1.9	(8)	93	(8)

Source: Ministry of Labour, *Statistics on Income, Prices, Employment and Production.* H.M.S.O.

The rank data in Table 3.3 yields a Spearman's rank correlation coefficient of 0.76 which is significant at the 5% level. The product moment correlation coefficient for the data, however, is extremely low at −0.18. Let us now explore this relationship or lack of relationship more thoroughly.

3

The basic hypothesis is that the relative level of regional earnings is related in some way to the conditions prevailing on the regional labour market. If there is a surplus of labour (or rather a deficiency of demand) in a particular region, earnings will be reduced by the absence of overtime working, and by the ability of employers to attract sufficient supplies of labour at the *national standard wage rate* without the necessity of making bonus payments above the negotiated wage rates. If there is a shortage of labour, the opposite conditions will hold with manufacturers making bonus payments to compete for labour and to keep their labour forces intact, and with high earnings also resulting from heavy overtime working. The dependent variable that is to be 'explained' by the condition of the regional labour market is therefore not the absolute value of average regional earnings but the deviation of average regional earnings from the average earnings for Great Britain.[12]

The average weekly earnings of male manual workers in the regions of Britain have been published since April 1960. As a time series, therefore, the period for analysis is somewhat restricted. The earnings figures are from the Ministry of Labour six monthly earnings enquiry with data for April and October of each year since 1960 (omitting unfortunately October 1960 for which no data is available on a regional basis). The ratios of regional earnings to national earnings $\left(\dfrac{E_r}{E_n}\right)$ are to be found in Appendix I.

Unemployment will be used as the main indicator of the condition of the regional labour market, although it is unlikely that in a region where a labour shortage is the general rule that the level of unemployment will reflect a short period recession in that businessmen will tend to hoard labour, allowing output per man to fall while the recession lasts.[13] The unemployment figures used are the published unemployment rates for April and October in each year commencing with April 1960.[14] In calculating the Unemployment/Unfilled Vacancy ratios $\left(\dfrac{U}{V}\right)$, the absolute number of *wholly* unemployed persons is expressed as a ratio of the absolute numbers of unfilled vacancies in each region.[15] The unemployment data for each region is also shown in Appendix I.

We will first examine four aggregate hypotheses (i.e. looking at all the regional data together). Hypothesis 1 is that there is a relationship between the relative regional earnings $\left(\dfrac{E_r}{E_n}\right)$ and the regional unemployment rate (U_r):

$$\frac{E_r}{E_n} = f(U_r)$$

(1)

The second hypothesis is that the $\dfrac{E_r}{E_n}$ ratio will not depend on the regional unemployment *per se* but on how the regional unemployment rate compares with the national unemployment rate. In other words that relative regional earnings will depend on relative regional unemployment $\dfrac{U_r}{U_n}$ where U_r is the regional unemployment rate and U_n is the national unemployment rate.

$$\frac{E_r}{E_n} = f\left(\frac{U_r}{U_n}\right)$$

(2)

The third hypothesis seeks to assess whether a consideration of the supply side only of the condition of the regional labour market gives misleading results. As a rough and ready measure of the balance of supply and demand conditions of the regional labour market the unemployment/unfilled vacancy ratio is used for each region $\left(\dfrac{U_r}{V_r}\right)$:

$$\frac{E_r}{E_n} = f \; \frac{U_r}{V_r}$$

(3)

In hypothesis (4) the regional unemployment/unfilled vacancy ratio $\left(\dfrac{U_r}{V_r}\right)$ is compared with the national unemployment/unfilled vacancy ratio $\left(\dfrac{U_n}{V_n}\right)$ so that the balance of demand and supply in the regional labour market is compared with that in the national labour market.

$$\frac{E_r}{E_n} = f \left(\frac{U_r}{V_r} \; \frac{V_n}{U_n} \right)$$

(4)

The data for these hypotheses has been used to construct Figures 3.1, 3.2, 3.3 and 3.4. From an initial inspection of Figure 3.1 there would seem little to support hypothesis 1 that there is a relationship between the deviation of regional earnings from national earnings $\left(\dfrac{E_r}{E_n}\right)$ and the regional unemployment rate (U_r). If, however, we ignore the three regions: Wales, the South West and Scotland, or rather make allowances for bias in the statistics for these regions, there would appear to be a stronger relationship apparent. For Wales the $\dfrac{E_r}{E_n}$ ratio is too high as an indicator of true regional average earnings in that the earnings figure is biased as a result of too much a weight being given to one or two high earning manufacturing industries in Wales (Metal Manufacture and Textiles). Also because of the low female activity rate in the working population and a greater propensity of male unemployed persons to register, the unemployment rate is likely to be higher relative to the other regions. In the South West, the importance of the service industry sector will mean that the $\dfrac{E_r}{E_n}$ ratio is below its true value and also that the unemployment rate will be under-estimated because of non-registration of people who seasonally withdraw from the labour force. For Scotland it is probable that the $\dfrac{E_r}{E_n}$ ratio and U_r is underestimated because of the nature of the industrial structure with a larger proportion than the other regions in Agriculture and in Mining and Quarrying.

If these three regions are ignored it is possible to fit a curve to the data for the remaining regions. The dotted curve in Figure 3.1 is hyperbolic in form: $y = a + \dfrac{K}{(x - b)^c}$ where K, a, b and c are constants. The implication of such a curve is that the relationship between the $\dfrac{E_r}{E_n}$ ratio varies according to the absolute level of unemployment experienced.[16] As the level of unemployment falls below 2 per cent the $\dfrac{E_r}{E_n}$ ratio rises more rapidly. In the case of London and the South East, in fact, it would appear that the $\dfrac{E_r}{E_n}$ ratio behaves independently of the rate of unemployment in that relative earnings increase even in times of recession. Regions where general experience is of unemployment rate between 1-2 per cent seem unlikely to show any downward trend of the $\dfrac{E_r}{E_n}$ ratio even in a recession because the labour market is still

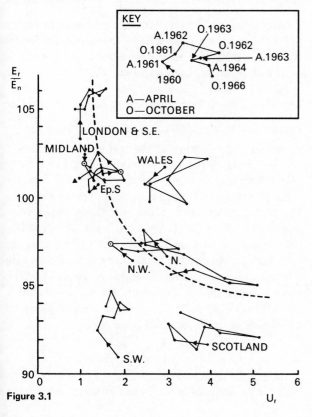

Figure 3.1

relatively 'tight' and because of the attitude that the recession is only temporary.

Figure 3.2 illustrates the hypothesis that $\frac{E_r}{E_n}$ ratio is a

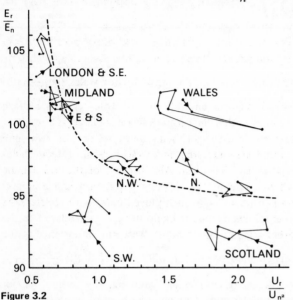

Figure 3.2

function of the $\frac{U_r}{U_n}$ ratio. Again a reasonable fit to a hyperbolic curve can be obtained if Wales, Scotland and the South West are ignored.

Hypothesis 2 illustrated in Figure 3.2 shows an improvement on Figure 3.1 in the relationship between the $\frac{E_r}{E_n}$ ratio and the unemployment measure over time for individual regions. The pattern in individual regions fits more closely the notion that when relative regional unemployment $\left(\frac{U_r}{U_n}\right)$ rises, then relative regional earnings $\left(\frac{E_r}{E_n}\right)$ will fall.

Figure 3.3 offers no evidence of an aggregate relationship between the $\frac{E_r}{E_n}$ ratio and the regional unemployment/unfilled vacancy ratio $\left(\frac{U_r}{V_r}\right)$. For individual regions the diagram suggests a 'perverse' relationship in the case of London and the South East, the East and South, Wales and the South West. There is, however, an improvement in Figure 3.4 when the regional unemployment/unfilled vacancy ratio is compared with the national ratio. A hyperbolic curve again is sketched in for the aggregate data but four of the eight regions can hardly be said to fit the curve! Changes of the $\frac{E_r}{E_n}$

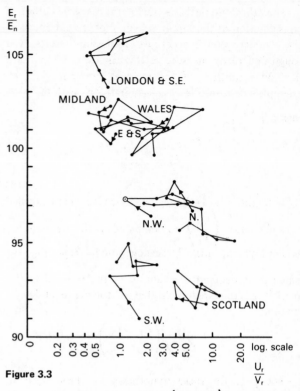

Figure 3.3

ratio with changes in the $\left(\frac{U_r}{V_r} \frac{V_n}{U_n}\right)$ ratio within individual regions do not conform as well as in Figure 3.2 – there are strong 'perverse' movements in Wales, Scotland, the North West and the North.

The data on an aggregate basis therefore does not suggest a strong relationship on any of the four hypotheses. By ignoring three of the regions a non-linear relationship of the Phillips curve type between the $\frac{E_r}{E_n}$ ratio and the condition of the regional labour market can be fitted. We cannot, however, ignore the three 'rogue' regions, and any adjustments in the data for these three regions is not likely to 'fit' the regions on to the dotted curve, because the hypotheses ignore completely the nature of the industrial structure of individual regions – some regions specializing in industries with high output per head and others in industries with low per capita net output. The four measures of labour market conditions in the hypotheses do not therefore provide a reliable indicator of the relative average level of earnings in the regions of Britain.

4

Although the aggregate regional data does not indicate a clear relationship between unemployment and relative

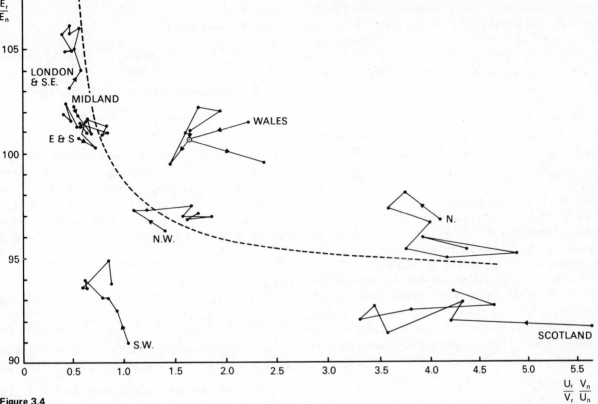

Figure 3.4

regional earnings, we must now examine whether any such relation exists for the data for each individual region. Whether for one region there is a relationship over time between changes in the $\frac{E_r}{E_n}$ ratio and the condition of the labour market. Because the range of unemployment experience within an individual region is limited, it is justifiable to treat any relationship for an individual region as linear in form (see Figure 3.1).

For each individual region five hypotheses have been examined:

A. $\quad \dfrac{E_r}{E_n} = f(U_r)$

B. $\quad \dfrac{E_r}{E_n} = f(U_r, \ U_n)$

C. $\quad \dfrac{E_r}{E_n} = f\!\left(\dfrac{U_r}{U_n}\right)$

D. $\quad \dfrac{E_r}{E_n} = f\!\left(\dfrac{U_r}{V_r}\right)$

E. $\quad \dfrac{E_r}{E_n} = f\!\left(\dfrac{U_r}{V_r} \ \dfrac{V_n}{U_n}\right)$

It will be noted that (A) above is comparable with (D) and that (C) is comparable with (E). The difference being that (D) and (E) indicate to some degree the balances of supply *and* demand on the labour market by using Unemployment/Unfilled Vacancy ratios.

For hypotheses (A), (C), (D) and (E) simple correlation coefficients have been calculated and these are shown in Table 3.4. The coefficients that are significant at the 5 per cent level are underlined. From Table 3.4 it can be seen that there is a general improvement in the

Table 3.4 Correlation Coefficients for Individual Regions

Region	Hypothesis			
	(A)	(D)	(C)	(E)
London & South East	+0.69	+0.51	−0.05	−0.15
East & South	+0.01	0	−0.79	−0.68
South West	+0.03	−0.08	−0.42	−0.59
Midlands & Yorkshire & Lincolnshire	−0.42	−0.47	−0.40	−0.73
North West	−0.03	−0.04	−0.30	−0.17
North	−0.87	−0.69	−0.85	−0.60
Scotland	−0.36	−0.43	+0.12	−0.14
Wales	+0.39	+0.66	−0.57	+0.09

degree of correlation (limited though it be) of hypotheses (C) and (E) over (A) and (D). The indication is that as an indicator of the deviation of regional earnings from national earnings the regional labour market conditions compared with the national condition is more relevant than considering the regional labour market condition alone.

All the regions where there is a significant correlation except London and the South East, and Wales show the expected negative correlation. In London and the South East there is a 'perverse' relationship between the $\frac{E_r}{E_n}$ ratio and the regional unemployment rate U_r. A similar perverse relationship is evident for Wales. The strong positive correlation for these two regions disappears however when the relative measures of labour market conditions are used (Hypotheses (C) and (E)).

For the hypotheses that gave significant correlation co-efficient simple regression equations have been calculated. The results are shown below with the standard error of the estimate for each equation (S.E.) and the standard error of the regression coefficients given in brackets.

Hypothesis (A)

(i)   London and South East

$$\frac{E_r-E_n}{E_n} = 1.5+0.03U_r \qquad \text{S.E.} = 0.67$$
$$(1.021)$$

(ii)   North

$$\frac{E_r-E_n}{E_n} = -0.19-1.03U_r \qquad \text{S.E.} = 0.50$$
$$(0.194)$$

Hypothesis (D)

(iii)   North

$$\frac{E_r-E_n}{E_n} = -2.49-0.178\left(\frac{U_r}{V_r}\right) \qquad \text{S.E.} = 0.73$$
$$(0.062)$$

(iv)   Wales

$$\frac{E_r-E_n}{E_n} = -16.65+5.4\left(\frac{U_r}{V_r}\right) \qquad \text{S.E.} = 0.69$$
$$(0.129)$$

Hypothesis (C)

(v)   East and South

$$\frac{E_r-E_n}{E_n} = 1.6-0.42\left(\frac{U_r}{U_n}\right) \qquad \text{S.E.} = 0.38$$
$$(2.805)$$

(vi)   North

$$\frac{E_r-E_n}{E_n} = 4.37-4.44\left(\frac{U_r}{U_n}\right) \qquad \text{S.E.} = 0.53$$
$$(0.902)$$

Hypothesis (E)

(vii)   East and South

$$\frac{E_r-E_n}{E_n} = 3.96-4.66\left(\frac{U_r}{V_r}\frac{V_n}{U_n}\right) \qquad \text{S.E.} = 0.46$$
$$(1.658)$$

(viii)   Midlands and Yorkshire and Lincolnshire

$$\frac{E_r-E_n}{E_n} = 3.09-2.64\left(\frac{U_r}{V_r}\frac{V_n}{U_n}\right) \qquad \text{S.E.} = 0.29$$
$$(0.822)$$

If the regression coefficients are compared with their standard errors, it will be seen that the rate of regional unemployment (U_r) is not a significant explanatory variable for the London and South East region (IV i) – the standard error of the regression coefficient being many times larger than the coefficient itself. The same is true for the $\frac{U_r}{U_n}$ ratio as an explanatory variable for the East and South Region (IV v).

Partial Regression Equations were calculated for hypothesis B: $\frac{E_r-E_n}{E_n} = f(U_r, U_n)$. This was done to enable a comparison of the results with the model using only the regional unemployment rate (U_r) and the model using the relative regional unemployment rate $\left(\frac{U_r}{U_n}\right)$. The results are given in Table 3.5 with the multiple correlation coefficient (R), the standard error of estimate (S.E.) and the standard error of the partial regression coefficients (in brackets). At the 5 per cent significance level only three of these equations are significant, those for London and the South East, the North, and for Wales – and only in the case of the North region are the standard errors and the standard error of estimate sufficiently low to suggest that the regional and national unemployment rates are good indicators of the deviation of the region earnings from national average earnings. The relationship shown in the partial regression equations for London and the South East and for Wales is again 'perverse' as was the case with the simple regression equations.

5. Conclusion

It has not been the aim of this paper to identify the true explanatory variables of the deviation of regional average earnings from national average earnings; but only to test whether the conditions of the regional labour market, as measured by the unemployment ratio or by the unemployment/unfilled vacancy ratio, were a good indicator of the $\frac{E_r}{E_n}$ ratio.

TABLE 3.5

37

Region	$\dfrac{E_r - E_n}{E_n} = a_1 U_r + a_2 U_n + b$	R	S.E.
London & South East	$\dfrac{E_r - E_n}{E_n} = 2.045 U_r + 0.60 U_n + 1.542$ $\qquad\qquad (0.434) \quad (0.804)$	0.67	0.684
East & South	$\dfrac{E_r - E_n}{E_n} = 0.60 U_r - 0.13 U_n + 1.391$ $\qquad\qquad (0.386) \quad (0.725)$	0.00*	0.617
South West	$\dfrac{E_r - E_n}{E_n} = -4.66 U_r + 3.04 U_n - 4.554$ $\qquad\qquad (0.644) \quad (1.154)$	0.48	0.982
Midlands & Yorkshire & Lincolnshire	$\dfrac{E_r - E_n}{E_n} = -0.95 U_r + 0.42 U_n + 1.832$ $\qquad\qquad (0.411) \quad (0.478)$	0.32	0.407
North West	$\dfrac{E_r - E_n}{E_n} = -0.04 U_r + 0.57 U_n - 3.891$ $\qquad\qquad (0.456) \quad (0.353)$	0.02	0.300
North	$\dfrac{E_r - E_n}{E_n} = -2.11 U_r + 2.72 U_n - 1.582$ $\qquad\qquad (0.905) \quad (0.412)$	0.94	0.351
Scotland	$\dfrac{E_r - E_n}{E_n} = -0.17 U_r - 0.91 U_n - 5.224$ $\qquad\qquad (1.054) \quad (0.665)$	0.33	0.566
Wales	$\dfrac{E_r - E_n}{E_n} = 0.27 U_r + 0.88 U_n - 1.582$ $\qquad\qquad (0.855) \quad (0.748)$	0.69	0.637

*The actual calculated coefficient was negative.

On an aggregate basis (i.e. considering all the regions together), there is little relationship shown between the actual published unemployment data and the $\dfrac{E_r}{E_n}$ ratio (see Figure 3.1, 3.2, 3.3 and 3.4). Although, if various allowances are made for bias in the data for Wales, Scotland and the South West compared with other regions, a closer fit might be obtained to the hyperbolic curves sketched in the three diagrams, it is hardly to be suggested on *a priori* grounds that a very close fit is to be found in data that incorporates no allowance for the very different industrial structures in each region.

It should, however, be remembered, that in Table 3.1 the average weekly earnings of male manual workers as a measure of regional income per head had several drawbacks compared with the other measures. These drawbacks led to the 'misplacing' of the South West region (too low in the ranking) and of Wales (too high in the ranking). If it had been possible to use the more accurate estimate of regional income per head on the basis of the Inland Revenue Estimates it seems likely that there would have been a more evident relationship between relative regional income per head and relative regional unemployment. In Figure 3.5 the $\dfrac{Y_r}{Y_n}$ ratio has been calculated from the Inland Revenue estimates of average total net income for 1959-60 where Y_r is Regional income per head and Y_n is U.K. Income per head. The $\dfrac{U_r}{U_n}$ ratio is for April 1960. A hyperbolic curve has been sketched for the data and provides a better fit than the curve sketched in the previous charts. Wales, Scotland and the South West do not figure as 'rogue' regions as they did when the average earnings measure was used. The aggregate relationship between unemployment and income per head may be stronger than our analysis with available data has suggested. A more frequent estimate of true regional income per head is necessary before this possibility can be explored further.

It has been shown that, if each region is considered individually there is little evidence that, for example, a fall in the $\dfrac{U_r}{U_n}$ ratio can be interpreted with any degree of certainty as indicating that the $\dfrac{E_r}{E_n}$ ratio has

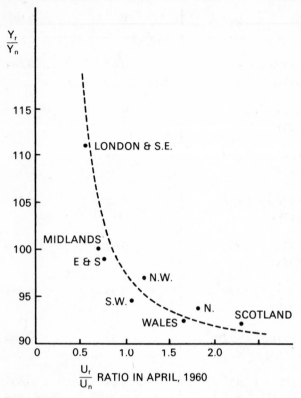

$\frac{Y_r}{Y_n}$

115 —

110 — •I LONDON & S.E.

105 —

MIDLANDS
100 —   •
E & S •

95 —   S.W. •
              • N.W.

                      • N.   SCOTLAND
           WALES •
90 —
    0   0.5   1.0   1.5   2.0

$\frac{U_r}{U_n}$ RATIO IN APRIL, 1960

Figure 3.5

risen. In fact in two regions, London and the South East and Wales, the statistical evidence suggests a strong relationship vice versa — not to be expected from theoretical reasoning. For the East and South and for the Midlands, Yorkshire and Lincolnshire, the simple regression analysis suggests that the relative unemployment unfilled vacancy ratio i.e. $\frac{U_r}{V_r} \frac{V_n}{U_n}$ is a reliable indicator of the deviation of the regional earnings from the national average earnings. The only region where one can feel confident about a relationship between the $\frac{E_r}{E_n}$ ratio and unemployment is the North region. For this region significant results, and results of the expected negative correlation nature, were obtained for four out of the five hypotheses tested. Again, however, it is possible that more significant results might be obtained if there were a more adequate time series of estimates of regional income per head than the inadequate indication given by the earnings data.

The results of this exercise have been negative in nature, but they do suggest that there is no justification for using unemployment measures as reliable indicators of the level of average earnings in individual regions and

of how the level of earnings in the region is changing over time.

It would seem desirable, therefore, if greater emphasis were placed on publishing and drawing attention to regional average earnings, rather than regional unemployment rates as the main indication to the public of the success (or otherwise) of government regional economic policies. More appropriate, however, would be the publication of more frequent data of *regional income per head* (to cover the many categories of income not covered by the Ministry of Labour's earnings enquiry).[17] It would then be possible to use a more adequate indicator of the level of regional economic development and to analyse further the possibility that in fact unemployment does or does not give some indication of the regional deviation of *income* per head from the national average *income* per head.

Notes and References

1 *The North East: A programme for regional development and growth,* H.M.S.O. Cmnd. 2206 para. 5, paras. 38-42.
Central Scotland: A programme for development and growth H.M.S.O., 1963, Cmnd. 21, para. 3 and paras, 101-111.
2 'Development Areas' in the 1945 Distribution of Industry Act. 'Development Districts' in the 1960 Local Employment Act.
3 *The North East,* H.M.S.O., 1963, Cmnd. 2206 and *Central Scotland,* H.M.S.O., Cmnd. 2188.
4 Gavin McCrone, *Scotland's Economic Progress 1951-60* (Allen & Unwin), p. 129.
5 The latest regional survey is to be found in *Survey of Personal Income (Before Tax)* in the 105th Report of the Board of Inland Revenue, H.M.S.O., 1963 (Cmnd. 1906), Appendix II. This provides estimates of regional income for 1959-60.
6 *Family Expenditure Survey Report for* 1963 (Min. of Labour, H.M.S.O. 1963), Table D, p. 6. Table 8, pp. 58-65.
Household Expenditure Enquiry Report for 1953-4 (Min. of Labour, H.M.S.O., 1957), Table 31, p. 150.
A Summary of the regional income estimates from these sources is to be found in 'Notes on Regional Labour Statistics,' No. 4, Income Expenditure and Characteristics of Households. *Ministry of Labour Gazette,* March 1965.
7 See *Ministry of Labour Gazette,* March 1965, p. 111.
8 See for example an early example of regional income estimates made by Phyllis Deane for 1948. Phyllis

Region and Date	Regional Earnings as % of U.K. Earnings (1)	% Unemployed in each Region (2)	% Unemployed in Region	Regional Unemploy-ment/Unfilled Vacancy Ratio (4)	Column (4) as Proportion of G.B. Ratio (5)
			% Unemployed in G.B. (3)		
London & South East					
April 1960	103.2	1.0	0.56	0.74	0.49
April 1961	103.9	1.0	0.67	0.61	0.59
October 1961	105.0	1.0	0.63	0.47	0.53
April 1962	106.0	1.2	0.60	1.10	0.59
October 1962	105.7	1.4	0.64	1.08	0.49
April 1963	106.1	1.6	0.59	1.96	0.49
October 1963	105.7	1.2	0.57	0.93	0.42
April 1964	104.9	1.1	0.61	0.73	0.52
October 1964	104.9	0.9	0.60	0.46	0.46
East & South					
April 1960	100.7	1.4	0.78	0.90	0.60
April 1961	100.2	1.2	0.80	0.78	0.76
October 1961	100.9	1.2	0.75	0.53	0.60
April 1962	101.5	1.5	0.75	1.23	0.65
October 1962	101.3	1.5	0.68	1.29	0.59
April 1963	101.3	1.9	0.70	2.21	0.56
October 1963	102.5	1.4	0.67	0.94	0.43
April 1964	101.6	1.2	0.67	0.73	0.52
October 1964	101.8	1.1	0.73	0.47	0.47
South West					
April 1960	91.0	1.9	1.06	1.58	1.05
April 1961	92.6	1.4	0.93	0.96	0.93
October 1961	93.2	1.5	0.94	0.75	0.84
April 1962	93.2	1.8	0.90	1.51	0.80
October 1962	93.9	1.9	0.86	1.40	0.64
April 1963	93.7	2.1	0.78	2.54	0.64
October 1963	93.7	1.9	0.90	1.38	0.63
April 1964	94.9	1.7	0.94	1.22	0.87
October 1964	93.8	1.6	1.07	0.89	0.89
Midlands & Yorkshire & Lincolnshire					
April 1960	102.2	1.1	0.61	0.78	0.52
April 1961	101.8	1.1	0.73	0.58	0.56
October 1961	101.0	1.3	0.81	0.61	0.69
April 1962	101.6	1.5	0.75	1.24	0.66
October 1962	101.3	1.9	0.86	1.85	0.84
April 1963	100.9	2.0	0.74	3.19	0.81
October 1963	100.9	1.5	0.71	1.86	0.85
April 1964	101.4	1.2	0.67	0.81	0.58
October 1964	101.0	1.0	0.67	0.63	0.63

APPENDIX I (Continued)

Region and Date	Regional Earnings as % of U.K. Earnings (1)	% Unemployed in each Region (2)	% Unemployed in Region	Regional Unemployment/Unfilled Vacancy Ratio (4)	Column (4) as Proportion of G.B. Ratio (5)
			% Unemployed in G.B. (3)		
North West					
April 1960	96.4	2.2	1.22	2.10	1.40
April 1961	97.3	1.7	1.13	1.12	1.09
October 1961	97.3	1.7	1.06	1.12	1.26
April 1962	97.3	2.4	1.20	2.54	1.35
October 1962	97.5	2.8	1.27	3.68	1.68
April 1963	97.0	3.3	1.22	6.29	1.59
October 1963	97.0	2.7	1.29	4.03	1.84
April 1964	96.9	2.3	1.28	2.28	1.63
October 1964	97.0	1.9	1.27	1.72	1.72
North					
April 1960	96.7	3.0	1.67	6.20	4.13
April 1961	98.2	2.4	1.60	3.84	3.73
October 1961	97.3	2.5	1.56	3.19	3.58
April 1962	96.7	3.4	1.70	7.53	4.01
October 1962	95·4	4.3	1.95	8.21	3.75
April 1963	95.0	5.1	1.89	16.51	4.17
October 1963	95.2	4.4	2.10	10.72	4.89
April 1964	95.9	3.6	2.00	5.49	3.92
October 1964	95.6	3.1	2.07	4.38	4.38
Scotland					
April 1960	91.7	4.0	2.22	8.46	5.64
April 1961	92.0	3.2	2.13	4.34	4.21
October 1961	92.9	3.0	1.86	3.87	4.35
April 1962	91.4	3.7	1.85	6.74	3.59
October 1962	92.7	3.9	1.77	7.59	3.47
April 1963	92.0	5.2	1.93	13.07	3.30
October 1963	92.5	4.2	2.00	8.32	3.80
April 1964	92.7	4.0	2.22	6.51	4.65
October 1964	93.4	3.3	2.20	4.21	4.21
Wales					
April 1960	101.5	2.9	1.61	3.33	2.22
April 1961	100.7	2.5	1.67	1.70	1.65
October 1961	99.5	3.5	2.19	1.31	1.47
April 1962	100.9	3.0	1.50	3.05	1.62
October 1962	102.2	3.4	1.55	3.78	1.73
April 1963	102.0	3.9	1.44	7.76	1.96
October 1963	101.1	3.0	1.43	3.62	1.65
April 1964	100.7	2.6	1.44	2.31	1.65
October 1964	99.6	2.6	1.73	2.39	2.39

Deane. 'Regional Variations in U.K. Income from Employment 1948.' *Journal of Royal Statistical Society* (Series A), Vol. CXVI, Pt. 11, 1953.

9 See *Ministry of Labour Gazette*, March 1965. Table 4, p. 111.

10 Female Activity rate in 1963 (aged 15 and over) in Wales was 28.2 percent compared with 38.8 per cent for Great Britain.

11 See for example H.A. Turner, measuring unemployment, *Journal of the Royal Statistical Society*, (Series A), Vol. 118, 1955, pp. 28-50.

12 The Great Britain average is used as a point of reference rather than the earnings of any one Standard Region.

13 See R.R. Neild, *Pricing & Employment in the Trade Cycle*, N.I.S.R. Occasional Paper XXI (1963), Chapter 3.

14 The October 1960 unemployment rate are omitted as there is no information on earnings for that month.

15 The inaccurate nature of unfilled vacancies statistics should be borne in mind, but is not considered an insuperable obstacle here where we are concerned with changes in the ratio as indicating general labour market conditions.

16 See A.W. Phillips, 'The Relation Between Unemployment and Rate of Change of Money Wage Rate in the U.K., 1861-1957.' Economica 1958, pp. 283-99, and R.G. Lipsey, 'The Relation between Unemployment and Rate of Change of Money Wage Rates in the U.K. 1862-1957: A Further Analysis' Economica 1960, pp. 1-31.

17 To enable for example, the more frequent publication of clearly understandable maps showing the pattern of regional income: See E.M. Rawstron and B.E. Coates, 'Opportunity and Affluence,' *The Guardian*, 26 July 1965.

Reprinted from *The Manchester School of Economic and Social Studies,* Vol. 34 (1), January, 1966, Manchester University Press, Manchester, with permission.

4 Regional Unemployment as a Cyclical Phenomenon

by A. P. Thirlwall

University of Kent at Canterbury

It is now 21 years since the White Paper on Employment Policy was published[1] which declared that checking of unemployment in particular areas of the country would be an integral part of the commitment to maintain a high and stable level of employment; and it is 20 years since the passing of the Distribution of Industry Act designed to help fulfil that commitment. Yet a glance at the regional unemployment statistics over this period reveals that here has been little real tendency for percentage regional unemployment rate differences to disappear. Taking the national unemployment rate as the norm, and considering the difference between the regional unemployment rate and the national rate as the measure of regional variation, it can be seen from Appendix I that, except in Wales, there has been little improvement in those regions which had positive differences at the beginning of the period.[2] The under-employed Administrative Regions in the nineteen-sixties have been the same as those in the nineteen-forties, and the Annual Reports by the Broad of Trade on the Local Employment Act 1960 reveal that the vast majority of the Development Districts created by that Act are situated within the boundaries of the old Development Areas (abolished by the same Act).[3] Since government policy in the post-war period has been concerned with reducing unemployment disparities between regions, it is the purpose of this paper to suggest a possible cause, which has not been seriously considered before, for its apparent failure. The main argument to be presented is that the persistence of regional unemployment discrepancies (commonly referred to as the 'regional problem') can be at least partially explained by the fact that fluctuations in the percentage level of national unemployment have tended to be associated with unequal changes in the percentage level of unemployment in different regions of the country. This is not a new hypothesis, but one that has not been sufficiently stressed in the light of the evidence that exists to support it. It conjunction with presenting the facts, reasons will be postulated why unemployment may fluctuate more in some regions than others, and attention will be drawn to the implications of regional unemployment as a cyclical phenomenon for future government policy.

The Persistence of the Regional Unemployment Problem

The degree to which unemployment can be considered to have become more or less of a regional problem can be measured by comparing the deviations of regional unemployment percentages from the national norm, at specific dates, to ascertain whether they have narrowed or widened. It can be said that if they have widened unemployment has become more of a regional problem, and if they have narrowed unemployment has become less of a regional problem (and more of a national problem). The standard deviation provides a precise statistical tool for measuring the dispersion of regional unemployment percentages around the national average, and the results of the calculation of these standard deviations for all Standard Administrative Regions and Development Areas are shown in Table 4.1.

The table suggests that the dispersion widens (i.e., the standard deviation rises) as the national unemployment percentage rises, lending support to the hypothesis that the regional problem is partially a cyclical one. It might be argued that, because a given percentage change in the mean will alter the standard deviation by the same per cent., the standard deviation ought to be adjusted to obtain a true measure of dispersion (i.e. that the standard deviation be divided by the mean to obtain the coefficient of variation). This is not necessary for the purpose of measuring the regional unemployment problem, however, because it is more important to know the absolute variations in regional unemployment percentages than the relative dispersion.[4] In other words, it is more realistic to measure the extent of the regional unemployment problem in terms of the pure standard deviation than the coefficient of variation. If this is done by using the figures presented in Table 4.1, it is apparent that, in the Administrative Regions of the country, the regional problem has shown no long run tendency to improve. Indeed, in 1964 the standard deviation was higher than in 1949. In the Development Areas, on the

Table 4.1 Standard Deviations of Regional Unemployment Percentages

Year	Admin. Regions*	Devel. Areas	Percentage Unemployed (U.K.)
(May)			
1949	1.78	2.03	1.5
1950	1.62	1.83	1.5
1951	1.50	1.19	1.0
1952	2.89	1.59	2.2
1953	2.10	1.27	1.6
1954	1.79	1.06	1.4
1955	1.83	1.01	1.0
1956	1.60	0.97	1.1
1957	1.85	0.86	1.5
1958	2.66	1.41	2.1
1959	2.04		2.2
1960	1.79		1.5
1961	1.97		1.3
1962	1.72		1.9
1963	1.98		2.4
1964	1.95		1.6

*All the Administrative Regions including Northern Ireland.
Source: Calculated from Appendix I.

other hand, improvement is discernible, despite a large rise in the deviation in 1958. The questions that need answering, however, are why government policy in the Development Areas was not more successful in reducing discrepancies in percentage unemployment rates from the national mean, and why the regional imbalance in the country as a whole has not been reduced.

Reasons for Persistence of the Regional Problem

Many hypotheses can be advanced to explain this seeming ineffectiveness of government policy in achieving its 1944 objective. During the nineteen-thirties, and the early post-war years, unemployment in the under-employed areas of the country used to be explained almost exclusively in terms of the industrial structure of these areas, i.e. the fact that they had higher percentages of their work force in contracting industries than in expanding industries. In 1939 Professor Dennison remarked, 'it seems that the important feature is not the rate of expansion in the expanding, nor the rate of decrease in the declining industries, but what may be termed the 'initial position' of the areas with respect to the relative importance of the two groups of industries. An area which has but a little of its activity centred on

the declining industries starts with a small problem however rapidly employment in the individual industries may be declining, while, because most industries are of the expanding type, a relatively slow rate of growth will soon solve the problem'[5] Those who stress this type of structural imbalance as the cause of the continuance of the regional problem argue that the main weakness of government policy has lain in its not securing a more even distribution of expanding industries throughout the country. Simple reasoning of this kind, however, overlooks many other derivations of regional unemployment rate differences. An examination of employment statistics, for example, reveals that several of the persistently underemployed areas have not only had a higher than average percentage of their work force in contracting industries, but have also experienced slower growth of employment in expanding industries compared with the country as a whole. This has undoubtedly reduced the ability of these regions to reabsorb unemployed workers, thrown out of work by adverse conditions in both contracting and expanding industries.

Regional unemployment discrepancies may also arise as a result of the percentage level of unemployment varying more in one region than another as the level of national unemployment fluctuates, but this possible cause of the continuance of the regional problem has either been neglected by economists or dismissed. Professor Lomax, for example, dismisses the cyclicality of different regions by combining the underemployed and overemployed regions and saying 'the relationship between the average unemployment rate in the north and that in the south shows no tendency to vary cyclically. In periods of both expansion and stagnation the percentage unemployed in the north has been on average about 2.7 times the average rate in the south'.[6] From the figures he presents this would appear to be so, but such aggregation can disguise significant differences between regions within these divisions of north and south. Dr. Oliver, likewise looking at regional unemployment as a cyclical phenomenon by calculating regional percentage unemployment as a ratio of national percentage unemployment, remarks, 'subject to exceptions, regional unemployment is closely related to national unemployment – in other words that general prosperity or recession affects all regions in much the same sort of way'.[7] However, this is not the conclusion to be drawn from looking at the deviations of regional unemployment rates from the national mean outlined in Appendix I, or from the analysis of the standard deviations of regional unemployment percentages outlined in Table

TABLE 4.2
RELATIONSHIP BETWEEN MOVEMENTS IN REGIONAL AND NATIONAL UNEMPLOYMENT PERCENTAGES

1. ADMINISTRATIVE REGIONS 1949-1964 (MAY)

(a) Areas with unemployment rates persistently below the national average.

	Equation			Level of Significance (2 degrees of freedom)
London & South East	$Y = +0.022 + 0.45$	X	$S_b = 0.17$	$r^2 = 0.704$ (5%)
East & South	$Y = -0.006 + 0.543$	X	$S_b = 0.047$	$r^2 = 0.815$ (1%)
South West	$Y = +0.008 + 0.534$	X	$S_b = 0.229$	$r^2 = 0.645$ (5%)
Midland	$Y = +0.045 + 0.535$	X	$S_b = 0.335$	$r^2 = 0.454$ (–)
North Midland	$Y = +0.028 + 0.798$	X	$S_b = 0.177$	$r^2 = 0.870$ (1%)
East & West Riding	$Y = +0.009 + 1.298$	X	$S_b = 0.267$	$r^2 = 0.885$ (1%)

(b) Areas with unemployment rates persistently above the national average

	Equation			Level of Significance (2 degrees of freedom)
Wales	$Y = -0.09 + 1.134$	X	$S_b = 0.55$	$r^2 = 0.574$ (5%)
Scotland	$Y = +0.096 + 1.066$	X	$S_b = 0.702$	$r^2 = 0.702$ (1%)
North	$Y = +0.030 + 0.873$	X	$S_b = 0.441$	$r^2 = 0.562$ (5%)
North West	$Y = -0.047 + 2.410$	X	$S_b = 0.753$	$r^2 = 0.769$ (1%)

2. DEVELOPMENT AREAS 1949-1958 (MAY)

	Equation			Level of Significance (2 degrees of freedom)
South Wales	$Y = 0.124 + 0.883$	X	$S_b = 0.782$	$r^2 = 0.333$ (–)
South Lancs.	$Y = -0.081 + 2.913$	X	$S_b = 0.951$	$r^2 = 0.786$ (1%)
Wrexham	$Y = -0.103 + 1.065$	X	$S_b = 0.426$	$r^2 = 0.711$ (5%)
West Cumberland	$Y = -0.188 + 1.845$	X	$S_b = 0.426$	$r^2 = 0.882$ (1%)
Scottish	$Y = -0.145 + 1.197$	X	$S_b = 0.348$	$r^2 = 0.717$ (1%)
North East	$Y = -0.136 + 0.722$	X	$S_b = 0.351$	$r^2 = 0.624$ (1%)
Merseyside	$Y = -0.110 + 1.005$	X	$S_b = 0.736$	$r^2 = 0.422$ (–)

Terminology

X = first differences in percentage unemployment in the U.K.

Y = first differences in percentage unemployment in region.

bx = regression coefficient of Y on X.

S_b = standard error of regression coefficient.

r^2 = coefficient of determination.

4.1. Indeed, the purpose of this analysis to follow is (1) to illustrate, more fully, that in the past there have been wide differences in the extent to which the percentage of unemployed in regions has varied with the percentage unemployed in the whole country; (2) to explain why this should be so; and (3) to suggest that the observed lack of improvement in the narrowing of regional unemployment deviations, and the dispersion of regional unemployment rates around the national mean, can perhaps be explained by this cyclical factor.

Variations in Regional Unemployment

On *a priori* grounds, there is no reason to believe that fluctuations in regional and national unemployment rates should be of the same magnitude. Each region has a different industrial composition which will make its sensitivity different when changes in business conditions take place in the country as a whole. Moreover, even if every region was a microcosm of the country as a whole, it is plausible to assume that an industry will differ in its sensitivity as between regions, as the economy alternates between boom and recession. Thus, while during periods of contraction theoretical reasoning and empirical evidence would suggest that employment rises more slowly and unemployment rises more rapidly than in periods of economic expansion, it would be incorrect to assume that all industries and geographic regions are affected in a like manner by the vagaries of the business cycle. The literature on regional unemployment, however, seems to pay scant attention to this fact.

An elementary approach to eliminate this deficiency is to regress a region's unemployment rate on the national unemployment rate to obtain a series of regression coefficients for each region, which can then be used as a measure of the unemployment sensitivity of regions. The results of this exercise for the Administrative Regions 1949-64, and the Development Areas 1949-58, are shown in Table 4.2. The influence of time and autocorrelation have been eliminated by taking the first differences of the successive observations.

The regions with a regression coefficient below the 5 per cent significance level can be ignored. These are: the Midland Administrative Region, and the South Wales and Merseyside Development Areas. Of the regions with percentage unemployment rates persistently below the national average only the East and West Riding Region can be described as cyclically sensitive, with a regression coefficient of bx, = 1.298 (S_b = 0.267). Of the regions with percentage unemployment rates persistently above the national average, only the North Administrative Region and the North East Development Area have a regression coefficient of less than unity, suggesting insensitivity. The bearing that these facts have on the regional problem will be discussed later.

Although the high standard errors of estimation make prediction of the future course of regional unemployment hazardous, it is nonetheless interesting to inquire into the reasons why there should be this marked difference between the sensitivity of regions to changes in national unemployment. The reasons are numerous and varied but can be grouped according to their influence on the two major determinants, (a) the industrial structure of regions, and (b) the sensitivity of an industry between regions. Industrial structure will play a part as a determinant because some industries are more sensitive than others, and the distribution of these industries between regions will therefore influence the sensitivity of regions. But industrial structure alone could not explain all of a region's sensitivity because industries differ in their sensitivity as between regions. In other words, a simple regression exercise of an industry's percentage unemployment rate on the national percentage unemployment rate might reveal that industry to be cyclically sensitive in the country as a whole, but a regression of that same industry's unemployment rate in a region on the national unemployment rate might reveal the industry to be insensitive in that particular region. To determine the influence of these two determinants on regional sensitivity, an assessment of the sensitivity of unemployment in different industries to changes in national unemployment is provided in Table 4.3, and this is followed by a quantitative assessment of the part played by industrial structure in influencing regional sensitivity. To calculate the unemployment sensitivity of industries the same elementary approach has been taken as previously in determining regional sensitivity. Namely, a first difference regression analysis has been performed between the percentage unemployed in an industry (y) and the percentage unemployed nationally (x), for the period 1949-1964.

A rank correlation analysis between the sensitivity of regions and the regional distribution of these industries with different sensitivities produced a coefficient of determination of 0.542 (r^2 = 0.542).[8]

The Sensitivity of Industries to Unemployment

The reasons why unemployment fluctuates more in some industries than others must be looked at from two angles. First, consideration needs to be given to the possibility of some industries being more prone to unemployment when economic activity in the whole economy slackens. Secondly, consideration needs to be given to the fact that it might be more difficult for the unemployed in some industries to be re-absorbed into the labour force, than those from other industries. Alternatively, the consideration is why, when workers from different industries are thrown out of work, some can find new employment more quickly than others.

With regard to the first consideration, some industries are more prone to unemployment than others in times of economic contraction because of the nature of the product they produce, or the service they provide. Durable consumption goods and capital goods are normally thought of as goods which have a relatively elastic demand compared with the demand for services and necessary consumption goods, when the country's level of income changes. One would expect, therefore,

TABLE 4.3
RELATIONSHIP BETWEEN MOVEMENTS IN INDUSTRY AND NATIONAL UNEMPLOYMENT PERCENTAGES 1949-1964 (MAY)

Industry*	Equation		Level of Significance (2 degrees of freedom)
Insurance, Banking & Finance	$Y = +0.042 + 0.129 \ X$	$(S_b = 0.063)$	$r^2 = 0.585$ (5%)
Gas, Electricity & Water	$Y = +0.015 + 0.214 \ X$	$(S_b = 0.100)$	$r^2 = 0.568$ (5%)
Mining & Quarrying	$Y = +0.065 + 0.217 \ X$	$(S_b = 0.177)$	$r^2 = 0.247$ (—)
Prof. & Scientific Sercices	$Y = +0.014 + 0.222 \ X$	$(S_b = 0.071)$	$r^2 = 0.739$ (1%)
Vehicles	$Y = -0.002 + 0.247 \ X$	$(S_b = 0.475)$	$r^2 = 0.081$ (—)
Transport & Communication	$Y = +0.011 + 0.395 \ X$	$(S_b = 0.175)$	$r^2 = 0.620$ (5%)
Agriculture, Forestry & Fishing	$Y = -0.091 + 0.470 \ X$	$(S_b = 0.389)$	$r^2 = 0.321$ (—)
Public Administration & Defence	$Y = -0.017 + 0.482 \ X$	$(S_b = 0.177)$	$r^2 = 0.708$ (5%)
Chemical & Allied Industries	$Y = -0.013 + 0.526 \ X$	$(S_b = 0.120)$	$r^2 = 0.867$ (1%)
Distributive Trades	$Y = +0.030 + 0.545 \ X$	$(S_b = 0.135)$	$r^2 = 0.736$ (1%)
Engineering & Electrical	$Y = -0.007 + 0.561 \ X$	$(S_b = 0.243)$	$r^2 = 0.632$ (5%)
Printing, Paper & Publishing	$Y = -0.005 + 0.645 \ X$	$(S_b = 0.131)$	$r^2 = 0.889$ (1%)
Food, Drink & Tobacco	$Y = +0.019 + 0.813 \ X$	$(S_b = 0.325)$	$r^2 = 0.661$ (5%)
Miscellaneous Services	$Y = -0.016 + 0.820 \ X$	$(S_b = 0.287)$	$r^2 = 0.726$ (5%)
Metal Goods not elsewhere specified	$Y = +0.024 + 0.854 \ X$	$(S_b = 0.408)$	$r^2 = 0.587$ (5%)
Bricks, Pottery, Glass & Cement	$Y = -0.021 + 1.015 \ X$	$(S_b = 0.263)$	$r^2 = 0.828$ (1%)
Metal Manufacturers	$Y = +0.112 + 1.159 \ X$	$(S_b = 1.000)$	$r^2 = 0.300$ (—)
Construction	$Y = +0.076 + 1.166 \ X$	$(S_b = 0.525)$	$r^2 = 0.615$ (5%)
Timber, Furniture	$Y = \qquad + 1.342 \ X$	$(S_b = 0.556)$	$r^2 = 0.653$ (5%)
Shipbuilding & Marine Eng.	$Y = +0.224 + 1.406 \ X$	$(S_b = 1.770)$	$r^2 = 0.286$ (—)
Other Manufacturing	$Y = -0.082 + 1.505 \ X$	$(S_b = 0.465)$	$r^2 = 0.772$ (1%)
Clothing & Footwear	$Y = +0.018 + 1.506 \ X$	$(S_b = 1.116)$	$r^2 = 0.396$ (—)
All Manufacturing	$Y = -0.043 + 1.676 \ X$	$(S_b = 0.395)$	$r^2 = 0.854$ (5%)
Leather, Leather Goods & Fur	$Y = -0.099 + 2.437 \ X$	$(S_b = 0.817)$	$r^2 = 0.743$ (5%)
Textiles	$Y = -0.360 + 7.758 \ X$	$(S_b = 4.320)$	$r^2 = 0.510$ (—)

*The figures for unemployment were adjusted to allow for the change in the Standard Industrial Classification 1958.

Terminology

X	=	first differences in percentage unemployment in the U.K.
Y	=	first differences in percentage unemployment in the industry.
bx	=	regression coefficient of Y on X.
S_b	=	standard error of regression coefficient.
r^2	=	coefficient of determination.

the Insurance, Banking and Finance industries to be less prone to unemployment than the Metal Manufacturing industries. Such an expectation might not be reflected in the statistics, however, if the workers thrown out of the Metal Manufacturing industries could find new employment with little delay, whereas the workers made redundant in Insurance, Banking and Finance found great difficulty in securing new employment. This is where the second consideration becomes important. In this respect, it is possible to cite many factors which will influence the degree to which the unemployed from an industry can be re-absorbed into the labour force. Perhaps the foremost centre around the nature of the industry, the type of worker it employs and the sociological environment in which the industry operates. If the unemployed labour is fairly specific to an industry, it is less likely to seek new employment in the knowledge that it would be difficult to find due to limitation of skills. The sociological environment in which the industry is situated, and in which the workforce lives, will influence the willingness of the unemployed to move geographically to a new place of work. The ease with which new jobs can be secured will depend on the rate at which employment is growing in alternative occupations, and the competition for jobs. This latter factor will be a function of the number of unemployed, the type of unemployment, and the number of new additions to the labour force in the form of school leavers and women seeking active participation in the labour force.

Bordering on both these considerations, which must be taken into account when discussing the unemployment sensitivity of an innustry, is the question of how an industry reacts to changes in business conditions with regard to the dismissal and recruitment of workers. Here, the nature of the industry becomes important again. An industry employing unskilled, wage labour is more likely to dismiss workers in bad times than an industry employing predominantly salaried staff and/or skilled labour. Professor Pigou contends than in industries with heavy fixed costs there will be a tendency towards instituting short-time rather than dismissing hands outright.[9] Beveridge also stresses this question of the reaction of industries as a determinant of the sensitivity of unemployment in industry in saying, '. . . unemployment depends not only on the demand for labour, but on the way industry responds to changes in demand'.[10]

The Sensitivity of an Industry between Regions

The correlation exercise between the sensitivity of regions and their weighted industrial composition, however, revealed that only one-half of the sensitivity of regions seemed to be accounted for by the uneven distribution of sensitive and insensitive industries.[11] The remainder of the variance, therefore, must be due to the fact that industries have different sensitivities as between regions. This is to be expected. It is quite possible that, due to sociological environment, the attitudes of the work force and the alternative employment opportunities etc., an industry will suffer proportionately more unemployment in one region than in another or in the country as a whole. Important in this connection is the fact that the nature of the industrial units is quite likely to vary from one region to another. One region might

have a predominance of branch plants in which production in bad times is slowed down earlier than in the parent firm situated in another part of the country. It may also be the case that the same industry produces different products in different regions, the demands for which differ during the phases of the business cycle.

To determine the sensitivity of the same industry in different regions, further first difference regression analysis could be undertaken between the percentage unemployment rate of an industry in the different regions and the national percentage unemployment rate. This is not attempted here because such an exercise would be of considerable magnitude, and divert attention from the major argument of the paper.

Implications of the Analysis for Government Policy

It has been shown that there seems to have been a tendency in existence, over the period 1949-64, for unemployment in the under-employed regions to vary more than in proportion to the national average; and unemployment in the overemployed regions to vary less than in proportion to the national average. Reasons have also been advanced as to why regions might differ in their sensitivity. What bearing do these facts have on the apparent lack of effectiveness of government policy in reducing the dispersion of regional unemployment rates around the national mean? Firstly, the theoretical implications of the analysis must be looked at. If some regions have higher unemployment percentages than the national average and are, at the same time, cyclically sensitive, this must mean that these areas will remain permanently underemployed in relation to the country as a whole unless, (a) the sensitivity of the region can be increased in the downward direction (i.e. when national unemployment falls), and decreased in the upward direction (i.e. when national unemployment rises), or (b) the higher unemployment percentage can be eliminated by government action which might, in turn, necessitate reducing the cyclical factor. Secondly, if there is a long-run upward trend in the national unemployment percentage, then the positive unemployment deviations of those underemployed regions, which are cyclically sensitive, can be expected to widen over time because the areas will experience falls in their rate of unemployment which are less than the rises. The graph in Figure 4.1 would seem to indicate that there has been such a long-run upward trend in national unemployment, and this would imply that government policy has been working against an unfavourable circumstance, not fully realised.

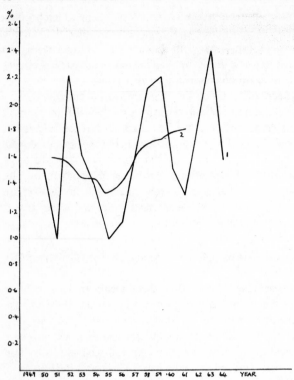

Figure 4.1 Percentage Unemployment in the U.K. 1949-1964 (May)

1. Annual percentage unemployment
2. Long-run trend (five year moving average).

Looking at this cyclical phenomenon in practice, it is possible to find many occasions on which the excessive sensitivity of regions, already underemployed, has offset the positive successes of government in reducing their unemployment differential. The most notable occasions have been during the recessions of 1951 to 1952, 1957 to 1958 and 1961 to 1963 when, taking the May figures, unemployment in the U.K. rose by 115 per cent., 43 per cent and 76 per cent respectively. In each of these recessions several of the underemployed areas experienced more than proportionate increases in unemployment compared with the increase for the U.K. Moreover, prior to these recessions, the deviations of many of the underemployed regions' unemployment rates from the national rate had been virtually eliminated, as can be seen in Appendix I.

If the magnitude of the regional unemployment problem can be measured in terms of the dispersion of regional unemployment rates around the national mean (and the regional problem worsens as the national unemployment rate rises), and government is concerned with maximising the efficacy of its policy to reduce the regional unemployment problem, then it would appear that government has two major courses open to it. Firstly, to pursue a combination of policies to ensure steady employment growth, so that fluctuations in the level of national unemployment do not become pronounced. Secondly, to take differential policy measures to ensure that regions suffer or benefit more equally as national conditions deteriorate or improve. This latter policy would necessitate a thorough survey into the precise reasons why some areas are more sensitive than others. Given that a region's sensitivity is a function of the behaviour of the industries that are to be found in it, however, it would appear that one of the government's tasks should be to exercise more care in deciding on the types of industries that it encourages to particular regions. Regions which are known to be sensitive should not, if possible, have a disproportionate amount of sensitive industries directed to them. It is these regions in which the more stable service industries need to be encouraged. The pursuance of these aims would not be easy, however. In the first place, the expansion of sensitive industries in underemployed areas provides valuable employment, and not to direct a sensitive industry to an underemployed area may condemn that area to permanent underemployment. The expansion of the Metal Manufacturing industry in Wales can be taken as an example of this dilemma. The direction of the industry to the region since 1945 has provided valuable employment for the unemployed, yet it was the excessive sensitivity of the industry in the 1957-58 recession that caused unemployment in both the South Wales Development Area, and Wales as a whole, to increase by more than in proportion to the national average, bringing the percentage unemployed in Wales to its highest level since 1949.[12]

The increased sensitivity of the North Region would also seem to reflect the industries that have moved and expanded there in the last decade.[13]

In the second place, the government cannot exert influence over the distribution of service industries without the statutory power to do so. At present, it does not possess this power. Furthermore, it would be optimistic to expect a natural disproportionate expansion of service industries in the underemployed, sensitive regions, because it is in these regions that the population is expanding least rapidly, and the growth of most service industries tends to be closely linked with growths of population and income.[14]

The long run solution to the problem of regional unemployment as a cyclical phenomenon will be found only when more research into the causes of sensitivity, as opposed to insensitivity, has been undertaken. Only then can appropriate policy be formulated.

Acknowledgement

I am indebted to Professor K. Lomax, Professor D.J. Robertson and Mr P. Harris for helpful comments on the draft of this paper.

Notes and References

1 Employment Policy, Cmnd. 6527, London H.M.S.O., May, 1944.
2 These areas are to be referred to as underemployed regions.
3 See, for example, *the Fourth Annual Report by the Board of Trade for the year ended 31st March, 1964.* London, H.M.S.O., 30th July, 1964, pp. 13-14.
4 This can be illustrated by the following example. Suppose that in year 1 national unemployment is 1.5 per cent.; the standard deviation of regional unemployment percentages is 1.8; the minimum regional unemployment deviation from the mean is −1.0 per cent, and the maximum regional unemployment deviation from the mean is + 5.0 per cent. Then suppose that, in year 2, all regions double their percentage unemployment rate causing the national unemployment rate to rise to 3.0 per cent; the standard deviation to rise to 3.6 per cent, and the minimum and maximum regional deviations from the mean to change to −2.0 per cent and + 10.0 per cent respectively. A use of the coefficient of variation would indicate no change in the state of the regional unemployment problem (i.e. $\frac{1.8}{1.5} = \frac{3.6}{3.0}$), despite the fact that the range of difference between regional unemployment percentages had become much greater (i.e. from −1.0 per cent + 5.0 per cent to −2.0 per cent = + 10.0 per cent).

5 S. Dennison, *Location of Industry and Depressed Areas*, London, O.U.P. 1939, p. 148.
6 K. Lomax, *The Less Prosperous Areas of the U.K.*, London and Cambridge Economic Bulletin No. 47, September 1963, p. xi.
7 F. Oliver, 'Interregional Migration and Unemployment 1951-61', *Journal of the Royal Statistical Society*, Series A, Vol. 1217, Part 1, 1964, p. 48.
8 By the t test, r^2 is significant at the 2 per cent level with 2 degrees of freedom. The technique used was to take the average percentage of the labour force in each industrial group in each region, and to weight this percentage by the industry's sensitivity index (ie. bx, for each industry). For all regions, the sum of these calculations, divided by the sum of the weights, was correlated with the regional sensitivity indices.
9 A. Pigou, *Unemployment,* London, William and Norgate, 1913, p. 197.
10 W. Beveridge *Full Employment in a Free Society*, London, George, Allen and Unwin, 1944, p. 51.
11 See footnote 9, p. 00.
12 Of the increase in unemployment of 12,981 in Wales between May, 1957, and May, 1958, 4,582 was due to unemployment in metal manufacturing. The increase in unemployment in metal manufacturing in Wales was 123 per cent more than in metal manufacturing in the U.K.
13 Between 1961 and 1963, unemployment increased 47 per cent more than in the U.K., whereas in the 1957-58 recession unemployment increased 42 per cent less than in the U.K.
14 A.P. Thirlwall, 'Reply to Mr. Holmans on "Restrictions of Expansion in S.E. England"'. *Oxford Economic Papers,* Vol. 17, No. 2, July 1965, p. 340.

Reprinted from *Scottish Journal of Political Economy*, Vol. 13 (2), June, 1966, Oliver & Boyd, Edinburgh, with permission.

Part II
Macro Analysis

Introduction

The purpose of this section is to present papers which examine the proposition that the prosperity of a region is often a consequence of its economic relations with other regions. The most important of these are commodity flows but there may also be capital transfers and invisible trades which contribute to a region's comparative affluence or poverty. Such an approach to inter-regional differences has parallels in the study of international trade and the supposed effects of a nation's trading performance on its rate of economic growth. For this reason many of the papers included in this selection represent borrowings and adaptations of international trade theory.

It is an established fact of both economic history and economic geography that inter-regional trading systems occur. Only on rare occasions can a region be considered as having developed in effective isolation. The reasons for the existence of inter-regional trade are explored in the paper by Ullman (p. 52). He argues first that complementarity between regions is a pre-condition of inter-regional trade. By complementarity he appears to be identifying the concept known to classical international trade theory as comparative advantage. Furthermore the concept might be extended to the use of 'back to back' supply and demand curves and of linear programming. Complementarity together with the concepts of transferability and intervening opportunity provides a sufficient intuitive understanding of why inter-regional trading systems exist (Bressler and King, 1970).

In the second paper Morawski (p. 67) demonstrates how difficult it is to monitor inter-regional exchanges within a single country even when that country has a commitment to central planning. The second part of Morawski's paper introduces the central theme of this section; that favourable inter-regional trading balances appear to be correlated with a higher than average share of the national income and higher than average regional growth rates. Other studies have identified similar balances and suggested similar associations in other countries but the problems of monitoring trade flows within a country often prove insurmountable (Hay and Smith, 1970; Finner, 1959); indeed in some countries more progress has been made by imputing inter-regional trade from known regional patterns of production and consumption (Boudeville, 1961). At this stage it must be stressed that, although for most regions commodity trade with other regions in the country is the most significant form of trade, some regions' favourable trading balances may be derived from trade with regions in other countries. Similarly, although in most cases commodity trade constitutes the major part of a region's imports and exports, some regions within a country may depend upon 'invisible imports and exports' to maintain a trading balance. For example there are regions which benefit greatly from tourist receipts.

Traditionally it was argued that all regions pass through a sequence of stages and that the sequence is marked by increasing industrialisation, increasing inter-regional trade, and increasing wealth (usually associated with Hoover, 1948), but the consideration of inter-regional economic relations led North (p. 76) to reject this approach and see inter-regional trade as a cause not a consequence of regional growth. North's argument focuses upon the 'export staples' or chief commodities produced by a region for export. He argues that not only does the success of export staples (collectively the 'export base') determine the level of absolute and per capita income in the region in the short term but that it also controls the economic growth of regions in the long run. Although there is no space to explore the wide literature to which this theory has given rise it must be noted that not all authors have accepted North's argument in its entirety. Tiebout in particular has suggested that reality is more complex than North supposes. Tiebout suggests two amendments to North's analysis. Firstly he claims that a region's income is not only affected by the size of its export base, but is also affected by both the amount of private and public investment in that region and the scale of residential industry. Secondly he stresses that the role played by the export base is dependent on the size of the region; the larger the region the less the importance of the export base as a determinant of regional economic growth (Tiebout, 1956).

If North's reasoning is accepted two types of region are identifiable. The regions with an expansion in staple commodity trades have a number of possible responses. In the short run the balances may be spent entirely in the expansion of consumption. Although such consumption may lead to an increase in imports it may also encourage the expansion of economic production within the region. If the short run balances are saved then the choice of a location for the investment of savings becomes significant. Investment within the region will tend to increase the region's productive capacity or improve its infrastructure. Investment outside the region on the other hand will, if successful, result in a flow of interest, profits and repayments to the region. In nearly all cases the region with a balance receives an increment of economic growth. On the other hand there is no guarantee that the positive balances will be maintained. Increased wealth within the region may divert the productive resources from the production of export staples to the satisfaction of local demand. An implication of this is that the relative cost advantage which previously favoured the region ceases to exist. In the slightly longer run the exports of the staple may decline due to the exhaustion of natural resources or declining world demand.

For a region with a trading deficit similar arguments apply. The deficit may show in declining profits or indebtedness of institutions and individuals within the region to investors outside the region. The possibilities of such short run adjustments taking place within a banking system are discussed in the paper by Ingram (p. 88). Smith (p. 96) takes the argument further for both surplus and deficit regions. He demonstrates that as long as the fundamental character of the inter-regional trading system remains unchanged the relative position of the regions will be unchanged even by the injection of investment or loans. Furthermore regions, unlike nations, have limited influence on imports, exports, and money supply and within a country, currency devaluation is not possible for a region with balance of payment problems.

The long run effects of export decline are to reduce incomes and living standards within the region. The response to such a decline may be two-fold. In the first place the region may seek a more successful export base. Such a diversification away from former export staples may be initiated by a fall in returns from investment or a fall in wage rates. In both cases there is evidence that decision makers are reluctant to initiate such changes of role. Miernyk's paper (p. 103) highlights the reluctance of a labour force to change in this way even when the alternative is lower wages or unemployment.

The second possible response is to initiate out-migration, although here too there is evidence of reluctance to change. The migration of people from a declining region is too often judged a 'good thing' or a 'bad thing' in simplistic terms but the paper by Okun and Richardson argues that the truth is more complex. In some regions out-migration will further damage a region's economy, in others it will assist it in staging a recovery. In discussing the effects of such migration it must be remembered that if the decline in a region's aggregate income is less than the decline in population, the net effect may be a rise in per capita incomes. Thus the absolute decline of a region does not necessarily imply a long-run decline in the welfare of those individuals who remain.

The final point to note is that these processes of adjustment are relatively slow but the economic decline can be relatively rapid. If this occurs there is considerable economic stress and perhaps personal suffering before any adjustment takes place. If this is acknowledged (and these effects are deemed undesirable) it constitutes a case for government intervention which will be explored in the final section.

Alan Hay

References

Boudeville, J.R. (1961) 'An operational model of regional trade in France', *Papers and Proceedings of the Regional Science Association, 7*, 177-87.

Bressler, R.G. and King, R.A. (1970) *Markets, prices and interregional trade*, Wiley, New York.

Finner, W.F. (1959) 'Inter-state and inter-region flows for agricultural products', *Journal of Farm Economics, 41*, 1050-64.

Hay, A.M. and Smith, R.H.T. (1970) *Inter-regional trade and money flows in Nigeria, 1964*, Oxford University Press, Ibadan.

Hoover, E.M. (1948) *The location of economic activity*, McGraw Hill, New York.

Tiebout, C.M. (1956) 'Exports and regional economic growth', *Journal of Political Economy, 64*, 160-5.

5 The Role of Transportation and the Bases for Interaction

by Edward L. Ullman
University of Washington at Seattle

Few forces have been more influential in modifying the earth than transportation, yet transportation itself is a result of other forces. Nor have the main results of transportation been the mere scratches of transport construction on the surface of the earth. Such traces, important locally and changing as we shall see, are really significant even on the habitable portions of the globe.

In order to define the role of transportation on the earth's surface, it is instructive to broaden the concept of transportation to the French *circulation*, which includes all movement and communication. Circulation, then, is basic to spatial interaction and thus to the geographic term 'situation.' Situation refers to the effects of phenomena in one area on another area. Specific processes relevant to situation include diffusion, centralization, migration, or transportation. Situation contrasts with 'site,' which refers to local, underlying areal conditions, such as type of soil correlated with type of agriculture. Site thus might be conceived as a vertical relationship; situation, as a horizontal one.

As early as 1890 Mackinder noted this dualism: 'The chief distinction in political geography seems to be founded on the facts that man travels and man settles.'

An example of alternate interpretation based, respectively, on site and on situation is provided by the age-old puzzle of assigning reasons for the growth of particular civilizations in particular places. Thus Toynbee, in his challenge-and-response theory, uses a site concept with a new twist — the challenging effect of a relatively poor environment. Gourou (1949), in reviewing this concept, poses the following query: Does the substitution of the effects of an unfavorable environment for the effects of a favorable one represent progress over previous interpretations based on environmental determinism? He poses as an alternate possibility a situation concept — the rise of civilizations in favored corridors for interaction, so that contact with other civilizations and contrasting ideas was facilitated, as in parts of Europe. Without going into the merits of either explanation, we would hold that undoubtedly site, situation, and other factors as well are all involved in any total understanding.

Basic to this process of interaction is the ease or difficulty of movement and communication. A host of authors justifiably, though perhaps not too critically, attest to the overwhelming importance of transportation and communication. With considerable logic, many scholars regard the early stages of the industrial revolution to be more properly labeled as the 'transportation revolution' (Taylor, 1951).

Economists and others have recognized through the ages that, in general, trade and improvements in transportation to facilitate it raise the standard of living of all parties concerned, although not necessarily equally. Thus Cammann writes (1951, p. 96) that Samuel Turner reported from his mission to Tibet in 1783 as follows:

> Necessity had developed a commerce that was only languidly conducted by a naturally lazy people. He felt, however, that once the Tibetans had become acquainted with the pleasures of luxury and the profits of commerce, they would be roused from their apathy and would feel the need for a higher standard of living.

Some Effects of Improved Transportation

Improvement in transportation and circulation has produced two contrasting and contradictory results: (1) In many cases it has made the world and its people more alike, since they are enabled to share ideas, products, and services; this aspect has been stressed most by social scholars and undoubtedly is of great importance. (2) Simultaneously, in many cases it has made areas more unlike, since each region has been enabled to specialize in activities it can do best, whether based on factors of production related to land, labor, capital, or simply economies of scale.

This latter has been emphasized by numerous students of transportation and economics and would appear to be the more important factor in the physical modification of the earth by man. Let us consider it in more detail.

Effect on Areal Specialization

Areal specialization promoted by improved transportation has resulted, in part, in the creation of large, monolithic, particularized production areas tied to distant markets. The wheat belts, corn belts, and truck areas in agriculture and the specialized manufacturing belts in industry have become the characteristic land-use features of the modern commerical world. This has produced a pattern drastically different from that of earlier subsistence economies, with little or no transportation, or even from the spatial economy envisaged in 1826 by von Thünen in his famous *Der isolierte Staat* as concentric rings of land use around a central-city market, their intensity being dictated by transport costs.

The chief change that transport improvement has wrought is in the scale of areal differentiation. Within the large specialized agricultural areas, for example, there is less subregional differention now than formerly, inasmuch as a wide range of subsistence or locally transportable crops need not be grown.

Some features of von Thünen's rings persist. Location near market is still important, as witness, for example, Bogue's (1949) studies on dominance and subdominance, wherein he shows that in the United States counties near metropolises tend to have denser population and greater development than counties farther out. This is due in part to easier access and in part, I am sure, to the fact that cities tend to be located near the middle of productive areas, in line with the 'central-place' theory (Christaller, 1935; Ullman, 1941). Bogue also notes that development tends to be greater in sectors along the main connecting transport lines, as would be expected and as is confirmed for most of the world by a mere glance at population maps.

The extraordinary development of steam navigation and steam railroads in the nineteenth century especially precipitated a drastic rearrangement of settlement patterns in much of the world. Wheat-growers in many parts of Europe were forced out of business by overseas competition. New England farmers abandoned their hill farms, particularly from the 1830's on, and moved to the superior farm lands of the Middle West or to new manufacturing opportunities in the cities. In much of New England the rural areas became among the least populous in America, the fields reverted to woodland, and only the indestructible stone walls remained as reminders that the land had once been farmed.

Conversely, in some cases transportation has enabled the natural environment to be 'corrected.' In France, for example, the construction of railroads permitted lime to be transported cheaply to poor fields and thus increased agricultural yields (Fromont, 1948, pp. 66-69). Fertilizer of course is now widely transported around many parts of the world and is a feature of modern agriculture.

Specialization, made possible by transportation, has also produced some of the evils associated with one-crop farming and excessive specialization. However, it seems reasonable to assume that such specialization, on balance, is probably more beneficial 'ecologically' than harmful. Steep slopes or other poor areas near markets, for example, no longer need be farmed. The forest is taking over such areas throughout the northeastern United States, as Klimm (1954) has shown.

Effect on Cities

Cities, the principal seats of population in the Western world, have long been intimately related to transportation. Their very existence on a large scale was made possible by the development of means to transport farm surplus to them. It was of course necessary that there first be a farm surplus, as Adam Smith (1937, p. 357) and others have noted (Sombart, 1916, pp. 130-31). This has been contingent on improvement in farming technique, a process still going on, as witness the declining number of farmers in much of the world. The specific city-building factor, however, is not the mere focusing of routes on a city but rather the transferring of goods from one form of transportation to another – a break in bulk as between land and water (Cooley, 1894; Harris and Ullman, 1945). Where goods must be handled, storage or further processing tends to develop.

Cities have long recognized their dependence on transportation and have sought to improve their connections. It has been standard practice for cities to subsidize transport routes to or through them. Some cities even built their own lines, for example, Cincinnati, which still owns the Cincinnati, New Orleans, and Texas Pacific, connecting the city with the South and now leased to the Southern Railway. Much of the historical geography of the eastern seaboard of the United States since independence is related to the struggles of the principal ports to gain access to the interior.

In newer parts of the country the railroads in many cases preceded extensive settlement and virtually created cities; on the other hand, some of them failed to touch major centers because of the multiplicity of competing lines. A somewhat chaotic geography is the result. In New England the rail pattern developed somewhat more rationally without a multiplicity of competing lines. Here the urban centers had been already established; the larger cities were able to put up more money than the smaller ones and thus obtained rail routes to reinforce their dominance (Kirkland, 1948). In many parts of Europe, also, the dominance of political capitals was strengthened by rail construction.

Effect of Freight Rates

The rate practices of transportation are often said to produce an artificial, 'unnatural' economic geography. To a degree this may well be true in many specialized cases. A well-established practice, for example, is to charge less than total-cost rates (sufficiently high to cover out-of-pocket or variable costs) for low-value commodities which cannot afford to pay high costs and to recoup the difference on higher-value commodities. In consequence, low-value, bulk commodities tend to be moved longer distances, and higher-value commodities shorter distances, than might otherwise be the case (Penrose, 1952).

How much the monopolistic rate practices cited by Penrose actually affect major flows in the United States is difficult to determine. The largest-volume haul of one commodity in the United States, for example, is coal from West Virginia and Virginia to the Middle West and the eastern seaboard (see Fig. 166, p. 874). The three principal coal-carriers (Norfolk and Western, Chesapeake and Ohio, and Virginian) obtain the overwhelming bulk of their revenue from this one commodity. It is likely, therefore, that their rates do cover total costs, since these three roads are the most profitable railroads in the United States (Lambie, 1954).

A generalized hypothesis that I would like to advance concerning the effect of freight rates is that they often tend to accentuate and perpetuate initial differences between areas. Most freight traffic, at least in the United States, moves on so-called 'commodity rates' specifically established from point of origin to point of destination. Low rates are granted on volume movements, which specialization tends to foster. Thus new areas or small producers may find it difficult to compete initially. Alexander found (1944) that the fertile, cash-grain area of central Illinois had low rail rates per mile to principal markets for its chief product — corn — and high rates on cattle, whereas rates in the less fertile cattle-producing area of western Illinois were reversed — low on cattle and high on corn. The rate structure thus tends to accentuate and perpetuate areal specialization based on natural conditions.

Much work remains to be done on interpreting the multiplicity of freight rates in meaningful geographical terms. Previous research has been concerned largely with regulatory or pricing aspects. Through new research the proposed generalization can be tested, and others may well emerge.

Effects of New and Varied Mediums of Transport

Improvements in transportation have tended to promote concentration and long hauls and thus to change the scale of the earth's regions. Rate structures, including former 'basing-point' systems, work in the same direction, as do the relatively low ton-mile rates applied to carloads, trainloads, and shiploads and on long hauls. This contributes to the growth of large cities, to large and more distant production areas, and to the elimination or reduction of, for example, small ports and some small producing areas.

Certain more recent developments, however, may be working in the opposite direction, namely, the use of the automobile in transportation and the telephone in communication, both of which are pre-eminently short-distance connectors. One of the main effects of the automobile is to provide uniform transport service throughout an area and thus to open all of it to interaction. In American cities the automobile has had the spectacular effect of opening up interstices between former transport 'spokes' on the periphery of cities and thus has increased the area available for urban settlement far more than the distance to work. Thus, if the radius of a city doubles during growth, the maximum length of journey to the center of the city also doubles, but the area available for settlement increased four-fold. Areas tributary to cities have become similarly accessible, and the spacing of cities thus has been made more regular. We are still adjusting to the effects of this revolutionary, universal transport medium.

Forms of transportation differ in their ability to overcome terrain and other features of the environment. When draft animals were used, forage was all-important, and routes were selected for good grazing conditions. The first railroad in South Africa, from Cape Town across the arid Cape Flats, was laid out partly because there was no forage for animals along this barren stretch (Goodfellow, 1931). To give but one more of possible examples, of all the forms of land transportation, if canals be excluded, railroads are the most sensitive to grades; hence the choice among alternative routes is more restricted for a railroad line than it is for a highway.

Developments in transportation have changed the impact on man of features of the natural environment. A mountain range is not the same phenomenon to canal-boats, steam locomotives, diesel engines, automobiles, trucks, jeeps, horses, yaks, pipelines, electric wires, airplanes, and radios. Advances in construction technology have also drastically altered the effects of terrain. Early railroads, built by men and animals, avoided extensive excavation and substituted curves or steep grades. The revolutionary improvement in earth-moving equipment in recent years has drastically cut excavation costs, in spite of great increases in labor and other costs. As a result, railroads and highways are realigning their routes; they are creating new and bolder marks on the earth's surface.

General Effects of Transportation Changes and the Effort Devoted to Movement

Interaction in the modern world has been enormously increased by improvements in transportation. The great trade routes of the past were mere trickles compared to today's volume flows. Bulk movements of raw materials even remotely comparable to the shipments which come daily to a modern steel plant were unknown. Each area of concentrated settlement, therefore, had to produce most of its own fuel, food, and other necessities, and trade was restricted largely to luxury items that could stand the high cost of shipment. To be sure, the relative cheapness of transportation by water permitted a certain amount of crop specialization even in sailing-ship days, as witness the dependence of Athens on the wheatlands of what is now the Ukraine and the dependence of Rome on grain shipped by sea from Egypt and other parts of North Africa. The partial dependence of Great Britain on specialized producing areas overseas also began before the development of modern forms of transportation. As just one example, the introduction of superior English ships into the Mediterranean in the fifteenth century in part made feasible winter navigation even in that inland sea (Braudel, 1949).

Transportation consumes an important part of the world's energy. In a modern industrial country like the United States, I estimate that about 20 per cent of the labor force is directly or indirectly employed in the operation, servicing, manufacturing, and selling of transportation and communication facilities. In a primitive society, equipped with little or no machinery, the daily output of energy is also great, as each person laboriously moves things from place to place within a small area. But the volume and distance of movement are small; the scale and range of spatial relations are likewise small.

It may be that the energy devoted to transport in primitive societies is as great as in modern ones, even though movement is negligible. Specialists in transportation operation or manufacture are few, and much movement is dependent on part-time efforts of others. For example, on the northern China plain in the 1930's great distances were not traversed by carts, in part because the farmers who provided the service were loath to leave their farms untended for more than three or four days (Yang, 1944). Even in the United States farmers not long ago had to devote much energy to local hauls, as the following statement of an Iowa farmer indicates (Moe and Taylor, quoted in Atherton, 1954, pp. 238-39):

> Years ago to haul hogs to market, I had to get the help of five of my neighbors. In 6 wagons we would carry 30 hogs. We went 5½ miles to the railroad stop in Irwin. I had to buy a meal for the men and myself. Generally it cost me about 50 cents apiece. Those men ate a real meal, not a lunch. That's $3. To put the 6 teams in the livery barn cost $1.20. Because I had the men come and help me, I had to go and help them, which meant 5 days of work off the farm for myself and my team. The cash cost alone was $4.50. Today, I can hire a trucker to take 25 or 30 hogs to Harlan, more than twice as far, for only $2.50. He can get them there and be back in 2 hours. And I don't have to spend any time off the farm.

The Bases for Transportation and Interaction

Transport is seldom improved without a demand. Many immigrants came to the United States before the steam-boat was perfected, and settlers began to push across the Appalachians before the Erie Canal or the railroads were built (Healy, 1947). Improvements in transportation alone, although important, were not as a rule responsible for the whole of increased interaction between places. What, then, are the conditions under which interaction develops? The following three-factor system is proposed for explanation.

1 Complementarity

It has been asserted that circulation or interaction is a result of areal differentiation. To a degree this is true, but mere differentiation does not produce interchange. Numerous different areas in the world have no connection with each other.

In order for two areas to interact, there must be a demand in one and a supply in the other. Thus an automobile industry in one area would use the tires produced in another but not the buggy whips produced in still another. Specific complementarity is required before interchange takes place.

So important is complementarity that relatively low-value bulk products move all over the world, usually utilizing, it is true, relatively cheap water transport for most of the haul. Some cheap products in the distant interior of continents, however, also move long distances. Thus, when the steel mills were built in Chicago, they reached out as far as West Virginia to get suitable supplies of coking coal, in spite of the fact that the distance was more than five hundred miles by land transport and that the coal was of relatively low value.

Complementarity is a function both of natural and cultural areal differentiation and of areal differentiation based simply on the operation of economies of scale (Ohlin, 1933). One large plant may be so much more economical than several smaller ones that it can afford to import raw materials and ship finished products great distances, such as specialized logging equipment from Washington to forest areas of the South. In this case the similarity of the two regions in other respects provides the market and encourages the interaction. This, however, is generally insufficient to affect significantly total interaction, because specialized products dominate the total trade of many regions. Thus total shipments from Washington to the southern states are low because of the dominance of forest products in each (Figures 5.1 and 5.2). On the other hand, flows of animals and products from Iowa to the complementary Industrial Belt and California are heavy, even though these are far away (Figures 5.3 and 5.4).

An example of similarity producing complementarity is provided by the overseas Chinese, who furnish a significant market for the export handicrafts and other products of the mother-country (Herman, 1954). The same occurs with Italians and other transplanted nationals. Perhaps we could generalize and say that similar cultures in different natural environments tend to promote interchange.

2 Intervening opportunity

Complementarity, however, generates interchange between two areas only if no intervening source of supply is available. Thus, sixty years ago, few forest products moved from the Pacific North-west to the markets of the interior Northeast, primarily because the Great Lakes area provided an intervening source. Florida attracts more amenity migrants from the Northeast then does more distant California. It is probable that many fewer people go from New Haven to Philadelphia than would be the case if there were no New York City in between. This, presumably, is a manifestation of Stouffer's law of intervening opportunity (1940), a fundamental determinant of spatial interaction.

Under certain circumstances intervening opportunity might ultimately help to create interaction between distant complementary areas by making construction of intermediate transport routes profitable and thus paying part of the cost of constructing a route to the more distant source. On a small scale this occurs with logging railroads: a line is extended bit by bit as timber nearer the mill is exhausted, whereas, if the line had had to be constructed over the long distance initially, it might never have been built. On a larger and more complex scale this is what happens in transcontinental railroads — every effort is made to develop way business, and, as this business develops, it contributes to some of the fixed costs for long-distance interchange.

3 Transferability

A final factor required in an interaction system is transferability or distance, measured in real terms of transfer and time costs. If the distance between market and supply is too great and too costly to overcome, interaction will not take place in spite of perfect complementarity and lack of intervening opportunity. Alternate goods will be substituted where possible; for instance, bricks will be used instead of wood.

Thus we might consider that the factor of *intervening opportunity* results in a *substitution of areas* and that the factor of *transferability* results in a *substitution of products.*

It is a mistake to assume that every place in the world is linked equally with every other place in the world. Distance and intervening opportunity drastically trim the relative quantity of such dramatic, long-distance relationships, which international trade enthusiasts like to emphasize. Great Britain and the United States provide contrasting examples. To reach enough complementary sources, Britain must trade with the world. The United States, on the other hand, has enough complementary areas within its own borders to account for the overwhelming bulk of its trade. Much of the remainder comes from Canada and the near-by Caribbean, although some of course comes from the farthest reaches of the world, and more will probably follow as the United States exhausts its own raw materials.

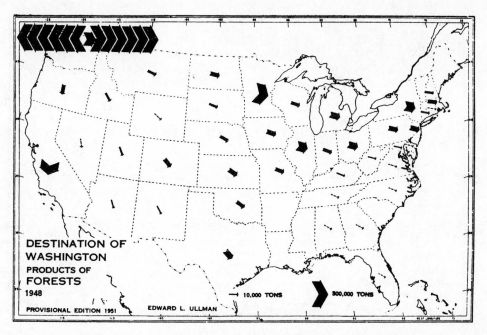

Figure 5.1 Destination, by states, of forest products shipped by rail from Washington, 1948. Width of arrows is proportionate to volume. Arrows within Washington represent intrastate movements. (Tons are short tons of 2,000 pounds.)

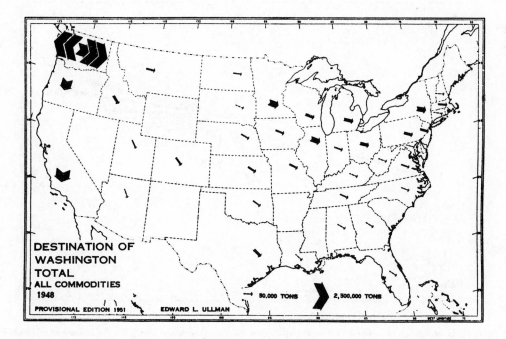

Figure 5.2 Destination, by states, of total commodities shipped by rail from Washington, 1948. Note scale of arrows is one-fifth that on Figure 5.1. (Tons are short tons of 2,000 pounds.)

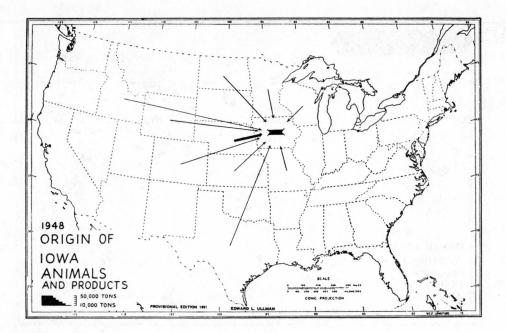

Figure 5.3 Origin, by states, of animals and products shipped by rail into Iowa, 1948. Width of lines is proportionate to volume on Figures 5.3 and 5.4. (Tons are short tons of 2,000 pounds.)

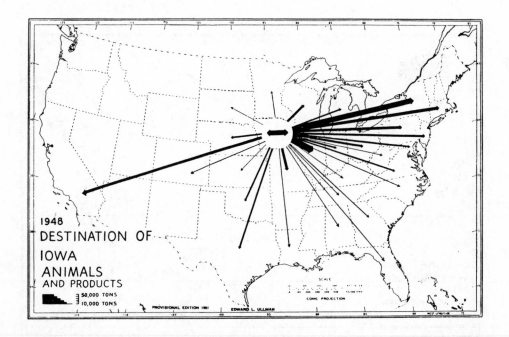

Figure 5.4 Destination by states, of animals and products shipped by rail from Iowa, 1948. Source of data for Figures 5.1 and 5.4 is Interstate Commerce Commission's 1 per cent sample of rail traffic reported in *Carload Waybill Analyses* (Washington, D.C., 1948) (statements: 4838, October, 1948; 492, January, 1949; 498, March, 1949; 4920, June, 1949). (Tons are short tons of 2,000 pounds.)

To sum up, a system explaining material interaction can be based on three factors: (1) *complementarity* – a function of areal differentiation promoting spatial interaction; (2) *intervening opportunity* (or intervening complementarity) between two regions or places; and (3) *transferability* measured in real terms, including cost and time of transport and effect of improvement in facilities.

The system proposed applies primarily to interaction based on physical movement, principally of goods but also to a large extent of people. It does not apply to spread of ideas or to most other types of communication, except as they accompany the flow of goods or people, which admittedly is often the case. Intervening opportunity, for example, would seem to facilitate rather than check the spread of ideas. Similarity of two regions also probably would facilitate the spread of ideas more than difference or complementarity, although the latter would be important in some cases.

An empirical formula often employed to describe interaction is a gravity model which states that interaction between two places is directly proportionate to the product of the populations (or some other measures of volume) and inversely proportionate to the distance (or distance to some exponent) apart of the two areas. This measure is often written $P_1 P_2/d$, where P is population place and d is the distance apart of the two places. This model, however, is useless in describing many interactions, because it assumes perfect or near-perfect complementarity, a condition which seldom obtains for physical flows. Some form of the model (with d modified by some exponent, n) apparently does come close to describing many interchanges, even for goods in a few cases, but apparently primarily for more or less universal, undifferentiated types of flow such as migration of some people or telephone calls between cities. It has been developed by Zipf (e.g. 1949), Stewart (e.g. 1947), Dodd (e.g. 1950), and others (Cavanaugh, 1950).

The three-factor system of complementarity, intervening opportunity, and distance, however, will cover, I believe, any case of material interaction of goods or people. The system should be kept in mind by investigators lest they be led astray by assigning exclusive weight to only one of the factors in attempting to explain past interaction or in predicting interaction under changed conditions.

Traffic versus Facilities as Generators of Interchange

Examples of erroneous single-factor explanations are numerous. One type concerns the role of traffic versus that of facilities as promoters of interchange, as has been noted earlier. Thus New York City was the largest port in the United States before the Erie Canal was built (Albion, 1939), and its size plus some settlement in the West made feasible construction of the Erie Canal, just as the opening of the canal had the effect later of drastically cutting real distance and enormously facilitating interchange and the growth of New York. Likewise, the great voyages of discovery were made in large part to tap the growing traffic between the Orient and Europe. Between these two centers were no significant intervening opportunities, although some were discovered as the routes were developed.

A more detailed example is provided by the opening of the St. Gotthard Pass across the Swiss Alps in the thirteenth century (Gilliard, 1929). According to an earlier, ingenious interpretation by the German historian Aloys Schulte, in 1900, it was the invention and construction of a suspension chain bridge along the vertical walls of the gorges of Schoellenen that opened up this best of all passes and produced a flood of traffic through Switzerland. Thus it was not William Tell who won independence for Switzerland but an unknown blacksmith who built the chain bridge which opened Switzerland to the currents of freedom from the south and the trade to support many people. Twenty-five years later careful research by scholars indicated that (1) before the hanging bridge was built, the precipitous gorge actually had been by-passed without too great difficulty via a longer route through Oberalp; (2) hanging bridges of the type noted were in reality common in the Alps by the thirteenth century; (3) the key bridge was not really the one credited but rather another farther downstream, which had been built of stone masonry by an unknown mason, requiring much more effort and capital than a mere suspension bridge; and, finally, and most important, (4) this key bridge and the rest of the route were not built until traffic was sufficient to pay for them! The traffic was generated by increased activity in the complementary regions of Flanders and the Rhineland, on the one hand, and the upper Po Valley, on the other hand, between which were few intervening complementary sources. Thus we must conclude that traffic was equally, if not more, instrumental in creating the route than was construction of the route.

A still different type of erroneous single-factor analysis concerns the role of certain features of the natural environment in promoting or retarding interchange. Mountain ranges, for example, are commonly thought of as barriers to interchange, but in many cases their barrier quality may be more than compensated for by the differentiation or complementarity which they produce. Thus climate, in many instances, differs on two sides of a mountain range; this difference may create interchange. More directly, the mountains themselves may be so different as to generate interaction, as in the case of transhumance – the moving of animals from lowland winter pastures to mountain summer pastures. Even more important in the modern world is the production of minerals in mountains associated with folding, faulting, uncovering of subsurface deposits by steam erosion, or other occurrences. The central Appalachians thus provide enormous quantities of coal, producing the largest single commodity flow in America. The Colorado Rockies, because of minerals, at one time had a denser network of rail lines than neighboring plains areas, in spite of formidable difficulties of penetration.

Potential Interaction

An example of the second reason for using the system — to predict or understand potential interaction under changed conditions – is provided by Portland, Maine, and Canada. At the end of the nineteenth century Portland was known as the winter outlet for Canada because it was the nearest ice-free port. The Grand Trunk Railroad built a line down from Canada to the city and also extensive docks at Portland. Canadian wheat was shipped out in quantity. Then Canada decided to keep the wheat flows within its borders and diverted the trade to the more distant, ice-free ocean ports of St. John and Halifax in the Maritime Provinces of Canada. Portland declined. Recently two changes have occurred. First, during World War II a pipeline for gasoline was constructed from Portland to Montreal to save long tanker trips from the Caribbean and Gulf of Mexico to Montreal through submarine-infested waters and to insure a year-round supply when the St. Lawrence River was frozen in winter. This gave Portland a shot in the arm and resulted in construction of large tank farms.

The second change can be illustrated by a story. In the summer of 1950, on a Sunday night, I stood on the international border between Derby Line, Vermont, and Rock Island, Quebec, and marveled at the constant stream of automobiles returning to Canada. I asked the customs inspector the reason, and he replied, 'Ninety per cent of the cars are bound for Quebec City and are coming from Old Orchard Beach, Maine.' Old Orchard

Beach is near Portland and is the ocean beach nearest to parts of eastern Canada, just as Portland is the nearest ocean port. The Dominion government in this case could hardly force tourists to drive a whole extra day to reach the Maritimes (once the Canadian economy had enough dollars). Thus (1) Portland's potential complementarity reasserted itself; (2) no intervening opportunity (ocean beach) occurs between Portland and Quebec; and (3) the distance is short enough so that it can be driven in a long weekend. Presumably if the distance were much greater, residents of Quebec would confine their swimming to the bathtub and use sun lamps. Needless to say, the underlying changes permitting both interactions were the invention and development of the automobile and, in conjunction with the tourist movement, increased leisure and higher standard of living, both fundamental trends, especially in Anglo-America.

A similar example, but one in the nature of a prediction, is the reasonable expectation by Professor Folke Kristensson of the Stockholm School of Economics that, as living standards rise in Sweden, Swedish diet will change, as the American diet has, and more fresh fruits and vegetables will be consumed the year round. This will result in increased interaction between Sweden and the nearest complementary sources – Italy, southern France, North Africa, etc. – just as occurred between the northeastern United States and Florida and California, today a fundamental feature of the American interaction pattern.

In fact, it is difficult to conceive of any changes – technical, political, social, or economic – which do not have some effect on interaction patterns and concomitantly on man's modification of the earth.

Transportation Pattern of the United States

The results of the forces noted above are summed up by Figure 5.5, which shows traffic flow on American and Canadian railroads.[1] The map is based on prewar data but on this scale is essentially correct today. Only lines carrying more than 1,000,000 net tons of freight per year are shown; these lines represent about 90 per cent of the American rail traffic measured in ton-miles. Highways are not shown, but their inclusion would hardly change the pattern, since highways even today carry only about 15 per cent of the ton-miles as compared to the railroads' more than 50 per cent, and the highways generally parallel the railways.

Cross-Grain Pattern of American Transportation

Note the cross-grain pattern of the flows in the United

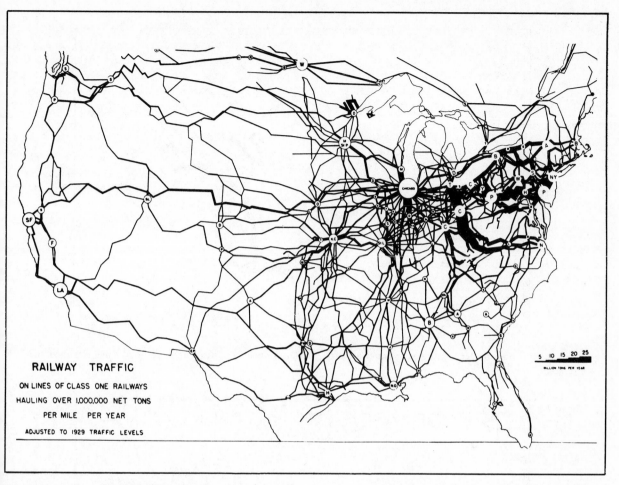

Figure 5.5 Traffic flow on United States and Canadian railroads. Figures are for late 1930's, adjusted to previous high level of 1929. (Prepared from data copyrighted by H.H. Copeland and Sons, New York; Canadian lines added and map adapted by Edward L. Ullman.)

States and Canada in Figure 5.5. Relief generally runs north-south, but traffic more generally moves east-west. Where possible, the railroads use *dioric* streams or gaps crossing some of the grain of the country, such as the Columbia, New, Kanahwa, Potomac, Susquehanna, Juniata, and, especially, Mohawk rivers (Ullman, 1951). Only the latter cuts entirely across the Appalachians, yet traffic through its gap via the New York Central, while heavy, is less than on the Pennsylvania or other lines which climb over the mountains. This cross-grain alignment of America is perhaps the major modification of the American earth due to transport. Transport connections are a more real feature of the geography of an area from a human-interaction viewpoint than is terrain. The inland waterways flow map (Figure 5.6), depicting less than 5 per cent of total United States traffic, reveals a

pattern geared more to the grain of the country. Prior to the opening of the Erie Canal in 1825 and the railroads thereafter, the American Middle West shipped goods south via the Mississippi and thence via coastal ships around to New York and other eastern seaboard ports (Taylor, 1951). The existence of this traffic spurred construction of the transappalachian lines and linked the East with the heart of America.

Transportation and the American Industrial Belt compared to Europe

The other major feature which emerges from this pattern is the focusing of the transport net on the Industrial Belt and on contiguous productive farm land (Figure 5.7). The Industrial Belt, because of its marked dominance in America, naturally has the greatest volume of transport-

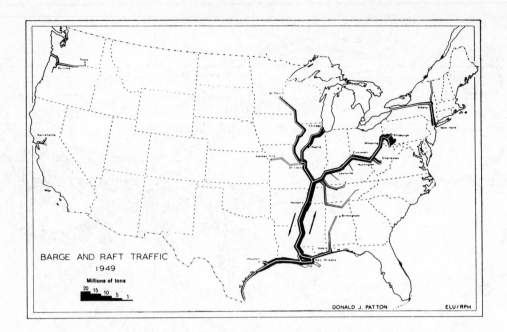

Figure 5.6 Traffic flow on United States inland waterways, 1949. (Donald J. Patton from Corps of Engineers data and field investigations.)

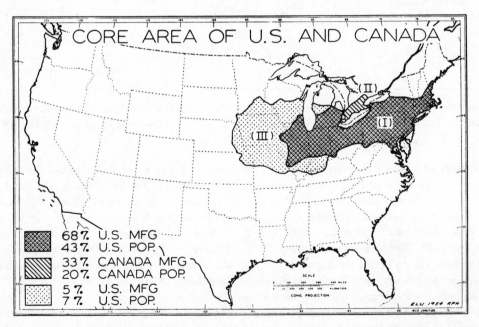

Figure 5.7 Core area of the United States and Canada. Additional data for these regions: Area I: 7.7 per cent U.S. area; 52 per cent U.S. income; 70 per cent of persons listed in *Who's Who*. Area III: 6.9 per cent U.S. area; 7.3 per cent U.S. income. Areas I and III combined: 14.6 per cent U.S. area; 50.3 per cent U.S. population; 59 per cent U.S. income; 73.3 per cent U.S. industrial employment. Area II: 0.4 per cent area of Canada; 19.8 per cent population; and 33 per cent Canadian industrial employment. Areas I and II combined percentage of U.S. and Canada: area 3.7; population 41.2; industrial employment 65.9. Areas I, II, and III combined per centage of U.S. and Canada: area 6.9; population 47.7; industrial employment 70.8.

ation; it also aligns the routes of the rest of the country, since it is the great market. Raw materials are shipped to it, and finished products are shipped out; as a result, traffic going into the belt is two or three times heavier than the return flows of lighter-weight, higher-value finished products. Note this phenomenon in Figures 5.3 and 5.4, where Iowa receives more animals and products from the West but ships more of them to the East, a standard feature of the United States pattern. The only other market area of even close intensity is the southern half of California, but it is tiny in comparison with the main belt (Harris, 1954). It is growing rapidly and affecting shipments; the only animals and products (mainly pork products) shipped west from Iowa in volume are, logically, to California, in spite of the great distance.

The Industrial Belt in one sense represents man's major modification of the American earth. It has its counterpart in Western Europe, the other heart of the world, and to a lesser extent in Russia, with other minor areas around the world. The American Industrial Belt, like Western Europe, is strongly dependent on coal which is in or adjacent to it and which furnishes the chief traffic to the railroads. Iron ore is also accessible in both cases in the United States, because cheap Great Lakes water transport is used to bring it to the belt. The heavy density of short lines on the northwestern end of Lake Superior (Figure 5.5) shows the rail haul of this ore from the Mesabi Range to Lake Superior for transshipment.

A new and vital resource which the Industrial Belt has in only negligible quantities is petroleum-natural gas, already the major source of energy in the United States. Fortunately for the Industrial Belt, oil is cheaply transported by pipeline or tanker, and gas by pipe; as a result, the 1,000-1,500-mile distance from the southwestern fields is no major handicap. This movement by pipeline and tanker has become an important feature of the American traffic pattern. Already natural-gas lines cover more route miles than railroads. Western Europe is in a parallel situation; it has little or no petroleum, but petroleum is available in the Middle East only slightly farther away than the American supplies are from the United States belt. Cheap tanker transport is employed, but natural gas as yet cannot be piped across conflicting political jurisdictions to Western Europe. This is a handicap; the market and supply are obviously both large, and the distance is not excessive. Will this strong complementarity triumph over the poor transferability resulting from political fragmentation, or will political barriers continue to prevent the substitution of the new fuel for the old?

Conclusion

The major modification of the earth by transport is the creation of large specialized agricultural and industrial areas, although improvement of transport has also created some uniformities. The major change has been in the scale of regional differentiation.

Transport improvement alone does not develop the increased interaction so characteristic of much of the modern world. Rather, a three-factor system of complementarity, intervening opportunity, and transferability (or distance) is suggested as a basis for explaining material interaction. The process of interaction links only certain areas, often in a quite specialized way, and leaves other areas relatively untouched. Bases for interaction with many hitherto relatively untouched areas, however, are growing, along with depletion of resources near markets, use of new ones by a changing technology, and extensions and improvements in transportation.

Some results of interaction processes are shown in (1) the predominantly cross-grain alignment of the United States and (2) the focusing of flows on the Industrial Belt, a phenomenon repeated somewhat in Western Europe and to a lesser extent in other parts of the world.

The study of interaction provides a fruitful field for investigation of the modification of the earth by man. It is evident even in the natural world (Whitaker, 1932), although it is the result of a quite different process probably requiring other explanations for sophisticated understanding. In the border zone between the natural and cultural worlds, as in the origin and diffusion of domesticated plants and animals, interaction is a rewarding field for investigation (e.g., Sauer, 1952).

In the cultural world interaction appears to be a topic of growing interest in many disciplines, although different labels may be attached to it. In economics, the term 'linkages' is commonly employed (Social Science Research Council, 1954). In sociology, interaction is extensively investigated, although it is often defined somewhat more narrowly and specifically. In political science, study of interaction patterns has been termed 'one of the two basic ways to describe and explain international politics,' the other being a decision-making approach (Snyder, in Deutsch, 1953). In history and other fields, the diffusion of ideas and their effects has been treated often and is considered by some to be a major unifying thesis (Highet, 1954). In geography and in understanding man's modification of the earth, interaction is implicit. A goal of this paper has been to make it more explicit.

Acknowledgement

Acknowledgement is gratefully made to the Office of Naval Research for support of research for this paper.

Notes

1 This map, based on private data collected by H.H. Copeland and Sons, has never been published before. It and numerous detailed origin and destination maps will be included in a forthcoming monograph on 'American Commodity Flow and Rail Traffic.' Additional analysis and maps for three states are in an article published in *Die Erde* (Ullman, 1955). Other maps showing facilities and more detailed analysis have been published (Ullman, 1949, 1951).

References

Abramovitz, Moses (1955) 'The Economic Characteristics of Railroads and the Problem of Economic Development,' *Far Eastern Quarterly*, XIV, No. 2, 169-78.

Albion, Robert (1939) *The Rise of New York Port*, New York: Charles Scribner's Sons.

Alexander, John (1944) 'Freight Rates as a Geographic Factor in Illinois,' *Economic Geography*, XX, 25-30.

Atherton, Lewis (1954) *Main Street on the Middle Border*, Bloomington: Indiana University Press.

Boggs, S.W. (1941) 'Mapping the Changing World: Suggested Developments in Maps,' *Annals of the Association of American Geographers*, XXXI, 119-28.

Bogue, Donald J. (1949) *The Structure of the Metropolitan Community: A Study of Dominance and Subdominance* (Contributions of the Institute for Human Adjustment, Social Science Research Project, University of Michigan), Ann Arbor: University of Michigan Press.

Braudel, Fernand (1949) *La Mediterranée et le monde mediterranéen à l'époque de Phillippe II*, Paris: Librairie Armand Colin.

Cammann, Schuyler (1951) *Trade through the Himalayas*, Princeton, N.J.: Princeton University Press.

Capot-Rey, R. (1946) *Géographie de la circulation sur les continents*, Paris: Gallimard.

Cavanaugh, Joseph A. (1950) 'Formulation, Analysis and Testing of the Interactance Hypotheses,' *American Sociological Review*, XV, 763-66.

Christaller, Walter (1935) *Die zentralen Orte in Süddeutschland*, Jena: Gustav Fischer.

Cooley, C.H. (1894) *The Theory of Transportation* ('Publications of the American Economic Association,' Vol. IX.)

Crowe, P.R. (1938) 'On Progress in Geography,' *Scottish Geographical Magazine*, LIV, 1-19.

Daggett, Stuart (1955) *Principles of Inland Transportation*, 4th ed., New York: Harper & Bros.

Daggett, Stuart, and Carter, John P. (1947) *The Structure of Transcontinental Railroad Rates*, Berkeley: University of California Press.

Deutsch, Karl W. (1953) *Political Community at the International Level: Problems of Definition and Meaurement*. (Introduction by Richard C. Snyder.) ('Organizational Behavioral Section, Foreign Policy Analysis Project,' Series No. 2.) Princeton, N.J.: Princeton University.

Dodd, S.C. (1950) 'The Interactance Hypothesis: A Gravity Model Fitting Physical Masses and Human Behaviour,' *American Sociological Review*, XV, 245-56.

Febvre, Lucien, and Demangeon, Albert (1931) *Le Rhin*, Strasbourg: La Société Générale Alsacienne du Banque, Imprimerie Strasbourgeoise.

Fromont, Pierre (1948) 'Les Chemins de fer et l'agriculture,' *L'Année Ferroviaire, 1948*, pp. 63-96. Paris: Librairie Plon.

Gilliard, Charles (1929) 'L'Ouverture du Gothard,' *Annales d'histoire économique et sociale*, I, 177-82.

Goodfellow, D.M. (1931) *A Modern Economic History of South Africa*, London: G. Routledge & Sons.

Gourou, Pierre (1949) 'Civilisations et malchance géographique,' *Annales, économies, sociétés, civilisations*, October-December, pp. 445-50.

Harris, Chauncy D. (1954) 'The Market as a Factor in the Localization of Industry in the United States,' *Annals of the Association of American Geographers*, XLIV, No. 4, 315-48.

Harris, Chauncy D., and Ullman, Edward L. (1945) 'The Nature of Cities,' *Annals of the American Academy of Political and Social Science*, CCXLII, 7-17.

Hartshorne, Richard (1939) *The Nature of Geography*, Lancaster, Pa.: Association of American Geographers.

Healy, Kent R. (1940) *The Economics of Transportation in America*, New York: Ronald Press Co. (1947) 'Transportation as a Factor in Economic Growth,' *Journal of Economic History*, VII, 72-88.

Herman, Theodore (1954) 'An Analysis of China's Export Handicraft Industries to 1930.' (Ph.D. dissertation, University of Washington, Seattle.)

Highet, Gilbert (1954) *The Migration of Ideas*, New York: Oxford University Press.

Hunter, Louis C. (1934) 'Studies in Economic History of the Ohio Valley,' *Smith College Studies in History*, XIX, Nos. 1-2, 1-32.

Kirkland, Edward C. (1948) *Men, Cities and Transportation*, 2 vols., Cambridge, Mass.: Harvard University Press.

Klimm, Lester E. (1954) 'The Empty Areas of the North-eastern United States,' *Geographical Review*, XLIV, No. 3, 325-45.

Kohl, J.G. (1850) *Der Verkehr und die Ansiedlungen der Menschen in ihrer Abhängikeit von der Gestaltung der Erdoberfläche,* 2nd ed., Leipzig: Arnold.

Lambie, Joseph T. (1954) *From Mine to Market: A History of Coal Transportation on the Norfolk and Western Railway*, New York: New York University Press.

Mackinder, H.J. (1890) 'The Physical Basis of Political Geography,' *Scottish Geographical Magazine*, VI, 78-84.

Mayer, Harold M. (1954) 'Great Lakes–Overseas: An Expanding Trade Route,' *Economic Geography*, XXX, No. 2, 117-43.

Ohlin, Berth (1933) *Interregional and International Trade*, Cambridge, Mass.: Harvard University Press.

Ouren, Tore, and Somme, Axel (1949) *Trends in Inter-war Trade and Shipping* ('Norwegian University School of Business, Geographical Series,' Publication No. 5), Bergen.

Penrose, E.F. (1952) 'The Place of Transport in Economic and Political Geography,' *Transport and Communications Review*, V, No. 2, 1-8. New York: United Nations.

Platt, R.S. (1949) 'Reconnaissance in Dynamic Regional Geography: Tierra del Fuego,' *Revista geografica*, V-VIII, 3-22. Rio de Janeiro.

Sauer, Carl O. (1952) *Agricultural Origins and Dispersals* (Bowman Memorial Lectures, Series Two), New York: American Geographical Society.

Scheu, Erwin (1924) *Deutschland's wirtschaftsgeographische Harmonie*, Breslau: F. Hirt.

Sestini, Aldo (1952) 'L'Organizzazione umana dello spazio terrestre,' *Rivista geografica italiana*, LIX, 73-92.

Siegfried, André (1940) *Suez and Panama*, trans. from the French by H.H. and Doris Henning, New York: Harcourt, Brace & Co.

Smith, Adam (1937) *The Wealth of Nations*, New York: Modern Library. (1st ed., 1776-79.)

Social Science Research Council (1954) *Interregional Linkages: Proceedings of the Western Committee on Regional Economic Analysis*, Berkeley, Calif.

Sombart, Werner (1916) *Der moderne Kapitalismus*, 2 vols. 2d rev. ed., Munich and Leipzig: Duncker & Humbolt.

Stewart, J.Q. (1947) 'Empirical Mathematical Rules concerning the Distribution and Equilibrium of Population,' *Geographical Review*, XXXVII, 461-85.

Stouffer, Samuel (1940) 'Intervening Opportunities: A Theory Relating Mobility to Distances,' *American Sociological Review*, XV, 845-67.

Taylor, George Rogers (1951) *The Transportation Revolution*, New York: Rinehart & Co.

Thünen, J.H. von (1910) *Der isolierte Staat in Beziehung auf Landwirtschaft und Nationalökonomie*, Jena: Gustav Fischer. (1st ed., 1826).

Ullman, Edward L. (1941) 'A Theory of Location for Cities,' *American Journal of Sociology*, XLVI, No. 6, 853-64. (1949) 'The Railroad Pattern of the United States,' *Geographical Review*, XXXIX, No. 2, 242-56. (1950) *United States Railroads: Classified According to Capacity and Relative Importance* (Map), New York: Simmons Boardman Pub. Corp. (1951) 'Rivers as Regional Bonds: The Columbia-Snake Example,' *Geographical Review*, XLI, 210-25. (1954) 'Transportation Geography,' pp. 147 and 310-32 in James, Preston E., and Jones, Clarence F. (eds.), *American Geography: Inventory and Prospect*, Syracuse, N.Y.: Syracuse University Press. (1955) 'Die wirtschaftliche Verflechtung verschiedener Regionen der USA betrachtet am Güteraustausch Connecticuts, Iowas and Washingtons mit den anderen Staaten,' *Die Erde*, Heft 2, pp. 129-64.

Whitaker, J.R. (1932) 'Regional Interdependence,' *Journal of Geography*, XXXI, 164-65.

Yang Ching-Kun (1944) *A North China Local Market Economy*, New York: International Secretariat, Institute of Pacific Relations.

Zipf, G.K. (1949) *Human Behavior and the Principle of Least Effort*, Cambridge, Mass.: Addison-Wesley.

This article is taken from *Man's Role in Changing the Face of the Earth*, ed. W.L. Thomas, 1956, University of Chicago Press, Chicago, and reprinted with permission of the publishers.

6 Balances of Interregional Commodity Flows in Poland: A Value Approach

by Wojciech Morawski

Institute of Geography, Polish Academy of Sciences, Warsaw

1 General Research Problems

The processes of production, consumption and economic growth are accompanied by numerous acts of exchange between the units involved in these processes. Three principal types of *object of exchange* can be identified. The first consists of *material goods*, i.e., raw materials, semi-finished goods and finished goods, the latter being produced for the processes of production, consumption and economic growth. Material goods are objects of sale and purchase according to current supply and demand conditions. A second group of objects of exchange is comprised of *services* such as tourist services.[1] Thirdly, there exist certain other manifestations of socio-economic activity which are collectively referred to as '*other benefits*.'[2]

The movement of material goods, services and 'other benefits' is an indispensable feature of a developed national economy. In many cases, the process of exchange involves the movement of an object over space from the point of production to the point of consumption. In effect, objects of exchange can be seen to exist as a spatial pattern of flows. These flows can be studied: a) from the standpoint of the individual units, e.g., enterprises or industries; b) from the standpoint of the individual objects of exchange themselves, i.e., goods or services; c) in terms of particular areal units such as centres, districts, or regions.

The phenomenon of interregional exchange is deeply rooted in the chain of causes and effects of economic processes. In the most general terms, it is the inequality within the regions between the level and structure of production and the level and structure of consumption which forms the basis for interregional exchange. This general statement can be developed by indicating the following four groups of factors which contribute to these inequalities:

a) the utilization and distribution of natural resources and the areal differentiation of other features of the physical environment;

b) the interregional division of labour (specialization) and the level of development and utilization of material and technical resources in the various regions;

c) the distribution of population and the level and structure of consumption in the regions:

d) the regional differences in the rate of economic growth.

Two approaches to the study of flows of objects of exchange can be identified. The first treats flows as the *object of research*. This approach considers first the various supply and demand functions in each region. It is then possible to determine existing or projected flows in the form of streams of commodities, of people, or of information. Having established the nature of present and future flows, one can begin to determine the extent to which these flows accord with the capacity of the transport system for accommodating them.[3]

The second approach to the study of flows reverses, to some extent, the order of reasoning, and in this case one can speak of the study to flows in space as an *instrument of research*. All information on the flows is treated as given and the objective is to speculate upon such features as: the degree of integration and differentiation of the nation's spatial structure, as has been carried out by Chojnicki (1961a, b), the openness or otherwise of regions, as Dziewonski (1961) has attemtped; and the extent of market areas for commodities and services, which can be determined by a variety of approaches well known in the methodology of location theory.

Of course, it is often difficult to distinguish between *flows as objects of research* and *flows as instruments of research*. A number of studies have been of significance for both approaches such as those undertaken by Ullman (1957). It appears that Isard (1960) treats the commodity flows (by volume) as an instrument of research. However, Isard differentiates among three types of research commodity flow analysis, money flow analysis, and balance of payments studies. Furthermore, he stresses the need for integration of these three types of analysis.

The study presented here deals only partially with the total process of interregional exchange. See Figure 6.1. The analysis has been limited to inter-regional flows of material goods by railways.[4] Thus, both the exchange of material goods by other modes of transport as well as

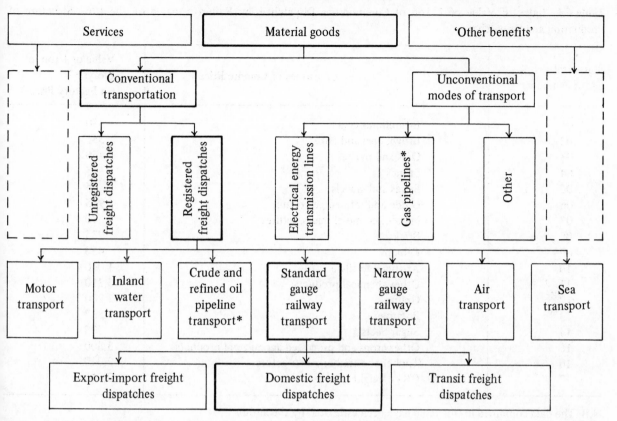

* The grouping of 'Gas Pipelines' with 'Unconventional Modes of Transport,' and 'Crude and Refined Oil Transport' with 'Conventional Transport' is arbitrary and represents the classification used by the official statistical agency, the Central Statistical Office of the Polish People's Republic.

Figure 6.1 Forms and Modes of Interregional Exchange.

N.B. The bold lines refer to the forms and modes of interregional exchange which are dealt with in this study.

the exchange of services and 'other benefits' have been excluded.

Classification of commodity flows which was used made it difficult to relate the findings of this study to other data on regional economic characteristics. In addition, this classification required a cautious formulation of the conclusions.[5] The data available were aggregated by economic-administrative regions, i.e., voivodships[6] and this factor automatically determined the *spatial level* of the analysis.[7]

In a previous work, I treated commodity flows as an instrument of research with the use of an *index of value*.[8] This measure is of limited value in transportation network analysis but it enhances the utility of flow data for regional and economic-geographic research. For these reasons, the effects of inter-regional exchange are analyzed and the criterion of *interregional linkages* is

applied in the delimitation of Poland's economic macro-regions. This criterion is preferred to those previously mentioned, which were concerned with resource endowment and with demographic and economic variables.

It is emphasized that no attempt has been made to deal with the causal relationships which exist in the interregional exchange process. To do so would involve such an abundance of analytical problems that it would obviously be beyond the scope of a single study.

2 Transformation of Data and the Problems of Distortion

Data from the official statistics of commodity flows between voivodships by railways in 1962 served as a starting point.[9] These data are published in the form of matrices, the volume of the flows being recorded in physical units of measurement (tons). The matrices

Table 6.1 Index of Value of 1 Ton of Commodities Dispatched by Railways, based on the 1962 Structure of Production and Dispatches

Statistical Group Number	Categories of Commodities	Value of 1 ton in Zlotys (in Factory Prices)
01	Bituminous coal	350
02	Brown coal and coke	555
03	Ores and pyrites	450
04	Stones	95
05	Sands and gravels	45
06	Crude and refined petroleum	1,985
07	Metals and metal manufactures	4,580
08	Bricks	235
09	Cement	450
10	Artificial fertilizers	1,060
11	Other chemical products	5,310
12	Grains	3,200
13	Potatoes	837
14	Sugar beets	505
15	Other crops and processed agricultural products	3,800
16	Timber and timber manufactures	2,040
17	Other freight	7,540

N.B. The data contained in this table have been estimated by the author.

contain commodity flows for each of the 17 groups of commodities as well as for their overall total.[10] As Isard, among others, has pointed out, data on the physical volume of flows have a definite descriptive value for regional research, aside from their significance in the study of transport systems.

However, there are obvious limitations in the conclusions derived from an analysis of interregional commodity flows in terms of physical volume. Roughly speaking, these limitations stem from the incomparability (in economic terms) of the various material goods when they are expressed in terms of physical volume. For these reasons, data on the physical volumes of flows have been transformed so as to achieve the estimated *monetary value of physical volumes*. This transformation of the data was carried out by the use of a *value index* for each of the 17 groups of commodities. These indices have been estimated in a separate study[11] and are presented in Table 6.1.

The index involved the use of simplifying assumptions which resulted in certain distortions. It should be remarked here that Isard (1960) notes the possibility of modifying statistical data on transport to this form.

However, he also draws attention to the difficulties involved and to the necessity of making simplifying assumptions. The establishment of the index used in this study was linked to the selection of a price base and to an estimate of the value of commodities in order to take advantage of the availability of a number of data-sources, including data other than transport statistics.

The problem of prices was solved by adopting *factory prices* as a base. Comparability among the component elements of interregional exchange was assumed to be indispensable. A further aim was to observe regional economies without the distortions caused by the 'two-level' sales price.[12] The sources of distortion in the value index for commodity groups consisted of the following:

a) the assumption that the number of dispatches of particular products is proportional to their production, which is a simplification in the case of non-homogeneous groups of commodities;

b) the assumption that there is no regional differentiation in the structure of production, which is also a simplification in the case of non-homogeneous groups of commodities although this problem is partly lessened by the two-level method of calculating the index:

c) the assumption that there is no regional differentiation in prices, which is false wherever there is regional dispersion of production with differences in production costs.

Consideration of the relations between regions and foreign nations has been excluded from the study. This was decided upon primarily because of the difficulty of assigning realistic prices to foreign imports. However, the complete lack of data in Poland on the regional components of foreign trade was an obvious additional factor.

3 Balances of Interregional Commodity flows: Definition and Interpretation

A study of the effects of interregional exchange is an essential element in the analysis of commodity flows from the standpoint of value. The inequality of exchange, apparent in this study, has led to a broad treatment of the balances of interregional commodity flows. A balance has been defined as the *difference between the outflows from the region and the inflows to the region*. The premises for this definition of a balance are the following:

a) the region is a part of a socio-economic whole, i.e., the nation;

b) the surplus of outflows over inflows implies a contribution of a part (the region) to the whole (the nation);

c) the reverse situation, i.e., a deficit, implies that a part (the region) draws from the whole (the nation).

By virtue of the definition and its premises, the following types of region can be recognized:

a) the *surplus region*: where outflows are *greater* than inflows and an active (positive) balance exists;

b) the *deficit region*: where outflows are *smaller* than inflows and an adverse (negative) balance exists.

c) the *balanced region*: where outflows are *equal* to inflows and a neutral balance exists.

If the sum of outflows of all material goods from a region exceeds the sum of inflows into it, such a situation can be regarded as favourable with respect to the regional system as a whole (the nation). In the transport balance of a region such categories as the regional output, current inputs to regional production, investment and consumption in the regions, and the state of regional reserves are not included. Only a balance containing all these components, as well as the outflows and inflows, could be regarded as a full regional balance.[13] In spite of these deficiencies in a regional balance constructed solely on the basis of transportation

data, it nevertheless approximately reflects the significant items in a full regional balance.

With respect to the whole regional system (the nation), there exists the requirement of equalizing the volume income and expenditures. Under certain conditions, the possible absence of such an equality can be compensated by foreign trade. This requirement is not formulated with respect to individual regions within the nation since the economy of a region need not necessarily be balanced, as Sulmicki (1962) has observed. In this connection, he draws attention to two phenomena: the 'divisibility of production within a country' and the 'free movement of capital.'[14]

An interpretative hypothesis has been formulated concerning the economic character of the balance of interregional commodity flows. This balance *approximately reflects the difference between the volumes of goods produced and consumed* within the region. In individual regions, differences in the volume and structure of goods produced and consumed are admissable. Naturally, the hypothesis presented here cannot be verified in terms of the data used in this paper, partly because of the latter's relatively simple character and partly because of the problem of aggregation. However, it is felt that the hypothesis may have some value as a preliminary investigation.

4 Balances of Interregional Commodity Flows

The calculation of total interregional commodity flows on the basis of the sums of the rows and columns of the matrix shows that a region's trade does not always balance exactly. Table 6.2 and Figure 6.2 indicate 7 surplus regions and 10 deficit regions. Each entry in column 4 of Table 6.2 indicates the magnitude of each region's total commodity flows relative to its regional balance.[15]

In terms of the present state of knowledge of the spatial structure of Poland, these are data of a new type. They tend to confirm what was previously known about the surplus character of the southern industrialized regions and the deficit character of the north-eastern and certain of the central regions. Furthermore, the scale of differentiation of active and adverse balances seems to be interesting. New light is thrown on the economy of Kielce and, to a lesser extent, on those of Bydgoszcz and Zielona Góra with their active balances. It is possible that a number of objections may be raised in connection with the deficit character which was shown to exist for the regions of Lódz, Poznan, Gdansk and Szczecin.[16]

The results presented here coincide with the estimates

TABLE 6.2 Interregional Commodity Flows by Railways and the Value of Regional Balances in 1962

| Regions (Voivodships) | Regional Balance | | Regional Balance Coefficient |
	Millions of Zlotys	Rank of Voivodship	
1	2	3	4
SURPLUS REGIONS			
Subgroup I, High Active Balances:			
Katowice	+13,134	1	11.4
Wroclaw	+ 9,729	2	18.0
Opele	+ 7,793	3	18.4
Kraków	+ 6,806	4	10.5
Lielce	+ 5,017	5	16.0
Subgroup II, Low Active Balances:			
Zielena Góra	+ 1,123	6	5.9
Bydgoszcz	+ 964	7	3.0
DEFICIT REGIONS			
Subgroup II, Low Adverse Balances:			
Bialystok	- 933	10	9.0
Keszalin	- 945	9	8.0
Olsztyn	- 969	8	7.8
Szczecin	- 1,633	7	9.4
Subgroup 1, High Adverse Balances:			
Rzeszów	- 2,918	6	14.3
Gdańsk	- 3,117	5	15.0
Poznań	- 4,861	4	12.2
Lublin	- 5,024	3	27.2
Lódz	- 7,871	2	28.0
Warsaw	- 16,294	1	36.9

N.B. 1) the data contained in this table have been estimated by the author. 2) The voivodships are ranked according to the value of the regional balances. Surplus and deficit regions are ranked separately.

of the regional system of Poland obtained by Prandecka (1965), (1966) in her studies of the regional breakdown of the national income produced and consumed. The two sets of findings are compared in Table 6.3. Naturally, data concerning national income cannot be directly related to data on commodity flows by railways. Hence, the regional balances have been compared with the *differences* between the regional shares of the national income produced and consumed. We can observe high correlations between the character of the balances (active and adverse) and the differences in the regional structure of the national income produced and consumed.

In addition, new insights into the regional balances are gained by analyses of their component structure. This is presented in Figure 6.3 with data aggregated into four groups.[17] In all deficit regions and in the majority of surplus regions, the situation in the 'industrial goods' group is decisive for the character of the total balance. In the region of Katowice, the overall surplus results from the surplus in the 'raw materials of mineral origin' group. In fact, the region of Katowice accounts for almost the entire surplus of all the regions in the 'raw materials of mineral origin' group. There is, however, a positive balance in the group in the region of Rzeszów but this is too small to appear in Figure 3. In the regions

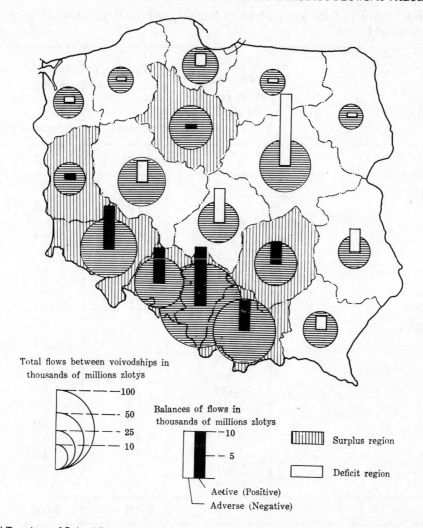

Total flows between voivodships in
thousands of millions zlotys

— 100

— 50

— 25

— 10

Balances of flows in
thousands of millions zlotys

— 10

— 5

Active (Positive)

Adverse (Negative)

Surplus region

Deficit region

Figure 6.2 A Regional Typology of Poland Based on the Balances of Commodity Flows by Railways in 1962.

of Bydgoszcz and of Zielona Góra, the source of the overall surplus consists of a combination of active balances in the 'industrial goods' group and in the 'field crops' or 'timber' groups.

5 Conclusions

It is hoped that the research findings presented here can be considered something more than a description of certain factual characteristics of Poland's space-economy. This discussion may have some significance for studies of the regional implications of economic growth theory, involving the introduction of spatial components. These studies are currently being carried out in some depth.

It appears that the possibility of utilizing transport data of the type presented here for the purposes of regional research is of limited significance. The problem that arises in Poland is that transport data have a spatial subscript only. They neither possess, nor make possible the derivation of, industry subscripts. However, in Poland, research into the regional pattern of the nation with the aid of input-output techniques has not been completed as yet. Moreover, there is a lack of statistical data for the elaboration of uniform economic balances for all regions. Hence, transport statistics are, and will continue to be, a valuable source of regional information. It is felt that further work in the field of commodity flows should focus on dynamic analyses of the interregional exchange of material goods. These analyses should be combined with data on the exchange

Table 6.3 Regional Balances of Commodity Flows by Railways and the Regional Structure of the Production and Consumption of National Income

Regions (Voivodships)	Regional Balance of Commodity Flows in 1962 (in Millions of Zlotys)	Structure of National Income in 1961 at Current Prices		Difference between Columns 3 and 4
		Produced (%)	Consumed (%)	
1	3	3	4	5
SURPLUS REGIONS				
Katowice	+13,134	14.9	13.3	+1.6
Wroclaw	+ 9,729	8.1	8.0	+0.1
Opole	+ 7,793	3.4	3.2	+0.2
Kraków	+ 6,806	8.9	8.6	+0.3
Kielce	+ 5,017	4.7	4.5	+0.2
Zielona Góra	+ 1,123	2.5	2.4	+0.1
Bydgoszcs	+ 964	5.6	5.5	+0.1
DEFICIT REGIONS				
Bialystok	- 933	2.5	2.8	- 0.3
Koszalin	- 945	1.7	2.3	- 0.6
Olsztyn	- 969	2.2	2.6	- 0.4
Szczecin	- 1,633	2.6	3.1	- 0.5
Rzeszów	- 2,918	4.5	4.6	- 0.1
Gdańsk	- 3,117	4.3	4.9	- 0.6
Poznań	- 4,861	8.5	8.2	+0.3
Lublin	- 5,024	4.6	4.9	- 0.3
Lódź	- 7,871	8.9	7.2	+1.7
Warsaw	- 16,294	12.1	13.9	- 1.8
Poland Total	0	100.0	100.0	0

N.B. 1) the data on regional balances have been estimated by the author. 2) The data on the structure of national income are taken from Prandecka (1966), with a slight modification. The income consumed has been subtracted from the income produced. This is a reversal of the procedure used by Prandecka.

of services and 'other benefits,' and also with data on the regional breakdown of such phenomena as production, consumption, foreign trade and economic growth processes.

Notes

1 As a rule, services are not objects of exchange among regions: they are consumed at the place of their production. However, a difference in the origin of the service and the location of the subject consuming it, *is* possible, as in the case of tourist services.

2 In the consideration of commodity flows, 'other benefits' have been singled out as one of the three principal forms of exchange. With respect to socialist economies, the following examples of 'other benefits' may be listed: pensions, scholarships, donations, education, results of scientific research, management and information.

3 For a discussion of spatial transportation research methods, see Morawski (1958), (1962), (1966b), (1967a).

4 The establishment of the role of railways in the total interregional exchange process is impossible, due to the lack of data, particularly in the fields of services

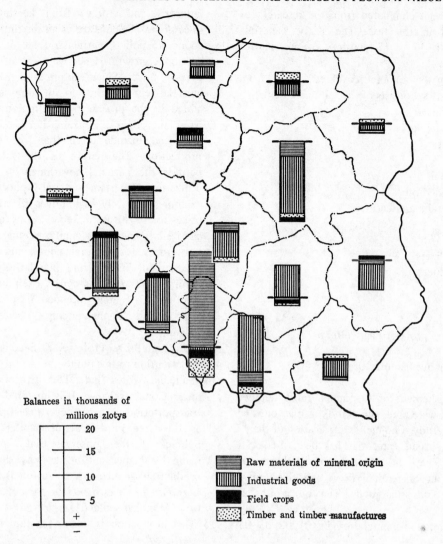

Balances in thousands of
millions zlotys

20

15

10

5

+

—

Raw materials of mineral origin

Industrial goods

Field crops

Timber and timber manufactures

Figure 6.3 The Generic Structure of Balances of Interregional Commodity Flows by Railways in 1962.

and 'other benefits'. As far as material goods are concerned, there are a number of indications which suggest that railways continue to play a decisive role in interregional commodity flows in Poland. One such indication can be seen in the results of a transport census undertaken by the Committee for Space Economy of the Polish Academy of Sciences and the Ministry of Transport.

5 See Morawski (1966a), (1967b) for a critical discussion of the classification of commodity flows and freight dispatches used by the various carriers (railways, road haulage concerns, etc.).

6 The term, 'region,' is used here according to Secomski's definition (1965).

7 As Dziewoński (1967) has stated, the study cannot, '. . . go beyond the frame of reference which, in this case, is this [regional] division.'

8 See Morawski (1966c).

9 From 1958 to 1965, the Central Statistical Office in Warsaw published a special series entitled: *Freight Dispatches between Voivodships and Voivodship Transport Balances*. The data contained therein referred to standard-gauge railway transport and inland water transport. It took into account 17 voivodships and city-voivodships and considered foreign exports and imports. In the study discussed here, the city-voivodships have been included in their respective voivodships and foreign exports and

imports have been eliminated from the research for reasons stated in the text. The study was thus concerned with 17 x 17 matrices of commodity flows.

10 The grouping of commodity flows, taken from transport statistics, consists of the following items:

01 Bituminous coal
02 Brown coal and coke
03 Ores and pyrites
04 Stones
05 Sands and gravels
06 Crude and refined oil
07 Metals and metal manufactures
08 Bricks
09 Cement
10 Artificial fertilizers
11 Chemical products
12 Grains
13 Potatoes
14 Sugar beets
15 Other crops and processed agricultural products
16 Timber and timber manufactures
17 Other freight

In the establishement of the index, more detailed statistical data were used, which took into account 81 items. In this study, Chojnicki's aggregation of the 17 items into 4 broad categories has been used. See Chojnicki [1]. The item, 'other freight' has been used to take account of residual flows and this item is grouped with 'industrial goods.' The four groups are as follows:

    I   raw materials of mineral origin (01, 02, 03, 05, 06);

    II   industrial goods (07, 08, 09, 10, 11, 17);

    III field crops (12, 13, 14, 15);

    IV timber and timber manufactures (16):

For a critical treatment of the classification discussed here, see Morawski (1966a), (1967b).

11 See Morawski (1967b).

12 In very general terms, there were two basic price categories used in Poland during the period under examination: factory prices and sales prices. The factory price is equal to the prime costs of production plus an average margin of 5 per cent. The sales price can be *either* higher, *or* lower than the factory price. If it is higher, the sales price is equal to the factory price *plus* a tax. If it is lower, the sales price is equal to the factory price *minus* a subsidy. This subsidy is refunded to the selling enterprise and is drawn from the state budget. The sales price thus constitutes an instrument of national economic policy, particularly in the stimulation of economic growth. Hence we speak of the 'two levels' of sales prices. Since the prices of investment goods are relatively low, they do not comprise the full-value added in the process of production. On the other hand, the prices of consumption goods are relatively high and include more than the value-added in production. The nature of the sales prices thus permits the national government to influence the utilization of certain material inputs by having, for example, relatively high prices for timber and low prices for substitute materials. Consumption patterns can be influenced in a similar manner. The relatively low prices for cultural goods and light industry products for children, and the relatively high prices of luxury goods such as spirits exemplify this policy. This note is merely intended to provide a general introduction to the pricing policies employed in Poland.

13 I am grateful to Professor K. Secomski for drawing my attention to this point.

14 Sulmicki writes that, 'This division is secured by interregional exchange. It is hindered by the costs of transportation, but it is nevertheless possible.' As far as the 'free movement of capital' is concerned, Sulmicki further observes that, '.. the decisions made by higher authorities may shift part of the production of region A to region B in the form of *subsidies for investments* or for collective consumption.' [Emphasis added].

15 This proportion is known as the *regional balance coefficient*.

16 The results obtained for these regions may have been influenced by the incomplete character of the data which were used. This might be due to the inclusion of certain outlays on production in the inflows. In addition, the outflows may have been underemphasized. This factor may have been important with respect to the foreign exports of the textile industry from the Lódz region; the exports of the machine industry and agricultural and food industry from the Poznań region; and the exports of the shipbuilding industry from the coastal regions.

17 Details of this aggregation are presented in note 10.

References

Chojnicki, Z. (1961a) 'Analizs przeplywów towarowych w Polsce w ukladzie miedzywojewódzkim,' [Analysis of Commodity Flows between Voivodships in Poland] *Studia KPZK PAN*, Vol. 1

Chojnicki, Z. (1961b) 'The Structure of Economic Regions in Poland Analyzed by Commodity Flows,' *Geographia Polonica*, **1**, 213-30.

Dziewoński, K. (1961) 'Elementy teorii regionu ekonomicznego,' [Elements of the Theory of Economic Region] *Przeglad Geograficzny*, **33**, 4, 593-613.

Dziewonska, K. (1967) 'Theoria regionu ekonomicznego,' [The Theory of the Economic Region] *Przeglad Geograficzny*, **39**, 33-50.

Isard, Walter *et al.* (1960) *Methods of Regional Analysis: an Introduction to Regional Science*, New York: The Technology Press of M.I.T. and John Wiley and Sons, Chapter 5.

Morawski, W. (1958) *Potoki ladunkow*. [Freight Flows] Instytut Geografii PAN, Dokumentacja, Geograficzna, No. 5.

Morawski, W. (1962) 'Metodyka badań przyszlego obciazenia linii kolejowych ruchem towarewym,' [Methods of Research for Future Railway Traffic] *Przeglad Komunikacyjny*, 10, 364-8.

Morawski, W. (1966a) 'reforme klasyfikacji ladunków w transporcie,' [On the Modification of Freight Classification in the Transport System] *Przeglad Komunikacyjny*, 12, 450-5.

Morawski, W. (1966b) 'Zagadnienia metodyki badań miedzyregionalnych przeplywów towarcwych (kolojami) w Polace.' [Methodological Problems in the Study of Interregional Commodity Flows by Railways in Poland] *Biuletyn KPZK PAN, 36* 101-42.

Morawski, W. (1967a) 'Methodological Problems in Transportation Research,' *Proceedings of the First Scandinavian-Polish Regional Science Seminar Szczecin, August 1965.* Warsaw: Polish Scientific Publishers, pp. 241-248.

Morawski, W. (1967b) 'Studium wartosói jednej tony towarów przemieszezanych transportem kolejowym i problem integracji klasyfikacji,' [A Study of the Per Ton Values of Commodities Transported by Railways and the Problem of Integrating the Classification] *Biuletyn KPZK PAN*, Series A, 4.

Morawski, W. (1966c) *Przeplywy towarowe i powiazania miedzyregionalne na obszarze polski*, [Commodity Flows and Interregional Connections in Poland] Doctoral dissertation, the Department of Space Economy and Regional Planning of the Institute of Geography, the Polish Academy of Sciences, Warsaw.

Prandecka, B.K. (1965) 'Analize tworzenia i podzialu dochodu naredowege Polski w ukladsie regionalynm,' [Regional Analysis of National Income Creation and Consumption in Poland] *Studia KPZK PAN, 9*.

Prandecka, B.K. (1966) 'Ogólna analiza struktury przestrzennej dechodu naredowege tworzonogo i polzielonego w latach 1960-1961 oraz uwagi na temat metody opracowanica GUS,' [A General Analysis of the Spatial Structure of National Income Produced and Consumed in 1960-61 and Remarks on the Method Used in the Central Statistical Office Publication] *Biuletyn KPZK PAN* 36, 7-32.

Sulmicki, P. (1962) 'Teoria roswoju regionów gospodarczych – próba aformulowania i wyznaszenia kierunków badań szczególowych,' [Theory of Development of Economic Regions – an Attempt to Formulate and Establish the Directions of Specific Research] *Biuletyn KPZK PAN*, 1 (10), 1-114.

Secomski, K. (1965) 'O niektórych problemach teorii rozmie szczenia sil wytwórczych,' [On Some Problems of the Theory of Distribution of Productive Forces] in K. Secomski (Ed.), *Teoretyezne problemy rozmieszczenia sil wytworczych*. [Theoretical Problems of Distribution of Productive Forces] Warsaw: Panstwowe Wydawniotwa Skonomiczne, pp. 11-71.

Ullman, E.L. (1957) *American Commodity Flow*, Seattle, Washington: University of Washington Press.

Reprinted from the *Regional Science Association Papers*, Vol. 20, Hague Congress, 1967, Regional Science Association, with permission.

7 Location Theory and Regional Economic Growth

by Douglass C. North

University of Washington, Seattle

I

During the past several decades there has been a growing interest in location theory in America. Building on the pioneering works of Thünen, Weber, Lösch, Palander, and others,[1] a number of economists and geographers have extended the analysis to apply to a wide range of problems and have attempted to synthesize location theory with other fields of economics.[2] However, very little work has been done in using the principles of location to analyze the historical growth of regions in America.[3] While economists concerned with location theory sometimes point out the implications of their analysis for the growth of regions, they have not followed up these discrete observations with any systematic analysis. A fundamental difficulty has been that the theory of regional economic growth[4] has little relevance for the development of regions in America. Not only does the sequence of stages outlined by the theory bear little resemblance to American development but its policy implications are also fundamentally misleading.

This paper will attempt to demonstrate the inadequacies of the existing theory of regional economic growth and will advance a number of propositions that may lead to a more useful theory, both for analyzing the historical development of the American economy and for understanding the contemporary problems associated with regional economic growth.

The analytical propositions advanced in this paper, though explicitly oriented to America's development, would apply equally well to other areas that meet the following conditions: (1) regions that have grown up within a framework of capitalist institutions and have therefore responded to profit maximizing opportunities, in which factors of production have been relatively mobile[5] and (2) regions that have grown up without the strictures imposed by population pressure.

II

Both location theory and the theory of regional economic growth have described a typical sequence of stages through which regions move in the course of their development.[6] E.M. Hoover and Joseph Fisher, in a recent essay entitled 'Research in Regional Economic Growth,'[7] point-out that 'there is now a fairly well accepted body of theory regarding the normal sequence of development stages in a region.'[8] This sequence may be outlined as follows:

1 The first stage in the economic history of most regions is one of a self-sufficient subsistence economy in which there is little investment or trade. The basic agricultural stratum of population is simply located according to the distribution of natural resources.

2 With improvements in transport, the region develops some trade and local specialization. 'A second stratum of population comes into being, carrying on simple village industries for the farmers. Since the materials, the market, and the labor are all furnished originally by the agricultural populations, the new "industrial superstructure" is located with reference to that "basic stratum." '[9]

3 With the increase of interregional trade, a region tends to move through a succession of agricultural crops from extensive grazing to cereal production to fruit-growing, dairy farming, and truck gardening.[10]

4 With increased population and diminishing returns in agriculture and other extractive industries, a region is *forced* to industrialize. 'Industrialization means the introduction of so-called secondary industries (mining and manufacturing) on a considerable scale.'[11] Typically the early stages of industrialization are based on the products of agriculture and forestry and include such activities as the processing of food, the manufacture of wood products, and the preparation of textile fibers. If industrialization is to continue, mineral and energy resources become critical.

As a second stage of industrialization, then, we see [in the regions possessing economically usable mineral resources] such industries as the smelting, refining, and processing of metals; oil refining; chemical industries based mainly on coal, petroleum, potash, salt, and other minerals; and glass and ceramics industries. Where cheap hydroelectric power is available,' industries requiring large amounts of cheap power (nonferrous metals refining, ferroalloys, and special steels, artificial abrasives, etc.) are possible, as in Norway, Switzerland, the Tennessee Valley, and the Columbia River Valley.[12]

5 A final stage of regional growth is reached when a region specializes in tertiary industries producing for export. Such a region exports to less advanced regions capital, skilled personnel, and special services.

The role of transport costs has been critical in the advancement through these successive stages of growth. Isard summarizes this effect as follows: 'Historically we find that reduced transport rates have tended (1) to transform a scattered, ubiquitous pattern of production into an increasingly concentrated one, and (2) to effect progressive differentiation and selection between sites with superior and inferior resources and trade routes.'[13]

III
When this sequence of stages is placed against the economic history of regions in America, two basic objections arise. (1) These stages bear little resemblance to the actual development of regions. Moreover, they fail to provide any insights into the causes of growth and change. A theory of regional economic growth should clearly focus on the critical factors that implement or impede development. (2) Furthermore, if we want a normative model of how regions should grow, in order to analyze the causes of arrested development or relative decay, then this sequence of stages is of little use and is actually misleading in the emphasis it places on the need for (and difficulties of) industrialization.[14]

The problems of industrialization will be explored later in this paper when the causes of regional growth are examined. Here we are concerned with the first objection: the lack of correspondence between the stages of the theory of regional economic growth and the economic history of regions in America. A major discrepancy is immediately evident; namely, that America was exploited in large part as a capitalist venture. Settlement in new regions and their subsequent growth were shaped by the search for and exploitation of goods in demand on world markets. The result was a kind of development very different from that implied by the theory of regional development in which regions gradually extended the market from a subsistence economy. From the early joint-stock companies on through the whole westward expansion, a basic objective was to exploit the land and its resources in order to produce goods that could be marketed 'abroad' and would bring in a money income. This is in marked contrast to the experience of Europe (which appears to be the model for the early stages of the theory of regional economic growth),

where a market-oriented economy emerged only gradually from the predominantly local economies of the manorial system. If a subsistence economy existed in a new region in America, it was solely because of a lack of means of transport, a condition that was swiftly remedied by the concerted efforts of the settlers.[15] This is not to deny that many homesteaders maintained a subsistence existance but only to affirm that such settlement was not significant in shaping the economic development of the region, any more than the modern subsistence farmer of the backcountry is shaping the development of contemporary agriculture.

This point may be illustrated briefly from the economic history of the Pacific Northwest.[16] Not only has this region never experienced a subsistence economy, but its markets from the very beginning have often been thousands of miles distant. Even before general settlement, the region was exploited for its furs by the Hudson Bay Company. With the decline of the fur trade and the coming of settlers, wheat, flour, and lumber were quickly developed as exportable commodities. They first found markets in California in the 1840's. With the gold rush the demand for both wheat and lumber expanded tremendously, and the region experienced rapid growth based on these two commodities. In 1868 the first wheat shipment went from Portland to Liverpool, and by the late 1870's Pacific Northwest soft wheat had become an important part of the world wheat trade; a fleet of ships sailed from the region around Cape Horn every year. In 1857 the first shipment of flour was made to Japan, and thereafter Pacific Northwest flour found markets in Australia, Hawaii, the Orient, Europe, British Columbia, and California.[17] In each decade after 1850 an increasing percentage of the crop was exported either as wheat or in the form of flour. Before the end of the nineteenth century over half the crop was being exported from the region.

The history of the lumber industry reflects a similar preoccupation with markets foreign to the region. The first lumber shipment went to California in 1847, and during the gold rush lumber exports from the Pacific Northwest expanded rapidly. The rate of growth of the lumber industry was directly related to the growth of the markets reached by water (primarily California, British Columbia, and some foreign markets). In 1894 James J. Hill established a 40 per cent per hundredweight freight rate on lumber to Minneapolis on his railroads, and the industry began to compete with the southern pine region for markets in the Middle West. With this rapid growth of markets the industry expanded many fold. In the first five years of the twentieth century output more than doubled, and thereafter in each successive decade Pacific Northwest fir increased its share of the national market at the expense of southern pine. The rate of growth of the region has been directly related to these basic exports. Between 1860 and 1920 lumber and flour milling accounted for between 40 and 60 per cent of the value of the region's manufacturing output. Almost all the rest of secondary industry (as well as tertiary industry) was passive in the sense that it served local consumer needs. Its growth therefore reflected the changing fortunes of the region's exportable commodities.[18] Wheat played a similarly critical role in the development of the region, although by the end of the nineteenth century the agricultural export base had broadened to include a number of other commodities.

This brief account of the development of the Pacific Northwest bears no resemblance to the theory of regional economic growth. There was no gradual evolution out of a subsistence economy. Instead the whole development of the region from the beginning was dependent on its success in producing exportable commodities. Nor was the Pacific Northwest's history exceptional. Furs and the products of mining were typically the early exportable commodities of western America. Colonial America exported such products as tobacco, rice, indigo, naval stores, ships, and fish. Even the well-worn historical generalization of location theorists that reduced transport rates will transform a scattered, ubiquitous pattern of production into an increasingly concentrated one is not true of America. Many new regions in America developed from the beginning around one or two exportable commodities and only widened their export base *after* transport costs had been reduced.[19] In short, both this generalization of location theorists and the early stages in the theory of regional economic growth appear to be taken uncritically from European experience rather than derived from the economic history of this country.

A basic starting point for reshaping our views on regional economic growth might well be the insights of the late Harold Innis in his studies of the growth of the Canadian economy.[20] Innis' early research had convinced him of the crucial importance of the export staple in shaping new economies. His subsequent studies of the growth of these staple exports were always directed toward attempting to understand 'how the Canadian economy had been generated and how it had been shaped as a working economy.'[21] An analysis of the export staples of the Canadian economy became the basis for understanding the character of that country's economic development. Moreover, it provided real insights into the political and social institutions of the country.

The term 'staple' refers to the chief commodity produced by a region. It is customarily thought of as describing products of extractive industry. Since my concept of the export commodities of a region may include products of secondary or tertiary industry as well, I shall use the term 'exportable commodities' (or service) to denote the individual items and the export base[22] to denote collectively the exportable commodities (or services) of a region. In young regions, typically dependent on extractive industry, my exportable commodities and Innis' export staples are synonymous.

Settlers in new regions typically experimented with a number of different crops before discovering one that was economically feasible.[23] The success of an industry in producing an exportable commodity can be understood in terms of the principles of location theory.[24] The development of an exportable commodity reflected a comparative advantage in relative costs of production, including transfer costs. Distributive transfer costs have served to limit the extent of the export market.

From the viewpoint of the region, the demand for the exportable commodity was an exogenous factor, but both processing and transfer costs were not. Historically new regions bent every effort to reduce these costs in their concerted drive to promote their economic well-being. The ceaseless efforts of new regions to get federally subsidized internal improvements, state aid for canal construction, federal and state aid for railroads, and river and harbor improvements were a part of the continuous effort of each region to reduce transfer costs to better the competitive position of its exports.[25]

As regions grew up around the export base, external economies developed which improved the competitive cost position of the exportable commodities. The development of specialized marketing organization, improved credit and transport facilities, a trained labor force, and complementary industries was oriented to the export base.

The concerted effort to improve the technology of production has been equally important. Agricultural experiment stations, state universities, and other local research groups become service adjuncts to export industries and conduct research in technological improvements in agriculture, mining, or whatever manufacturing comprises the region's export base.

The purpose of this concerted effort is better to enable the region to compete with other regions or foreign countries for markets. In new regions highly dependent on extractive industry, these external economies and technological developments tend to more than counteract diminishing returns in the staple product.[26] As a result, these efforts tend to reinforce a region's dependence on its existing staples rather than promote changes in the export base. This conservative bias is further reinforced by the role of capital. Capital is typically imported into new regions in the development of the export staple industries. Indeed, until a region develops sufficient income to provide a substantial share of its own investment capital, it must rely upon outside sources. External suppliers of capital tend to invest primarily in existing export industry rather than in new, untried enterprises.[27]

IV

The following section will deal with the way in which regions grow; first, however, we must explore the significance of the export base in shaping the whole character of a region's economy.

At the outset, export industries must be clearly distinguished from 'residentiary industries.'[28] The term 'residentiary' is used to designate industry for the local market which develops where the consuming population resides. In order to determine the market area of each industry more precisely than can be done by a priori classification, the 'location quotient' developed by Hildebrand and Mace[29] is employed. The location quotient measures the concentration of employment in a given industry in one area (the 'subject economy,' which for our purposes is the region) with another area (the 'benchmark economy,' which for our purposes is the nation).

Formally the location quotient is the numerical equivalent of a fraction whose numerator is employment in a given industry in the subject economy relative to total employment in the subject economy and whose denominator is employment in the given industry in the benchmark economy relative to total employment in the benchmark economy. *A priori* a location of 1.00 means no greater relative specialization in the subject economy than in the benchmark economy, for the particular industry. In each industry values significantly below 1.00 indicate much greater relative specialization in the benchmark eco-

nomy; or if well over 1.00 much greater relative specialization in the subject economy.[30]

Thus industries producing for export will show values significantly above 1.00.[31]

We are now in a better position to examine the role of the export base in shaping the economy of the region.

Clearly the export base plays a vital role in determining the level of absolute and per capita income of a region. While the return to factors of production[32] in the export industries indicates the direct importance of these industries for the well being of the region, it is the indirect effect that is most important. Since residentiary industry depends entirely on demand within the region, it has historically been dependent on the fate of the export base.[33] Vining's analysis indicates that employment in residentiary industry tends to bear a direct relationship to employment in export industries. The median figure for employment in residentiary industry in individual states was approximately 55 per cent of the total employment.[34]

The export staple plays an equally vital role in the cyclical sensitivity of the region; it acts as the 'carrier' in diffusing changes in the level of income from other regions to the subject region. Furthermore, the sensitivity of the region to fluctuations depends on the income elasticities of the export staples. Clearly regions that specialize in a few products with high income elasticities will have more violent fluctuations in income than more diversified regions.[35]

When we turn to the role of exports in shaping the pattern of urbanization and nodal centers,[36] we are on ground that has been more thoroughly explored by location theorists and geographers.[37] Again, however, the pioneering work has been done by German location theorists who have extended the implications of each stage of economic growth to embrace the logical pattern of urbanization that would ensue.[38] Since these stages do not fit the American development, the pattern of American urbanization likewise differs in many respects from the German models. However, it is beyond the scope of this article to explore the whole question of urbanization and the export base. We may note in passing the observations of August Lösch that in such areas as Iowa, with a rather even distribution of production of agricultural staples, the distances between towns increase with their size.[39] In contrast, cities in the English coal districts are the same distance from each other irrespective of size.[40]

While discussion of the spatial distribution of urban areas would take us too far afield, the role of the export base in shaping the growth of nodal centers deserves some attention. Nodes grow up because of special locational advantages that lower the transfer and processing costs of exportable commodities. Nodal centers become trading centers through which exports leave the region and imports enter for distribution throughout the area. Here special facilities develop to implement the production and distribution of the staples. Subsidiary industries to service the export industry, as well as specialized banking, brokerage, wholeselling, and other business services, concentrate in these centers and act to improve the cost position of the export.[41]

The character of the labor force will be fundamentally influenced by the export industries. The types of skills required, the seasonality and stability of employment, and the conditions of work will shape the social attitudes of the working force.

As already noted, the political attitudes of the region will be largely directed toward improving the position of its export base. The extent of such activity is too well known historically and too obvious in the contemporary American political scene to require extended discussion.

V

Previous sections of this paper have examined the significance of the export base for a region's economy. I have tried to indicate the primary role that such exports have played historically, but I have not yet touched on the critical question of the causes of the growth of a region. It is evident that this growth is closely tied to the success of its exports and may take place either as a result of the improved position of existing exports relative to competing areas or as a result of the development of new exports. However, a major question that must first be examined is whether a region must industrialize if it is to continue to grow. Such a necessity has been a major tenet of the theory of regional economic growth. Moreover, industrialization has been regarded as a difficult stage to achieve, so that it is the source of problems of arrested regional development. Hoover and Fisher stress three factors that make this transition difficult: (1) the need for greatly improved transportation facilities, which call for large scale capital investments; (2) the need for intensification of the geographic division of labor; and (3) the fact that industrial technology is novel to an agricultural region.[42] If these statements are correct, then the implications for our analysis are clear. At some point regions must shift from an extractive to an industrial export base, and this shift will be fraught with diffi-

culties. However, the contention that regions must industrialize in order to continue to grow, as well as the contention that the development of secondary and tertiary industry is somehow difficult to achieve, are both based on some fundamental misconceptions.

The importance of industrializing is based upon the notion that, with increased population and diminishing returns in extractive industry, the shift to manufacturing is the only way to maintain sustained growth (measured in terms of increasing per capita income). This argument has been buttressed by evidence such as that gathered by Dr. Louis Bean correlating per capita income with percentage of the labor force engaged in primary, secondary, and tertiary occupations by states for 1939.[43] Bean's figures purport to demonstrate that increased industrialization leads to higher per capita income, and he goes so far as to say that 'a 10 point [per cent] increase in industrial progress in the east and south . . . apparently tends to add $100 to $150 (1939 prices) per capita and in the western states substantially more.'[44] In fact, Bean's statistics do not prove this, and the policy implications of such generalizations may be misleading and dangerous.

We may note first of all that his correlation is not very impressive. There were eleven states in which the percentage of the labor force in primary occupations was above the national average whose per capita income either exceeded the national average or was close enough to the average so that annual variations could well place it on one side or the other. Indeed, had the correlation been made for postwar years, it would have been substantially different.[45]

Furthermore, money income data significantly understate the real income of the farmer,[46] because of the great variety of goods and services produced on the farm that require cash payment in the city.[47]

However, the real source of error has resulted from a basic misunderstanding of the nature of the economy. A state whose export base consists mostly of agricultural products may have a low percentage of its labor force in primary activity and a high percentage in tertiary occupations and *yet* be basically dependent upon agriculture for the high per capita income it enjoys. It is the agricultural export staples that provide the high income that enables the state to support a substantial level of services. In such a case both the secondary and the tertiary activities are 'residentiary' and can survive only because of the success of the basic agricultural export staples. In short, a percentage shift in such a state from primary to secondary and tertiary employment does not necessarily reflect a shift away from dependence on agriculture to dependence on manufacturing and services. Instead, it may reflect the simple fact that farmers are receiving high incomes for their staple crops and therefore buy more goods and services from residentiary industry.

This brings us to the related question of the difficulty of industrialization. The implication of the preceeding paragraph is that a substantial amount of secondary industry of the residentiary variety will develop automatically as a result of high incomes received from the exportable commodities. Nor is this the only kind of manufacturing that can be expected to develop. We may distinguish four different kinds of manufacturing that will develop:[48]

1 Materials-oriented industries which, because of marked transfer advantages of the manufactured product over the raw material, locate at the source of the latter. Among the industries in this category are sugar-beet refining, flour-milling,[49] and lumbering.[50] Such industries may develop further stages of vertical integration until transfer cost advantages become equalized. Such industry is typically part of the export base.

2 Service industries to the export industry. Foundries and establishments that make machine tools, specialized agricultural implements, and logging and lumbering equipment are illustrations.

3 Residentiary industry producing for local consumption.

4 Footloose industries, where transfer costs are not of significant importance in location. A great many such industries develop purely by chance in some location.[51]

While footloose industries have typically developed by chance, the other three types of secondary activity develop naturally because of locational advantages in a society responsive to profit-maximizing stimuli. There is nothing difficult about the development of such industries. The difficulties arise when promoters seek to develop in a region industries which simply are unsuited for the area and which can therefore only be maintained under hothouse conditions.[52]

The argument may be advanced that the kinds of industry described above do not constitute industrialization. How much and what kind of secondary industry must a region possess to be termed 'industrialized'? By 1950 census classification, the state of Oregon had almost 24 per cent of its labor force in manufacturing, which was only slightly under the United States average (25.9 per cent) and exceeded the United States average in durable goods (16.7 per cent as compared with the national average of 13.8 per cent). It was well ahead of the neighboring states of Washington and California, despite the fact that these two states had a variety of manufacturing industries, in contrast to Oregon's specialized dependence on the Douglas fir lumber industry. Is such a state industrialized? Implicit in the concept appears to be the notion that industrialization is somehow tied up with steel and the capital goods industries. However, historically, the locational pull of coal and iron ore has shaped the development of the steel producing centers, which in turn have attracted and concentrated heavy industry.[53] While locational influences in the steel industry have been changing significantly in the last half-century with the growing importance of scrap and the changing composition of inputs,[54] nevertheless, the possible areas for the development of efficient large-scale steel production[55] and, therefore, capital goods industry are severely circumscribed. A more useful concept of industrialization for our purposes is a region whose export base consists primarily of finished consumers' goods and/or finished manufactured producers' goods.

We may summarize the argument up to this point as follows: (1) There is no reason why all regions must industrialize in order to continue to grow. (2) A great deal of secondary (and tertiary) industry will develop automatically either because of locational advantages of materials-oriented industry or as a passive reflection of growing income in the region resulting from the success of its exportable commodities. (3) The concept of industrialization is an ambiguous one that needs further clarification if it is to be useful.

Since the growth of a region is tied to the success of its export base, we must examine in more detail the reasons for the growth, decline, and change in the export base. Clearly, the decline of one exportable commodity must be accompanied by the growth of others, or a region will be left 'stranded.'[56] Among the major reasons[57] for the decline of an existing exportable commodity have been changes in demand outside the region,[58] exhaustion of a natural resource,[59] increasing costs of land or labor relative to those of a competing region,[60] and technological changes that changed the relative composition of inputs.[61] A historically important reason for the growth of new exports has been major developments in transport (in contrast with mere cost-reducing improvements in transport, which may reinforce dependence on existing exports). Such developments have often enabled a region to compete with other regions in the production of goods that were previously economically unfeasible because of the high transfer costs.[62] Growth in income and demand in other regions[63] and technological development[64] have also been important. The role of the state and federal government in creating social overhead benefits has created new exports in many regions,[65] and the significance of war in promoting industries that may either continue or leave a residue of capital investment for peacetime use has also been important.

A region may expand as a result of increased demand for its existing exportable commodities, whether due to an increase in the income of the market area or to a change in taste. An improvement in the processing or transfer-cost position of the region's staples vis-à-vis competing regions will likewise promote growth.

Historically, in a young region, the creation of a new export or the expansion of an existing export has resulted in the influx of capital investment both in the export industry and in all the kinds of passive and supporting economic activity described above. Meier has described this process for the Canadian economy in the first decade of the twentieth century, when increased world demand for wheat not only led to an expansion of warehousing, transport, public utilities, and construction in the Prairie Provinces, but also, by increasing income, augmented demand for secondary products and thereby induced investment in a host of other industries.[66] As a result the growth of a region will, in all likelihood, be uneven, coming in spurts of increased investment rather than proceeding at an even pace.

Increased capital investment in the export industry will go toward achieving optimum size of the enterprise, increased mechanization of the processes, and further development of the specialized services to the export. The source of capital will play an important part in the region's growth. Typically, the capital in young regions comes from outside. Profits (and some other nonwage income) flow out of the region. To the extent that the export base is profitable, a part of this income will be reinvested in the expansion of this base.

With the growth of population and income, indigenous savings will increase. Both indigenous savings and the reinvested capital can pour back into the export industries only up to a point, and then the accumulated capital will tend to overflow into other activity. As described above, some will go into residentiary industry and industries subsidiary to the export; but it is also very likely that some will go into locationally 'footloose' industries, which may start out to serve only the region, but which can expand into export industries.

At this point a region is no longer young. The social overhead benefits that have been created through political pressure or as a part of the pattern of urban development and the development of a trained labor force and indigenous capital make it far easier to develop new exports. Whether such industries were originally residentiary and, by gradually overcoming transfer cost disadvantages, became export industries, or were originally footloose industries not significantly affected by transfer costs, the result is to broaden the export base. As such a region matures, the staple base will become less distinguishable, since its production will be so varied.

We may expect, therefore, that the differences between regions will become less marked, that secondary industry will tend to be more equalized, and indeed in economic terms that regionalism will tend to disappear.

VI

The purpose of this paper has been to re-examine location theory and the theory of regional economic growth in the light of the historical development of regions in America and to advance some propositions that may lead to a new theory of regional economic growth.

It has been argued that the stages outlined in the theory of regional economic growth bear little relationship to the character of American development and more specifically do not focus on the crucial elements that will enable us to understand that growth. Furthermore, the traditional theory has policy implications that may be fundamentally in error.

The first stage of subsistence has been relatively unimportant, and, to the extent that it existed at all, it was because means of transport were lacking rather than because of a nonmarket orientation. In Europe a subsistence or a village economy with local markets was built into the social and economic structure for centuries. In America subsistence was only a frontier condition to be overcome as rapidly as means of transport could be built.

The second stage of the theory is based on a gradual widening of the market area with improved transport and the development of a second stratum to service the basic agricultural stratum. Far from moving through such a gradual progression American regions, as soon as any transport permitted, developed goods for export often to markets thousands of miles away. The early town centers were located not only so as to service the agricultural stratum but so as to implement the export of the region's staples. The prosperity of the region depended on its success in competing with other areas producing the same staple exports. Therefore, the region's economic and political efforts were oriented toward the reduction of processing and transfer costs. The struggle for internal improvements by the West, the agrarian pressure for inflation and cheaper credit, and the campaign for free coinage of silver were fundamentally economic movements. Their objectives included increasing the supply of capital, eliminating real or fancied transport discrimination, reducing interest rates, and improving the market for silver, however much they may also have been concerned with social justice.

The third stage of regional growth has been described as the gradual shift from extensive to intensive farming. While it is true that rising land values promoted such a shift, there were many other reasons for a shift in the staple base. New means of transport, changing demand, new technological developments, changing cost relationships vis-à-vis competing regions, government subsidization of social overhead benefits, and war have all been important.

The shift from an agricultural to an industrial base has been looked upon as the difficult, but indispensable, step for sustained economic growth. It is a major argument of this paper that such a step may be neither necessary nor desirable and that the evidence customarily advanced to support this argument proves nothing of the sort. There is nothing to prevent population and per capita income from growing in a region whose export base is agricultural. Moreover, there is nothing difficult about developing secondary and tertiary industry in such a region. Indeed, it will develop automatically, often to such an extent that analysis of the region in terms of distribution of employment will lead to the conclusion that it is an industrial region.

The final stage has typically been conceived to be the mature regional economy exporting capital, skills, and specialized services to less-well-developed regions. While this may be true for some regions, it is unlikely to be a final stage for all. Indeed, one would presume that some sort of balanced relationship would emerge among regions as transfer costs become less significant and income differentials tend to be ironed out by long-run factor mobility.

The major propositions that emerge from this paper are:

1 For economists' purposes the concept of a region should be redefined to point out that the unifying cohesion to a region, over and beyond geographic similarities, is its development around a common export base. It is this that makes it economically unified and ties the fortunes of the area together. This tends to result in the interdependent development within the region of external economies and unified political efforts for government assistance or political reform. The geographer has emphasized the distributive functions of the nodal centers of a region, but the role of the nodal center in providing external economics for the export industries has been equally important.

2 The success of the export base has been the determining factor in the rate of growth of regions. Therefore, in order to understand this growth, we must examine the locational factors that have enabled the staples to develop.

3 The importance of the export base is a result of its primary role in determining the level of absolute and per capita income in a region, and therefore in determining the amount of residentiary secondary and tertiary activity that will develop. The export base has also significantly influenced the character of subsidiary industry, the distribution of population and pattern of urbanization, the character of the labor force, the social and political attitudes of the region, and its sensitivity to fluctuations of income and employment.

4 In a young region dependence on staples is reinforced by the concerted efforts of the region's residents to reduce processing and transfer costs through technological research, and state and federal government subsidization or social overhead benefits, as well as the tendency for outside suppliers of capital to reinvest in the existing staple base.

5 Some regions, because of locational advantages, have developed an export base of manufactured products, but this is not a necessary stage for the sustained growth of all regions. A great deal of secondary and tertiary industry will result from the success of the export base. This residentiary industry will, in all likelihood, provide for widening the export base as a region develops.

6 The growth of regions has tended to be uneven. A given increase in demand for the region's exports (or a significant reduction in processing or transfer costs) has resulted in a multiple effect on the region, inducing increased investment not only in the export industry but in all other kinds of economic activity as well.

7 As a region's income grows, indigenous savings will tend to spill over into new kinds of activities. At first, these activities satisfy local demand, but ultimately some of them will become export industries. This movement is reinforced by the tendency for transfer costs to become less significant. As a result, the export bases of regions tend to become more diversified, and they tend to lose their identity as regions. Ultimately, we may expect with long-run factor mobility more equalization of per capita income and a wider dispersion of production.

Notes

1 A summary of earlier contributions to location theory may be found in E.M. Hoover, *Location Theory and the Shoe and Leather Industries* (Cambridge: Harvard University Press, 1937).

2 In addition to Hoover's valuable study cited above, see his *The Location of Economic Activity* (New York: McGraw-Hill Book Co., 1948). See also Bertil Ohlin, *Interregional and International Trade* (Cambridge: Harvard University Press, 1935); National Resources Planning Board, *Industrial Location and National Resources* (Washington, D.C.; Government Printing Office, 1943); and the articles by Walter Isard cited below.

3 A significant exception is Walter Isard's 'Transportation Development and Building Cycles,' *Quarterly Journal of Economics*', LVII (November, 1942), 90-112. See also William H. Dean, *The Theory of the Geographic Location of Economic Activities (Selections from the Doctoral Dissertation)* (Ann Arbor: Edward Bros, Inc., 1938).

4 See Sec. II below.

5 Obviously both profit maximization and factor mobility are relative notions and nowhere perfectly met. However, there is a vast difference between the response of an underdeveloped area where the social and economic structure is not fundamentally geared to capitalist stimuli and the kind of response one can expect in a basically capitalist society. The reluctance of the economic historian to make more extensive use of the tools of the theorist reflects in good part the fact that most of the world's economic history falls outside our first condition and that therefore economic theory is of little use in analyzing a large part of its development. On the other hand, the joint efforts of economic theorists and historians applied to the development of the United States and of some other areas hold out the promise of yielding valuable insights.

6 See August Lösch, 'The Nature of Economic Regions,' *Southern Economic Journal*, V (July, 1938), 71-78; Hoover, *Location Theory and the Shoe and Leather Industries*, pp. 284-85, and *The Location of Economic Activity*, pp. 187-88.

7 Universities — National Bureau Committee for Economic Research, *Problems in the Study of Economic Growth* (New York: National Bureau of Economic Research, 1949), chap. v.

8 *Ibid.*, p. 180.

9 Hoover, *Location Theory and the Shoe and Leather Industries*, p. 284. The second stage of regional growth has been elaborated by Hoover and Fisher to include some further specialization and interregional trade (*op. cit.*, p. 181).

10 The theory of location diverges here from the theory of regional economic growth in stressing the historical pattern of the emergence from feudalism. Since this pattern has little meaning for American development, it is omitted here. However, it will be an important part of my argument that American location theorists have implicitly accepted a good deal of this stage sequence based on the European experience of emergence out of feudalism without recognizing the significant difference between this pattern and the pattern of American development.

11 Hoover and Fisher, *op. cit.*, p. 182.

12 Hoover, *The Location of Economic Activity*, p. 193.

13 Walter Isard, 'Distance Inputs and the Space Economy. Part I. The Conceptional Framework,' *Quarterly Journal of Economics*, LXV (May, 1951), 188-98.

14 Hoover and Fisher stress the difficulties of achieving an industrial stage and maintain that most of the bottlenecks and problems of arrested development occur in moving from an agricultural to an industrial economic base (*op. cit.*, pp. 182-84).

15 More often than not, this concerted effort was directed toward getting the government to provide the necessary internal improvements.

16 This brief summary of the development of the Pacific Northwest is condensed from a larger research project that I am currently undertaking. Support for the data presented here may be found in John B. Watkins, *Wheat Exporting from the Pacific Northwest* (State College of Washington Agricultural Experiment Station Bull. 201 [May, 1926]; the Silver Anniversary Number of the *Commercial Review* (Portland, Ore.), July 1, 1915; E.S. Meany, Jr., 'History of Northwest Lumbering' (Ph.D. dissertation, Harvard University, 1935); and R.W. Vinnedge, *The Pacific Northwest Lumber Industry and its Development* (New Haven: Yale University School of Forestry, 1923).

17 A substantial amount of the wheat and flour sent to California was exported to Europe.

18 This point will be elaborated and qualified in the following section.

19 In the Pacific Northwest the export base (particularly of agricultural commodities) only broadened after the advent of the railroad.

20 See *The Fur Trade in Canada* (New Haven: Yale University Press, 1920); *The Cod Fishery: The History of an International Economy* (New Haven: Yale University Press, 1940); *Problems of Staple Production in Canada* (Toronto: University of Toronto Press, 1933); and, in collaboration with A.R.M. Lower, *Settlement and the Forest and Mining Frontier* (Toronto: Macmillan Co., 1936).

21 W.A. Mackintosh, 'Innis on Canadian Economic Development,' *Journal of Political Economy*, June, 1953, p. 188. This article provides an excellent summary of Innis' views.

22 The use of the term 'base' has become popular among urban land economists and city planners in the concept of the urban economic base, which refers to those activities of a metropolitan community that export goods and services to other areas. For a history of the development of the concept see Richard B. Andrews, 'Mechanics of the Urban Economic Base: Historical Development of the Base Concept,' *Land Economics*, XXIX (May, 1953), 161-67.

23 The experiments with silkworm culture in the Southern Colonies are a famous case in point.

24 For our purposes it is convenient to follow Hoover's breakdown of costs into procurement, processing and distribution costs (see *The Location of Economic Activity*, pp. 7-9, 15-115). While processing costs reflect factor-input coefficients and factor prices, procurement and distribution costs depend fundamentally on transfer costs.

Isard has done a great deal of work attempting to introduce the problems of space into economic theory through the concept of distance inputs (the movement of a unit weight over a unit distance). The price of a distance input is the transport rate and, as in the case of capital inputs, a reduction in price has both a scale and a substitution effect. Distance inputs are conceived to be simply another factor of production whose price is the transport rate and whose optimum combination with other factors can be determined by the principles of substitution (see his 'Distance Inputs and the Space Economy,' *op. cit.*)

25 Such efforts have not been confined to pressure-group activity but have erupted into political movements. The Grangers and the Populists were fundamentally concerned with a number of economic measures that would, for example, improve the position of American wheat on the world wheat market or provide the western miner with a better market for his silver.

26 In the case of mining this statement probably would not hold.

27 This outside capital often comes in waves associated with (or in anticipation of) substantial reductions in costs or increases in demand. As a result the growth of regions tends to be uneven. This whole subject of the growth of regions is dealt with in more detail in Sec. V.

28 The term 'residentiary industry' was first used by P. Sargent Florence in National Resources Planning Board mimeographed releases. Rutledge Vining subsequently employed the concept in 'Location of Industry and Regional Patterns of Business Cycle Behavior,' *Econometrica*, XIV (January, 1946), 37-68.

29 George Hildebrand and Arthur Mace, Jr., 'The Employment Multiplier in an Expanding Industrial Market: Los Angeles County, 1940-47.' *Review of Economics and Statistics*, XXXII (August, 1950), 341-49.

P. Sargent Florence developed the concept of a coefficient of localization. He first computed a 'location factor' for each industry by computing the ratio of the percentage of employment in the given region found in the given industry to the corresponding percentage for the nation as a whole. If all industries were perfectly evenly distributed among regions, the location factor would be unity. 'The coefficient of localization for a given industry is obtained by computing the weighted average deviation from unity of the location factors for all regions, the weight for a local region being the proportion of total national employment found in that region. This measure divided by two varies between zero and unity' (Vining, *op. cit.*, pp. 40-51). Completely even geographic distribution would give a coefficient of zero, while increasingly greater concentration of industry in a region would give a coefficient approaching unity. Although this method is somewhat different from that of Hildebrand and Mace, the result is the same.

30 Hildebrand and Mace, *op. cit.*, p. 243. In their study

of Los Angeles County these authors varied the subject and benchwork economies. Using the United States as the benchmark economy, they used successively the twelve western states, the eleven counties of southern California, and Los Angeles County as subject economies. Then using the eleven western states as the benchmark economy, they used southern California and Los Angeles County as subject economics and finally used Los Angeles County relative to southern California. As a result, they were able to delimit precisely the extent of the market for each export (while exports out of the country would increase the location quotient, they would not of course be isolated by this technique).

31 Hildebrand and Mace allowed for differences in demand functions, which might make some residentiary industry appear with a location quotient above 1.00. They came to the conclusion that 1,508 was the boundary line in their study (*ibid.*, p. 246).

This location quotient is not too well adapted to use in agriculture. There I have used a coefficient of specialization in which the numerator is the region's physical volume of production relative to the physical volume of production of the agricultural good for the nation. The denominator is the region's absolute population relative to the nation's absolute population. While such a coefficient has some obvious limitations and must be used with care, it is more adaptable to the available data than the one discussed above.

32 Obviously the disposition of nonwage income to residents of the region or outside the region is important here. It will be further considered in the next section.

33 This statement requires both substantiation and careful qualification. This article is primarily concerned with the historical development of the American economy, and here the statement needs little qualification. The fortunes of regions have been closely tied to their export base. However, it is conceivable that a region with a large influx of population and capital might simply 'feed upon itself' and thereby account for a substantial share of its growth. Moreover, in older 'mature' regions, economic activity may become so diversified as to make the export base less significant. This question will be dealt with in the next section.

34 Vining, *op. cit.*, p. 49.

35 For further discussion of this subject see Vining, *op. cit.*

36 The concept of nodes is one that has been extensively used by geographers. The term refers to *sites* that have strategic transfer advantages in reference to procurement and distribution costs and therefore become processing centers. Such advantageous points are limited in number and tend to develop into major metropolitan areas. For further discussion of nodes see Hoover, *The Location of Economic Activity*, pp. 119-30.

37 For a summary of recent developments in this area see Walter Isard, 'Current Development in Regional Analysis,' *Weltwirtschaflliches Archiv*, LXIX (September, 1952), 81-91.

38 An excellent summary of the German contributions is contained in Isard's 'The General Theory of Location and Space Economy.' Quarterly Journal of Economics, LXIII (November, 1949), 476-506.

39 Lösch, *op. cit.*, p. 75. In this article Lösch advances an interesting theoretical model of spatial location.

40 *Ibid*, p. 75. A summary of the development of concepts of spatial organization may be found in Isard's 'Distance Inputs and the Space Economy,' *op. cit.*

41 These specialized facilities provide economies in addition to the general economies of urban concentration resulting from such things as fire and police protection, lower utility rates, and a specialized labor force. For further discussion of these aspects of urban concentration see Ohlin, *op. cit.*, pp. 203-4.

42 *Op.cit.*, p. 182. Hoover and Fisher go on to point out that 'further difficulty arises from the fact that when a non-industrial region reaches a limit of growth it is likely to retrogress or decay' (*ibid.*, p. 184).

43 *Studies in Income and Wealth*, VII (New York: National Bureau of Economic Research, 1946), 128-29.

44 *Ibid.*, p. 167.

45 See 'State Income Payments in 1950,' *Survey of Current Business*, August, 1951, p. 18.

46 There is also evidence to indicate that money incomes are disportionately understated.

47 See Margaret Reid, 'Distribution of Non money Income,' *Studies in Income and Wealth*, Vol. XIII (New York: National Bureau of Economic Research, 1951). See also Jacob Viner, *International Trade and Economic Development* (Glencoe, Ill.: Free Press, 1952), pp. 63-73. Professor Viner provides a number of trenchant criticisms of Bean's argument.

48 This classification is similar to that of E.J. Cohn, Jr., in *Industry in the Pacific Northwest and the Location*

Theory (New York: Columbia University Press, 1954), pp. 42-44.

49 However, milling-in-transit privileges may modify this materials orientation.

50 See National Resources Planning Board, *op. cit.*, chap. vi, for a further account of such industries.

51 For further discussion of such industries see National Resources Committee, *The Structure of the American Economy*, Part I: *Basic Characteristics* (Washington, D.C.: Government Printing Office, 1939), p. 36.

52 This does not mean that there is no room for appropriate public policy that may create the social overhead benefits that will make certain industries feasible. I can do no better here than to quote Viner: 'There are no inherent advantages of manufacturing over agriculture, or, for that matter, of agriculture over manufacturing. It is only arbitrarily in fact that the line separating the two can be drawn. The choice between expansion of agriculture and expansion of manufacturers can, for the most part, be left to the free decisions of capitalists, entrepreneurs and workers. To the extent that there is need for government decision, it should be made on national grounds, in the light of considerations of costs and comparative returns from alternative allocation of scarce national resources, human and material' (*op. cit.*, p. 72).

53 National Resources Planning Board, *op. cit.*, p. 162.

54 Walter Isard, 'Some Locational Factors in the Iron and Steel Industry since the Early Nineteenth Century,' *Journal of Political Economy*, LVI (1948), 213-17.

55 The extensive utilization of scrap makes possible small scale steel production as a residentiary industry wherever the local market achieves sufficient size.

56 The cut-over region in the Great Lakes area is a case in point.

57 For further discussion on shifting industry see National Resources Planning Board, *op. cit.*, pp. 92-104.

58 Such as the decline in the demand for beaver hats, which affected the fur trade.

59 Exemplified by the Great Lakes lumber industry.

60 The most famous example is the decline in the New England cotton textile industry.

61 Such as the case of steel cited above.

62 The whole history of canal and railroad development contains innumerable illustrations of such developments (see Isard, 'Transportation Development and Building Cycles,' *op. cit.*).

63 The growth in demand for wheat in England and on the European continent in the last half of the nineteenth century is a famous example.

64 The development of the petroleum industry is a typical illustration.

65 The development of hydroelectric power in the Pacific Northwest and the resultant development of the aluminum industry is an example.

66 G.M. Meier, 'Economic Development and the Transfer Mechanism,' *Canadian Journal of Economics and Political Science*, XIX (February, 1953), 1-19. M.C. Daly has attempted to work out a geographic multiplier between 'localized' and 'non-localized' industry, using data for Britain for the years 1921-31 ('An Approximation to a Geographic Multiplier,' *Economic Journal*, L [June-September, 1940]), 248-58. See also Hildebrand and Mace, *op. cit.*

Reprinted from *Journal of Political Economy*, 43, 1955, University of Chicago Press, Chicago, with permission.

8 State and Regional Payments Mechanisms
by James C. Ingram
University of North Carolina

The close similarity between interregional and international trade has long been recognized, and the theory of balance-of-payments adjustment has been thought applicable to regions within a nation as well as to separate nations. So it is, in a general sense, but general statements of the theory tend to become taxonomic.[1] Such a variety of circumstances may exist that the number of policy alternatives becomes unmanageably large.

The purposes of this paper are, first, to examine the payments mechanism for a single state within the United States in order to see how policy alternatives are limited by the position in which the state finds itself; and, second, to examine the implications of the analysis developed in the case of a state for the nation-member of a customs union.

I
When we take a single state of the United States as our geographic entity, many of the policy variables in ordinary balance-of-payments analysis are fixed by the legal and political structure in which the state exists. This fact considerably reduces the number of possibilities and enables us to talk more concretely about what the probable mechanism of adjustment will be.

Specifically, the following assumptions become 'reasonable' ones to make for the purpose of analyzing the balance of payments of a state. (In what follows we use North Carolina as our example.)

(a) The exchange rate is fixed at a par of unity. No exchange controls exist. Convertibility is complete and unhampered.

(b) The money supply is outside the control of state authorities. It will tend to respond 'automatically' to conditions of trade and payments. While the total supply will be determined by a supra-state agency (the Federal Reserve System or Treasury), it is unlikely to be varied because of the balance-of-payments conditions existing in North Carolina.

(c) Commercial policy is not available as a tool for balance-of-payments adjustment. Certain barriers exist, largely in forms of agricultural and administrative protection, but there is little or no scope for manipulation of these restrictions in order to exert a deliberate influence on trade.

(d) Prices are in large part fixed in the 'world' market. North Carolina is assumed to comprise so small a part of the total market for U.S. and world goods that variations in her demand will not affect their price. Similarly, North Carolina output is so small relative to the world market that the prices of North Carolina exports will not change in balance-of-payments adjustment. In short, foreign demand for North Carolina goods and foreign supply of North Carolina imports are both assumed to be perfectly elastic.[2]

(e) Labor is largely immobile in the short run because of cultural factors. Although wage rate differentials between North Carolina and the United States will induce movements of labor in the longer run, we will omit the effect of such movements in the following discussion. Wages are sticky in both directions.

(f) Some goods, and a number of services, do not or cannot enter into trade between North Carolina and the United States. The prices of such goods and services may change in the process of balance-of-payments adjustment.

These assumptions, along with a little casual empiricism, imply that North Carolina's marginal propensity to import is large, and that the rate of interest will differ only marginally in North Carolina from its level in the United States, especially for securities sold in national financial markets. Interest rate differences on such securities will be quickly erased by movements of funds, which are highly fluid and virtually costless.[3]

Within the framework of these assumptions, we shall analyze in a conventional way the mechanism of adjustment to a disturbance in the balance of payments. As the first example, let us take the classic case of a long-term capital movement. Starting from an initial equilibrium in which both internal and external balance exist, suppose U.S. capitalists decide to invest $1.0 billion in new plants to be constructed in North Carolina. (This is an addition to whatever capital flows existed in the initial equilibrium.)

As the new plants are constructed, expenditures are made for domestic North Carolina resources and for imported machinery and supplies. The former will cause incomes to rise in North Carolina and, to the extent that these expenditures are for nontraded materials and services, North Carolina prices will tend to rise. The reserves of North Carolina banks will rise by approximately the same amount as North Carolina demand deposits, thus increasing excess reserves of North Carolina banks. Since this increase in reserves is likely to be regarded as temporary, and since North Carolina banks may not be able or willing quickly to expand local loans, the banks are likely to acquire short-term assets through U.S. money markets. Consequently, the North Carolina money supply will not have a tendency to expand by a multiple of the increased reserves resulting from the capital movement, nor will the U.S. money supply tend to contract by such a multiple.

As domestic sellers of materials and services dispose of their increments of income, imports will rise. A large fraction of the increased consumption outlays is likely to be spent on imports, since North Carolina is highly specialized and dependent upon U.S. suppliers for much of her consumer goods. A portion will also be spent on goods previously exported. Thus the banks will soon find it necessary to sell their newly acquired short-term assets to cover the drain of reserves to the United States. However, it may take some time for the induced rise in imports to equal the increase in reserves resulting from the initial outlays for domestic material and services; and, to the extent that North Carolina residents save their income increments, North Carolina banks will be left with increased reserves (or foreign assets).[4]

The remainder of the planned construction outlay will be spent for imports of machinery and supplies for installation in North Carolina. To this extent the real capital inflow occurs immediately. (Labor and other services required from North Carolina factors have been included in the first category, above.) No direct change in North Carolina income or money supply is associated with this part of the capital inflow.

So far this descriptive account of the capital movement suggests that the bulk of the 'real transfer' is effected through the shift in purchasing power and the rise in North Carolina incomes. Only a small role is played by the price effect of classical price-specie-flow analysis. Our two regions are so closely linked that the disparate price movements of classical theory cannot occur, except in a small way as prices of nontraded goods and services rise in North Carolina. Similarly, the monetary systems are so closely linked that North Carolina banks, having acquired excess reserves, are content (or even prefer) to acquire U.S. short-term assets, thus preventing disparate movements in the money supply such as would be expected under the gold standard. To the extent that it involves an increase in expenditure in North Carolina, the capital movement brings about a rise in North Carolina money income, but a cumulative rise is quickly stopped by a high marginal propensity to import. Meanwhile, a large part of the capital inflow is initially spent for imported capital goods, thus producing no (immediate) income effect in North Carolina.[5] The institutional structure makes possible a smooth and rapid real transfer of capital with almost no price effect, not much of an income effect, and with no monetary phenomenon that is exactly equivalent to a gold flow. Equilibrating capital movements perform a much larger role in the adjustment process than was true in the classical gold standard case.[6]

As our second example, let us suppose that an increase in North Carolina domestic investment of $1.0 billion occurs, but without a prior decision by U.S. capitalists to finance the investment. The key question then becomes: How is the new investment financed? Several possible answers may be given:

(a) North Carolina owners of U.S. assets may decide to sell them, using the proceeds to finance domestic plant construction.

(b) The North Carolina state government may float a bond issue in U.S. money markets, and use the proceeds to finance domestic plant construction (either directly or by lending to private firms).

(c) North Carolina banks may decide to make loans to North Carolina business to finance the new construction. Without initial excess reserves, they will have to liquidate other assets such as U.S. securities. This then becomes a special case of (a) above.

(d) Funds for new investment expenditure may be released by reductions in consumption or current government expenditures. This might occur through: a spontaneous and voluntary increase in private savings out of given incomes, increased taxes which force such reduction in consumption, reduction in current government expenditures, or through a combination of these possibilities.

The first three of these alternatives, (a), (b), and (c), essentially involve a long-term capital inflow into North Carolina, and the analysis developed above will apply. The only difference – an important one – is that the initiative is taken by a different group or agency. In our original example foreign (U.S.) capitalists held the initiative. In (a), (b), and (c), respectively, the initiative is taken by North Carolina capitalists, the North Carolina government, and North Carolina banks. Only in the case of government initiative is any deliberate planning for a large-scale expansion of North Carolina domestic investment likely to be feasible. North Carolina capitalists and banks are likely to respond to about the same incentives as U.S. capitalists, and if one is willing to finance new investments the other will also be willing.

The fourth possibility is, of course, the traditional prescription for capital accumulation. In the case of a state, however, it is unlikely that the fiscal weapons will be effective. Both increased taxes and reduced current expenditures are likely. to frighten away as much foreign and domestic capital as they encourage or facilitate by releasing resources from other uses. Furthermore, if a spontaneous reduction of consumer expenditures occurred, North Carolina residents would be as likely to purchase U.S. assets as to finance North Carolina capital formation, if not more so. Where the saver and investor (purchaser of real capital) are one and the same person, a spontaneous reduction in consumption will probably mean an increase in North Carolina capital formation. This condition will hold where capital formation takes place in small business units, but it will rarely hold where large-scale plants are involved. Financing of the latter is likely to be dispersed (where it involves security sales to a wide public) or concentrated in business organizations whose decisions to invest are little affected by the geographic location of the physical plant (so long as it is within the United States).

We may conclude that, where a single state is concerned, the supply of capital is much less critical than the expected rate of return in determining the rate of investment. Paraphrasing Keynes, one may say that if Opportunity and Incentive are present, Thrift and Investible Funds will take care of themselves. Or, in other words, a state has access to a large pool of investible funds whose owners, both in the United States and in North Carolina, will respond to clear economic opportunities. When such funds are attracted to a state, existing institutions allow a smooth and rapid real transfer to occur. No 'transfer problem' exists.

It also seems to follow that a state can do little to promote capital formation within its borders. The main thing it can do is to make itself as attractive as possible to the owners of investible funds. That states have recognized this rudimentary fact is apparent when one examines the activities of state and local development-planning agencies. The only difficulty seems to lie in determining what will please the prospective investor. Some put their faith in low taxes, cheap labor, and free land or buildings, while others rely on good schools, abundant public services, and skilled labor. Unfortunately, our analysis furnishes no clues to this problem.

But what if North Carolina rejects this passive and waiting role? What if state authorities are determined to take positive steps to expand capital formation? We have noted that the North Carolina government could issue bonds and use the proceeds for domestic investment. This constitutes a long-term capital inflow (if bonds are sold through the national capital markets) and presupposes sound state credit and willingness on the part of U.S. residents to buy the bonds. We have also noted that North Carolina could raise taxes or lower current state expenditure in order to raise funds for investment. Both of these seem limited in scope, especially since they may cause a drop in the existing rate of capital inflow from the United States.

A third approach is more similar to plans and proposals now being advanced by underdeveloped nations anxious to promote economic growth. The state government might *create* additional loanable funds within North Carolina by reducing reserve requirements for state banks (not members of the Federal Reserve System), or by permitting such banks to count new issues of North Carolina bonds as part of their reserves.[7] Both actions enable nonmember banks in North Carolina to expand their loans and deposits.

Let us suppose that reserve requirements are lowered sufficiently to create $10 million of excess reserves in North Carolina banks, and that loans of this magnitude are made to finance domestic investment. As before, we assume that the new expenditure is used partly for direct purchases of imports and partly for domestic goods and service. Both direct and induced imports will cause North Carolina banks to run adverse clearing balances with U.S. banks. It is now necessary to discuss several cases:

(a) Imports are paid for with checks drawn on nonmember North Carolina banks.

(1) Nonmember North Carolina banks keep their reserves in U.S. banks. In this case adverse clearings will reduce reserves of North Carolina banks. In the limiting case, adverse clearing balances will reach the amount of initial excess reserves (and thus equal the amount of new loans made), and the North Carolina money supply will return to its former level. The increased imports will

have been paid for with a reduction in short-term assets abroad – i.e., with a short-term capital inflow.

It is possible that this limit will not be reached – i.e., that the North Carolina money supply will remain higher than before, in which case part of the initial excess reserve will become required. Imports will have risen by less than the amount of new loans made.

(2) Nonmember North Carolina banks keep their reserves in North Carolina member banks. In this case adverse clearing balances of nonmember North Carolina banks will reduce their reserves. But North Carolina member banks, which must settle the checks drawn in favor of U.S. residents, will suffer a drop in their reserve deposits with Federal Reserve Banks. To cover the deficiency in reserves they will probably sell short-term (U.S.) assets in the necessary amount. Thus the net effect is that increased imports are financed by the short-term capital inflow, as before.

(b) Imports are paid for with checks drawn on North Carolina member banks. This case is the same as (a. 2) above, except that the preliminary clearings between nonmember and member banks are omitted. The net effect is to reduce U.S. assets held by member banks in an amount sufficient to cover increased imports.

None of these cases is likely to appear in pure form. Instead, a mixture of them, along with other variations and complications, is to be expected. It seems clear, however, that North Carolina holdings of short-term assets in the United States will decline.[8] If no such assets are available for this purpose, a balance-of-payments 'problem' will arise.

The description of the last alternative – deliberate expansion of credit within a single state – probably suffices to show its impracticality. The reserves of nonmember state banks are small;[9] the expanded deposits (and excess reserves) would quickly be lost through adverse clearings resulting from a high marginal propensity to import; the action could not be repeated; and such a move would frighten away foreign capital and probably cause a net decline in North Carolina capital formation.

The interregional payments mechanism is thus marvelously effective in facilitating the transfer of capital. Given the motivation for capital to move into a state, its transfer can take place smoothly and efficiently; but the existence of this mechanism for transfer does nothing to set in motion a flow of long-term capital. The determinants of such a flow are not to be found in a study of the short-run mechanism of adjustment in the balance of payments.

II

The above analysis suggests that one of the chief reasons why 'transfer problems' and other balance-of-payments pressures are not currently a source of much concern in the United States is the existence of a large stock of financial claims, readily transferable from place to place. The growth of such a stock of 'generalized' claims may indeed be of more importance than the Federal Reserve System in promoting smooth regional balance-of-payments adjustments. While the rediscount facilities of the Federal Reserve enable banks to convert 'local' claims into transferable funds, a strong banking tradition has limited the use of this method. The other contribution of the Federal Reserve that is often mentioned in this connection – namely, the provision of rapid clearing facilities – is to be attributed more to developments in communication than in banking. It is, indeed, an interesting coincidence that the Federal Reserve System came into existence at about the same time that commercial banks began to hold significant stocks of 'generalized' financial claims. Thus the Federal Reserve may have been credited with improvements in interregional payments which actually belong to other institutional developments. The relative importance of 'generalized' claims is shown in Table 8.1 for selected dates. The liquidity of 'other securities' has probably increased considerably since 1914, as the capital market has developed and matured.

Table 8.1 All Commercial Banks: Ratio of 'Generalized' Claims to Total Loans and Investments

Date	U.S. Securities	All Securities
June 30, 1914	4.9 per cent	21.9 per cent
June 30, 1919	16.2 per cent	29.6 per cent
June 30, 1925	11.2 per cent	28.3 per cent
June 30, 1930	10.2 per cent	29.4 per cent
June 30, 1935	36.8 per cent	56.9 per cent
June 30, 1940	40.2 per cent	57.7 per cent
June 30, 1950	54.0 per cent	63.2 per cent
June 30, 1958	35.6 per cent	46.7 per cent

Sources: Banking and Monetary Statistics, 1943, Board of Governors, Federal Reserve System, p. 19; *Federal Reserve Bulletin*, various issues.

That interregional payments problems existed prior to 1913 is well known. The nature and causes of these disturbances may be interpreted in terms of the analysis so far developed. Along the moving frontier the demand for capital was intense. Some capital movements did take place from the older regions to the developing regions, but institutional arrangements had not yet been developed to allow absentee capitalists to participate in many types of investment. The capitalist and entrepreneur were still one and the same person, to a large extent, and most eastern capitalists were not inclined to expose themselves to frontier life.

The intense demand for investible funds, not being satisfied through autonomous capital movements, exerted great pressure upon banks and state governments. When these agencies yielded to the temptation to create loanable funds, money incomes and imports swiftly rose in the expanding regions. The rise in imports was augmented by price and accelerator effects. The necessity to remit funds to U.S. banks to pay for the rising volume of imports caused reserves to fall in frontier banks. Since their assets were almost wholly in 'local' claims, these banks had no way to settle the drafts to U.S. banks except by drawing down their reserve balances in those banks. A regional 'dollar shortage' therefore appeared. Sporadic efforts were made to develop institutions to bridge this gap. For example, in the nineteenth century mortgage dealers bought mortgages from frontier banks in the central northwest and sold them to eastern banks and investors. Such mortgages '... were, in fact, readily salable and in many cases were considered a secondary reserve. Whenever the demand for so-called commercial loans in the territory increased, the banker sold real-estate mortgages to raise funds for local loans.'[10]

Had a Federal Reserve System existed at this time, the frontier banks could have converted local claims into funds for settling adverse clearings through the rediscount operation. But this would have simply underwritten the creation of credit by frontier banks. If the tradition of quick repayment of bank debt to Federal Reserve Banks had been in force, no real solution would have been provided by the Federal Reserve, per se. On the other hand, if the assets of frontier banks had included 'generalized claims,' or if eastern banks had been willing to hold claims on frontier firms and persons, the payments problem would have been readily handled. While this is a short-run argument, with clear limits to its usefulness, it seems legitimate to argue that the present easy transfer relations among U.S. regions is due less to the Federal Reserve System than to the development of a huge stock of 'generalized' financial claims.[11]

Even in fairly recent times, equilibrating short-term capital movements have sometimes not performed their vital role. For example, just after World War I, commercial banks in the Ninth Federal Reserve District were faced with large and persistent adverse clearing balances because of the sharp decline in prices of the agricultural exports from this district. 'If the banks had owned some exportable assets, such as Government securities, the persistent deposit outflow might have been accommodated without the large number of bank failures which were actually suffered. As it was, the earning assets of most district banks consisted almost entirely of paper with a very limited market, paper which could not be exported or sold in other districts to help minimize the clearing house deficits which were encountered.'[12]

It thus appears that the disappearance of the kind of regional payments pressures formerly experienced within the United States is the result of the development of large holdings of 'generalized' claims and the attendant development of an integrated capital market. These developments have caused the payments position of individual states and regions to be less like that of separate nations (as usually analyzed in international trade textbooks), and more like that of parts of a fully integrated economy. Thus the multiple expansions and contractions of money so often stressed in balance-of-payments theory are not experienced by U.S. states and regions.[13]

III

The regional adjustment mechanism within the United States appears to lie midway between the mechanism of adjustment for separate nations and the mechanism in a completely integrated economy. The chief difference involved in this comparison concerns the nature of the banking system. In an integrated economy, where a small number of banks have nationwide branch-banking facilities, payments from one region to another create no difficulties because total reserves and deposits are unaffected. In the U.S. system, payments from North Carolina to the United States reduce North Carolina reserves and deposits and increase U.S. reserves and deposits, but North Carolina banks can forestall any pressure toward multiple contraction by selling U.S. securities or other secondary reserves in the United States. Because of this equilibrating capital movement, the net effect is the same as in an integrated economy. But when payments are made from one nation (A) to another (B), the fall of A's reserves and deposits is more likely to set in motion a multiple contraction because the assets of A-banks may not be readily saleable in B, or because of restrictions on such sales by A-authorities, or because B-banks and other financial institutions are not allowed to hold 'foreign' securities. In short, financial claims tend to be 'localized' rather than 'generalized,' and this operates to separate the two economic systems in such a way as to produce payments pressures.

Our analysis serves to throw into sharp relief the crucial role of the capital market in balance-of-payment adjustment.[14] It carries with it policy implications for any group of nations, such as the European Common Market, anxious to minimize payments pressures among its members. First, this analysis implies a need for an integrated capital market with facilities for quick sales of securities, for establishing standard measures of investment quality for widely different types of securities, and for establishing ethical codes to govern dealers and issuing firms and agencies. Second, eligibility rules for asset-holdings of banks, insurance companies, pension funds, and other financial institutions need to be modified to enlarge the market for the securities of any single nation and thus to convert localized (national) claims into generalized (internationally acceptable) claims. Third, restrictions on capital movements need to be removed, since they directly conflict with the mechanism by which payments pressures may be lessened. Existing provisions of the International Monetary Fund are, of course, in conflict with this requirement.

Equilibrating capital movements are likely to be most effective under a regime of fixed exchange rates. This is likely, not for theoretical but for institutional reasons. If exchange rates are free to fluctuate, it is less likely that the regulatory authorities of a nation will allow financial institutions to hold securities denominated in foreign currencies. Since the free movement of such securities is a vital part of the adjustment process, fixed rates are also vital.

In a recent article, Meade discusses prospective balance-of-payments problems in a European free-trade area, and mentions several possible solutions.[15] Four of these are the traditional alternatives: (a) an increase in international reserves, (b) the gold standard approach, (c) direct controls on payments, and (d) exchange-rate adjustments. Meade approves of (a) and (d), at least in some degree, and he prefers (c) to (b), which is his bête-noir. His antagonism to the gold standard approach is based on the belief that it requires a multiple contraction of money in the deficit country, with this monetary stringency leading to lower incomes and prices, in order to correct a deficit. 'This solution is dangerous,' he writes, and 'the probable outcome ... would in fact be the breakdown of the free-trade arrangements.'[16]

Meade's fifth alternative is to integrate European financial arrangements 'so as to make it as easy for a Frenchman to pay a German ... as it is for a Welshman to pay an Englishman ...'[17] To achieve this goal, Meade thinks it would be necessary to have a single currency and banking system and a single authority to fix uniform monetary and fiscal policies, control the over-all balance-of-payments, and remedy any 'depressed-area problems' that may arise. Because these requirements imply a single European government, Meade doubts that this alternative is now feasible.

Our analysis implies that considerably less stringent requirements may be sufficient to make it as easy for a Frenchman to pay a German as it is for a Tarheel to pay a Texan. Integration of capital markets in the several partner countries, plus removal of restrictions on the movement of claims, will enable equilibrating capital movements to perform their vital role. This involves a vast increase in 'liquidity,' but not in the usual sense. The entire stock of securities held by a nation's banking system (or other financial institutions) becomes a potential source of foreign exchange to settle a deficit. It also involves a part of the gold standard mechanism, but neither the multiple contraction feature nor the cumulative deflation of income and prices is necessary. While close co-ordination of fiscal and monetary policies would be highly desirable in any case, this proposal does not require a single authority. A nation could engage in deficit financing, although it would have to pay the going rate of interest to attract buyers for its bonds. For example, individual states pursue widely different fiscal policies within the United States. Total debt of state and local governments rose from $14.4 billion to $46.7 billion between 1947 and 1957. This is considerably larger than the net increase in federal debt over the same period.[18]

It would be a mistake to minimize the difficulties in the way of such a proposal, however. Much study and negotiation would be necessary to determine the exact scope for independent monetary and fiscal policies in each country, and to specify the kinds of institutional adjustments necessary to make this payments system function smoothly. Our present argument is that it can work, that it is consistent with recent moves toward economic integration, and that it would be a pity to see no proper hearing given merely because of fears associated with past experience with the gold standard.

Acknowledgement

The author wishes to thank the North Carolina Business Foundation for financial assistance during the preparation of this paper, and Professor Maurice W. Lee for reading and criticizing the paper.

Notes

1 See J.E. Meade, *The Balance of Payments* (London: Oxford University Press, 1951), and the review by H.G. Johnson, 'The Taxonomic Approach to Economic Policy,' *Economic Journal,* LXI (Dec. 1951).

2 This may not be true of some states – e.g., Texas in oil, Michigan in automobiles, or even North Carolina in tobacco – but it is a convenient place to begin.

3 Interest rate differentials on 'local' loans may persist, just as do wage differentials. These do not much affect the following analysis, however, unless the size of the differential varies significantly.

4 North Carolina banks will be willing to hold large quantities of U.S. assets, even for long periods of time. The failure of equilibration to be 'complete' in this sense therefore need cause no difficulties, either in theory or practice. Cf. F. Machlup, *International Trade and the National Income Multiplier* (Philadelphia: Blakiston, 1943), pp. 41-42.

5 Income in the United States will rise as a result of these capital goods purchases, unless U.S. domestic investment outlays fall when the new investment in North Carolina is made. We ignore the 'foreign repercussions' since they are likely to be very small in any case. (E.g., if U.S. income rises, the marginal propensity to import North Carolina goods is likely to be so small that little further change in North Carolina income will be induced.)

6 While it is true that the classical mechanism allowed for equilibrating short-term capital movements, their motivations (movement of the exchange rate toward the gold points, interest rate differentials in the two money markets) were not the same as in the present case. It is essentially the institutional structure that makes the difference.

7 This is, of course, not offered as a 'practical' proposal, but merely for illustrative purposes. The scope for such action is small, in any case, and it would be violently opposed as an extremely radical move. In earlier times, before the federal government achieved clear supremacy in the monetary field, states sometimes used such means to expand the supply of money. These experiments often ended disastrously, as was the case in 1858 when Minnesota, anxious to promote railway construction, made a special issue of state bonds eligible to be used as collateral for the notes of state banks. These bonds dropped far below par and were finally defaulted. Cf. Charles S. Popple, *Development of Two Bank Groups in the Central Northwest* (Cambridge, Mass.: Harvard University Press, 1944), pp. 11-12.

8 Of course, the definition of 'short-term' is arbitrary, and any claim linking North Carolina and the United States could serve the purpose.

9 As of Dec. 31, 1958, North Carolina had 156 nonmember state banks with cash and demand balances totaling $240 million, and deposit liabilities (demand and time) totaling $1,216 million. (Figures supplied by Mr. Ben R. Roberts, North Carolina Commissioner of Banks.)

10 Popple, *op. cit.,* pp. 58-59. Such arrangements were likely to break down just when they were most needed.

11 After showing that reserve and correspondent balances do not perform this function, Douglas Hellweg asks: '... What other assets ... can banks liquidate to accommodate a deposit outflow? What assets are held by the First National Bank of Podunk which are readily marketable in other districts and thus can be used to produce credits at the interdistrict settlement fund? Government securities, of course, have the necessary characteristics.' See Douglas Hellweg, 'Comments on Task Force Report,' in *Record of the Federal Reserve System Conference on the Interregional Flow of Funds* (Washington, D.C, 1955).

12 *ibid.*

13 'Under the fractional reserve system, primary losses or gains of deposits and reserves would lead to multiple swings in bank deposits within the region if the process of banks' liquidating secondary reserves (or borrowing) outside the region to meet the primary losses ... did not result in an equilibrating flow.' – Norman N. Bowsher, J. Dewey Daane, and Robert Einzig, 'The Flows of Funds between Regions of the United States,' *Regional Science Proceedings,* III (1957), 140.

14 This has been stressed in a similar context by T. Scitovsky, 'The Theory of the Balance of Payments and the Problem of a Common European Currency,' *Kyklos,* X (1957) No. 1.

15 J.E. Meade, 'The Balance-of-Payments Problems of a European Free-Trade Area,' *Economic Journal LXVII* (Sept. 1957).

16 *Ibid.*, p. 385.

17 *Ibid.*

18 *Economic Report of the President*, January 1958, p. 170.

Reprinted from *The Quarterly Journal of Economics*, 73, 1959, Harvard University Press, Cambridge, with permission.

9 Markov Chains, Exchange Matrices, and Regional Development

by Paul E. Smith

University of Missouri

In light of the recent attention paid to the appearance and discovery of so-called depressed areas in the United States, and to cold war developments in Latin America and Southeast Asia, it has become understandably fashionable among economists and political decision makers to be concerned with regional economic development. Unfortunately, it is not always clear just what is meant by either 'depressed' or 'region,' although the former term is usually taken to imply that the area in question has a lower per-capita income than other similarly defined areas. We shall adopt this definition for the lack of a better one and avoid the political, geographical, and economic pitfalls of the second problem by merely defining a region as a bordered topological space. Hence, we specify that the inhabitants of some regions enjoy a higher level of living than the residents of others and that it is deemed socially desirable to narrow the income gaps between regions.

Two broad types of solutions, both entailing the geographic reallocation of resources, are often proposed. The first or market solution is in the classical tradition and suggests that, if impediments to labor mobility are absent, human resources will move from the low-income regions to the high-income regions until the income differentials within competing groups are wiped out. In the case of noncompeting groups, public subsidized training programs are sometimes advocated, e.g., West Virginia coal miners are converted into California real estate brokers at government expense. However, recent legislation, possibly due in part to lobbying activities by 'California real estate brokers', has been aimed in the direction of subsidies to the inhabitants of depressed regions and the raising of the income base in those areas via capital investment.

The purpose of this paper is to explore the possibility of increasing the incomes of some regions relative to those of others. We shall not be concerned so much with the techniques of growth *per se*, but rather with whether such development can be attained within the framework of a model of interregional trade. For this purpose we will find it convenient to employ stochastic or Markov matrices as a useful mathematical tool. The problem will be briefly considered first from the standpoint of comparative statics and then within the context of a dynamic model. Numerical examples will be used extensively.

1 Comparative Statics

Consider n geographic regions $R_1, \cdots, R_n$ which may or may not trade with each other. Each region R_i has income Y_i which it spends either on its own output or the output of other regions, with domestic consumption and imports having linear and homogeneous relationships with its own income.[1] Hence a_{ij} may be said to be the marginal and average propensity of R_i to spend in R_j. Therefore, we can write the exchange matrix

$$A = \begin{pmatrix} a_{11}a_{12} \cdots a_{1n} \\ a_{21}a_{22} \cdots a_{2n} \\ \cdots\cdots\cdots \\ a_{n1}a_{n2} \cdots a_{nn} \end{pmatrix}$$

Clearly A is a square matrix with nonnegative elements and with row sums equal to unity, i.e., $a_{ij} \geq 0$ and $\sum_{j}^{n}{}_{=1} a_{ij} = 1$. This is because no region can make negative expenditures in any region and in equilibrium each region spends all of its income. Therefore A may be called a stochastic or Markov matrix of transition probabilities.

We shall cut the subset of regions $R' \subset R$ closed if no region in R imports from any region in $(R - R')$ so that $a_{ij} = 0$ for $i \epsilon R'$ and $j \epsilon (R - R')$. If $a_{ii} = 1$, then R_i spends all of its income on its own output and is said to be an absorbing state or region. Moreover if R contains more than one closed set, the rows and columns of A can be rearranged into A^*. A^* is partitioned with closed sets of coefficients along the main diagonal, i.e.,

$$A^* = \begin{pmatrix} A_1 & 0 & 0 & \cdot & \cdot & \cdot & 0 \\ 0 & A_2 & 0 & \cdot & \cdot & \cdot & 0 \\ 0 & 0 & A_3 & \cdot & \cdot & \cdot & 0 \\ \cdot & & \cdot & \cdot & \cdot & \cdot & 0 \\ \cdot & & & & & & \\ \cdot & & & & & & \\ 0 & & \cdot & \cdot & \cdot & \cdot & A_k \end{pmatrix}$$

where the $A_i (i = 1, \cdots, k)$ are indecomposable or irreducible subsets of coefficients of the decomposable or reducible parent set A.

The total income of each region R_i is given by summing its sales to itself and all other regions, i.e.,

$$y_i = \sum_{j=1}^{n} a_{ji} y_j$$

(1)

Hence an equilibrium income vector is a vector $y = (y_1, y_2 \cdots, y_n)$ which satisfies the equation

$$A'y = y$$

or

$$(I - A')y = 0,$$

(2)

where I is the identity matrix of order n. Equation 2 is seen to be equivalent to the set of n homogeneous linear equations

$$(1 - a_{11})y_1 - a_{21}y_2 - \cdots - a_{n1}y_n = 0$$
$$- a_{12}y_1 + (1 - a_{22})y_2 - \cdots - a_{n2}y_n = 0 \quad (3)$$
$$\cdots\cdots\cdots\cdots\cdots\cdots\cdots\cdots\cdots\cdots$$
$$- a_{1n}y_1 - a_{2n}y_2 - \cdots + (1 - a_{nn})y_n = 0,$$

whose matrix is $(I - A)$. A basic theorem of linear algebra asserts that a nonzero solution vector y of these equations exists if and only if $(I - A)$ is a singular matrix. We assume this to be the case and concern ourselves only with whether y is non-negative as well. That such an equilibrium vector exists and that all of its elements are positive has already been proven by Gale (1960). For a more general discussion of existence and uniqueness theorems, see Baumol (1961).

If A is indecomposable, the equilibrium income vector y is trivially nonunique in that any scalar multiple of a solution vector is also a solution vector. If A is decomposable with indecomposable subsets $A_1, A_2, \cdots, A_k$ and if y is an equilibrium solution vector for A, then $y = (y_1^*, y_2^*, \cdots, y_m^*, \cdots, y_k^*)$ where y_m^* is an equilibrium solution vector for the set of regions with the non-decomposable submatrix A_m. That is, a solution vector can be found for each submatrix, and these can be suitably ordered so that they are also solution for A. Furthermore, a vector, say cy^*, found by multiplying any solution subvector by a positive scalar c is also an equilibrium solution vector. Hence for decomposable matrices the general solution vector is nonunique from the standpoint of relative incomes since any non-negative linear combination of the subsolutions is also a solution.

A simple numerical example may help to illustrate the problem. Consider the three regions represented by the indecomposable matrix

$$A = \begin{pmatrix} 0.5 & 0.2 & 0.3 \\ 0 & 0.6 & 0.4 \\ 0.2 & 0 & 0.8 \end{pmatrix}$$

Inasmuch as each region receives its income from sales either to itself or to other regions, the equilibrium income vector y can be found by simultaneously solving the system of homoneous linear equations

$$0.5\,y_1 \qquad\quad + 0.2\,y_3 = y_1$$
$$0.2\,y_1 + 0.6\,y_2 \qquad\quad = y_2$$
$$0.3\,y_1 + 0.4\,y_2 + 0.8\,y_3 = y_3$$

which can be rewritten

$$-0.5\,y_1 \qquad\quad + 0.2\,y_3 = 0$$
$$0.2\,y_1 - 0.4\,y_2 \qquad\quad = 0$$
$$0.3\,y_1 + 0.4\,y_2 - 0.2\,y_3 = 0$$

The solution vector is

$$\bar{y} = (y_1, 0.5\,y_1, 2.5\,y_1),$$

where y_1 may be any arbitrary positive real number. In general, the equilibrium income vector will always take the form

$$\bar{y} = (y_i, b_1 y_i, \cdots b_{n-1} y_i)$$

(4)

for any indecomposable model with n regions.

Two tentative conclusions can be derived at this point. In the first place it becomes immediately apparent in the static equilibrium model that if the elements of A are held constant no improvement in a region's relative share of the total available income is possible. Therefore, it follows that any increase in the absolute level of income for a poor region, say Region 2 in the numerical example, must be accompanied by an even greater absolute increase in the incomes of its wealthier trading partners if the exchange model is to remain in equilibrium. The result is a widening of the absolute income gaps between regions.

Secondly, equilibrium growth can take place in the linear exchange model, the limiting requirement being that the growth rate must be the same for each region.

As noted above, however, the basic problem is not solved since depressed regions become even more depressed relative to their wealthier neighbors. We remark that this may not be true in terms of utility, depending upon the elasticities of the marginal-utility-of-income schedules of the regions' inhabitants.

The situation is somewhat less hopeless if it is possible to reduce the regional complex into a set of indecomposable subsets of regions. To consider another numerical example, take a five-region model whose exchange matrix, after suitable reorganization, can be written

$$A^* = \begin{bmatrix} 0.5 & 0.5 & 0 & 0 & 0 \\ 0.2 & 0.8 & 0 & 0 & 0 \\ 0 & 0 & 0.6 & 0.4 & 0 \\ 0 & 0 & 0.1 & 0.9 & 0 \\ 0 & 0 & 0 & 0 & 1.0 \end{bmatrix}$$

Note that Region 5 neither exports to nor imports from any other region and that subsets $A_1 = \begin{pmatrix} 0.5 & 0.5 \\ 0.2 & 0.8 \end{pmatrix}$ and $A_2 = \begin{pmatrix} 0.6 & 0.4 \\ 0.1 & 0.9 \end{pmatrix}$ are irreducible submatrices. Proceeding as before, we find that the equilibrium income vector is

$$\bar{y} = (y_1, 2.5\, y_1, y_3, 4\, y_3, y_5),$$

where y_1, y_3, and y_5 again are any nonnegative real numbers.

The conclusions are now less rigid than before. Clearly, Region 1's income cannot be increased relative to the income of Region 2, but the combined incomes of Regions 1 and 2 can be raised relative to the incomes of the three remaining regions. The same result is apparent in the case of Regions 3 and 4, and Region 5's income, being independent of the income of any other region, can be increased unilaterally without violating the equilibrium condition. Hence through a suitable process of aggregation, regions can be redefined in a manner such that regional growth is possible in a manner consistent with trade equilibrium. This solution, however, merely amounts to sweeping the income discrepancies under the rug and does not eliminate the original problem.

2 Dynamic Regional Growth

We now consider the dynamic properties of the model. In particular, we shall begin with a trade equilibrium as defined in the previous section and then examine the consequences of some exogenous shock, e.g., either a one period injection of income into a depressed region or an increase of autonomous investment which increases that region's income for all subsequent periods. As before, we first investigate the situation for an indecomposable trade matrix.

If we wish to find the interregional distribution of income after t time periods, we know that

$$\sum_{j=1}^{n} v_{ij}(t) = 1 \tag{5}$$

and

$$v_{ij}(t+1) = \sum_{j=i}^{n} v_{ij}(t)a_{ij}, \tag{6}$$

where the number in parentheses dates the associated variable, and the v_{ij} denote the elements of the ith row in A^t. Hence the row elements still sum to unity, and Equation 6 introduces a dynamic situation in that a region's income in any time period is given by the total of its sales to all other regions and itself during the previous periods. It follows that the income distribution vector in any period is given by

$$\begin{aligned} y(1) &= y(0)A \\ y(2) &= y(1)A = y(0)A^2 \\ y(3) &= y(2)A = y(0)A^3 \end{aligned}$$

and, in general,

$$y(t) = y(t-1)A = y(0)A^t. \tag{7}$$

A few definitions are in order at this point.

1 A state, say i, is called *periodic* with period h if a return to i is possible in gh steps, where g is a positive integer and $h > 1$ is the largest integer with this property. Thus $a_{ii}^{(t)} = 0$ where t is not divisible by h. A state which is not periodic is called *aperiodic*.

2 A state i is called *recurrent* or *nontransient* if a return to that state is certain. If the probability of a return is less than unity, the state is said to be *transient* or *nonrecurrent*. If the expected recurrence time for i is infinite, the state is said to be *recurrent null*. If the expected recurrence time is less than infinite, the state is called *positive*.

3 A recurrent state i which is neither null nor periodic is called *ergodic*.

4 An income vector $\bar{y}$ will be called an *equilibrium income vector* if it satisfies the property

$$\bar{y} = \bar{y}A. \tag{8}$$

The corresponding matrix A will be called *stable*.

We find it extremely convenient in the initial period to divide each region's income by the summed income of all the n regions so that

$$\sum_{i=1}^{n} y_i = 1 \tag{9}$$

for the interregional distribution of income in period 1.

We next state without proofs two basic limit theorems of the theory of discrete Markov chains with a denumerable number of states, and then consider their implications for regional economic development. The proofs are to be found in Bharucha-Reid (1960).

Theorem 1: If the state j is either transient or recurrent null, then

$$\lim_{t \to \infty} a_{ij}^{(t)} = 0 \tag{10}$$

for all i, where $A^t = (a_{ij}^{(t)})$.

Theorem 2: If the exchange matrix A is ergodic, then for every pair of states i and j

$$\lim_{t \to \infty} a_{ij}^{(t)} = v_j, \tag{11}$$

independent of i, and the v_j satisfy the equation

$$v_j = \sum_{i=1}^{n} v_i a_{ij} \tag{12}$$

as well as Equation 4. Moreover, the v_j are unique.

The importance of these two limit theorems for Markov chains and their implications for the convergence of regional incomes to an equilibrium is obvious. The theorems assert that if all of the states of A are aperiodic and A is indecomposable then all of the elements of A^t converge toward limiting values as t approaches infinity. Another theorem follows, therefore, that the elements of $y(t) = y(0)A^t$ also converge toward limiting values as t increases without bound.

3 Aperiodic Chains

For example, consider a simple model consisting of two regions R_1 and R_2 with the exchange matrix

$$A = \begin{pmatrix} p & 1-p \\ q & 1-q \end{pmatrix}$$

where p and q lie between zero and one. Using the method of generating functions, we calculate A^t to be

$$A^t = \frac{1^t}{1-p+q} \begin{pmatrix} q & 1-p \\ q & 1-p \end{pmatrix} + \frac{(p-q)^t}{1-p+q} \begin{pmatrix} 1-p & p-1 \\ -q & q \end{pmatrix}$$

Since $|p - q| < 1$,

$$\lim_{t \to \infty} A^t = \begin{pmatrix} \dfrac{q}{1-p+q} & \dfrac{1-p}{1-p+q} \\ \dfrac{q}{1-p+q} & \dfrac{1-p}{1-p+q} \end{pmatrix}$$

Clearly, by Equation 7,

$$\bar{y} = y_1, \quad \frac{(1-p)}{q} y_1 \tag{13}$$

A discussion of generating functions and their use is provided in Howard (1960) and Saaty (1959).

Suppose now that income is increased for one period only in R_1 by an amount to x. The interregional income distribution converges over time to a new equilibrium given by

$$\bar{y} = \left((1+x)y_1, \frac{(1-p)(1+x)}{q} y_1 \right) \tag{14}$$

An examination of Equation 14 reveals that for the income of Region 1 to increase more than that of Region 2, it is necessary and sufficient that $q > 1 - p$, i.e., that Region 1 spends a greater proportion of its income at home than does Region 2. But from Equation 13 this would make Region 2 the initially depressed area so that the result is same as for the static model.

A simple numerical example is given by

$$A = \begin{pmatrix} 0.5 & 0.5 \\ 0.4 & 0.6 \end{pmatrix}$$

The equilibrium income vector is

$$\bar{y} = (y_1, 1.25\, y_1).$$

Since we want total income to equal unity,

$$\bar{y} = (\tfrac{4}{9}, \tfrac{5}{9}).$$

In order to illustrate theorem, we assume a transfer from Region 2 to 1 in the initial period so that

$$y(0) = (0.5, 0.5)$$

and examine the behavior of $y(n)$ as t increases indefinitely.

$$\lim_{t \to \infty} A^t = \begin{pmatrix} \frac{4}{9} & \frac{4}{9} \\ \frac{5}{9} & \frac{5}{9} \end{pmatrix}$$

and, therefore,

$$\lim_{t \to \infty} y(t) = \bar{y} = (0.5 \ 0.5) \begin{pmatrix} \frac{4}{9} & \frac{5}{9} \\ \frac{4}{9} & \frac{5}{9} \end{pmatrix}$$

$$= \left(\frac{4}{9}, \frac{5}{9} \right)$$

If income is raised by x in period 0 in Region 1 we get

$$y(0) = (\tfrac{1}{2} + x, \tfrac{1}{2}),$$

and

$$\bar{y} = (\tfrac{4}{9}(1+x), \tfrac{5}{9}(1+x)).$$

Hence y converges to a unique equilibrium with the same relative interregional distribution as formerly.

If $q = 0$, then Region 2 spends all of its income at home, and Region 1 is a transient state such that the equilibrium income vector is

$$\bar{y} = (0, 1),$$

and all of the benefits of any one-shot injections will have accrued to Region 2 once the new equilibrium is attained.[2]

However, if the aid to the depressed region is in the form of capital investment such that the area's output and income are increased during the current and all subsequent periods, the income gap will be partially closed, the amount of the change depending upon the amount of the initial investment and the capital-output ratio. Thus, if model is in equilibrium in period 0 and income in Region 1 is increased in periods $1, 2, \ldots, n$ by an amount equal to x,

We conclude that in the case of aperiodic states and indecomposable matrices it is possible to raise the relative incomes of depressed regions through continual and constant injections by an amount equal to the injection.[3]

4 Periodic Chains

In the case of periodic chains the components of A^t do not converge toward limiting values as n becomes very large but tend to oscillate indefinitely, resulting in an oscillation in the componets of the regional income distribution vector. These oscillations, however, are predictable. As defined on paper 12, a periodic chain is a recurrent chain such that for every fixed state the chain will occupy that state with probability equal to one after $h, 2h, 3h, \cdots$ transitions, where h is an integer denoting the periodicity of the chain.

Consider again the simple two-regional model with $p = 0$, and $q = 1$, i.e.,

$$A = \begin{pmatrix} 0 & 1 \\ 1 & 0 \end{pmatrix}$$

That is, Region 1 spends all of its income in Region 2 and vice versa. We have

$$A^2 = \begin{pmatrix} 1 & 0 \\ 0 & 1 \end{pmatrix}$$

$$A^3 = \begin{pmatrix} 0 & 1 \\ 1 & 0 \end{pmatrix}$$

In general, using an appropriate generating function,

$$A^t = \begin{pmatrix} 0.5 & 0.5 \\ 0.5 & 0.5 \end{pmatrix} + (-1)^n \begin{pmatrix} 0.5 & -0.5 \\ -0.5 & 0.5 \end{pmatrix}$$

where $h = 2$.

Hence the system does not move toward an equilib-

$$y(0) = \left(y_1, \frac{(1-p)}{q} y_1 \right)$$

$$y(1) = \left((y_1 + x), \frac{(1-p)}{q} y_1 \right)$$

$$y(2) = (y_1 \ (1)A + (x, 0)) = \left[((1+x)y_1 + x), \left(\frac{(1-p)}{q}(y_1 + x) \right) \right]$$

$$y(3) = (y_1 \ (2)A + (x, 0)) = \left[((1+2x)y_1 + x), \left(\frac{(1-p)}{q}(y_1 + 2x) \right) \right]$$

. . . .

rium in the sense that the $a_{ij}^{(t)}$ converge to any limiting values. If the initial income vector is $y(0) = (y_1, 1 - y_1)$, we have

$$y(1) = y(0)A = ((1 - y_1), y_1)$$
$$y(2) = y(0)A^2 = (y_1, (1 - y_1))$$
$$y(3) = y(0)A^3 = ((1 - y_1), y_1)$$
. . . .

and the interregional distribution of income fluctuates indefinitely for any $y_1 \neq 0.5$.[4]

Suppose next that a one-shot attempt is made to increase income in Region 1. We see that

$$y(0) = ((y_1 + x), (1 - y_1))$$
$$y(1) = y(0)A = ((1 - y_1), (y_1 + x))$$
$$y(2) = y(0)A^2 = ((y_1 + x), (1 - y_1))$$

Once more we note that while Region 1 is better off in an absolute sense it has not gained relatively. Moreover, the amplitude of the oscillation has increased.

If, on the other hand, the injection x is continued indefinitely we have

$$y(0) = ((y_1 + x), (1 - y_1))$$
$$y(1) = y(0)A + (x, 0) = ((1 - y_1 + x), (y_1 + x))$$
$$y(2) = y(0)A^2 + (x, 0) = ((y_1 + 2x), (1 - y_1 + x))$$

We conclude once more, therefore, that the only way a depressed region's income can be increased relative to the income of the other regions of an irreducible exchange matrix, periodic or not, is via either a capital investment program or some other program designed to maintain a continuous flow of new income in the low-income region.

5 Decomposable Chains
We now consider the exchange matrix

$$A = \begin{pmatrix} 0.5 & 0.5 & 0 & 0 & 0 & 0 & 0 \\ 0.4 & 0.6 & 0 & 0 & 0 & 0 & 0 \\ 0 & 0 & 0.5 & 0.5 & 0 & 0 & 0 \\ 0 & 0 & 0 & 1.0 & 0 & 0 & 0 \\ 0 & 0 & 0 & 0 & 0 & 1.0 & 0 \\ 0 & 0 & 0 & 0 & 1.0 & 0 & 0 \\ 0 & 0 & 0 & 0 & 0 & 0 & 1.0 \end{pmatrix}$$

The indecomposable submatrices A_1, A_2, A_3, and A_4 are

all familiar to us by this time. The equilibrium income vector is

$$\bar{y} = (y_1, 1.25\, y_1, 0, y_2, y_3, y_3, y_4).[5]$$

As in the static case a single injection will increase the income of all the regions in any indecomposable submatrice relative to the incomes of other regions. However, in order to raise the income of any single region which is a proper subset of one of the irreducible submatrices, relative to the incomes of all other regions, it is necessary to make the stream of new income in that region continuous. Otherwise, the equilibrium requirements would force relative incomes within each submatrix back to their former relationship.

6 Conclusions
In summary, if the economic development of a region is defined as an increase in that region's income relative to the incomes of other regions, such growth is consistent with trade equilibrium, and hence possible, only under special circumstances. In the first place, the relative incomes of an indecomposable trading bloc of regions can be increased by a once-and-for all injection. However the income of a region or regions within such a bloc can be raised relative to the incomes of other regions within the bloc only by continuous injections, hence necessitating either a continuous flow of payments into the depressed region or capital outlays designed to enlarge the region's income base.

We have assumed throughout the propensities to spend remain constant. Buy-at-home campaigns and import duties, where possible and in the absence of retaliation, can change the components of a trade matrix in a manner favourable to the depressed region. Moreover, beneficial adjustments in the a_{ij} are apt to take place if the capital projects are designed to produce exported or import-competing commodities, especially if the region enjoys a comparative advantage in those areas. This points out the principal difficulty of such a program; the need for retraining the labor force exists, whether the solution entails relocating the workers in other regions or the development of new industries in the depressed region.

Notes
1 We assume that prices are held constant so that all variables are expressed in real terms.
2 In a typical Markov process Region 1 would clearly be a transient state inasmuch as its limiting state

probability is zero. Furthermore, Region 2 is called a *trapping* or *absorbing* state since $a_{22} = .1$, i.e., all income ends up in R_2.

3 We implicitly assume that no opportunity costs are connected with the initial investment. Hence an increase in the capital stock of depressed regions is not accompanied by a reduction in the income base of other regions.

4 If Equations 6 and 7 are used to find an equilibrium income vector, $\bar{y} = (0.5, 0.5)$, in which case both regions would have stable income over time. However, $y(n)$ does not converge to these values as n → ∞.

5 See note 4 with respect to the solution of A_3.

References

Baumol, W.J. (1961) *Economic Theory and Operations Analysis,* Englewood Cliffs: Prentice Hall, Chapter 16.

Bharucha-Reid, A.T. (1960) *Elements of the Theory of Markov Processes and Their Applications*, New York: McGraw-Hill, pp. 28-30 and Appendix A.

Gale, D. (1960) *The Theory of Linear Economic Models*, New York: McGraw-Hill, Chapter 8.

Howard, R.A. (1960) *Dynamic Programming and Markov Processes*, New York: Wiley, pp. 7-12.

Saaty, T.L. (1959) *Mathematical Methods of Operations Research*, New York: McGraw-Hill, pp. 77-84.

Reprinted from *Journal of Regional Science*, Vol 3 (1), 1961, Regional Science Research Institute, Philadelphia, with permission.

10 Labor Mobility and Regional Growth
by *William H. Miernyk*
University of West Virginia

A number of years ago Allen G.B. Fisher and Colin Clark called attention to the structural changes in employment which accompany the industrialization of under-developed economies.[1] The thesis developed by Clark and Fisher is that technological progress reduces labor requirements in the primary sector of the economy, thereby making available a larger proportion of the labor force to the secondary sector. Later, technological progress in the secondary sector permits an increasing proportion of the labor force to be employed in tertiary activities.[2]

More recently, Lewis H. Bean has pointed out that there is a close relationship between per capita incomes in various countries and the stage and pattern of industrialization.[3] Bean and others have also tried to explain the relative per capita incomes of regions in the same terms.[4] There is general agreement that incomes rise as dependence upon the primary sector is reduced. Clark and Bean argued, however, that incomes will rise still further as there is a progressive shift from the secondary to the tertiary sector. This conclusion was accepted by Hyson and Neal.[5] The core of this argument is that the successive shifting of the labor force from primary to secondary, and later to tertiary, occupations is the essence of economic development. Professor Seymour Harris, however, has questioned this. He has suggested that gains in tertiary employment 'do not always reflect a rising standard of living, as Colin Clark claims, but frequently reflect a deterioration in manufacturing ...'[6] Professor Harris's position has been supported by Jean Fourastié, a French political scientist, who believes that a shift in the labor force from the secondary to the tertiary sector which is not induced by technological progress is evidence not of economic development but of economic retrogression.[7] Fourastié's position is that a nation is not wealthy because it has a large tertiary sector; rather, it is the inverse. As the wealth of a nation increases it can afford to have a progressively larger proportion of its labor force engaged in trade and service activities. If the shift of the labor force from the secondary to the tertiary sector proceeds too rapidly, i.e., without a significant increase in productivity in the secondary sector, the result may be what Fourastié terms a 'tertiary crisis.' This he considers to be the case in France.[8] Similarly Professor Garnsey has pointed out that a region may have a larger proportion of its labor force engaged in tertiary activities than the nation and yet its per capita incomes may be below the national average.[9] Evidently, as Professor Harris has suggested, the progressive shifting of a region's labor force into the tertiary sector need not be an indicator of economic development.

One should emphasize that the shifts in the labor force discussed in the preceding paragraphs relate to the long-run; the same workers are not necessarily involved in the transition from one sector to another. In general, such changes have occurred slowly, and in large measure they represent the movement of succeeding generations of children into new occupations.[10] In those countries where new generations have not been bound by occupational traditions, the shifts have proceeded fairly smoothly.

It is necessary, however, to distinguish between such long-run *shifts* in the labor force and short-run labor *mobility*. By the latter we mean 'changes of job, of employer, of occupation, of industry, of locality or region, and also changes of status, such as entrance to or exit from the labor market, and shifts from employment to unemployment or vice-versa,'[11] where all changes refer to a given worker or a given group of workers. The present paper is concerned with labor mobility and immobility in the short-run, and with their influence on long-run shifts in the labor force and regional economic development.

In the United States, as the regional economy of the South has shifted from dependence upon agriculture and other primary activities to increasing dependence upon manufacturing, labor has moved readily from the farm to the factory. Manufacturing establishments located in the South have offered unusually good employment opportunities to the children of southern farmers. And labor in the South has been available in abundance.[12] Even before the tempo of industrialization in the South was accelerated by World War II and its aftermath, technological progress in agriculture had reduced man-hour requirements, and the agricultural sector was characterized by chronic under-employment. When factories were located in southern rural communities they were swamped with job applicants. It is not uncommon even today for hundreds of applicants to leave their names with the employment office of a new establishment which can hire at most one-tenth their number.

Southern workers seeking industrial employment are typically the younger members of the labor force.[13] Older workers who have spent a lifetime in agriculture may not readily make the transition to manufacturing industry, but their children make the transition easily.[14] Although many other factors must be considered in explaining the rapid industrialization of the South in recent years, one of the most important was the availability of a large pool of relatively young and adaptable workers. This, in turn, was the result of a high degree of long-run labor mobility between the primary and secondary sectors.

The situation is quite different, however, in an older industrial region such as New England. The industrial structure of New England has been changing in recent years. The precipitous decline in textile employment is well known, but this has been offset to some extent by the growth of durable goods industries in the region, and total manufacturing employment has not declined as much as textile employment.

There has been, however, an absolute as well as a relative decline in manufacturing employment in New England. The gains resulting from the expansion of new industries, notably electronics and apparel, have not been sufficient to offset the decline in textile employment. As a consequence there has been a long-run shift to tertiary occupations, but there has not been enough of a demand for labor in the trades and services to absorb new entrants into the labor force as well as the displaced textile workers, and as a result there is a relatively high level of chronic unemployment in the region which is concentrated for the most part in those areas hardest hit by the decline of textiles.[15]

Case Studies of Displaced Workers

Most discussions of the transition in New England have been based upon highly aggregated data, and have dealt with the changing pattern of industrial employment in the region from the long-run point of view. Although to a large extent the problems of short-run labor mobility have been avoided, some have simply assumed that workers displaced by the liquidation of textile mills are finding jobs in electronics factories, apparel shops, and other industries in which employment has been expanding in New England. To test this hypothesis, the present writer and others have made a series of case studies of the post-liquidation employment experience of displaced workers in some of the major textile areas of Massachusetts and Rhode Island.[16]

In all, six case studies were made, each consisting of a sample of workers who had been displaced by the liquidation of a textile mill in one of the communities listed in Table 10.1.[17] The population in each case consisted of the workers employed in the mill during the last full quarter of operation. From payrolls completely random samples, stratified by sex, were selected. The

Table 10.1 Workers included in Survey by Labour Market Area

	Interviews		Mail Returns		Total	
	Number	Per Cent of Total in Each Case	Number	Per Cent of Total in Each Case	Number	Per Cent of Grand Total
Lowell	205	88.4	38	15.6	243	14.3
Fall River	302	88.3	40	11.7	342	20.1
Lawrence	360	81.1	84	18.9	444	26.0
Non-Textile Areas	291	82.2	63	17.8	354	20.8
Providence	103	78.0	29	22.0	132	7.7
New Bedford	163	85.8	27	14.2	190	11.1
Total	1,424	–	281	–	1,705	100.0

Source: *Inter-Industry Labor Mobility,* p. 13.

size of the samples varied with the size of the mills. In some cases a 50 per cent sample was selected (where the mill was relatively small) and in others a 10 per cent sample was drawn. Where it was possible to do so the age and sex distribution of sample workers was compared with that of the population.

Following this, the addresses of the sample workers were plotted on large maps. Field interviewers then attempted to contact each member of the sample using lists prepared from the maps.[18] A standard interview schedule was employed, and in addition the interviewers attempted to elicit information about workers' attitudes which were recorded as nearly verbatim as possible. Those who could not be reached personally were sent a mail questionnaire similar to the interview schedule employed. The response to the mail survey was good.

After the interviews and mail surveys were completed, frequency distributions of the two sets of samples were made to compare them with the populations in terms of age and sex distributions, the two control factors used (see Table 10.2). In all cases the comparisons were close with no deviations larger than those which could be explained by sampling variation. Hence, the interviews and mail surveys were combined for purposes of analyzing the post-liquidation experience of the sample workers.

The case approach would not have been appropriate if the cases analyzed were unique in some respect. Cases were not selected solely because information about the liquidated mills was readily available, but rather to obtain a good distribution of displaced textile workers geographically and over time. While we do not claim that

Table 10.2   Age and Sex Distribution of Former Mill Workers

	Interviews						Mail Returns						Total					
	Male		Female		Total		Male		Female		Total		Male		Female		Total	
	Number	Per Cent	Number	Per cent	Number	Per Cent	Number	Per Cent	Number	Per Cent	Number	Per Cent	Number	Per Cent	Number	Per Cent	Number	Per Cent
24 and under	22	3.4	13	1.7	35	2.5	6	4.3	2	1.4	8	2.8	28	3.6	15	1.6	43	2.5
25-35	119	18.3	130	16.8	249	17.5	27	19.6	32	22.4	59	21.0	146	18.6	162	17.6	308	18.1
36-45	136	21.0	161	20.8	297	20.9	30	21.7	33	23.1	63	22.4	166	21.1	194	21.1	360	21.1
46-55	147	22.7	244	31.5	391	27.5	31	22.5	43	30.1	74	26.3	178	22.6	287	31.3	465	27.3
56-65	159	24.5	189	24.4	348	24.4	36	26.1	26	18.2	62	22.1	195	24.8	215	23.4	410	24.0
66 and over	65	10.0	34	4.4	99	7.0	6	4.3	5	3.5	11	3.9	71	9.0	39	4.2	110	6.5
Unknown	1	.2	4	.5	5	.4	2	1.4	2	1.4	4	1.4	3	.3	6	.7	9	.5
Total	649	100.0	775	100.0	1,424	100.0	138	100.0	143	100.0	281	100.0	787	100.0	918	100.0	1,705	100.0

Source: *Inter-Industry Labor Mobility*, p. 14.

Table 10.3   Subsequent Experience of Former Mill Workers

Employment Experience	Male		Female		Total	
	Number	Per Cent	Number	Per Cent	Number	Per Cent
Presently employed: one job since layoff	301	38.2	214	23.3	515	30.2
Presently employed: several jobs since layoff	153	19.4	110	12.0	263	15.4
Unemployed now, had job at one time	101	12.8	113	12.3	214	12.6
Unemployed since layoff	166	21.1	345	37.6	511	30.0
Withdrawn from labour force	66	8.4	136	14.8	202	11.8
Total	787	100.0	918	100.0	1,705	100.0

Source: *Inter-Industry Labor Mobility*, p. 17.

the samples of workers studies are completely represent-ative of all displaced textile workers in New England, there is a strong presumption at least that their experience is representative of a much larger group.

Summary of Findings

The average displaced textile worker in New England is relatively old compared with the average worker in the Massachusetts civilian labor force. The modal age group for female workers in the civilian labor force is less than 24 years, and for males it is between 25 and 35 years. But the modal age group of female workers in our sample is between 46 and 55 years, and for males between 56 and 65. Only 2.5 per cent of the sample workers were 24 years of age or younger, while 17 per cent of the civilian labor force in Massachusetts con-sisted of workers in this age group.[19]

Subsequent Experience of Former Mill Workers.

Forty-six per cent of the sample workers contacted were employed when interviewed. A substantially larger pro-portion of men than women had found new jobs (Table 10.3). Forty-three per cent of the sample workers contacted were unemployed, although about 13 per cent had been employed at some time since their original layoff. The remaining 12 per cent had withdrawn from the labor force with a larger proportion of women withdrawing than men.

The age distributions of employed and unemployed workers are compared in Figure 10.1. It is clearly evident that younger workers were more successful in finding new jobs than those, for example, past the age of 45. This is particularly true of the male members of the samples. It appears that the greatest barrier to re-employment of this group of displaced textile workers was their age.

Inter-Industry Labor Mobility.

Recent employment trends in selected Massachusetts industries, during the period covered by our survey, are given in Figure 10.2. It is apparent that the drop in textile employment was much greater than the increase in employment in apparel and communication equip-ment. Nevertheless, the latter two industries were expanding. To what extent did the displaced textile workers find jobs in the expanding industries?

The distribution of employed sample workers by industries is given in Table 10.4. Despite the very substantial decline in textile employment, textile mills offered the best source of job opportunities to the displaced workers with more than 35 per cent of all the employed sample workers once again at work in a textile mill.[20] It is interesting to note that only 6 per cent of the sample workers, almost all of them females, found jobs in the apparel industry. And only 7 per cent, again mostly women, were employed by the electrical machinery *industry group*. Since there are other indus-tries than communications equipment in this group, it is highly probable that less than 7 per cent were employed by this growth industry.

After textiles, service occupations absorbed the largest number of displaced workers. Most service jobs were relatively low-paying and unskilled, and they include such occupations as chambermaids, janitors, porters, hospital attendants, nursemaids, etc. Most of the remaining workers found jobs in manufacturing estab-lishments, and they were employed by a wide variety of industries as indicated in Table 10.4. Labor mobility and immobility are matters of degree, but given the employ-ment trends in New England during the relevant period, the displaced textile workers exhibited a remarkably low degree of inter-industry mobility. We also found relat-ively little evidence of geographic mobility among the workers included in our survey.

An earlier study of the mobility of textile weavers lends support to these conclusions. Professor Gladys Palmer found that 'the degree of mobility . . . is limited . . . in times of prosperity as well as depression.'[21] And she concluded that the 'relative immobility of weavers may be considered representative of that of most textile workers.'[22] In a later study Carrie Glasser and Bernard N. Freedman concluded that 'like the coal miners of Wales . . . and like many miners in this country during the great depression, textile workers show a strong attachment to their trades and their communities.'[23]

Does this mean that textile workers are unable or unwilling to transfer to other industries or occupations? And are they unwilling to move to other areas where jobs might be more plentiful? The geographic im-mobility of our sample workers is undoubtedly a function of age rather than occupation. The average age of the sample workers was high, and many of them had spent a lifetime in the communities in which they had worked, or in nearby communities from which they could commute to their jobs. Geographic immobility is probably characteristic of older workers in general, and should not be considered as a unique attribute of textile workers. The willingness of workers to migrate tends to decline as they become older and feel bound to their

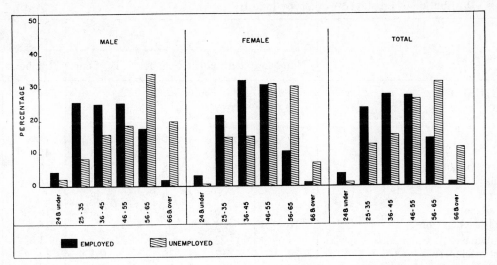

Figure 10.1 Age distribution, by sex, of employed and unemployed workers. (Source: *Inter-Industry Labor Mobility*, p. 14.)

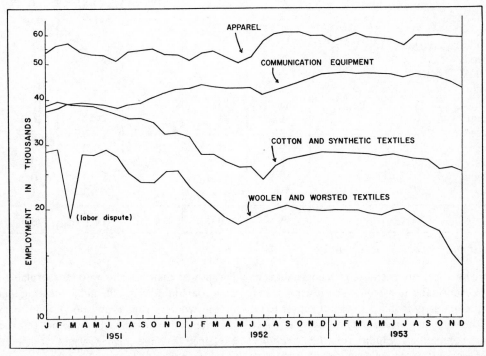

Figure 10.2 Employment trends in selected Massachusetts industries, 1951-1953 (Source: *Inter-Industry Labor Mobility*. Data from U.S. Department of Labor, Bureau of Labor Statistics.)

Table 10.4   Distribution of Employed Workers by Industry

	Male		Female		Total	
	Number	Per Cent	Number	Per Cent	Number	Per Cent
MANUFACTURING:						
Ordnance	3	.7	—	—	3	.4
Food	12	2.6	5	1.5	17	2.2
Textiles	167	36.8	110	34.0	277	35.6
Apparel	4	.9	43	13.3	47	6.0
Rubber and products	12	2.6	8	2.5	20	2.6
Chemicals	11	2.4	5	1.5	16	2.1
Paper, etc.	13	2.9	9	2.8	22	2.8
Fabricated metals	12	2.6	2	.6	14	1.8
Non-electrical machinery	16	3.5	—	—	16	2.1
Primary metals	1	.2	—	—	1	.1
Electrical machinery	24	5.3	30	9.3	54	6.9
Leather and shoe	16	3.5	26	8.0	42	5.4
Printing and publishing	8	1.8	3	.9	11	1.4
Furnishings and Fixtures	8	1.8	1	.3	9	1.2
Transportation equipment	11	2.4	1	.3	12	1.5
Instruments (watches)	1	.2	1	.3	2	.3
Jewelry	5	1.1	6	1.9	11	1.4
Toys	2	.4	2	.6	4	.4
Lumber	1	.2	—	—	1	.1
Photographic equipment	1	.2	—	—	1	.1
Miscellaneous	1	.2	4	1.2	5	.6
NON-MANUFACTURING:						
Construction	21	4.6	—	—	21	2.7
Service	65	14.3	53	16.4	118	15.2
Government	6	1.3	—	—	6	.8
Armed forces	3	.7	—	—	3	.4
Retail trade	19	4.2	13	4.0	32	4.1
Warehousing	2	.4	—	—	2	.3
Miscellaneous	9	2.0	1	.3	10	1.3
Unknown	—	—	1	.3	1	.1
Total	454	100.0	324	100.0	778	100.0

Source: *Inter-Industry Labor Mobility,* p. 19.

communities by ties of friendship, membership in organizations, and similar non-economic influences. But the lack of inter-industry mobility does not appear to be the result of unwillingness or inability to move to other industries or occupations. Studies of the *voluntary* movement of workers among jobs and occupations have demonstrated that 'the amount of voluntary movement has been, *without question*, primarily dependent upon the existence of job opportunity.'[24] One may assert with equal confidence that had job opportunities existed a much larger proportion of the displaced textile workers would have been employed in other industries.

Because of their age the only jobs available to many of them were in other textile mills. It is true that a majority of the workers who found non-textile jobs indicated a preference for textile employment, but this is largely explained by the higher wages and better working conditions they had enjoyed in the mills.[25]

Significance for Regional Development
What is the significance of these findings as far as long-run regional development is concerned? There is little question about the long-run mobility of labor either within or between sectors. But our survey, which

is supported by several earlier studies, suggests that there is considerable immobility in the short-run; that displaced industrial workers do not easily transfer to new industries largely because of the absence of job opportunity,[26] and that older workers in particular do not exhibit a high degree of geographic mobility. As a consequence, the migration of labor-oriented industries from an older industrial region, such as New England, to regions which are now industrializing might result in a transfer of under-employment from the latter to the former.

We should distinguish clearly between the relative decline in the secondary sector of our national economy which is the result of technological progress and a consequent reduction in man-hour requirements, and a relative decline in the secondary sector of a regional economy which is the result of inter-regional competition. In the former case total output has risen as labor has been shifted into the tertiary sector. More efficient machinery has permitted us to turn out more goods with less human effort, and workers have been released to provide us with more services. All this has led to a steadily rising national income.

In the regional case, however, the results might be entirely different. To the extent that the relative decline in the secondary sector is due to technological progress the results are no different from those discussed above. But if, in addition, the relative decline is partly due to the inability of manufacturing employers to compete with those in other regions, unemployment in the region will rise. Because of the short-run immobility of manufacturing workers this unemployment may persist even when there is 'full' employment in the nation as a whole.[27] This, in turn will tend to depress wages not only in the secondary sector, but also in the tertiary sector where employers are faced with less competition from manufacturing industry for new entrants into the labor force.[28] Where this occurs, a region may experience a relative decline in its income position.[29]

As wages in such a region fall, in relation to national wage levels, there may well be expansion of employment in both the secondary and tertiary sectors, although not necessarily enough to approach an optimum utilization of the region's labor force. The expansion of employment in some industries while employment in other industries is declining, we should repeat, is primarily a long-run shift in the labor force and is not evidence of a high degree of short-run mobility.

The present paper has been primarily concerned with a particular occupational group in a given region. But the conclusions are not equally restricted. In a dynamic economy there will always be some shifting about of industry.[30] Other regions are now beginning to experience some of the transitional problems New England has been faced with for some time. If regional development is to proceed smoothly these problems must be minimized.

To date, the operation of the labor market has received scant attention from regional scientists and others concerned with regional development. In part this is due to the emphasis on long-run change, and a preoccupation with the development of backward regions and areas. But in the United States at least the problems of structural change in older industrial regions should command greater attention in the future.

There is some evidence that positive efforts to encourage short-run labor mobility can smooth the adjustment to structural change. Some communities have initiated programs, involving the cooperative efforts of state divisions of employment security and industrial development agencies, to retrain displaced workers and place them in new jobs.[31] While no one has yet come up with a panacea for all the problems engendered by structural changes in employment, positive programs to encourage labor mobility have demonstrated that the short-run problems can be mitigated. At least they offer something more tangible than the vague and often illusory hope that displaced workers will on their own be able to find jobs by shifting to new industries or occupations.

Notes

1 Allen, G.B. Fisher: *The Clash of Progress and Security,* London, 1935; Colin Clark: *The Conditions of Economic Progress*, London, 1940.

2 The primary sector includes agricultural, pastoral, forest, fishing, and hunting industries. The secondary sector includes manufacturing, electric power production, mining, building, and construction. The tertiary industry is defined as all other economic activities. See Colin Clark: *The Economics of 1960*, London, 1942, p. 22n.

3 Lewis H. Bean: 'International Industrialization and Per Capita Income,' Part V of *Studies in Income and Wealth*, National Bureau of Economic Research, 1946, p. 121. 'By stage of industrialization is meant the proportion of a country's working population engaged in the primary occupations – agriculture, forestry, and fishing; by pattern of industrialization, the relative importance of secondary occupations –

manufacturing, mining, and construction; and of tertiary, occupations – trade and services.' *loc. cit.*

4 See Morris E. Garnsey: *America's New Frontier: The Mountain West*, New York, 1950, pp. 141-153; Charles D. Hyson and Alfred C. Neal: 'New England's Economic Prospects,' *Harvard Business Review,* Vol. 26, March, 1948, pp. 156-180; and Lewis H. Bean, *op. cit.*

5 *Op. cit.*, p. 168.

6 Seymour E. Harris: *The Economics of New England*, Harvard University Press, 1952, p. 286.

7 Jean Fourastié: *le Grand Espoir du XXe Siecle*, Presses Universitaires de France, Paris, 1950, pp. 92-93. A summary of Fourastié's ideas may be found in his *Esquisse D'Une Théories Générale de L'Evolution Economique Contemporaine*, Presses Universitaires de France, Paris, 1947.

8 On this point, Colin Clark would evidently agree: 'In France . . . there appears to have been almost a complete cessation of economic growth since the beginning of the present century. Until very recently at any rate this was certainly not attributable to unemployment.' See *The Conditions of Economic Progress*, p. 148.

9 *Op. cit.*, p. 146.

10 Cf. Fisher, *op. cit.*, pp. 117-118.

11 Gladys L. Palmer: *Labor Mobility in Six Cities,* Social Science Research Council, New York, 1954, pp. 4-5.

11 See *Economy of the South*, Report of the Joint Committee on the Economic Report, U.S. Government Printing Office, Washington, 1949, pp. 4-5.

13 *Ibid.*, p. 5.

14 Cf. Fisher, *op. cit.*, pp. 117-118.

15 Arthur A. Bright, Jr., and George H. Ellis (Eds.): *The Economic State of New England*. Report of the Committee of New England of the National Planning Association, Yale University Press, 1954, pp. 312-316.

16 For the complete results see William H. Miernyk: *Inter-Industry Labor Mobility*, North-eastern University, Bureau of Business and Economic Research, Boston, 1955.

17 In the Lowell case the mill had not been liquidated but had permanently curtailed its work force to about one-fourth the number employed before the downturn in textile employment started in New England in 1948.

18 The maps also gave some indication of the distances mill workers traveled to their jobs.

19 See, *Inter-Industry Labor Mobility*, p.15.

20 Even during a period of declining employment in an industry there are some job openings created by normal labor turnover. In addition, employment in all textile industries does not decline at the same time nor at the same rate. In some cases workers displaced by one textile industry were absorbed by another.

21 Gladys L. Palmer: 'The Mobility of Weavers in Three Textile Centers,' *Quarterly Journal of Economics,* May, 1941, p. 486.

22 *Ibid.*, p. 485.

23 'Work and Wage Experience of Skilled Cotton-Textile Workers,' *Monthly Labor Review*, Vol. 63, July, 1946, p. 13.

24 George P. Shultz: 'Recent Research on Labor Mobility,' reprinted from *Proceedings of the Fourth Annual Meeting, Industrial Relations Research Association*, as M.I.T. Publications in Social Science, Series 2, No. 34, p. 1. See also Lloyd G. Reynolds: *The Structure of Labor Markets*, New York, 1951, p. 32.

25 There was a substantial decline in earnings between old and new jobs, and a downgrading in skill classifications. For example, while 12 per cent of the sample workers reported no significant change in earnings and 21 per cent reported higher earnings, 64 per cent were earning less in their new jobs than they had prior to their displacement. Some of those who were earning less were still employed in textiles, but in lower skill classifications.

26 A further contributing factor to labor immobility is a lack of information about labor market conditions. See Lloyd G. Reynolds, *op. cit.*, pp. 84-85; and George P. Shultz. *op. cit.*, pp. 5-6.

27 See William H. Miernyk: *Chronic Unemployment in New England from 1947 to 1951*. Committee of New England of the National Planning Association, Staff Memorandum Number 2, Boston, May, 1952.

28 For a discussion of New England's relative wage position see *Wage Differentials and Rate Structures Among 40 Labor Markets*, U.S. Department of Labor, Bureau of Labor Statistics, Bulletin No. 1135, April 1953.

29 The argument that New England has maintained its income position in spite of a decline in manufacturing employment is not convincing. It is true that the *absolute* difference between regional and national per capita incomes has remained nearly constant, but the *relative* difference between the two has diminished.

30 The long-run trends described by Clark and Fisher will also continue and probably will be accelerated by

recent developments in the automatization of manu-facturing industry.

31 For further details see *Inter-Industry Labor Mobility,* pp. 145-149.

Reprinted from *Economic Geography*, 31, October 1955, Clark University, Worcester, with permission.

11 Regional Income Inequality and Internal Population Migration

by *Bernard Okun and Richard W. Richardson*

Brooklyn College, New York   Western Michigan University, Kalamazoo

Introduction

Recent literature on economic growth evidences increasing concern over what appears to be ever-widening economic inequality between the advanced and the backward countries of the world. While some countries have in a relatively short time effected enormous improvements in economic performance and generally commensurate gains in levels of living, other countries have failed to keep pace.[1] Less attention is paid to the fact that disparities in growth rates are equally typical among regions and areas within a country, whatever its overall state of economic development.

The factors governing the levels and trends of per capita income have been a major concern of the literature on economic growth. One traditional approach attempts to relate the size of a country's population to the objective of maximizing per capita income. A country, region or area is said to be 'underpopulated' or 'over-populated' if, respectively, an increase or a decrease of population would contribute to a rise of per capita income. Any 'over' or 'under' population must of course occur relative to one or more other economic variables, e.g., the supply of natural resources, the stock of capital, the state of technology, or the size of the labor force.

This paper is concerned with the effect of internal migration on regional inequality of per capita income. The use of population size as the reference variable is a very convenient analytic device for this purpose, for the immediate effect of net internal migration is obviously to change the population size of the region concerned. In order to assess the effect of migration on a region or area, we analyze the effect of the change in population on regional per capita income by examining the relation of the new population size to the other relevant economic variables noted above. In addition, an attempt is made to draw some inferences on the short and the long run effects on regional inequality of per capita income.

Internal Migration and Economic Growth

As a preliminary to our central theme, let us briefly explore the general relationship between internal migration and economic growth, in order to stress the extreme importance of one phenomenon in the growth process – the mobility of human resources.

Assume, for the sake of simplicity, an economy with a closed population – that is, one in which no emigration or immigration takes place. A simple demand and supply model can be developed to explain the economic rationale for internal migration. Consider first the supply side. It is unlikely that rates of natural increase of population will be the same in all regions of the country. Though there are probably only small differences in mortality rates among regions in an advanced country, it is likely that regional differences in fertility rates are larger, causing regional differences in the natural rate of increase.[2] There is, similarly, no reason to believe that the natural rate of increase is the same in all regions of the typical underdeveloped country. Many factors account for regional differences in fertility and consequent differences in the natural rate of increase. Among these are regional differentials in the degree of urbanization, in the relative weight of agriculture vs. manufacturing activities, in the religious composition of the populations, in the level of education, etc. These and other factors help to account for the fact that some regions are, quantitatively speaking, more efficient producers' of people than other regions.

On the demand side, it is historically true that economic growth is typified by shifts in the relative importance of industries: from agriculture to manufacturing, from manufacturing to services. Equally characteristic are changes in the relative importance of activities within the broad industrial groupings, e.g., from textiles to automobiles, electronics and aircraft. The fact that natural resources are not homogeneously distributed geographically throughout an economy means that shifts in the importance of different activities, and consequent changes in relative resource demands, will generally be associated with shifts in the economic importance of different regions. Economic growth, with its concomitant and characteristically rapid changes in economic structure, will generally have an uneven impact on the different regions within an economy. Changing inter-regional differentials in the marginal productivity of labor, and in economic opportunities more generally, are a necessary by-product of the process of economic growth.

It is possible that those regions of an economy that demand relatively more labor are those which have relatively higher natural rates of population increase. If there were a close conformity between natural rates of increase and the growth of economic opportunity, then the need for internal migration would be diminished. But differential rates of natural increase cannot be counted upon to redistribute population in the optimal way. Crude death rates are not a function of economic opportunity. Also, the birth rate may fail to respond positively to economic growth. Even if it did, the time lag between new births and new entries into the labor force is longer than a region enjoying rapid economic growth is willing or able to wait for additional labor. It would, in fact, be necessary for the crude birth rate to lead movements in a region's demand for labor by twenty years.

Far from reducing the need for migration, regional patterns of natural population increase and growth of economic opportunity generally enhance the importance of mobility. For while the agricultural regions typically have the higher rate of natural increase, it is in the non-agricultural regions that the demand for labor grows more rapidly.

Internal Migration and Equilibrium Theory

From what has been said, it is clear that population migration must be the predominant force making for redistributions of human resources in response to changing relative opportunities among regions. Its role as a catalyst in the growth of the entire economy is apparent. The major part of this paper is addressed to an examination of the effect of such migrations on the economies of the individual regions.

Gunnar Myrdal has recently asserted that traditional economic theory suffers from what he terms an 'equilibrium bias.' According to him, traditional economic theory argues or implies that movements of capital and labor (as well as trade) all tend to reduce inequalities of per capita income among countries and among regions within a country. In the face of generally widening inequalities, Myrdal submits that theory is blind to reality, largely because of its use of unrealistic assumptions – particularly the notion of stable equilibrium.[3]

Myrdal seems to have misconstrued some of the propositions of traditional theory, and consequently much of his criticism is levelled against a non-existent body of doctrine. A fundamental proposition of general equilibrium theory and the theory of the competitive market is that discrepancies in factor payments, caused by shifts in supply and demand schedules, will lead to an appropriate reallocation of productive factors until equilibrium is restored. In the particular case in which we are here interested, theory asserts that inter-regional factor mobility is a force which tends to equalize prices for homogeneous factors in different regions.

Myrdal's critique appears to be based on a confusion between the concepts of equilibrium and equality. Equilibrium analysis addresses itself to the problem of equality, but only with respect to *factor payments*. Factor mobility is an instrument for the elimination of factor price differentials; nothing can logically be inferred from this, however, about the impact of spatial factor mobility upon the per capita income differentials between the geographical units which are the sources or recipients of the factors themselves. In other words, while spatial factor mobility tends to equalize the returns to homogeneous factors residing in different areas, it may or may not tend to reduce the differential in per capita income between these areas. Whether or not the effect is equalizing depends upon several variables: the income of the mobile factor relative to the average incomes in the regions of origin and destination; the direction of the migratory movement (from a lower to a higher per capita income region, or vice versa); and other variables which will be considered presently. Myrdal states that 'according to the classical doctrine movements of labour and capital between countries would not be necessary to bring about a development towards and equalization of factor prices and, consequently, incomes.'[4] The soundness of this observation, however, does not justify the inference, which Myrdal first establishes and then criticizes, that the process of trade and growth reduces international and inter-regional inequalities of per capita income.

Internal Mobility and Regional Inequality

Though he fails to make the important distinction between equilibrium and equality, Myrdal nevertheless raises a question of considerable interest in his analysis of the process of growth: does internal mobility tend to widen or to narrow income inequality? Myrdal asserts that mobility widens inequality:

> The localities and regions where economic activity is expanding will attract net immigration from other

parts of the country. As migration is always selective, at least with respect to the migrant's age, this movement by itself tends to favour the rapidly growing communities and disfavour the others.[5]

It is generally the case that the age distribution of migrants tends to favor the 20-40 age bracket relative to the population as a whole. Therefore, it probably would follow that migration tends to increase the proportion of the population in the labor force of the receiving region, and to decrease its proportion in the region of origin. From this, Myrdal infers that migration benefits the economy of the receiving region, and debilitates the economy of the originating region.

So strong an inference from the age-selectivity argument may prove seriously misleading. The beneficial effects upon the receiving regions of age-selective migration may be exaggerated, while it may on the other hand be possible that emigration of any age distribution whatsoever may be helpful, rather than detrimental, to the region of origin. Consider first the region of origin. In the first place there appear to be areas in the world where the marginal productivity of labor is zero, or very low.[6] Even if all the emigrants from such areas were members of the labor force, there would result no or little diminution of total income, and per capita income might well rise. A second possible consequence of such emigration – indeed, a likely consequence – is that the capital-labor ratio would rise, and this would also tend to increase per capita income.[7] Thus there is a strong presumption that when the marginal productivity of labor is zero or very low – and this is not, apparently, uncommon for backward agricultural regions in underdeveloped countries and perhaps even in some advanced countries – emigration from such regions, regardless of age distribution, is likely to increase the region's per capita income.

With respect to the receiving region, the age-distribution argument is similarly not so complete or straightforward as Myrdal suggests. Two obvious points come to mind. First, the in-migrants may be of such inferior quality as to lower the average output per worker in the region, perhaps to an extent which more than offsets the positive influence of the rise in the proportion of the population in the labor force. Second, the age distribution of the migrants is such that it tends to raise the proportion of the population in the child-bearing age groups. Most of the migrants are or will be married, and have or will bear children. This factor will, of course, tend to reduce the proportion of the population in the labor force, somewhat offsetting the

positive effect on this proportion of the workers themselves.

Similarly, the proportion of the population of child-bearing age in the region of origin will be reduced, and this will tend to reduce the region's crude birth rate; consequently, the proportion of this population which is in the unproductive pre-labor force age will also fall. Such a consequence would, in the short run, have a salutary effect upon the per capita income of this region – the more so if it happens, as is not unlikely in backward agricultural regions, to be suffering from too high a birth rate.

These few counter-examples alone suffice to demonstrate that a simple interpretation of the age-distribution argument does not adequately deal with the complexities inherent in the relationship between migration and inequality of per capita income. To provide a fuller treatment of this problem, a model will be developed which, though it will not in all instances yield definitive conclusions, will point to the relevant variables that must be considered.

The Model

We assume a closed economy, not subject to international migratory movements, and composed of four paradigm types of region: (1) low per capita income and stagnant (LS); (2) high per capita income and stagnant (HS); (3) low per capita income and growing (LC); and (4) high per capita income and growing (HG).

Some elaboration of these concepts is in order. A 'stagnant' region is here defined as one in which there occurs, over time, relatively little or no increase in per capita income; a growing region, correspondingly, is one in which there is sustained secular improvement in per capita income. Growing regions are generally characterized by advances in productive organization and techniques, and changes in industrial structure. Such characteristics are typically lacking in stagnant regions.

The 'low' and 'high' concepts are of course concerned, not with the rate of growth, but with the level of per capita income at a point in time. A low per capita income region is here defined as one in which per capita income is low by comparison with other regions in the same country, *and/or* by comparison with some median per capita income level prevailing among advanced countries. It follows that a high per capita income region is defined so by comparison *both* with income levels in other regions of the same country *and* with some median level among the advanced countries. (The latter condition makes it possible that *all* regions in an underdeveloped country may be classified as low.)

In the United States, to which we shall continually refer for illustrative purposes, the Pacific Coast would be described as 'high growing' (HG); parts of New England as 'high stagnant' (HS); the East South Central region (particularly Mississippi) as 'low stagnant' (LS); and Texas and North Carolina as 'low growing' (LG).

Our model considers only migratory movements from one region to another of a different category, since nothing of economic interest can be discerned in the cause or nature of migration between similar regions. Since there are four categories, the direction of migration can theoretically vary in twelve ways:

$$
\text{I.}\quad \text{LS} \quad \text{to} \diagup\!\!\!\!\begin{array}{l}\text{LG}\\ \text{—HS}\\ \diagdown\text{HG}\end{array}
\qquad
\text{II.}\quad \text{LG} \quad \text{to} \diagup\!\!\!\!\begin{array}{l}\text{LS}\\ \text{—HS}\\ \diagdown\text{HG}\end{array}
$$

$$
\text{III.}\quad \text{HS} \quad \text{to} \diagup\!\!\!\!\begin{array}{l}\text{LS}\\ \text{—LG}\\ \diagdown\text{HG}\end{array}
\qquad
\text{IV.}\quad \text{HG} \quad \text{to} \diagup\!\!\!\!\begin{array}{l}\text{LS}\\ \text{—LG}\\ \diagdown\text{HS}\end{array}
$$

It is clear that the characteristics of the migratory group with respect to occupation, education, etc., and the consequences of the migration for regional inequality of per capita income, will depend on the direction taken by the migratory stream.

The Low Stagnant Region

For reasons which will presently be made apparent, the low stagnant region will tend to experience a net outflow of population. In 1950, for example, there were 442, 500 native whites who were born in Mississippi but living elsewhere in the United States, while there were at the same time only 178,900 native whites living in Mississippi who were born in other states.[8] Assuming the quality of the in-migrants in such a case does not differ substantially from that of the out-migrants, we may treat Mississippi as an originating state, and need not be concerned with it as a recipient state. As a general proposition for present purposes, we shall regard the low stagnant region as a region of origin only.

In order to weigh the consequences of out-migration from a low stagnant region, it is necessary to specify certain characteristics typical of such a region. In both developed and underdeveloped countries, a stagnant and low per capita income region is generally agricultural. Labor-intensive methods of agricultural production are used, capital and modern equipment may be lacking, and per capita arable land tillage is low. These factors help to explain the low marginal productivity of labor which typically prevails in such a region. It is conceivable, in the extreme case, that marginal productivity of labor is zero – the case of disguised unemployment. Such a condition, however, is much more likely to be encountered in underdeveloped countries. This type of region also tends to have a relatively high fertility rate and natural rate of increase. This condition, combined with an excess labor supply, militates strongly in favor of out-migration, to the extent that any migratory movement at all takes place. It seems reasonable, moreover, to assume that the out-migration will consist primarily of unskilled laborers and their families, because this is the segment of the labor force which is here relatively abundant. Now, if the marginal product of the out-migrants is lower than the average for the region as a whole, it is evident that per capita income will rise, provided that not too drastic a reduction in the proportion of the population in the labor force has resulted from their exit. Moreover, the out-migration of workers may cause the marginal productivity of the remaining workers to rise, because of the resulting increase in capital-labor and in arable land-labor ratios. For these reasons, a fair presumption may be said to exist that *current* out-migration will in general tend to help rather than hinder a low stagnant region, both in the immediate and the distant future.

The Low Growing Region

The case of the region with low, but nevertheless growing, per capita income is somewhat more complicated than the first. To begin with, the issue of whether there is likely to be net in-migration or out-migration is not clear-cut. Much depends on the economic status of the other regions of the country. If the low growing region is part of a country which is otherwise typically low stagnant, then it is likely to be a net recipient of population. This case is, of course, ruled out for an advanced country, which, by definition, must have at least one advanced region. For some underdeveloped countries, however, the greatest economic opportunities may, well lie in the low growing region, thus tending to make it a recipient of population migration. On the other hand, in the advanced countries there may be regions – presumably high growing – which provide relatively greater economic inducements than the low growing region. In this case, the latter might be a net loser of population, though not to so great an extent as the low stagnant region in similar circumstances.[9]

Let us consider the case where the low growing region is a net loser of population. It is now necessary to distinguish two patterns of growth that may emerge in this region. The first involves progress chiefly in the agricultural sector; for example, more capitalistic techniques of production may be employed. In this situation, because capital serves within wide limits as a substitute for labor, the amount of labor employed per arable acre of land will decline; and because the available quantity of land is relatively fixed, a decline in the population and the labor force as a result of out-migration will probably not have deleterious effects, in either the short or the long run, upon the potential economic growth of the region. On the contrary, a reduction of population will probably facilitate the introduction of more capitalistic techniques, and accelerate the mechanization of agriculture.

A second possible growth pattern involves a shift from agriculture to manufacturing production. Assuming that this is an agricultural region with a high labor-to-land ratio, it is unlikely that investment of even a relatively labor-intensive variety will be sufficiently great in the early phases of the shift to absorb fully the excess population of the region. Furthermore, it is probable that population will continue to grow in this region in the short run despite out-migration, because of the high natural rate of population increase that is historically characteristic of such situations. Hence, it is likely that a sufficiently large labor force will continue to exist in the face of out-migration, so that the demand for labor can be met at a wage which will not deter investment. For these reasons, it is unlikely that out-migration would in the short run prove harmful to the growth of the region.

For the long run, it is not possible to reach firm conclusions about the effect of migration on a low growing region with changing economic structure. Even the question of whether there would be net out-migration in the long run is in doubt. Such a situation could prevail, however, if there are other regions in the country which offer even greater economic opportunity, because their growth rate is higher and per capita incomes are higher, and/or they have a lower natural rate of population increase. If out-migration should indeed continue over a prolonged period, it would prove harmful to the region of origin if labor shortages developed which kept the long-run actual rate of growth of income per capita below the potential rate of growth. The possibility of labor shortages is increased if the

out-migration is accompanied by the secular decline in the birth rate which so often attends a transformation from agricultural to manufacturing structure.

In the special case of a low growing region sparsely populated to begin with, any significant out-migration would impede the growth of manufacturing in the short as well as the long run. But this is an unlikely case. It is doubtful that such a region, with a limited labor supply, would attract manufacturing activity. Moreover, even if it did, the marginal productivity of labor would rise to such a degree that the region would probably become a net recipient of population.

In the low growing region which is not sparsely populated, it is also uncertain that out-migration will always prevail. We have remarked that in underdeveloped countries, which consist predominantly of either low stagnant or low growing regions, the low growing region can be expected to be a net recipient of migration. Even in an advanced country, if a region of low per capita income is growing sufficiently rapidly, a large demand for labor will often result in net in-migration. In the United States, for example, personal per capita income in Texas was 90 per cent of the national average in the period 1949-1951, and had been growing rapidly to that time.[10] As a result of its rapid growth rate, Texas — which would here be characterized as low growing — had been (and still is) experiencing net in-migration. It is possible, therefore, that a low growing region may, as in the case of Texas, more than offset its population losses to other, higher per capita income regions by gains from low stagnant regions.

Whether or not such in-migration is helpful or harmful to the growth of such regions will depend on the actual rate of in-migration relative to the rate of regional investment and the availability of land. It is more likely to be harmful in the shorter run, when capital is probably not available in quantities adequate to absorb the suddenly enlarged population. With the passage of time, however, in-migration may prove fruitful for the regional economy, as it becomes better able to use the new arrivals efficiently.

Whereas the propositions concerning the low growing regions which are net-migration recipients are relatively straightforward, those dealing with the net migration losers are, as we have seen, less so, and therefore warrant a brief summary. It was noted that low growing regions are likely to experience out-migration only in advanced countries. In the short run, net out-migration is likely to prove beneficial, except in the special case of sparsely populated areas. In the long run, increasingly limited supplies of labor could well retard the rate of growth. But severe limitations of the labor supply would probably be a consequence, not merely of the out-migration itself, but of birth rate reductions accompanying a structural transformation of economic activity. If the economic changes that characterize the region are predominantly modernization and capitalization of agricultural production, the supply of labor is likely to remain adequate – indeed, more than adequate; out-migration might accelerate the rate of growth of regional per capita income. But if the changes are characterized predominantly by a shift from agricultural to manufacturing activity, then it is possible that out-migration will deter the rate of growth in the long run.

The High Stagnant Region

As in the previous case, two basic regional types are distinguishable in the high per capita income category. The first is the 'old' region, in which the rate of growth of income has markedly declined. The second is the high per capita income region which continues to grow at a rapid rate.

Stagnation in a high per capita income region is usually associated with the presence of industries which enjoyed their secular peaks of activity at an earlier date, and the failure of a sufficient number of newer and rapidly growing industries to appear. An obvious empirical example of this type is provided by parts of New England. The decline and partial withdrawal of the textile industry from this region was a prominent factor in its economic retardation, and was not by any means offset by the appearance of some electronic and other firms. Large portions of the region have over a period of years experienced stagnation.[11]

A high stagnant region is likely to be a net exporter of people, particularly in countries which also have high growing regions, for the pull of economic opportunity from the high growing regions is likely to more than offset any in-migration which originates in the low stagnant or low growing regions. There are a number of forces operating in a high stagnant region which tend to push people in the direction of high growing regions, and which act simultaneously to thwart in-migration from the low per capita income regions. Why is this so?

A number of observations can be made concerning the characteristics of the inhabitants of a high per capita income region. First, if a high growing region elsewhere is offering improved economic opportunities – as is likely to be the case – many residents of the high stagnant region are likely to know about it. In this region, as contrasted with low per capita income regions, the communication of information – in this case concerning job possibilities elsewhere – is likely to be relatively efficient. The educational standard of the population of a high stagnant region is such that information media such as newspapers are relatively better utilized than they are in isolated rural areas in low income regions. Moreover, the sheer number of such sources of information is likely to be larger.

Another factor of importance in contrasting the migratory potential of low and high per capita income regions is that the potential migrant from the latter is likely to possess the economic resources to move himself and his family to new areas of opportunity, whereas migrants from regions of the former type are more likely to find such resources unavailable. Finally, the general training of the high income potential migrant would tend to strengthen the demand for his services in high growing regions, as compared with the services of migrants from low per capita income regions.

While the high stagnant region is a likely origin of migration, particularly to high growing regions, it is not a likely candidate for migratory inflows from low per capita income regions. What inflow does occur is likely to originate predominantly in low income regions, however, the very fact of stagnancy implies that despite high per capita income, the region does not offer sufficiently promising economic horizons to attract large numbers from elsewhere, particularly when compared to horizons in high growing regions. Even though per capita income may be high, its composition may not be such as to encourage significant in-migration. For example, property income per capita may be relatively high in high stagnant regions. Many families accumulated wealth in earlier periods when the region was economically dynamic. Although the rate of growth of the region has now declined, these families are still receiving returns for their past accumulations, in the forms of rent, interest, and dividends, all of which contribute to regional per capita income. But these income components provide no direct inducement to potential migrants who would be unable to share in it.

The recent Study of Population Redistribution and Economic Growth by the University of Pennsylvania provides some interesting figures bearing on this argument. The data in Tables 11.1, 11.2 and 11.3 are for the period 1949-1951 in the United States, and are taken as percentages of the national average.[12]

It is interesting to note, from Tables 11.1 and 11.2, that in New England property income per capita is

Table 11.1 Property income Per Capita in the United States, 1949-1951

	(percent of United States average)
Maine	105.0
New Hampshire	111.9
Vermont	96.8
Massachusetts	131.4
Rhode Island	118.2
Connecticut	174.2

Table 11.2 Service Income Per Worker in the United States, 1949-1951

	(percent of United States average)
Maine	82.8
New Hampshire	82.9
Vermont	81.1
Massachusetts	102.0
Rhode Island	93.4
Connecticut	109.6

greater than service income per worker, relative to the United States as a whole. This indicates that property income accounts for a larger proportion of total income in New England than in the United States at large. Moreover, the near-average figures for service income per worker in the three southern New England States suggest that these states really enjoy their high economic status almost solely because of the property component of its income, as is borne out by the figures on total per capita income in Table 11.3

Table 11.3 Total Personal Per Capita Income, 1949-1951

	(percent of United States average).
Maine	82.4
New Hampshire	88.8
Vermont	81.0
Massachusetts	111.0
Rhode Island	106.1
Connecticut	125.1

Another factor that is probably significant in maintaining for a considerable period the high per capita income of relatively stagnant regions is the occupational distribution of the population. A lengthy previous history of growth and high income will probably have left the region with an endowment of superior educational facilities. In addition, high incomes will have permitted the inhabitants to postpone entrance into the labor force longer than would otherwise have been

possible, meanwhile enabling them to acquire additional schooling and pre-job training. For these reasons, it is probable that, on the average, there are in high stagnant regions relatively more labor force members of professional and skilled status than in low stagnant or low growing regions. In such a region, there is also a greater demand for such workers than in regions of low capita income. These factors, taken together, provide further explanation for a current higher per capita income in the high stagnant region. However, such sources of income would, as in the previous case of property income, fail to provide inducement to the potential out-migrant from low per capita income regions, who tends to fall in the unskilled, or at best semi-skilled category. Neither high property nor high service incomes per capita provide powerful inducements for in-migration.

Some in-migration into high stagnant regions may occur, nevertheless, for different reasons. Potential out-migrants from low stagnant or low growing regions might find a high stagnant region attractive because the services offered by state and local government, particularly in the areas of education and welfare, may far surpass those available in the originating regions. There may, too, be a fairly substantial demand in the receiving region for certain types of service – for example, domestic help – which can be met by the untrained migrant. In general, however, limited opportunities for the relatively unskilled laborer in a stagnant region, for the reasons enumerated above, will usually reduce any population inflow to insignificant levels.

On balance, a high stagnant region is likely to be a net exporter of population. Aside from purely quantitative considerations, however, some extremely interesting consequences of a qualitative type may emerge from this case, which makes inadmissable the analytic netting of inflows against outflows. Consider, for example, the question of educational selectivity. As noted earlier, a region of historically high per capita income will probably have developed, over the years, a strong and ubiquitous educational tradition, which will have had the effect of creating a large amount of educational capital. The average educational level of the indigenous population will be higher than that of the economically more backward areas, and the out-migrants from such a region will tend to be of higher 'quality' and potential productivity than the average for the country as a whole. At the same time, the existence of a population of this educational and productive quality, in a stagnant region where the demand for such a population is not growing very rapidly, will very likely mean that whatever in-migration does occur will not be of similar quality. The inflow will consist predominantly of the unskilled, who seek to improve their status in the high stagnant region.

What are the consequences for the high stagnant region of this 'quality exchange?' The in-migration, in whatever numbers, of the unskilled and semi-skilled laborers and their families probably has a depressing effect on per capita income, for two reasons – one merely arithmetic and the other economic. In the first place, it is apparent that the average income of the in-migrant will be lower than the average for the region, given the presumption that he tends to be of lower 'quality.' This will necessarily reduce the average income of the recipient region. Secondly, because this is not a growing region, the capital-labor ratio will probably fall as a result of any increase in unskilled or semi-skilled labor, and this will tend to diminish the marginal productivity of these classes of labor. Thus, any net increase in the numbers of lower-quality workers through migration will probably have a detrimental effect on per capita income. One cannot, however, predict whether or not an increase of population of this category will result from inter-regional migration. While it is probable that the average quality of the out-migrant will be higher than that of the in-migrant, the *number* of low quality out-migrants may or may not exceed the number of low quality in-migrants.

The net out-migration of professional and highly skilled labor from the high stagnant region will operate upon per capita income of that region in the same downward direction as the inflow of the less skilled, as their exodus constitutes a reduction of the average productivity of the remaining population.[13] These considerations, taken together, point to the conclusions that inter-regional migration will prove detrimental to the per capita income of a high stagnant region. This conclusion is valid for both the short and the long run, assuming the persistence of stagnation in the region.

The migration figures for the New England states, in Table 11.4, illustrate some of the points mentioned above. Four of the six New England states had, in the decade 1940-1950, significant migratory losses. In Rhode Island there was no significant change. Connecticut, as a real exception, experienced significant net in-migration. This exception, however, strengthens the argument presented above. As Harris has noted, 'Connecticut, with its close relations with the Middle Atlantic States and its concentration on thriving industries in the last generation, is a manufacturing state with a much

better record than the rest of the region.'[14] This state, therefore, should not be classed as a high stagnant area, and it is therefore not surprising that it experienced net in-migration.

Table 11.4 Net Intercensal Migration by Nativity and Race, for the New England States, 1940-1950*

	Native Whites	Negroes	Foreign-Born Whites	Totals
Maine	-41,600	- 100	5,900	-35,800
New Hampshire	-12,600	300	3,300	- 9,100
Vermont	-25,800	- - -	2,000	-23,800
Massachusetts	-73,800	10,600	33,600	-29,500
Rhode Island	200	1,200	1,700	2,700
Connecticut	49,000	13,000	27,500	89,500
Totals	-105,000	25,000	74,000	- 6,000

* The data are derived from figures in Lee *et al., op. cit.,* I, 119-21, 149-51, 154-56, 174-76, 199-201, 214-16. The totals do not all check because of rounding. The figures for the foreign-born include international as well as domestic migration.

The breakdown of Table 4 also supports our contention concerning the 'quality exchange' that characterizes migration in high stagnant areas. While New England (except for Connecticut) experienced a large net loss of native whites, it gained considerable numbers of foreign-born whites and Negroes. Presumably, the occupational status and per capita income of the native white out-migrants was higher than that of the foreign born and Negro in-migrants. This undoubtedly tended to depress the per capita income of the region.

It would, however, be incorrect to conclude that migration is an important prime cause of the plight of a high stagnant region. In the main, causality runs the other way. Because of the failure of old industries to grow rapidly, and of new ones to appear, growth rates have declined. It is this which causes the migration streams to behave as they do – contributing to, but not initially responsible for, the impairment of the region's economy.

High Growing Regions

Finally, we must consider the direction and effects of migration for a region characterized by relatively rapid growth of per capita income, starting from levels already high. It should be immediately evident, from what has already been said about the low per capita income regions and the high stagnant region, that the high growing region will be a net recipient of significant migratory inflows. All of the other regional types are likely to be contributors, in one or another degree, to the population of the high growing region. Because of its level and rate of growth of income, there is in this region a substantial and growing demand for labor, thus creating a wage structure which will prove attractive to labor in other regions. A further attraction is the educational and welfare facilities made possible by the already high per capita income.

The long-run effects of migration into such a region are fairly clear. This region is characteristically composed of relatively youthful industries, growing at a rapid pace, which have located there for some economic or other advantage. This is a region in which the birth rate (and hence the natural rate of increase) will be relatively low, particularly in comparison to the low-income rural areas of more backward regions. Typically, a substantial amount of population growth is required to facilitate the long-run expansion of the region's industries to their full potential. In the absence of a high rate of natural increase, in-migration at least partially fulfills this function and thus in the long run is conducive to higher levels of per capita income.

The situation is less clear in the short run. The entry of quantities of unskilled and semi-skilled labor mainly from the regions of low per capita income could in the shorter period have a depressing effect on per capita income; this is an arithmetic proposition to which we have already alluded. These migrants, whose average income is below the average income of the receiving region, tend in the short run to lower per capita income for the receiving region as a whole. For example, the influx of population into the state of Michigan in the 1920's very probably had a depressing effect on Michigan's per capita income during that decade. There were about 550,000 net in-migrants into the state between 1920 and 1930, representing about 15 per cent of the average Michigan population in that decade, which was 3,769,900. Of the total migratory inflow, about 86,100 were Negro, and 224,000 were foreign-born.[15] Thus a large proportion were, we may infer, either unskilled or semi-skilled, and this probably had a depressing short run effect on per capita income.

Because of the enormous influx of population into Michigan, a heavy demand for housing and public facilities undoubtedly developed quickly. To the extent that this caused a diversion of resources into these sectors, where the capital-output ratio is relatively high,

and away from other activities of lower capital-output ratios, the short run effect of the heavy in-migration may have been adverse. However, this may have been partially or wholly offset by a capital inflow from other regions which had been attracted by the economic prospects of the new automobile industry.

But despite any unfavorable initial impact of this migration of the twenties, it is evident that the subsequent phenomenal growth of the automobile industry, and the consequent growth of the state's per capita income, were directly contingent upon this influx of unskilled labor from other regions. The role of migration was highlighted by the fact that the natural rate of increase in Michigan during this period was relatively low.

The case of Michigan is particularly interesting in that it points to a close relation which sometimes exists between migration and technology. The assembly-line technique of automobile production could not have been successfully instituted without the presence of an adequate supply of unskilled and semi-skilled labor, and the economic opportunity generated by the introduction of this technique was probably responsible for encouraging and absorbing the large-scale unskilled in-migration.

California provides another illustration of a high growing region. The secular growth of the aircraft industry, as well as the growth of the rest of the state's economy, was made possible by the in-migration – the role of in-migration again being highlighted by the fact that before 1940 the fertility rate in the state was among the lowest in the nation.

We may conclude from these observations that the significant in-migration probably experienced by high growing regions may have an unfavorable effect on per capita income in the short run. In the long run, however, it is bound to have a beneficial effect on the region's economy, for it provides the labor required for sustained growth.

Conclusions

On the basis of the foregoing analysis of regional migration, we may now attempt to assess the effects of such migrations on regional inequalities of per capita income.

It has been noted that low stagnant regions are quite likely, over time, to experience a net outflow of population. This outflow, it was argued, would in the short and probably in the long run prove beneficial to the region, whether it is in an advanced or in an underdeveloped country. When this outflow is in the direction of low growing regions, this will tend in the short run to retard the rate of growth of the latter regions, though in the long run the result may be either retardation or acceleration of the growth rate. We may therefore conclude that in the short run, migration from low stagnant to low growing tends to diminish the rate of widening inequality between the low stagnant and low growing regions. In the long run, out-migration is of benefit to the originating low stagnant region, but at the same time may prove to be either an aid or a detriment to the receiving low growing region. Thus, it is not certain whether in the long run migration will contribute to a widening or a narrowing of inequality in per capita incomes between the low stagnant and low growing regions.

A second important stream of migration flows from the low stagnant to the high growing regions. In the short run, the inflow of persons of probable 'low quality' (in terms of educational and occupational status) to the high growing region tends to depress per capita income there, while the outflow from the low stagnant region reduces its excess labor supply, tending here to raise per capita income. It is evident, therefore, that in the short run migration from low stagnant to high growing regions will tend to narrow inequality between these regions. In the long run, however, because net in-migration probably is of benefit to the high growing region, nothing definite can be concluded regarding the effects upon inequality of per capita income.

A third important migratory stream flows from the high stagnant to the high growing regions. It was argued that the out-migrants may tend to be of relatively 'high quality' in terms of occupation and education; hence, in this case, quality deterioration in the labor force of the high stagnant region is linked to quality improvement in the labor force of the high growing region. It follows that this migration will tend to accelerate the growing inequality in per capita income between the high stagnant and high growing regions.

It was also noted that there may be some migration of relatively 'low quality' labor from the low stagnant to the high stagnant regions. Hence, migration may adversely affect the high stagnant region in two distinct ways – through a loss of relatively high-productivity labor to the high growing regions, and through a gain of relatively low-productivity labor from the low stagnant regions.

Finally, a migratory stream may flow from the low growing to the high growing regions. This case is the most difficult to assess in terms of its effects on per capita income inequality. In the short run, this movement probably contributes to lesser inequality. This is based on the assumption that the quality of the in-migrants is such as to depress the average level of labor productivity of the high growing region, thus tending to depress per capita income. On the other hand, the out-migration is not likely to prove detrimental to the low growing region, particularly since there may be a partially compensating inflow from the low stagnant region. Moreover, in the short run, with limited capital available, the low growing region is unlikely to experience a relative scarcity of labor.

What should now be abundantly clear is that no general proposition can be formulated concerning the effect of internal migration on regional inequality of per capita income. Any general statement, such as Myrdal's conclusion that migration widens regional inequality, based as it is only on an age-selectivity argument, is not valid. As we have shown, the effect on inequality depends on the direction of the migration, on whether one considers the short or the long run, and on whether the country involved is advanced or underdeveloped. And even when all of these factors are specified, there are important cases where the outcome in indeterminate.

Acknowledgement

This study was undertaken with financial assistance from the Ford Foundation.

Notes

1 Simon Kuznets, 'Under-developed Countries and the Pre-industrial Phase in the Advanced Countries: An Attempt at Comparison,' *Proceedings of the World Regulation Conference* (Rome, 1954), and G. Myrdal, *Economic Theory and Under-developed Regions* (London, 1957).

2 For figures on state fertility rates in the United States, see Bernard Okun, *Trends in Birth Rates in the United States Since 1870* (Baltimore, 1958), pp. 33-34.

3 Myrdal, *op. cit.*, pp. 12-13, 142-146.

4 *Ibid.*, p. 148.

5 *Ibid.*, p. 27.

6 Ragnar Nurkse, *Problems of Capital Formation in Underdeveloped Countries* (Oxford, 1957), pp. 32-36.

7 John D. Black, for example, shows that for the period 1925-30, the southern regions had, in agri-

culture, the lowest monthly wage rates and the lowest value of capital goods per worker of all regions in the United States. Cf. 'Agricultural Wage Relationships: Geographical Differences,' *Review of Economic Statistics* XVIII, No. 7 (May, 1936), 74.

8 Everett S. Lee *et al.*, *Population Redistribution and Economic Growth, United States, 1870-1950* (Philadelphia, 1957). I, 271.

9 For example, North Carolina, with a population in 1940 of about 2.5 million native whites, had a net loss of 81,600 native whites between 1940 and 1950; Mississippi, with about 1.1 million in 1940, lost 94,300 in the same period. Data from *ibid.*, 1, 162, 185.

10 Data derived from *ibid.*, I, 753.

11 Cf. Seymour Harris, *The Economics of New England:* *Case Study of an Older Area* (Cambridge, Mass.).

12 Data derived from Lee *et al., op. cit.*, 1, 253, 757.

13 Of course, the average income of the remaining higher-quality labor will presumably benefit from the depletion in the numbers of the highly trained, but the average income of the region as a whole will be reduced.

14 Harris, *op. cit.*, p. 73.

15 Lee *et al., op. cit.*, I, 157-159. The foreign-born figure also includes persons coming to Michigan directly from foreign countries.

Reprinted from *Economic Development and Cultural Change*, 9, 1961, University of Chicago Press, Chicago, with permission.

Part III
Micro Analysis

Introduction

The analysis of trade, monetary and migration flows between dimensionless regions is one method of studying interregional variations in economic structure and prosperity. Part III sets out an alternative micro frame of analysis, in which differences in wage levels, production costs or regional demand are conceived of as differences between points on continuous cost or demand surfaces. The conceptualisation of land values as a continuous economic surface with marked peaks over the centre of cities is well known, but similar surfaces can also in theory be constructed for wage levels, commodity prices and other economic phenomena. Figure 1 shows a land value surface drawn by D.M. Smith for Lancashire. Locations with the same land price per acre are joined by isocost lines to form a series of cost contours. It only requires a little imagination to realise that a map of this type could easily be turned into a relief model dominated by two peaks over Liverpool and Manchester and a ridge of high prices running between them.

D.M. Smith's paper (p. 126) provides a framework for identifying the minimum cost location of firms and the spatial margins of profitability within which they can operate. The margins are determined by the locus of points at which the cost of producing and delivering goods exactly equals the price being charged for them. The minimum cost location for a firm is somewhere within this margin contour, although its exact position will vary with the case being analysed. Around this optimum location a whole series of contours can be drawn, each of them representing a given increment of production cost above that of the optimum. Thus a cost surface is produced the lowest point of which represents the cost-minimisation location, while the set of viable locations for factories is bounded by the margin contour.

The paper by Harris (p. 141) attempts to identify not the point of minimum production cost but the location at which a firm can expect to experience the maximum demand for its goods. He assumes that for most purposes the location and size of population is a good indicator of the spatial distribution of potential demand and that the actual level of demand which a firm experiences for its goods is a function of the distance between the market and the producing point. Thus a firm which locates nearest to most major markets will maximise its sales. Harris produces a series of demand surfaces for the United States both for aggregate demand and for individual segments of the economy.

It will be clear that few firms are concerned only with minimising costs or maximising demand for their products. More realistically they will be concerned with maximising their profits. A location where this can be done may be neither the minimum cost or the maximum demand point. Hence the cost surfaces of Smith and the demand surfaces of Harris need to be combined into a cost and demand surface. This is done by Stafford (p. 155), who demonstrates that the point of maximum profit is where the height of the demand or revenue surface above the cost surface is at a maximum.

Naturally cost and revenue surfaces are abstractions produced by generalising the differences in costs and revenue found at a whole series of locations. These costs and revenues are produced by the locations and activities of individual firms, large corporations and ordinary people. If a firm chooses to expand at location A the demand for labour may increase. This will lead to an increase in cost and the labour cost surface will rise at that point. Similarly if large numbers of people move into a new suburb then the demand for retail goods in that area will rise and this can be conceptualised as a change in the retail demand surface.

Although individuals and firms produce changes in cost and revenue surfaces they are more often influenced by them in making location decisions. A firm seeking to build a new factory in a city may move out of the city and down the slopes of the land value surface until it finds land at a price per acre which it can afford. Similarly an individual, anxious to improve his real income, may seek a point on the wages surface higher than the one he at present occupies.

The combined effect of people and firms perceiving the differences in the form of cost and demand surfaces is to produce locational change. Fuchs' paper (p. 159) describes how the redistribution of manufacturing in the

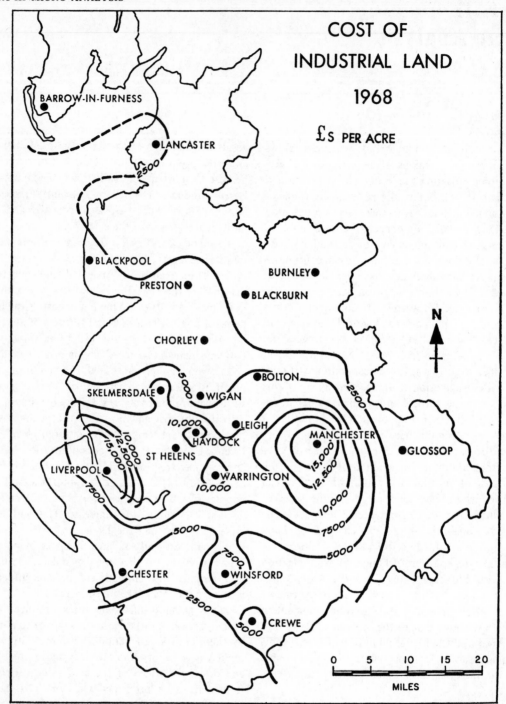

Figure 1 A generalised land-cost surface, based on the cost of representative industrial sites.
(Source: Lamida.) In the case of rented land, purchase price is taken to be ten times the annual rental.

This figure is reprinted here with the author's permission. It has also appeared as Figure 22, page 123 in *The North West*, 1968, David and Charles, Newton Abbott, and as Figure 15.1, page 281, in *Industrial Location: An Economic Geographical Analysis*, 1971, John Wiley & Sons, New York.

USA since 1929 has been away from the Manufacturing Belt and towards the South and West. He tries to identify why this locational change has taken place.

On a smaller spatial scale Pred (p. 176) examines how the growth of manufacturing industry and population in urban centres has set in process a cycle of cumulative growth which has progressively lowered the production cost surface of firms by enabling them to achieve scale and agglomeration economies. At the same time the demand surface has risen due both to the movement in of population and to the rise in real incomes. In the USA the expansion of the rail network in the last part of the nineteenth century allowed larger and strategically located centres to invade the markets of smaller towns and syphon off demand to permit their own more rapid expansion. This naturally accentuated differences in cost and revenue surfaces.

The paper by Lever (p. 194) actually focuses upon the process of industrial relocation within the city. He makes a case study of the movement of firms from the inner areas of Glasgow out to the suburbs and suggests that as this process continues the peak of property values and rents at the urban core may diminish while the values in suburban locations rise. He thus suggests that decentralisation of industry will reduce inequalities in the cost surface. Keeble (p. 206) in contrast examines the process of relocation from the city to towns or cities elsewhere in the country. He argues that shortage of land in North West London and high land prices is forcing firms to move out of London altogether. Some move to satellite towns while others move to development areas, where the capital cost surface is artificially lowered by government subsidy.

Firms are not the only type of decision making unit which is influenced by the form of the cost and revenue surfaces. Parsons (p. 220) points out that in some cases the decision maker can be the large multi-plant corporation. Such corporations can easily transform profits earned in one region or at one location on the surface into capital investment in a new place in a different region. Hence the economic performance of a plant and the revenue it earns can be reflected in changing demands for labour, changing investment decisions and changing land values many miles away.

Wolpert's paper (p. 224) provides a theoretical framework for the examination of a family's decision to migrate. He suggests that the decision maker only knows of a limited number of places other than the one he now occupies. Characteristically these are clustered around his existing location. His information about these places is often imperfect, but he tries to rate them in terms of the increased utility they offer him. This could be interpreted as an assessment of which places are higher on the wage surface and hence offer greater fiscal rewards. However this would be a simplification since 'utility' embraces the social as well as the economic incentives to migrate.

Wolpert's paper emphasises, as does Parsons', that the reaction which a decision maker is likely to have to inequalities in economic and social surfaces is determined in large measure by the character and attitudes of the decision making unit itself. It also of course follows that the character of the unit will also determine the effect it has in changing the form of socio-economic surfaces. Hence the key task of micro regional analysis is to determine the form of economic and social surfaces and to examine their evolution in response to the location decisions of bodies or people with which they interact.

12 A Theoretical Framework for Geographical Studies of Industrial Location

by D.M. Smith

University of Southern Illinois

One of the most important requirements in geographical research today is a sound theoretical basis for studies in economic geography. The belief that economic activity can be explained as a response to the physical environment is no longer regarded as an adequate interpretation of the spatial arrangement of economic phenomena, but an alternative set of principles with a firm foundation of economics has not yet gained general acceptance. The basis which is needed is what William Warntz has described as 'macro analysis,' the aim of which is to develop 'concepts at a more meaningful level of abstraction so as to make possible the understanding of the whole economic system and to provide a conceptual framework into which to put the micro-descriptions.'[1]

The need for some such theoretical base is particularly urgent in industrial geography. Much empirical research remains to be done in the field of industrial location, and an understanding of the factors influencing the siting of factories is becoming increasingly important in national and regional planning. Any attempt to explain the location of a particular industry or the industrial geography of a particular region or to solve local or regional employment problems requires some knowledge of how locations are arrived at in general. Geographers are well aware of the factors which influence industrial location, but they seem less certain of precisely how these operate and how the relative importance of particular causal factors can be assessed in any specific case.

Industrial geography is concerned with the description and interpretation of the real world rather than with the derivation of abstract theory. Consequently, the student of industrial location has to go to the work of economists such as Hoover, Lösch, Isard, and Greenhut for a thorough grounding in location theory. But much of this work is aimed at bringing the space dimension into conventional economic theory rather than providing a background from which to embark upon empirical studies of industrial geography. If the geographer seeks a theoretical basis for his examination of the real world, he will only achieve it by adapting or reformulating existing location theory for his own particular purposes.

To provide the background he needs, the industrial geographer must examine the location problem afresh – he must return to first principles. This study is an attempt to approach industrial location in elementary theoretical terms by constructing a series of simple models to demonstrate the influence of various factors on the location of plants and industries. The approach developed here embodies contributions of various other writers whose work is alreadu well known to the geographer, but some of the means of analysis and illustration employed here may be less familiar. The aim is to provide a theoretical background from which a more realistic way of looking at location problems in the real world may emerge.

First Principles

In setting up a factory a businessman has to make a number of decisions, one of which is where to put the plant. On the assumption that he is in business to make money, he will, other things being equal, choose the location at which he can make maximum profits. The locational decision is not, of course, taken in isolation, but is related to other considerations such as scale of operations, combination of factors of production, and market conditions. The maximum profits location may be different for different sizes of factories or different combinations of factors, and demand may vary with the choice of location. The interrelation of all these factors makes the analysis of location an extremely complex matter, but by making certain simplifying assumptions the problem may be reduced to elementary terms.

In any industry, costs vary from place to place in accordance with variations in the cost of the necessary factors of production and in the cost of marketing. The total revenue obtainable also varies from place to place according to variations in demand and price. The most profitable location will clearly be where total revenue exceeds total costs by the greatest amount. The effect of spatial variations in cost and price are illustrated in Figure 12.1, which indicates the sort of conditions which exist, in a far more complicated form, in any industry in the real world. The spatial cost/price situations as shown here represent the simplest possible conditions, and are based on the assumption that cost and price are fixed and cannot be altered by the individual firm by, say, large-scale production, changes of technique or factor combination, and entrepreneurial skill. For simplicity of presentation it is also assumed that output is constant in space, and that variations in demand, if they exist, are reflected in variations from place to place in price. Cost and price (£) are plotted on the y axis, and distance on the x axis.

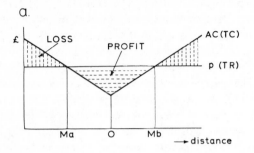

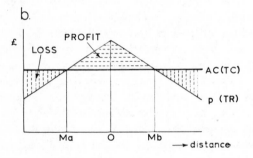

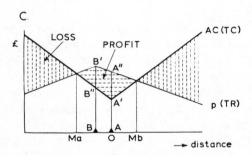

Figure 12.1 Optimum location and spatial margins to profitability in different cost/price situations.

The effect of variation in cost and price on location can best be seen by assuming one to be variable and the other constant. In Figure 12.1a, costs are variable in space while demand is constant and the price obtainable (p) is the same everywhere. The average cost per unit of production at any point is indicated by the appropriate

value on the line AC, which rises in both directions from point O. This line may be termed the *space cost curve* (not to be confused with the cost curve of conventional economic theory), and is the basic analytical tool in the more detailed discussion which follows. O represents the point of minimum costs and Ma and Mb the points where the average cost is just equal to the price obtainable. The vertical distance between p and AC where price is above average cost (i.e., between Ma and Mb) indicates the average profit on each unit of production. As it is assumed that output does not vary from place to place, the spatial average cost/price situation indicated in Figure 12.1a also holds good for the total situation, with the appropriate adjustment of values on the y axis.[2] Average cost thus becomes total cost (TC) and the price line shows total revenue (TR), all values having simply been multiplied by a constant representing total output. The vertical distance between AC(TC) and p(TR), where the revenue line is above the cost line, now represents total profits, so O becomes the point of maximum profits, or the optimum location.

But Figure 12.1a shows more than simply the derivation of optimum location in a given cost/price situation. It also indicates limits to the area in which profitable operation is possible. These spatial limits, or *margins*, to profitability[3] are indicated by Ma and Mb, which correspond with the points where TC = TR, i.e., where firms can just break even. Beyond the margin, where costs exceed revenue, firms can only operate at a loss, the size of the loss being indicated by the vertical distance between TC and TR.

Figure 12.1b represents the reverse of the situation illustrated in Figure 12.1a, with costs assumed to be the same everywhere but with spatial variations in price. These price variations reflect variations in demand, p being highest where demand is greatest. Again O is the location where average profit per unit of output is greatest, and Ma and Mb are the break-even points. As with Figure 12.1a this diagram can be taken to represent the total situation, as output is assumed constant and cannot respond to spatial variations in demand. AC thus becomes TC, and p becomes TR. O is now the point of maximum profits — the location at which TR exceeds TC by the greatest possible amount — and Ma and Mb represent the margin to profitability beyond which a loss would occur. This is, of course, only one possible way of representing a situation with spatial variation in demand; alternatively, price could have been held constant and output allowed to vary, with the possibility of economies of scale introduced. But the simple situation illustrated in Figure 12.1b is sufficient to show that the concepts of optimum and marginal locations apply in just the same way as in a situation in which demand is constant.

In reality, of course, both cost and demand (as reflected in price in this simplified presentation) are likely to vary from place to place. This sort of situation is shown in Figure 12.1c, where the average cost rises away from point A, and where price is reduced away from B as demand falls off. Again the assumption of constant output enables TC to be substituted for AC and TR for p. An examination of the vertical distance between TR and TC now shows that the maximum profit point is A, where costs are lowest. Profit here $(A' - A'')$ is greater than at the point of highest price, or greatest demand $(B' - B'')$, and the manufacturer seeking maximum profits will therefore choose the least cost location despite the lower total revenue obtainable there. The reverse situation, with maximum profits at the high price (i.e., demand) location, could be illustrated simply by altering the gradients of the price and cost lines.

From the foregoing analysis it is possible to state the fundamental principle underlying industrial location in any cost/price situation. Spatial variations in total cost and total revenue impose limits to the area in which any industry can be undertaken at a profit. Within this area the amount of possible profit is likely to vary, and unless maximum profits are sought, the individual manufacturer is free to locate anywhere. It is further evident from Figure 12.1 that the steeper the gradient of the cost or price lines (i.e., the greater the spatial variation), the more localized the industry is likely to be, and the shallower the gradient, the more dispersed will be the distribution pattern.

Further generalization would be possible from a more detailed analysis of the relationship between cost and price lines in Figure 12.1, but the value of this is restricted by the simplifying assumptions which have been made. It is now necessary to introduce some of the complications which exist in the real world and to consider the implications of changes in the spatial cost/price situation through time. This can be done within the analytical framework set up in this section, but before proceeding it is necessary to examine certain alternative approaches briefly in order to establish the most suitable theoretical model.

The Least Cost and Market Area Approaches

Until about ten years ago the various attempts on the part of economists to develop a theory of industrial location could be divided fairly rigidly into two types. These may be termed the 'least cost' and the 'market area' approaches.[4]

The least cost approach arises largely from the work of Alfred Weber,[5] and is directed toward the determination of the least cost location. It assumes that costs vary from place to place, largely in accordance with transport costs, and that a market exists at a particular point. Demand is assumed constant or unlimited, and cannot be influenced by the action of individual firms. The situation envisaged is, in fact, similar to that depicted above in Figure 12.1a.

The market area approach, the best-known exponent of which was August Lösch,[6] is based on conditions of monopolistic competition, as opposed to the perfect competition existing in the least cost theory. Costs are assumed constant in space and the market widely scattered. Producers seek the location giving them greatest profit by attempting to control the largest possible market area, thus maximizing sales and total revenue. Within their market area they will have a monopoly position. Away from the point of production the delivered price to consumers rises with transport costs, and the boundary of the market area is reached when the price becomes so high that consumers buy from an alternative source. If the manufacturer maintains a uniform price, he will not normally sell beyond the point where the cost of distribution absorbs his profit.

Melvin Greenhut has attempted to fuse these two approaches, and Walter Isard[7] has developed a general theory based on the principle of substitution. However, the acceptance of spatial variations in demand as well as cost makes the formulation of a theory of plant location an extremely complex matter, particularly when it is recognized that each firm influences and is affected by the locational decisions of other firms. In attempting to demonstrate in simple graphical terms how locational decisions are governed and freedom of choice restricted, it is clearly necessary to simplify the complex situation which exists in the real world. This can most readily be done by assuming either costs or demand conditions constant in space.

The approach adopted here is fundamentally the least cost approach, with demand and price held constant. In attempting to formulate a way of looking at location problems which has practical application in empirical research, the least cost approach has certain advantages. The most important of these from the geographical point of view is that it enables the effect of the location of spatially variable supplies of materials and labor to be considered, which is impossible under Löschian assumptions of a uniform plain with scattered population. Despite the value of the concept of market areas, its application to the interpretation of industrial patterns in a country like Britain, or in the more heavily industrialized parts of the United States, is strictly limited. Some industries, like brewing and grain milling, may comprise a series of individual plants surrounded by their own market area, but most leading industries in Britain, for example, are concentrated in particular localities and serve a national or world market. Few firms making cotton yarn, clothing, machine tools, or motor cars would claim to have their own market area with some degree of local monopoly.

Under the conditions operating in an advanced industrial economy with a high degree of geographical specialization, the least cost approach to the search for the most profitable location, therefore, seems the most realistic one. However, in theoretical analysis the simplifying assumption of constant demand conditions must always be borne in mind, and the possibility of spatial variations in the size of the potential market must always be considered in the interpretation of specific cases.

Spatial Variations in Costs: Some General Considerations

Before attempting to develop a simple model to illustrate the effect of spatial variations in costs on locational decisions, it is necessary to consider in general terms how costs come to vary from place to place. In order to produce a given quantity of any goods, the manufacturer must assemble at one point the necessary amount of the four factors of production — land, labor, capital (including materials and machines), and enterprise. The cost of each of these is likely to vary from place to place. In considering the cost of factors of production it is useful to distinguish between basic cost and locational cost. The basic cost is the sum which must be paid irrespective of location, e.g., the cost of a raw material at source, or the cost of labor at its cheapest point. The locational cost is the additional expenditure incurred in bringing the factor to the place where it is needed (i.e., the factory), which varies according to where the factory is situated. Just as each factor of production has its basic and locational cost, so these two elements can be

distinguished in the total cost of any firm or industry. This is illustrated in Figure 12.2, an adaptation of Figure 12.1a. It is obvious that the least cost (maximum profit) location will be where total locational costs (the sum of the locational cost of all factors) is at a minimum, for each factor's basic cost is, of course, constant in space.

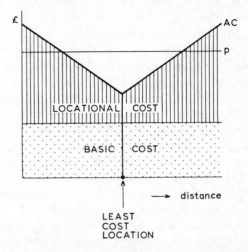

Figure 12.2 The distinction between basic and locational cost.

It is unnecessary to describe in detail how the cost of the various factors of production differs from place to place.[8] Some brief comments may be helpful, however, in explaining what is included in the cost of each factor. The cost of land includes any particular physical attributes of the site, such as flatness or the presence of a stream for water power. A level site or a water-power site can be created anywhere providing the financial inducement is great enough, but if they occur naturally costs will be reduced. The cost of labor varies from place to place according to wage rates and efficiency; labor costs may be less with highly paid and highly efficient workers than with cheap but unskilled labor, but this is not necessarily always the case. In areas of labor shortage additional costs may be incurred in providing welfare facilities, bonus schemes, etc., in order to attract labor. The capital item may for the purposes of location analysis be seperated into financial capital equipment, and materials (including power). Financial capital for certain types of enterprise may be more easily (i.e., cheaply) obtained in some places than in others — in the Industrial Revolution in Britain, for example, capital to back new inventions in textile machinery was generally more forthcoming in existing textile manufacturing towns. The cost of machinery, materials, and power varies from place to place largely in accordance with transport costs. To what extent the cost of managerial skill varies from place to place it is difficult to say, but it could be argued that the same skill would cost more in an area with an unattractive environment than in a pleasant town with many social attractions. A comparison between southeastern England and parts of the northern industrial areas may be relevant in this respect, greater inducements being needed to attract skilled management north.

In order to evaluate the influence of individual factors of production in any specific locational study, it is necessary to know not only how their costs vary from place to place, but also their relative importance in the cost structure will, of course, be an average figure for the industry as a whole, as it will differ for each firm according to location and combination of factors. As a general rule, the factor or factors making up a relatively large share of total cost variations are likely to have the greatest influence on variations in total cost and thus on location. A small component of total costs may have an important influence on location if its cost varies from place to place to a much greater extent than that of other factors. A factor which is ubiquitous in space, and therefore has no locational cost, will not influence location, no matter how high a proportion of total cost it comprises.[9]

A Simple Locational Model

The ground has now been prepared for a more detailed examination of the way in which industrial location is influenced by spatial variations in costs. This can be done with the help of a simple hypothetical model, which can be used to illustrate how the space cost curve introduced above can be derived in practice, and how optimum location and spatial margins arise. The model can also be adapted to illustrate the effect of certain influences on industrial location which have not yet been considered.

Assume that an imaginary manufacturing industry exists and that for production it requires land, a certain amount of labor, and a given quantity of a single raw material. It sells its products to a dispersed market. Assume that the material is found at point A, the labor is concentrated at B, and the centre of the market is at C.[10] Assume further that to manufacture and market each unit of product, a firm requires £40 worth of materials, £30 worth of labor (both these figures representing basic cost at source, i.e., at A and B respectively), and £10 worth of land (which is the same price anywhere), and that sales costs are £20 at a

location at the center of the market. The *basic* cost structure of the industry, per unit of production is thus:

Item	Cost (£)
Land (ubiquitous)	10
Marketing (at C)	20
Labor (from B)	30
Material (from A)	40
Total	100

Locational cost must now be considered. Assume for the sake of simplicity that the cost of transporting £40 worth of material increases proportional to distance at £1 per mile, that labor costs rise £1 per mile away from B (perhaps additional wages have to be paid to attract workers from their home town), and that the average cost of marketing one unit increases by £1 per mile the farther away from the center of the market (C) the factory is established. Land costs are assumed constant in space, so no locational costs arise. If it is also assumed that points A, B, and C are in a certain situation in relation to one another (say, equidistant from each other and 30 miles apart), then cost isopleths can be constructed and a space cost curve can be derived graphically.[11]

Before proceeding further it is necessary to state certain fundamental simplifying assumptions which underlie this analysis. Any model which attempted to take into account all variables likely to have a bearing on locational choice would be very complex indeed, and in order to reduce the location problem to its basic essentials, some causal factors must be eliminated or held constant. Such an approach is perfectly valid as long as the extent of the simplification adopted is made clear, so that the limitations of any conclusions drawn can be fully understood. The assumptions which have been made through this and the following section (for reasons which should be self-evident) are as follows:

1 All producers are in business to make a profit (but not necessarily maximum profit), and choose their location with this in mind.

2 They are all aware of the spatial variations in costs and profits which exist in their industry.

3 Sources of factors of production are fixed, supply is unlimited, and substitution between factors is impossible.

4 Demand and price are constant in space.

In deriving a space cost curve applicable to an entire industry (i.e., to every firm) it is also necessary to assume that returns to scale are constant so that no firm can take advantage of economies of scale, that firms do not influence each other's location and no advantages are to be derived from agglomeration, that all entrepreneurs are equally skillful, and that no location is subsidized. These assumptions will later be relaxed in turn to show the locational effect of the various considerations involved. It is also necessary to emphasize that this is a static analysis at one point in time, and that price, costs, combination of factors, and techniques cannot be changed. Some dynamic aspects of industrial location will be considered in the next section.

The spatial cost situation in the hypothetical case outlined above is illustrated in Figure 12.3. Here a series of concentric circles have been drawn about points A, B, and C at five mile intervals (the thin lines) each circle indicating an increase of £5 in the cost of the necessary material, labor, and marketing. From this the total cost per unit of production at any point can be worked out, and a series of isopleths joining points of equal cost can be derived (the thick lines).

Figure 12.3a shows that costs rise away from a point 0. Because of the particular values chosen for the combination of factors and their cost variations, this is exactly in the middle of the triangle formed by points A, B, and C. The solution of the problem of least cost site within a so-called 'locational triangle' has been attempted in a number of ways. Weber regarded each corner as exerting a force pulling the least cost location toward it and showed how the point could be found by geometry and by Varignon's mechanical model.[12] Isard approaches it as a substitution problem, analyzed through his *transformation lines*.[13] But the derivation of cost isopleths seems the most direct and realistic method, and it has the important advantage of also revealing the spatial margin to profitability when price is introduced into the analysis.

This is illustrated in Figure 12.3a. Assume that for each article produced a price of £165 is obtainable. The £165 cost isopleth thus becomes the margin — inside the line a profit can be made, outside it firms will operate at a loss. Profitable operation is possible at the source of material (A), at the least cost labor point (B), and at the center of the market (C), but there are other more advantageous sites nearer to O. In Figure 12.3b a space cost curve for the situation under review has been derived simply by taking a cross-section through Figure 12.3a along the line PQ. The introduction of a price line shows the area of profitability between Ma and Mb. At the optimum location costs are minimized at £151 per unit of production, giving a (maximum) profit of £14. At this point the basic cost, as everywhere, is £100, while the locational cost is, of course, £51.

It must be emphasized that although in this simple model the optimum location is within the triangle ABC, this need not be the case. In practice the least cost location is very often at the source or least cost point of one factor of production. It can easily be shown (for example, by Varignon's mechanical model) that if the pull exerted by one corner of the triangle is greater than that exerted by the other two corners together, least cost location will be at that corner. In terms of the present model, the force exerted by each corner is equivalent to the gradient of the space cost curve of its own factor, which in each case is £1 per mile. Expressed another way, the pull is equal to the cost of the required quantity of the factor in question at source multiplied by the percentage increase in cost per unit of distance. This is illustrated by the following figures:

Item	Cost of required quantity at source (a)	Percentage cost increase per mile (b)	Locational pull (a x b)	Gradient of space cost curve (£'s/mile)
Land	10	nil	nil	nil
Marketing (C)	20	5.0	100	1
Labor (B)	30	3.3	100	1
Material (A)	40	2.5	100	1

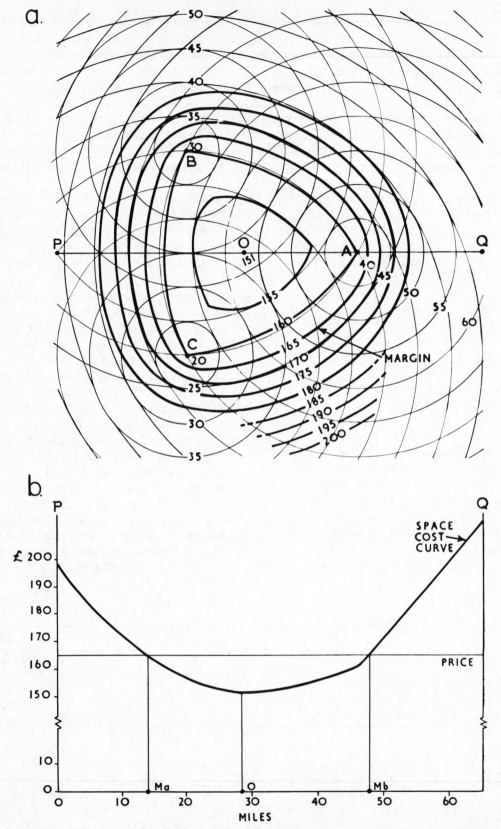

Figure 12.3 A simple locational model illustrating the derivation of cost isopleths and a space cost curve.

No pull is exerted by land, with no cost variation, but the forces exerted by A, B, and C are equal; therefore, the least cost location is centrally placed between these points. If, however, £100 worth of material has been needed, with its cost still increasing by 2.5 per cent per mile, a x b for point A would have been 250 (more than twice that at B and C) and least cost location would have been at A. Similarly, if the cost of moving £40 worth of material had increased to, say, 6 per cent per mile, the pull (240) would again have been dominant.

The model worked out in Figure 12.3 illustrates the value of the concept of cost isopleths. This idea appears to have originated with Alfred Weber's *iso-dapanes* — lines joining places of equal transport costs — and was extended by (in particular) Palander and Hoover.[14] It is undoubtedly one of the most valuable analytical tools yet devised for the study of industrial location in theory and in practice. The construction of maps of 'cost contours' should commend itself to the geographer as an application of a familiar technique, though in practice the lack of complete statistical data limits its use in empirical research. If sufficient material were available, it would no doubt reveal different patterns of contours for different industries, varying from the steep mountain and valley topography of an industry with large spatial cost variations to the almost level plain of the 'footloose' industry with a wide range of locational choice.

The derivation of space cost curves — sections through the contour map — is a logical extension of the idea of cost isopleths. Again, the shape of the curves will differ from industry to industry. A line showing a number of v-shaped depressions (like sections of steep-sided valleys) separated by more elevated areas would indicate a series of separate low-cost locations, perhaps coinciding with isolated towns in a rural area. A single broad depression bounded by areas of higher costs might represent a more extensive area with cost advantages, coinciding with a regional concentration of industry. Information on the likely form of cost isopleth maps and the gradient of space cost curves is of fundamental importance in both the interpretation of existing industrial location patterns and the formulation of plans for the future.

Variations in the Simple Model

Having shown how optimum location and the spatial margins to profitability are dervied from a set of cost isopleths and a space cost curve in a simple set of circumstances, it is now possible to introduce some of

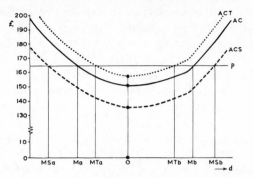

Figure 12.4 The effect of differences in entrepreneurial skill

the complications of the real world which were earlier assumed not to exist. These are differences in entrepreneurial skill, subsidy of certain location, and the effect of external economies arising from agglomeration. The element of chance and the purely personal factor in locational decisions must also be considered.

Entrepreneurial Skill

In practice, the degree of skill possessed by businessmen will vary from one to another, and this will influence freedom of locational choice. With entrepreneurial skill as a variable, there is, in effect, a separate spatial cost situation for each firm, with wide margins for the highly efficient entrepreneur and only a narrow range of choice around the most profitable location for the less efficient firm.

This can be illustrated simply by using the space cost curve derived in Figure 12.3. Assume that this represents the average situation in the industry as a whole (AC in Figure. 4). Within the industry the firm S has a management which through its high efficiency can produce at a cost 10 per cent below the average. The space cost curve for this firm (ACS) shows that a profit is possible anywhere between MSa and MSb — wider limits than for the average firm (Ma-Mb). Similarly, if firm T has a less efficient management and operates at 5 per cent above the industry's average cost its cost curve (ACT) will indicate only a small area where a profit can be made (MTa-MTb).

In theory, the limiting cases would be where management is so efficient that a profit could be made in any location, or where a firm was so inefficient that it could not remain in business anywhere. However, the former situation is far less likely to happen in practice than the latter: there are spatial limits beyond which even the most efficient entrepreneur is unlikely to succeed.

The fact that certain industrial pioneers were highly

skilled entrepreneurs helps to explain why the initial location of certain industries appears to have been determined by fortuitous circumstances. The location of the Morris motor works at Oxford, the founder's home town, is a case in point, and other examples readily come to mind. But these men operated within wide spatial margins created by their personal enterprise, and freedom of choice as to precise location was therefore relatively great. An observation by Lösch is relevant in this context: 'Imitating entrepreneurs easily forget that this range [of locational choice] is more restricted for them than for their abler pioneers. A location that may yield the latter some profit, though not the greatest possible, may result in losses to the former.'[15]

Subsidy

Firms can operate in relatively high-cost locations if they are subsidized. A subsidy, in effect, reduces costs, thus increasing the profit obtainable at the point in question if it is within the margin, or changing a loss to a profit if the location is beyond the margin.

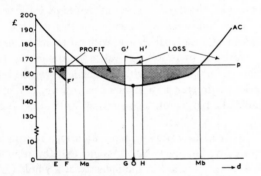

Figure 12.5 The effect of a subsidy beyond the margin and of a tax imposed in an advantageous location.

This can be illustrated by using the space cost curve for our hypothetical industry. Assume that for social reasons, perhaps high unemployment, it is felt necessary to attract the industry to the area E-F outside the normal margin (Figure 12.5). This can be made a profitable location by providing a subsidy sufficient to bring the cost curve below the price line between E and F. If, for example, a subsidy of £20 per unit of production were offered, a new section of the cost curve (E'-F') would operate between E and F, offering an average profit ranging from about £2.50 at E to £10 at F. This artificially created situation could, then, attract new industrial development.

The effect of increased taxation at a certain point, perhaps imposed to restrict industrial expansion in a

congested location, can be illustrated in a similar way. Assume that it was considered necessary to restrict new industrial growth in the area G-H round the optimum location. The imposition of a tax which had the effect of increasing cost per unit of output by £20 would raise the cost curve to G'-H', making the area no longer a profitable location for new firms or branch factories.

These illustrations help to emphasize that the attraction of industry into a high-cost location by offering a subsidy, or the possible alternative of restricting industrial growth in certain areas is not a simple matter. In the case of a subsidy, the desired end will not necessarily be achieved by offering all firms and all industries the same arbitrarily chosen grant relating to, for example, the cost of their factory or machines. If plans for industrial relocation are to succeed in a predictable way the appropriate subsidy must be worked out carefully for each industry in relation to the prevailing spatial cost situation. Only if the subsidy is large enough to make the location in effect intra-marginal and competitive with other locations will the plan succeed, and this cannot necessarily be achieved by guesswork. An analysis of spatial variations in costs (and by implication profit potential) industry by industry is the essential prerequisite to the formulation of realistic plans for selective industrial redistribution, for it is only with this knowledge that the subsidy needed can be calculated with any precision.

External Economies

Like entrepreneurial skill and financial subsidy external economies derived from the congregation together of firms in the same industry can operate as cost reducing factors. These economies are derived from such things as collective marketing and research facilities, and the existence of specialized ancillary trades like machine repairers or (in textiles) finishing plants. If, for example such considerations operated at point A in our model (Figure 12.3) to the extent of reducing the average cost per unit at that place from £160 to £140, this would become the least cost location.

In practice, of course, the reduction in costs attributable to the existence of external economies is difficult, if not impossible, to measure. But in investigations of particular industries the possible operation of such factors must always be considered. They may distort the general cost/price situation in space and may be significant in explaining the persistence of an industry in a location which no longer seems to be advantageous from the point of view of low-cost assembly of factors or productions under present conditions.

The influence of external economies on industrial location is closely related to scale of operations. In general, the location of large firms is less likely to be determined by the operation of external economies than is the location of small firms, for large firms can create their own internal economies of scale. This helps to explain the high degree of localization of some industries with a relatively small size of plant — the manufacture of sporting guns, jewelry, and clothing in Britain, for instance. This provides just one example of the fact that in practice the locational decision cannot be examined in isolation without reference to scale, for there may be different optimum locations and margins for plants of different sizes.

Chance and Purely Personal Factors

The operation of chance and personal non-economic factors in no way inhibits the theoretical analysis of locational problems. Lösch mentioned briefly that as long as capricious choice of location costs no more than the entrepreneurial profit it is still consistent with theory,[16] though he did not elaborate the point. Greenhut, however, gives full weight to the influence of purely personal considerations, introducing to location theory the concept of 'psychic income' as a measure of the non-pecuniary satisfaction that a particular choice of location might offer to the individual manufacturer.[17] Greenhut suggests that each entrepreneur will choose the location at which his total satisfaction in terms of financial and psychic income is maximized. The logical extension of this argument is that the location theorist should regard the maximization of personal satisfaction as the entrepreneur's goal rather than the maximization of financial profit, but, as Greenhut points out, this creates difficulties. To say, in effect, that man puts his factories where it pleases him is clearly an inadequate basis for a theoretical framework aimed at assisting the interpretation of business behavior. Useful though the concept of the maximization of total satisfaction may be in the explanation of particular cases, it is with the economic forces influencing locational choice that the theorist is primarily concerned.

The intention here is simple to integrate the operation of chance and personal factors into the theoretical framework developed above, based as it is on the profit motive. This is assisted by the recognition of spatial margins to profitability, for it can be stated as a general principle that within the margin freedom of choice exists, and the exact location of any plant may be

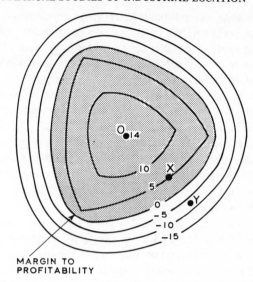

MARGIN TO
PROFITABILITY

Figure 12.6 An illustration of the operation of personal non-economic factors.

determined by non-economic considerations or by pure chance.

The operation of personal factors on plant location may be illustrated with the help of Greenhut's 'psychic income,' and Weber's concept of forces diverting factories from the least (transport) cost location.[18] Figure 12.6 shows a map of isopleths of average profit per unit of output derived from Figure 12.3. The maximum profit (least cost) location is in the center (O), and the margin line is where profit is nil. The negative figures beyond this indicate a loss. Let X be a point within the margin which has certain personal attraction for one manufacturer — perhaps a golf course or an attractive house available. If the numbers on the isopleths in Figure 12.6 are now taken to refer to 'units of satisfaction' and not to money (e.g., £5 profit gives 5 units of satisfaction), the situation can be analyzed theoretically in terms of psychic income. The manufacturer will site his factory at X if the psychic income obtainable there (measured in units of satisfaction) exceeds the loss of satisfaction (i.e., 9 units) resulting from getting a profit of £5 on each of his products instead of the £14 possible at O. The plant is thus diverted from the maximum profit location by personal factors offering higher total satisfaction. If the psychic income at X is 9, then, in Weberian parlance, X would be exactly on the 'critical isodapane,' for the 5 isopleth indicates a loss of 9 units of satisfaction by moving from maximum profit location. In these circumstances the businessman would be indifferent as to whether he locates at O or X. If X (= 9) had been beyond the critical cost isopleth, then the least cost location would still have been preferred despite the non-economic attraction of the alternative site.

In theory, of course, there is no reason why a manufacturer may not operate outside the margin, at a loss, if he maximizes his satisfaction by so doing. A firm at Y in Figure 12.6 might be in this position, if his psychic income was, say, 25 units, or greater than the sum of the pecuniary satisfaction he is foregoing by not being at O (14 units) and the loss of satisfaction incurred by producing at a loss of £8 (8 units).

It could be argued that a philanthropist running a factory to provide work in an isolated location is in this position, but this kind of situation can best be explained as subsidizing an extra-marginal location. It is conceivable that an individual might derive satisfaction in certain other circumstances from operating a factory at a loss, but the interpretation of such behaviour would hardly come within the sphere of location theory.

Some Dynamic Aspects of Industrial Location

The analysis of the previous sections was confined to one point in time. It is only under this condition that the least cost or maximum profit site and the spatial limits to profitability can be regarded as having a definite location, for their position is constantly changing through time with changes in the spatial cost/price situation. As Lösch put it: 'Dynamically there is no best location, because we cannot know the future.'[19] In practice, a manufacturer is unlikely to go to great lengths to find the most profitable location, because he knows that it will not always be in the same place. He is more likely simply to ensure that his location is within the margin in the long run, relying on his efficiency and enterprise to build up profits.

At this point it is worth stressing that the present distribution of an industry, or its distribution at some point in the past, represents but a single stage in a long process of evolution. The interpretation of distribution patterns as they are found in the real world requires an understanding of the evolutionary process. A theoretical background is just as important in this context as in static investigation of industrial location. The theoretical framework developed above can easily be adapted to illustrate the effect of changes in price, costs, techniques, and combination of factors of production, introducing further realism into the simple basic model. This kind of analysis may assist in the interpretation of

locational change in reality, where something more than merely a description of the evolutionary process is required.

Changes in Price

The effect of a change in price can be illustrated easily by returning to the model developed in the previous sections. In Figure 12.7 the original space cost curve is shown, together with the price line (p) at £165. If the price is raised by £10, a new price line (p') can be drawn at £175. This of course changes the position of the spatial margin, the area in which a profit can be made being extended to Ma' and Mb'. A reduction in price would have the opposite effect, narrowing the area in which the industry can be undertaken successfully. But as long as the change in price is uniform in space, the position of the optimum location will remain unchanged.

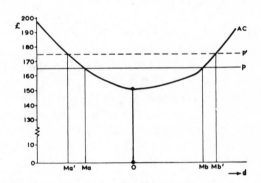

Figure 12.7 The effect of a change in price.

Changes in Cost

A uniform change in cost has exactly the same effect as a change in price. If, for example, £10 is added to the cost of each unit of production irrespective of location, a new cost curve (AC') can be drawn above the original curve (AC), as shown in Figure 12.8. The new positions of the spatial margin (Ma' and Mb') indicate a contraction of the area in which a profit can be made. A reduction in costs results in a widening of the margin. As in the case of a uniform change in price, the optimum location remains the same.

The effect of changes in costs which are not uniform in space and of changes in the cost of individual factor of production can best be examined in the context of changes in technique and in factor combination, for this enables the fundamental reason for the changes in cost to be introduced into the analysis.

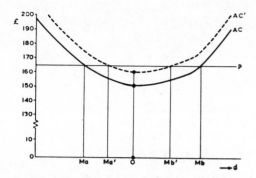

Figure 12.8 The effect of a change in average cost.

Changes in Factor Costs, Techniques, and Combination of Factors

Changes in the cost of individual factors of production, in techniques, and in the combination of factors influence industrial location through their effect on cost structure and on the spatial cost/price situation. This could be illustrated with further adaptations of the model which has been used already, but it is more convenient to use a slightly different framework. Assume that an industry exists using two factors of production, the basic cost of each being £10 per unit of output. Let the source or least cost point of these factors be A and B respectively (Figure 12.9). The cost of the factors rises away from A and B, the space cost curves having identical shallow 'U' shapes.[20] A curve for total cost per unit (ATC) can be derived from the two factor cost curves (ACA and ACB), and when a price line at £30 is introduced the limits of the area of profitability can be indicated by Ma-Mb. Optimum or least cost location is at O.

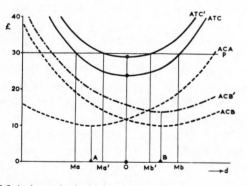

Figure 12.9 A change in the basic cost of one factor of production.

The first case to be examined is a change in cost structure resulting from a uniform increase in the basic

cost of one factor. Assume that the cost of factor B at source is increased by 50 per cent (perhaps the result of a rise in the cost of extraction of a mineral), resulting in an increase of £5 in the cost of each unit of output. The new cost curve for factor B is ACB′, and the average total cost curve becomes ATC′. The spatial margin contracts to Ma′-Mb′, but the position of the optimum location remains the same. The effect is thus the same as in the cases of the uniform change in price or cost considered above.

The effect of a change in the locational cost of one factor is illustrated in Figure 12.10. Assume that the cost of moving factor B from its source doubles as a result of a change in freight rates. The new cost curve ACB′ is drawn, and from it a new average total cost curve ATC′. The result of this is not only a contraction in the margin (from Ma-Mb to Ma′-Mb′) but also a shift in optimum location to O′. The least cost point has moved toward the source of factor B, in response to its increase in locational cost.

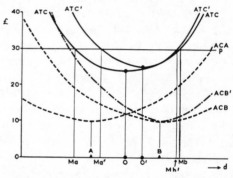

Figure 12.10 A change in the locational cost of one factor of production.

The two cases examined in Figures 12.9 and 12.10 reveal an important distinction between the effect on location of changes in basic costs and locational costs, which can be stated as a general principle. A change in the basic cost of a factor of production will, other things (including price) remaining the same, lead to a change in the spatial margin to profitability, but will leave optimum location unaltered, whereas a change in locational cost is likely to affect the position of both the margins and the optimum location.

In many instances in the real world a simultaneous change in both basic and locational cost may take place. In Figure 12.11 the quantity of factor B required in the productive process is halved, perhaps by an improvement in technique. As a result basic and locational costs are both halved, giving a new cost curve (ACB') below the old one. ATC' becomes the new average total cost curve, which indicates a widening of the margin, and there is a shift in the optimum location toward the source of factor A, the locational pull of which has been strengthened.

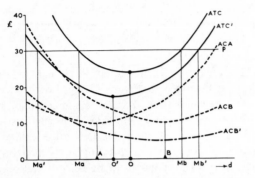

Figure 12.11 A change in both basic and locational cost of one factor of production.

A final example indicates the result of the replacement of a factor with considerable locational cost by one which is ubiquitous. This may arise from technical innovation, such as the introduction of electricity as an alternative to steam power based on coal as a source of motive power in industry. In Figure 12.12 let factor B be coal, the cost of which increases away from its source. The use of electricity is introduced, the cost involved being, say, £13 per unit of output irrespective of location. The cost 'curve' for electricity is therefore a horizontal line (ACE). The figure of £13 has been chosen to introduce a complication, namely that the cost of coal at source (£10) is cheaper than electricity, and that between the points R and S (perhaps representing the coalfield) it is in fact cheaper to continue to use coal than to change to electricity. The new cost curve for 'power' as opposed to either electricity or coal would therefore follow electricity's horizontal line as far as R but then dip down to follow the coal curve to S. This is also reflected in the new total cost curve (ATC'), which corresponds with the original curve (ATC) between R and S. The general effect of the introduction of electricity is, however, to reduce costs over a large area, resulting in a widening of the margin. But the margin is extended in only one direction; on the coalfield the original cost situation still obtains, and the margin remains unaltered. The introduction of electricity results in a shift of the optimum location to the source of factor A under the conditions postulated in this simple model.

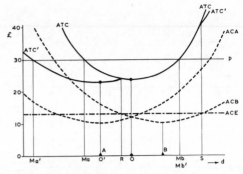

Figure 12.12 The replacement of a spatially variable factor of production by one which is ubiquitous.

Many other situations could be illustrated in the way those considered above have been. Increasing realism could be introduced, with more complex situations illustrated by three-dimensional diagrams if necessary. However, these four cases are sufficient to show that locational changes may be analyzed in the same way as a static situation, with space cost curves indicating optimum and marginal locations as the basic tools.

Conclusion

The approach to industrial location outlined and illustrated here has been expressed in abstract theoretical terms. The models which have been introduced are extremely simple, with many of the complexities of the real world assumed not to exist. As has been emphasized a number of times, it is only by simplifying that the location problem can be reduced to fundamentals. As each of the simplifying assumptions is relaxed the situation more closely resembles reality, but it also becomes steadily more complex. For example, it is easy to visualize the difficulty of analyzing the sort of situations considered above if the assumption of constant demand were relaxed and potential sales varied from place to place as well as costs and could be influenced by the action of individual firms.

How far is the theoretical approach demonstrated here of value in the interpretation of the real world? It is highly unlikely that in reality the student of industrial location can construct precise sets of cost isopleths and space cost curves. This may be possible for a single factor of production, but the absence of statistics may make it impossible for total costs. However, the same is true of the economist's average cost, marginal cost, and marginal revenue curves and so on, but this does not prevent suggestions as to their likely form from being used in the interpretation of business behavior in the real world.

The value of theoretical analysis in the field of economics has been suitably expressed by R.B. McNee: 'Economics has attained great intellectual heights in the building of abstract models, though these models have not always been tested in the real world. Perhaps many of them are not testable. Nevertheless, these models are of great value in interpreting, if not predicting, economic behavior in the real world. As guiding hypotheses, they are superior to anything else thus far developed in the social sciences.'[21] It is precisely in this light that the present study, or any similar work of a theoretical nature, should be viewed. In any industry at any time a spatial cost/price situation similar to, though far more complex than, those illustrated here actually exists, and even the most incomplete statistical data may give a clue to the nature of this situation in the case being studied. A point of departure for realistic interpretation may thus be established.

What is offered here is an *approach* to industrial location rather than a set of formulae or laws which can provide the immediate solution to particular cases. What is offered is simply a way of thinking around practical locational problems, based on deductive knowledge of the nature of locational problems in general. If the application of such an approach does no more than indicate in the broadest possible way how far the location of a particular industry is restricted, and how this restriction is imposed, it may at least provide some insight into the reasons behind industrial patterns which have so far only been explained in terms of an undifferentiated list of 'favorable factors.' In addition, it may provide some guidance to planners concerned with regional employment problems and the redistribution of industry, if only by helping to reveal something of the nature and complexity of the situations which they face.

Acknowledgement

The author is grateful to Mr. E.M. Rawstron, Reader in Economic Geography at Queen Mary College, University of London, for reading this paper in draft, and for a number of helpful suggestions.

Notes

1 W. Warntz: Progress in Economic Geography, *in* P. James, Edit.: New Viewpoints in Geography (Washington, 1959), p. 55.

2 If this assumption of constant demand had not been made, the point of least average cost need not have been the point of least total cost (TC = AC x output), and the line of total revenue would not have remained horizontal. This would have complicated the diagrammatic representation without any compensating advantages in realism or clarity

3 The concept of spatial margins to profitability is developed in E.M. Rawstron: Three Principles of Industrial Location. *Trans. and Papers, Institute of Brit. Geogrs.*, No. 27, 1958, pp. 135-142. Much of the thought underlying the discussion of margins in the present study is derived from Rawstron's writing and teaching.

4 For a full comparison between the two approaches, see M. Greenhut: Plant Location in Theory and Practice (Chapel Hill, 1956), pp. 3-100 and 253-272.

5 A. Weber: Theory of the Location of Industries (1909), translated by C.J. Friedrich (Chicago, 1929).

6 See A. Lösch: The Economics of Location (New Haven, 1954).

7 W. Isard: Location and Space Economy (Cambridge, Mass., 1956).

8 This is considered in detail elsewhere, the most useful discussion being in Greenhut, *op. cit.,* Part Two (pp. 103-177). See also E.M. Hoover: The Location of Economic Activity (New York, 1948), Part One (pp. 15-141), and R.C. Estall and R.O. Buchanan: Industrial Activity and Economic Geography (London, 1961), Chapters 2, 3, and 4 (pp. 24-101).

9 For further discussion of these points, and for illustrative examples, see Rawstron, *op. cit.*, pp. 136-140.

10 The assumption of a dispersed market with the cost of marketing rising from a central point is a convenient device for overcoming the Weberian assumption of a punctiform market without having to introduce the concept of market areas.

11 The assumptions that A, B, and C are equidistant from each other and that the cost of the necessary quantity of labor, materials, and marketing all vary spatially to the same degree (£1 per mile), have been made in order to simplify graphical presentation. The assumption that the cost of transportation is proportional to distance is also unrealistic, and has been made for the same reason. None of these simplifying devices invalidate conclusions drawn from the model.

12 Weber, *op. cit.*, pp. 53-58 and 227-239.

13 Isard, *op. cit.*, pp. 95-104 and 119-125.

14 T. Palander: Beitrage zur Standortstheorie (Uppsala, 1935); and E. Hoover: Location Theory and the Shoe and Leather Industries (Cambridge, Mass., 1937).

15 Lösch, *op. cit.*, p. 16 (note 1).

16 Lösch, *op. cit.*, p. 16 (note 2).

17 Greenhut, *op. cit.*, pp. 175-176.

18 This is the basis of Weber's analysis of agglomeration economies and the effect of a cheap labor location. See Weber, *op. cit.*, pp. 102-104.

19 Lösch, *op. cit.*, p. 16 (footnote 3).

20 This assumption of a 'U' shaped space cost curve, which may be realistic when related to average total cost (as in Figure 12.3b), is not realistic when the cost of individual factors is considered. Transport costs are the main determinants of spatial cost variations for most factors, and freight rates tend to fall off with increasing distance. (For further details on this point, see Hoover: The Location of Economic Activity, pp. 15-26, and Isard, *op. cit.*, pp. 104-112).

The 'U' shaped cost curve has been adopted in this model simply as a device for ensuring that optimum location lies initially between the sources of the two factors, so that their relative pull under different circumstances can be considered. The same situation could, of course, be created under more realistic conditons, but the model would be too complex for the present purpose.

21 R.B. McNee: The Changing Relationships of Economics and Economic Geography, *Econ. Geog.*, Vol. 35, 1959, p. 191.

Reprinted from *Economic Geography*, 42 (2), 1966, Clark University, Worcester, with permission.

13 The Market as a Factor in the Localization of Industry in the United States

by Chauncy D. Harris

University of Chicago

Manufacturing in the United States is highly localized as a result of a complex of many factors. In the Manufacturing Belt of the Northeastern United States, which occupies only a twelfth of the country, is concentrated half the entire national market, seventy per cent of the industrial labor force, and the sources of supply of most materials and parts directly used in manufacturing. It should be made clear at the outset that the existence of this historically evolved belt, with its markets, labor force, factories, mines, transportation, and other established facilities, is far more important that the distribution of any particular raw material (such as iron ore) or of fuel (such as coal or petroleum), or of any other single factor such as labor or markets. The interrelationship between growth of this and other manufacturing areas and location of markets has been reciprocal; manufacturing has developed partly in areas or regions of largest markets and in turn the size of these markets has been augmented and other favorable conditions have been developed by the very growth of this industry. It is good to focus attention on man, as the active agent who develops tools, cultures, and technologies to satisfy his wants from whatever natural resources he can find and be able technically or economically to utilize. A coalfield is useless until it falls within the technological capabilities of specific human groups and until it can be utilized in a favorable economic environment. Geographers can learn much from economists with their emphasis on wants and markets and their flexibility in considering alternative resources that can be substituted for one another in the satisfaction of human needs.

Individual industries vary, of course, in their locational requirements both in respect to processing costs and to transfer (transport) costs.[1] The location of some factories is strongly affected by regional differences in processing costs, either of labor (cotton textiles) or of power (aluminum reduction). In order to minimize total transport costs other factories are best located between sources of raw materials and markets. Factories that sharply reduce either the bulk or perishability of the materials in processing minimize total costs by locating near the source of raw materials; such are ore concen-

trating plants, sugar beet factories, creameries, cheese factories, ice works, gas works, bottling plants for soft drinks, building construction, newspaper printing. Such industries, though large in total volume, are ubiquitous and do not contribute substantially to regional differentiation.

A large and very significant fraction of manufacturing in the United States is not tied to local raw materials, local markets, or to current regional differences in power or labor costs; this segment, typified by the automobile and agricultural machinery industries, appears to be concentrated in areas having maximum accessibility to national or regional markets for such products. These markets typically are associated with a considerable industrial labor force, with numerous other factories, and with well-developed facilities of many kinds. It is with such markets and associated phenomena that this paper is concerned.

The following questions seem pertinent to an analysis of the rôle of regional and national markets. Is the importance of the market as a location factor generally increasing or decreasing? Where are the markets? How can accessibility to them be measured? What are their divisions in terms of regions or of specialized activities such as mining, agriculture, or manufacturing? Does recent industrial growth indicate any attraction to markets and their associated phenomena? Such questions might be posed about any area or about the entire world, but the United States has been selected for investigation here. It embodies a widespread and very large market characterized by relatively homogeneous cultural and economic conditions, by a dense and interconnected transport network, by considerable national distribution, and by the absence of major internal trade barriers. Furthermore, comparable statistical materials are available.

Importance of the Market

Economic activities tied to the location of raw materials are waning in relative importance; activities carried on near markets or in intermediate positions are surging upward. In contrast to falling employment in raw-material-oriented primary activities, employment in secondary and tertiary activities is rising rapidly. Primary, secondary, and tertiary as here used refer broadly to the production of raw materials, to the processing of materials, and to the performance of services, and not to basic or service function in the economic support of a given area.[2] Between 1940 and 1950 the number of workers in agriculture in the United States diminished from 8.4 million to 7.1 million or about 15 per cent.[3] During this same period employment in secondary activities grew from 13.5 to 18.6 million or 37 per cent and in tertiary activities from 22.3 to 29.3 million or 31 per cent. These shifts are part of a long-run trend. Between 1820 and 1950 the proportion of occupied persons in primary activities in the United States shrank from 72 to 13 per cent, while that in secondary activities expanded from 12 to 33 per cent, and in tertiary from 15 to 53 per cent.[4] The location of the now dominant secondary and tertiary activities is not tied primarily to the distribution of raw materials, but exhibits a correspondence to the disposition of regional and national markets; yet these very markets are partly an outgrowth of the historical development of these self-same activities.[5]

In the location of manufacturing, as in economic activities in general, the distribution of raw materials is of decreasing weight. Materials undergo many processing stages from the crude raw material to the final product; in general the first stages are near the sources of raw materials, the intermediate stages somewhat footloose in location, and final stages close to the market.[6] Products are becoming more highly fabricated with the result that the initial treatment of raw material is diminishing in relative importance; the automobile is more intricate than the buggy and the mechanical refrigerator than the ice box. Within related industries employment in the final processing segments typically is growing more rapidly than in early or intermediate stages. Between 1939 and 1947, for example, the rate of increase of production workers in the apparel industries (final stage) was nearly five times as high as in textiles, and in machinery nearly three times as high as in primary metals.[7]

The production of iron and steel illustrates the decreasing significance of the location of raw materials in manufacturing. In the middle of the eighteenth century each ton of pig iron produced in Britain required about 8 tons of coal and 3 tons of iron ore.[8] In the United States in 1952 for each ton of steel produced, only 1.2 tons of iron ore, 0.9 tons of coal,

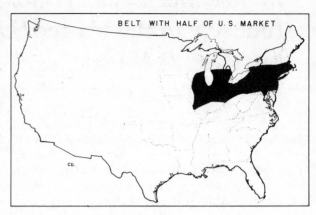

Figure 13.1 Belt with half the retail sales in the United States in 1948. This belt occupies only 8 per cent of the country.

and 0.6 tons of scrap were consumed.[9] But about half the scrap comes from the market areas (the rest is produced within each plant). Excluding limestone, which is widely distributed, the ratio of the mined raw materials such as coal and iron ore to market-oriented materials such as purchased scrap and produced steel has sunk from 11 to 1 to a low of 1.6 to 1, or only a seventh as high. During this same period transportation and mechanized handling have become more efficient and much cheaper for bulky materials. Especially dramatic is the use of pipelines for the transmission of oil and natural gas. In general finished products do not lend themselves to bulk handling, but involve high labor cost in transportation. The truck, however, has benefitted short hauls of finished products.

The production of iron and steel, even though a raw-material-processing industry, exhibits the importance of the market factor.[10] At times the steel industry of Pittsburgh has been considered as 'based mostly on the coking coal of the Connellsville district;'[11] it is equally an expression of superb central location amidst the huge markets of the American Manufacturing Belt. Malcolm Keir demonstrated that the iron industry of Pittsburgh arose in relation to the market; iron-using factories, such as rolling mills and plow works, preceded by many decades the production of pig iron in the city.[12] The conspicuous growth of the steel industry has been near markets, as symbolized by the founding of Gary near Chicago half a century ago and the recent construction of the Fairless Steel Works on the Delaware River convenient to New York City; both have low total transport costs by virtue of the cheapness of water carriage of distance ores and the proximity to markets.[13] In spite of the favorable juxtaposition of local coking coal, iron ore, and limestone, Birmingham, Alabama, has remained a small producer. The small size of the Southern markets has been one factor stunting its growth. Duluth near the iron ore deposits of Minnesota has stagnated because of distance from markets.[14] The general world distribution of the iron and steel industry exhibits a congruity with markets rather than with the distribution of coal, iron ore, or any other raw material.

Location of Markets

Population and markets are unevenly distributed over the United States. Many factors contribute to this irregularity; scanty rainfall in the western half, hence less agricultural settlement there; spotty distribution of other resources such as coal, petroleum, metalliferous ores, forests, level land, rich soil, water power; history of settlement, which advanced from the Eastern Seaboard, at which arose the main seaports and urban concentrations; the development of transportation facilities by water (canals, rivers, and the Great Lakes) and by land (road and railroad); the sequence of the rise and spread of modern manufacturing from New England westward into the present Manufacturing Belt; and many other factors.

Population is one measure of the market, but income or retail sales provide more adequate indices. For international comparisons national income serves well. Within the United States sharp regional differences in income level occur. In 1949 the median income per family in New Jersey was $3,670 or more than three times as high as in Mississippi, $1,198.[15] Thus the average family in New Jersey has about three times as much money to spend as the average family in Mississippi. Retail sales approximate the ultimate market for goods sold commercially to consumers. In spite of certain limitations, these sales appear to provide the most valuable single index of the total final market for commercial goods. Fortunately such figures are readily available by countries from the Census of Business, 1948.[16]

Half the retail sales in the United States are made in a small belt in the Northeast, extending from Boston to St. Louis (Figure 13.1). A manufacturer distributing to a national market is likely to make about half his sales here. The development of industries in the South or the West has sometimes been considered evidence of a trend toward location near markets. Insofar as such developments represent branch plants to serve regional markets this interpretation is correct. Distribution costs from

these areas to the total national market, however, run higher than in most parts of the Manufacturing Belt (Figure 13.7 below).

In terms of total size of market the Northeastern states dominate the entire country. On Figure 13.2 the area of each state has been made to vary with the size of the retail market in the state. The country appears to be afflicted with a hospital case of hydrocephalus, in which the head (from Illinois to Massachusetts) has swelled six times normal size to exceed in bulk the rest of the body. The shriveled Southeast hangs limply like the forelegs of a kangaroo. The Mountain States have atrophied and nearly disappeared. The giant New York Metropolitan Area is larger than all the Southern States on the Atlantic south of the Potomac. The Chicago Metropolitan Area takes the measure of Texas. Massachusetts equals the combined Mountain States.

Some states in the Northeast have a density of market several hundred times as high as other states in the West. The United States may be divided into five grades of decreasing intensity of market as follows (Figure 13.3): 1) the Eastern Seaboard states extending from Massachusetts to Pennsylvania with very high densities, five to fifteen times the national average; 2) the western half of the Manufacturing Belt from Ohio to Illinois with densities several times the national average; 3) most of the rest of the eastern half of the United States with densities about the national average; 4) the central and southern Great Plains with low densities; and 5) the Mountain States and Dakotas with very low densities,

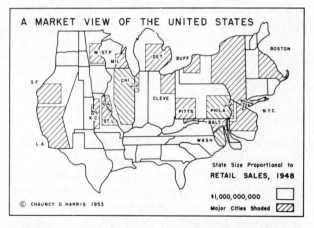

Figure 13.2 A market view of the United States. The area of each state is proportional to the amount of retail sales in 1948. Sales of important metropolitan areas are indicated by shading. Some, such as New York City and Chicago, extend into more than one state. The Mountain states have been grouped as a single unit east of California.

only a twentieth to a fourth the national average.

In order to determine more exactly and quantitatively the relative accessibility of various parts of the United States to the widespread markets, two new measures are proposed in this paper: 1) the market potential and 2) the point of lowest transport cost to market. These will be discussed in turn.

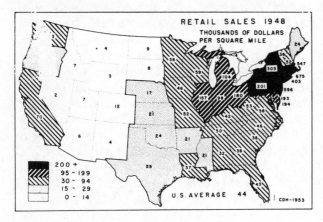

Figure 13.3 Intensity of the American market as measured by density of retail sales in 1948 by states.

The Market Potential

The term market potential, suggested by Colin Clark, is analogous to that of population potential as proposed and mapped by John Q. Stewart.[17] It is an abstract index of the intensity of possible contact with markets. The concept is derived ultimately from physics, in which similar formulas are used in calculating the strength of a field, whether electrical, magnetic, or gravitational.

The market potential (P) is defined as the summation (Σ of markets accessible to a point (M) divided by their distances from that point (d)

$$P = \Sigma \left(\frac{M}{d} \right)$$

Two measures need to be selected and tabulated, one of the market and the other of distance.

A good measure of the over-all ultimate market for goods in the United States is provided by the figures for retail sales. These data have been tabulated on a county by county basis to give the values of M in the equation.

With respect to a measure of distance (d), for this purpose transport cost is superior to sheer miles. With the help of Harold M. Mayer, Colin Clark and I calculated generalized formulas for estimating transportation costs by road, rail or water between any two

points in the United States. On the basis of studies in the Chicago area typical terminal and running costs were established and utilized. Thus it was found that local truck delivery within a city costs about $6 per ton and that running costs approximate an additional 4 cents per ton-mile.[18] Trucking costs thus are set at $6 for local delivery, $8 for movements up to 50 miles, $10 for 100 miles, $18 for 300 miles, etc. Beyond this distance railroad transport costs were utilized. These were calculated at $5 per ton rail terminal costs plus 2½ cents per ton-mile, plus truck delivery cost of $6 per ton at destination.[19] The rail rates work out at $22 per ton for 440 miles and $40 for 1160 miles, etc. Total costs per ton-mile decrease with distance because of the lessening proportion of terminal costs in long hauls. Thus the *total* cost including railroad terminal costs, truck delivery costs, and a constant running cost per ton-mile declines from 5 cents per ton-mile for 440 miles to 3½ cents per ton-mile for 1160 miles. For intercoastal water transportation in the United States total terminal costs are estimated at $18 ($6 for terminal ship costs in the port; $6 for truck collection on land, and $6 for delivery by truck at destination). The running costs are very low, only ¼ per cent per ton-mile. On the other hand the distances by sea may be much greater than by land. Inland waterways have not been included in the calculations.

It should be emphasized that these figures are estimated transport *costs* for simple manufactured goods not actual *rates* for any specific article.[20] Rates for bulk commodities, such as coal, are much lower. Whether a particular product takes a higher or lower rate would not affect the calculations significantly since the distance ratios would remain approximately the same.

To determine the market potential (P) for a given city, one simply makes a summation (Σ) of the market potentials for that city of all counties in the area under consideration (the United States or a major region). The market potential of each county is the retail sales of that county divided by the transport cost of reaching the city for which the market potential is being calculated $\left(\frac{M}{d} \right)$.

In making the calculations two assumptions are made: 1) that because the United States is covered by a dense network of highways and railroads, the shortest distances on a map are proportional to actual route miles and therefore it is not necessary to tabulate data for individual routes; and 2) that because of the large number of counties involved figures can be grouped into class intervals. In the actual computations concentric circles are drawn on tracing paper around each selected city representing transport costs of 6 (local county), 8, 10, 12, 14, 18, 22, 30, 40, 50, 60, 70, and 80 dollars. The retail sales of each concentric circle are calculated by simply adding the retail sales of all counties within the band included by that circle and not by a smaller circle. (The county figures are recorded on a base map that can be used over and over again.) The market potential of each band is then calculated by dividing the total sales of the band by the cost of reaching it from the city under consideration. The total market potential for this city is then obtained by adding the market potentials for all the bands or concentric circles. Dots on the maps indicate the cities for which these detailed calculations were made. On the basis of the values determined for these points, lines of equal market potential are drawn on maps, much as one draws contours or isotherms. For easier comparisons the figures are expressed as percentages of the city with the highest value (Figure 13.4).

A fixed volume of retail sales within a city (transport cost $6) provides ten times as much market potential to this center as would the same volume of *total* retail sales in a county 1960 miles away (transport cost $60 by land).

Validity for the concept of market potential as a meaningful index of accessibility to markets would seem to rest on a progressive decline in quantity of goods moved with increasing distance. Market potential appears to gauge the possible spatial interaction between producers and markets, of the likely flow of goods from a point to accessible regions.[21] A number of studies indicate that freight movement as well as many other types of relationships between any two points varies directly with their size and inversely with their distance apart.[22] Actually there is a complex hierarchy of distribution areas from any given city; some products may have national or international distribution, others regional, and many local only. The aggregation of these various distribution areas results in a large volume of local and nearby movement with amounts decreasing with distance, just as in a contour relief model of a hill, all layers are represented at the center, but a decreasing number as one moves outward to the edge. Walter Isard, who has undertaken research on the decrease of shipments with distance, estimates that within the United States the total tonnage of Class I railroad shipments varies inversely with distance raised to roughly the 1.7 power when a straight line is fitted to the data plotted on double log scale.[23] If the exponent were as low as 0,

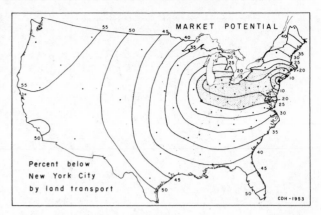

Figure 13.4 Distribution of market potential for the United States, based on retail sales in 1948 and on land transportation only. The points for which calculations were made are indicated by dots on this and on following similar maps. For method of calculation see the text.

distance would have no effect. If it were as high as 3 (distance cubed), only nearby markets would have much weight. In total shipments utilized by Isard, bulky raw materials loom large. In the calculations of this paper I have used an exponent of 1, which may be approximately correct for manufactured goods. Research needs to be undertaken to calculate the actual values for different types of commodities and for different areas.

Areas of high market potential furnish especially suitable conditions for the development of manufacturing. Industries in which economies of scale are important find in the immense nearby markets a particularly favorable environment. The existence of a large and diversified labor force, the presence of many specialized services, the ease of obtaining components or sub-assemblies nearby, the presence of large industrial markets for new parts and gadgets, the ability to deliver quickly to the markets, and a host of other factors reinforce the transport advantages.

Areal Distribution of Market Potential

The market potential for the United States reaches a very high level in a broad belt between Massachusetts and Illinois and attains its maximum at New York City (Figure 13.4, which is calculated on the basis of land transportation). The belt of high market potential extending east-west nearly coincides with the Manufacturing Belt. It stretches from Boston on the east to the Mississippi River on the west and from mid-Michigan on the north into Kentucky on the south. One of the interesting features of the westward extension of the

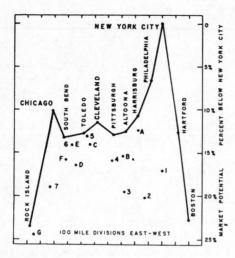

Figure 13.5 Market potentials for cities on or near the ridge of high potential between New York City and Chicago. Cities north of the ridge are indicated by numbers: 1, Albany; 2. Syracuse; 3. Buffalo; 4. Erie; 5. Detroit; 6. Battle Creek; and 7. Milwaukee. Cities south of the ridge are identified by letters: A. Baltimore; B. Cumberland, Md; C. Columbus, Ohio; D. Cincinnati; E. Fort Wayne; F. Indianapolis; and G. St. Louis. Cities are aligned according to position on an east-west axis.

area of high potential is the ridge of maximum potential, away from which the level drops sharply both to north and to south (Figure 13.5). This ridge extends from New York City westward through Philadelphia, Harrisburg, Altoona, Pittsburgh, Cleveland, Toledo, and South Bend, to Chicago. Omitting the high peak for New York City on the east and the lower peak for Chicago on the west, the ridge is remarkably even, varying less than 2 per cent in height between Altoona on the east and South Bend on the west, and reaching its highest point in this section at Cleveland (Figure 13.5). Baltimore (A in Figure 13.5) lies south of the ridge and Detroit and Upper New York State (1.5 in Figure 13.5), north of it. West of Chicago or east of New York City the market potential falls precipitately; in the 150 miles between Chicago and Rock Island or in the 180 miles between New York City and Boston it declines by a greater amount than anywhere in the 750-mile ridge of high potential between New York City and Chicago.

That the apex of market potential occurs in New York City reflects both the size of the city and its central position within the early settled, densely populated, highly urbanized Atlantic Seaboard extending from Boston on the north to Washington on the south.[24] A compact coastal belt includes Boston, New

York City, Philadelphia, Baltimore, and Washington, 5 of the 11 cities in the United States with retail sales of more than 1 billion dollars in 1948 (Figure 13.2). It contains 45 other counties with retail sales of more than 100 million dollars each. With a little more than 1 per cent of the area of the country it accounts for nearly one-fourth of the total retail sales.[25] In this diminutive area more retail sales are made than in the 60 per cent of the United States west of the Mississippi River, excluding the Pacific Coast.[26] Another expression of the importance of the large compact market on the Eastern Seaboard is the market potential for the area within 200 miles of various cities. The market potential for New York City of the area within 200 miles only of the city is about eight times as great as for any Southern city within a similar area.[27]

The Southeastern United States is characterized by moderate market potentials. The belt of highest potential extends east-west and the Atlantic Coastline trends southwesterly. Coastal Georgia lies due south of Ohio, mid-way in the belt. Greenville, S.C., for example, is closer to both New York City and Chicago than they are to each other.

The eastern corners of the country in Maine and in Florida have low market potentials. All their market support must be derived from a sector of less than a quarter of a circle, whereas inland points may draw sustenance from all directions.

The western areas have very low potentials. A minimum occurs in the Pacific Northwest, which is farther than the Southwest from eastern markets and which also contains a smaller local market.

The market potential rises in Southern California, the only major break in the otherwise persistent and regular

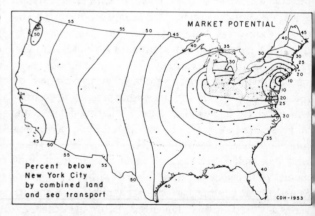

Figure 13.6 Distribution of market potential for the United States, by combined land and sea transport.

decline away from New York City and the ridge of high market potential. The large local market accounts for this rise.

The differential between the market potential of the Eastern Seaboard ports and of Midwestern cities is heightened by the utilization of water transport, where cheaper (Figure 13.6). Use of the sea roughly halves the cost of shipment between the Pacific Coast and the Atlantic Seaboard although ocean routes are much longer than land routes. Water transportation gives the Gulf Coast cheaper access to the immense markets of both the east and west coasts. The Pacific Coast potentials, although still lower than those of the East, rise above other parts of the West. By combined land and sea transport the Mountain States form a trough of low potential in contrast to a continuous decline to the Pacific Coast for land transport. Most of the goods move by rail, but the rates on the coast are lowered by the competition of water transport. The sharp impact of cheap ocean transportation shows more clearly in the second measure of accessibility, the point of lowest transport costs to market.

Comparative Transport Costs to Market

Assume that a manufacturer is to serve an entire market area, is to absorb the costs of shipment, and wishes to locate so as to minimize his freight costs to market or, to use Isard's term, his distance inputs.[28] What will his location be?[29] Here instead of maximizing the summation of sales divided by distance as in market potential, one sets out to minimize the summation of sales multiplied by the transport costs, according to the formula.

$$T = \Sigma (Md),$$

where T is total transportation costs to an aggregate of market areas, M is the size of the market in each unit (county in this case), and d is the distance in transport costs from any given city to the market in this unit (county). The same transportation cost figures, assumptions, and methods are utilized as in the calculation of the market potential.

In contrast to market potential, the point of lowest transport costs is only slightly affected by cheap local deliveries and is dominated by expensive distance shipments.[30] For example, the retail sales of the Pacific Coast amount to 11.4 per cent of the total sales for the United States, yet because of their distance account for only 4.6 per cent of the market potential for Chicago, but for 22.0 per cent of the freight cost of serving a

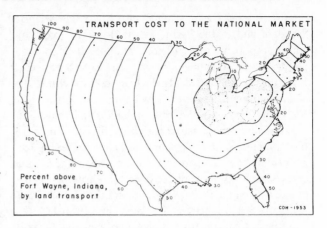

Figure 13.7 Transport cost to the United States national market (as measured by retail sales in 1948) by land transport only. For method of calculation see the text.

national market from Chicago. Market potential presupposes a declining market with distance, whereas the transport cost calculations postulate that the size of the market is unaffected by distance within the area being measured.

Areal Distribution of Comparative Transport Costs

The area with lowest transport costs to serve the entire United States market by land transportation has an interior position centered on Fort Wayne, Indiana (Figure 13.7). It lies within the belt of high sales in the northeastern United States, but in the western part of it because of the small, yet distant, markets west of the Mississippi River. The area with transport costs less than 10 per cent higher than Fort Wayne extends from Harrisburg on the east to St. Louis on the west. Beyond this, transport costs rise regularly in all directions to reach 50 per cent higher costs in eastern Maine or southern Florida and 100 per cent higher costs along the Pacific Coast.

Philadelphia, at the point where the Chicago-New York axis of largest market intercepts the margin of cheap sea carriage, has the lowest transport costs to the national market by combined land and sea movement (Figure 13.8). Most parts of the Manufacturing Belt fall within the area with transport costs less than 10 per cent above Philadelphia. This area reaches on the north to Albany and Detroit, on the west to Chicago, and on the south to Cincinnati and Roanoke.

The Gulf and Pacific coasts are especially benefitted by water transport (cf. Figures 13.7 and 13.8). The Gulf

Coast possesses cheap water transport to the Atlantic Seaboard and to the Pacific Coast. Houston, Texas, by land transport has costs 40 per cent above the minimum point, but by combined land and sea only 18 per cent. Nevertheless, it is still higher than points within the Manufacturing Belt, for even by water transport, freight costs are heavy to the belt of high retail sales. San Francisco by land transport has costs 102 per cent above the minimum point, but by combined land and sea only 56 per cent higher. The sharp difference between land and sea costs is probably a major factor in the clustering of the population on the Pacific Coast around the seaports: Los Angeles, San Francisco, Portland, and Seattle. The Mountain States constitute a plateau of highest transport costs by combined land and sea transport — more than 70 per cent above the minimum point.

The large size of the market on the Pacific Coast and its remoteness and consequent high transport cost from other parts of the country encourage the development of an independent market area. James J. Parsons has noted the rise of industries here in response to the Western market.[31] On the basis of the possibility that the Pacific market may become somewhat independent, let us re-examine our figures. Since the area is relatively distant from the eastern United States its removal will not greatly affect figures for market potential, but its separation would sharply reduce the freight bill for many Eastern concerns. The points of lowest transport costs to the national market, excluding the Pacific Coast, have interior locations, whether transport is by land alone or by combined land and sea (Figure 13.9). Fort Wayne and Cleveland have the lowest costs. The Gulf Coast, the Atlantic Seaboard, and Florida benefit from sea transport but not enough to offset more central location of interior points.

The Midwestern parts of the Manufacturing Belt combine central position within the belt of high retail sales with fair access to the markets of the South and the West. Points outside this belt have higher transport costs to national markets simply because they have to ship so much into the belt. St. Louis, for example, at the western edge of the belt, has a high freight bill because of having to transmit large amounts long distances to the huge markets of the Atlantic Seaboard. Boston, on the other end, has much freight moving long distances into the big markets of the Midwest, Ohio, Indiana, and Pennsylvania in the central part of the belt of high retail sales have the most favorable position for minimizing transport costs to market. The automobile industry is localized in this area. Its development to the north of

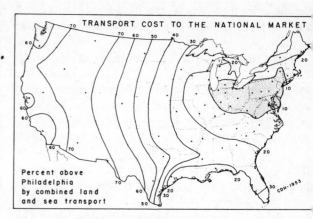

Figure 13.8 Transport cost to the United States national market by combined land and sea transport.

the center of the area may be due in part to historical circumstances and possibly in part also to the pull of the Canadian market in this direction. Within the Manufacturing Belt, New England with costs 10-20 per cent above those of the central part lies in a disadvantageous position for industries in which cost of transportation to market is a significant localizing factor. It is interesting that the shift of textile industries from New England to the South has not significantly altered the transport cost to market. Figure 13.9 is thought to be a fair approximation of the relative favorableness of various areas for the location of industries to serve the national market (excluding the Pacific Coast), insofar as these industries are transport oriented with respect to market.

Thus far the market has been considered in national terms and for all products taken together. Now we turn first to an analysis of regional markets, and secondly to the various segments of the national market.

Regional Markets

The general decline in market potential outward from New York City is interrupted by a slight rise in only three places, each of particular significance: Cleveland, Chicago, and Los Angeles (Figures 13.5 and 13.6). Cleveland represents the area in northern Ohio with lowest transport costs to serve the national market (excluding the Pacific Coast) (Figure 13.9) and also the point with lowest land transport costs to manufacturing markets or sources of supply. Chicago and Los Angeles, in addition to many other functions, serve as regional centers for the Central and Western segments of the country. New York City, although the center of the most intense markets (Figure 13.2 and 13.3), has a coastal peripheral position for the country as a whole. It

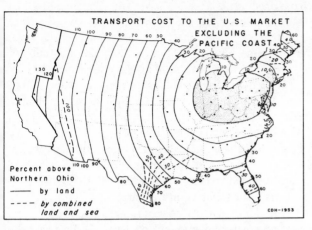

Figure 13.9 Transport cost to the national market excluding the Pacific Coast by land transport only (solid lines) or by combined land and sea transport (dashed lines where different from lines for land transport only).

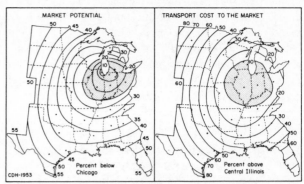

Figure 13.10 Market potential within the Central states only and transport cost to this market, based on retail trade 1948.

was natural therefore that an interior point such as Chicago should arise at some favorable location for inland markets, and should become the center of the railroad network. As noted, the Pacific Coast offers favorable conditions for the rise of independent sources of supply; Los Angeles is becoming its center.

The largest convenient areal subdivision of the country is into three great regional segments: the East served by New York City, the Central area served by Chicago, and the West served by Los Angeles. It is suggestive that these three cities constitute in themselves the largest metropolitan markets in the United States (Figure 13.2). If divisions are drawn at points approximately mid-way between the three centers, the Eastern area includes the New England, Middle Atlantic, and South Atlantic states, except for Georgia and Florida. The Central Area includes the Central states — East North Central, West North Central, East South Central, and West South Central (the census names are significant) plus Georgia and Florida. The West includes the Pacific and Mountain states. The retail sales in 1948 in each of these three areas were East, 47.1 billion dollars; Central, 64.0; and West, 19.5. These three areas will be considered in turn.[32] Then the South, which poses special problems, will be treated separately.

The Central Market
The point of highest market potential within the central area is at Chicago (Figure 13.10). The entire Midwestern part of the Manufacturing Belt possesses a relatively high potential, less than 20 per cent below Chicago. The

potential declines more or less regularly to the corners in North Dakota, Texas, and Florida with minima of less than 50 per cent of the Chicago potential.

The point of lowest transport cost to the central area lies south of Chicago in central Illinois (Figure 13.10). Decatur has the lowest transport cost to the central market of any city calculated, but some uncalculated point might have slightly lower costs. The area with transport costs less than 10 per cent above central Illinois extends from mid-Ohio on the east to mid-Missouri on the west, and from southern Wisconsin and Michigan on the north, to the Tennessee line on the south. Beyond this, costs rise in all directions to the corners, with El Paso and Miami having transport costs to the central market 80 per cent higher than central Illinois.

The East
New York City has by far the highest market potential

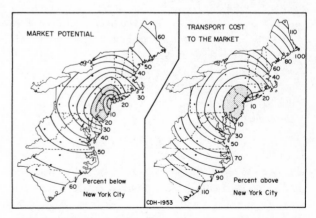

Figure 13.11 Market potential within the East only and transport cost to this market.

in the East, just as it has in the entire country (Figure 13.11). The Eastern part of the Manufacturing Belt has a market potential, for the most part, less than 40 per cent below New York City. Beyond it northern New England and the Carolinas extend as two wings of much lower potential. New York City also has the lowest transport cost to serve the Eastern market.

The West

Los Angeles increasingly dominates the West. It now has by far the highest market potential in the west (Figure 13.12). In spite of its peripheral position it also has the lowest transport costs to reach the western markets. One-third of the retail sales of the entire West are made to the nearby markets of Southern California (Figure

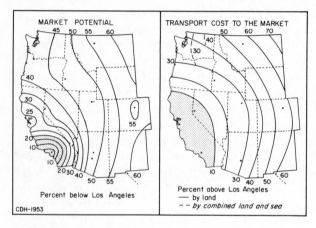

Figure 13.12 Market potential within the West only and transport cost to this market.

13.2). The next largest market, in the San Francisco area, is only half as large. These two small areas contain half the markets of the West. Unlike the East, where settlement is more or less continuous (although, of course, differing in density), the West is made up of a series of oases, which contain most of the population and the bulk of the markets. The largest of the areas of dense settlement has become the main center for the entire region.[33]

The South

The Central area, the largest, might be split into two areas, a North Central and a South Central. Since the North Central has a market more than twice as large as the South Central (43.9 billion dollars of retail sales in 1948 compared with 20.1) it predominates in the

combined area. Separate maps for the potential and transport costs of the North Central do not differ substantially from those of the *whole* central area, except that Chicago becomes the point not only of highest potential, but also of lowest transport cost.

The South Central area lacks a commanding center. The highest potential for this area occurs in Dallas, Texas, in the western part, but much of the area has a potential at least 90 per cent as high (Figure 13.13). Closer examination reveals a secondary peak farther east. This secondary peak occurs at Birmingham, Alabama, within the area here defined, but shifts eastward to Atlanta if the Carolinas are included.

The South falls naturally not into one market area, but into two, separated by the lesser markets near the Mississippi River in the states of Arkansas and Mississippi. In income level they are the lowest states in the Union with median family incomes in 1949 of $1501 and $1198 respectively, compared with $2248 for the South as a whole and $3073 for the entire country.[34] In terms of another measure, density of market as measured by retail sales per square mile, they are the lowest states in the eastern half of the United States and also in the South; their level is lower than Oklahoma and Texas on the west, both of which have large arid and semiarid regions; and is only about half as high as either Tennessee or Louisiana (Figure 13.3).

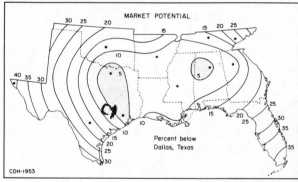

Figure 13.13 Market potential within the South Central states.

The Southwest (Texas, Oklahoma, Louisiana, and Arkansas) has a clear focus in Dallas, which has both the highest market potential and the lowest transport costs in this market (Figure 13.14). Dallas is well located to compete also in the adjoining states of New Mexico and Kansas.

For the Southeast as a separate area, including the Carolinas,[35] the clear focus is Atlanta with both the highest potential and the lowest transport costs to

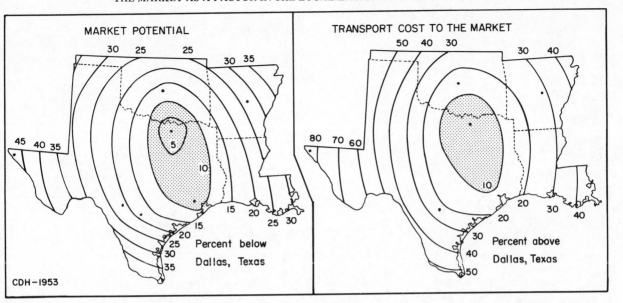

Figure 13.14 Market potential and transport cost, West South Central states.

market (Figure 13.15). If one were to include the border states of Kentucky, West Virginia, and Virginia to form yet a larger Southeast, Atlanta would retain its position as the center with the highest market potential, but the point of lowest transport cost would shift to Knoxville, Tennessee. But the main markets of Kentucky face the Ohio River and most of the state is an area of poor market, comparable with Mississippi and Arkansas. Just as the tails of comets point away from centers of gravity, so tributary areas tend to have their greatest extent away from competing centers of higher market potential. Thus, Kentucky, West Virginia, and Virginia tend to be drawn into the orbit of the high potential to the North.

Acknowledgement
The author is grateful to John W. Alexander, Colin Clark, Alice Foster, William L. Garrison, Walter Isard, Harold M. Mayer, James J. Parsons, Thomas R. Smith, Edward L. Ullman, and Alfred J. Wright for ideas or suggestions that have been incorporated in this paper.

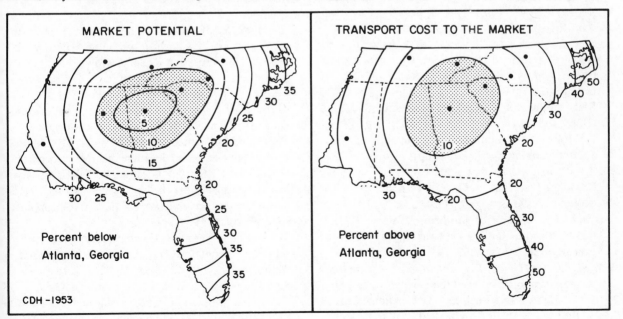

Figure 13.15 Market potential and transport cost, the Southeast.

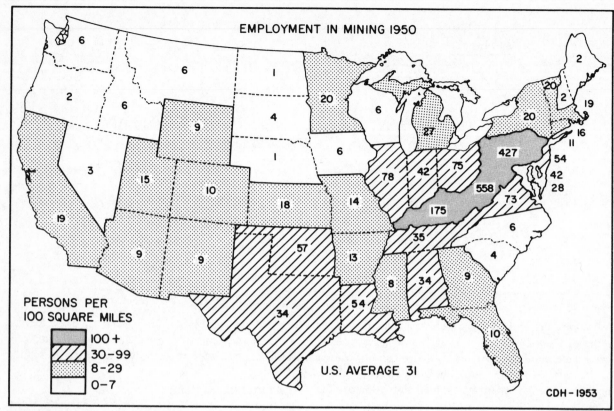

Figure 13.16 Density of employment in mining in the United States in 1950 by states.

Notes

1 Edgar M. Hoover, *The Location of Economic Activity*. New York, 1948. Especially Part One, 'Locational Preferences and Patterns,' pp. 27-141; Richard Hartshorne, 'Location as a Factor in Geography,' *Annals of the Association of American Geographers,* xvii (1927): 92-99; Robert S. Platt, 'A Classification of Manufacturers, Exemplified by Porto Rican Industries,' *Annals of the Association of American Geographers,* XVII (1927); 79-91; and H.H. McCarty, 'Manufacturing Trends in Iowa,' *Iowa Studies in Business*, VII (July 1930): 1-79.

2 Cf. Richard B. Andrews, 'Mechanics of the Urban Economic Base: The problem of Terminology,' *Land Economics*, XXIX (August 1953): 266.

3 *Statistical Abstract of the United States, 1952*, p. 185. During the same period farm output rose 24 per cent (*Agricultural Statistics, 1953*, p. 584).

4 See Colin Clark. *The Conditions of Economic* of Secondary and Tertiary Productivity,' Chapter III, pp. 22-32; and P.K. Whelpton, 'Occupational Groups in the United States 1820-1920,' *Journal of the*

Progress. London, 1940. 'The Flow of Labour to Tertiary Production,' Chapter V, pp. 176-219; *idem., The Economics of 1960*. London, 1942. 'The Trend *American Statistical Association*, XXI (Sept. 1926): 339-340.

5 The location of certain of these activities shows an increasing effect of amenity factors (Edward L. Ullman, 'Amenities and Regional Growth,' abstract in International Geographical Union, *XVIIth International Geographical Congress, United States, 1952. Abstracts of Papers,* 'Publication No. 6.' Washington, D.C., 1952. p. 92; full paper in the *Geographical Review*, XLIV (January 1954): 119-132. The importance of the market as a locational factor is recognized in Thomas R. Smith, 'Locational Analysis of New Manufacturing Plants in the United States,' *Tijdschrift voor Economische en Sociale Geographie*, XLV (February 1954): 46-50.

6 U.S. National Resources Committee, *Structure of the American Economy, Part I, Basic Characteristics*. Washington, 1939. Chapter IV, 'The Structure of Production – Geographical Structure,' pp. 33-59.

7 Production workers in textiles increased 1939-1947 from 1,082 to 1,147 thousands or 6 per cent, in

apparel industries from 753 to 973 thousands or 29 per cent; in primary metals from 672 to 1,010 thousands or 50 per cent; in machinery from 784 to 1,883 thousands, or 140 per cent. (U.S. Bureau of the Census, *Census of Manufactures: 1947, Vol. II, Statistics by Industry*. Washington, 1949. p. 22.)

8 Walter Isard. 'Some Locational Factors in the Iron and Steel Industry since the Early Nineteenth Century,' *The Journal of Political Economy*, LVI (June 1948): 203-217, citation on p. 204. See also L. Dudley Stamp and Stanley H. Beaver, *The British Isles*. 3rd ed., London, 1941, p. 333.

9 Production of steel 93 million tons; consumption of iron ore, 112 million tons, of coal (all purposes) 87 million tons (78 for coke), and of scrap 53 million tons (American Iron and Steel Institute, *Annual Statistical Report 1952*. New York, 1953. pp. 7, 15, 18, and 23. In addition fuel oil, natural gas, and purchased electric power supply significant amounts of energy.)

10 Cf. Richard Hartshorne, 'The Location of the Iron and Steel Industry,' *Economic Geography*, IV (1928): 242-252; and Allan Rodgers, 'Industrial Inertia, A Major Factor in the Location of the Steel Industry in the United States,' *Geographical Review*, XLII (January 1952): 56-66.

11 L. Rodwell Jones and P.W. Bryan, *North America, An Historical, Economic and Regional Geography*. London, 1933. p. 289.

12 Malcolm Keir, 'The Iron and Steel Industry,' *Manufacturing Industries in America, Fundamental Economic Factors,* Chapter V. New York, 1920. pp. 142-172, Pittsburgh on pp. 114-116. The opening sentence in this chapter announces Keir's theme, 'The story of iron and steel in the United States turns about one central theme, the market for the products.'

13 Walter Isard and William M. Capron, 'The Future Locational Pattern of Iron and Steel Production in the United States.' *Journal of Political Economy*, LVII (April 1949): 118-133.

14 Langdon White and George Primmer, 'The Iron and Steel Industry of Duluth: A Study in Locational Maladjustment,' *Geographical Review*, XXVII (1937): 82-91.

15 U.S. Bureau of the Census, *County and City Data Book 1952*. Washington, 1953. p. 3, col. 20.

16 *Ibid.*, col. 67. The 1949 edition giving the same data in column 2 was actually used in the tabulation for this paper.

17 John Q. Stewart, 'Empirical Mathematical Rules Concerning the Distribution and Equilibrium of Population,' *Geographical Review*, XXXVII (1947): 461-485, esp. 471-482; *idem.*, 'Demographic Gravitation: Evidence and Application,' *Sociometry*, XI (1948): 31-58; *idem.*, 'A Basis for Social Physics,' *Impact of Science on Society,* III (1952): 110-133, esp. 118-122.

18 These generalized truck cost figures are based on studies by Colin Clark and Harold M. Mayer, checked against a series of rates for specific items. The rates have been analyzed to separate out running costs from terminal costs. For example the rate on barbed wire, nails, and steel sheeting is estimated at 74c a hundred pounds for 100 miles, 92c for 200 miles, $1.12 for 300 miles (*Montgomery Ward Fall and Winter Catalogue* 1952-1953, p. 1041). The difference in rate between 100 and 200 miles is 18c, and between 200 and 300 miles is 20c, an average of 19c. Multiply this figure for 100 pounds by 20 to get tons or $3.80 per ton for 100 miles or 3.8c per ton-mile for running costs. Subtact 19c running costs from 74c (for 100 miles) to get 55c terminal costs per 100 pounds or $11 per ton. For another example, the rates by public carrier for an 8-ton truckload of books from the Midwest Inter–Library Center in Chicago for delivery to the University of Chicago (½ mile) or to Illinois Institute of Technology (4 miles) is $56. (*Midwest Inter-Library Center Newsletter*, February 28, 1953, p. 8.) Both may be considered local delivery and the rate works out at $7 per ton. For delivery to the University of Minnesota at Minneapolis the rate is $208, or $26 per ton. Subtract $7 per ton for terminal charges and divide the remaining $19 per ton for running costs by 419 miles to get about 4½c per ton-mile for running costs.

19 By the Illinois Central Railroad the rate on plows by carload lots from Chicago to St. Louis is 78c per 100 pounds, to Memphis $1.18, and to New Orleans $1.46. The corresponding figures per ton are $18.50, $28.00, and $34.60. It is 284 miles to St. Louis, 536 to Memphis, and 719 to New Orleans. The difference in rate from Chicago between St. Louis and Memphis is $9.50 per ton (252 miles hence 3.8c running costs per ton-mile) and between Memphis and New Orleans is $6.60 per ton (183 miles hence 3.6c running costs per ton mile). Taking figure of 3.6c per ton-mile running costs for the 284 miles between St. Louis and Chicago gives a figure of $10.22 for running costs between the two cities; this subtracted from the

$18.50 rate leaves just over $8.00 for terminal costs. On this route for this commodity one could use figures of $8.00 per ton terminal and 3.6c per ton-mile additional running cost.

20 For a series of maps and graphs showing actual rates for specific commodities as affected by distance see Stuart Daggett and John P. Carter, *The Structure of Transcontinental Railroad Rates*. Publications of the Bureau of Business and Economic Research, University of California, Berkeley, Calif., 1947.

21 See Edward L. Ullman, 'Human Geography and Area Research,' *Annals of the Association of American Geographers* XLIII (March 1953): 54-66; *idem.*, *Maps of State-to-State Rail Freight Movement for 13 States of the United States in 1948*, Office of Naval Research, Contract N50RI-07633, Report No. 3, Harvard University, Cambridge, Mass., 1951 (preliminary); *idem.*, 'Advances in Mapping Human Phenomena,' reproduced in the same series as Report No. 5; *idem.*, and Walter Isard, *Toward a More Analytical Economic Geography: The Analysis of Flow Phenomena*, Report No. 1, in the same series. For a discussion of the relationship of population and distance in retail trade see: William J. Reilly, 'Methods for the Study of Retail Relationships,' *University of Texas Bulletin* No. 2944 (Bureau of Business Research, Research Monograph No. 4), November 22, 1929; *idem.*, *The Law of Retail Gravitation*, New York, 1931, P.D. Converse. 'New Laws of Retail Gravitation,' *Journal of Marketing*, XIV (October 1949): 379-384; and Robert B. Reynolds, 'A Test of the Law of Retail Gravitation,' *Journal of Marketing*, XVII (January 1953): 273-277.

22 See George K. Zipf, *Human Behavior and the Principle of Least Effort*. Cambridge, Mass., 1949. 'The Factor of Distance,' pp. 386-409; and Donald J. Bogue, 'Distance from the Metropolis,' chapter IV, *The Structure of the Metropolitan Community, A Study of Dominance and Subdominance*. Ann Arbor, Michigan, 1949. pp. 67-78.

23 Walter Isard and Merton J. Peck, 'Location Theory and International and Interregional Trade Theory,' *Quarterly Journal of Economics, in press.* cf. Rutledge Vining, 'Delimitation of Economic Areas: Statistical Conceptions in the Study of Spatial Structure of an Economic System,' *Journal of the American Statistical Association*, XLVIII (March 1953): 44-64, especially charts 2 and 5.

24 See Jean Gottmann, 'La Région Charnière de l'Économie Américaine,' *Revue de 'La Porte Océane.'*

VII (March 1951) No. 71: 9-14 and VII (April 1951) No. 72: 11-20.

25 38,000 square miles or 1.3 per cent of the area of the United States; $29.9 billion in retail sales in 1948 or 22.9 per cent of the total for the United States.

26 The eight Mountain States, seven West North Central States, and four West South Central States with an area of 1,798,000 square miles and retail sales of $28.6 billion in 1948.

27 Knoxville, Tenn., Greensboro, N.C., Atlanta, Ga., and Greenville, S.C., in that order, have the highest market potentials within 200 miles in the South. Houston and Dallas, by virtue of their size, have higher potentials within 100 miles, but less intense markets in the intermediate umlands.

28 Walter Isard, 'Distance Inputs and the Space-Economy,' *Quarterly Journal of Economics*, LXV (1951): 'Part I: The Conceptual Framework,' 181-198; 'Part II: The Locational Equilibrium of the Firm,' 373-399. Isard is concerned with total distance inputs on materials as well as products.

29 Cf. Leonard C. Yaseen, *Plant Location*. Roslyn, N.Y., 1952. Chapter III 'Competitive Advantages in Raw Materials, Sources and Markets,' pp. 21-38.

30 In this it is similar to the 'center of population' as calculated by the U.S. Bureau of the Census. See 'Center of Population of the United States: 1950,' *U.S. Bureau of the Census, Geographic Reports*, No. 2. Washington, September 30, 1951. See also E.E. Sviatlovsky and Walter Crosby Eells, 'The Centrographical Method and Regional Analysis,' *Geographical Review*, XXVII (April 1937): 240-254.

31 James J. Parsons, 'California Manufacturing,' *Geographical Review*, XXXIX (1949): 240.

32 For an analysis of major industry groups into those with national, regional, sub-regional, or local market areas see Walter Isard, 'Some Empirical Results and Problems of Regional Input-Output Analysis,' Chapter 5 in *Studies in the Structure of the American Economy by* Wassily Leontief and others. New York, 1953. pp. 116-181.

33 Cf. Chauncy D. Harris, 'Location of Salt Lake City,' *Economic Geography*, XVII (1941): 204.

34 *County and City Data Book 1952.* p. 3, col. 20.

35 The removal of the Carolinas does not greatly alter the patterns of market potential or transport costs of the East (Figure 13.12).

Reproduced by permission from the *Annals* of the Association of American Geographers, Volume 44, 1954.

14 Comparative Cost and Revenue Models

by Howard A. Stafford

University of Cincinnati

Conceptualising

To a question of why manufacturing is located as it is, the common response is to consider first the factors which make up the cost of production. That an implicit least-cost approach seems most normal, even to those who never seriously consider the 'whys' of industrial location, is to be expected, for at least the following reasons:

1 Our traditional understanding and teaching of the history of the Industrial Revolution, and the location of manufacturing activities lay heavy emphasis on the exploitation of place-specific 'raw' materials.

2 within this context, the existence of an accessible, even though perhaps dormant, market is either consciously or unconsciously assumed

3 spatial variations in demand often are difficult to visualise and measure, while the cost factors are much more tractable since they derive directly from the production process and are usually subject to accounting procedures. It is not surprising that most of our industrial location rationale, both in theory and in practice, is couched in a least-cost framework.

The opposite to a strict least-cost approach to location theory is to consider spatial variations in demand, and to assume costs, rather than revenues, spatially constant. The usual approach is to take the three-dimensional demand surface as given, and the problem is to maximise sales via strategic location vis-à-vis the locations of the competitors. Thus, the maximum demand formulation is also often known as an interdependence approach.

The simple or extended least-cost models are commonly associated with Weber (1929) and many others who have followed. The maximum-demand models likewise have had many contributors, with the underlying framework based on the initial work of Hotelling (1929). Although both classes of models abstract greatly from reality, neither is simple in the sense of being incapable of considerable extension and refinement. This, along with their elegance, and when coupled with the operational difficulties of fusing the two, accounts for the continued popularity of, and concern with, these approaches.

Both the least-cost and maximum-demand models may be termed 'maximum profit' models if their assumptions are accepted. However, it is best to reserve the label 'maximum profit' to those models which effectively integrate both costs and revenue variations. In line with Greenhut (1956, 286), the optimum location (L) is that spatial position where there is the greatest spread between total costs and total revenues. Symbolically, $L = f(R - C)$, where R = total revenues and C = total costs: $C = f((SR)(Ca))$, where SR = sales radius (by definition, proportionate to sales) and Ca = average cost, exclusive of freight, and $R = f((SR)(m))$, where m = profit-maximising net-mill price.

Such a maximum profit model seems eminently reasonable, but it is deceptively simple, even in a static, let alone a dynamic, situation. As always, the difficulty is that the variables are simultaneously interdependent. Thus, the profit-maximising product price may not be external to the system as implied above. Rather, price may itself depend on the location of production and the location of competitors and markets, as for example, when the existence (or perception) of a spatial monopoly may suggest varying optimum pricing policies (see Greenhut, 1956, 288-91, for additional thoughts, and Beckmann, 1968, 30-41, for a recent review of spatial price policy).

Likewise, average cost is not calculated simply by the addition of the cost inputs at various locations, but may also involve the consideration of scale economies, the magnitude of which in part depend on the location selection vis-à-vis the spatial demand surface faced by the concern. The optimum location of a plant may in part be a function of economies of scale, both internal and external, which in turn are a function of the demand curve faced by the plant, which is in turn a function of the location of the plant.

An illustration may help to clarify some of these issues. The case treats the integration of minimum cost, economies of scale, and demand in the location decision when input prices, scale and revenues all vary between sites. (For more complete treatments of this case see Moses, 1958, and Nourse, 1968.)

Imagine a simple manufacturing process which involves only two inputs: a raw material at location m, some distance from the centre of the market, and man-hours of labour. Assume that the price of labour decreases towards the centre of density of the market, and that materials cost less at the material site. Considering only raw material and market sites, the combinations purchasable for a given outlay may vary as in Figure 14.1 (after Nourse, 1968, 27). Assume that UV represents the combinations of materials and labour purchasable for a given amount of money if production is at the material site. XY represents the combinations purchasable for the same amount of money if production is located at the market centre. Likewise, PQ and RS are paired isocost lines representing, respectively, a material and a market location, but with some greater amount of total cost than UV, XY.

From knowledge of the production process, it should be possible to compute the varying mixes of materials and labour (assuming substitution) which will produce a given amount of product. Curves representing these combinations — isoquants, or lines of equal quantity — also may be placed on Figure 14.1, e.g. Q_1 and Q_2.

It is apparent from Figure 14.1 that the least-cost combination of materials and labour to produce an output level of Q_1 is given by the tangency point A.

Since point A falls above Z on a segment of the original materials location UV line, the least-cost site of production, given production level Q_1, should be at the material site. The same outlays for labour and materials (costs) at the market site (line XY) obviously will permit only a lower rate of production.

The same sort of analysis can indicate in this simple example where the larger volume of production represented by isoquant Q_2 should be located. In this instance, we postulate that scale changes occasion a modified production process, with a different mix of materials and labour. In the case of Q_2 the least-cost-maximum-production location is at the market since the tangency point B is along the original RS market site line.

These least-cost solutions determine the least-cost combinations of inputs for each rate of production at each site and at which site costs would be least for each rate of production. Since the actual site depends on profitability, not least cost, the next step is to combine cost with revenues. (Nourse, 1968, 28.)

Using the same type of procedure, the revenue curves may be added to the graph containing the cost curves. For example, we might assume that the greatest sales (revenues) can be obtained by a location at the market, and that a location at the material site represents some revenue penalty by virtue of its being somewhat away from the centre of density of the market. Again, as for costs, revenues can also be represented as a function of the scale of production. In this case it might be because of a pricing policy of lower per unit charges in order to create sufficient demand for increased production levels.

In Figure 14.2 (after Nourse, 1968, 28), curve TR_p represents total revenues if production is located at the market site; TR_m is the total revenue curve if the production is materials oriented. Similarly, carrying the cost data forward from the previous step produces the total cost-related-to-output curve TC_p when production is at the market; likewise, TC_m is the total cost curve for production at the material site.

Substracting total costs from total revenues so as to calculate maximum profits, it is clear that the greatest profitable difference between the materials site curve is the distance BD. Thus, if production is to be materials-oriented, then production level Q_1 is most profitable. However, even though at production level Q_1 the material site possesses the least costs (TC_m falls below TC_p), it is apparent that a market site for production at level Q_1 is more profitable since $AC > BD$. Finally, it is

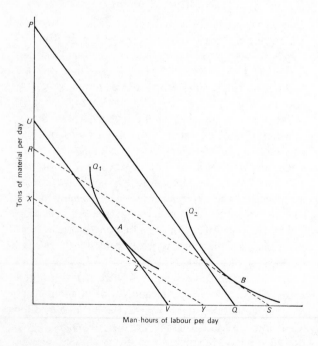

Figure 14.1 *After Nourse (1968,27)*

apparent that the *maximum* profit situation is again a market orientation, but with production at level Q_2, since here line segment *EF* portrays the greatest difference between costs and revenues of the entire graph.

Although very simple this two-point case effectively illustrates the maximum-profit principle of industrial location. Subsumed under the general headings of costs, revenues and economies of scale are all of the factors commonly considered in manufacturing geography. For example, transport costs are included in the consideration of the price of labour (because workers near the centre of the market have lower average commuting costs), and in the lower costs of materials at the material site, and in the increased transport costs to consumers as the plant is located farther from the centre of density. In the same way any of the other traditional location factors can be explicitly considered.

local supply and demand curves. Similarly, we might expand the interpretation of the shifts in the revenue curves to considerations beyond the usual spatial variations in the marketing transportation costs. For example, shifts in revenue curves might also reflect price concessions necessary to maintain output in the face of competitive locational and pricing strategies.

Another attraction of this schema is that it is easy to visualise many more cost and revenue lines on the graph — a pair for each feasible plant location. Given a very large number of possible locations and a finite number of production levels for which costs and revenues are calculated, it is then possible to visualise over space a set of pairs of cost and revenue surfaces, one pair for each feasible level of output. In Figure 14.3, the 'strata' of the block diagram, $TR_1 - TC_1$, and $TR_2 - TC_2$, represent paired total costs and revenues curves for

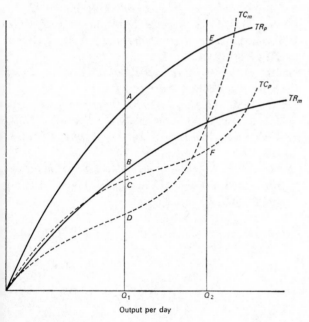

Figure 14.2 *After Nourse (1968, 28)*

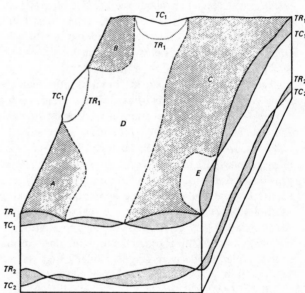

Figure 14.3

Also, it is possible within this general framework to conceptualise location strategies in which the location of the factory itself has an impact on input prices, in contrast to the simplifying assumption that factor prices are independent of the operation of the enterprise in question. Thus, the total cost curve might be constructed to reflect the expected effect on input prices through the influence of a newly located plant on the

two different levels of production. If the costs and revenue curves are visualised as alternatively intersecting surfaces, as illustrated along the 'edges', then it is possible to imagine a three-dimensional profitability surface. We might conceive areas A, B and C as those where $TR > TC$ and thus profitable location of production is feasible. Areas D and E, where $TC > TR$, would represent unprofitable locations. The boundary lines between the profitable and unprofitable areas, that is, those places where $TR = TC$, delimit the 'spacial margins' of the economically feasible locations. Conceptually, at least, the maximum profit location could be determined by 'coring' each production surface within the feasible areas to find the location where $TR - TC$ is at a maximum.

Thus, all we require are the following: sufficient data on the individual cost and revenue factors; perfect foresight to anticipate accurately the effects of competitive locational strategy, and to anticipate spatial shifts in the underlying factors (for example, regionally differential growth or decline in the distribution of the market) so to incorporate properly such predictions in the computation of the future receipts and costs at each site, and, finally, appropriate algorithms and adequate computers to perform the arithmetic.

At the present time, none of the above conditions can be satisfied. Less ambitious models do exist now, however. For example, 'location decisions under these conditions [uncertainty about the policies of rivals] are amenable to the use of game theory' (Hamilton, 1967, 379). Also, uncertainty may be considered in a broader context than when it is possible to construct a pay-off matrix as is necessary in a game theoretic system. Increasingly, substantial behavioural approaches are being suggested. Also, sophisticated linear programming models — even though they must utilise inadequate data, and assume that forecasting the future is outside the realm of operations research (Jandy, 1968, 198) — are being employed. In his recent book Smith (1971) provides a review of many of the current models, and illustrates how the cost-surface approach to industrial location can be extended to more realistic situations. Also included are discussions of the application of regression models, linear programming, and input-output analysis, plus a relatively simple model based on the work of Hoover (1966; 1967) and originally reported by Smith and Lee (1970).

References

Beckmann, M. 1968: *Location theory*. New York: Random House.

Greenhut, M.L. 1956: *Plant location in theory and practice*. Chapel Hill: University of North Carolina Press.

Hamilton, F.E.I. 1967: 'Models of industrial location'. In Chorley, R.J. and Haggett, P., editors, *Models in geography*, London: Methuen.

Hoover, E.M. 1966: *Computerized location models for assessing of indirect impacts of water resource projects*. St Louis: Institute for Urban and Regional Studies, Washington University.

Hoover, E.M. 1967: 'Some programmed models of industry location'. *Land Economics* 43.

Hotelling, H. 1929: 'Stability in competition'. *Economic Journal* 39.

Jandy, G. 1968: 'Problems of location in operations research models'. *Papers of the Regional Science Association* 22.

Moses, L.N. 1958: 'Location and the theory of production'. *Quarterly Journal of Economics* 72.

Nourse, H.O. 1968: *Regional economics: a study in the economic structure, stability and growth of regions*. New York: McGraw-Hill.

Smith, D.M. 1971: *Industrial location: an economic geographic analysis*. New York: Wiley.

Smith, D.M. and Lee, T. 1970: 'A programmed model for industrial location analysis'. *Southern Illinois University, Department of Geography Discussion Paper 1*.

Weber, A. 1929: *Theory of the locations of industries*. Chicago: University of Chicago Press. (Translated by Friedrich, C.J.)

This article first appeared as Section Two of 'The Geography of Manufacturers' from *Progress in Geography*, Volume 4, eds. C. Board, R. Chorley, P. Haggett, D. Stoddart, 1972, Edward Arnold, London.

15 Statistical Explanations of the Relative Shift of Manufacturing among Regions of the United States

by Victor R. Fuchs

Yale University, New Haven, Connecticut

1 Introduction

Since 1929 there has been a substantial change in the location of manufacturing in the United States. The direction of redistribution has been fairly consistently from north to south and from east to west. In 1929 the South and West together accounted for less than one out of every four U.S. manufacturing employees and for only one-fifth of value added by manufacture. By 1958[1] their share of U.S. manufacturing had increased to one-third as measured by either variable.

These changes have had a significant impact on the political, social, and economic life of the nation. The consequences for businessmen, labor leaders, and government officials have been strong, direct, and sometimes painful. For the economist and regional scientist these changes provide a splendid opportunity to test hypotheses, improve techniques of measurement, and increase our understanding of locational change. Hermann Schumacher has noted, 'Effective location factors are ... most clearly indicated when industries move' (Schumacher, 1937, p. 586), and August Lösch has written, It is easier to discuss such migrations of industry than to give reasons for their original locations because as a rule they (the migrations) are more clearly and rationally motivated' (Lösch, 1954, p. 377).[2]

Given a set of industries, a set of areas, and the distribution of these industries in these areas in different periods of time, two principal foci of location analysis are possible. One alternative is to concentrate on questions concerning differentials among *industries*. Which industries have changed location most, and which least? What relation is there between geographical redistribution (mobility) and industry rate of growth? Or between mobility and concentration of ownership? Is it true that 'light' industries change location more readily than 'heavy' ones, or that industries with high labor costs are more prone to shift than are others? For tentative answers to these and related questions, see Fuchs (1961).

The other possibility, followed in this paper, is to analyze *area* differentials in growth of manufacturing and related variables. To what extent is differential growth attributable to differences in industrial structure?

What relation is there between growth of manufacturing and wage differentials? Or between growth of manufacturing and extent of unionization? What other factors seem to affect growth and structure? In addition to examining these questions, I use the data to test hypotheses concerning population migration and changes in relative wage levels.

These are important questions, but the limits of this inquiry should be noted. This is not an attempt to discover 'universal' or 'general' solutions to the 'location problem'; instead I hope to gain a better understanding of a quarter century of important locational change in the U.S. and to add to that small fund of empirically tested theory upon which wise policy must rely.

The design of this study presented many of the familiar problems of coverage, scope, definitions, and methodology that are usually encountered in such work. Difficult decisions had to be made. These are summarized below, but limitations of time and space preclude discussion of the underlying theoretical and practical considerations.[3]

The basic source of data is the U.S. Bureau of the Census, *Census of Manufacturers*. The basic method is comparative statics. I look at the distribution of manufacturing (as measured by value added and by total employment) in 1929, and again in 1954, and take the differences between the two distributions as a reflection of net changes in location between the two dates. There is no attempt to study the 'dynamics' of change or the 'process' of growth. The geographical units are the 48 states.[4] Manufacturing establishments are classified in a 221 industry classification specially prepared for this study in order to achieve comparability between the Bureau of the Census classifications of 1929 and 1954. The following notations and definitions are employed:

Primary Notation

Let X_{si} = value in initial year (e.g. 1929) of industry i in state s

X_s = value in initial year (e.g. 1929) of all industries in state s

$X_{.i}$ = value in initial year (e.g. 1929) industry i in the U.S.

$X_{..}$ = value in initial year (e.g. 1929) all industries in the U.S.

Let $Y_{si}, Y_{s.}, Y_{.i},$ and $Y_{..}$ represent the same values in the terminal year (e.g. 1954)

Secondary Notation

Let $\quad H_{s.} = X_{s.}\dfrac{Y_{..}}{X_{..}}, \qquad H_{si} = X_{si}\dfrac{Y_{i}}{X_{i}}, \quad H'_{s.} = \sum\limits_{i} H_{si}$

and $\quad B_{s.} = Y_{s.}\dfrac{X_{..}}{Y_{..}}, \qquad B_{si} = Y_{si}\dfrac{X_{.i}}{Y_{.i}}, \quad B'_{s.} = \sum\limits_{i} B_{si}.$

Definitions

(1) $Y_s - H_s =$ Comparative Gain or Loss, All Manufacturing, State s (number of employees or dollars of value added)

(2) $\dfrac{Y_{s.} - H_{s.}}{Y_{s.} \text{ or } H_{s.}} =$ Comparative Gain or Loss, All Manufacturing, State s (per cent)

(3) $\dfrac{1}{2}\left[\dfrac{Y_{s.} - H'_{s.}}{Y_{s.} \text{ or } H'_{s.}} + \dfrac{B'_{s.} - X_{s.}}{B'_{s.} \text{ or } X_{s.}}\right] =$ Comparative Gain or Loss, All Manufacturing, Adjusted for Industrial Structure, State s (per cent).

(4) $\dfrac{1}{2}\left[\dfrac{H'_{s.} - H_{s.}}{H'_{s.} \text{ or } H_{s.}} + \dfrac{B_{s.} - B'_{s.}}{B_{s.} \text{ or } B'_{s.}}\right] =$ Comparative Industrial Structure, State s (per cent)

The measures defined above should be interpreted as follows:

(1) This is the difference between the actual value in 1954 in a given state and what the value would have been if the state had grown at the U.S. rate. For example, the figure for total employment in the state of Illinois is $-70,051$, indicating that Illinois had that many fewer manufacturing employees in 1954 than might have been expected on the basis of its employment in 1929 and the U.S. rate of change of manufacturing employment between 1929 and 1954. In the terminology of this paper, these employees are said to have been 'lost' by Illinois.

(2) Because states differ greatly in absolute size, and because I wish to compare results using different variables, it is useful to have a measure of comparative gain or loss expressed as a percentage. There are various ways to accomplish this. In this study the percentage is always calculated by using the larger of the two terms of the numerator as the denominator; i.e., if the numerator is positive, the first term is used as the denominator; if the numerator is negative, the second term is used. This method was chosen because it limits the range from plus 100 per cent to minus 100 per cent, it is easy to interpret, and it results in a distribution which is symmetrical around zero if comparative growth is randomly distributed. The resulting figure for the state of Illinois in 1954 was -5.7 per cent, which means that manufacturing employment in Illinois was 5.7 per cent less than it would have been if Illinois had grown at the same rate as the U.S. If the figure had been +5.7 per cent, it would have meant that 5.7 per cent of the actual employment in Illinois in 1954 represented a gain over what the state would have had if Illinois had grown at the same rate as the U.S. This percentage measure is not affected by the fact that 1929 is the base and that the comparison is in terms of a forward projection, 1954 could be used as a base and a hypothetical figure calculated for 1929 ($B_{s.}$). This could then be compared with the actual figure for 1929. The results in percentage terms are identical.[5]

(3) and *(4)* The next two measures are somewhat more complicated. It is true by definition that the relative growth of manufacturing in a state will depend upon a) the rate at which specific industries grow in the state as compared with the growth of these industries in the U.S., and b) the industrial structure of the state, i.e. whether the state has, on balance, industries which at the national level are growing faster or slower than manufacturing in general. It would be very useful to have a measure of the relative growth of manufacturing in each state, *adjusted for the direct influence of its industrial structure*, and to have a measure of the extent to which the state had a favorable or unfavorable structure.

To accomplish this, a hypothetical figure is calculated for each state based on the U.S. rate of growth of each industry taken separately, and weighted by the industrial structure of the state, i.e.H'_s. The difference between the actual figure and this hypothetical one measures comparative gain or loss, adjusted for industrial structure. The difference between this hypothetical and the hypothetical based on treating manufacturing in the aggregate (H_s) yields a measure of the comparative industrial structure of the state. Both these measures, however, refer to the industrial structure in the initial year. The calculations could be reversed and a hypothetical value computed for 1929 based on the structure for 1954 (i.e. $B_{s.}$). The results of these alternative measures would be different if the state's comparative industrial structure had changed between 1929 and 1954. There is no logical basis for choosing one set of weights rather than the other; I have, therefore, taken the arithmetic mean of the two as being a useful compromise.[6] For the state of Illinois for 1929-54 the results are as follows: comparative growth adjusted for industrial structure is −12.8 per cent, and comparative industrial structure is +7.5 per cent. These figures should be interpreted as follows: the first one means that if the U.S. had had the same structure in 1929 and 1954 as did Illinois, that state's comparative loss would have been −12.8 per cent instead of the −5.7 per cent described in (2) above. The second figure means that if every industry in Illinois had grown at its national rate, the state would have had a comparative gain of +7.5 per cent as measured by (2) above.

This adjustment for comparative structure yields important insight into the comparative growth of manufacturing in various states and regions. For example, when Pennsylvania and New Jersey are compared on an unadjusted basis, we find that Pennsylvania did very poorly during 1929-54 with a comparative loss of −18.8 per cent (total employment), while New Jersey had a dip of only −2.2 per cent. The comparative growth adjusted for structure, however, shows that their experience was almost identical, −13.6 per cent for Pennsylvania and −13.8 per cent for New Jersey. Or consider North Carolina. This state shows a comparative loss of −14.1 per cent for value added on an unadjusted basis, but a comparative gain of +35.1 per cent on an adjusted basis. This means that North Carolina's industrial structure was very heavily weighted with slow growing industries, but that these industries grew relatively rapidly in North Carolina compared with the rest of the U.S.

Table 15.1 at the end of this paper presents measures (1), (2), (3) and (4) for each state for 1929-1954.

2 Analysis of Area Differentials

As has been noted above, area differentials in growth of manufacturing may be attributed to area differences in industrial structure or area differences in the rates of growth of specific industries. For the period 1929-1954, the latter was by far the more important factor. Comparative growth of manufacturing employment, unadjusted, was highly correlated with comparative growth adjusted for industrial structure ($r = + .79$), whereas the coefficient of correlation between comparative growth, unadjusted, and comparative industrial structure was only $+ .16$. It may be noted that comparative growth, adjusted, and comparative industrial structure were negatively correlated ($r = − .46$).

Comparative growth of manufacturing, adjusted, is a summary measure of changes in the location of indivi-

dual industries. These changes are caused by a great variety of factors, some peculiar to only one or a few industries. In the following analysis the aggregate result of shifts of individual industries is examined and an attempt is made to discover which area characteristics were significantly associated with the comparative gain or loss of manufacturing among the 48 states. I do not mean to suggest by this that the treatment of industries in the aggregate is the only or even the preferred way of studying comparative growth. On the contrary, I would stress the need for analyzing shifts of individual industries and groups of industries specially selected according to important location criteria, such as degree of market orientation, labor intensity, etc. Neither do I suggest that the regression and correlation analyses described below should be used to the exclusion of other descriptive and analytical techniques. In a larger work (Fuchs, 1961), I attack the data by several different methods, but in this brief paper it is feasible to develop only this single approach.

The analysis is based on the fitting of multiple regression equations of the form $X_1 = a + b_2 X_2 \ldots + b_n X_n$ by the method of least squares. This approach is desirable because many of the state characteristics are interrelated, and useful tests of significant relationship can be made only if these interrelations are taken into account. Multiple regression analysis provides a convenient, systematic, and familiar method of accomplishing this objective. It is best not to exaggerate the importance of high partial coefficients, however, since there may be relations with other variables not included in the equation, or subtle non-linear relations among the included variables which contribute to these results. Furthermore, although the equations are cast in the form of a 'dependent' and several 'independent' variables, high partial coefficients do not *prove* that a causal relation exists between the variables. Table 15.2 at the end of this paper presents zero order coefficients of correlation between a large number of state variables in order to permit the reader to explore many possible interrelations in addition to those discussed below.

I have fitted multiple regression equations with comparative growth of manufacturing, adjusted, as the dependent variable and state measures of various factors alleged to influence location and comparative growth as the independent variables. The variables examined most closely in the multiple regression analysis are wage levels, extent of unionization, space (land), and climate. In addition, the 'catching up hypothesis,' which maintains that the states that have been experiencing rapid growth in recent decades have been doing so primarily because of a late start, will also be tested. A brief discussion of each variable follows.

Wage levels

Interregional differentials in wage levels have long occupied a prominent position in discussions of locational change in the U.S. This is readily understandable since regional differentials of as much as 20 to 30 per cent are frequently encountered, and payrolls are typically one-fourth of total manufacturing costs. The relative wage level of each state, adjusted for structure, is defined as the ratio of the actual wage bill to what the wage bill would have been if every production worker in the state had received an annual wage equal to the national average for his industry.[7]

Such an index of wage levels is not a perfect measure of relative wage costs for identical work. It may reflect interarea intraindustry differences in productivity, occupational mix, or per cent of plant utilization. These differences would not significantly bias the index, however, unless they were large, and consistently in one direction for most industries. With a few exceptions (notably Lumber) this does not seem to be the case.[8] Earnings per man-hour would be preferable to annual earnings for this index, but the former were not available for 1929. Moreover, a comparison of the results obtained using man-hour earnings and the four-digit Standard Industrial Classification with the indexes for 1947 based on annual earnings and the special 221 industry classification shows a very high correlation (Spearman's rho = + .961).[9] The hypothesis to be tested, of course, is that manufacturing growth and relative wage levels are negatively correlated.

Extent of unionization

The frequency with which the 'union issue' is mentioned in connection with manufacturing shifts by both businessmen and union leaders suggests that this may have been a factor of major importance during the period studies. The relative extent of unionization in each state is highly correlated with relative wage levels, but the hypothesis to be tested is whether each of these variables has been associated with comparative growth of manufacturing, *ceteris paribus*. It has frequently been alleged that manufacturers who seek to avoid unions are not primarily motivated by a desire to find cheap wages. They may be trying to escape from the rules and regulations imposed by unions and from the type of governmental 'climate' usually found in highly organized

states.[10] The relative extent of unionization in 1939 and 1953 is measured by the actual union membership in a state divided by a hypothetical union membership based on the number of workers in each broad industry group in the state multiplied by the national rate of union membership for each industry group.[11] The change in relative unionization between 1939 and 1953 is also measured. It should be noted that this measure of unionization refers to all types of industry in each state and not only to manufacturing. This is appropriate, as it reflects the relative importance of organized labor in the state generally. States in which organized labor is strong will typically have higher unemployment compensation and workmen's disability benefits, and stricter regulations of working conditions, especially for women and children (De Vyver, 1951). These factors may affect location decisions even when the industry in question is not highly unionized in any area.

Climate

It has probably always been true that businessmen and workers have preferred locations with mild and equable climates, but this factor may have become more important in the U.S. in recent decades for several reasons. First, climate has been an important location determinant for the aircraft industry, which finds mild, clear weather to be an asset in production, testing, storage, and delivery (Cunningham, 1951, pp. 29, 30, 170, 194). This industry has grown at a phenomenal rate since 1929 to a point where, in the 1950's it provided more employment than any other manufacturing industry. In 1954, for example, total employment in Aircraft and parts was 822,470 compared with 695,475 in Motor vehicles and equipment and 530,051, in Blast furnaces and steel mills. Second, the rapid growth of air transportation tends to favor areas with good year-round flying weather. A third reason is the growing importance of older people seeking mild climates for retirement. The increase in the number of older people who have independent incomes is particularly significant, because they have greater freedom of choice of location than if they were dependent on others. Increased real income is also important because of its effect on the demand for winter vacations. Finally, the armed forces, an important source of income in recent years, have favored warm locations for training fields, air bases, testing areas, etc. As a measure of climate, I use the average *monthly* temperture deviation from 65 degrees Fahrenheit (18.3 Centigrade) for the largest city in each state. Sixty-five degrees Fahrenheit was chosen arbitrarily as representing a mild climate which necessitates a minimum of expenditure for either heating or air conditioning. Substantial departures from 65 degrees Fahrenheit in either direction were felt to be disadvantageous for manufacturing from the viewpoint of cost and efficiency.[12] A more complex measure of climate, which takes humidity into account and which allows for intrastate variations in the larger states, would be desirable for a detailed analysis but is not necessary for a rough test of association.

Space

The search of manufacturers for abundant inexpensive space, which has received considerable attention in the post-war period, is related to intraarea shifts from the central city to the suburbs as well as to interarea change, but only the latter is considered here. Probably the most important reason why low-cost space has become so important for factory owners is the increased use of automobiles by factory workers. This development has fundamantally altered the economics of plant location with respect to the potential area from which the plant can expect to draw its labor supply. Whereas factories formerly found it necessary to locate in heavily populated localities, or near public transit lines, it is now possible for a plant to be set down in open country and draw its labor supply from an area of 70 to 80 miles (120 kilometers) in diameter. This has increased the relative advantage of uncongested areas with low land costs, compared with areas of high population density. Factory owners prefer the more efficient one-story type of plant, which is only practical where land is abundant. Provision must be made for parking facilities, which in many cases require more land than the plant itself. Many factories in the future will also make provision for air transportation (New York Times, 1960, p. 1). Another contributing factor may be that some factories find it necessary to avoid heavily populated areas because of problems of waste disposal or objectionable noises and odors. As a rough measure of congestion and relative lands costs I use the population per square mile for each state in 1940. As in the case of climate, more precise measures should be employed if this factor is to be investigated in detail, but a rough measure will serve to indicate whether or not this variable is significantly associated with comparative growth.

The 'catching up' hypothesis

This hypothesis is tested in three ways. First, the absolute level of manufacturing value added in 1947 is used. If it is true that the rapidly growing states are simply those that started from low levels, there should be a significant relation between the absolute level and comparative growth. As an alternative version of this hypothesis, the date of admission to the U.S. as a state is' used as an independent variable. Finally, this hypothesis is tested by using relative manufacturing employment per capita, 1929, which should be negatively correlated with comparative growth of manufacturing, 1929-1954.

Two other location factors not included in this regression analysis which should be mentioned are consumer demand and raw material supply.[13] The role of raw materials in attracting some manufacturing industries is a familiar and, I believe, an important one, but its relative weight cannot be appraised in an analysis of the shifts of manufacturing industries treated in the aggregate. It is not feasible to assign a single simple measure of raw material availability to each state which would meaningfully describe the diverse products of forests, fields, and mines that form the basis of much manufacturing activity.

Consumer demand also does not lend itself to regression analysis, but for a different reason. It is clear that comparative growth of manufacturing is highly correlated with comparative growth of income and population. The respective coefficients are + .73 and + .51. We should not, however, conclude that the shifts of manufacturing were in response to shifts of final markets, as some writers have done.[14] Manufacturing is a prime source of employment and income in most areas, and it is at least as plausible to suggest that the shifts in manufacturing were responsible for changes in population and income. Using other techniques of analyses, I have concluded that regional shifts of consumer demand were not a primary determinant of locational change in the United States since 1929, except in a few areas such as Florida and some of the Mountain states (Fuchs, forthcoming).

Regression results

With comparative growth of manufacturing, adjusted, as the dependent variable, various equations were fitted with different combinations of independent variables. These equations revealed that the data are not inconsistent with three of the above hypotheses and fail to support two of them.

The three variables that are significantly related to comparative growth of manufacturing are: 1) Relative extent of unionization (negative relationship) 2) Deviation from 65 degrees Fahrenheit (negative relationship) 3) Population per square mile (negative relationship).

These three variables alone 'explain' a considerable portion of all interstate differentials in the growth of manufacturing, adjusted. The coefficient of multiple correlation, R, is .804. The multiple regression equations, the standard errors of the regression coefficients, the Beta coefficients and the coefficients of partial correlation are shown at the end of this paper in Table 15.3, equations 1 and 2. Subject to the limitations mentioned previously, these results provide some support for the hypotheses that the absence of unions, a mild climate, and low population density have been factors favorable to the growth of manufacturing since 1929, while the opposite conditions have been associated with comparative loss of manufacturing.

The data do not support the view that relative wage levels have been significantly associated with interstate differentials in rates of growth of manufacturing.[14] Also, the 'catching up' hypothesis is not supported by the data. (See equation 2.) The absolute level of manufacturing is not significantly related to comparative growth when the other variables are taken into account nor does the date of admission as a state nor relative manufacturing employment per capita, 1929, show any significant relation to growth, *ceteris paribus*.

An examination of the comparative growth of individual states indicates why the 'catching up' hypothesis has little to recommend it. The five-state area North Dakota-South Dakota-Nebraska-Montana-Wyoming should have been 'catching up' under any interpretation of the hypothesis, yet this area actually showed a comparative loss of manufacturing, 1929-1954. This hypothesis also contributes nothing to an understanding of why the Kansas-Oklahoma-Texas-New Mexico-Arizona-Nevada-California area grew so much more rapidly than the Idaho-Colorado-Utah-Washington-Oregon area, nor does it help to explain the retardation of the Middle Atlantic states relative to the Delaware-Maryland-West Virginia area.

The direction of the correlation (negative) between comparative growth and relative wage levels conforms with the prediction based upon economic theory, but the small partial coefficients do not provide significant support for the hypothesis that comparative growth has been determined by wage differentials. It is difficult to explain these small coefficients; they may be the result of the strong influence of the unionization factor. Wage levels and extent of unionization are highly correlated ($r = + .65$), but the latter evidenced a much closer correlation with comparative growth than did the former variable.

The dominance of unionization over wage levels in the regression analysis can be illuminated by reference to the experience of particular states. Some of the most rapidly growing Western states, e.g. Arizona, Nevada, had relatively high wage levels but low levels of unionization. On the other hand, several highly unionized states such as Pennsylvania, Wisconsin, and West Virginia, all experienced comparative losses in manufacturing despite relative wage levels, adjusted, which were slightly below the national average.

In the regression analysis each state is treated as a single unit of observation, without regard to its size or importance relative to other states. Nevada, New Mexico, North Dakota and Wyoming, for example, have as much influence on the regression coefficients as do states such as New York, Ohio, and Illinois, which have a hundred or more times as much manufacturing. Would a regression equation based on the same observations weighted by the amount of manufacturing in the various states yield different results? I have calculated such an equation and find that it is strikingly similar to the one obtained with unweighted observations. (See equation 3W). In the weighted version, the relative extent of unionization and population per square mile are slightly more important and the temperature variable slightly less important that in the unweighted equation. On the whole, however, the correspondence between the two equations is very close. The coefficient of correlation between the calculated values obtained with equations 1 and 3W is + .990.

It is also of interest to ask whether the results would be significantly different if comparative growth of manufacturing was measured by total employment instead of by value added. The answer is again in the negative. The coefficients of partial correlation are very similar as may be seen in Table 15.4 at the end of this paper. This table also presents comparable coefficients for comparative growth, adjusted, 1947-1954, and these too are similar. Finally, as an example of how this analysis may be extended, Table 15.4 presents the corresponding partial coefficients of correlation for two separate groups of industries — those with above average labor intensity (as measured by the ratio of wages to value added) and those with below average labor intensity. We find that the relative extent of unionization was *not* significantly associated with the comparative growth of the non-labor intensive industries. These variables were significantly related for the labor intensive group.

This concludes the examination of comparative

growth of manufacturing, adjusted. In the remainder of the paper we shall look briefly at comparative industrial structure, population migration, and changes in relative wage levels.

Regression analysis: Comparative industrial structure

The comparative growth of manufacturing in a state depends in part on the industrial structure of the state, i.e., whether it has, on balance, fast or slow growing industries. In this section I examine several variables that might be used to explain and predict comparative industrial structure as measured by growth.

Comparative industrial structure measured by wages

This is the ratio of what the wage bill for a state would be if every worker in the state received the national average wage for his industry to what the wage bill would be if every worker in the state received the national average wage for manufacturing taken as a whole.[15] The hypothesis is that states which have high wage industries, on average, will also have a favorable industrial structure with respect to growth. Rapidly growing industries usually find it necessary to offer higher wages to draw labor away from other industries.

Relative patents per capita

(This is an average for the years 1929, 1930, 1931, 1952, 1953, 1954.) The hypothesis is that high patents per capita will be associated with favorable industrial structure in terms of growth. States in which there is a great deal of research and development work, as evidenced by patents, are likely to have a large proportion of rapidly growing industries.[16]

Climate and population per square mile

Two other variables that were found to be closely correlated with comparative growth, adjusted, were also included. They are the monthly deviation from 65 degrees F. and population per square mile. The hypothesis is that since these were favorable factors for comparative growth of manufacturing, adjusted, they may also be favorable factors for comparative industrial structure, when other variables are taken into account.

Equations four and five in Table 15.3 reveal a significant positive correlation between structure as measured by wages and structure as measured by growth. The data are also consistent with the hypothesis

of a positive relation between patents per capita and structure. There is a strong negative correlation between deviations from 65 degrees F. and structure, but population per square mile shows no relation to structure. The significant relation between climate and structure is particularly interesting because climate was also significantly related to comparative growth, adjusted, and the latter is negatively correlated with comparative industrial structure. The states with mild temperatures were not only growing more rapidly on an industry-by-industry basis, but they also tended to have the growth industries, *ceteris paribus.*

Regression analysis: Population migration

The data on the comparative growth of manufacturing, relative wage levels, and other state characteristics can be used to test certain hypotheses regarding the migration of population in the United States. In this analysis the dependent variable is the net cumulative migration out of or into a state, of persons still living in 1950. It is computed as follows:

> All persons living in the state, born in other states, minus all persons born in the state living in other states, divided by the population of the state in 1950. A plus figure indicates that there has been a net inflow to a state as measured by people still living in 1950. A minus figure indicates a net outflow.[17] The independent variables and hypotheses to be tested are;

Comparative growth of manufacturing (total employment)

The hypothesis is that people have been attracted towards states experiencing comparative gains in manufacturing as this indicates an increase in job opportunities.

Relative wage levels adjusted

The hypothesis is that people have been attracted to states with relatively high wage levels.

Deviations from 65 degrees F. temperature

The hypothesis is that migration has been towards the states with mild climates.[18]

Degree of west longitude of principal city

This was included to test the naive hypothesis that migration can be explained simply in terms of 'western movement' without regard to climate, wage levels, or growth of manufacturing.

The results shown in equations six and seven suggest that the relative wage level has been the most significant factor determining the direction of net interstate population migration in recent decades. The evidence pointing to a movement from the low wage to the high wage states is very impressive, especially in view of the slight importance assigned to wage differentials by most labor economists.[19]

Of 14 states that had above national average relative wage levels (average 1929-1954), only two experienced net out-migration, and this amounted to only three-tenths of one per cent from New York and five-tenths of one per cent from Illinois. Of the 34 states that had below average wage levels, all by six experienced a net cumulative outflow.[20] The coefficient of partial correlation between population migration and relative wage levels was + .71. This result, and the absence of a significant relation between comparative growth of manufacturing and wage levels, suggests that the movement of surplus labor to industry may have been at least as important as the movement of industry to labor in recent decades.[21]

Temperature was also significantly related to migration, although its influence was not as great as that of wage levels. People have apparently been seeking milder climates independently of the growth of manufacturing in these areas.

The comparative growth of manufacturing was moderately correlated with migration, but the relation was not as strong as between migration and wage levels or climate. The hypothesis regarding a western movement abstracted from other factors is not supported by the data. There was no significant relation between migration and longitude when the other factors are taken into account.[22]

Regression analysis: Change in relative wage levels, adjusted

Between 1929 and 1954 some states experienced substantial increases in their relative wage level (adjusted) while others experienced decreases. Several hypotheses regarding this differential rate of change of wages may be tested. The variables examined and the expected relation to wage change are:

Comparative growth of manufacturing
The hypothesis is that states that have gained manufac-

turing also experienced a rise in relative wages because the growth of manufacturing increased the demand for labor.

Comparative growth of population
While there is not a perfect correspondence between labor force and population, the hypothesis is that wage changes were negatively related to relative growth of population, *ceteris paribus*, because the latter is a rough indication of changes in the supply of labor.

Changes in the relative extent of unionization
It has been claimed by some writers, and denied by others, that increases in unionization result in higher wages. The hypothesis tested here is that the change in relative unionization has been positively related to the change in relative wage levels.[23]

The actual level of wages
This variable is included to take account of the general hypothesis that wages have tended to become more equal throughout the United States and that this change is for reasons other than those given above.

According to equation eight, the hypothesis regarding the influence of unionization on wage levels is not supported. there does not appear to be any significant relation between the changes in these two variables. Many states in the South Atlantic and East South Central divisions experienced large increases in relative wage levels, adjusted, without accompanying increases in relative extent of unionization. In New England there were very substantial increases in relative unionization while relative wage levels were actually declining.

The comparative growth of manufacturing emerges as a significant factor in wage level change. The comparative growth of population does not. There also was a marked tendency for wage level changes to result in greater equality of wages; those states with extreme values, either high or low, tended to change toward the mean.

3 Summary
The direction of redistribution of manufacturing in the U.S. since 1929 has been away from the Northeast and towards the South and West. This was true both for manufacturing, unadjusted, and after adjustment for industrial structure.

Area differentials in the growth of individual industries were much more important in determining differential growth of manufacturing than were area differentials in industrial structure.

The factors most significantly related to the differential rates of growth of manufacturing, adjusted, were:

(a) Population per square mile (negative relation)

(b) Average deviation from 65 degrees F. (negative relation)

(c) Relative extent of unionization (negative relation) The data, therefore, are not inconsistent with the hypotheses that manufacturing grew most rapidly in the states with low population density, milder climate, and freedom from unions and the 'business climate' of highly-organized states. The association between growth and unionization, however, was true only for the group of industries with above average labor intensity.

The hypothesis that wage levels were a significant factor influencing the differentail rates of growth of manufacturing is not supported by the data. This does not mean that wage levels may not have been important for particular industries, but the factor was not significant for the general redistribution of manufacturing. Wage levels and the relative extent of unionization are highly correlated, but the 'net' influence of the latter appears to have been more important.

The hypothesis that differential growth was merely the result of the less industrialized states catching up with the more industrialized ones is not supported by the data. Neither the date on which statehood was granted, nor the absolute level of manufacturing, nor manufacturing employment per capita emerges as significantly related to growth when the other factors are taken into account.

The regression results are substantially the same when the equations are calculated with the states weighted by the amount of manufacturing in the state as when they are unweighted. The results based on growth of total employment are similar to those based on value added, and the 1947-54 period shows results similar to those for 1929-1954.

Comparative industrial structure (in terms of industry growth) was closely related to comparative industrial structure as measured by industry wages. Those states with high wage industries were also the states with rapidly growing industries. Relative patents per capita was also positively related to comparative industrial structure (in terms of growth).

There was a significant negative relative between comparative industrial structure and deviations from 65 degrees F. temperature. Thus, both structure and adjusted growth had the same relationship to climate despite the fact that they were negatively related to each other.

Interstate migration of population was very pronounced toward states with relatively high wage levels (adjusted for industrial structure). This was probably as important in bringing about greater interregional equality of wages as was the movement of industry to low wage areas. The consistency of net migration in the direction predicted by economic theory is impressive. There is, perhaps, less reason to be complacent about the magnitude of the movement since large interregional differences in average wages still persist (Fuchs and Perlman, 1960).

Population migration was also towards states with the least amount of deviation from 65 degrees F. temperature, *ceteris paribus*. This lends some support to the hypothesis that people have been seeking milder climates. The hypothesis that migration has represented a westward movement independent of climate, wage levels, and manufacturing growth is not supported by the data.

There was a very strong tendency for regional wage differentials to narrow since 1929. This narrowing appears to have been unrelated to changes in relative extent of unionization. Wage level change was significantly related to comparative growth of manufacturing, but there were also other narrowing factors at work, not identified in this analysis. They probably were related to the New Deal and World War II since nearly all of the narrowing occurred prior to 1947 (Fuchs and Perlman, 1960).

Table 15.1   Comparative Gain or Loss of Manufacturing, by State, Unadjusted and Adjusted for Industrial Structure, and Comparative Industrial Structure, 1929-54

State	Comparative Growth, Unadjusted				Comparative Growth, Adjusted for Industrial Structure		Comparative Industrial Structure	
	Value Added (millions of dollars)	Total Employment (hundreds of employees)	Value Added (per cent)	Total Employment (per cent)	Value Added (per cent)	Total Employment (per cent)	Value Added (per cent)	Total Employment (per cent)
New England								
Maine	− 74	− 152	− 11.7	− 12.9	+ 6.3	+ 14.8	− 17.2	− 25.9
New Hampshire	− 127	− 339	− 23.8	− 30.8	− 2.4	− 5.0	− 21.9	− 27.1
Vermont	− 74	− 129	− 26.7	− 28.0	− 5.7	− 5.6	− 22.3	− 23.7
Massachusetts	− 1874	− 3167	− 30.6	− 32.4	− 26.4	− 26.2	− 5.8	− 8.4
Rhode Island	− 492	− 959	− 42.2	− 44.2	− 26.1	− 27.4	− 21.0	− 23.1
Connecticut	− 90	− 387	− 3.1	− 8.9	− 14.8	− 16.0	+ 12.1	+ 7.7
Middle Atlantic								
New York	− 4215	− 1814	− 23.9	− 9.0	− 24.0	− 19.0	+ .2	+ 11.0
New Jersey	− 151	− 178	− 2.3	− 2.2	− 13.2	− 13.8	+ 11.1	+ 11.8
Pennsylvania	− 2453	− 3204	− 20.3	− 18.8	− 15.3	− 13.6	− 5.9	− 6.0
East North Central								
Ohio	− 485	− 524	− 4.6	− 4.0	− 12.1	− 10.5	+ 7.8	+ 6.7
Indiana	+ 454	+ 306	+ 10.1	+ 5.4	+ 7.3	+ 1.7	+ 2.9	+ 3.6
Illinois	− 931	− 701	− 9.0	− 5.7	− 13.1	− 12.8	+ 4.5	+ 7.5
Michigan	+ 1045	+ 632	+ 12.3	+ 6.4	+ 2.9	− 3.0	+ 9.6	+ 9.3
Wisconsin	− 284	− 552	− 8.4	− 11.8	− 15.2	− 17.0	+ 7.3	+ .5
West North Central								
Minnesota	+ 52	+ 108	+ 3.5	+ 5.8	+ 7.7	+ 5.2	− 4.3	+ .5
Iowa	+ 63	+ 221	+ 5.3	+ 14.2	+ 1.7	+ 8.0	+ 3.6	+ 6.7
Missouri	− 246	− 82	− 8.9	− 2.3	− 6.7	− 4.4	− 2.4	+ 2.1
North Dakota	− 13	− 1	− 27.9	− 2.2	+ 11.9	+ 16.3	− 36.6	− 18.3
South Dakota	− 2	+ 2	− 2.5	+ 1.5	+ 20.8	+ 10.0	− 22.7	− 8.6
Nebraska	− 60	+ 34	− 14.9	+ 6.7	− 2.5	+ 1.5	− 12.6	+ 5.3
Kansas	+ 331	+ 524	+ 32.2	+ 41.2	+ 12.4	+ 11.0	+ 22.6	+ 33.9
South Atlantic								
Delaware	+ 97	− 13	+ 29.1	− 3.5	+ 18.8	− 12.8	+ 12.0	+ 9.6
Maryland	+ 343	+ 203	+ 19.1	+ 8.4	+ 13.2	− .6	+ 6.7	+ 8.9
Virginia	+ 300	+ 499	+ 18.8	+ 21.4	+ 34.0	+ 33.7	− 18.6	− 15.5
West Virginia	+ 117	− 131	+ 12.0	− 10.1	− 7.5	− 13.3	+ 18.6	+ 3.5
North Carolina	− 355	+ 708	− 14.1	+ 17.0	+ 35.1	+ 46.8	− 44.4	− 35.9
South Carolina	+ 465	+ 434	+ 44.9	+ 19.9	+ 61.4	+ 48.4	− 29.9	− 35.6
Georgia	+ 551	+ 439	+ 34.9	+ 14.7	+ 49.5	+ 30.7	− 22.3	− 31.9
Florida	+ 299	+ 134	+ 39.3	+ 11.3	+ 53.7	+ 39.0	− 23.8	− 31.2
East South Central								
Kentucky	+ 249	+ 128	+ 24.1	+ 9.8	+ 42.1	+ 24.0	− 23.7	− 15.6
Tennessee	+ 511	+ 462	+ 31.4	+ 18.3	+ 34.7	+ 31.4	− 4.7	− 16.0
Alabama	+ 401	+ 237	+ 30.8	+ 11.0	+ 39.9	+ 30.6	− 13.1	− 22.0
Mississippi	+ 84	+ 57	+ 18.1	+ 6.3	+ 36.5	+ 33.4	− 22.4	− 28.8
West South Central								
Arkansas	+ 111	+ 49	+ 25.7	+ 6.6	+ 31.4	+ 22.5	− 7.7	− 16.9
Louisiana	+ 258	− 64	+ 23.2	− 4.4	+ 26.2	+ 8.5	− 4.1	− 12.7
Oklahoma	+ 34	+ 212	+ 5.9	+ 27.4	+ 14.1	+ 25.4	− 8.6	+ 2.7
Texas	+ 1784	+ 1785	+ 52.9	+ 45.3	+ 53.6	+ 45.4	− 2.2	− .7

State	Comparative Growth, Unadjusted				Comparative Growth, Adjusted for Industrial Structure		Comparative Industrial Structure	
	Value Added (millions of dollars)	Total Employment (hundreds of employees)	Value Added (per cent)	Total Employment (per cent)	Value Added (per cent)	Total Employment (per cent)	Value Added (per cent)	Total Employment (per cent)
Mountain								
Montana	− 67	− 34	− 33.6	− 16.4	− 2.9	+ 14.4	− 31.5	− 28.4
Idaho	+ 21	− 18	+ 11.9	− 7.2	+ 39.1	+ 23.2	− 30.8	− 28.7
Wyoming	− 58	− 15	− 54.0	− 20.6	− 42.7	− 8.6	− 19.5	− 13.0
Colorado	+ 28	+ 66	+ 6.3	+ 11.0	+ 17.2	+ 11.1	− 11.4	− .2
New Mexico	+ 87	+ 84	+ 74.6	+ 61.7	+ 75.5	+ 64.2	− 6.1	− 7.6
Arizona	+ 73	+ 84	+ 40.8	+ 34.0	+ 51.0	+ 40.3	− 17.2	− 10.2
Utah	+ 79	+ 33	+ 28.9	+ 11.4	+ 44.8	+ 24.6	− 22.3	− 14.9
Nevada	+ 38	+ 34	+ 65.0	+ 64.4	+ 70.8	+ 70.3	− 16.6	− 16.5
Pacific								
Washington	+ 178	− 69	+ 12.0	− 3.6	+ 4.5	− 9.7	+ 7.4	+ 6.3
Oregon	+ 289	+ 214	+ 28.5	+ 16.3	+ 43.2	+ 35.3	− 20.5	− 22.8
California	+ 3746	+ 4855	+ 46.2	+ 49.5	+ 38.8	+ 38.8	+ 11.2	+ 16.9

Note: *Comparative gain or loss* measures the extent to which an area exceeded or fell short of the level it would have had if it had grown at the U.S. rate between the indicated years. *Comparative gain (per cent)* shows this comparative gain as a percentage of the area's actual level in 1954; comparative loss (per cent) shows the comparative loss as a percentage of the hypothetical or expected 1954 level based on the U.S. rate of growth. *Comparative industrial structure* shows what the comparative gain or loss would have been if each industry in the state had grown at its national rate.
Source: U.S. Bureau of the Census.

Table 15.2   Zero Order Coefficients of Correlation, 27 State Variables

	1	2	3	4	5	6	7	8	9	10	11	12	1
1.													
2.	− .378												
3.	− .530	.082											
4.	− .505	.002	.004										
5.	− .422	.363	− .059	.427									
6.	− .345	.652	.253	.138	.304								
7.	− .345	.356	− .138	.242	.414	.205							
8.	− .486	.319	.361	.118	.323	.377	.611						
9.	− .566	.275	.126	.708	.583	.491	.537	.441					
10.	− .389	.353	.041	.168	.422	.298	.887	.755	.519				
11.	.158	.336	− .293	.034	.107	.615	.182	.178	.356	.159			
12.	.771	− .188	− .473	− .469	− .173	− .161	.081	.010	− .350	.156	.274		
13.	.406	.365	− .112	− .559	− .331	.420	− .126	.079	− .319	.027	.430	.500	
14.	.799	− .363	− .395	− .460	− .394	− .131	− .371	− .466	− .351	.305	.732	.732	.4
15.	− .153	.645	.129	.043	.267	.950	.228	.303	.430	.300	.661	.027	.4
16.	.626	− .311	− .457	− .279	− .223	−.630	.017	− .292	− .419	− .075	− .267	.548	− .0
17.	.494	.099	− .444	− .116	− .001	.301	.095	.007	.127	.031	.863	.514	.3
18.	.132	− .657	.036	.218	− .190	− .255	− .099	− .158	.073	− .161	− .073	− .003	− .3
19.	− .570	.164	.093	.764	.505	.277	.316	.118	.801	.158	.142	− .588	− .6
20.	.233	.224	.171	− .542	− .400	.311	− .106	.267	− .356	.087	.244	.360	.8
21.	− .427	.341	− .061	.444	.996	.269	.390	.296	.567	.387	.074	− .198	− .3
22.	.916	− .362	− .436	− .570	− .417	− .304	− .471	− .438	− .647	− .456	.148	.792	.4
23.	.766	− .393	− .389	− .466	− .409	− .277	− .327	− .337	− .462	− .350	.134	.588	.3
24.	− .122	.371	− .122	.022	.325	.206	.825	.662	.334	.852	.297	.320	.1
25.	.005	.285	− .124	− .092	.166	.277	.636	.555	.208	.790	.364	.479	.3
26.	.802	− .130	− .540	− .423	− .310	− .081	− .152	− .220	− .355	− .203	− .547	.729	.4
27.	.301	− .300	− .197	− .285	− .107	− .467	.127	− .013	− .373	.266	− .497	.526	.0

Column
  1. Comparative growth of manufacturing, adjusted, value added, 1929-54
  2. Relative extent of unionization, 1939
  3. Average monthly deviation from 65°F.
  4. Population per square mile, 1940
  5. Value added by manufacture, 1947.
  6. Relative wage level adjusted, average, 1929-54
  7. Comparative industrial structure, (growth) value added, average, 1929-54
  8. Relative industrial structure (wages), 1947
  9. Relative patents per capita, average, 1929-30-31-52-53-54
  10. Comparative industrial structure, (growth) total employment, average, 1929-54
  11. Net cumulative migration (still living in 1950)
  12. Comparative growth of manufacturing total employment, 1929-54
  13 Degree of west longitude, principal city

14	15	16	17	18	19	20	21	22	23	24	25	26	27
− .020													
.285	− .391												
.512	.427	.106											
.145	− .270	.058	− .015										
− .545	.220	− .300	− .013	.179									
.387	.297	− .179	.175	− .254	− .650								
− .399	.231	− .207	− .024	− .181	.522	− .436							
.847	− .145	.505	.410	.088	− .656	.287	− .422						
.840	− .189	.369	.405	.159	− .517	.212	− .409	.739					
− .195	.247	.043	.268	− .182	.028	.118	.293	− .222	− .224				
.029	.317	− .039	.300	− .152	− .176	.334	.125	− .032	− .076	.844			
.721	.093	.457	.802	− .042	− .410	.260	− .322	.757	.663	.058	.163		
.244	− .396	.504	− .388	.020	− .461	.130	− .111	.343	.219	.136	.239	− .023	

14. Comparative growth of manufacturing adjusted, total employment, 1947-54
15. Relative wage level, adjusted, average, 1947-54
16. Change in relative wage level, adjusted, 1929 to 1954
17. Comparative growth of population, 1929-54
18. Change in relative unionization, 1939 to 1953
19. Relative manufacturing employment, per capita, 1929
20. Date of entry to the U.S. as a state
21. Total manufacturing employment, 1947
22. Comparative growth of manufacturing, adjusted, total employment, 1929-54
23. Comparative growth of manufacturing, adjusted, value added, 1947-54
24. Comparative industrial structure, (growth) value added, average, 1947-54
25. Comparative industrial structure, (growth) total employment, average, 1947-54
26. Comparative growth, personal income, 1929-54
27. Change in relative manufacturing employment per capita, 1929 to 1954

Table 15.3   Partial Regression and Correlation Coefficients, State Comparative Growth Adjusted, and Related Variables

Equation	Dependent Variable	Constant Term	Independent Variables					Coefficient of Multiple Correlation R (N = 48)
(1)	X_1'	96.61	$-.2343X_2$ $(.0628)$ $-.336$ $-.490$	$-3.258X_3$ $(.586)$ $-.500$ $-.642$	$-.095X_4$ $(.017)$ $-.502$ $-.644$			.804
(2)	X_1	68.89	$-.2539X_2$ $(.0856)$ $-.364$ $-.416$	$-3.554X_3$ $(.599)$ $-.546$ $-.675$	$-.0846X_4$ $(.0189)$ $-.447$ $-.568$	$-231\times10^{-8}X_5$ (140×10^{-8}) $-.176$ $-.247$	$+.3821X_6$ $(.3187)$ $+.147$ $+.182$	.823
(3W)	X_1	96.25	$-.3136X_2$ $-.422$	$-3.0484X_3$ $-.462$	$-.0901X_4$ $-.576$			
(4)	X_7	−117.29	$+1.278X_8$ $(.257)$ $+.589$ $+.604$	$-1.444X_3$ $(.370)$ $-.401$ $-.512$	$-.0119X_4$ $(.0149)$ $-.114$ $-.121$	$+.00804X_9$ $(.00311)$ $+.408$ $+.366$		.779
(5)	X_{10}	−154.68	$+1.61X_8$ $(.24)$ $+.712$ $+.715$	$-.974X_3$ $(.345)$ $-.260$ $-.395$	$-.018X_4$ $(.014)$ $-.165$ $-.192$	$+.00728X_9$ $(.00291)$ $+.354$ $+.357$		.827
(6)	X_{11}	−105.64	$+.2282X_{12}$ $(.1179)$ $+.255$ $+.283$	$-1.7829X_3$ $(.5065)$ $-.378$ $-.473$	$-.0925X_{13}$ $(.1792)$ $-.068$ $-.078$	$+1.4715X_6$ $(.2202)$ $+.780$ $+.714$		.795
(7)	X_{11}	−118.15	$+.360X_{14}$ $(.186)$ $+.234$ $+.283$	$-1.4358X_3$ $(.4878)$ $-.305$ $-.410$	$-.0997X_{13}$ $(.1754)$ $-.073$ $-.087$	$+1.5202X_{15}$ $(.2346)$ $+.740$ $+.703$		.787
(8)	X_{16}	35.53	$+.1151X_1$ $(.0359)$ $+.441$ $+.439$	$+.01686X_{17}$ $(.05103)$ $+.045$ $+.050$	$-.0651X_{18}$ $(.0485)$ $-.134$ $-.201$	$-.3585X_6$ $(.0873)$ $-.526$ $-.531$		.777

Legend. See notes to Table 15.2

Explanation: Line 1 = partial regression coefficients
Line 2 = unbiased standard errors of regression coefficients
Line 3 = standardized regression or 'Beta' coefficients
Line 4 = partial correlation coefficients

Table 15.4   Partial Coefficients of Correlation Between Comparative Growth of Manufacturing, Adjusted and Unionization, Climate, and Population Density

Comparative growth of manufacturing, adjusted	X_2 (Unionization)	X_3 (Climate)	X_4 (Population density)
	(second order coeffients)		
Value added, 1929-1954	−.490	−.642	−.644
Total employment, 1929-1954	−.468	−.550	−.677
Value added, 1947-1954	−.454	−.449	−.546
Labor intensive industries, total employment, 1929-1954*	−.408	−.572	−.450
Non-labor intensive industries, total employment, 1929-1954*	−.075	−.467	−.440

= 48

This grouping and analysis is based on 20 major industry groups rather than 221 individual industries.

Notes

1 Census data for 1958 became available as this paper was nearing completion. Preliminary inspection suggests that the paper's conclusions, based on analysis of data through 1954, would apply for 1958 as well.

2 It should be noted that this paper does not rest upon Lösch's assumption of 'adaptive' behavior on the part of businessmen. As Alchian has suggested, changes in location may be the result of an 'adoptive' process in the environment (Alchian, 1950).

3 A brief discussion of these choices appears in Fuchs (1959a) and a more complete review in Fuchs (1961).

4 Alaska and Hawaii are not covered. For a note on the use of states, see Fuchs (1959b).

5 That is $\dfrac{Y_{s.} - H_{s.}}{Y_{s.} \text{ or } H_{s.}} = \dfrac{B_{s.} - X_{s.}}{B_{s.} \text{ or } X_{s.}}$.

6 There is an extensive literature dealing with this problem of standardization and interaction. For a recent summary discussion, see Hanna, 1959, (Appendix B).

7 Let X_{is} = number of production workers in industry i in state s

$X_{.s}$ = number of production workers in all manufacturing in state s

$X_{i.}$ = number of production workers in industry i in U.S.

$X_{..}$ = number of production workers in all manufacturing in U.S.

And W_{is}, $W_{.s}$, $W_{i.}$, and $W_{..}$ equal the same for average annual earnings per production worker. Then relative wage level adjustment equals

$$\frac{X_{.s}W_{.s}}{\sum_i X_{is}W_{i.}}.$$

8 See Hanna (1959) p. 155, also Lester (1946).

9 The source for relative wage levels, adjusted, based on man-hour data and the SIC is Hanna (1959) p. 153.

10 L.R. Boulware, Vice President of General Electric, in a speech to the Phoenix Chamber of Commerce on May 21, 1958, said, 'Incidentally, a very important factor in General Electric's decision favoring Arizona over the other contenders for our computer business was the combination of the fact that you *do* have a Right to Work law and the fact that a *growing majority* of the citizens are so obviously coming to appreciate and support volunteerism as opposed to compulsion in union membership.' (*not added*) This may not be a new phenomenon. A generation ago Hermann Schumacher observed, 'Of late the search for tractable labor had induced perhaps as many shifts in location as the quest for low paid labor,' (Schumacher, 1937, p. 589).

11 The source for this data is Troy. The percentage of non-agricultural employment that is unionized is over 40 per cent in some states and below ten per cent in others.

12 Edward L. Ullman suggests a 'best' climate of about 70 degrees Fahrenheit and no rain, but this is in the context of general amenities rather than manufacturing *per se* (Ullman, 1954, p. 122).

13 Other factors that have been considered important by some observers, but for which I have not found supporting evidence, include tax differentials, the plant dispersal policy of the Federal government, the condemnation by the U.S. Supreme Court of 'basing point pricing,' and shifts in the direction and composition of U.S. foreign trade.

14 This statement is not meant to apply to individual industries, some of which have probably been influenced by wage differentials, but applies only to manufacturing in the aggregate. Moreover, the individual industry pattern of comparative gain and loss varies from area to area in a manner which *is* related to wage level differentials (Fuchs, forthcoming).

15 It is $\dfrac{\sum\limits_{i} X_{is} W_{i.}}{X_{.s} W_{..}}$.

16 The data on patents were supplied by Professor Jacob Schmookler of the University of Minnesota. This measure provides only an approximate index of inventive activity, and more sophisticated ones should be developed if this factor is to be examined in detail (Thompson, 1960).

17 The analysis is limited to persons born in the United States.

18 See Ullman (1954) for the increased importance of amenities. According to Ullman, 'Climate is probably the most important regional amenity' (1954, p. 123).

19 For example, Lloyd G. Reynolds has written, '. . . there are indications that geographical movement is mainly job oriented rather than wage oriented and migration sometimes occurs even in the face of adverse wage differentials' (Reynolds, 1957, p. 218).

20 The six states were Delaware and Maryland (both had wage levels almost equal to the national average), Florida, Texas (very small inflow), Colorado, and New Mexico.

21 In a study of regional trends in per capita income from 1880 to 1950, Richard A. Easterlin found that migration from low income to high income areas was one of the most important factors contributing to the narrowing of regional differentials in per capita income (Easterlin, 1958, p. 321).

22 Population per square mile is also not correlated with migration when wage level, temperature, and relative growth of manufacturing are held constant. The coefficient of partial correlation is + .067. Unlike comparative shifts of manufacturing, which do show a high negative correlation with population density, there was no tendency for population movement to be toward the sparsely populated states, *ceteris paribus.*

23 The data are not completely comparable. The change in unionization is from 1939 to 1953, while the change in wage levels is from 1929 to 1954.

References

Alchian, A.A. (1950) 'Uncertainty, Evolution, and Economic Theory,' *The Journal of Political Economy*

Cunningham, W.G. (1951) *The Aircraft Industry: A Study in Industrial Location,* Morrison, Los Angeles.

De Vyver, F.T. (1951) 'Labor Factors in the Industrial Development of the South,' *Southern Economic Journal*, October.

Easterlin, R.A. (1958) 'Long Term Regional Income Changes: Some Suggested Factors,' *Papers and Proceedings of the Regional Science Association.* 4.

Fuchs, V.R. (1959a) 'Changes in the Location of U.S. Manufacturing Since 1929,' *Journal of Regional Science*, No. 1, Spring.

Fuchs, V.R. (1959b) 'States or SMA's When Studying the Location of Manufacturing *Southern Economic*, January.

Fuchs, V.R. and Perlman, R. (1960) 'Recent Trends in Southern Wage Differentials,' *Review of Economics and Statistics*, August.

Fuchs, V.R. (1961) *Changes in The Location of Manufacturing in the United States Since 1929,* Yale University Press, New Haven, Conn.

Fuchs, V.R. 'The Determinants of the Redistribution of Manufacturing in the United States Since 1920,' *Review of Economics and Statistics,* forthcoming.

Hanna, F.A. (1959) *State Income Differentials, 1919-54,* Duke University Press, Durham N.C.

Lester, R.A. (1946) 'Effectiveness of Factory Labor, South-North Comparisons,' *Journal of Political Economy*, February.

Lösch, A. (1954) *The Economics of Location*, Translated from the second revised edition, Yale University Press, New Haven, Conn.

New York Times (1960) April 17, Section 8.

Perloff, H.S., Dunn, E.S., Jr., Lampard, E.E., and Muth, R.F. (1960) *Regions, Resources and Economic Growth,* Johns Hopkins Press, Baltimore.

Reynolds, L.G. (1957) 'The Impact of Collective Bargaining on the Wage Structure in the United States,' in *The Theory of Wage Determination*, J.E. Dunlop, ed., St. Martin's Press, New York.

Schumacher, H. (1937) 'Location of Industry,' *Encyclopaedia of the Social Sciences,* **9** The Macmillan Company, New York.

Thompson, W.R. (1960) 'Locational Differences in Inventive Effort and Their Determinants,' Conference on the Economic and Social Factors Determining the Rate and Direction of Inventive Activity, University of Minnesota, May.

Troy, L. National Bureau of Economic Research, unpublished worksheets.

Ullman, E.L. (1954), Amenities as a Factor in Regional Growth,' *The Geographical Review,* **44**, January.

Reprinted from *Regional Science Association Papers*, vol. 8, Hague Congress, 1961, Regional Science Association, Philadelphia, with permission.

16 Industrialization, Initial Advantage, and American Metropolitan Growth

by Allan Pred

University of California, Berkeley

The spatial, as well as the economic and social, processes of nineteenth and twentieth-century urbanization and industrialization are not independent. The phenomena that led to the concurrent emergence of the modern American metropolis and large-scale manufacturing are dynamically involuted and nearly always inseparable.[1] Urbanization, as in the case of Washington, D.C., is not inexorably associated with industrial growth;[2] yet, conversely, the multiplication of factories, product output, and markets since 1860 is virtually synonymous with city development. That the largest urban concentrations have played a monumental role in American industrial expansion is underscored by the fact that, in 1961, 37.5 percent of the nation's value added by manufacture was accounted for by ten metropolises, which in turn contained 27.0 percent of the total 1960 population.[3]

The complex reciprocals of urbanization and industrialization are crucial girders in the superstructure of economic growth. Perhaps because capital formation and investment are viewed as this entity's most significant components, economists and others have logically and legitimately emphasized their part in the growth process, and have conducted only limited theoretical inquiries into the spatial interaction of urban and manufacturing growth.[4] Within this context, the concentration of much of American manufacturing and population in ten metropolises leads one to pose at least two basic questions: How and why do cities expand precipitately during periods of rapid industrialization? Why do some cities grow more rapidly than, and at the expense of, other cities? No fewer than three traditional frameworks of locational thinking provide theoretical ammunition with which to assault these two questions.

Underlying Theoretical Themes

Superficially, intellectual derivations from Weber's and Marshall's agglomeration and scale economies provide the most potentially fruitful source of theoretical concepts. The unique array of scale, localization, and urbanization economies available at urban industrial sites is frequently employed to explain the industrial growth and specialization of metropolitan centers. The city's internal and external manufacturing economies were presumably of particular importance during the nineteenth century. At that time individual firms were in a position both to minimize the internalization or absorption of external diseconomies and to maximize the reduction of per unit input costs 'through acquisitions, combinations, or mergers with closely interdependent economic activities.'[5] While these observations contribute to an understanding of why manufacturing grows in cities, they are inadequate for a comprehension of the precise dynamics of city-size growth, though agglomeration economies imply that manufacturing on a grand scale must be limited to a few cities. Even if these observations were of more definite assistance, 'the concept of external economies is at best only one among a number of possible keys to the understanding of modern city development.'[6]

The possible interrelationships between central-place theory and the urbanization-industrialization syndrome are somewhat less obvious, especially in view of the criticism that has been leveled at Christaller's theory for its failure to deal with the location of manufacturing activities. Attempts to apply central-place theory to the problem of urban growth have admittedly exaggerated the role of business and service activities and have generally emphasized small urban places at the expense of the multimillion metropolis.[7] However, these shortcomings aside, central-place theory may be combined with Löschian market-area hypotheses to provide two basic avenues of approach. One is the threshold concept, from which it can be inferred that industries 'oriented' toward local or regional markets will not appear in cities until their local or regional thresholds are attained. Secondly, if the schema of a hierarchy of market areas is extended to include manufacturing activities, the largest or most nodal cities will logically have the greatest variety of manufacturing functions. Although both the detailed implications of, and the supporting evidence for, this elementary translation of central-place theory from tertiary to secondary activities remain to be spelled out, such a translation cannot in itself provide complete insight into the interlocking spatial processes of urbanization and industrialization.

Of the several other ingredients to be added to this theoretical amalgamation, the concept of initial advantage is probably most important. Initial advantage is here employed as an umbrella to cover three overlapping ideas: that existing locations are usually characterized by tremendous inertia and a temporal compounding of advantages; that existing locations often exert considerable influence on plant-location decisions; and that once concentration is initiated it is self-perpetuating.[8] These ideas contribute substantially to one of the major themes of this paper, namely that some urban centers, through rapid industrialization, generate their own conditions for growth into multimillion metropolises, and that such centers are usually those possessing relative initial advantages. A rationale for viewing urban and industrial growth as an interrelated process, with each stage of development a function of previous stages, is contained in Myrdal's 'principle of circular and cumulative causation.' He contends that 'in the normal case a change does not call forth contradicting forces but, instead, supporting changes, which move the system in the same direction but much further. Because of such circular causation a social process tends to become cumulative and often to gather speed at an accelerated rate.'[9] Of course, all cities would grow indefinitely if urban-industrial growth were merely a process of circular and cumulative causation. Therefore it is imperative to elaborate explicitly the means by which initial advantages favor some cities at the expense of others.

American Urbanization and Industrialization, 1860-1910

If it is contended that the emergence of inordinately large concentrations of manufacturing in the United States' greatest metropolises is a function of agglomeration economies, the fulfillment of successive market thresholds, and initial advantage, then the period when these forces were most operative should be identified and outlined; for there comes a time when tertiary activities supplant manufacturing as the principal determinant of urban-size growth.[10]

Table 16.1   Urbanization and Industrialization in the United States, 1860-1910*

	1860	1870	1880	1890	1900	1910	% Increase
1. Total U.S. population (1000's)	31,513	39,905	50,262	63,056	76,094	92,407	193.2
2. Total urban population (1000's)	6,217	9,902	14,130	22,106	30,160	41,999	575.6
3. Population in cities > 100,000 (1000's)	2,639	4,130	6,211	9,698	14,208	20,302	669.3
2 as % of 1	19.7	24.8	28.1	35.1	39.6	45.5	—
3 as % of 1	8.4	10.3	12.4	15.4	18.7	22.0	—
Miles of railroad operated[1]	30,626	52,922	93,262	166,703	206,631	266,185	769.1
Rails produced (1000's of long tons)	183	554	1,305	1,885	2,386	3,636	—
Pig-iron production (1000's of long tons)	821	1,665	3,835	9,203	13,789	27,304	——
Steel ingots and castings produced (1000's of long tons)	11.8	68.8	1,247	4,277	10,188	26,095	—
Index of Manufacturing production (1899= 100)	16	25	42	71	100	172	975.0

* Compiled from 'Historical Statistics of the United States' [see text footnote 53 below], pp. 7, 14,427 and 429; and Edwin Frickey: Production in the United States, 1860-1914 (Harvard Economic Studies, Vol. 82; Cambridge, Mass., 1947), pp. 10-11 and 54.

[1] Not including yard tracks and sidings.

The early 1860's are generally regarded as a turning point in American urban and manufacturing growth (Table 16.1). In the decades after 1860 the economy completed its transition from a commercial-mercantilistic base to an industrial-capitalistic one. Concomitantly, the top of the urban hierarchy became characterized more and more by industrial, multifunctional cities, and less and less by cities dominated by mercantilistic wholesaling and trading functions. 'By the 'fifties the more far-sighted leaders of midwestern communities had realized that potential growth was limited so long as it was based exclusively on commerce';[11] and demands created by the Civil War provided a considerable stimulus to previously initiated industrialization, and to the momentum of urban growth throughout the country. Before this crucial period, and before the nation's railroad network was fully articulated, markets for manufactured goods were not a primary concern of urban business interests. But by 1865 the attention of the financial solons of Boston, New York, and other mercantile cities was 'no longer focused primarily upon foreign commerce,' and had instead 'turned to manufacturing and the distribution of its products in domestic markets.'[12]

Table 16.2   Population Growth in Ten United States Cities, 1860-1910*

	Population 1860	Population 1910		Population 1860	Population 1910[a]
New York	1,174,799[b]	4,766,883	Cleveland	43,417	560,663
Chicago	112,172	2,185,283	Pittsburgh	49,221	533,905
Philadelphia	565,529	1,549,008	Detroit	45,619	405,766
St. Louis	160,773	687,029	San Francisco	56,802	416,912
Boston	177,840	670,585	Los Angeles	4,385	319,198

* Derived from the 'Census of Population: 1960' [see text footnote 3], pp. 1-66.

a This column understates metropolitan growth, since it includes only the population within the municipal boundaries. In 1860 transport facilities permitted a negligible degree of development beyond the central city; but by 1910, although suburbanization was still in its initial stages, there was considerable integration between these cities and the areas contiguous to their boundaries. The figures do particular injustice to Boston and Pittsburgh, both of which had long possessed a number of factories in their essentially rural surroundings.

b 'New York and its boroughs as constituted under the act of consolidation in 1898' ('Census of Population: 1960' [op. cit.], pp. 1-67).

By 1910 evolving systems of mass production had been made economical by the development of mass domestic markets, despite periodic interruptions by inflation, protracted deflation, and depression. Within a span of fifty years, much of which Rostow might term 'the drive to maturity,'[13] the United States rose from its position as one of the world's secondary industrial nations to manufactural preeminence.[14] Clark went so far as to state that the experience of these years constituted 'a greater quantitative expansion of industry than [that] in all the previous history of the race.'[15]

Clearly, then, by 1910 the modern industrialization of the United States was an accomplished fact and its major metropolises were more than commercial entrepôts. Within this context it is not surprising to find the contention that before 1910 'industry rather than commerce was the chief source of urban growth.'[16]

Although this observation is elementary, its recognition is crucial to acceptance of the urban-size growth model to be presented. That urban growth since World War I has been perpetuated more by tertiary activities than by manufacturing is most clearly reflected by the fact that the percentage of population gainfully employed in the latter has been decreasing at the expense of the former.[17] Because manufacturing continued to be the prime inducer of urban expansion for a few years beyond 1910, it was not until the appearance of the 1930 census that it became apparent 'that the factors involved in metropolitan growth . . . were primarily commercial and institutional, with industry playing a relatively smaller role.'[18] Economists usually attribute this shift in sectoral employment to the different income elasticities of demand for the goods and services of industrial and tertiary activities, and to simultaneous increases of real product per man-hour in manufacturing greater than those in other sectors of the economy.

Table 16.1 reveals that manufacturing output between 1860 and 1910 increased at a pace exceeding the growth rates of national population, urban population, and population in large cities. Manufacturing also outstripped the railroad development vital to its raw-material assembly and finished-product distribution. However, the extension of markets and the alterations in average scale of production, which were the outward expressions of rapid industrial growth, can be seen in their proper perspective only in relation to certain railroad developments: intensification of trunk lines, spread of feeder lines, and integration of fragmented operating units; technical improvement of freight-car carrying capacity, motive power, rails, roadbeds, and terminal facilities; financing innovations adopted by industrial enterprises; precipitation of an enormous demand for steel rails, steam engines, and rolling stock; and elaboration of consumer demand through wages paid to line employees and construction workers.[19]

A generous part of post-Civil War urban growth occurred in those cities which are now the country's ten most important industrial metropolises (Table 16.2). Except for Los Angeles, these cities were, to one degree or another, established commercial centers, and in the capacity of financial and transport nodes they served as logical foci for industrial development. However, commercial supremacy in 1860 was obviously not prophetic of future industrial significance: Baltimore, New Orleans, Cincinnati, and Buffalo, among the ten largest cities of 1860, are not among today's ten more important urban-industrial concentrations.

A Model of Urban-Size Growth in Periods of Rapid Industrialization

It is commonly acknowledged that 'there are close relations between urban growth and changes in the structure of urban activities,'[20] Through the use of a simple descriptive model, such relationships for major American cities from 1860 to 1910 can be tersely expressed.

Imagine a mercantile city, with some minor industrial functions, which is indiscriminately located in space and unengaged in market-area competition with other cities (though it does import some goods that are not locally produced). Assumption of these isolated aspatial and monopolistic conditions permits concentration on the growth process itself and defers inquiry into the interplay of initial advantages and the growth of some cities at the expense of others.

Further imagine the introduction into this city of one or more large-scale factories, whose location may have been determined either rationally or randomly. Sooner or later this event evokes two circular chains of reaction (Figure 16.1).

New manufacturing functions, whether or not they primarily serve local markets, will have an initial multiplier effect; that is, new local demands created both by the factories themselves and by the purchasing power of their labor force will call into being a host of new business, service, trade, construction, transport-

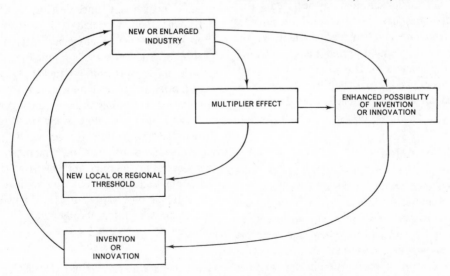

Figure 16.1 The circular and cumulative process of industrialization and urban-size growth.

ation, professional, and miscellaneous white-collar jobs. The combined effect of new industrial employment and an initial multiplier effect will be an increase in population, or growth in urban size, and the probable attainment of one or more new local or regional industrial thresholds. These higher thresholds will support new manufacturing functions as well as additional plants in existing industrial categories. Once production facilities have been constructed in accordance with the new thresholds, a second round of growth is initiated, and eventually still higher thresholds are achieved. Plant construction in response to these thresholds again generates a multiplier effect and higher thresholds, and the process continues in a circular and cumulative manner until interrupted or impeded.[21]

A second circular sequence of reactions occurs at the same time and compounds and reinforces the effects of the first. This chain stems from the continually more complex network of interpersonal communications and confrontations that derives from an expanding population. The multiplication of interactions among the growing number of individuals engaged in the manufacturing and tertiary sectors enhances the possibilities of technological improvements and inventions, enlarges the likelihood of the adoption of more efficient managerial and financial institutions, increases the speed with which locally originating ideas are disseminated, and eases the diffusion of skills and knowledge brought in by migrants from other areas.[22] Although, as Schumpeter[23] would have it, inventions and ideas are not immediately implemented but await an imaginative entrepreneur to exploit them, once implementation has occurred – that is, once new factories have been erected or old ones enlarged – employment and population increase, the web of interpersonal communications is again extended and densened, the chances for invention and innovation are further enhanced, and the circular process continues, perhaps even at an accelerated pace, until diverted or hindered.

Components of the Model

As so far explained, this descriptive model suffers from glaring omissions and imprecisions, and from the other shortcomings commonly associated with high-order generalizations. However, only in rare circumstances can models pertaining to the past be explicit, and therefore 'the insight furnished by the simplest of models makes the effort involved in . . . more complicated theories economically unsound.'[24] Hence expansion of this capsuled theory is limited to examination of the single

components presented, identification of additional impetuses to the circular and cumulative process, and, most important, introduction of the ambivalent forces that influence the selective growth of cities.

The Multiplier Effect

To avoid unnecessary rigidities in our hypothesized process of urban-size growth, the multiplier has been defined rather vaguely. Little controversy can result from an assertion that the multiplier is not a constant, that it varies from industry to industry, and from place to place and time to time within a single industry.[25] However, any implication that *all* new or expanded industrial activities generated some multiplier effect in the era from 1860 to 1910 is open to immediate contention.

The original expositions on the multiplier emphasized solely the effect of investment in the capital-goods industries on employment in other sectors of the economy.[26] Later, others independently developed a modified and broadened version, the basic/nonbasic ratio, and maintained that export (basic or city-forming) industries were the primary determinants of regional and urban growth.[27] If this is the case, how can the association of a multiplier effect with all new manufacturing be rationalized? For one thing: 'There is no reason to believe that exports are the sole or even the most important autonomous variable determining regional [or urban] income.'[28] In fact, it has been empirically demonstrated that local-market industries, by perpetuating income flow within the city, further generate income and hence development.[29] Secondly, a multiplier effect restricted to export industries would often suppress the development-instigating qualities of local industries that provide inputs for the exporters. Or factories might shift from producing exclusively for local consumption to serving a more extensive area.[30] Further support for dispensing with the basic/nonbasic distinction, and for conceding some multiplier effect to virtually all new manufacturing, may be gained from the common argument that the importance of exports dwindles as the economic unit (metropolis) grows in area and population. Finally, one may point to the somewhat mercantilistic observation that 'a city may also grow by purchasing something locally that it has previously imported.'[31]

Thresholds and the Urban Hierarchy

As employed here, the threshold concept may be interpreted as an economic phenomenon. A threshold is the minimum population or volume of sales required to support a new factory or an addition to existing facilities; and until the city attains this demand level, it must import the industry's products from a more complex center. However, thresholds may also be placed in a sociological context; that is, new industrial capacity is created through a sequence of events determined by a locality's 'dominant value system' and initiated 'when elements in the population express a dissatisfaction with industrial productivity.'[32] In either case it is obvious that ease of entry into the market varies enormously from industry to industry. Both modes of thinking, until modified by the introduction of the question of selective urban growth, are consistent with Weber's assumption that small production units will agglomerate whenever the minimum requirements for a larger scale of production are satisfied.[33]

It might legitimately be asked what evidence supports the theoretical interconnection (implied in the model and logically derived from Lösch and Christaller) between city size and the fulfillment of a succession of market thresholds. The evidence available, though far from definitive, is not inconsiderable. The measurement in American cities of minimum requirements, or 'k' values (the minimum percentage of economic activity in a particular industry in all cities of a given size), has revealed that manufacturing categories infrequently encountered 'in small cities become more or less ubiquitous in large cities.'[34] Rodgers' diversification index demonstrates that the diversity of manufacturing in metropolitan areas is to some degree a function of population,[35] and Beckmann[36] has shown the rank-size concept to be compatible with the idea of an urban-centered hierarchy of market areas. All this is not tantamount to saying that industries are only market oriented; nor does it follow that similar-sized metropolises will have nearly identical manufacturing structures, for no two centers are likely to possess equivalent initial advantages for the same industries.[37]

Invention and Innovation

The number of applications registered in the United States Patent Office skyrocketed from 120,000 before 1870 to more than a million by 1910, and most of these requests were of urban origin. Although this simple fact grossly substantiates the role of inventiveness in encouraging urban-industrial growth, one step further should be taken. Since the model implies that a multiplication of personal contacts and the importation of nonlocal skills and knowledge were fundamental to

urban-size growth, and since a good part of American urban growth from 1860 to 1910 was the consequence of a great influx of European migrants and an 'urban implosion' of the domestic rural population (brought about by agricultural surpluses, the downfall of rural population manufactures, and 'the lure of the city'), it is critical to emphasize that *knowledge of the labor market and destinations of previous migrants are two of the most important determinants of individual migration decisions.*[38] It follows logically that new industries and their multiplier effects created the employment opportunities which attracted migrants to the infant metropolises, and eventually led to additional manufacturing growth through the enhanced possibility of invention and innovation and the attainment of new market thresholds. Migrants, such as Pittsburgh's British and Dutch glassmakers and St. Louis' German brewers, often introduced new industries to the larger cities; and not infrequently 'the larger and better established industrial centers' proved to be the most fertile 'germinating grounds for new industries.'[39]

The increasing complexity of the network of interpersonal communications does more than merely induce innovation within specialized industrial activities, because innovations usually constitute an addition to the existing repertory of know-how in a city. Put in slightly different terms, the communication-invention cycle of the model is validated by the fact that industrialization during the period under discussion 'was characterized by the introduction of a relatively small number of broadly similar productive processes to a large number of industries.'[40] Many production techniques could be converted with little or no adjustment from the manufacture of one commodity to that of another. The chain of linked innovations is vividly illustrated by 'the Leland, Faulconer and Norton Company (later the Cadillac Automobile Company) of Detroit, which was founded in 1890 as a producer of machine tools and special machinery, introduced machinery for producing bicycle gears during the brief heyday of the bicycle, switched to building gasoline engines for motor boats when the bicycle industry began to decline, and by 1902 had undertaken the production of automobile engines.'[41]

This last point also casts light on the anchoring of so-called 'footloose' industries in existing manufacturing complexes, and the further reinforcement of the hypothesized circular process of urban-size growth. Theoretically, the cost structure of footloose manufactures permits them to locate as economically in one area or city as in another. Since such industries generally serve a market area of vast or national dimensions, the fulfillment of local or regional thresholds is immaterial to economical operation. Therefore, the manufacture of special machinery, machine tools, and other products of high value per unit weight is likely to flourish at the place of invention, regardless of its size, though an already industrialized city is the most likely location of new technological conceptions. This line of reasoning regarding the adaptability of techniques and footloose industries is consistent with the traditional argument that additional opportunities for industrial specialization are associated with every increment in manufactural differentiation.[42] It should be added that the random inception of footloose manufactures is a major cause of dissimilar industrial structures among metropolises of similar size.

Finally, it is not to be inferred from the model that invention on the part of the laborer or the entrepreneur inevitably met with success and another round of job and investment opportunities. Innovators were constantly confronted with 'the appearance of equally good alternative solutions,' and few 'were fortunate to withstand the rigors of competition, substitution, technological obsolescence, and senescence.'[43] However, the model is not invalidated by these conditions; for its soundness rests on the successful materialization of only *some* inventions and newly introduced skills and ideas.

Additional Stimulants to Urban-Size Growth

A number of factors other than those already enumerated provided momentum to the circular and cumulative process of industrialization and urban-size growth. Although it is not feasible to catalogue them exhaustively, identification of the most important is almost mandatory.

Natural population increase is perhaps the most obvious omission. Although it is generally conceded that migration dominated metropolitan population growth in the late nineteenth century, it is undeniable that natural increase also contributed to the aggregate demand of the metropolis and the realization of higher thresholds. Barring emigration from the city, natural increase of itself would have generated some enlargement of food processing and other essential local industries.

Average wages per manufacturing employee in the United States rose from $378 in 1869 to $512 in 1909 (data in current dollars).[44] The absolute increase of wages and real buying power meant that with the passage of time the multiplier effect of most manufac-

turing increments became more extensive, and thereby the speed of urban-size growth was accelerated. Higher average levels of per capita consumption were particularly stimulating to the expansion of industries whose products had a high income elasticity of demand. The ramifications of higher average earnings were compounded by the fact that total family incomes were also being increased through the more widespread employment of women; that is, the female working force was increasing more rapidly than total employment.

The growth process may also be accelerated because all 'urban qualities which can be construed as providing external economies would seem in some measure to increase with size.'[45] In other words, the locational attraction exerted by external agglomeration economies (or localization and urbanization economies) increases functionally rather than arithmetically. Furthermore, since agglomeration diseconomies also mount and eventually become oppressive, external economies were of 'unique importance' in the period 1860-1910 to the urban concentration of manufacturing.[46] The multiplication of external economies at that time amounted to more than the benefits usually associated with more efficient interfirm communication and the sharing of facilities and urban 'social overhead capital.' Urban linkages and concentration were also the consequence of an increasing vertical disintegration of production and concomitant decreases in the locational influence of primary raw materials. As technology progressed there was a greater specialization of manufacturing functions, which often dictated locational proximity of successive stages of production.[47] This increasing interdependence was accompanied by an increasing complexity of inputs both of raw materials and of semifinished products, and a reduction in importance 'of any one material in the locational calculus.'[48] The advantages of urbanization economies and market accessibility were further enhanced by the establishment of higher freight rates on manufactured goods than on raw materials, and by the introduction, in the late 1890's, of cheap, easily transmitted electrical energy.

Finally, acceptance of an adaptive-adoptive dichotomy of locational processes provides additional insight into the size growth of cities. Two polar viewpoints exist: one affirms that economic activities rationally adopt themselves to the conditions of the society in which they exist (firms rationally locate in cities because of the size of the local market or the availability of localization and urbanization economics); the other asserts that activities react to their environment in ignorance, with the 'lucky ones' being adopted by the system.[49] In other words, the adaptive-adoptive dichotomy represents a conflict between purely random and economically rational forces. Acknowledgment of the concurrent operation of these two processes permits the addition of new productive capacity, with attendant multiplier effects and perpetuation of the circular and cumulative growth process, even before higher thresholds are attained or new innovations become economically sound. The long-term adoption or survival of some firms that have thus located purely by chance or in an effort to minimize their uncertainty (risk of input shortages is minimized in large metropolitan areas) is also a key to disparate industrial structures in metropolises of nearly equal size.

Selective Growth of Cities in Periods of Rapid Industrialization

If the circular and cumulative process of urban growth during rapid industrialization functioned flawlessly, and if all cities were isolated units not in market-area competition with one another, then every city would expand indefinitely, or at least as long as available natural resources permitted. However, between 1860 and 1910 some cities in the United States grew more rapidly and at the expense of others. Only a few attained supremacy in the urban hierarchy, others grew moderately, some became stultified and declined. Today's ten leading industrial centers had already been singled out by 1910 (Table 16.2), and although their individual importance has varied, as a group they continue to dominate the urban hierarchy.[50] Clearly then, within an interacting system of cities in an expanding space economy, the circular and cumulative growth process does not persist indefinitely for all places. A number of ambivalent forces simultaneously break the circuit of cumulative growth in some instances and precipitate the emergence of multi-million metropolises in others. The most conspicuous of these forces may be construed as geographical expressions of initial advantages.

Transport Improvements

Railroad developments probably had the most profound influence on the growth of some centers at the expense of others. Reductions in the price of transport inputs, and expansion and intensification of the railroad net, both brought many repercussions for the relative importance of American cities.

On a representative railroad innovations in motive power, carrying capacity, and operating procedure reduces average freight charges per ton-mile from 3.31 cents in 1865 to 0.70 cent in 1892.[51] Cheaper transport inputs 'meant a spreading out of critical isodapanes, and an opportunity to realize previously untapped scale economies – even in the absence of advances in production technology.'[52] This extension and enlargement of the firm's market area increased the feasibility of agglomeration and large-scale production (a tendency compounded by concurrent innovations in production technology), created the possibility of still further divisions of labor and mass-production economics, and increased the practicability of satisfying national and regional demands from a limited number of cities. Theoretically, then, *the spatial lengthening of production raised the threshold of some industries by increasing their minimum optimal scales of operation, and this, by extension, favored the growth of already efficiently producing centers over inefficient and nonproducing cities.* The occurrence of this phenomenon is crudely mirrored by an increase in the average length of railroad hauls from less than 110 miles per ton in 1882 to about 250 miles per ton in 1910,[53] and by the fact that some industries have historically not responded as quickly as others to regional redistributions of population and income; inertia, partly in the form of rising thresholds, reduced the locational mobility of some industries.[54]

Cheaper transport inputs presumably also worked to the advantage of cities with plants having large market areas. Diminished transport rates normally favor growth – with attendant multiplier effects – of the firm 'which already has a larger market area because of its lower marginal cost of production,' since 'the firm with a larger market area, and therefore more transport inputs, has its total costs reduced more by a lowering of transport rates than any of its competitors.'[55]

Efficient factories (cities) tended to be favored also by the expansion of the railroad net, and specifically by the spread of feeder lines. Feeder-line construction, like cheaper transport inputs, extended the market area of the producer, usually increased returns through scale economies, and restricted the growth of nonproducing cities by raising the threshold.

As transport improvements turned out to be more and more conducive to large-scale manufacturing, specialized production in a limited number of cities became to some extent self-generating. Large-scale production brought ton-mile or freight-volume economies to a firm, enabled still greater extension of its market area, and continued the accretion of initial advantages. Freight volume economies also accrued to cities as a whole, since ton-mile costs on railroads are usually a function of the total traffic per unit distance of track. Thus the availability of lower freight rates in a relatively few cities on the major trunk lines acted as an urbanization (agglomeration) economy and further diminished the importance of less favored points. The traffic volume radiating out of some cities grew so rapidly that as early as the eighties much railroad construction was in response to existing, rather than anticipated, demand.[56]

Large-scale production and specialized manufacturing agglomerations, and hence the growth of some cities at the expense of others, also gained impetus as it became apparent that railroad terminal and transshipment costs could be spread out by dividing them over increased distances. Realization of this cost relationship normally tended to promote a decrease in freight rates 'for long hauls in comparison with short hauls' and encouraged the 'movement of materials and products over longer distances.'[57] Terminal and transfer costs also contributed to the polarization of manufacturing activity around trunk-line terminals and major rail intersections by inspiring both the elimination of multiple transshipments of product mixes and the locational adjacency of successive stages of fabrication. The paramount importance of initial rail and terminal-facility advantages to urban-industrial growth is best exemplified by Chicago. In 1860 Chicago was a city of moderate size (Table 16.2), with about 5500 workers employed in industries that catered primarily to local markets. Within fifty years the industrial working force in the physically expanded metropolis had grown to more than 325,000, many of them in firms serving distant markets.[58] Chicago's phenomenal rise was foreshown by 1860, when the city had emerged as the nation's most important railroad center, a terminus for eleven trunk roads and twenty branch and feeder lines.

An expanded railroad net, decreasing freight tariffs, and lower volume rates also strengthened the initial advantages of efficient producers and added to their scale and external economies, by broadening possible supply areas and providing access to superior raw materials or semifinished goods. In effect, transport improvements permitted large producers, or agglomerations with low marginal outlays per unit of product, to usurp the potential raw-material consumption of non-producing cities and firms with higher production costs. In general, this ultimately resulted in a still larger scale of output, some multiplier effect, and additional growth of the favored city.

None of these repercussions of improved transportation can be divorced from the historical distinction between cities with superior, and those with inferior, trade routes. Traditionally, the selective growth of cities was interpreted almost entirely in terms of site and situation,[59] and this is understandable; for eight of today's ten most important industrial metropolises occupy superior Atlantic, Great Lakes, or Pacific coastal sites, and the remaining two, Pittsburgh and St. Louis, thrive at or near a strategic river confluence. However, site and situation fail to shed light on the *processes* underlying the selective growth of cities. As Dean[60] has pointed out, transport advances do not bring equal benefit to all existing routes but instead increase the relative importance of a few 'primary nodes' by precipitating either 'a radical change in the strategy of the flow of traffic' or 'an intensification in the utilization of certain routes and sites.' Radical changes in traffic media and prevailing routes certainly contributed to stunt the growth of New Orleans and Cincinnati (the fifth and sixth cities of the country in 1860[61]); on the other hand, intensified use of the route through the Hudson and Mohawk Valleys strengthened New York's dominance in the late nineteenth century. In short, by definition highly nodal points on superior routes offer better accessibility to materials and markets, and these favorable conditions are usually translated into scale and agglomeration economies, which in turn perpetuate growth and initial advantages. Finally, the theoretically critical importance of some nodal points is consistent with the fact that manufacturing growth in the United States from 1860 to 1910 was most marked in some of the already developed commercial, mercantile cities.

Agglomeration Economies and Reduction of Production Costs

Production innovations, like transport improvements, conferred advantages on a few cities rather than on all. Advances in American industrial technology during the period under discussion almost inevitably conduced diminished production outlays per unit. New machinery and new techniques also required large capital investment and an increase in the optimal size of operation. Thus the avalanche of innovations brought a tremendous impetus toward shifts in manufacturing scale and an attendant urban concentration of production, involving both the expansion of existing plants and the establishment of new facilities. The pronounced scale shifts in American manufacturing between 1860 and the outbreak of World War I were partly reflected by size of establishment. For example, the average establishment in 1860 had about nine employees and a product value of $13,420, as compared with more than twenty-five employees and nearly $88,000 product value in 1914. More revealing and imposing is the fact that, in 1914, 3819 out of 275,791 establishments accounted for 35.2 per cent of the nation's industrial wage earners and 48.6 per cent of the product.[62]

In Weberian terminology, the reduction or 'compression' of per unit production costs permitted a substitution of transport outlays for labor and other production outlays, and therefore prompted a greater extension of market areas than would have occurred if only transportation improvements had been present. Augmentation of market areas again promised the division of fixed costs over an increasing volume of production, which induced still larger optimal scales of production and higher thresholds.

Consequently, *technical innovations that yielded lower per unit production costs tended to favor growth and industrial agglomeration in those few cities which had originally initiated efficient production, and at the same time arrested the development of nonproducing and inefficient centers.* As thresholds reached higher and higher levels, the possibilities of entry into the market or expansion of existing facilities became confined to a smaller and smaller number of cities, and many functions shifted from lower-order to higher-order urban places. A study contemporary to these events described the decline of small-town industry in an area stretching from Detroit to Des Moines; and the disappearance of local machine shops, sawmills, flour mills, furniture workshops, and agricultural-implement manufacture was attributed partly to 'the substitution of production on a large scale.'[63] Except for anomalies due to competitive strategy, the area in which large-scale urban producers could theoretically eliminate less efficient establishments was limited only by the locus of points where their marginal production costs plus transport inputs equaled market price. For specific industries, detailed capabilities for market expansion can be put in the cost structure and relative location terms used to develop a typology of modern manufacturing flows.[64]

Since a single cost-reducing invention was often applicable to a number of industries, innovation bred innovation, and the vertical disintegration of production often compelled proximity of successive stages of production. And since, in addition, a sequence of lower prices and greater demand frequently accompanied production-cost decreases, it is easy to understand why metropolises with innovation-implementing entrepreneurs grew at the expense of lesser cities. In fact, it once again becomes clear that the scale and external economies associated with urban-industrial activities are not 'simply additive,' but 'multiplicative in a complex fashion.'[65]

It must be repeated that urban diseconomies also accumulated and eventually became oppressive to some types of industries. Nothing that has been said should be interpreted as meaning that advantages accrued indefinitely to the major metropolises. In the half century following 1860 urban diseconomies mounted — 'diseconomies engendered by rises in the cost of living and money wages, in the costs of local materials produced under conditions of diminishing returns, in time-cost and other costs of transportation, and in land values and rents.'[66] If it had not been for the continued accumulation of these diseconomies, and for the maturing of automotive transportation, new raw-material requirements, and regional population growth leading to the more widespread attainment of specific thresholds, it is probable that the ten largest industrial metropolises would account for even more than their present 37.5 per cent of national value added by manufacturing.

Relative Accessibility

Relative accessibility, here defined as the accessibility of a city to the population or market of the country as a whole,[67] also influences the selective growth of cities. In general, *transportation improvements and lower unit production costs work to the advantage of points with high accessibility as opposed to points with low accessibility.*[68] This is partly because, by definition, low-accessibility areas have relatively small aggregate populations and incomes and consequently encounter difficulties in meeting scale thresholds for other than essential consumer goods. In addition, in serving a regional market of given sales volume, manufacturers in low-accessibility cities would have longer average shipments, and greater allocations for transport, than their counterparts in high-accessibility cities. The late-nineteenth-century low-accessibility firm, being in a comparatively undeveloped area, was probably further hampered by a small-mileage railroad network with few connections and intersections.[69]

Despite these handicaps, some large metropolises should eventually arise in low-accessibility areas, even in the absence of the mass population shifts that have been characteristic of the United States in the twentieth century. Large metropolises are not totally alien to low-accessibility areas, but their potential numbers are limited. Growth of urban centers in such areas is possible partly because transportation economies may be substituted for production diseconomies; that is, for some goods lower scales of production, and consequently higher unit costs, are compensated by avoidance of the trans-continental freight costs that would be incurred if the product were imported from high-accessibility cities. Expressed somewhat differently, a small number of low-accessibility cities can achieve metropolitan proportions because they are beyond the critical isodapanes of many market-oriented industries in high-accessibility centers, or, alternatively, because they are at great distances from cities with equal rank in the urban hierarchy. Regardless of these circumstances, the low-accessibility centers that do grow quickly during periods of rapid industrialization, like the corresponding cities in older high-accessibility areas, almost invariably possess some pertinent initial advantages.

The influence of relative accessibility on American urban development in the late nineteenth century is roughly indicated by Figures 16.2 and 16.3. In 1860 the four largest cities in the country, New York (including Brooklyn), Philadelphia, Baltimore, and Boston, were in the highest-accessibility area. By 1900 centers such as Chicago, St. Louis, Cleveland, and Detroit had achieved large populations, though they were not in the area of highest accessibility. Agricultural development of the Midwest and the Great Plains, as well as urban-industrial growth itself, had created levels of accessibility between the Mississippi and the northern Appalachians that far exceeded those of any of the Atlantic Coast cities in 1860. The steady growth of the older eastern metropolises (Table 16.2) is understandable in the light of the more than doubling of their accessibility during the forty years. By the same token, no city on the low-accessibility Pacific Coast, including San Francisco and Los Angeles, had grown to the size of the largest midwestern and eastern cities, though the rise of the two had been impressive.

Combination and Competition

The growth of trusts and mammoth corporations, the vertical and horizontal integration of previously independent firms, and the consolidation of small railroads into vast systems also had ramifications that confirmed the ascendancy of a few cities at the expense of others. The previously cited size-of-establishment statistics provide only an inkling of the combination activity that gathered momentum after business recovered from the panic and depression of the seventies. The proliferation of limited-divident manufacturing corporations, almost nonexistent in manufacturing in 1860 and numbering more than forty thousand in 1900, was another manifestation of the increasing concentration of industrial capital. Limited-divident corporations 'comprised barely a tenth of all establishments, [but] they produced 60 per cent of the value, and almost completely dominated the metal and technical branches.'[70]

Although risk and other factors sometimes prevented response to small local demands and prompted dependence on larger producers in big cities, the consequences of corporate manufacturing were particularly far-reaching in the industries with distribution to a large regional or national market. In such industries excess-profit taking and the strategies of oligopolistic competition often prevented the appearance of new plants when minimum thresholds were fulfilled, and hence reality ran counter to Lösch's idealistic equilibrium conditions. In other words, the piratical competitive strategies of a few industrial giants frequently hindered entry into the market and generally favored the growth of producing cities to the detriment of inefficient and nonproducing centers. Moreover, it was often possible under oligopolistic competition that no single corporation could monopolize threshold markets in the South and West, and therefore exploitation of the threshold of scale economies was occasionally restricted to producers in the somewhat older, high-accessibility cities in the Manufacturing Belt.[71] As consolidation sometimes limited production in such industries to a handful of plants, and as opportunity costs, or even chance or entrepreneurial whim, sometimes determined locational decisions within the older industrialized area of the country, it is still more comprehensible that similar-sized metropolises have asymmetrical manufacturing structures.

Preferential and discriminatory freight rates were an important by-product of railroad combination and competition, and they too had repercussions on the selective growth of cities. In spite of the formation of the Interstate Commerce Commission in 1887, it was some decades before discriminatory rates began to be abolished on a wide scale. Throughout the period under discussion, below-average unit cost and below-operating-cost freight rates were not uncommon. Deficits were recouped on noncompetitive commodities and in areas where rivalry was lacking.

In general, rates were most propitious for terminal cities within 'Official Territory' (a rate zone that

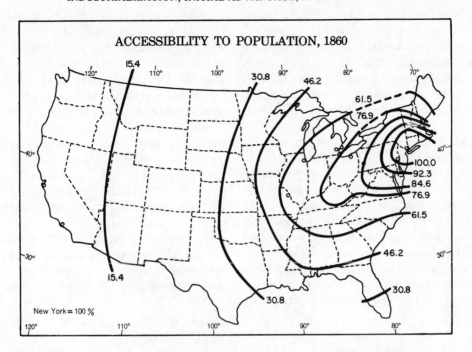

Figure 16.2 Accessibility to population, 1860. Adapted from John Q. Stewart and William Warntz: Macrogeography and Social Science, *Geogr. Rev.,* Vol. 48, 1958, pp. 167-184, Fig. 7 (p. 181).

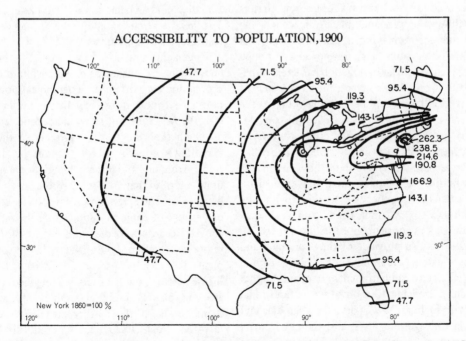

Figure 16.3 Accessibility to population, 1900. Adapted from Stewart, Empirical Mathematical Rules Concerning the Distribution . . . Population [see text footnote 67 for reference] , Fig. 11 (p. 479).

included the first eight cities in Table 16.2). Rates were low for raw materials coming into the territory and high for goods manufactured outside it, and this arrangement 'undoubtedly discouraged and retarded the diffusion of manufactures into outlying regions.'[72] Typically, for a time, the 'railroads west of Chicago followed the general policy of maintaining, as their share of all through tariffs, the rate charged for the transportation of products from interior points to Chicago or from Chicago to interior points.'[73] This policy inevitably reduced through traffic and promoted manufacturing and other economic activities in the metropolis. In fact, for all benefiting cities, discriminatory rates had the tumbling-domino effect of lessening the significance of distance, of permitting greater scale economies and multiplier effects through a widening of the market, of generating higher thresholds for nonproducing centers, of eliminating small-scale inefficient competition, and of perpetuating the circular and cumulative size-growth process.

Availability of Labor and Capital

The external economies of labor and capital availability also operated as initial advantages favoring the growth of existing commercial foci over smaller places.

Many new or expanding industries may be viewed as having minimum labor as well as market thresholds. Therefore, older commercial and manufacturing centers were often the most probable places in which the undecided entrepreneur, making a marginal locational decision, would seek skills and manpower. Although semiskilled and unskilled labor might have been duplicated fairly easily from place to place, the significance of the size of the local labor pool became magnified as the average size of establishment increased. The singular advantages of established industrial cities were even more pronounced with respect to skilled labor; for location or expansion elsewhere put the firm in the dilemma of finding 'a labor market big enough to provide an adequate number of workers with the necessary aptitudes' or resigning itself 'to a prolonged training period for a major segment of its labor force.'[74]

Capital availability (a province of the economist and only cursorily treated here) and knowledge of capital outlets were crucial to industrial entrepreneurs. Capital was more readily available to innovators in traditional banking capitals such as New York, Philadelphia, and Boston, and in Chicago and St. Louis, the new central reserve cities created by law in 1887. The diffusion of knowledge regarding investment opportunities was most efficient in these and other centers, such as Cleveland, Detroit, and San Francisco, where the lines of commercial communication were of comparatively long standing. It follows that these few cities exerted a strong attraction on the undecided marginal locator, and that the chances for a new round of growth in smaller places were correspondingly diminished. As the size of the capital-goods sector became more important vis-à-vis the consumer-goods sector,[75] capital availability also became more important, since, on the whole, 'the food and clothing industries need less capital to build and equip their factories . . . than such industries as iron, steel and engineering.'[76] According to the logic of the circular and cumulative growth model, investment in new or expanded capital-goods factories created additional local capital outlets, since the multiplier effects of these new facilities called forth a greater demand for ubiquitous industries and tertiary activities.[77]

Other Considerations

The compilation of an encyclopedic roster of other factors and initial advantages affecting selective urban growth is hardly feasible, for the fabric of reality is woven of an infinitely complex warp and woof. Moreover, to go beyond the vital and most conspicuous, to interpret imprecisely the plethora of apparently irrelevant minutiae, would be to indulge in unnecessary turgidity, and to becloud the vivid pattern of that fabric. The enumeration of additional influences is therefore restricted to a minimum.

The achievement of a given threshold, and the consequent establishment or expansion of equal scales of production in different geographical locales, are not normally followed by exactly equivalent patterns of growth. All cities and firms are unique, and the manner in which their singularities interact in the circular and cumulative growth process cannot be duplicated like prints from a lithographic plate. Some plants expand more rapidly than others in the same industry, either because of entrepreneurial aggressiveness and ingenuity or because of some permutation of the factors discussed above. Because variable rates of establishment growth imply variable multiplier effects, the selective growth of plants is logically both an instigator and a corollary of the selective growth of cities. Not uncommonly, faster-growing plants obtain economics of scale that allow them to usurp the market area of slowly expanding factories. Such a sequence of events likewise tends to favor some cities at the expense of others. Different rates of plant growth also contribute to the dissimilar industrial structures of multimillion metropolises.

The circular and cumulative growth of smaller cities with limited initial advantages is often, but not always, impeded and short-circuited because their new or enlarged manufacturing does not have a multiplier effect capable of drawing a train of higher thresholds and new innovations. When such stagnancy occurs, many local demands must be satisfied with goods produced in regional and national metropolises whose growth is unobstructed.

Finally, no inquiry into the growth of some cities at the expense of others would be complete without passing mention of the part played by factor immobility. Because management is more prone to augment existing facilities than to relocate where large initial capital expenditures would be necessary, 'the ability of a locality to hold an industry greatly exceeds its original ability to attract.'[78] On a grander scale, large cities themselves 'are much less subject to relocation than are individual units of production.' This is because 'the accumulated fixed investments of an urban mass in conjunction with its vested social institutions entail major geographic immobilities and rigidities.'[79] These immobilities, as much as any other factor, lie at the crux of initial advantage.

The evolution of a system of cities in the United States, and of a disproportionate concentration of manufacturing in the highest-order centers of that system, has been, and continues to be, a process of fog-enshrouded and gigantic complexity. No pretense to originality is made for any of the ideas presented here, though it is hoped that their juxtaposition gives them new ramifications. Nor is it argued that the logical cement holding these eclectic conceptual bricks together is flawless, lacking in conjecture, uncontroversial, or unrepetitious. It is also conceded that there are numerous other shortcomings. Historical intricacies have been impressionistically sketched in an over-simplified manner; business cycles and other contingencies are unmentioned; the empirical evidence presented is minimal; the roles of capital, the entrepreneur, migration, and tertiary activities have been underplayed; the intra-urban locational shifts of manufacturing that accompanied the growth of cities are ignored;[80] and no parallel is drawn with the experience of West European countries that also underwent rapid urbanization and industrialization within a framework of capitalistic institutions.

Although these and other criticisms are justifiable, it should be acknowledged that broad generalizations always have their imperfections, exceptions, and drawbacks, and that the countless interlocking pieces of the locational mosaic are not easily reassembled in verbal abstractions.

Notes

1 Some of the more cogent statements concerning the interrelationships between urbanization and industrialization in the United States are contained in Eric E. Lampard: The History of Cities in the Economically Advanced Areas, *Econ. Development and Cultural Change*, Vol. 3, 1954-1955, pp. 81-136; and in R.D. McKenzie: The Rise of Metropolitan Communities, *in* Recent Social Trends in the United States: Report of the President's Research Committee on Social Trends (2 vols.: New York and London, 1933), Vol. 1, pp. 443-496.

2 The bonds between urban and manufacturing expansion are obviously less pronounced in non-Western societies. For statistical comparisons see Thomas O. Wilkinson: Urban Structure and Industrialization, *Amer. Sociol. Rev.*, Vol. 25, 1960, pp. 356-363.

3 Based on *1961 Annual Survey of Manufactures* and 'Census of Population: 1960,' Vol. 1, Part A, pp. 1-66 and 1-67 (Table 28) (U.S. Bureau of the Census, Washington, D.C., 1962 and 1961 respectively).

4 This is not to imply that the spatial aspects of economic growth have been totally ignored. For some of the efforts in this area see Lampard, *op. cit.* [see footnote 1 above]; Wolfgang Stolper: Spatial Order and the Economic Growth of Cities, *Econ. Development and Cultural Change,* Vol. 3, 1954-1955, pp. 137-146; John R.P. Friedmann: Locational Aspects of Economic Development, *Land Economics,* Vol. 32, 1956, pp. 213-227; Walter Isard: Location and Space-Economy ([Cambridge, Mass.] New York and London, 1956), pp. 1-23; and Benjamin Chinitz: The Effect of Transportation Forms on Regional Economic Growth, *Traffic Quart.,* Vol. 14, 1960, pp. 129-142.

5 Albert O. Hirschman: The Strategy of Economic Development (Yale Studies in Economics, No. 10; New Haven, 1958), p. 58.

6 Alexander Gerschenkron: City Economics – Then and Now, *in* The Historian and the City (edited by Oscar Handlin and John Burchard; Cambridge, Mass., 1963), pp. 56-62; reference on p. 58.

7 See, for example, Richard L. Morrill: The Development of Spatial Distributions of Towns in Sweden: An Historical-Predictive Approach, *Annals Assn. of*

Amer. Geogrs., Vol. 53, 1963, pp. 1-14.

8 See Edward L. Ullman: Regional Development and the Geography of Concentration, *Papers and Proc. Regional Science Assn.,* Vol. 4 (Fourth Annual Meeting, 1957), Philadelphia, 1958, pp. 179-198.

9 Gunnar Myrdal: Rich Lands and Poor (World Perspectives, Vol. 16; New York, 1957), p. 13. For related statements on cumulative growth and initial advantage see Bertil Ohlin: Interregional and International Trade (Harvard Economic Studies, Vol. 39; Cambridge, Mass., 1933), pp. 235-236; Harvey S. Perloff and others: Regions, Resources, and Economic Growth (Baltimore, 1960), p. 82; and Joseph A. Schumpeter: The Theory of Economic Development (translated by Redvers Opie; new printing; New York, 1961, pp. 9 and 64).

10 The importance of manufacturing is merely subordinated, not completely replaced, once business, service, and professional activities have become the principal stimulus to metropolitan growth. Although significant, the mechanisms through which tertiary activities induce the growth of some cities and not others are not treated in this paper. Presumably, tertiary activities play an important role even when the industrial sector dominates the urban-growth process.

11 Lampard, *op. cit.* [see note 1 above], p. 121.

12 Edward Chase Kirkland: Men, Cities and Transportation: A Study in New England History 1820-1900 (2 vols.: Cambridge, Mass., 1948), Vol. 2, p. 268.

13 W.W. Rostow: The Stages of Economic Growth (Cambridge, England, 1960), p. 59.

14 'It has been estimated that in 1860 the value of manufactured goods in each of the three leading countries, the United Kingdom, France, and Germany, was greater than in the United States. By 1890 the United States had not only moved into first place, but the value of its manufactures nearly equaled the combined output of the three former leaders' (L.C.A. Knowles: Economic Development in the Nineteenth Century [London School of Economics and Political Science Monographs: Studies in Economics and Political Science, No. 109; London, 1932], p. 201). See also George Rogers Taylor and Irene D. Neu: The American Railroad Network 1861-1890 (Cambridge, Mass., 1956), p. 1.

15 Victor S. Clark: History of Manufactures in the United States (3 vols.; New York, 1929), Vol. 2, p. 6.

16 Blake McKelvey: The Urbanization of America (1860-1915) (New Brunswick, N.J., 1963), p. 45.

17 See the vast collection of data in H. Dewey Anderson and Percy E. Davidson: Occupational Trends in the United States (Stanford University, 1940). McKelvey, although arguing that manufacturing was the principal urban-growth stimulus until a date beyond the turn of the.century, points out that after 1890 most large industrial cities began 'to show a more rapid increase in tradesmen and white-collar workers than in factory hands' (*op. cit.* [see note 1 above], pp. 50-51).

18 McKenzie, *op. cit.* [see note 1 above], p. 493. McLaughlin noted that the rate of manufacturing growth in most industrial metropolises had slumped by 1919 (Glenn E. McLaughlin: Growth of American Manufacturing Areas [University of Pittsburg, Bureau of Business Research Monographs, No. 7; Pittsburgh, 1938], pp. 203-204).

19 Although the role of the railroad as an initiator of economic growth has recently been a subject of contention, even the skeptics are willing to grant that the part it played was most dramatic in the era immediately following the Civil War. See Paul H. Cootner: The Role of the Railroads in United States Economic Growth, *Journ. of Econ. History,* Vol. 23, 1963, pp. 477-521; Leland H. Jenks: Railroads as an Economic Force in American Development, *ibid.,* Vol. 4, 1944, pp. 1-20; and Taylor and Neu. *op. cit.* [see note 14 above].

20 Brian J.L. Berry and William L. Garrison: A Note on Central Place Theory and the Range of a Good, *Econ. Geogr.,* Vol. 34, 1958, pp. 304-311; reference on p. 311.

21 For specific related statements on the cumulative effect of new manufacturing on regional rather than urban growth see Myrdal, *op. cit.* [see note 9 above], pp. 23-26; and Perloff and others, *op. cit.* [see note 9 above] pp. 94-96. Note also H[ans]Carol: Die Entwicklung der Stadt Zürich zur Metropole der Schweiz, *Geogr. Rundschau,* Vol. 5, 1953, pp. 304-307, and observations on the effect of industrial growth 'on the size of local industrial populations' in E.A. Wrigley: Industrial Growth and Population Change (Cambridge, England, 1961).

22 For a discussion of urban growth and the flow of ideas see Richard L. Meier: A Communications Theory of Urban Growth (Cambridge, Mass., 1962). See also Torsten Hägerstrand: The Propagation of Innovation Waves, *Land Studies in Geography,* Ser. B. Human Geography, No. 4, 1952, and the review of the diffusion literature in Everett M. Rogers: Dif-

fusion of Innovations (New York, 1962). The mechanisms by which innovations are spread must have operated with particular efficiency in late-nineteenth-century American urban environments, which were characterized by relatively small and cohesive built-up areas and a close relationship between place of work and place of residence.

23 *Op. cit.* [see note 9 above].

24 Cootner, *op. cit.* [see note 19 above], p. 478.

25 'The time element is important because technology and organization influencing activity interaction within any given industry is subject to change ...' (Perloff and others, *op. cit.* [see note 9 above], p. 94). See also Walter Isard: Methods of Regional Analysis ([Cambridge, Mass.] New York and London, 1960), p. 227.

26 John M. Keynes: The General Theory of Employment, Interest and Money (New York, 1936), pp. 113-131; and Richard F. Kahn: The Relation of Home Investment to Unemployment, *Econ. Journ.*, Vol. 41, 1931, pp. 173-198.

27 See, for example, Douglass C. North: Location Theory and Regional Economic Growth, *Journ. of Polit. Economy*, Vol. 63, 1955, pp. 243-258; and Gunnar Alexandersson: The Industrial Structure of American Cities (Lincoln, Nebr., and Stockholm, 1956), pp. 15-17.

28 Charles M. Tiebout: Exports and Regional Economic Growth, *Journ. of Polit. Economy,* Vol. 64, 1956, pp. 160-164 and 169; reference on p. 161.

29 Ralph W. Pfouts: An Empirical Testing of the Economic Base Theory, *Journ. Amer. Inst. of Planners*, Vol. 23, 1957, pp. 64-69. As a case in point, Los Angeles' manufacturing growth before World War I was almost wholly confined to industries producing for a virtually local market.

30 Industries catering to purely local or nonlocal markets are exceptional. For further comments and a review of the literature concerning the conceptual and technical difficulties of the economic base as a multiplier see Isard, Methods of Regional Analysis [see note 25 above], pp. 194-205.

31 Robert L. Steiner: Urban and Inter-Urban Economic Equilibrium, *Papers and Proc. Regional Science Assn.,* Vol. 1 (First Annual Meeting, 1954), 1955, pp. C1-C10; reference on p. C8.

32 Neil J. Smelser: Social Change in the Industrial Revolution (Chicago, 1954), p. 3; see also pp. 32-33 ff.

33 Alfred Weber: Alfred Weber's Theory of the Location of Industries: English Edition, With Introduction and Notes by Carl Joachim Friedrich (Chicago, 1929), p. 140.

34 Irving Morrisett: The Economic Structure of American Cities, *Papers and Proc. Regional Science Assn.,* Vol. 4 (Fourth Annual Meeting, 1957), Philadelphia, 1958, pp. 239-256; reference on p. 246. See also Edward L. Ullman and Michael F. Dacey: The Minimum Requirements Approach to the Urban Economic Base, *ibid.*, Vol. 6 (Sixth Annual Meeting, 1959), 1960, pp. 175-194.

35 Allan Rodgers: Some Aspects of Industrial Diversification in the United States, *Econ. Geogr.*, Vol. 33, 1957, pp. 16-30; reference on pp. 21-22. See also Otis Dudley Duncan and others: Metropolis and Region (Baltimore, 1960), pp. 15, 65, and 69.

36 Martin J. Beckmann: City Hierarchies and the Distribution of City Size, *Econ. Development and Cultural Change*, Vol. 6, 1957-1958, pp. 243-248.

37 Differences in manufacturing structure between cities in the same size group are further commented on later. See also Stolper, *op. cit.* [see note 4 above], especially p. 140.

38 See Esse Lövgren: The Geographical Mobility of Labour, *Geografiska Annaler*, Vol. 38, 1956, pp. 344-394, reference on p. 352; Morrill, *op. cit.* [see footnote 7 above] p. 13; and Torsten Hägerstrand: Migration and Area, *in* Migration in Sweden, *Land Studies in Geography*, Ser. B, Human Geography, No. 13, 1957, pp. 27-158, reference on p. 130. For an analysis of the voluminous literature relating industrialization, cityward migration, and migration theory see Allan Pred: The External Relations of Cities during 'Industrial Revolution,' *Univ. of Chicago, Dept. of Geogr., Research Paper No. 76,* 1962, pp. 57-68.

39 Edgar M. Hoover: The Location of Economic Activity (New York, Toronto, London, 1948), p. 176.

40 Nathan Rosenberg: Technological Change in the Machine Tool Industry, 1840-1910, *Journ. of Econ. History,* Vol. 23, 1963, pp. 414-443; reference on p. 422. Rosenberg also cites the recent literature that stresses the importance of technological change, as opposed to capital accumulation, in American economic growth.

41 *Ibid.*, pp. 442-443.

42 See Allyn Young: Increasing Returns and Economic Progress, *Econ. Journ.*, Vol. 38, 1928, pp. 527-542, reference on pp. 529-539; and Lampard, *op. cit.* [see

note 1 above], p. 99. See also subsequent comments in the present paper on vertical disintegration and linkages, and Simon Kuznets: Retardation of Industrial Growth, *Journ. of Econ. and Business History*, Vol. 1, 1929, pp. 534-560, especially p. 548.

43 Richard L. Meier: The Organization of Technological Innovation, *in* The Historian and the City [see note 6 above], pp. 74-83; reference on p. 76. The role played by entrepreneurs as implementers and initiators of innovations is not discussed in the present paper but is covered by Schumpeter, *op. cit.* [see note 9 above], and others.

44 Simon Kuznets, Ann Ratner Miller, and Richard A. Easterlin: Analyses of Economic Change ('Population Redistribution and Economic Growth: United States, 1870-1950,' Vol. 2). *Memoirs Amer. Philos. Soc.*, Vol. 51, 1960, p. 129. For a detailed breakdown of wage increases by industry and state see Clarence D. Long: Wages and Earnings in the United States, 1860-1890 (National Bureau of Economic Research Publs., General Ser. No. 67; New York, 1960).

45 Aaron Fleisher: The Economics of Urbanization, *in* The Historian and the City [see note 6 above], pp. 70-73; reference on p. 72. This contention is supported by Lösch's logic regarding the coincidence of market networks in regional metropolises (August Lösch: The Economics of Location [translated from the 2nd rev. edit. by William H. Woglom with the assistance of Wolfgang F. Stolper; New Haven and London, 1954], p. 77).

46 Shigeto Tsuru: The Economic Significance of Cities, *in* The Historian and the City [see note 6 above], pp. 44-55, especially p. 49.

47 See Lampard, *op. cit.* [see note 1 above], pp. 90-91; and George J. Stigler: The Division of Labor Is Limited by the Extent of the Market, *Journ. of Polit. Economy*, Vol. 59, 1951, pp. 185-193, reference on p. 192.

48 Raymond Vernon: Production and Distribution in the Large Metropolis, *Annals Amer. Acad. of Polit. and Soc. Science,* Vol. 314, 1957, pp. 15-29; reference on p. 20. See also comments by Friedmann, *op. cit.* [see note 4 above], pp. 222-227; and Norton Ginsburg: Natural Resources and Economic Development, *Annals Assn. of Amer. Geogrs.*, Vol. 47, 1957, pp. 197-212.

49 See Charles M. Tiebout: Location Theory, Empirical Evidence, and Economic Evolution, *Papers and Proc. Regional Science Assn.,* Vol. 3 (Third Annual Meeting, 1956), Philadelphia, 1957, pp. 74-86; and Armen A. Alchian: Uncertainty, Evolution, and Economic Theory, *Journ. of Polit. Economy,* Vol. 58, 1950, pp. 211-221.

50 See related remarks by Carl H. Madden in his 'On Some Indications of Stability in the Growth of Cities in the United States,' *Econ. Development and Cultural Change,* Vol. 4, 1955-1956, pp. 236-252, and 'Some Spatial Aspects of Urban Growth in the United States,' *ibid.,* pp. 371-387; and by McLaughlin, *op. cit.* [see note 18 above], pp. 193-251 (Chap. 5).

51 Figures refer to the New York Central and Hudson River Railroad. See Edward Atkinson: Productive Industry *in* The United States of America (edited by Nathanial Southgate Shaler; 2 vols; New York, 1894), Vol. 2, pp. 671-734; reference on p. 712.

52 Pred, *op. cit.* [see note 38 above], p. 31. 'Critical isodapanes' for a production site, or agglomeration point, refer to the locus encompassing all alternative production points at which the transport advantages, in terms of inputs and costs, are equal to, or less than, agglomeration or labor economies at the production site (or city).

53 Atkinson, *op. cit.* [see note 51 above], p. 708; 'Historical Statistics of the United States, Colonial Times to 1957' (U.S. Bureau of the Census, 1960), p. 431.

54 Kuznets, Miller, and Easterlin, *op. cit.* [see note 44 above], pp. 110-115.

55 Pred, *op. cit.* [see note 38 above], p. 38.

56 Jenks, *op. cit.* [see note 19 above], p. 15. Railroad freight traffic in the United States increased from 13 billion ton-miles in 1870 to 255 billion ton-miles in 1910 (Arthur F. Burns: Production Trends in the United States since 1870 [National Bureau of Economic Research Publs., No. 23; New York, 1934], pp. 302-303).

57 William Henry Dean, Jr.: The Theory of the Geographic Location of Economic Activities (Cambridge, Mass., 1938), p. 32.

58 [Eighth Census of the United States, 1860: Book 3] Manufactures (Washington, 1865), p. 87; Thirteenth Census of the United States, 1910: Vol. 10, Manufactures, 1909 (U.S. Bureau of the Census, Washington, 1913), p. 917. For a discussion of the impact of the railroads in the earlier decades of this expansion see Wyatt Winton Belcher: The Economic Rivalry between St. Louis and Chicago, 1850-1880 (Columbia University Studies in History, Economics and Public Law, No. 529; New York, 1947).

59 See, for example, Lawrence V. Roth: The Growth of

American Cities, *Geogr. Rev.*, Vol. 5, 1918, pp. 384-398.

60 Dean, *op. cit.* [see note 57 above], p. 41; see also pp. 35-38. Remarks on the evolution of 'high-priority' transport linkages and on the circular growth of transport demands and transport construction, and other useful ideas, are contained in Edward J. Taaffe, Richard L. Morrill, and Peter R. Gould: Transport Expansion in Underdeveloped Countries, *Geogr. Review.*, Vol. 53, 1963, pp. 503-529.

61 Brooklyn, which was the third-largest city in the United States in 1860, is here included with New York.

62 Isaac Lippincott: Economic Development of the United States (New York and London, 1922), pp. 476-477.

63 Adna Ferrin Weber: The Growth of Cities in the Nineteenth Century (Columbia University Studies in History, Economics and Public Law, Vol. 11; New York, 1899), p. 188, citing H.F. Fletcher: The Doom of the Small Town, *Forum*, Vol. 19, 1895, pp. 214-223.

64 Note subsequent comments on relative accessibility, and Allan Pred: Toward a Typology of Manufacturing Flows, *Geogr. Rev.,* Vol. 54, 1964, pp. 65-84.

65 Isard, Location and Space-Economy [see note 4 above], p. 188.

66 *Ibid.*, p. 183. Isard's statement does not specifically refer to the period 1860-1910, but it nonetheless applies to the conditions of that period.

67 Relative accessibility is measured in terms of population potential or market potential. See John Q. Stewart: Empirical Mathematical Rules Concerning the Distribution and Equilibrium of Population. *Geogr. Rev.*, Vol. 37, 1947, pp. 461-485; and Chauncy D. Harris: The Market as a Factor in the Localization of Industry in the United States, *Annals Assn. of Amer. Geogrs.*, Vol. 44, 1954, pp. 315-348.

68 It has been demonstrated that similar-sized cities 'with high accessibility tend to have higher levels of manufacturing activity than those with low accessibility' (Duncan and others, *op. cit.* [see note 35 above], p. 128). Alfred Weber was also cognizant of the relationship between population concentration and degree of industrial agglomeration (*op. cit.* [see note 33 above], p. 168).

69 Cf. K.J. Kansky: Structure of Transportation Networks, *Univ. of Chicago, Dept. of Geogr., Research Paper No. 84,* 1963, pp. 93-104 (Chap. 6).

70 McKelvey, *op. cit.* [see note 16 above], p. 41.

71 See Ullman, *op. cit.* [see note 8 above], pp. 186-187.

72 Perloff and others, *op. cit.* [see note 9 above], p. 219. See also Fletcher, *op. cit.* [see note 63 above], p. 219.

73 Belcher, *op. cit.* [see note 58 above], p. 198.

74 Martin Segal: Wages in the Metropolis (Cambridge, Mass., 1960), p. 20.

75 In 1860 the clothing, shoemaking, and food-processing industries were typically of primary importance in the manufacturing structure of most large cities, but by 1910 the metal-fabricating and machinery industries usually predominated.

76 W.G. Hoffmann: The Growth of Industrial Economies (translated from the German by W.O. Henderson and W.H. Chaloner; Manchester, England, 1958), p. 38.

77 Obviously, investment in ubiquitous industries and tertiary activities 'has to be located where the demand is' (James S. Duesenberry: Some Aspects of the Theory of Economic Development, *Explorations in Entrepreneurial History*, Vol. 3, 1950-1951, pp. 63-102; reference on p. 97).

78 Ohlin, *op. cit.* [see note 9 above], p. 236.

79 Isard, Location and Space-Economy [see note 4 above]. p. 183.

80 The relationships between manufacturing growth and urban morphology are discussed in Allan R. Pred: The Intrametropolitan Location of American Manufacturing, *Annals Assn. of Amer. Geogrs.*, Vol. 54, 1964, pp. 165-180.

17 The Intra-Urban Movement of Manufacturing: A Markov Approach

by W. F. Lever

University of Glasgow

A recent view of models of urban growth and structure drew attention to the way in which they concentrated upon residential land use and retail location and to the relative absence of both static and dynamic models of industrial location at the intra-urban scale (Colenutt, 1970). Models of industrial location have most commonly dealt at the regional level with the criteria which determine the unique optimal location for a single plant and few have dealt with the spatial distribution of large numbers of manufacturing plants in aggregate (Pred, 1964). One result of this is that physical planners have often found it difficult to envisage what the total result of many separate decisions will be with respect to industrial land use needs. To meet this need a model has been developed to predict the likely future distribution of manufacturing plants within the Clydeside conurbation.

Decentralization of Manufacturing

The overall trend in the changing pattern of manufacturing location within urban areas has been one of decentralization. Older manufacturing areas in the city centres have been abandoned, converted to office space or warehousing, or cleared for re-use. At the same time suburban manufacturing has become commonplace. The reasons for this outward movement of manufacturing firms have been well described by Moses and Williamson (1967) and by Meyer, Kain and Wohl (1965) and need little reiteration here. Demand for space for manufacturing has increased considerably. As capital has been substituted for labour with increased automation, factories have needed to expand their floorspace (Tulpule, 1969). At the same time changes in handling techniques have created a widespread demand for single-storey premises. Increased demands for transport space, predominantly for car parking, office and landscaping have further increased the overall demand for manufacturing space. The scale of this increase in demand for industrial land was calculated by Best (1961) from development plans covering the period approximately from 1950 to 1975. The increases of 40 per cent in the county boroughs and 60 per cent in the large towns were almost twice as great as the increases in residential and recreational land use.

Such large demands for industrial space could not be met close to the city centre and only on the urban periphery were large sites in sufficient numbers to be found at reasonable rents. Just as planners realized the advantages of zoning land for manufacturing in the form of industrial estates on or near the urban periphery, so manufacturers realized the external economies they might derive from such locations. As these advantages were drawing firms to the periphery of cities, other factors were forcing them to leave the city centres. Increased road congestion began to cause high costs from 1950 onwards and access to city central stations was being replaced as a locational incentive by access to peripheral airports. The change from the clearance of sub-standard housing to the more comprehensive redevelopment of all land uses in and around the city centres was forcing firms to re-evaluate their central locations (Cameron and Johnson, 1969). Many found that the external economies available at the city centre were insufficient to outweigh the differential in rent between central and peripheral sites.

The Markov Process

While the outward movement of manufacturing establishments is an obvious feature of large urban areas in Britain, no model has been developed to predict how long the trend is likely to continue and what will be the most probable final result. Harvey (1967) has suggested that industrial location and relocation are probability processes and, consequently stochastic rather than deterministic models should be used in describing them. Of the range of stochastic models, those based upon the Markov process, and in particular the Markov chain model, seem most suitable to describe and predict industrial location at the intra-urban scale.

The Markov process is based on the assumption that the probability that any state s_i will occur in a time sequence at t_n is dependent upon the state of the system at t_{n-1} and independent of all other states of the system. The transition between the state of the system of t_{n-1} and the state of the system at t_n can be mathematically described as a set of probabilities arrayed in matrix form. Thus the distribution of manufacturing establishments in, say, 1969 is some function of their distribution in 1959 modified by some component of change which covers the intervening period.

The Markov chain forms one type of Markov process. It conforms to the same set of basic assumptions but has the added property that any state s_i occurring at time t in a particular sequence T, is independent of its position in that sequence. A Markov chain is therefore a Markov process with the additional condition of stationarity (Olsson and Gale, 1968). The condition of stationarity is only met if the matrix of transition probabilities does not change from one time period to the next. Thus, as Brown (1970) pointed out in a recent critical review of Markov chain models in movement research, studies of population migration which use Markov chains do not conform to the condition of stationarity because, with the gravity model implicit in the formulation of such models, the fastest growing towns are likely to attract migrants at an increasingly rapid rate (Anderson, 1954). There is reason to believe, however, that the process of industrial movement at the intra-urban scale does conform to the condition of stationarity. The attractive force of agglomeration economies is much less important at the intra-urban scale than at the regional or national scale so that concentrations of manufacturing within the city are unlikely to attract further establishments at an increasing rate (Richardson, 1969). At the same time, diseconomies resulting from increased spatial concentration of manufacturing, such as increased traffic costs from congestion and costs imposed by the scarcity of land for expansion, also support the hypothesis that the movement of manufacturing establishments does not conform to a gravity model and that the condition of stationarity demanded by the Markov chain model is not transgressed. Empirical evidence from the case study area, the Glasgow conurbation, is presented below to support the assumption of stationarity.

Brown (1970) also points out that the nature of the dynamic process being modelled affects the formulation of the Markov chain model. Strictly speaking, the Markov chain model should be applied only to the process of relocation where the number of elements in the system does not change between t and $t + 1$. Where the model is used to describe the process of contagion, as in studies of diffusion, or to describe differential growth rates, the model must be modified. As the

movement of manufacturing location within urban areas is a process of differential growth, the basic mover-stayer model must be elaborated to take account of differential rates of establishment creation and closure.

The operation of a Markov chain model of industrial location depends upon the definition of a set of mutually exclusive and comprehensive states, which in this instance will be spatial zones which do not overlap and which together comprise the whole of the urban area under study, and upon the definition of a set of probabilities that any manufacturing establishment will move between any two such zones within a fixed period of time. These transitional probabilities can be expressed in the form of a square transitional probability matrix (P) with the form

$$P = \begin{array}{c} a_1 \\ a_2 \\ a_3 \end{array} \begin{array}{ccc} a_1 & a_2 & a_3 \\ \begin{pmatrix} p_{11} & p_{12} & p_{13} \\ p_{21} & p_{22} & p_{23} \\ p_{31} & p_{32} & p_{33} \end{pmatrix} \end{array}$$

The value p_{21} in the matrix represents the probability that a unit, which in this case would be a manufacturing establishment, in zone a_2 at a point in time t, will be in zone a_1 at a later point in time $t + 1$ (Kemeny and Snell, 1960, 1962). The value p_{11} in the matrix represents the probability that a unit will remain in a_1 either by staying in the same place during the time period which extends from t to $t + 1$ or by moving only within a_1 during that time.

The states through which the system passes may be of three types and the values of p in the matrix define these three types. If every state can be entered from any other and the system can be left, the system is transient and the values of one or more horizontal lines in the matrix will total less than 1.0. If every state can be entered from any other but the system cannot be left, the system is ergodic. In this case the total value of every horizontal line will be 1.0. Thirdly, if one or more states are ergodic, the system is absorbing and in this case all the values except 1 on one or more horizontal lines will equal o and the value on the diagonal, $p_{11} \ldots p_{22} \ldots p_{33} \ldots p_{nn}$, will be 1.0. In the case of industrial movement the system is transient because it is theoretically possible for any manufacturing establishment to move from one zone to any other but the system can be left by the closure of the establishment. A method is demonstrated below, however, which converts the system to an ergodic one and which considerably simplifies the operation of the model.

Sources of Data

The main sources of data for the model were the Post Office postal directories of the greater Glasgow area for 1959, 1964 and 1969. Although these directories cover an area larger than the continuous built-up area of Glasgow, coverage of the physically separate towns such as Paisley, East Kilbride and Renfrew is incomplete and such towns were omitted from the survey. The area covered by the survey therefore comprises the city of Glasgow together with the contiguous towns of Barrhead, Clydebank, Bearsden, Milngavie, Bishopbriggs, Cambuslang and Rutherglen. To make the data easier to handle all manufacturing establishments were located on a 16 x 21 km square grid which is shown in Figure 17.1. The outer solid line effectively marks the limits of the continuous built-up area and the two gaps in the grid (D 15, E 15; K 8, K 9, L 8, M 8) represent the only kilometre squares which are completely without any urban development. The former represents Little Hill golf course and Springburn Park; the latter represents Pollok Grounds and Cow Glen golf course.

The Post Office postal directory distinguishes between manufacturing establishments, offices and establishments engaged in wholesaling and retailing. A comprehensive list of manufacturing establishments was drawn up and, after those establishments located outside the continuous built-up area had been eliminated, a 20 per cent sample was taken. As the establishments were listed first by type of manufacturing process and then alphabetically, the selection of the fifth, tenth, fifteenth, etc., establishments formed a stratified random sample of all establishments in which industries with five or more establishments were certain to be represented. In total, the sample yielded 419 firms which were then located on the kilometre square grid. Figure 17.1 shows the distribution of manufacturing establishments in the sample. The most striking feature of the diagram is the clustering of establishments in the central squares, H 12 and I 12, which together contain seventy-seven of the 419 firms. From this peak there is a steady decline in most directions until, on the urban fringe, there are large blocks of squares without a single establishment. Prominent among these are the two large housing estates of Drumchapel south-west of Milngavie and Castlemilk west of Cambuslang. The only major exception to this steady decline in firms with increasing distance from the city centre is square H 5 which has nineteen establishments. This square is almost wholly occupied by Hillington Industrial Estate which was established in 1936 and which in 1969 contained 113 establishments. Table 17.1

demonstrates how the number of sample establishments falls from 26.5/km^2 at the city centre to less than 0.4/km^2 at a radius of 6.5 km from the city centre.

For these purposes the centre of Glasgow is taken to be the intersection of gridlines H/1 and 12/13 which is the nearest intersection point to the land value peak (Diamond, 1962). At radii greater than 6.5 km, the kilometre-wide bands become too discontinuous to permit further calculations.

Typology of Manufacturing Firms and Definition of Zones

Although a proportion of the manufacturing establishments included in the sample were branch plants of national companies, the great majority (82 per cent) were locally owned single-plant companies. It is therefore not too misleading if the cumbersome term 'establishment' is from this point replace by 'firm'. The 419 firms in the 1969 sample were traced back to 1959 by using the Post Office directory for that year. The firms were then allocated to one of three categories. Two hundred and thirty-two firms occupied the same premises in both 1959 and 1969: thus 56 per cent of the firms could be called 'stayers'. Ninety-three firms moved from one location to another within greater Glasgow between 1959 and 1969: thus 22 per cent of the firms could be called 'movers'. Lastly, ninety-four firms in the 1969 sample could not be traced in the 1959 directory even when changes in name, in ownership or in company structure had been taken into account. These 'new' firms are of two types. There are some which were established spontaneously within the region and there are others which have moved into the region either as branch plants or less commonly as total relocations (*Board of Trade*, 1968). In some cases the directory records the previous location or head offices of these immigrant firms but, as it does not do so in all cases, all 'new' firms whether spontaneous or immigrant must be classified together. It is possible that under-recording in the 1959 directory would lead to firms being wrongly classified as new but a check in a different directory and subsequently with the Glasgow University Register of Manufacturing Establishments (Firn, 1970) revealed no such under-recording and this possibility was discounted.

Having made the distinction between stayers, movers and new firms, their different distributions can be used to define several concentric zones around the city centre. Figure 17.2 maps the distribution of kilometre squares in which stayers form a larger proportion of all firms than they do throughout the city as a whole. The

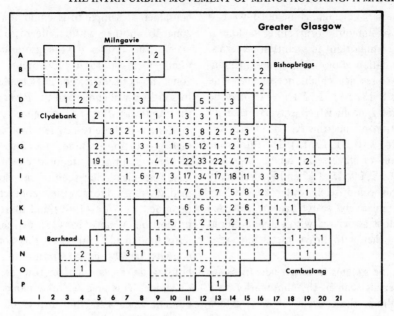

Figure 17.1 Distribution of sample firms, 1969

Table 17.1 The distribution of manufacturing establishments in the sample, 1969

Mean distance from city centre (km)	0.5	1.5	2.5	3.5	4.5	5.5	6.5
Establishments per km²	26.5	8.8	4.0	2.0	1.5	0.5	0.4

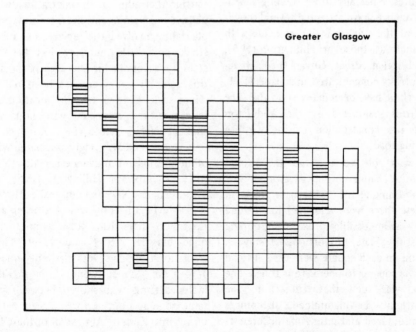

Figure 17.2 Grid squares with immobile firms, 1969

most distinct feature of the diagram is the north-west to south-east alignment of immobile firms along the line of the River Clyde. More important in quantitative terms, however, is the demarcation of our major zones differentiated by the relative presence or absence of immobile firms. Squares H 12, H 13, I 11, I 12 and I 13 may be identified as a central zone in which stayers make up only a small proportion of all firms (G 10, 11, 12, 13, 14; H 10, 14; I 10, 14; J 10, 11, 12, 13). The third zone has a high proportion of stayers and includes squares E 9, 10, 11, G 9, H 9, 15, I 9, 15, J 15 and K 15. Finally the remaining squares comprise an outer zone where immobile firms are relatively scarce except for two groups, one of which is associated with shipbuilding at Clydebank and the other with heavy metal industries north of Cambuslang.

Figure 17.3 maps the squares in which new firms are relatively more numerous than in the conurbation as a whole. This map is almost the converse of the previous one in that new firms are common in Zones 2 and 4 and relatively scarce in Zones 1 and 3. The absence of new firms from the city centre is a marked feature while several new housing areas such as Milngavie and Bishopbriggs in the north have attracted new industry.

Figure 17.4 maps those squares in which mover firms are relatively more numerous than in the conurbation as a whole. The patterns are less easy to discern than in Figures 17.2 and 17.3 but certain trends are apparent. The major radial routes, especially those running southwards from the city centre, have attracted several mover firms as have most of the squares which coincide with industrial estates such as those at Hillington (H 5), Balmore (D 12) and Helen Street, Govan (I 8). Movement in the city centre is concentrated in squares H 11, I 11 and I 12 where there have been many short-distance moves made by firms dislocated by the Anderston redevelopment and the construction of the western sector of the inner ring road.

Bourne (1969) was able to use the transitional probabilities of land-use change to identify groupings of intra-urban areal units among the 135 census tracts in Toronto. Because few firms were relocated in any one kilometre square, it was impossible to use this grouping technique in this study. The proportions of stayers, movers and new firms in each square were used instead to allocate each of the squares to one of four zones. The grouping procedure was such that, subject to the constraint that contiguity be maintained, differences within zones were minimized and inter-zone differences were maximized. No grid squares other than those which contained no sample firms could be transferred from one zone to another without decreasing inter-zone differences. The results of the grouping are presented in Figure 17.5 and Table 17.2. Figure 17.5 shows that the zones are concentric, but not circular, as the north-west to south-east alignment of the River Clyde is reflected in the elliptical pattern of the zones.

Zone 1 is the city centre which is characterized by a high proportion of immobile firms (69 per cent) many of them in printing, tailored clothing, guns and jewellery, the classic city-centre industries relying on immediacy of face-to-face contact with customers described by Wise (1949) and Martin (1964). The low proportion of new firms (12 per cent) shows how high rents have made entry into this zone difficult. Zone 2 consists largely of a mixture of industry and poor housing in areas such as Bridgeton, Cowcadens and Cessnock. This area has undergone widespread redevelopment since 1966 but many old industrial premises remain. The high proportions of movers and new firms in this zone reflect the shuffling around of small firms within the area and the relative cheapness of premises for new firms who need access to the city centre. Zone 3 is more mixed in character, containing some high class residential areas, older town centres such as Govan which have become incorporated within Glasgow, some poorer housing and some specialist land users such as Glasgow University and several hospitals. The area is outside the radius of the central roadworks and comprehensive redevelopment. Such redevelopment as has taken place has involved the replacement of obsolete housing stock and little industry has been displaced. This stability accounts for the high proportion of stayers in this zone. Where there has been redevelopment on a wider scale, as in Govan, the location of new firms and movers is often associated with industrial estates such as that at Helen Street (I 8). Zone 4 with its greater reserves of land is strongly associated with the attraction of new firms and movers especially to industrial estates such as those at Hillington (H 5), Balmore (D 12), Thornliebank (N 7) and Queenslie (H 19).

Table 17.3 lists by zone the origin and destination of the ninety-three firms in the sample who moved at least once between 1959 and 1969. There is a steady transition from a net loss of twenty-one firms from Zone 1 to a net gain of twenty firms in Zone 4. The Table includes firms who moved between points within the same zone accounting for the seemingly high number of moves into Zone 1. Almost all of these in-movers were in fact already located in Zone 1 in 1959. The largest single

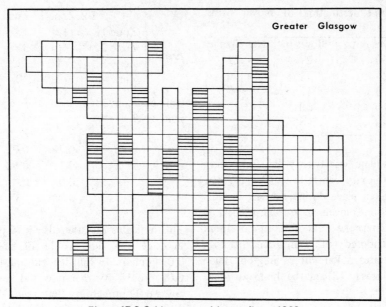

Figure 17.3 Grid squares with new firms, 1969

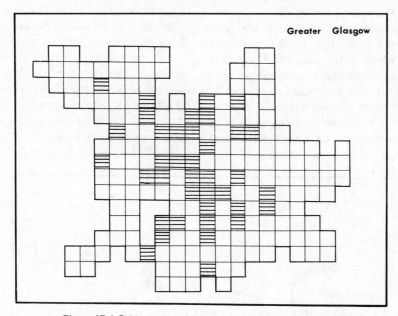

Figure 17.4 Grid squares with intra-urban migrant firms, 1969

Table 17.2 Types of firm by zone, 1969

	Movers	Per cent	New	Per cent	Stayers	Per cent
Zone 1	28	19	17	12	99	69
Zone 2	18	26	24	34	28	40
Zone 3	17	17	17	17	67	66
Zone 4	30	32	35	37	29	31
Older areas	0	0	1	10	9	90
Total	93	22	94	22	232	56

Table 17.3 Origin and destination of mover firms, 1959-69

	Moves out	Moves in	Net change
Zone 1	50	29	- 21
Zone 2	25	19	- 6
Zone 3	8	15	+ 7
Zone 4	10	30	+ 20
Total	93	93	

loss from any one square was twenty-one firms from H 12, the sector of the city centre in which most new office building has taken place during the last decade. The squares with a net out-movement are sharply peaked around this square whereas the areas of net in-movement are more widely distributed with some concentration upon (a) industrial estates at Balmore, Hillington, Helen Street and Dixon's Blazes (J 13) and (b) the major roads south of the city centre.

The Basic Closed Markov Chain Model

On the basis of the movement of these ninety-three firms, it is possible to provide values for the transitional probability matrix which is the basis of the Markov chain model. At first we treat this as a closed system in which the total number of firms remains fixed from t_0 to t_1. Although we are concerned with the movement of firms the stayers must be included on the top left to bottom right diagonal of the matrix. Thus the numerical matrix

$$From \begin{cases} & \text{To: Zone 1} \quad \text{Zone 2} \quad \text{Zone 3} \quad \text{Zone 4} \\ \text{Zone 1} & 118 \qquad 13 \qquad 4 \qquad 14 \\ \text{Zone 2} & 6 \qquad 33 \qquad 8 \qquad 6 \\ \text{Zone 3} & 1 \qquad 1 \qquad 68 \qquad 5 \\ \text{Zone 4} & 2 \qquad 0 \qquad 3 \qquad 43 \end{cases}$$

can be converted into the transitional probability matrix P:

$$P = \begin{array}{c} Z_1 \\ Z_2 \\ Z_3 \\ Z_4 \end{array} \begin{pmatrix} Z_1 & Z_2 & Z_3 & Z_4 \\ 0.79 & 0.09 & 0.03 & 0.09 \\ 0.11 & 0.63 & 0.15 & 0.11 \\ 0.01 & 0.01 & 0.91 & 0.07 \\ 0.04 & 0.00 & 0.06 & 0.90 \end{pmatrix}$$

This indicates that there is a 0.79 probability that a firm in Zone 1 in 1959 would still be in Zone 1 in 1969, a 0.09 probability that it would have moved to Zone 2, a 0.03 probability that it would have moved to Zone 3, and a 0.09 probability that it would have moved to Zone 4. As these four values total 1.00, the firm must occupy one, and only one, of the four zones in 1969. The high values on the diagonal show the high level of inertia in the system. In every case the probability is much greater that a firm will stay where it is than that it will move to another zone. The fact that the values below the diagonal are lower than those above it shows the overall outward trend in the movement of firms. The model, however, is not absorbing as there is some movement of firms towards the city centre.

In 1959 Zone 1 contained 46 per cent of all stayer

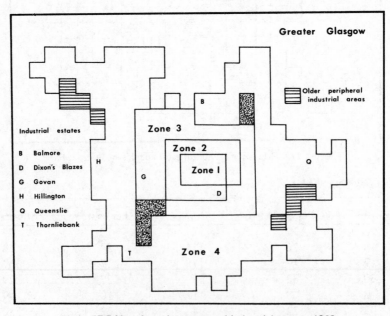

Figure 17.5 Manufacturing zones and industrial estates, 1969

and mover firms in the sample, Zone 2 had 16 per cent, Zone 3 had 23 per cent and Zone 4 had 15 per cent. These values can be expressed as a probability vector with the form

$$0) = (p_1(0), p_2(0), p_3(0), p_4(0)) = (0.46, 0.16, 0.23, 0.15)$$

Subsequent states of the system are predicted by multiplying this initial probability vector by the transition probability matrix.

$$p(1) = p(0)P = (0.39, 0.14, 0.26, 0.21)$$

Thus in terms of movers and stayers only in 1969 Zone 1 has 39 per cent of the firms, Zone 2 has 14 per cent, Zone 3 has 26 per cent and Zone 4 has 21 per cent. Successive states of the system at equal time intervals are generated by the following sequence:

$$p(2) = p(1)P; p(3) = p(2)P; p(4) = p(3)P \ldots$$

Table 17.4 lists the successive distributions of firms from t_0 to t_6 predicted by the model. Over the period $t_0 - t_6$ as a whole, the number of firms in Zone 1 declines by 54 per cent, in Zone 2 it declines by 50 per cent, in zone 3 it increases by 48 per cent and in Zone 4 it increases by 147 per cent. The decline in the number of firms in Zone 1 slows down from 1.4 per cent a year to 0.7 per cent a year in the later decades. The steady rate of outmigration of firms from Zone 2 is partially offset by the movement of firms from Zone 1. Both Zone 3 and Zone 4 gain firms at rates which gradually decrease. The rates of gain differ so that it is only after t_4 that Zone 4 contains more firms than Zone 3.

Table 17.4 Predicted distribution of firms: Model 1 (percentages)

	Zone 1	Zone 2	Zone 3	Zone 4
t_0 (1959)	46	16	23	15
t_1 (1969)	39	14	26	21
t_2	33	13	28	26
t_3	29	11	30	30
t_4	25	10	32	33
t_5	23	9	33	35
t_6	21	8	34	37

The slowing down in the rates of loss from Zones 1 and 2 and in the rates of gain by Zones 3 and 4 suggests that there is some stable end-state towards which the system is progressing. The limiting probability vector, $p(t)$ which holds the system in equilibrium can be obtained by solving a set of $m + I$ simultaneous equations where m is the number of states (zones). This solution is found to be: $p(t) = (0.16, 0.05, 0.39, 0.40)$,

and it follows that this limiting structure must satisfy the expression $p(t) = p(t)P$. The significant point about this equilibrium is that it is achieved irrespective of the original state of the system. The original distribution of firms is immaterial as only the transitional probabilities are used in calculating the unique limiting probability vector, $p(t)$. Thus the model predicts that stability of location of manufacturing firms will come when Zone 1 contains 16 per cent of all firms, Zone 2 has 5 per cent, Zone 3 has 39 per cent and Zone 4 had 40 per cent. At this point, the higher probability that some of the small number of central firms will move outwards is balanced by the lower probability that some of the large numbers of peripheral firms will move inwards. The end-state, therefore, does not imply that no firms will relocate within the urban area but that the proportion of firms in each zone will not change.

Conversion from a Closed to an Open System

Up to this point the model has been used as though it were a closed system in which the same firms present at t_0 are still there at t_1 when the system reaches equilibrium. In reality, however, there is an open system within which firms are created, firms go out of existence and firms move into and out of the region. One solution to the problem of the system's 'openness' was suggested by Blumen, Kogan and McCarthy (1955) in their study of labour mobility. They assumed that all incomers to the system were identical in every respect with those they replaced. While such an assumption is valid in the case of workers entering and leaving different types of industrial employment, it is certainly not valid in a study of manufacturing change where newly created firms are likely to be different (a) in number, (b) in industry, (c) in size, and (d) in location, from firms leaving the system either through death or relocation (Hart and Prais, 1956).

To close the system an additional state, here termed X to distinguish it from $Z_1 Z_2$, etc., must be created. Firms are assumed to leave this state when they are founded or move into the region and to move into it when they go out of business or move out of the region. From the first survey, data are already available on 'births' between 1959 and 1969 allocated to zones occupied in 1969. As the sample was drawn from firms in existence in 1969 it is clear that data on 'deaths' between 1959 and 1969 cannot be derived in this way. These data can, however, be provided by reversing the procedure, taking a 20 per cent sample of 1959 firms and tracing them in the 1969 directory, thereby identifying the firms which died in the interim and their location in 1959. A second numerical matrix can now be drawn.

	Z_1	Z_2	Z_3	Z_4	X
Z_1	118	13	4	14	63
Z_2	6	33	8	6	20
Z_3	1	1	68	5	24
Z_4	2	0	3	43	17
X	17	24	17	36	–

In this matrix, the bottom row represents the 1969 location of births and inmovers which are most common in Zone 4, and the right-hand column shows the 1959 location of deaths and out-movers which are most common in Zone 1. The bottom right-hand square of the matrix presents the problem of finding a meaningful value for the number of firms not in existence in 1959 which were also not in existence in 1969. Adelman (1958) provided mathematical proof that the size of the number of firms in X at t_0 does not affect the final prediction of the model and empirical proof is provided below. The value of X at t_0 is assumed to be 1000, this choice being guided by the desire to keep the source of new firms large in comparison with the number of those actually in being. The value 906 can therefore be placed in the right-hand square in order that the elements of the bottom row total 1000. The second transitional probability matrix is therefore

$$P = \begin{array}{c} \\ Z_1 \\ Z_2 \\ Z_3 \\ Z_4 \\ X \end{array} \begin{array}{ccccc} Z_1 & Z_2 & Z_3 & Z_4 & X \\ \left(\begin{array}{ccccc} 0.56 & 0.06 & 0.02 & 0.07 & 0.29 \\ 0.08 & 0.41 & 0.11 & 0.08 & 0.27 \\ 0.01 & 0.01 & 0.69 & 0.05 & 0.24 \\ 0.03 & 0.00 & 0.05 & 0.66 & 0.26 \\ 0.02 & 0.02 & 0.02 & 0.04 & 0.90 \end{array}\right) \end{array}$$

As the numbers of sample firms in the four zones in 1959 were 212, 73, 99 and 65 respectively and X has been arbitrarily given the value 1000, the initial probability vector, $p(0)$, is (0.147, 0.050, 0.068, 0.043, 0.692). To derive $p(1)$, the initial probability vector is multiplied by the transitional probability matrix $p(1) = p(0)P = (0.100, 0.047, 0.072, 0.073, 0.708)$. This can be interpreted that, of the 447 actual firms in existence in 1959 and the 1000 potential entrants in 1959-69, there is a 0.100 probability that a firm will be in Zone 1 in 1969, a 0.047 probability that it will be in Zone 2, a 0.072 probability that it will be in Zone 3, a 0.073 probability that it will be in Zone 4 and a 0.708 probability that it will not be in existence.

Table 17.5 lists the successive probability vectors $p(0)$, $p(1)$, etc., up to $p(8)$ which is found to be the terminal probability vector holding the system in equilibrium. In this case, $p(t)$ is found to be (0.049, 0.034, 0.080, 0.115, 0.722). Comparison between $p(0)$ and $p(t)$ shows that the values of Z_1 and Z_2 have declined, those of Z_3 and Z_4 have increased and, because deaths have outnumbered births, X has increased. At this point, X can be disregarded as the model is only concerned with those firms which are actually in existence, the proportions of which are given solely by the relative sizes of Z_1, Z_2, Z_3 and Z_4. Table 17.6 transforms these relative probabilities into percentages to show how the city centre rapidly loses firms both by death and outmigration so that, from containing 48 per cent of all firms in 1959, it declines to containing only 18 per cent of all firms at t_t. Zone 2 suffers a slow outward drift of firms with deaths only slightly outnumbering births and the proportion of firms declining from 16 per cent in 1959 to 12 per cent at t_t. Zone 3 had 22 per cent of the 1959 firms but by t_t this will have grown to 29 per cent. The really massive increase, however, is experienced by Zone 4 whose share rises from 14 per cent in 1959 to 41 per cent both through migration and through a substantial excess of births over deaths.

Criticism has been levelled at the use of Markov chain models for prediction because of the length of time taken to achieve the equilibrium state. In the model described here, t_t is found to be 2039 as equilibrium is reached after seven successive 10-year iterations of the model from 1969. It is arguable that predictions over such time periods are unlikely to have any real validity but, because the rates of growth or decline fall off over time, the system reaches a point half-way between the 1969 stage and equilibrium, not half-way between t_4 (1999) and t_5 (2009), but half-way between t_2 (1979) and t_3 (1989). Thus from the policymaker's point of view, it is important to realize not only what the final state of the system will be in 2039 but also that the most rapid changes will occur within the next decade.

In order to demonstrate that the arbitrary value assigned to X at t_0 has no effect on the model's predictions, the calculations were repeated with the initial value of X increased to 2000. Table 17.7 lists the successive proportions of firms in each of the four zones up to t_8 when equilibrium is reached. No value in the Table differs by more than one percentage point from the corresponding value in Table 17.6 and such minor differences may well be caused by rounding errors.

Table 17.5 Successive values of $p(n)$. Model II

	Zone 1	Zone 2	Zone 3	Zone 4	X
$p(0)$	0.147	0.050	0.068	0.043	0.692
$p(1)$	0.100	0.047	0.072	0.073	0.708
$p(2)$	0.077	0.043	0.075	0.090	0.715
$p(3)$	0.064	0.040	0.078	0.100	0.718
$p(4)$	0.057	0.038	0.078	0.105	0.721
$p(5)$	0.054	0.037	0.079	0.109	0.721
$p(6)$	0.051	0.035	0.080	0.112	0.722
$p(7)$	0.050	0.034	0.080	0.113	0.723
$p(8)$	0.049	0.034	0.080	0.115	0.722

Table 17.6 Predicted distribution of firms (percentage). Model II ($X = 1000$)

	Zone 1	Zone 2	Zone 3	Zone 4
t_0 (1959)	48	16	22	14
t_1 (1969)	34	16	25	25
t_2	27	15	26	32
t_3	23	14	28	35
t_4	20	14	28	38
t_5	19	14	28	39
t_6	18	13	29	40
t_7 (2029)	18	12	29	41
t_8 (t_t) (2039)	18	12	29	41

Table 17.7 Predicted distribution of firms (percentages). Model II ($X = 2000$)

	Zone 1	Zone 2	Zone 3	Zone 4
t_0 (1959)	48	16	22	14
t_1 (1969)	34	16	25	25
t_2	27	15	26	32
t_3	23	14	27*	36*
t_4	20	13*	28	39*
t_5	19	13*	28	40*
t_6	19*	12*	29	40
t_7	18	12	29	41
t_8 (t_t)	18	12	29	41

Note: *value differs from Table 17.6

Possible Changes in the Rates of Interzonal Transition

The importance of the condition of stationarity was stressed above and some general reasons why the process of industrial movement at the intra-urban scale should conform to this assumption were advanced. More detailed information from the Glasgow study is now offered to support this assumption which is basic to the use of a Markov chain model. Intuitively there are two

main reasons why the rates of interzonal movement might change, thereby conflicting with the assumption of stationarity. First, the removal of manufacturing firms from the city centre will free resources there which may in turn attract other firms, thereby slowing the rate of outward movement. Secondly, migration from the city centre may continue until all the firms who remain cannot move because they are engaged in industries which demand the city centre's uniquely accessible location.

The freed resources are largely in the form of buildings and labour as other resources such as capital and information either die with the firm or are easily transferred to another location. There was little evidence from the sample of firms that premises left vacant were reoccupied by new or mover firms. Of the seventy-five industrial premises vacated by mover firms and the eighty-three industrial premises vacated by the death of firms in Zones 1 and 2, only 3 per cent had been reoccupied by new or mover firms by 1969. Of course, if a 100 per cent survey had been made, the proportion of reoccupancies would have been greater but if the 20 per cent sample is representative a complete survey would have found only twenty-four reoccupancies per 158 vacancies (16 per cent) within the two central zones. This is not to suggest that the other 84 per cent of the buildings left by movers and dying firms remained vacant. Many were pulled down and their sites redeveloped for housing, offices or roads while others were converted to office space, warehousing or retail uses.

The labour freed by firms moving from the city centre is unlikely to attract other firms. Labour is increasingly mobile, the journey-to-work within cities is becoming longer and reverse commuting is becoming more common (Taaffe, Garner and Yates, 1963; Boyce, 1965). At the same time, the suburbanization of manufacturing is being matched by the outward movement of residence often as a result of central housing redevelopment. For example, Hutchesontown Gorbals held 27,000 people before redevelopment began in 1958 but the same site after redevelopment is completed will hold only about 11,000 people (*City of Glasgow Corporation*, 1960).

The argument that industries such as printing and clothing which traditionally have been located in the city centre cannot move outwards as they rely on immediacy of contact seems to suggest that, when a core of such firms is reached, emigration rates from the city centre will fall. Evidence from Hall's work on the New York Metropolitan Region (1959) confirms, however, that even these manufacturing processes can be moved out and only the service functions such as dress design need remain in the city centre. Even if the rate of out-movement in these industries is below average, this is compensated for by their higher-than-average death rates. In addition, Keeble (1969) has provided evidence that such industries as foodstuffs, chemicals and printing can move from city central locations, either abandoning central linkages and establishing new linkages at the peripheral sites or accepting the higher costs incurred by the increase in the length of linkages back to the city centre.

Empirical evidence for the period 1959-69 suggests that the transitional probabilities over this period remained stable although this is no guarantee that they will remain so. By using the 1964 directory it was possible to generate and compare separate transitional probability matrices for the periods 1959-64 and 1964-69. These were tested against matrices devised to conform with the assumption of stationarity. The X^2 test, developed for testing the similarity between transitional matrices by Anderson (1954) and Goodman (1962) was used and the expected and observed matrices were found to be similar at the 95 per cent level.

Implications of the Model's Prediction and Future Development

The model predicts that, within 30 years, the number of manufacturing firms in the city centre will have declined by more than half and the number in the current area of extensive redevelopment will have declined by a fifth. The number of firms in Zone 3 will have increased by 27 per cent and the number in the suburbs and on the urban fringe will have almost trebled. The decentralization of manufacturing on this scale has important implications especially for transport and physical planners. Large-scale shifts in the location of place of work will affect journey-to-work patterns. Existing public transport systems are usually nodal in character and, while it is possible to re-route public road transport to take account of the outward shift of jobs, other forms of transport such as surface rail and underground may be obsolescent. Secondly, the assumption of centrality of place of work is basic to several conceptual urban models. The idea, for example, that residential preference is based on a trade-off between rent, which is high near city centres because of access to place of work, and transport costs which are high near the urban periphery because of distance from place of work, may well need revision in light of the outward movement of manufac-

turing employment (Knos, 1968; Muth, 1969). If employment becomes peripheral while services remain central, rents, as a function of total accessibility, may level out across the urban area or even dip towards the city centre. Lastly, the increasing suburbanization of manufacturing industry will have important implications for city financing. Where the suburban areas lie outside the central city administrative area, as they do in Glasgow's case, rateable income will fall in the central city and rise in the surrounding towns and counties. This tendency will be intensified if central industry is replaced by such land uses as roads or public recreational space which do not directly earn revenue.

The simple Markov chain model developed here has been concerned only with predicting the distribution of manufacturing establishments in a single British conurbation. No allowance has been made for the increase in the average size of firms with increasing distance from the city centre (Goldberg, 1970). Had this been taken into account, the employment totals rather than the number of manufacturing establishments would have emphasized even further the process of suburbanization of manufacturing. The next development of the model as presented here may be the inclusion of data concerning the movement of establishments not only in space but between size classes. Markov models of this type have already been developed by Adelman (1958) and more recently by Norcliffe (1970). Multi-dimensional Markov models of the type required have been developed by Clark (1965) and by Olsson and Gale (1968). The combination of the spatial and size class Markov models would, if data were available, provide a more comprehensive method of predicting the location of manufacturing employment in urban areas.

Acknowledgements
This research project was carried out with the assistance of a research grant from the Social Science Research Council, which is gratefully acknowledged.

References

Adelman, I.G. (1958) 'A stochastic analysis of the size distribution of firms', *J. Am. statist. Ass.* 53, 893-904.

Anderson, T.W. (1954) 'Probability models for analyzing time changes in attitudes' in P.F. Lazarsfeld, *Mathematical thinking in the social sciences* (Glencoe).

Bartholomew, D.J. (1967) *Stochastic models for social processes.*

Best, R.H. (1961) 'The urbanization of Teesside', *Plann. Outl.* 3, 15-36.

Blumen, L.,M. Kogan and F.J. McCarthy (1955) *The industrial mobility of labour as a probability process.*

Board of Trade (1968) *The movement of manufacturing industry in the United Kingdom, 1945-65.*

Bourne, L.S. (1969) 'A spatial land-use conversion model of urban growth', *J. reg. Sci.* 9, 261-72.

Boyce, D.E. (1965) 'The effect of direction and length of person trips on urban travel patterns', *J. reg. Sci.* 6, 65-80.

Brown, L.A. (1963) 'The diffusion of innovation: a Markov chain approach', *Discussion Paper Ser. 3, North-western Univ., Dept of Geography.*

Brown, L.A. (1970) 'On the use of Markov chains in movement research', *Econ. Geogr.* 60 (Supplement), 393-403.

Cameron, G.C. and K.M. Johnson (1969) 'Comprehensive urban renewal and industrial relocation' in J.B. Cullingworth and S.C. Orr, *Regional and urban studies.*

City of Glasgow Corporation (1960) *First quinquennial review of the development plan: survey report.*

Clark, W.A.V. (1965) 'Markov chain analysis in geography: an application to the movement of rental housing areas', *Ann. Ass. Am. Geogr.* 55, 351-6.

Colenutt, R.J. (1970) 'Building models of urban growth and spatial structure', *Progr. Geogr.* 2, 109-52.

Diamond, D.R. (1962) 'The central business district of Glasgow' in K. Norberg (ed.), *Proceedings of the IGU symposium in urban geography (Lund).*

Firn, J. (1970) 'The Glasgow University register of manufacturing establishments in the central Clydeside conurbation', *mimeo.* (Univ. of Glasgow).

Goldberg, M.A. (1970) 'An economic model of intra-metropolitan industrial location', *J. reg. Sci.* 10, 75-9.

Goodman, L. (1962) 'Statistical methods for analyzing processes of change', *Am. J. Sociol,* 68, 57-78.

Hall, M. (ed.) (1959) *Made in New York* (Cambridge, Mass.).

Hart, P.M. and S.J. Prais (1956) 'The analysis of business concentration: a statistical approach', *J.R. statist. Soc.,* Ser. A, 119, 150-75.

Harvey, D.W. (1967) 'Models of the evolution of spatial patterns in human geography', in R.J. Chorley and P. Haggett, *Models in geography.*

Keeble, D.E. (1969) 'Local industrial linkage and manufacturing growth in outer London', *Tn Plann. Rev.* 40, 163-88.

Kemeny, J.G. and L. Snell (1960) *Finite Markov chains* (Princeton).

Kemeny, J.G. and L. Snell (1962) *Mathematical models in the social sciences* (Englewood-Cliffs, N.J.).

Knos, D.S. (1968) 'The distribution of land values in Topeka, Kansas', in B.J.L. Berry and D.F. Marble, *Spatial analysis* (Englewood-Cliffs, N.J.).

Martin, J.E. (1964) 'Three elements in the industrial geography of Greater London', in J.T. Coppock and H.C. Prince (eds.), *Greater London.*

Meyer, J.R., J.Kain and M. Wohl (1965) *The urban transportation problem* (Cambridge, Mass.).

Moses, L. and H.F. Williamson (1967) 'The location of economic activities in cities', *Am. econ. Rev.* 57, 211-22.

Muth, R.F. (1969) *Cities and housing* (Chicago).

Norcliffe, G.B. (1970) 'Industrial location dynamics', Unpubl. Ph.D. thesis, Univ. of Bristol.

Olsson, G. and S. Gale (1968) 'Spatial theory and human behaviour', *Pap. Proc. reg. Sci. Ass.* 21, 229-42.

Pred, A.J. (1964) 'The intrametropolitan location of American manufacturing', *Ann. Ass. Am. Geogr.* 54, 165-80.

Richardson, H.W. (1969) *Elements of regional economics.*

Taaffe, E.J., B.J. Garner and M.H. Yates (1963) *The peripheral journey to work* (Evanston, Ill.).

Tulpule, A.H. (1969) 'Dispersion of industrial employment in the Greater London area', *Reg. Stud.* 3, 25-40.

Wise, M.J. (1949) 'On the evolution of the jewellery and gun quarters in Birmingham', *Trans. Inst. Br. Geogr.* 15, 57-72.

Reprinted from *Transactions*, 56, 1972, Institute of British Geographers, London, with permission.

18 Industrial Migration from North-West London 1940-64[1]

by D. E. Keeble
University of Cambridge

Introduction

Within the area covered by the former boroughs[2] of Acton, Brentford and Chiswick, Wembley and Willesden, together with certain neighbouring parts of Ealing, Heston and Isleworth, and Hendon, is to be found the most important industrial zone of outer London (see Figure 18.1).[3] This area, referred to here as North-West London, contained only a handful of manufacturing firms before 1914[4]; yet by 1960, manufacturing industry had expanded so considerably as to employ 240,000 workers.[5] Part of this vast increase has occurred since the second world war, no less than 29,000 industrial jobs having been created in the area during the decade 1950-60 alone[6]; yet despite this growth, a number of firms have decided that N.W. London is no longer suitable for their activities, and have either established branch factories elsewhere, or even moved completely out of the area. The extent and significance of the resultant industrial migration has hitherto received little attention, even from local planning authorities concerned with the development of industry in the area[7]; and indeed this paper, utilising data obtained in the course of a wider investigation into industrial growth and change in N.W. London, represents the first attempt at comprehensive analysis of post-war industrial movement from any part of the Greater London area.[8]

The information obtained in this investigation reveals that industrial migration from N.W. London has been on a quite considerable scale. Since 1940, no less than 267 factories have been established by firms from the area in United Kingdom locations ten miles or more away from their former or main factories. Of these, some 147 represented complete moves, the firm closing down its factory in N.W. London altogether, and transferring its production lock, stock and barrel to another area. The remaining 120 factories represent branch plants, set up in other areas by firms which have nonetheless retained their main manufacturing units in N.W. London.[9] Altogether, these 267 factories involved a gain to the reception areas concerned of at least 67,000 jobs – a figure based only on the 135 or so plants for which employment data are known, and therefore undoubtedly underestimating the actual number of workers involved. It is true that this total number of factories does include some – 37 all told – which are now no longer operating; but since no employment figures are available for these, their inclusion in the total does not affect the employment value given above. This value, of 67,000 jobs, represents over one-quarter of the present total employment in manufacturing industry in N.W. London; and inasmuch as these jobs may be thought of as having been lost to N.W. London, industrial migration can be seen to have been of considerable importance to the post-war employment situation in the area.

The Causes of Industrial Migration

So much for the broad facts of this industrial migration from N.W. London. Why, however, has it occurred at all, particularly from an area in which, at least up to 1960, industry was expanding rather than declining?

The answer to this is that migration is in fact directly linked to expansion; for the growth of certain firms has been so great that it has outstripped the capacity of the area to contain it. Put in another way, expanding firms in N.W. London have come up against a 'ceiling', imposed by conditions existing in the area, beyond which they can continue to grow only with difficulty. In order to expand further, to overcome this ceiling, many have found that they are forced to move the whole or part of their production out of the area, to new locations where at least initially this ceiling does not exist. In the case of c. 85 per cent of all the factories set up by N.W. London firms outside the area since the war, locational shift was a direct result of the growth of the individual firm concerned.[10]

The ceiling on industrial expansion in the area is made up of a number of different elements. The most important one is the inadequacy of existing factory premises, particularly in terms of available space.[11] Expanding firms, after all, sooner or later require additional space, for production, storage or administration. All else being equal, the simplest solution to this problem is to extend the factory buildings; but with the passage of time and the very considerable expansion of

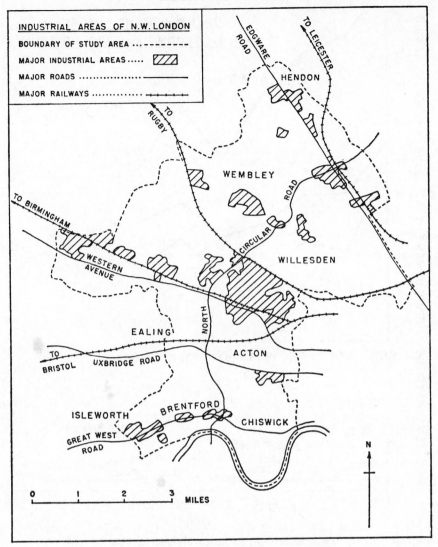

Figure 18.1 The North-West-London Industrial Zone.

industry in N.W. London since the 1930's, the c. 1,800 acres at present occupied by industry[12] has become so crowded with factories that there is by now little or no room for such extensions, except on a very few sites. Instead of extending their premises, therefore, many expanding firms are forced to look for new, larger factories in the area. Here, however, they encounter a second element in the ceiling on expansion — that of the high cost of factory space. In part a response to the lack of open land available for new factories in such a built-up area, in part a direct reflection of government policy which has deliberately restricted new factory-building in N.W. London, the construction of new factories within the area has in no way kept pace with the growth in demand for premises from local industrial

firms. As a natural result, the cost of both freehold and leasehold factories has risen enormously, chiefly since the last war. In 1930, for example, an average rental for a modern factory in the great Park Royal industrial estate of Acton and Willesden was 10d. per sq. ft. per annum; by 1939 it had risen only to about 1/1d per sq. ft. per annum; today, however, the *same* factory, now twenty-five years older, would cost between 50p and 62½p per sq. ft. per annum, a tenfold increase since 1939.[13] The same is true of freehold premises. As a result, many expanding firms are unable to afford the larger premises that they need; and they are forced to move out of the area altogether, to localities where the cost of premises is lower.

A third factor hindering industrial expansion in N.W.

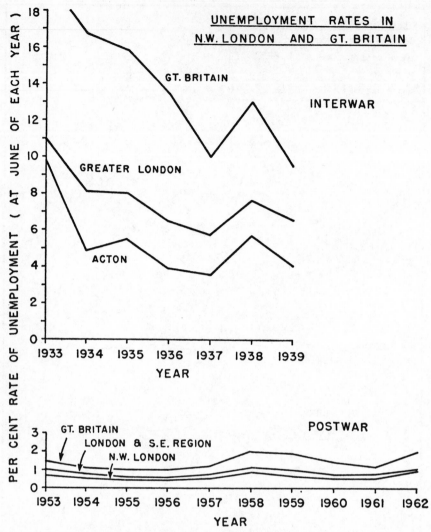

Figure 18.2 Post-war and Inter-war Unemployment Rates, Great Britain and N.W. London.

Source: Inter-war Rates, from the Local Unemployment Index, published monthly by Ministry of Labour, Statistics Division, 1933-9. Post-war Rates: Gt. Britain, and London & S.E. Region, *Monthly Digest of Statistics*, Central Statistical Office; N.W. London, calculated from employment and unemployment data provided by Ministry of Labour from unpublished records.

London is that of shortage of labour, a situation clearly illustrated by Figure 18.2, showing unemployment rates in N.W. London and Great Britain. It should be emphasised that although all other rates are from published sources, that for N.W. London during the post-war period has been calculated by the author from data supplied by the Ministry of Labour. The graphs show, however, that during the 1930's N.W. London, although much better off than most other parts of the country, nonetheless had a fairly high rate of unemployment. Most firms in the area therefore had no difficulty in obtaining all the labour they needed. Since the war,

on the other hand, the unemployment rate in N.W. London has been very low indeed, reflecting both the expansion of industry in the area, and the Government's policy of full employment. As a result, expanding firms have found it very difficult to obtain extra labour; while competition for what workers are available has forced up wages and labour costs and increased labour turnover, in the area. The result has been a further restriction on industrial expansion.

Finally, government policy has itself deliberately sought to control industrial growth. Both the Middlesex County Planning Authority and the Board of Trade have

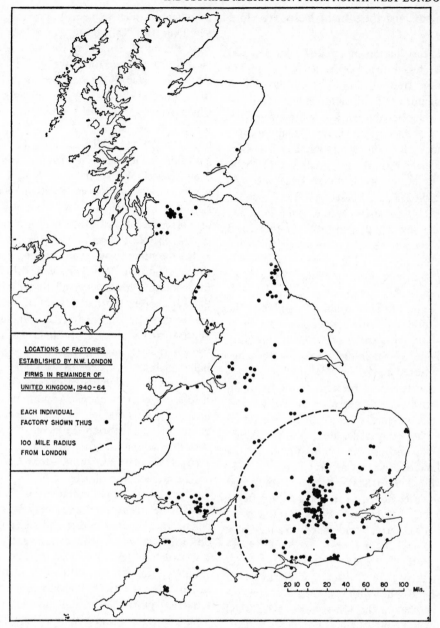

LOCATIONS OF FACTORIES
ESTABLISHED BY N.W. LONDON
FIRMS IN REMAINDER OF
UNITED KINGDOM, 1940-64

EACH INDIVIDUAL
FACTORY SHOWN THUS   •

100 MILE RADIUS
FROM LONDON

20 10 0   20   40   60   80   100
Mls.

Figure 18.3 The Geographical Distribution of Branch and Relocated Factories established by N.W. London firms, 1940-64.

acted in this way since the war, the former following the recommendations of the Greater London Plan 1944,[14] the latter those of the 'Barlow' Commission Report of 1940.[15] Armed with powers given them by post-war legislation, they have refused permission to new firms to build factories in the area, prevented existing firms, even those with space available, from extending their factories, and displaced so called 'non-conforming' firms from sites regarded as unsuitable for manufacturing industry. In all these ways, government controls have provided a very important element in the ceiling on industrial expansion in N.W. London.

So much, then, for those factors which together or individually constitute a ceiling on industrial growth in the area, and have therefore stimulated a migration of industry from N.W. London. The remainder of this paper will be concerned with analysing the locational and other characteristics of this migration.

The Geographical Distribution of Relocated and Branch Factories

The geographical distribution of the 267 relocated and branch factories, taken together, is shown in Figure 18.3. Each factory, irrespective of its size, is shown by a single dot. One important qualification is that as already mentioned only factories ten miles or more away from the main or former factory are shown – and the map therefore excludes the very large number of short distance moves which have occurred within N.W. London and the county of Middlesex since the war. Another is that although partly based on official records, the data from which the map has been drawn is more the result of personal investigation in N.W. London, and therefore cannot claim to be exhaustive. Given the scope of this investigation, however,[16] it does seem reasonable to conclude that the great majority of moves have been discovered and recorded.

Two main features of this distribution stand out. The first and most noticeable one is the concentration of factories within 100 miles radius of London. If slightly extended to include the whole of East Anglia, this area, which will be referred to as the 'Metropolitan zone', contains 159 factories, or 59 per cent of the total. On the other hand, within it, the overwhelming majority of such factories are concentrated in a belt lying between 15 and 50 miles from central London; and within that belt, the greatest numbers are to be found to the north-west of London, in a segment enclosed by lines joining central London to Salisbury in the south and Peterborough in the north. The second significant feature about the distribution is the grouping of factories outside this Metropolitan zone into a relatively small number of areas. The five most important of these areas – Central Scotland including Ayrshire; the North-East; South-East Lancashire, Cheshire and North Wales; South Wales; and the South-West peninsula – contain by far the greater number of the 108 factories established beyond the 100-mile radius from London – that is, within the remainder of the United Kingdom, an area which will be referred to as the 'Provincial zone'.

Provincial Zone Migration – Background and Characteristics

This second feature is best explained in relation to the general distribution of manufacturing industry, and particularly of the industrial labour force, within the United Kingdom. Apart from the London and Home Counties area itself, this labour force is largely concen-

trated into a relatively small number of areas – Central Scotland; the North-East; South-East Lancashire; the West Riding of Yorkshire; the Midlands, especially the West Midlands; and South Wales.[17] It is therefore clear that when establishing factories in the Provincial zone, N.W. London firms have on the whole chosen areas which already possessed a substantial industrial labour force. Yet not *all* such areas have attracted them. In both the West Midlands and the West Riding of Yorkshire conditions for manufacturing industry have been very similar to those in N.W. London in recent years; and these areas have not only failed to attract N.W. London firms, but have themselves provided many of the emigrant firms which have moved to locations such as the North-East or South Wales since the war.[18]

On the other hand, the remaining industrial areas, in which conditions have been very different, have benefited considerably. Nearly all of these areas have since the war experienced higher rates of unemployment that the average for the country as a whole, as has also the South-West peninsula. This alone means that for those firms requiring large quantities of semi-skilled or unskilled labour, particularly for the manufacture of standardised products such as washing machines, transistors, or electric meters, conditions are much better than in N.W. London. Workers are much more easily obtainable, competition for labour from other firms and therefore labour turnover are not as great, and labour costs as a whole are sometimes lower.[19]

The availability of labour in these areas, then, has undoubtedly attracted a number of N.W. London firms; but the relatively high unemployment rate which lies behind this has also worked indirectly to the same end. Since the war, successive Governments concerned about this situation have extended various inducements to manufacturing firms setting up or extending their activities in these areas. Not only have reasonably priced, modern factories been built in them by the Board of Trade, but loans and grants of many kinds have been made available to industrialists commencing manufacture there. During the recent period 1st April 1960 to 31st March 1964, for example, the Board of Trade, acting under the provisions of the 1960 and 1963 Local Employment Acts, provided no less than £798 in the form of loans, grants and building costs for each new job to be created by a factory-building project in a so-called 'Development District', most of which lie in these areas.[20]

On the whole, it would seem that these relatively short-term financial inducements have been less impor-

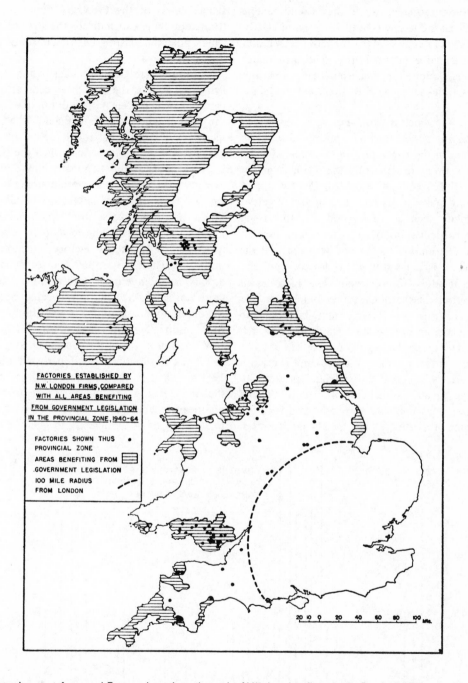

Figure 18.4 Unemployment Areas and Factory Locations chosen by N.W. London firms in the Provincial Zone.
Source: Unemployment areas (i.e. all Development Areas, DATAC Areas, and Development Districts listed or scheduled by the Board of Trade, 1940-Dec. 1963) from maps and information supplied by Map Library, Ministry of Housing & Local Government, and the Board of Trade.

tant in attracting N.W. London firms to these areas than the long-term prospect of available labour. It is however not surprising that having decided on a new factory in the Provincial zone, a large majority of N.W. London firms also chose localities in which they would benefit from the financial inducements available, a point clearly illustrated by Figure 18.4 showing the close correlation in the Provincial zone between areas scheduled under government legislation for financial help, and the locations of factories set up by N.W. London firms, since the war.

A further point which is worth noting is that a small but significant number of firms were prompted to set up branch factories in the Lancashire and Cheshire area, by the desire to serve more efficiently the regional market of the north of England and Scotland. Chiefly true of firms producing bulky goods such as cylinders of gas, or perishable goods such as food products, this trend indicates the particular advantages which that area has for industrial distribution to the northern parts of the United Kingdom, as London itself has for the southern.

The characteristics of Provincial zone factories in many ways reflect the locational forces which have just been discussed. For one thing, such factories are comparatively large in size. Considering those for which employment data are available, the average labour force is 720 workers per factory, much higher than the average for factories in N.W. London itself, and presumably linked to the greater availability of labour in the Provincial zone. It is probably also connected with the fact that a large proportion of Provincial zone factories,

some 64 per cent, are branch factories, most of which have been set up by the larger firms of N.W. London, and planned from the start as large-scale, self-sufficient production units.[21] Such branch factories indicate the attractiveness of the Provincial zone to N.W. London firms; but they also indicate the strength of the forces which hold the existing main factories of such firms to the London area.

A third characteristic peculiar to the factories of the Provincial zone is the high proportion of them, some 47 per cent, which were set up during the five years after the second world war (see Figure 18.5). This pheno-menon was largely due to the action of the Board of Trade; for during that period, when the post-war boom in demand was stimulating many N.W. London firms to expand production, the continuation of wartime con-trols over raw materials and factory building enabled the Board drastically to restrict industrial expansion in London, channelling it instead to the Provincial zone, where existing, vacant factory premises were more readily available. By 1950, however, industrial con-ditions and competition were beginning to return to a more normal level, and firms became much less willing to submit to Board of Trade pressure in this direction. As a result, the rate of establishment of factories by N.W. London firms in the Provincial zone fell to a very low level, a situation which persisted throughout the 1950's. Whether the apparent increase in movement shown by Figure 18.5 for very recent years denotes a significant change in this pattern is as yet very difficult to say. Part of it, particularly in 1962, is very probably

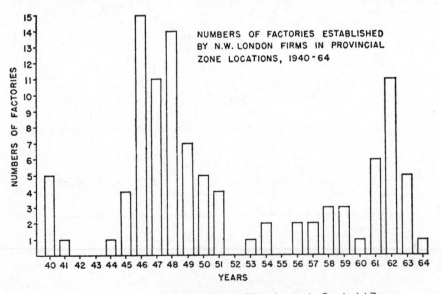

Figure 18.5 Post-war Rates of Industrial Migration to the Provincial Zone.

due to the inclusion in the figures of types of movement which may not have been recorded for earlier years. However, given the increasing rate of migration as a whole from N.W. London, some increase may possibly have occurred.

Metropolitan Zone Migration – Background and Characteristics

Factories established by N.W. London firms in the Metropolitan zone have rather different characteristics from those which have just been discussed. As has been shown, these factories are more numerous – 159, as compared in 108 in the Provincial zone; but at the same time, they are on average much smaller. In terms of employment, the average number of workers in the 85 Metropolitan zone factories for which data are available is only 360 per factory – exactly half that for Provincial zone factories, and much closer to that for N.W. London firms as a whole. It seems clear, in fact, that smaller N.W. London firms, if forced to move at all, prefer to move to the Metropolitan rather than to the Provincial zone, possibly because they regard the much greater dislocation of a long-distance move as more than their limited financial and managerial resources can sustain.[22]

Linked to this is a second characteristic – the fact that a much higher proportion of Metropolitan zone factories, some 64 per cent in all, are complete relocations. Rather than duplicate overhead and management costs by the establishment of a separate branch factory, the smaller firms migrating to the Metropolitan zone have preferred to expand production by moving completely – a factor which in turn has reinforced their unwillingness to move too far into the 'terra incognita' of provincial Britain.

The third and perhaps most important characteristic is the much greater dependence of Metropolitan zone factories upon London. Although impossible to establish quantitatively, it appears that Provincial zone factories, many of which are large, relatively independent branch factories of firms with a headquarters factory in London anyway, require much less direct contact with London than do the smaller ones of the Metropolitan zone. The great majority of the latter are still closely dependent on the metropolis for a host of needs, ranging from the buying of materials and components, to the recruiting of skilled labour, and the all-important marketing of finished goods.[23]

This dependence renders a location as close as possible to London extremely important; why then did Metropolitan zone firms move out of N.W. London at all? The answer to this is the same in nearly all cases; as expanding firms, they were unable to find in N.W. London the extra factory space, at a reasonable price, which they needed. Factory premises, or industrially-zoned land on which to build them, are available in the Metropolitan zone, constituting by far its greatest attraction. The net result is that N.W. London firms have moved into the Metropolitan zone, but only as far as is

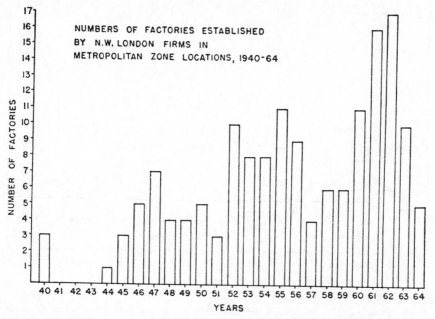

Figure 18.6 Post-war Rates of Industrial Migration to the Metropolitan Zone.

absolutely necessary to obtain the larger premises, or sites, they need.

This situation is of course not new. An exactly similar set of forces acting upon the industry of inner London during the inter-war period was responsible for rapid industrial growth around the fringes of the conurbation, accelerating the steady extension of the built-up area into the Home Counties.[24] Since the war, however, the continued operation of these forces has failed to produce this effect, owing to the intervention of Town and Country Planning legislation, and the creation of the so-called 'Green Belt' around London (see Figure 18.7).[25] N.W. London industrialists, searching for indus-

trial land as close as possible to London, have either been refused permission to build factories within this area, or have only been allowed to do so in its existing urban centres.

Those refused permission, particularly in very recent years, have had to look further afield to more isolated towns at a greater distance from the metropolis. In this, they have been deliberately aided by the Government's New Town and Expanded Town policies,[26] aimed at transferring people and industry from a congested London to both new and expanding urban centres situated within 50, or at the most 100 miles of London. In these centres, new factories and subsidised housing

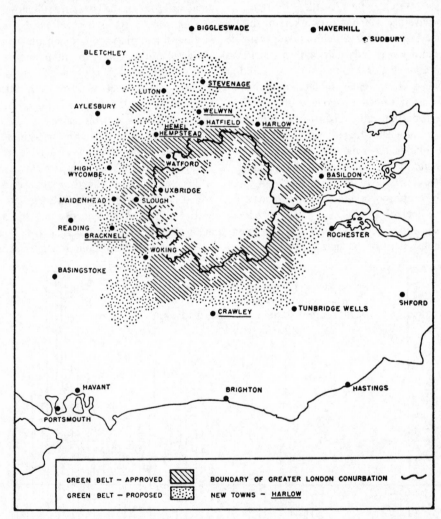

Figure 18.7 The London Geen Belt

Redrawn from the Ministry of Housing & Local Government, *The South East Study 1961-1981,* Fig. 25, p.88, with the sanction of the Controller of Her Majesty's Stationery Office.   Extent as at Dec. 1963.

for employees have been major attractions to industrialists anxious to move from N.W. London, but fearful of losing the skilled workers on whom the very existence of the firm often depends. The success of these policies, particularly as they concern the New Towns, has been very considerable. But what must be realised is that the New and Expanded towns are only one element, though the most publicised one, in a steady migration of firms from N.W. London to a wide range of urban centres in the Metropolitan zone, most of which have not benefited as directly as the New and Expanded towns from government-promoted schemes. In fact, of the 159 Metropolitan zone factories, 114, or 72 per cent, were set up in towns unaffected directly by New or Expanded town legislation; only 18 per cent went to New Towns; and only 10 per cent to Expanded towns. In each category, however, this migration has benefited most those towns, such as Watford, Hemel Hempstead, and High Wycombe, which are closest to London; and the great majority of factories have been established within the belt lying between 15 and 50 miles from the centre of the metropolis.

The Significance of Radial Migration into the Metropolitan Zone

It has already been pointed out that within this belt, factories set up by N.W. London firms are found on all sides of London; but Figure 18.3 also shows that such factories are far more concentrated to the north-west and west of London than in other directions. This very interesting preference clearly invites comparison with trends in industrial migration to outer London during the inter-war period, when, as Hall has demonstrated,[27] firms moving from the west and north-west of inner London exhibited a similar preference for new locations further out, but in the same direction from the centre – that is, for areas such as N.W. London itself. The fact that N.W. London during the post-war period has in turn been 'exporting' industrial firms still further to the north-west of London not only establishes conclusively the importance of radial movement in the geographical spread of industrial London over the last fifty years, but also suggests that the factors accounting for such movements today may well be closely comparable to those which were important during inter-war years. These factors, as far as post-war migration is concerned, are fourfold. The most important is the need for continuing close contact with N.W. London itself; for given the communications pattern of the inner Metropolitan zone, with major routes radiating outwards

from London like spokes from a wheel, it is obvious that locations with the greatest accessibility to N.W. London lie in the north-west segment. For both branch factories, needing close managerial and other contacts with parent factories still in N.W. London, and for those which have moved completely but still find in N.W. London their customers, raw material supplies, or even some of their workers, ease of contact with N.W. London is very important. Hence the channelling of branch and re-located factories to the north-west segment. A second factor reveals the close connexion between the movement of population and the movement of industry; for during the post-war years, many towns twenty or more miles from London have been developed as residential areas for the managers and directors of London firms. Naturally enough, given the communications pattern, the directors of many N.W. London firms have tended to settle in areas to the north-west of the area, commuting daily via the A40 or the Great West Road from localities such as Gerrards Cross, Chesham and Burnham Beeches. The desire to cut down this daily travel on their part has been an important, thought often unadmitted, factor in their decision to move production north-west or west, rather than south, north or east.[28] Government policy has also to some extent reinforced radial movement. It was expected, for example, that N.W. London firms considering a New Town location would move to Hemel Hempstead, to the north-west of their old locations, in preference to any other New Town; and the resultant publicity given to Hemel Hempstead by local authorities in N.W. London helps to account for the concentration of factories from N.W. London in it (see Figure 18.3).[29] Finally, it must be noted that a factory relocated to the north-west of London has extremely good access not just to London, with its concentrated market, but to the wider national market beyond. From areas to the north-west of London, first-class road and rail communications, many of them recently improved, give directly onto the other great population centres of the country, providing greater accessibility to these centres from the north-west than from any other segment of the Metropolitan zone. This factor has definitely attracted some firms to move in that direction,[30] although the factors listed earlier appear to be more important reasons for such a preference.

Conclusions

These, then, are some of the most significant aspects of industrial migration from N.W. London in the post-war period. Three important conclusions can be drawn from them. Firstly, the amount of manufacturing industry moving out of N.W. London has been greater, in number of firms and jobs involved, than perhaps has hitherto been expected. Recent local and national government publications have tended to stress the difficulties of persuading firms to move[31]; yet quite considerable numbers, equivalent to about a quarter of the total number of firms employing over ten workers in N.W. London today, have been establishing factories outside N.W. London in recent years. This trend is of great importance as far as N.W. London itself is concerned; for although, as pointed out earlier, industrial employment in the area expanded by some 29,000 workers, or 19.5 per cent, during the 1950's, the three years 1960-3 actually witnessed a decline of over 5,000 workers from the peak reached in the former year.[32] This decline, almost certainly the first ever recorded in the twentieth-century history of industrial growth in N.W. London, would appear to be more than a temporary pheno-menon, since it was preceded by a steady falling-off in the rate of expansion of industrial employment in the area during the five years 1955-60[33]; and its coincidence in time with an increasing rate of industrial migration, as evidenced by Figure 18.6, strongly suggests that the latter trend provides one major reason for it.

The second conclusion relates to the movement of firms to the older industrial areas of the Provincial zone; for just such a migration from London as a whole has been a major objective of government policy over the last twenty years, provoking the expenditure of a great deal of taxpayers' money and of the energies of Board of Trade officials. It is clear from this analysis of post-war movement that as far as N.W. London's industry is concerned, these policies have met with some success. At least 33,000 jobs have been provided by factories set up by N.W. London firms in the Provincial zone, nearly all of which are in areas regarded by the government as being in particular need of new employment. However, although this is true, it must be emphasised that most of these jobs are in factories established only during the abnormal conditions of the immediate post-war years; and that without much stronger and more ruthless governmental pressure, it seems unlikely that N.W. London firms can be persuaded in greater numbers in the future to set up factories in the Provincial zone,[34] particularly when in many cases the alternative — and it is an alternative — of establishing factories in the Metro-politan zone is open to them.

The third and most important conclusion concerns the migration of N.W. London firms to the Metropolitan

zone; for not only does this migration involve more firms than that to the Provincial zone, but, more important, it is a much more recent and rapidly-growing phenomenon. Unlike movement to the Provincial zone, which reached its peak just after the war, the rate of movement to the Metropolitan zone is still rising, having been doing so more or less steadily ever since 1945 (Figure 18.6). It would seem probable that conditions for expanding firms in N.W. London are becoming increasingly difficult; while at the same time, the publicity given to the New and Expanded Town schemes, and the success of those firms which have already moved out, have opened the eyes of many industrialists in N.W. London to the possibility of expanding into the Metropolitan zone. There seems no reason therefore, why a high and possibly increasing rate of movement into this zone from N.W. London will not continue, a trend which, as the latest governmental study of employment and population trends in the area, *The South-East Study, 1961-1981*,[35] recognises, would be of great value as far as regional planning within south-east England is concerned. On the basis of the facts already presented, it is reasonable to expect that this movement will benefit principally the belt around London lying between 15 and 50 miles from the centre, although more migration will occur to areas beyond this than has been the case in recent years; and that both within this belt and beyond, the greatest growth zone as far as N.W. London firms and probably many inner London firms as well are concerned, will be the west and north-west segment. In this connexion, it is surely no coincidence that two of the three major new 'growth centres' suggested by *The South-East Study* lie precisely within this very segment of the Metropolitan zone.[36]

Finally, the effect of this migration upon the human and economic geography of the Metropolitan zone is of the greatest importance; for in view of the close links which most of these firms retain with London, the parallel outward movement of London population,[37] and the ease of communication by road and rail with the metropolis, it is clear that what we are seeing in south-east England is the spread of London, in a new way, over a much wider area. This new London is taking the form of a great Metropolitan Region, within which formerly isolated towns and villages expanding by infusions of London firms and population, are becoming increasingly bound in an economic sense to the centre.[38] In terms of industrial migration, this Region already extends up to at least 50 miles from central London, and on the crucial north-west side will soon be meeting the expanding city-region dominated by Birmingham, London's nearest rival.[39] Within it, both employment in manufacturing industry and, as a result, population, are increasing at a rapid rate, particularly in the belt just beyond 15 miles from the centre, a situation largely attributable to just such an industrial migration as the one which has been considered.[40] The establishment of factories by N.W. London firms in the Metropolitan zone, therefore, is helping to bring about great changes in its human and economic geography, changes which can confidently be expected to continue, probably at an increasing rate, during the next fifteen to twenty years.

Notes

1 This paper was first presented, with slight differences, to Section E of the British Association at its Southampton Conference, 1964, under the title of 'Why Leave London?'; and a summary of this is included in A.A.L. Caesar and D.E. Keeble (eds.), 'Regional Planning Problems in Great Britain', *Advancement of Science*, Vol. 22, 1965.

2 Following the recommendations of the Royal Commission on Local Government in Greater London 1957-60, all former Municipal and Metropolitan Boroughs in Greater London have been regrouped, as from 1st April 1965, into larger Greater London Boroughs. Thus in N.W. London, the former boroughs of Wembley and Willesden have been amalgamated as the new borough of Brent; those of Acton, Ealing and Southall as Ealing; and those of Brentford and Chiswick, Heston and Isleworth, and Feltham (urban district) as Hounslow. Hendon is now part of Barnet. For further reference, see, M.J. Wise, 'Reforms in Local Government in Britain', *Geography*, Vol. 49, Part 3, No. 224, July 1964, pp. 259-62.

3 This is corroborated both by P. Abercrombie, *Greater London Plan 1944*, H.M.S.O., 1945, p. 42; and by P.G. Hall, 'Industrial London: A General View', Chapter 9 in J.T. Coppock and H.C. Prince (eds.), *Greater London*, London, 1964, pp. 237-8. Detailed figures are presented in the latter case.

4 See M. Robbins, *Middlesex*, London, 1953, pp. 56-57.

5 Calculated from data supplied by the Ministry of Labour, from unpublished employment records.

6 Source as above. Comparability of the 1950 and 1960 figures was achieved by detailed checking of original record sheets for each National Insurance Office Area of N.W. London, and reallocation of employment affected by 1958 classificatory and other changes.

7 In 1962, the former Middlesex County Planning Department knew only of 48 firms which had *either* moved out of the County *or* ceased to operate altogether. These were all firms displaced by planning developments. Most of these were in fact in the second category. See, Middlesex County Council, *First Review of the Development Plan, Report of the Survey 1962*, 1963, Vol. 1, p. 21.

8 The only publication presenting original data on this theme is E.J.L. Griffith, 'Moving Industry from London', *Town Planning Review*, Vol. 26, 1955-6, pp. 51-63. However, this dealt only with those Greater London firms known to have transferred their entire production to a New Town, Expanded Town or Out-County Estate in south-east England by the end of 1953. For other general comments, see also D.L. Munby, 'The Cost of Industrial Dispersal from London', *Planning Outlook*, Vol. 2, No. 3, 1951, pp. 5-16; P. Self, 'Congested London; Can employment be dispersed?', *Times Review of Industry*, 16, July 1962, pp. 34-35; C.H. Cuttriss, 'The Relocation of Industry with reference to both the Human and Economic Factors', *Town and Country Planning Summer School*, 1955, pp. 50-60; L.P. Bevan, 'An Industrialist's Experience', unpublished paper read to the Town and Country Planning Association conference on Town Development: Achievements and Obstacles, Aylesbury, 2nd Oct. 1962, 5 pp. Several important studies of actual costs of industrial movement in post-war Britain have recently been carried out under the National Institute of Economic and Social Research. Chief of these is, W.F. Luttrell, *Factory Location and Industrial Movement*, London, 1962, 2 vols., which includes a number of unnamed Greater London firms among the case studies listed. However, inasmuch as it does not attempt to relate its findings to Greater London, and studies only cases of long-distance branch factory migration, it is only of background relevance to this paper.

9 These facts cast considerable doubt on the suggestion by L. Needleman and B. Scott, 'Regional Problems and Location of Industry Policy in Britain', *Urban Studies*, Vol. 1, No. 2, Nov. 1964, p. 158, that 'in Britain most relocations are probably' of the kind in which 'it is only a branch of the firm that moves, rather than the whole firm'.

10 Griffith, op. cit., p. 56 reaches a similar but more

qualitative conclusion. For the significance of expansion as far as the establishment of branch factories is concerned, see G. Picton, 'Diversification of Industry', *Economic Journal*, 61, 1951, pp. 658-60.

11 See E.M. Hoover and R. Vernon, 'Locational Pressures on Manufacturing', Chapter 2, in *Anatomy of a Metropolis*, Cambridge, Mass., 1959, pp. 29-36.

12 Source, Middlesex County Council, *First Review of the Development Plan, Proposals for Alterations and Additions to the Written Statement*, 1962, Table 11, p. 33.

13 Personal communication, Mr R.W. Diggens, Chairman, Allnatt London Properties Ltd. This company was responsible for much of the inter-war and post-war development of the Park Royal industrial estate.

14 Abercrombie, op. cit., 221 pp.

15 Royal Commission on the Distribution of the Industrial Population, *Report* (Chairman, A. Montague-Barlow), Cmd. 6153, H.M.S.O., 1940, 320 pp.

16 Information on migration was obtained in the course of visits to 219 manufacturing firms at present or formerly operating in N.W. London, from discussions with officials in all the Employment Exchanges and Factory Inspectorate Offices in the area, and from many other local sources. In very nearly every case, a further detailed check was made with the firm concerned, or in some other way, to verify the fact of migration.

17 See Map 'Industrial Employment in the United Kingdom', p. 259, Central Office of Information, *Britain: An Official Handbook*, H.M.S.O., 1962 edition.

18 See, for example, B. Loasby, 'The Experience of West Midlands Industrial Dispersal Projects', *Town and Country Planning*, Vol. 29, 1961, pp. 309-13.

19 See, particularly, J. Cole, 'How to avoid High Labour Costs', *The Guardian*, 3rd Jan. 1962, p. 3; also Luttrell, op. cit., Vol. 1, p. 116.

20 Source, Board of Trade, *Local Employment Acts, 1960 and 1963, Fourth Annual Report*, H.M.S.O., July 1964, Table IIIB, p. 7.

21 This point has been noted by Luttrell, op. cit., Vol. 1, pp. 342-3.

22 See C. Hill, 'Some Aspects of Industrial Location', *Journal of Industrial Economics*, Vol. 2, No. 3, Aug. 1954, pp. 184-92.

23 For an excellent analysis of the advantages which a London location offers industrial firms, see M.J. Wise, 'The Role of London in the Industrial Geography of

Great Britain', *Geography*, 41, 1956, pp. 219-32.

24 See Abercrombie, op. cit., pp. 44-48. Fringe development of this type has been the common experience of most large manufacturing centres in developed countries, and many studies of very similar trends have been made outside Great Britain – see, for example, E. Kitigawa and D.J. Bogue, *Suburbanisation of Manufacturing Activities within Standard Metropolitan Areas*, Miami, 1955; L. Reeder, 'Industrial Deconcentration as a Factor in Rural-Urban Fringe Development', *Land Economics*, Vol. 31, pp. 275-80; G.J.R. Linge, 'The Diffusion of Manufacturing in Auckland, New Zealand', *Economic Geography*, Vol. 39, No. 1, 1963, pp. 23-39; and M.L. Logan, 'Manufacturing Decentralisation in the Sydney Metropolitan Area', *Economic Geography*, Vol. 40, No. 2, April 1964, pp. 151-62.

25 For aims and objectives of Green Belt policy, see D. Thomas, 'London's Green Belt: The Evolution of an Idea', *Geographical Journal*, Vol. 129, Part 1, March 1963, pp. 14-24.

26 For summaries of these policies, see Griffith, op. cit., pp. 33-34; also K.C. Edwards, 'The New Towns of Britain', *Geography*, Vol. 49, Part 3, No. 224, July 1964, pp. 279-85.

27 P.G. Hall, *The Industries of London since 1861*, London, 1962, pp. 136-7.

28 The connexion between radial journeys-to-work in Greater London and the outward movement of industry is discussed in J.E. Martin, *The Location of Industry in Inner North East London: a study in industrial geography*, Ph.D. thesis, University of London, 1961, pp. 395-9.

29 See J.C. Morris, *The Willesden Survey 1949*, Corporation of Willesden, 1950, pp. 90-92.

30 This same point was singled out by inter-war authorities to explain industrial development in N.W. London itself – see Greater London Regional Planning Committee, *Second Report*, 1933, p. 55.

31 Middlesex County Council, *First Review of the Development Plan, Report of the Survey 1962*, 1963, Vol. 1, p. 21; also the significant comments in Ministry of Housing and Local Government, *London. Employment: Housing: Land*, Cmnd. 1952, H.M.S.O., Feb. 1963, p. 3 – 'Wholesale removal of existing concerns is certainly impracticable'; and Ministry of Housing and Local Government, *The South-East Study 1961-1981*, H.M.S.O., 1964, p. 81 – 'there is little mobile expanding industry in London itself'.

32 Source, Ministry of Labour, unpublished employment records.

33 Source, Ministry of Labour, op. cit.

34 This view is strongly corroborated by A.E. Holmans, 'Industrial Development Certificates and Control of the Growth of Employment in South-East England', *Urban Studies*, Vol. 1, No. 2, Nov. 1964, pp. 138-52.

35 Ministry of Housing and Local Government, *The South-East Study 1961-1981*, H.M.S.O., 1964, 145 pp. esp. Part 2.

36 Ministry of Housing and Local Government, op. cit., pp. 73-74. The third major expansion was suggested for the Southampton-Portsmouth area, to which also there has been some considerable industrial migration from N.W. London. For analysis of this, including the presentation of data on the motives of the migrant firms involved, see, D.E. Keeble, 'The Migration of Metropolitan Industry into Wessex 1945-64', *Wessex Geographer*, No. 5, April 1964, pp. 52-60.

37 See A.G. Powell, 'The Recent Development of Greater London', *Advancement of Science*, Vol. 17, No. 65, 1960, pp. 79-81.

38 See A.G. Powell, op. cit.; P.G. Hall, *London 2000*, London, 1963, Chapters 1-5; and W. Thomas, 'The Growth of the London Region', *Town and Country Planning*, 29, May 1961, pp. 185-93.

39 This of course is a reflection of the very small size of the effectively populated area of the United Kingdom. For a penetrating analysis of trends affecting industrial and economic growth in the whole of this area, viewed in a national setting, see A.A.L. Caesar, 'Planning and the Geography of Great Britain', *Advancement of Science*, Vol. 21, No. 91, Sept. 1964, pp. 230-40.

40 Powell, op. cit., pp. 79-85.

Reprinted from *Urban Studies*, Vol. 2 (1), May, 1965, Oliver and Boyd Ltd, Edinburgh, with permission.

19 The Giant Manufacturing Corporations and Balanced Regional Growth in Britain

by G. F. Parsons

University College, University of London

British post-war manufacturing growth has been accompanied by increases in the size of both individual units of production (establishments) and enterprises. A part of this general growth has been an increase in the numbers of multi-establishment, multi-enterprise firms, whose operations are recorded in the press as mergers, take-overs or nationalization. The extent of this dominance of 'big-business' is recorded in Table 19.1, in which the establishments-per-enterprise column reveals the existence, in the 5000-and-over employment class, of the multi-plant corporation that accounted for nearly 50 per cent of the total net output in 1963. Over the period 1958-63 this particular indicator of corporate growth increased by over 35 percent.

Some evidence relating to the current policies of British corporations

A review of the 300 largest companies in Great Britain as determined by the *Times Review of Industry*, revealed 224 predominantly manufacturing corporations. These firms were surveyed to identify the geographic source of particular functions,[2] the likelihood of certain areas generating these activities, and the geographic distribution of the corporations within the U.K.

Survey data revealed that in the field of professional services[3] the large corporation showed little demand for the fractional use of local labour near the factory, and indeed transferred a section of the demand for these functions, through the internal policies of the corpor-

Table 19.1 Enterprises by employment size, United Kingdom, 1963

Size of enterprise by No. of persons employed	No. of enterprises	No. of establishments	Estabs/ enterprise	per cent of total employment	per cent of total net output
5000 and over	210	6,031	28.72	42.79	47.60
1000-4999	767	5,368	7.00	20.43	20.78
25- 999	18,114	26,530	1.47	31.10	27.37
less than 25	45,276	45,845	1.02	5.70	4.27

Source: Board of Trade, Census of Production 1963 (1970)

A neglected area of discussion has been the impact of these corporate structures upon regional growth. In a situation where multi-plant, multi-enterprise firms have an increasing market dominance, the internal operational policies of the whole group of firms (henceforth called a corporation) and their geographic distribution may well constitute critical factors in regional growth that are not wholly controllable or compatible with externally applied location of industry policies. This note briefly explores the regional effects of the increasing corporate dominance in British industry which, although at times obscured by the many national benefits of corporate scale,[1] do provide the spatial disparities that remain central to geographic enquiry.

ation, to the head office or specialist division often located in another region from the factory.

With respect to the maintenance labour[4] involved in any factory's operation, the great majority of corporations, 79 per cent, assured their supplies of this labour by hiring internally. Such a policy differs radically from that adopted by the typical small business described by Vernon (1957), where maintenance labour would be hired on demand, and does nothing to encourage the development of services around a factory of which fractional use could be made. The very existence of such small firms may be seen as a useful pre-condition for the development of additional small-scale entrepreneurs (Taylor, 1970).

The removal of decisions to a head office or specialist division extends to investment and the purchasing of capital equipment and raw materials. Business theory indicates that local factory profits are returned to the head office, where decisions are made on a corporate basis, which will not always result in a reinvestment at the local level if higher rates of return exist elsewhere. Even given a positive decision to invest in the local factory, this does not imply that the side effects of this capital investment will accrue to the local area. Survey results showed that 60 per cent of the corporations purchased heavy capital equipment for a factory at least partially through a central buying division, while over 25 per cent relied entirely upon this facility. In spheres of raw materials and fuels purchasing, the closer control required at the factory level is exhibited by over 70 per cent of the corporations relying on direct factory purchasing and only 40 per cent making use of the central buying division.

The removal of investment and spending decisions to the head office or specialist division effectively alters the geographic range over which any decision will be made. If the corporation has a national distribution, the head office's normal operating area will be national and it is more likely to take into account, or implement choices from within, this larger geographic area. For the smaller businessman located in one region, this is not an alternative since his information will be limited to that of his local area and/or other major production centres.

In other areas of corporate activity the internal transfer of local functions that would have existed externally under a single-plant, single-establishment industrial structure is seen to continue. Ninety per cent of the corporations provided warehousing facilities, 80 per cent cafeteria or restaurant facilities and 75 per cent their own transport facilities within their local factory organization; while nearly 40 per cent made use of specialist transport divisions servicing a whole corporation.

A geographic analysis of corporate structure

Whether the policies operated by the corporations benefit or detract from regional growth depends in large part upon the cumulative geographic distributions of the operating and control units of the corporations (Tornqvist, 1970). These are shown in Table 19.2 which reveals a greater degree of regional concentration between control units than operating units. London and the South East emerge as the main beneficiaries from this concentration, although the regional disparities decline

from the group head office, to the central services, to research and development, to the divisional head offices; the last control group being nearly twice as concentrated as the operating units.

The West Midlands was also favoured by the corporations for the location of corporate control, divisional head offices and research and development facilities. However, a predicted distribution of control functions based upon the actual distribution of operating units indicated that this region contained less than its share of group head offices. These results are similar to those presented by Buswell and Lewis (1970) who, in an examination of the geographic distribution of industrial research activity in the United Kingdom, also identified the South East and West Midlands as areas with a 'marked and disproportionate concentration of research establishments'. Apart from these areas, only the East Midlands exhibited an ability to increase its share of a control facility, and this only for research and development. Thus, upon the evidence of Table 19.2 the majority of the United Kingdom is failing to acquire corporate control facilities. In some regions such as East Anglia, Wales and the North, the deficiencies may be marginal, whilst in the North West and Yorkshire/Humberside they must be considered significant.[5]

The implications of corporate distribution for regional growth

Given the policies of corporate industry and its geographic distribution, one can assess the likely impact of high regional corporate concentration in the U.K. today. Any region other than the South East and the West Midlands, where the numbers of corporate control units are in surplus, is likely to be experiencing a deflationary tendency on the basis of the regional effects of corporate power already outlined. The converse of these arguments holds true for the surplus areas such as London and the South East.

These tendencies arise from several features associated with simple demand and supply models of regional economies. Simple demand models are affected by the action of corporate concentration, when the removal to a head office outside the region of professional functions reduces local spending through a decreasing regional wage packet, leading to a decline in the level of regional consumption. The provision of specialist facilities on a national basis may increase the level of regional imports. Finally, with the transfer of investment and purchasing decisions to another area the probability of regional investment and purchasing may diminish leading to a fall

Table 19.2 The regional distribution of the control and operating units of a sample of large corporations, 1970[1]

	South East	London[4]	South West	East Anglia	Wales	West Midlands	East Midlands	North West	Yorks/ Humberside	North	Scotland
Control Units											
Group Head Office											
No.	51	40	0	1	1	6	3	3	1	1	2
%	73.9	58.0	0	1.4	1.4	8.7	4.3	4.3	1.4	1.4	2.9
Central Services[2]											
No.	15	9	0	0	0	12	0	2	0	1	1
%	48.4	29.0	0	0	0	38.7	0	6.5	0	3.2	3.2
Corporate Control[3]											
No.	66	49	0	1	1	18	3	5	1	2	3
%	66.0	49.0	0	1.0	1.0	18.0	3.0	5.0	1.0	2.0	3.0
Divisional Head Office											
No.	86	58	7	2	5	53	10	20	9	3	11
%	41.7	28.2	3.4	1.0	2.4	25.7	4.7	9.7	4.4	1.5	5.3
Research and Development											
No.	41	23	4	2	0	19	8	5	2	3	2
%	47.7	26.7	4.7	2.3	0	22.1	9.3	5.8	2.3	3.5	2.3
Operating Units											
No.	507	180	97	54	62	264	146	286	174	68	124
%	28.45	10.10	5.44	3.03	3.47	14.81	8.19	16.05	9.76	3.81	6.95

1 Northern Ireland was omitted from the investigation.
2 Central Services were defined as those functions concerned with administering the Corporation at a geographically distinct location from the Group Head Office. Usually these included accounts, computers, etc.
3 Corporate Control is Group Head Offices plus Central Services.
4 London is also included in the South East.

n investment and an increase in regional imports. Together the net effect will be a fall in the level of the regional income. Supply models of regional economies are also affected by a decline in capital sources of investment, resulting in a decline in regional output. Perhaps of more significance is the impact of corporate concentration upon total factor productivity. Here are found the residual causes for output deviation not explicable in terms of capital and labour supply, including such features as 'applied technical and organizational knowledge and external factors' (Deakin and Seward, 1969), and containing the external economies identified by Vernon (1957) and others. In reducing the regional labour supply by the removal of some professional functions outside the region, and the internalization of other professional and maintenance functions, the regional economy will have less demand for, and less supply of, the specialist services. This will reduce total factor productivity and in turn output.

This latter feature has significance outside the limits of the supply model. In an alternative assessment of growth procedures, external economies are held to play a role in the generation and transfer of innovations to the production process, from which point they may be developed individually or taken over by a corporation Lichtenburg, 1960). With decreases in these specialist services from which external economies may accrue, and a removal in the demand for much of the professional regional labour force – a potential source of competent management – it must remain doubtful whether the deficit regions can regain a comparative advantage in these respects, from which to generate further non-corporate growth.

The findings of this brief investigation do suggest that the policies and geographic distributions of private, large manufacturing corporations are not wholly compatible with balanced regional growth. At a time when Britain's imminent membership of the EEC may well suggest an increase in the amount of corporate activity in the U.K, not always presumably with head offices in London and the South East, it would seem worthwhile exploring the regional impact of these large institutions further than has been the case to date. Indeed, as far as public policy favours corporate scale through the decisions of the Monopolies Commission and government ministries, and unless the distributions of nationalized industries, civil servants and the non-manufacturing private corporations differ radically from the sample investigated, one may expect this force for regional inequality of development to continue and to curb the alleged aims of regional development policies.

Notes

1 Corporate scale generates many benefits in terms of research, productivity, remuneration, exports, etc., which to some extent all regions of the nation may share.
2 The functions included professional labour, maintenance labour, transport facilities, cleaning, warehousing, the purchase of new materials and capital.
3 The professional services were defined as accountancy, advertising, architecture, computers, economics, legal services, marketing, market research, printing facilities and public relations.
4 Maintenance labour was defined as bricklayers, electricians, joiners, mechanics, plumbers, welders, factory cleaners, office cleaners, and window cleaners.
5 The consistently negative nature of the signs in these 'deficit regions' supports this interpretation of the data in spite of the small sample size in some of these regions.

References

Buswell, R.J., and Lewis, E.W., 1970. The geographical distribution of industrial research activity in the United Kingdom. *Regional Studies*, 4, 297-306.

Deakin, B.M., and Seward, T. 1969. *Productivity in transport.* Cambridge University Press.

Lichtenburg, R.M., 1960. *One-tenth of a nation.* Harvard University Press.

Taylor, M.J., 1970. Location decisions of small firms. *Area*, 1970, No. 2, 51-4.

Tornqvist, G. 1970. *Contact systems and regional development.* Lund.

Vernon, R., 1957. Production and distribution in the large metropolis. *The Annals of the American Academy*, No. 314.

Reprinted from *Area*, Vol. 4 (2), 1972, Institute of British Geographers, London, with permission.

20 Behavioral Aspects of the Decision to Migrate

by Julian Wolpert

University of Pennsylvania

During the decade 1950-60, there were sufficient changes from previous patterns of migration streams in the United States to warrant some reexamination and reevaluation of model building attempts in migration analysis. It must be admitted that the gravity model and its elaborations appear to lose explanatory power with each successive census. When flows are disaggregated, the need becomes greater selectively to determine unique weights for areas and unique distance functions for subgroups of in- and out-migrants. The Stouffer model of 'competing migrants' (Stouffer, 1960) provided a rather poor prediction of migration streams for the 1955-60 period. Perhaps the most successful of spatial interaction models, which does take into consideration the spatial arrangement of places of origin and destination, is sufficiently rooted in the 1935-40 depression-period movements so as to present serious deficiencies when applied to recent streams. Plots of migration distances defy the persistence of the most tenacious of curve fitters.

The defenders of the wage theory of economic determinism find some validity for their constructs, so long as net, and not gross, migration figures are used and regional disaggregation does not proceed below the state level, thereby neglecting much of the intrastate heterogeneity (Blanco, 1964; Bogue, et. al, 1957; Bunting, 1961; Raimon, 1962, and Sjaastad, 1960).

The extremely scanty empirical evidence of the 'friends and relatives effect' in directing migration has given birth to a generation of models which, although offering the solace of a behavioral approach, provide little explanation of the actual process involved (Kerr, 1942, Nelson, 1959). Perhaps the most serious gap occurs in the transition from micro- to macro-model and in the selection of appropriate surrogates for testing. Here, the inadequacy of published data in the United States appears to have its most telling effect. Though almost every conceivable method of combining existing data into useful indicators has been tried, explanation through surrogates hardly provides an analysis which is independent of the bias which is introduced.

A good deal of useful information has come from the analysis of migration differentials by categories of occupation, income, race, and, especially, age (Bogue et al., 1957; Eldridge and Thomas, 1964; Thomas, 195? and Wilber, 1963). However, predictive models have not been designed to include these findings and to consider the interdependence of these characteristics in migration behavior. Demonstrating the potential usefulness of the migration differential approach is one of the objectives of this paper.

A composite of interesting ideas about migration behavior has been incorporated within Price's ambitious proposed simulation model (Price, 1959). On the basis of selected characteristics of individuals and of places of origin and destination, migration probabilities are generated reflecting empirically observed regularities. As far as is known, the model has not become operational — the task for simulating United States migration would overtax the most modern computer. The only successful attempt in this direction has been Morrill's study of the emerging town development in south central Sweden (Morrill, 1962).

The use of Monte Carlo simulation models in migration analysis does offer a viable and promising approach, especially considering the rather persistant tendencies for critical elements or parameters to remain stable over time. Thus, although the streams show considerable variation over time, and the characteristics of the population and of places continuously change, stability persists in migration behavior.

To illustrate this observation it may be noted that Bogue, Shryock, and Hoermann (1957), in their analysis of the 1935-40 migration streams, summarize with the following statements that could as well be applied to the 1955-60 streams:

1 Basic shifts in the regional and territorial balance of the economy guided the direction and flow of migration streams.

2 The two factors that seem to contribute most to the mobility of the population are above average educational training and employment in white collar occupations.

3 Any theory of economic determinism in migration

s inclined to be incomplete.

It appears, therefore, that understanding and prediction of migration streams require determining of the constants in migration behavior and distinguishing these from the variables with respect to population composition and place characteristics which evolve differentially over time.

As indicated, attempts at model buildings in migration research have largely focused on variables and surrogates such as distance and ecological characteristics of places exerting 'push and pull' forces (Bogue et. al., 1957; Burford, 1962), to the exclusion of behavioral parameters of the migrants. The model suggested here is of doubtful usefulness as an exact predictive tool. It borrows much of its concepts and terminology from the behavioral theorists, because of the intuitive relevance of their findings to the analysis of mobility. Verification will be only partial because of the general absence in this country of migrational histories. Instead, greater reliance will be placed upon evidence from a variety of sources and special studies. The framework of the analysis must be classified as descriptive or behavioral and partially dynamic.

Clearly, the focus must remain with the process of internal migration, i.e., a change of residence which extends beyond a territorial boundary. Some attempt will be made, however, to relate this process of 'long distance' movement to the more general topic of mobility which encompasses not only shifts within areal divisions but also movement between jobs and social categories. This larger zone of investigation is referred to as the 'mover-stayer' problem Goodman (1961).

Central Concepts of Migration Behavior

The central concepts of migration behavior with which we shall be concerned are: 1. the notion of place utility, 2. the field theory approach to search behavior, and 3. the life-cycle approach to threshold formation.

Before translating these concepts into an operational format·within a proposed model, some attempt will be made to trace their relevance to migrational decisions.

Place Utility

Population migration is an expression of interaction over space but differs in certain essential characteristics from other channels of interaction, mainly in terms of the commodity which is being transported. Other flows, such as those of mail, goods, telephone calls, and capital also reflect connectivity between places, but, in migration, the agent which is being transported is itself active and generates its own flow. The origin and destination points take on significance only in the framework in which they are perceived by the active agents.

A degree of disengagement and upheaval is associated with population movements; thus, households are not as readily mobile as other phenomena subject to flow behavior. Yet, it would be unrealistic to assume that sedentariness reflects an equilibrium position for a population. Migrational flows are always present, but normally the reaction is lagged and the decision to migrate is nonprogrammed. Thus, migration is viewed as a form of individual or group adaptation to perceived changes in environment, a recognition of marginality with respect to a stationary position, and a flow reflecting an appraisal by a potential migrant of his present site as opposed to a number of other potential sites. Other forms of adaptation are perhaps more common than change of residence and job. The individual may adjust to the changing conditions at his site and postpone, perhaps permanently, the decision to migrate. Migration is not, therefore, merely a direct response or reaction to the objective economic circumstances which might be incorporated, for example, within a normative transportation model.

In designing the framework for a model of the migration decision, it would be useful at the outset to enumerate certain basic descriptive principles which have been observed to have some general applicability and regularity in decision behavior. To a significant degree these principles have their origin in the studies of organizational theorists.

We begin with the concept of 'intendedly rational' man (Simon, 1963) who, although limited to finite ability to perceive, calculate, and predict and to an otherwise imperfect knowledge of environment, still differentiates between alternative courses of action according to their relative utility or expected utility. Man responds to the perception of unequal utility, i.e., if utility is measured broadly enough to encompass the friction of adaptation and change.

The individual has a threshold of net utitility or an aspiration level that adjusts itself on the basis of experience (Cyert and Marsh, 1963; Lewin, 1951; McGuire, 1964; Siegel, 1957; Simon, 1963 and Starbuck, 1963). This subjectively determined threshold is a weighted composite of a set of yardsticks for achievement in the specific realms in which he participates. His contributions, or inputs, into the economic and social systems in terms of effort, time, and concern are rewarded by actual and expected attainments. The threshold functions as an evaluative mechanism for distinguishing, in a binary sense, between success or failure, or between positive or negative net utilities. The process is self-adjusting because aspirations tend to adjust to the attainable. Satisfaction leads to slack which may induce a lower level of attainment (Cyert and Marsh, 1963). Dissatisfaction acts as a stimulus to search behavior.

Without too great a degree of artificiality, these concepts of 'bounded rationality' (Simon, 1963) may be transferred to the mover-stayer decision environment and a spatial context. It is necessary, only, to introduce a place subscript for the measures of utility. *Place utility*, then, refers to the net composite of utilities which are derived from the individual's integration at some position in space. The threshold reference point is also a relevant criterion for evaluating the individual's place utility. According to the model, the threshold will be some function of his experience or attainments at a particular place and the attainments of his peers. Thus, place utility may be expressed as a positive or negative quantity, expressing respectively the individual's satisfaction or dissatisfaction with respect to that place. He derives a measure of utility from the past or expected future rewards at his stationary position.

Quite different is the utility associated with the other points which are considered as potential destinations. The utility with respect to these alternative sites consists largely of anticipated utility and optimism which lacks the reenforcement of past rewards. This is precisely why the stream of information is so important in long-distance migration – information about prospects must somehow compensate for the absence of personal experience.

All moves are purposeful, for an evaluation process has preceded them, but some are more beneficial, in an *ex post* sense, because of the objective quality of search behavior, the completeness of the information stream and the mating of anticipated with realized utility. If migrations may be classified as either successes or failures in a relative sense, then clearly the efficiency of the search process and the ability to forecast accurately the consequences of the move are essential elements.

Assuming intendedly rational behavior, then the generation of population migration may be considered to be the result of a decision process which aims at altering the future in some way and which recognizes differences in utility associated with different places. The individual will tend to locate himself at a place whose characteristics possess or promise a relatively higher level of utility than in other places which are conspicuous to him. Thus, the flow of population reflects a subjective place-utility evaluation by individuals. Streams of migration may not be expected to be optimal because of incomplete knowledge and relocation lag but neither may we expect that individuals purposefully moved in response to the prospect of lower expected utility.

The process of migration is conceived in the model as: 1 proceeding from sets of stimuli perceived with varying degrees of imperfection, and 2 involving responses in a stayer-mover framework.

The stayers are considered lagged movers postponing the decision to migrate for periods of time extending up to an entire lifetime. Thus, the mover-stayer dichotomy may be reduced to the single dimension of time – when to move.

Distinction must clearly be made between the objective stimuli which are instrumental in generating response originate in the individual's action space which is that part of the limited environment with which the individual has contact (Lewin, 1951). Thus, the perceived state of the environment is the action space within which individuals select to remain or, on the other hand, from which to withdraw in exchange for a modified environment.

Field Theory Approach to Search Behavior

Though the individual theoretically has access to a very broad environmental range of local, regional, national and international information coverage, typically only some rather limited portion of the environment is relevant and applicable for his decision behavior. This immediate subjective environment of action space is the set of place utilities which the individual perceives and to which he responds. This notion of the action space is similar to Lewin's concept of life space – the universe of space and time in which the person conceives that he can or might move about (Lewin, 1951). Some correspondence may exist with the actual external environment but there may also be a radical degree of deviation. The life space is a surface over which the organism can locomote and is dependent upon the needs, drives, or goals of the organism and upon its perceptual apparatus (Simon 1956). Our concern is with man in terms of his efficiency or effectiveness as an information collecting and assimilating organism and thus with his ability to produce an efficient and unbiased estimation or evaluation of the objective environment. It is suggested that the subjective action space is perceived by the individual through a sampling process whose parameters are determined by the individual's needs, drives, and abilities. There may not be a conscious and formal sampling design in operation, but, nevertheless, a sampling process is inherently involved in man's acquisition of knowledge about his environment.

Both sampling and nonsampling errors may be expected in the individual's perceived action space — a spatial bias induced by man's greater degree of expected contact and interaction in his more immediate environment, as well as sampling errors introduced because of man's finite ability to perceive and his limited exposure and observation. The simple organism which Simon describes has vision which permits it to see, at any moment, a circular portion of the surface about the point in which it is standing and to distinguish merely between the presence or absence of food within the circle (Simon, 1956).

The degree to which the individual's action-space accurately represents the physically objective world in its totality is a variable function of characteristics of both man and the variability of the environment. Of primary emphasis here are the consequences of man's fixity to a specific location — the spatial particularism of the action space to which he responds.

What is conspicuous to the individual at any given time includes primarily information about elements in his close proximity. Representing the information bits as points, the resulting sampling design most closely resembles a cluster in the immediate vicinity of the stationary position. The individual may be considered at the stationary position within the cluster of alternative places, each of which may be represented by a point on a plane. The consequences of this clustered distribution of alternatives within the immediate vicinity of the individual is a spatially biased information set, or a mover-stayer decision based upon knowledge of only a small portion of the plane.

Cluster sampling may be expected to exhibit significantly greater sampling bias for a given number of observations than random sampling; its most important advantage is in the reduction of the effort or cost in the collection of information. In the absence of a homogeneous surface, however, the difference in cost may be more than outweighed by the loss in representativeness of a given cluster.

The local environment of the individual may not, of course, be confined purely to his immediate surroundings. The action space may vary in terms of number and intensity of contacts from the limited environmental realm of the infant to the extensive action space within which diplomats, for example, operate. The degree of contact may perhaps be measured by the rate of receipt or perception of information bits (Meier, 1962). Mass communications and travel, communication with friends and relatives, for example, integrate the individual into a more comprehensive spatial setting but one which is, nevertheless, still biased spatially. Mass communications media typically have coverage which is limited to the service area of the media's transmission center. Here a hierarchy of nodal centers exists in terms of the extent of service area and range of coverage. Thus the amount of transmission and expected perception of information by individuals is some function of the relative position of places within the network of communication channels. The resident in the area of a primary node has an additional advantage resulting from his greater exposure to information covering a relatively more extensive area of choice. His range of contact and interaction is broader, and the likelihood of an unbiased and representative action space is greater.

The Life Cycle Approach to Threshold Formation

Another significant determinant of the nature and extent of the individual's action space (i.e., the number and arrangement of points in the cluster) consists of a set of factors which may be grouped under the heading of the 'life cycle.' Illustrative of this approach is Hägerstrand's analysis of population as a flow through a system of stations (Hägerstrand, 1962). Lifelines represent individuals moving between stations. The cycle of life almost inevitably gives rise to distinct movement behavior from birth, education, and search for a niche involving prime or replacement movements. Richard Meier also has examined this notion of the expanding action space of the individual from birth through maturity (Meier, 1959, Meier, 1962). The action space expands as a function of information input — and growth depends on organization of the environment so that exploration becomes more efficient. Associated with the evolution of the individual's action space through time is a complex of other institutional and social forces which introduce early differentiation. Differences in sex, race, formal education, family income, and status are likely to find their expression early in shaping the area of movement and choice. Although the action space is unique for each individual, still there is likely to be a good deal of convergence into a limited number of broad classes. The congruity and interdependence of the effects of race, family income, education, and occupation are likely to result in subgroups of individuals with rather homogeneous action spaces.

In Lewin's concept, behavior is a function of the life space, which in turn is a function of the person and the environment (Lewin, 1951). The behavior-influencing aspects of the external (physical and social) environment are represented through the life space. Similarly, but in a more limited fashion, the action space may be considered to include the range of choice or the individual's area of movement which is defined by both his personal attributes and environment. Most prominent among the determinants of the alternatives in this action space which are conspicuous to the individual is his position on one of divergent life cycles and location in terms of the communication networks linking his position to other places. His accumulated needs, drives, and abilities define his aspirations — the communication channels carry information about the alternative ways of satisfying these aspirations. To illustrate this structure in terms of the simple organism, we may turn to Simon's model of adaptive behavior (Simon, 1956). The organism he describes has only the simple needs of food getting and resting. The third kind of activity of which it is capable is exploration for food by locomotion within the life space where heaps of food are located at scattered points. In the schema, exploration and adaptive response to clues are necessary for survival; random behavior leads to extinction. The chances of survival, i.e., the ability to satisfy needs are dependent upon two parameters describing the organism (its storage capacity and its range of vision) and two parameters describing the environment (its richness in food and in paths). Of course, with respect to the human organism, aspirations require the fulfillment of many needs, and thresholds are higher. Exploratory search is aided by clues provided by the external environment through communication channels which extend the range of vision.

Other Behavioral Parameters

The discussion was intended to develop the concept of action space as a spatial parameter in the mover-stayer decision. Thus the action space of the individual includes not only his present position but a finite number of alternative sites which are made conspicuous to him through a combination of his search effort and the transmission of communications. The action space refers, in our mover-stayer framework, to a set of places for which expected utilities have been defined by the individual. A utility is attached to his own place and relatively higher or lower utility has been assigned to the alternative sites. The variables here are the absolute number of alternative sites and their spatial pattern or arrangement with respect to his site. The sites may consist of, alternative dwellings within a single block, alternative suburbs in a metropolitan area, or alternative metropolitan areas. The alternatives may not all present themselves simultaneously but may appear sequentially over time.

There are other components of behavioral theories which are relevant in the analysis of migration, especially with respect to the problem of uncertainty avoidance. We have already mentioned the sequential attention to goals and the sequential consideration of alternatives (Cyert and Marsh, 1963). The order in which the environment is searched determines to a substantial extent the decision that will be made. In addition, observations appear to confirm that alternatives which *minimize uncertainty* are preferred and that the decision maker *negotiates for an environment of relative certainty* (ibid.). Evidence shows also that there is a tendency to *postpone decisions* and to rely upon the *feedback of information*, i.e., policies are reactive rather than anticipatory (ibid.). Uncertainty is also reduced by imitating the successful procedures followed by others (ibid.).

The composite of these attempts to reduce uncertainty may be reflected in a lagged response. A lapse of time intervenes in a cause and effect relationship — an instantaneous human response may not be expected. As with other stimulus-response models, events are paired sequentially through a process of observation and inference into actions and reactions, e.g., unemployment and outmigration. As developed in economics, a lag implies a delayed, but rational, human response to an external event. Similarly, with respect to migration, responses may be measured in terms of elasticity which is in turn conditional upon factors such as complementarity and substitutability. A time dimension may be added to measures of elasticity, and the result is a specific or a distributed lag — a response surface reflecting the need for reenforcement of the perception of the permanence of change.

Framework of a Proposed Operating Model

The model which is proposed attempts to translate into an operational framework the central concepts with which we have been concerned: the notion of place utility, the field theory approach to search behavior, and the life cycle approach to threshold formation.

The model is designed to relate aggregate behavior in terms of migration differentials into measures of place utility relevant for individuals. The objective is a prediction of the composition of in- and out-migrants and their choice of destination, i.e., by incorporating the stable elements which are involved in the changes in composition of population of places.

Inputs into the system are the following set of matrices:

1 Matrix A, defining the migration differentials associated with the division of the population by life cycles and by age, represented respectively by the rows and columns.

2 Matrix B, representing the distribution of a place's population within the life cycle and age categories.

3 Matrices C, D, E, and F, representing respectively the gross in-, out-, and net-migration and 'migration efficiency'[1] for each of the cell categories corresponding to Matrix B.

The rates for the A matrix are determined on an aggregate basis for the United States population by means of the 'one in a thousand' 1960 census sample. These rates are then applied to the B matrix entries for specific places to predict the expected out-migration rates of profile groups at these places. The differences between the expected rates and those observed in the C, D, E and F matrix tabulations are then used to provide a measure of the relative utility of specific places for the given profile groups which may be specified as a place utility matrix. The net migrations, whether positive or negative for the given cell, represent the consensus of cell members of the utility which the place offers relative to other places which they perceive. The migration efficiency measures not only the relative transitoriness of specific subgroups of the population but also the role of the specific place as a transitional stepping stone or station for certain groups.

There is an additional matrix, Matrix G, representing the parameters of search behavior which are characteristic of the subgroup populations. These are specified in terms of the number of alternatives which are perceived and the degree of clustering of these alternatives in space. The destination of the out-migrants predicted by means of the G matrix entries are tested against the observed migration flows in order to derive measures of distance and directional bias.

The concepts of place utility, life cycle, and search behavior are integrated, therefore, within the classification of the population into subgroups. Preliminary testing has revealed a significant degree of homogeneity of migrational behavior by subgroup populations in terms of differential rate of migration, distance, and direction of movement. The classification procedure, involving the use of multivariate analysis, is designed to provide a set of profile or core groups whose attributes may be represented by prototype individuals. The differential migration rates of Matrix A are assumed, therefore, to be parameters in the migration system, at least for the purposes of short-term forecasting. Individuals move along each row as they grow older and, to some extent, move in either direction along age columns as socio-economic status changes over time, but the migration rates for the cells remain relatively constant.

Similarly, the utility to the population subgroups of the specific places of origin and destination shift over the long-term but remain relatively constant in the short-run. For long-term forecasting, exogenous measures of economic trends in specific places would be necessary inputs.

Acknowledgement

The support of the Population Council and of the Regional Science Research Institute is gratefully acknowledged.

Notes

1 Migrational efficiency refers to the ratio of net migration to total gross migration (Shryock, 1959).

References

Ajo, Reino (1954) 'New Aspects of Geographic and Social Patterns of Net Migration Rate,' *Svensk Geografisk Arsbok*, Lund, Sweden.

Blanco, Cicely (1964), 'Prospective Unemployment and Interstate Population Movements,' *Review of Economics and Statistics*, XVLI, pp. 221-22.

Bogue, Donald J, Shryock, Henry S., Hoermann, Siegfried (1957), 'Streams of Migration between Subregions,' *Scripps Foundation Studies in Population Distribution* No. 5, Oxford, Ohio.

Bogue, Donald J. (1959), 'Internal Migration' in Hauser, P.M. and Duncan, O.D., eds, *The Study of Population*. Chicago: The University of Chicago Press.

Bunting, Robert L. (1961), 'A Test of the Theory of Geographic Mobility,' *Industrial and Labor Relations Review*, 15, pp. 76-82.

Bunting, Robert L. (1962) 'Labor Mobility in the Crescent,' in Chapin, F. Stuart, Jr., and Weiss, Shirley F. eds, *Urban Growth Dynamics in a Regional Cluster of Cities*. New York, Wiley.

Burford, Robert L. (1962), 'An Index of Distance as Related to Internal Migration,' *Southern Economic Journal,* XXIX, pp. 77-81.

Cyert, R.M. and Marsh, J.G. (1963). *A Behavioral Theory of the Firm.* Englewood Cliffs, N.J.: Prentice-Hall.

Eldridge, Hope T. (1964), 'A Cohort Approach to the Analysis of Migration Differentials,' *Demography* 1, pp. 212-19.

Eldridge, Hope T. and Thomas, Dorothy Swaine (1964) *Population Redistribution and Economic Growth, United States 1870-1950.* Philadelphia: American Philosophical Society.

Goodman, Leo (1961), 'Statistical Methods for the Mover-Stayer Model,' *Journal of the American Statistical Association.* 56, pp. 841-68.

Hägerstrand, Torsten (1962), 'Geographical Measurements of Migration,' *Entretiens de Monaco en Sciences Humaines.*

Kerr, Clark (1942), 'Migration to the Seattle Labor Market Area; 1940-42,' *University of Washington, Publications in the Social Sciences,* 11, pp. 129-88.

Lewin, Kurt (1951) *Field Theory in Social Science.* New York: Harper and Row.

Meier, Richard L. (1959), 'Measuring Social and Cultural Change in Urban Regions,' *Journal of the American Institute of Planners,* XXV, pp. 180-90.

Meier, Richard L. (1962) *A Communications Theory of Urban Growth.* Cambridge: Massachusetts Institute of Technology Press.

McGinnis, Robert and Pilger, John E. (1963) 'On a Model for Temporal Analysis' and 'Internal Migration as a Stochastic Process,' (mimeo). Department of Sociology, Cornell University.

McGuire, Joseph W. (1964), *Theories of Business Behaviour,* Englewood Cliffs, N.J.: Prentice-Hall.

Morrill, Richard L. (1962), 'The Development of Models of Migration,' *Entretiens de Monaco en Sciences Humaines.*

Morrill, Richard L. and Pitts, Forest R. *Marriage,* 'Marriage, Migration and the Mean Information Field', *Annals,* Association of American Geographers, forthcoming.

Nelson, Phillip (1959), 'Migration, Real Income and Information,' *Journal of Regional Science,* 1, pp. 43-74.

Oliver, F.R. (1964), 'Inter-Regional Migration and Unemployment, 1951-61,' *Journal of the Royal Statistical Society,* Series A, 127, pp. 42-75.

Price, D.O. (1959), 'A Mathematical Model of Migration Suitable for Simulation on an Electronic Computer,' *Proceedings, International Population Conference,* Vienna, pp. 665-73.

Raimon, Robert L. (1962), 'Interstate Migration and Wage Theory,' *Review of Economics and Statistics,* XLIV, pp. 428-38.

Rosen, Howard, (1961), 'Projected Occupational Structure and Population Distribution,' *Labor Mobility and Population in Agriculture.* Ames: Iowa State University Press.

Rossi, Peter, (1955), *Why Families Move.* The Free Press of Glencoe, Illinois.

Shryock, H.S. Jr. (1959), 'The Efficiency of Internal Migration in the United States,' *Proceedings, International Population Conference,* Vienna, pp. 685-94.

Siegel, S. (1957), 'Level of Aspiration and Decision Making.' *Psychological Review,* 64, pp. 253-63.

Simon, Herbert A. (1956), 'Rational Choice and the Structure of the Environment,' *Psychological Review,* 63, pp. 129-38.

Simon, Herbert A. (1963), 'Economics and Psychology,' in Koch, Sigmund, ed., *Psychology: A Study of a Science,* 6, New York: McGraw-Hill.

Sjaastad, Larry A, (1960), 'The Relationship Between Migration and Income in the United States,' *Papers and Proceedings, Regional Science Association,* VI, pp. 37-64.

Sjaastad, Larry A. (1961), 'Occupational Structure and Migration Patterns,' *Labor Mobility and Population in Agriculture.* Ames: Iowa State University Press.

Starbuck, William H, (1963), 'Level of Aspiration Theory and Economic Behavior,' *Behavioral Science,* 8, pp. 128-36.

Stouffer, Samuel A. (1960), 'Intervening Opportunities and Competing Migrants,' *Journal of Regional Science,* 2, pp. 1-26.

Taeuber, Karl E. and Taeuber, Alma F. (1964), 'White Migration and Socio-Economic Differences between Cities and Suburbs,' *American Sociological Review,* 29, pp. 718-24.

Ter Heide, H. (1963), 'Migration Models and Their Significance for Population Forecasts,' *Milbank Memorial Fund Quarterly,* XLI, pp. 56-76.

Thomas, Dorothy S. (1959), 'Age and Economic Differentials in Internal Migration in the United States: Structure and Distance,' *Proceedings, International Population Conference,* Vienna, pp. 714-21.

Thomas, Dorothy S. (1958), 'Age and Economic Differentials in Interstate Migration,' *Population Index, pp. 313-24.*

Webber, Melvin M. (1969), 'The Urban Place and the Nonplace Urban Realm,' *Explorations into Urban Structure*, Philadelphia: University of Pennsylvania Press.

Wilber, George L. (1963), 'Migration Expectancy in the United States,' *Journal of the American Statistical Association*, 58, pp. 444-53.

Reprinted from the *Regional Science Association Papers*, Vol. 15, 1965, Regional Science Association, Philadelphia, with permission.

Part IV
Government Intervention

Introduction

These papers are grouped together with the common editorial purpose of showing how governments of widely differing political complexion and socio-economic conviction have set about tackling their regional problems. They specifically refer to three contrasting groups of countries; those whose economies are centrally planned and ideologically founded ostensibly on Marxist principles as in the case of Poland; those whose foundations are essentially democratic but within a relatively free enterprise economy indulge in some centralised planning which has important socio-economic connotations — here emphasis is placed on Britain but with general reference to western European countries; and finally the developing countries where both papers deal with the situation of an emerging post-colonial territory which also has a 'mixed economy', Nigeria.

Given the inevitability of the difference in approach of each of the writers, a picture of common aim by the governments of the three contrasting groups of countries does emerge from a reading of these papers. The objectives of regional development can be broadly summarised in all cases as the reduction or even elimination of a number of imbalances which give rise to social difficulties, wasteful costs and economic and technical anomalies. It would also be generally agreed, however, that their aim was not the elimination of some degree of regional diversity in terms of culture or way of life so long as these do not conflict with the general development of the nation as a whole.

However, another generalisation that might be assumed in the mind of the reader before coming to grips with the collection of papers in Part IV should be corrected at once, and it is that those responsible for regional development in Iron Curtain countries will somehow be more concerned in their decision making with socialist principle and less governed by subjective foible and personal prejudice. Any such assumptions are rapidly scotched by F.E.I. Hamilton's paper (p. 235) on eastern Europe. Although he identifies ten so-called 'objective and rational' socialist principles which determine the spatial disposition of industrial development, he suggests that regional planning is also influenced by

other considerations such as the imperfections of the total information base, a growing tendency towards allowing freer play to purely economic forces and the personal proclivities of those involved in the decision making process. Andrew Dawson's study (p. 249) of Polish industry from 1949 to 1965 implicitly mirrors some of these points through a spatial analysis of the growth (by county) of industrial development over time with particular emphasis on the relationship between evolving distribution patterns of industrial employment and population. He also stresses the unevenness of industrial development which he explains in terms of changes in policy by the Polish government in the period of study, often conflicting aims (not least the dichotomy between those of a national kind and those at a more localised level), and the inherent pull of agglomerative forces inasmuch as they draw new industry towards areas of pre-existing growth. Part of the problem of dealing with regional inequality is seen to be the contrasting regional levels and types of industrialisation inherited from the pre-war period of capitalism in Poland (even where material resources were similar). The notion of an inherited industrial spatial pattern, the residue of a past political order, is taken up in Aboyade's paper (p. 265) on the significance of industrial location in terms of regional development in Nigeria. But here we are dealing with relatively marginal changes that have been wrought in the last two decades on an industrial pattern which emerged to serve the commercial needs of the colonial power, not least through its mining activities, its electrical and mechanical workshops and its few agricultural processing activities. Thus, as Aboyade points out, at the achievement of political independence there were only 150 plants of medium to large scale in the industrial sector.

Since then growth has been rapid with the emphasis moving away from production rooted in local raw materials. However, the colonial legacy has given the ports of Lagos and Port Harcourt an industrial pre-eminence based on foreign financed and foreign trade oriented activities. Present government administration and entrepot commerce has led, for example, to industrial development in the Kaduna – Zaria – Kano zone. In spite of the need within the regions of the state for greater locational diversification in order to combat regional inequality, the agglomerative forces of the old industrial areas have been hard to resist. Unfortunately many attempts at the establishment of new regional industry, mostly as joint public and foreign private partnerships, have not been successful. Given the political character of Nigeria with its tribal undertones and its administrative machinery, 'the substance of a development strategy' as Aboyade says, 'is likely to be missed by the rulers for the shadow of narrow self-interest.' However, perhaps more important than these immediate malfunctions is the lack of any real industrial location policy for the economy as a whole, the federal government relying on tax reliefs and high capital allowances to attract plant to new locations. The active persuasion of firms to come to a specific area had been left until recently to the regional governments, though now increasing industrial crowding in federal territory around Lagos, as well as regional political pressure, has led them to more positive statements about industrial dispersal. But even at regional level governments who have actively tried to promote industrial estates have done so not with a view to a spatial disposition most suited to the socio-economic needs of their peoples, but so as to best compete with other regions of the state.

The essential lack of any clear cut strategy for regional industrial development at federal level which can be related to the real needs of the individual states is then evident enough. A remedy may be a complete appraisal at national level of regional resources both physical and human, married to a policy of giving to locations within them those activities to which they are best suited bearing in mind all the economic and social variables.

The paper by M.I. Logan (p. 283) is also designed to offer a coherent programme for regional development in Nigeria. As with Aboyade, he points to the inadequacies of the space economy of the colonial era in meeting the present needs of the people, though he deals with this matter in greater detail. He then postulates a new form of spatial organisation which would counter the dominance of the present large urban areas which have increased in size in recent years through the agglomeration factors mentioned by Aboyade. This would involve the allocation of national resources to build up a number of second tier cities selected on the basis of their growth potential and their location and the extension and consolidation of organisational links between these cities

and their hinterlands. This system of urban/rural linkage would result in the dissemination of better agricultural practices, which would in turn provide greater farm outputs, a factor which Logan rightly stresses as of vital importance in the proper development of a nation such as Nigeria. The new twelve state structure of Nigeria (not in being at the time Aboyade wrote his paper) might provide a framework for the selection of these urban centres.

The choosing of specific urban nodes as centres for the application of development assistance of the kind outlined by Logan has been the philosophy of regional planning in West Germany since 1959. Such regional policies are generally conceived in such a way as to enable them to be analysed under several headings. Within the first of these Wright (p. 292) intends to encompass the whole range of 'stick and carrot' legislation whose purpose is to encourage the provision of additional employment in particular areas. Their effectiveness as far as the U.K. is concerned is also the subject of a paper by Beacham and Osborn (p. 303) who look at the interregional movements of industry from 1945 to 1965 and conclude that the government policies of incentives in development areas and restrictions in congested urban areas have had some influence. However, having considered reasons for variations in the amount of out-migration from 'origin' regions, the authors say that they are unable to identify hypotheses to explain the factors that determine the pattern of regional destinations for moves. Keeble, (p. 311), in a supplement to their paper, finds spatial variations in migration to the peripheral regions can be largely explained by variations in labour availability and distance from major origin regions, while relative proximity to regional and national markets appears to have exerted an influence on the migration pattern.

Wright's other headings include policy declarations, and here he cites the co-ordinated action programmes published by the British Government for the various regional divisions of the U.K.; regional economic studies designed to enable central government to compare the social and economic circumstances and prospects of different regions; and feasibility studies aimed at providing an outline plan for the rapid growth of new or existing settlements. However, Wright finds it possible to criticise all these attempts at coming to terms with regional imbalance in the U.K., as well as those of western Europe. He expresses a need for an examination of the inter-related economic, physical and administrative problems which have to be solved in guiding programmes of regional development over a number of years. Future lines of action, he suggests, must take account of two powerful forces which are making for regional change in Europe – the demand for higher living standards and movement into the city, and the demand for more living space and migration to the suburbs. The development of new urban regions will be needed to counteract the growth rate of the present dominant regions. New machinery will be required to choose suitable future urban growth areas, to prepare a relevant national communication net and to translate regional economic plans into physical planning based on regional hierarchical networks.

In his attempts to look at the inadequacies of current regional policies in western Europe and his suggestions regarding the development of a Christaller-like framework on which to base future growth, his thesis is not dissimilar to that of Logan and indeed is really an elaboration of the somewhat more nodally based planning concepts extant in West Germany for a decade or so.

Whether Wright's thesis does point towards a logical framework or not, it is likely for the future that a coherent regional development plan will be a major concern of the newly enlarged EEC. Certainly the gap between the richer regions, mostly within the 'golden triangle' between Paris, London and north Germany, and the poorer ones, mostly but not all situated at the periphery, is still widening. Although Wright correctly identifies the broad similarities in regional policies in Europe as revolving around the provision of financial and taxation advantages for the poorer regions whose common denominator is that they amount to a subsidy to undertakings prepared to set up in underprivileged areas, he fails to make the important comment that the sums allocated by the various countries for regional development vary widely. In Britain spending on this item is ten times as high as that of France; half-way between the two comes Italy whose budget allocation for such expenditure is double that of Germany. Thus, inevitably, were a common policy not evolved, the free movement of goods and labour and eventually capital would accentuate these regional contrasts still further, notwithstanding other strong forces that will lead to the continued accretion of wealth by the richer regions. However, the present looseness of the federation of EEC members in political terms and the knowledge that the Italians and the British are likely to make the greatest demands on any system of aid for regional development have already led the Germans and the French to seek ways of preventing their contribution to it exceeding what they take from it. If this is the attitude at the outset the establishment of a community regional policy is going to be a long and painful task.

It may be fairly pointed out, then, by way of a summary of the papers in Part IV, that although problems of regional development do vary between countries according to their politico-economic colour and state of development, there are more common factors than disparate ones. Attempts to formulate policies to redress imbalance, whether they rely on direct central planning or financial and other means of persuasion, are always subject to the competence of those who are responsible for them and constrained by the frameworks inside which they work, whether they be ideological or administrative. More often than not governments concerned with regional policy are faced with the problems of imbalance arising from the inability of some areas to shrug off, unassisted, out-worn economic or industrial systems that are more relevant to an earlier period and the difficulties of countering the agglomerative attractions of regions already enjoying economic prosperity.

John Blunden

21 Decision-Making and Industrial Location in Eastern Europe

by F. E. Ian Hamilton

London School of Economics, University of London

Environment, properly defined, consists of 'the whole complex of climatic, edaphic and biotic factors . . .' as well as 'the aggregate of social and cultural conditions (customs, laws, languages, religions, and economic and political organization) that influence the life of an individual or community'.[1] Until recently, geographers generally formulated their hypotheses on the assumption that an objectively existing environment explained man's quest for optimal spatial patterns of settlement, production and servicing. Increased attention is now being paid to the ways in which subjective environments, as they are perceived by man,[2] explain the essentially satisficer or behavioural decisions that really determine locational patterns. All decisions to locate industrial production, including decisions to effect zero change in production in particular places, are expressions of each decision-maker's (or each group of decision-makers') perception of the environmental variables pertinent to his (or their) industry and enterprise. In this context, decision-making behaviour is synonymous with perception of environment properly defined plus certain individual or group attributes. Reduced to fundamentals, each decision about location primarily reflects a decision-maker's sources of information and his level of perception, and his use of either information which he seeks or information which is readily available. Stated another way, politics, prejudice, primordial loyalties, or nationalism can and do shape the character and content of the information field as perceived by a decision-maker quite as much as transport and production economies or demand and supply. This is no less true of decision-making in the so-called 'planned economies' than in the so-called 'free market economies'. Any review of the literature, however, reveals that research on entrepreneurial behaviour in industrial location decision-making is limited for capitalist economies and virtually non-existent for planned economies.[3]

The Objectivity of Socialist Location Principles

One basic reason why little research in Eastern Europe concerns itself with behaviour is that decisions are considered officially to be 'planned' and planned according to 'the objective laws of socialist location.'[4] The laws, better termed principles, are in existence to guide all planning decisions on industrial location. These principles are explained elsewhere,[5] but it is essential that they be noted here briefly. They state that industry should be located within a nation in such a manner as to (1) ensure national military security, (2) improve the socio-economic conditions of minority ethnic population groups, (3) develop rapidly the 'backward regions' in the state, (4) achieve an 'even' dispersion throughout the national territory, (5) eliminate socio-economic differentials between urban and rural areas, (6) process available natural resources and use energy near their production sources, (7) serve market areas from central places, (8) achieve regional specialization of production, (9) achieve regional self-sufficiency in industrial output; and last, but not least, (10) industry should be located internationally to facilitate greater international division of labour (specialization) within the COMECON organization.

Party members and planners, at least officially, believe that these laws are objective on two grounds. First, each law *per se* is objective and rational. Two examples must suffice to illustrate this point. Location of industry near sources of raw materials, fuel and power (principle 6) is a law intended to fulfil certain economic efficiency goals: (i) economy of transport of bulky, perishable, low-value or 'gross' (weight-losing) materials, just as elsewhere; (ii) maximization of production since the presence of manufacturing facilities stimulates the full use locally of natural resources; and (iii) maximization of productivity since factories can process efficiently the waste or by-products that derive from exploiting or processing those natural resources. The spatial allocation of industrial investment so that backward or underdeveloped regions receive their fair share of state economic growth is also considered *per se* to be an objective law. It contributes to the achievement of full employment of surplus rural labour in overpopulated regions, increasing national production and, potentially and often actually, increasing labour productivity and *per capita* income. In addition, however, this law is a fundamental tool in the attainment of socialist equality in economic, social and cultural opportunity on both the macro-geographical and the micro-geographical scales. When backward regions are inhabited by minority or non-majority ethnic peoples, such as the Macedonians or Albanians living in south-eastern Yugoslavia, the Slovaks or Hungarians living in Czechoslovakia, then the law of rapid development of these regions has, as an additional objective, the long-term stability in internal political relations necessary to the maintenance of national or federal strength.[6] Secondly, all ten laws are viewed collectively as an objective *set* since they are key spatial instruments in, and are thus consistent with, the fulfilment of socialist planning goals, namely, rapid national economic growth, full utilization of resources, human equality and an impregnable defence system.

Such a viewpoint begs three crucial and interrelated questions. How do decision-makers select the principle that is, or the principles that are, pertinent to one particular, or to a set of, locational decisions? How is a compromise, if any, effected between the needs of socialist policy and the technical and economic requirements of each and every industry? How do the decision-makers resolve conflicts between essentially economic laws (that is, principles 6, 7, 8, 9 and 10) and essentially non-economic laws which have significant political and social implications (principles 1, 2, 3, 4 and 5)? In short, can the principles be *applied* objectively? At present, insufficient evidence does not permit conclusive answers to these questions. However, some light may be thrown upon the answers through an analysis of five *selected* types of environment by which locational behaviour is conditioned. These are, respectively, the ideological, the decision-makers', the economic, the spatial and the information environments.

The Ideological Environment

Scholars have frequently assumed, or concluded, that Communist ideology, as theorized and practised, imparts to the Communist world a uniqueness which qualifies it, or parts of it, as a special study area. Throughout the social sciences, including geography, this view is being challenged by the quest for nomothetical approaches, involving model- and theory-building. Specifically, it is being challenged by research into the interaction between ideology, individual and group decision-making behaviour and the other environments outlined in this paper.[7] Evidence is beginning to show the existence and operation of sets of processes which are common to all economic, political and social behaviour, and that Communist systems constitute a sub-set within general social scientific theory.[8] Such research is essential to end current conflicts among social scientists as to the precise role of official ideology in actual decision-making, to remove the 'unique' approaches of individual disciplines and to begin to frame ideology in a theoretical context.[9]

Hitherto, five viewpoints of the role of ideology in decision-making have been accepted. First, anthropologists claim that ideology is invoked by decision-makers to maintain their ego, prestige or credibility, and hence, ideology is applied consistently and rigidly in all decision-making. Political scientists, secondly, and especially Kremlinologists, assign ideology little, if any, role in making decisions, asserting that it is merely a polemical tool used to justify decisions which are really motivated by political manoeuvring to maintain individual or group-power status. Thirdly, geopolitical theorists assume that ideology is subservient to strategic motives. By contrast, fourthly, sociologists argue that ideology is applied sometimes, but at other times is solely polemical. Finally, historians are wont to stress the continuity of traditional Slavic behaviour patterns and institutions in present-day decision-making. Such beliefs[10] are of little help to the geographer who is seeking to establish the nature and extent of ideological influence upon locational decisions.

It is, however, but a step from the beliefs of social scientists to the beliefs of decision-makers. Recent social research has established that ideology is a sub-set of beliefs within the broad 'belief-disbelief systems' of individuals and groups.[11] These belief-disbelief systems also contain highly personalized pre-ideological and post-ideological beliefs,[12] so that it is insufficient to study merely the character of the ideological system to explain human behaviour. One must examine, first and foremost, the character of individual entire belief systems.[13] These systems are organized in a hierarchical manner, ranging from specific, isolated opinions of the lowest order, through habitual opinions of an intermediate order, to 'clusters of attitudes' of the highest order in the hierarchy. Ideological beliefs may be held at any or all levels by the individual. The importance of ideology in individual belief-disbelief systems is a function of the interaction of the nature of society, personal characteristics, personal function in society and the immediate social environment as it affects the individual as he is reared, educated and socialized.[14] Nevertheless there is a tendency for ideological beliefs to comprise habitual opinions or attitude clusters, and to be held at the higher orders of the belief hierarchy. This is particularly true of Party members and politically committed non-Party members who comprise a substantial proportion, if not a majority, of the decision-making group.[15] Moreover, the higher the level at which a belief is held, the greater the value the individual attaches to that belief, and hence, the greater is his vested interest in it.[16]

Certain conclusions emerge from this research which are pertinent to any assessment of the role of ideology in decision-making or, indeed, what constitutes the perceived ideological environment. First, the personalities and social experience of decision-makers cannot be dissociated from the nature and degree of their ideological beliefs. Secondly, varying personalities, beliefs and ideological commitments interact with certain ideological or functional (i.e., role or job) vested interests in decision-making. Thirdly, the socio-economic diversity of families and individuals and the ethnic, linguistic and cultural groups to which they belong in East Europe yield significant spatial variations within the region (and vis-à-vis the Soviet Union) both in the importance attached to, and in the understanding or interpretation of, ideology among even those who become the leaders or members of the decision-making group.[17] Fourthly, the role of ideology in decision-making varies from decision to decision so that its locational impact is very variable.[18] Yet one can argue that decisions on industrial location have been more susceptible to ideological argument than other economic activities, on account of the key role that industry plays in economic development, socialization and defence. Nevertheless, in no way does this reject the arguments that either non-ideological factors may determine locational decisions or ideology may be merely a polemical tool on occasions. Fifthly, ideological applications may not be necessary in attempting to achieve development goals: means to this end may be justified economically, socially or politically, for example, the question of allocating development to Albanian-inhabited areas of Yugoslavia. Sixthly, a related argument asserts that ideology played little or no role in decision-making until Marxist-Leninist-Stalinist concepts were challenged by economists who stressed the need to apply criteria of economic efficiency in the making of decisions.[19] Finally, the motives for making particular decisions are often complex.

Given that the perceived ideological environment has not necessarily been all-pervasive, or even important, in decision-making in East Europe, nevertheless it may be reasonably claimed that the following ideological tenets have been potential influences upon decisions of industrial location. First, production and services should be nationalized and managed collectively to eliminate capitalism and private ownership. Secondly, strong, centrally organized economic management, planning, advancing technology and Party will, give decision-makers free will or independent discretion as to how, and how much, environment should be used or altered for productive purposes. Thirdly, long-term modernization of society should achieve socio-economic equality both structurally and spatially as the basis of a classless society. Fourthly, populations must be proletarianized and socialized so that individualistic attitudes may be replaced by collective attitudes progressively over time. And fifthly, the Marxist theory of surplus value was considered for many years to be a superior guide in economic decision-making over 'bourgeois' theory of profit.

At this juncture, detailed analysis of the first, third and fifth ideological beliefs is inappropriate. The first belief — nationalization — essentially resulted in the replacement of private entrepreneurial decision-making by bargaining among decision-makers in the planning and management processes; this is discussed in the subsequent section of this paper entitled 'the decision-makers' environment' (p. 240). The impact of the third belief is discussed elsewhere,[20] while the fifth belief is incorporated below (p. 241) under 'the economic environment'.

How different evolving Communist spatial patterns of industrial production may be from their capitalist or pre-capitalist (feudal) antecedents depends clearly upon how far these ideological beliefs are translated into practice, i.e., upon the degree to which decision-makers have applied location principles 2, 3, 4 and 5 in choosing locations for industry in East Europe since 1945. The greater the Marxist-Leninist-Stalinist ideological content of the individual's, or the group's aggregate, belief-disbelief system, the more often these four principles as a set will be examined first as locational guidelines, and chosen secondly as locational determinants, by decision-makers. Conversely, the lower the ideological content of their belief-disbelief system, the less likely are decision-makers to begin and end their search for locational criteria among those principles in comparison with the attention they pay to non-ideological principles. It would seem that ideology reached its peak impact upon locational decisions in the 1950s when, concurrently, four conditions attained their maximum importance: the need to demonstrate the superiority of socialism over capitalism; a belief in man's free will over environment;

the concentration of decision-making and management power in the hands of a small, central élite; and Soviet economic aid and political influence.[21] Subsequently, the collective importance of locational principles 2, 3, 4 and 5 has decreased with the securing of socialist society, some realization of environmental constraints, decentralization of decision-making, the concomitant innovation of economic efficiency criteria, and the increasing independence of East Europe from the U.S.S.R. Internationally, however, the de-emphasis upon the ideological location principles began much earlier in Yugoslavia (after 1950), Poland and Hungary (after 1956) than in East Germany, Czechoslovakia, Rumania and Bulgaria (after 1963-66). These evolutionary changes are the product of two trends: (1) changing personal experience (e.g., in attempting to attain certain economic goals) and environmental conditions (e.g., external, such as Soviet relationships) interacting with individual and group belief-disbelief systems to cause frequently some significant substitution of non-ideological (e.g. economic) beliefs for formerly dominant ideological beliefs; and (2) increasing numbers of individual participants in the planning and decision-making processes, many of them specialists or technocrats, whose lower ranking of ideological beliefs *vis-à-vis* their higher ranking of technical, economic or social beliefs, leads to a gradual shift in the aggregate balance of the decision-making group from a more to a less ideological aggregate belief-disbelief system.

Complexity of analysis increases when attention is focused upon individual ideological principles. Their aggregate application yields decisions which disperse, as opposed to concentrate, industrial production. Yet conflict of principles may occur. At the state level, for example, Czechoslovak planners are confronted by principle 4, which requires wide industrial dispersion throughout the nation and by principles 2 and 3 which require priority industrial investment in the background minority region of the nation – Slovakia.[22] Since no individual, or group of decision-makers, holds more than one belief – and hence principle – at any one level in their belief hierarchies,[23] ceteris paribus, low rates of industrial development in Slovakia would occur when the most influential decision-makers held principle 4, ensuring adequate industrial expansion in Bohemia and Moravia as well as Slovakia, higher in their aggregate belief systems than principles 2 and 3. By contrast, it is unnecessary for location principle 2 to be present at even the lowest level in the belief systems of Bulgarian, East German, Hungarian or Polish decision-makers since

minority ethnic populations are absent from their national planning territories. Principles 3, 4 and 5 probably form an important part of these decision-makers' ideological beliefs, but certain constraints have restricted their translation into practice. Development of backward regions to achieve more locational evenness demanded priority industrialization in East Germany of areas north of Berlin and along the western Oder and Neisse valleys, yet such policy has been constrained by economies of redeveloping and expanding industry within the already highly industrialized Erfurt-East Berlin-Dresden triangle.[24] In Poland the principle to develop the backward regions delimited 'Poland B' – south-east, east and north of the Vistula river – as the region of priority industrialization; its application in reality was restricted by economies of industrial expansion in Upper Silesia and by the need to invest large sums of money in the reconstruction and industrialization of the 'western and northern territories', i.e., the areas that Poland regained from Germany in 1945 and which have functioned as a frontier region of pioneer Polish settlement since that year. Hungarian planners who hold high-ranking ideological beliefs have been concerned to decentralize existing, and to disperse new, industrial development from Budapest. Yet despite the concurrence of principles 3, 4 and 5 towards this common end, Budapest has continued its rapid industrial growth. On the other hand, the virtually undeveloped nature of all of Bulgaria created an environment which generally elevated principles 4 and 5 to higher ranks in the Bulgarian planners' belief systems than principle 5. As the less developed region of East Europe (i.e., all but East Germany, Silesia and Bohemia-Moravia)[25] became more industrialized, however, the growth of urban settlements at locations selected for industry increased the differentials between town and country. If decision-makers held strong ideological beliefs on this score, one can suppose that they might take action to restrict or reverse this trend. In reality, principle 5 seems to have been applied to locational decisions only rarely, except possibly in Bulgaria.

By contrast, a high correlation in Czechoslovakia, Rumania and Yugoslavia between backward areas and distinct, economically poorer ethnic groups undoubtedly explains the substantial efforts to develop such areas in these nations. In Czechoslovakia, the Slovaks, a large minority group, inhabit the major underdeveloped eastern region. Yugoslav backward regions, however, are settled by the large, dominant Serb people, and by the Macedonians, Montenegrins and Albanians. In Rumania, however, the poorer people are the majority group, the Rumanians. The best economic conditions are enjoyed in Yugoslavia and Rumania by small minorities, the Slovenes, by the large minority Croat people, and the Hungarians and Germans. This same problem of backwardness, however, may be a socio-environmental variable which has different impacts upon the content and structure of decision-makers' belief systems as between different ethnic groups and between different-sized (i.e., large, small, majority, minority) ethnic groups. That these interactions occur serves to underline the complexities of the situation.

Any discussion of the ideological environment would be incomplete without reference to the Communist notion of man's free will or independent discretion in making decisions. Belief in this notion is the greater, the higher the Marxist-Leninist ideological beliefs rank in the individual's belief-disbelief system. Party members and decision-makers are often convinced of the correctness of the belief. Frequently they have a sense of unbounded optimism in what the Party can do with its control over the use of planning, economic, social, administrative and technological tools to alter society both structurally and spatially. People who advocate that Party policy must take into account constraints such as hostile physical environment, scarce natural resources, poor infrastructure or inadequate skilled labour supply in regional development policies or industrial location choices are severely reprimanded for their 'bourgeois sabotage tactics'. Exercise of independent discretion is interrelated with the possession of very great decision-making power by an individual or by a group of individuals, i.e. with the highly centralized power associated with the command economy that prevailed in East Europe generally until the early 1960s (in Yugoslavia only to 1951). Operation of free will resulted then in a greater frequency than in the later 1960s (1950s and 1960s in Yugoslavia) of so-called 'adoptive' locational decisions. These constitute decisions which (1) overrule expert advice as to the scale, type or location of a project; or (2) minimize or ignore the importance of constraints which threaten the economic or technological success of a project; or (3) represent drastic measures to open serious bottlenecks (e.g., in capital supply, in transport, in non-agricultural employment opportunities) or to break vicious poverty circles at the regional or local levels; or (4) are designed to secure a 'technical demonstration effect' to show opponents (e.g. the Church or apathetic peasantry) how far a planning system is capable of altering ways of

living; or (5) show in the location chosen a poor perception of the environmental conditions that are required by a given project.

The growth of the East European iron and steel industry and its ancillaries abounds in examples of essentially adoptive locational decisions. If we ignore the operation of market-orientation factors at the international level which required the location of steel industries in each and every East European country, then within several nations many steel and related industries were located in areas which did not necessarily possess the right quantities or qualities of iron ore or coal, infrastructure (power, transport, water supply), or skilled labour to support them efficiently or economically. Iron and steel plants located after 1948 at Eisenhüttenstadt (then called Stalinstadt) in East Germany, Košice in Czechoslovakia, Dunaujvaros (then called Sztalinvaros) in Hungary, Nikšić and Skopje in Yugoslavia[26] are examples of decisions which fulfilled criteria 1 to 3 above, i.e., the over-ruling of advice, the minimization of constraints and drastic measures to change local economies. The first four plants depend upon costly hauls of materials from distant or foreign regions, the fifth has been hampered in its operation by technical difficulties associated with the use of very low-grade ores and brown coal-bituminous coal mixes for coking coal production. The location of Poland's second largest integrated steel plant at Częstochowa is frequently cited as an example of the fourth type of adoptive decision, in this case the need to show the strength of the state's industrialization – proleterianization – socialization policies at the gate of the pilgrimage centre of the Polish Catholic Church. How far this was really so is difficult to judge without further evidence. Częstochowa is sited upon Poland's only iron ore field and is situated near Upper Silesian coking coal supplies. Development of plants at Schwarze Pumpe (East Germany), Lukavac and Zenica (Yugoslavia) to manufacture coking coal from local brown coal – a process which failed and threw the plants into costly dependence upon brown coal-bituminous coal mixtures or long haul coking coal imports – illustrates poor environmental perception under pressure from Party demands for rapid industrialization. To conclude that all adoptive decisions yield poor location choices, however, would be erroneous. Sometimes the location of a project in an underdeveloped area, at first unprofitable, in the long run renders profitable other industries which eventually yield positive feedback to the original project, justifying it economically *ex post facto*. The growth of metal-fabricating industries in Macedonia and south Serbia-Kosmet in relation to the Skopje steel plant is a good latent example.

The Decision-Makers' Environment

For long in the West it was assumed, in effect, that East European economic decision-making was, by analogy with the U.S.S.R., subject to total control by a monolithic Communist party, whose members' belief systems were similar and largely undifferentiated in their thinking and behaviour. The whole party and its members were conceived as commanding independent discretionary powers in decision-making *vis-à-vis* non-party persons while co-operative interdependence (harmony, agreement) prevailed within the party. Such a totalitarian concept, which excludes group interests and conflicts, is no longer appropriate to any analysis of East European decision-making.[27] It is now agreed that conflict interdependence, the interaction of conflicting interests, really characterizes decision-making behaviour both within the party and between party and non-party members. Conflict between group interests arises from the interaction of two complex elements: (1) strong groups whose members are commonly bound, and yet differentiated from other groups, by interests vested in their (a) social status, i.e., functioning in the state, collective or private sectors; (b) job and career identity consequent upon division of labour between industry, agriculture, services, administration and their sub-groups such as electric power or chemicals; (c) income levels; (d) participation in decision-making, as between Communists, non-party persons, managers, workers; (e) ethnic affiliation and (f) territorial identity with a region, a place or an administrative unit.[28] (2) Aggregates of individual belief-disbelief system structures and hierarchies, each having common characteristics in thought, ideology and motivation, and yet differing from other aggregates of belief systems. (3) These interactions cause conflicts between groups or individuals for two scarce factors — finance for economic development and political power — since 'the struggle over who gets what when and how . . . takes place entirely within the public domain . . .' so that '. . . individuals and groups are compelled to focus their attention and pressure on the decision-making process if they hope to maintain or improve their status.'[29]

East European industrial location patterns, therefore, have been powerfully shaped by the outcome of conflict interdependence among individuals and groups whose power positions have been institutionalized as part of the administrative and planning machinery. Such individuals and groups form a hierarchy from the most influential top party organs (e.g. the executive, leadership), down through the highest state officials (especially ministers, economic planners, regional planners, or, in Yugoslavia, heads of the six autonomous republics and two autonomous regions),[30] industrial enterprise managers and the military to the regional, local or city political and economic representatives. Conflict occurs between these groups and among members of each group and influences industrial location decisions in several ways.

The more powerful individuals and groups determine which laws of socialist location are applied most frequently to the spatial allocation of industrial capacity in accordance with their quest to satisfy their vested interests. The long-term dominance among East European decision-makers of supporters of the growth of heavy industry[31] over supporters of a shift towards greater expansion of light industries has had profound long-term locational implications. Supported by top party leaders, ministers of various heavy industries (who may be a large group), planners, military experts and parliamentary representatives from regions with industrial resource potentials, heavy industrialization has favoured industrial growth in regions with, or highly accessible to (1) formerly under-utilized mineral and energy resources, particularly brown coal, water power, petroleum, gas, metallic ores and certain non-metallic minerals located in and around the Balkan, Carpathian, Dinaric and Rhodope mountain systems and (2) existing heavy industrial complexes in Upper Saxony, Upper and Lower Silesia and Bohemia-Moravia. This has given great weight in all East European nations to the application of location laws 6 and 8, requiring, respectively, that industry be locationally orientated towards sources of raw-material/energy, and regional industrial specialization on the lines of Kolossovsky's 'energy resource cycles' or of the Soviet 'territorial production complex'.[32] By contrast, the supporters of light industry — some party leaders, certain ministers, parliamentary representatives of regions with large pools of rural labour or without natural resources or both — have occupied weaker ideological and power positions and have been able to attract less support from other potentially interested groups. This weakness has been rooted in (a) what party leaders perceive as a preoccupation with 'bourgeois consumer preference', (b) the dominance of the leadership with its 'national' vested interests over rank-and-file parliamentary representatives with their essentially 'local' vested interests, and (c) the poorer bargaining position of less developed regions with fewer industrial managers and hence less interaction with economic ministers and planners in the planning process[33] vis-à-vis the greater bargaining power of more industrialized regions where there are more industrial managers who interact more frequently with top economic leadership. In addition, however, it is not possible to dissociate the poor bargaining position of representatives of underdeveloped, labour-surplus regions – such as eastern Poland, the Great Alföd of Hungary, Wallachia and Moldavia and Banat in Rumania, much of northern and eastern Yugoslavia – from the dominance of industrial over agricultural interests which, by severely restricting investment in agriculture, has had a negative feedback effect on the growth of food-processing and of farm-serving (machinery, fertilizer) industries in such predominantly agricultural regions. Clearly this power hierarchy among the decision-makers participating in the planning process in East Europe explains the neglect of, or insufficient attention paid to, the application of principles 3, 4 and 5 to industrial locational problems.[34]

Not all individual or group interests, however, necessarily maintain long-term positions of influence. For instance, the military seem to have exercised a good deal of influence upon location decisions until 1954 when the advent of long-range missiles began to undermine arguments for strategic factory location in East Europe. Nevertheless between 1947 and 1954 the military ensured that industrial growth, especially in engineering and chemicals, was dispersed among many locations in a belt from eastern Poland, through Slovakia and the eastward-curving Carpathians in Rumania to central and eastern Bulgaria. On the other hand, after the June 1948 Cominform Resolution, the Yugoslav army succeeded in persuading the planners in Belgrade into re-locating most planned industrial capacity from the northern cities to quite inaccessible areas in the Dinaric-Rhodope mountain systems. Such behaviour gave short-term emphasis to location principles 1 (national security) and 4 (even dispersion); since 1955, military influence on industrial location seems to have waned.

A more fundamental shift in the power balance since the mid-fifties in Eastern Europe has been the product of interaction between three trends: (1) the substitution for the 'cult of personality' by larger, more collective leadership among whom policy conflicts are more frequent, (2) the growing economic and technical complexity of developing societies and (3) the consequent decentralization of management of the economy. As a result, the leadership's consultation and interaction with, and dependence upon, expert advice from scientists, technocrats, economists, industrial managers and regional representatives, has increased rapidly – restricting or eliminating avenues of independent discretion, opening new avenues of conflict interdependence among experts and among party officials, ministers and planners vying for expert support. This broadening of conflict has brought many lower échelons in society into more influential positions concerning policy issues or locational choices. It is interrelated also with the increased flow of information and with the increased need for information which themselves reflect the growing need for 'invisible hand' criteria, such as economic mechanisms, to guide decisions. This subject is pursued later in the sections on the economic, spatial and information environments. For the present, however, it may be noted that these trends have raised the relative importance of the more economic principles 6, 7, 8, 9 and 10 compared with the more ideological principles and it has stimulated greater interest in the spatial aspects of industrial development.

In part, this interest is associated with frequent conflict over location choices among decision-makers who have different personal spatial identities (e.g., Wallachian vs. Moldavian in Rumania, Mazurian vs. Silesian in Poland) or who represent in parliament different electoral areas and who identify themselves and their success with the economic and social progress of their areas. The impact upon locational decisions of such spatial identity, however, is the greater the more that identity is also associated with different ethnic groupings. In other words the 400,000 Montenegrins, 2.5 per cent of the Yugoslav population, have had more influence upon Yugoslav industrial location decisions than has an equivalent percentage of the Polish population living in either Szeczcin or Zielona Góra voivodships. Such influence may be both direct and indirect. The Slovenes and Croats in Yugoslavia have not only been powerful in decision-making but the outcome of the decision to decentralize economic management has essentially worked to the advantage of their growth.[35] These questions will be referred to later in the section on 'the spatial environment'.

The Economic Environment

To shake off vestiges of capitalism, the Communist governments of Eastern Europe acted, between 1947 and 1948, to convert economics from its traditional role as an 'invisible hand' guiding locational decisions through pricing (and hence, costs and profits), to a mere accounting device. Another motive for the change was the elimination of constraints which economic criteria – as guides to the efficient allocation of scarce resources – might impose upon the free will of the Party in attempting to apply the social, political and strategic principles of location policy. In effect, as the preceding section showed, this action, together with the establishment of a formalized planning system and command economy, substituted bargaining between interest groups for economic criteria in determining the allocation of resources. Despite some decentralization in economic decision-making and management since 1957, necessitating the adoption of criteria of economic efficiency, the economic environment in Eastern Europe (except Yugoslavia since 1964) still continues to suffer from the major defect of the command economy: non-market, or arbitrary, pricing which confers neither utility nor scarcity values on goods and services. These prices, nevertheless, constitute the economic environment to which ministers, planners and industrial managers respond in attempting to fulfil locational plans or maximize output on fixed budgets. To do this, they require knowledge of costs, revenue and profits, which they calculate using the arbitrary prices; questioning the rationality of the prices lies outside their sphere of authority.

Use of arbitrary prices for cost-benefit calculations has been enhanced by the conflicts between interest groups, each of which seeks sources of, or arguments in, support of their locational interests. In most East European countries until the early or mid-sixties, for example, ministers frequently argued strongly for the expansion of existing plants or the location of new plants in already industrialized regions on account of the lower investment and operating costs in these regions as compared with the higher plant investment and operating costs associated with new factories in virgin areas. The minister's high-ranking position, combined with this powerful argument, permitted ministers to have their own way. In most countries, therefore, manufacturing growth has been greater in the larger cities such as Warsaw, Poznań or Wroclaw in Poland, Prague, Brno and Bratislava in Czechoslovakia, Budapest in Hungary, Bucharest and Braşov in Rumania, and Ljubliana, Zagreb and Belgrade in Yugoslavia – than in smaller cities. Often this ran counter to the application of the ideological – strategic principles which were supported more by regional planners. The latter advocated control over large city growth and greater dispersion to avoid the high social costs of large cities. The small number of

such planners and their inferior position *vis-à-vis* the ministers (who were supported also by national economic planners) combined with the lack of social cost data and the difficulties of predicting investment and operating costs in virgin areas to weaken the regional planners' opposition. Not until better data became available in the 1960s, permitting regional planners to show that, economically and socially, cities are optimal in the size range of 50,000-300,000 and become high social cost burdens when their population exceeds one million, has this ministerial dominance and industrial agglomeration been somewhat mitigated. The impact of the regional planners has been the greater since they have been able to draw on broadening sources of support for their position, as decentralization of decision-making and the involvement of technocrats grew. Formerly, when conflict occurred in the narrower upper échelons, the only checks on ministerial behaviour came from top party leaders, more 'ideological' ministers, powerful planners and regional representatives who might insist on some dispersion.

This shift of influence, interacting with the growing concern for economic efficiency, has significantly altered patterns of industrial location. Recent industrial location trends in Poland are a good illustration of this point. Until 1960, Polish industrial growth had been spatially allocated to two types of location: (1) the localized mineral-resource and energy-resource region of Upper Silesia (coal, iron ore, lead, zinc, limestone) where plants were agglomerated, though subject to some intra-regional dispersion on account of land scarcity; (2) the major cities with their distributional, transport and infrastructural facilities, although some decentralization of plants to, or of industrial expansion in, smaller satellite cities had been achieved, especially around Łódź. From 1960, however, industrial growth in larger cities and in Upper Silesia slowed significantly, with the exception of certain key plants such as the Nowa Huta steel combine. Indeed, industrial capacity has actually declined in Warsaw as manufacturing was moved out from the city to nearby satellite cities. By contrast there has been a rapid rise in the number of large plants located in the medium-sized cities of 40,000 population or over. Much of this dispersion has been achieved in central Poland where industrial growth has focused upon energy-using and chemical industries. Some use local resources such as the thermal-electricity plants based on Konin brown coal that supply new alumina/aluminium smelter and aluminium-fabricating industries at Konin, Koło and Kłodawa or the ore-concentration plant at

Leczyca north of Łódź using local low-grade iron ores. Others are based directly on imported material inputs. The best example is Poland's first modern oil refinery which is located on the Friendship-pipeline (which runs from the Soviet Volga oilfield at Kuybyshev to Schwerin on the Oder in East Germany) and the Vistula river at Płock, a city of 50,000 people located 80 km west of Warsaw. Another is the nitrogen fertilizer combine located at Puławy some 120 km south of Warsaw, along the Vistula river, which uses eastern Polish and western Soviet natural gas. The Płock oil refinery and petrochemicals complex is the source of semi-processed chemicals which are being further manufactured by a whole series of other chemical industries located in small cities (e.g., Toruń, Swiecko) within the region bounded by Warsaw, Łódź, Poznań and Gdańsk.

High prices on consumer goods, fixed to yield high profits for capital re-investment and to restrict consumer demand, encouraged planners for most of the post-war period to apply socialist principles to, and to pay less attention to comparative locational costs in, the location of new consumer-goods factories. Often high-value consumer-goods production was located in backward areas where high value and low transport costs of hauling light materials and products offset poor accessibility and labour quality. Growth of textile, light metals and plastics industries in the Yugoslav Karst and islands provides an excellent example. Conversely, low subsidized prices for energy, materials and basic producers' goods (cement, steel, sulphuric acid, etc.) have encouraged planning institutes to undertake research into comparative location costs to an extent unheard of in the higher-order manufacturing sector. Particular attention is paid, since the introduction of economic efficiency criteria, to marketing costs as well as to production cost variables. Perhaps the cement industry has been subject to more computer-programmed research than any other industry.

Until the advent of economic efficiency criteria (1954 in Yugoslavia, after 1960 elsewhere), planners frequently paid insufficient attention to *which* costs required analysis in order to make a location decision. For long – though not now – products had the same price wherever they were sold, irrespective of the locational relationships between production and consumption locations. Decision-makers were genuinely misled, it seems, at least in the less developed Balkan states, into believing that transport costs were zero or inconsequential. The perception of a zero-transport-cost environment by decision-makers allowed them to focus attention upon the socialist principles *per se* for guid-ance, to disperse plants more freely according to principles 2, 3, 4 and 5 and to concentrate in cost calculations purely on the production function. When transport costs were included after 1952 in Yugoslavia and 1955 elsewhere, all the idiosyncrasies of subsidized and 'deviational' tariffs (i.e., special transport rates for particular articles or for transport to and from particular factories) evoked responses from ministers, planners and managers in the same manner as did pricing. For example, although the Yugoslav government called for greater use of under-utilized waterway capacity (Sava, Danube rivers), few industrial concerns located along those waterways used them, as longer rail journeys for their materials and products were often cheaper because rail rates were heavily subsidized. Labour costs are not considered a locational variable since employment is a planned factory norm and wages are fixed nationally to reflect basic living needs. Labour, however, has had powerful indirect influences upon location through social investment (housing) requirements and skills. The Marxist theory of surplus value appears not to have been at all significant in locational decisions except indirectly through low capital charges which encouraged investment more in capital-intensive than in labour-intensive industrial processes. Hence the rapid growth of mountain-located hydro-electricity stations throughout central and south-eastern Europe and the lag in the development of thermal power stations using the major fuel resource of the region – brown coal or lignite – in the plains.

The Spatial Environment

In searching for locations for planned industrial expansion, each planner or minister (in Yugoslavia, each workers' council) must become acquainted with the set of locations which should be investigated to establish optimal or satisficer suitability. In reality, decision-makers have poor innate spatial perception. Search for a location thus tends to end with the first or easily found location if it fulfils a desired socialist location law, a desired interest, or the criterion of economic efficiency when this is applied. Three conflicting factors operate to influence the locational search procedures. First, the acute pressure on planners' time that characterizes planning offices restricts the depth of locational analysis that is feasible: the theory of least effort may thus be highly relevant to the planner's search behaviour. Secondly, it is characteristic of the developing East European countries, where modernization is recent, that many planners (and other decision-makers who put pressure on planners) retain a strong sense of spatial or territorial identity with their home area. They may thus have an urge to steer projects to that area and hence begin their locational search there or neglect to search in other areas. Such behaviour is undoubtedly much more likely and more complex in Yugoslavia where ethnic and hence spatially identified conflicts are ever present than in ethnically homogeneous states. It can be argued, therefore, that when a planner or group of planners with marked territorial identity hold great power – as they did during the period of highly centralized management – they were in a good position to channel investment into 'their' region. Further research is required to prove or disprove this hypothesis, yet Yugoslav industrial location patterns during the period 1947-57 seem to indicate the strong influence of Boris Kidrič, the chief planner, in facilitating rapid growth of industry in Slovenia. Thirdly, the broader the participation by different groups in the planning process, the larger the number of interests with specific spatial identities, so that planners have been subjected to more and more interaction with other decision-makers, from managers and city government representatives to top party leaders with particular spatial preferences, regarding the range of possible locations. The outcome of this interaction may well reflect the degrees of influential power which various spatially identified individuals and groups represent. Yet, combined with a growing involvement of expertise and a concern for economic efficiency, it seems unlikely that location choices since 1960 express individual or group pressure which has no or only poor economic foundations. By contrast, before 1960, there were fewer checks on top decision-makers so that industrial location choices *could* have represented the spatial preferences of the planners, ministers of top leadership. At present, the inadequacy of evidence does not permit any conclusive statements on this score. Further research is necessary to establish or revoke any link between decision-makers, their spatial identities and actual locational decisions. Such research would require an analysis of the level upon which spatial identity occurs in the individual's belief-disbelief system in comparison with other locational variables such as economic, social or ideological awareness.

The Information Environment

A major variable in this discussion of spatial perception for purposes of planning industrial location at the national or regional level is the spatial pattern of information sources, their quality and quantity, and the flows of information between the source points and the 'consumption' (i.e., decision-making) points. In the model of a highly centralized economy, efficient location choices, *ceteris paribus*, require perfect information from all areas of the state whether developed or undeveloped. Yet this assumes that the quantity and quality of information supplied must be the greater, the more imperfect is the spatial perception of the state area by the decision-makers who are localized in the central capital city. As a general rule, therefore, information should be increasingly better for areas at increasing distances from that city, that is, it will be inversely related to the decreasing perfection of the spatial perception that decision-makers have of territory and its attributes with increasing distance from the central city. Of course, their spatial identity with regions other than the capital city provides some correction of the information picture, yet detailed scientific data are still essential from all points of the nation. A model of decentralized decision-making such as the most far-reaching Yugoslav example, by contrast, attempts to achieve perfection of information supply from many small areas to their central points – capitals of the six republics, district or commune centres, industrial enterprises – where the information is processed.

In reality, the supply of information is imperfect. Inevitably, as scientific knowledge and methodology progress, there are at any given point in time either insufficient data on, or awareness of, relevant problems. In the earlier post-war years in the region, secrecy and manipulated statistics provided planners and other decision-makers with poor data. This was not unconnected with the behaviour of ministers or factory managers to inflate or deflate their productive capabilities in order to gain prestige (and income) by overfulfilling plans. Lines of communication for collecting data and applying planning decisions are still dominantly vertical and the horizontal links at proper spatial levels are usually weak. Information relevant to the coordination of essentially linked activities at the local or regional level, therefore, has often been unavailable, with a resulting loss of external economies. However, basically the problem is that information is of poor quality as long as price, and hence cost and profit, remain arbitrary: success indicators and investment criteria are of little real value.

In addition, the spatial and group interaction patterns of decision-makers with vested interests inevitably condition the type, quality and locational preference of the information that planners receive concerning any given project. There is no guarantee, therefore, that there will not be (1) considerable variation in the information available as between different areas of the state or region; (2) similar variability is likely in the information environment for the alternative locations relevant to any given project; (3) some relationship between the frequency of information flows, the degree of pressure of vested interests and distance to the capital city where the decisions are made. This is a whole field for investigation; yet the probability of its importance must be established in order to complete the environmental picture pertaining to decisions about industrial location in East Europe. For the present, it is important to establish that, in the centralized decision-making systems of the East European nations (except Yugoslavia), most decision-makers (party leaders, ministers, planners), and those influencing decisions (parliamentary and economic representatives of the regions of the state, most experts on geographical, economic, technical and scientific matters located in the centralized Academics of Sciences) are all located in the central city. One may suppose then that the information environment is more susceptible to the effects on information flows of vested interests and group conflict, and that its quality depends upon the influential standing of the Academicians, than in the more decentralized system of Yugoslavia where economic criteria operate more effectively to influence decentralized decisions. Nevertheless, in the other nations there are certain group or individual interests which do not necessarily have their seats of representatives in the capital city, namely, the city governments, industrial managers and, say, the church. The question which must be raised but cannot be answered here is this; does the friction of distance between the locations of these individuals and groups and the central city affect their ability to influence centrally-made decisions? The answer would probably be 'yes' since influence is likely to be greater the more personal contact and interaction there is and this is clearly the prerogative of the higher ranks of the decision-making hierarchy. Conversely, decision-makers located at increasing distances from the capital city are in increasingly inferior positions to influence central decisions, unless they have personal contact and friendship with influential participants in the decision-making process who are located in the central city.

What information has been available has often been poorly processed. Emphasis upon the appointment of politically reliable people at all levels of administration, from the Planning Commissions down, has restricted the inflow of the necessary economic expertise into appropriate offices. Decisions have thus been based sometimes upon superficial or naïve analysis as, for example, of inter-regional growth rates in Yugoslavia. However, the régime alone cannot be blamed for this. The fundamental problem has been the overall lack of even secondary school education among the first generation of planners, let alone any real planning experience. Universities have now produced a new crop of experts who are eager to apply modern computational methods to planning and locational problems. The introduction of efficient data processing is being restrained, however, by politicians who fear that linear programmes and computers, in producing optimal planning solutions, undermine their own authority and credibility.

Even given perfectly rational pricing, data collection, data processing and decision-taking, there is still no guarantee that optimal location solutions could be produced. The reason lies in the serious limitations upon the time, financial resources and comprehension of planners to devise exhaustive alternative plans and projects for objective socio-economic comparison. There are also serious limitations on the ability of planning bodies to compare competing projects satisfactorily. During the years of the open competition for investment in Yugoslavia, the investment bank was flooded with 250- to 750-page project proposals which received little more than adequate analysis at the cost of two or three years' delay in reaching a decision. Moreover, given efficient evaluation of competing projects, there is, in Yugoslav experience, little guarantee that the projects proposed will be either properly documented or objectively assessed. Two points are relevant: (a) factory workers' councils, regional councils, industrial associations usually have insufficient expertise and knowledge to produce really sound economic projects; (b) people devising projects have insufficient education to understand the books available that give lengthy instructions on how to cost projects and how to establish their likely profitability or rentability.

Conclusion

Industrial location decisions in the planned economies of the Eastern European Soviet-bloc states, and of Yugoslavia prior to 1954, result officially from the impartial application of objective socialist laws. It is evident that many of the laws are applied in practice, but the extent to which they are so depends basically upon several environmental conditions. First, the ideological environment stresses the social, political and strategic virtues of dispersed industrial location patterns, and yet the importance of ideology for decision-making is strongly influenced by the level at which Marxist-Leninist (and at one time Stalinist) beliefs are held in individual and aggregated belief-disbelief systems. Broadly, the immediate post-war Stalinist phase and the socialist revolutionary atmosphere brought the ideological beliefs to a peak of acceptance and application around 1950-51, from which they have subsequently declined. Secondly, that decline is interrelated with some decentralization or 'collectivization' of decision-making and the growth in the numbers of individuals, groups and interests which conflict both within and outside the normal channels of decision-making interaction. In the last analysis, this establishes that conflict interdependence determines how far and which location principles are applied in any given decision. Over time and especially since 1956, the association of rising groups of experts with, thirdly, the changing nature and the growing importance of the economic environment in decision-making has increasingly shifted the balance of power towards the application of economic criteria in industrial location decision-making and to a more rigorous assessment of the applicability of the more ideological principles to location decisions. Indeed, the principles are being subordinated more and more to economic considerations, though the decision-makers' response to the economic environment made it somewhat more important even between 1948 and 1956 than is often realized. Finally, the interaction between the perception of the spatial environment and the information environment, may hold key answers to the understanding of certain agglomerative tendencies in Eastern European industrial location patterns, but this cannot be established for the present. A major problem is that, frequently, there is an apparent spatial coincidence between the aims of the socialist location principles and the various environments within which they operate. Industrial dispersion on the one hand results from the operations of principles 1, 2, 3, 4, 5, and 9 interacting with the influential ascendance of the military, ideological planners and party leaders, ethnic minority pressures, diversity in the spatial identities of many participants in decision-making, and regional planners with good comparative socio-economic cost-benefit data. Industrial concentration appears, on the other hand, to be associated with principles 6, 7, 8 and 10 interacting with the ascendance of ministers, sector planners, managers of larger industrial enterprises, more centralized decision-making involving fewer participants. This results in a reduced supply, both in terms of

quantity and quality, of information (or better ec[o]nomic data) concerning locational alternatives and da[t] for selection of the best locations.

Notes

1 *Webster's Third New International Dictionary of th[e] English Language* (1968), 760. This definition o[f] 'environment' is held throughout the paper, unles[s] specified.

2 The following are selected works which give both [a] review and an extensive bibliography of the subject o[f] environmental perception: P. Ambrose (ed.) *Analy[t]ical human geography* (1969), part 5; H.C. Brook[-] field, 'On the environment as perceived', *Progr[.] Geogr.* 1 (1969), 51-80; D.L. Lowenthal (ed[.] 'Environmental perception and behavior', *Univ. o[f] Chicago, Department of Geography, Res. Pap.* 10 (1967); T.F. Saarinen, 'Perception of environment[,] *Ass. Am. Geogr. Commn on College Geograph[y] Resource Pap.* 5 (1969).

3 Studies which touch upon this problem in regard t[o] capitalist economies include: Melvin L. Greenhu[t,] *Microeconomics and space economy* (1964); M.[L.] Greenhut and M.R. Colberg, *Factors in the locatio[n] of Florida industry* (1962); W. Isard and T.E. Smit[h,] 'Location games: with applications to classic locatio[n] problems', *Pap. reg. Sci. Ass.* 19 (1967), 45-80; [C.] Krumme, 'Toward a geography of enterprise', *Eco[n.] Geogr.* 45 (1969) 30-40; W. Isard *et al., Gener[al] theory; social, political, economic and regional wit[h] particular reference to decision-making analys[is]* (1969); P.J.D. Wiles, *The political economy o[f] Communism* (1962). The only substantial studies [of] enterprise functioning in the planned economies [of] East Europe are: G. Feiwel, *The socialist enterprise: [a] case study of a Polish firm*, but this is economic, n[ot] spatial; and N.J.G. Pounds, 'Fabryka in Julian[a] Marchlewskiego: a textile plant in Łódź, Poland' [in] R.S. Thoman and D.J. Patton (eds.), *Focus o[n] geographic activity: a collection of original studi[es]* (1964), but this is historical, not behavioural.

4 Another reason is the widespread use of 'norms' [of] technical, economic, social or cultural character i[n] planning future change. Such use gives much weig[ht] to normative models which, together with plannin[g] notions, have inhibited the introduction of stochast[ic] models.

5 F.E.I. Hamilton, 'Planning the location of industry i[n] East Europe: the principles and their impact', *Eco[n.] Plann.* 6 (1970), 3-7.

6 Recent unrest in the Albanian-inhabited Kosovo region of south-eastern Yugoslavia and the Yugoslavian government's long overdue response in greatly increased industrial investment in this poverty-stricken region merely serves to substantiate the reality of this objective.

7 The author's discussions of the content of a preliminary version of this paper with staff and students at several American universities indicated that there may well be many similarities in decision-making processes and decision-making behaviour between (i) planned socialist economies and (ii) bureaucratic organizations (federal and state agencies, large corporations, city governments, universities) in the U.S.A. Since this paper was written, broad support has been given to this viewpoint by J. Wolpert, 'Departures from the usual environment in locational analysis', *Ann. Ass. Am. Geogr.* 60 (1970), 220-9.

8 So far this has been most clearly brought out in two recent publications: F.J. Fleron (ed.), *Communist studies and the social sciences* (1969); and R.E. Kanet (ed.), *The behavioral revolution and Communist studies: applications of behaviorally-oriented political research on the Soviet Union and East Europe* (1970).

9 R.M. Kelly and F.J. Fleron, 'Motivation, methodology and communist ideology' in R.E. Kanet (ed.), op. cit.

10 Recently some attention has been paid to the importance of beliefs in establishing scientific viewpoints and methodological 'fashion'. For a comment pertinent to geography see D. Harvey, *Explanation in geography* (1969).

11 M. Rokeach, *The open and closed mind* (1960), 35; S.H. Barnes, 'Ideology and the organization of conflict: on the relationship between political thought and behavior', *J. Politics* 28 (1966), 513-30.

12 These are beliefs acquired from experience and social environment respectively before and after exposure to education in Communist ideology. They may complement or conflict with ideological beliefs which individuals acquire through the socialization process in childhood, educational training, party indoctrination and later functioning in society.

13 R.M. Kelly and F.J. Fleron, op. cit. 4.

14 M.B. Smith, 'A map for the analysis of personality and politics', *J. soc. Issues* 23 (1968), 15-28; H.H. Hyman, *Political socialization: a study of the psychology of political behavior* (1959).

15 This is an important point because it is frequently alleged that it is difficult to gain membership of the Communist Party in East Europe and the Soviet Union — a fact expressed in the low percentages of the working population who are members. Therefore, not only are many 'politically committed' people left outside the CP but some of them do not wish to become members.

16 H. Eysenck, *The psychology of politics* (1900)

17 This is an avenue of further research which lies outside the scope of this paper. Any results of such research must take account, however, of Soviet influence and its impact upon international or Slav/non-Slav variations in the importance and nature of ideological commitments. Nevertheless, it is also true that these same variables in East Europe have provided selective 'filters' of Soviet ideology which have been influential in yielding variegated interpretations of official ideology.

18 This does not mean, however, that individual decisions, which must be investigated, are unique, but it does mean that empirical evidence from many case studies is essential to be able to test adequately, to embellish or to reject existing sociological, psychological and group behavioural hypotheses which at present are invoked to evaluate the role of ideology in decision-making.

19 R.M. Kelly and F.J. Fleron, op. cit., 15. It seems hard to accept this statement as it stands, even though it contains a certain truth. East European leaders and decision-makers, for example, went to considerable pains to state, and to try to demonstrate, the superiority of the ideological concepts of Communism over their capitalist competitors several years before economists began to urge the application of economic scientific tools to decision-making. On the other hand, the evolution and practice of Yugoslav ideology clearly was in response to the challenge of Soviet-dominated Communist ideology.

20 F.E.I. Hamilton, 'Some aspects of spatial decision-making in planned economies', *Pap. reg. Sci. Ass.* 25 (1970).

21 This latter point is discussed briefly in F.E.I. Hamilton, 'The location of industry in East-Central and South-east Europe' in G.W. Hoffman (ed.), *Eastern Europe: essays in geographical problems* (1971).

22 Of course there need not be any conflict as regards Slovakia where priority investment allocations from the Czechoslovak state budget might still be dispersed

within Slovakia. This kind of phenomenon may be called 'dispersed localization'. See F.E.I. Hamilton in G.W. Hoffman, op. cit.

23 H. Eysenck, op. cit.

24 See this author's discussion of a new concept, the 'spatial elasticity of investment planning' in G.W. Hoffman, op. cit., for a summary view of this problem as it pertains to East Europe.

25 For a discussion of the main industrial area of East-Central Europe before the second world war, see G.W. Hoffman, op. cit.

26 For details see F.E.I. Hamilton, 'The location of the Yugoslav iron and steel industry', *Econ. Geogr.* 40 (1964), 46-64.

27 See, for example, M. Lodge, 'Groupism' in the post-Stalin period', *Midwest J. polit. Sci.* 12 (1968), 330-51; S.I. Ploss, *Conflict and decision-making in Soviet Russia* (1965); H.G. Skilling, 'Interest groups and Communist politics', *World Politics* 18 (1966), 435-51.

28 See R. Conquest, *Power and policy in the U.S.S.R.* (1961); R. Pethyridge, *A key to Soviet politics* (1962); and especially the Slovak theorist M. Lakatos, 'K niektorym problemom struktury nasej politickej sustavy' (On some problems of the structure of our political system). *Pravny Obzor* 1 (1965), 26-36, in Slovak.

29 J.J. Schwartz and W.R. Keech, 'Group influence and the policy process in the Soviet Union', *Am. polit. Sci. Rev.* 62 (1968), 313-14.

30 The six republics are Bosnia-Hercegovina, Croatia, Macedonia, Montenegro, Serbia and Slovenia. The two autonomous areas located within the republic of Serbia are, respectively, Kosovo-Metohija (Kosmet) in the south and Vojrodina in the north.

31 Heavy industry in the Communist world is a hood term which is synonymous with 'producers'-goods industries'. It includes all mining, electricity generation, fuel-processing, metallurgy, engineering (frequently termed 'machine-building' from the Russian language), chemicals and some timber-processing industries.

32 These are discussed in R.E. Lonsdale, 'The Soviet concept of the territorial production complex', *Am. Slavic Rev.* 24 (1965), 466-78.

33 For an outline discussion of interaction between decision-makers in the planning process, readers are referred to this author's article in *Pap. reg. Sci. Ass.*, op. cit. (1970).

34 This has been true even of Yugoslavia where strong ethnic and nationalist pressures have influenced industrial location. See F.E.I. Hamilton, *Yugoslavia: patterns of economic activity* (1968).

35 F.E.I. Hamilton, op. cit. (1968), Chapters 8 and 16.

Reprinted from *Transactions*, 52, 1971, Institute of British Geographers, London, with permission.

22 The Changing Distribution of Polish Industry, 1949-65: A General Picture

by Andrew H. Dawson

University of St. Andrews

Since 1945 the communist government of Poland has expanded manufacturing and extractive industry in the belief that 'industrialization is the chief factor in economic progress', and accepted that 'policy on the location of industrial investments is an integral part of the general policy of industrialization – especially in a planned economy'.[1] This study was undertaken to discover what general changes have occurred in the distribution of this group of industries against the background of the locational policies of the Polish government.

Two approaches have been used. After an account of the chief elements of Polish industrial policy, the major trends of industrial growth and changes of population over the country are outlined, and the developing pattern of industrialization is analysed through the use of trend surfaces. The dense-space method of cluster analysis is then employed in an attempt to divide the country into regions with similar patterns of development between 1949 and 1965.

The Data

The scope of the study was limited by the availability of data. In studies of the changing distribution of economic activity, A. Kukliński, S.E. Brown and C.E. Trott, and S. Leszczycki,[2] among others, have all used the twenty-two *województwa* (provinces), for which much information has been published, but a finer division is required if homogeneous areas within provinces, or which straddle provincial boundaries, are to be revealed. The *gromada* (parish) and *powiat* (county) are two such administrative divisions, and details of industrial employment and population in 1949/50, 1960 and 1965 have recently been published on a constant areal basis for the 317 counties, seventy-four county and five provincial towns.[3] It is from this source that the data have been drawn.

The data have been modified to take account of the administrative separation of towns of medium and large size in Poland from the surrounding counties. While small towns are incorporated within counties, those with populations of approximately 20,000 or more have

independent county status. But this separation from the surrounding rural areas has no validity in the context of the industrialization of Poland for, while new industry has frequently been located in towns, workers have often been recruited from villages and farms. Administrative restraints or their permanent settlement in cities where housing has been in short supply, or the lack of incentive to move house where cheap or free transport between residence and workplace has been provided by the employing enterprise, have encouraged a pattern of short-distance, village-to-town commuting on a large scale. Planning authorities have generally attempted to reduce the distance of journeys only where they have exceeded 45 minutes in each direction. Thus, large numbers of the rural population began to work in near-by towns between 1945 and 1965, and in many villages the role of agriculture declined as the populations became industrialized.[4]

In order that this situation should be reflected more accurately than in the original data, county and provincial towns have been incorporated with the surrounding counties and, where a town is contiguous with more than one county, the values for the town have been proportionally divided between the counties according to the population of each county in the same year.

Thus modified, the data have been used to investigate the following four aspects of change:

(a) Changes in the number of workers in manufacturing and extraction in each county between 1949 and 1965. Although industrial growth began in 1945 as the war ended, 1949 is a suitable starting point, for it marked both the end of the programme of reconstruction which re-established the pre-war levels of employment and output (though not of the rebuilding of all damaged industrial plant), and also the beginning of a conscious effort to alter the distribution of industry. 1965 is the year in which the third part of the programme of industrialization and redistribution, the Second Five-Year Plan, was completed. There are no published statistics showing the division of employment by branch of industry or between manufacturing and mining at the county level for the post-war years.

(b) Changes in the population of each county between 1950 and 1965 have been included because they affect the proportion of the total population which is employed in industry, that is, the degree of industrialization of any county. The population variable is one to which the Polish government has paid considerable and increasing attention, attempting to tailor the supply of industrial jobs to the demand for employment in all parts of the country. Indeed, some Polish writers have gone so far as to adopt the number of new jobs created as the most appropriate measure of the yield from industrial investments.[5] Changes in the size of the working-age group, which would have been more appropriate than changes in the total population, are not available for the whole period.

(c) Changes in the index of industrialization, that is, in the proportion of the population employed in manufacturing and extraction, combine the effects of (a) and (b) into one value. This is expressed in workers per thousand of the total population. In a situation in which the government has been attempting to restrain industrial growth in some areas and to increase its role in the economy of others, changes in the index provide an appropriate measure of success, but they give no indication of the strength or direction of the constituent, causal changes in *(a)* and *(b)*.

(d) The relationship between the patterns of change (a), (b) and (c) in each county was examined by cluster analysis,[6] and the clusters were transferred to the map for analysis of their areal arrangement.

Although the four aspects of change produced only a skeletal picture of the changing role of manufacturing and mining, the presentation of these basic parameters at the county level permitted a detailed analysis of the changing distribution of industry and of the changing pattern of industrialization to be made.

Polish Industrial Policy

Changes in the distribution of industry since 1949 have been made almost entirely at the behest of the government. Three aspects of policy which have had areal consequences have been the desire to build up heavy industry, to distribute industry more widely, and to obtain the highest yield from investments.

Both strategic needs, associated with East-West hostility, and the autarkic policy of the early 1950s, led to the expansion of the basic, producer-goods industries, while, since the late 1950s, the emphasis on this branch of the economy has been maintained through COMECON plans for Polish specialization upon coal, coke, primary metallurgy and associated chemical products.[7] Such policies have inevitably resulted in substantial growth among the already-existing centres of mining, metallurgy and heavy engineering, with their close locational ties

Figure 22.1 Location of places mentioned in the text

with sources of raw material, and this trend has been strengthened in a country with meagre resources because t has been cheaper almost everywhere to enlarge existing factories or locate new plant in existing industrial districts than to build anew in rural areas lacking the basic infrastructure of transport, water and other services. Furthermore, experience has shown that the costs of production are raised by the low level of labour productivity in areas with no tradition of factory employment or industrial skill.

In this situation, the effort to escape from the dichotomy of acute industrial congestion in limited regions and severe rural over-population across the larger part of the country, which was the legacy of the pre-war private enterprise economy, has been limited. Only the rising social costs of industrial growth in such areas as Upper Silesia, Łódź and Warsaw in the late 1950s

(Figure 22.1), expressed in shortages of housing and water, congestion and pollution, produced a more vigorous attempt to deflect expansion to the perimeters of built-up areas or away from them altogether, and a greater emphasis upon taking industry to labour.[8]

The effect of these policies upon individual counties has been the establishment or enlargement of industry where underemployment has existed among farm workers, where employment other than in agriculture has required long-distance commuting, or where important deposits of raw materials have hitherto been neglected. Labour-intensive investments in food-processing, timber and building-material plants have been a common means of industrializing such areas, related to locally supplied and bulky raw materials, to the small size of the available labour force, and to its limited skills. Large factories have been built where surpluses of labour

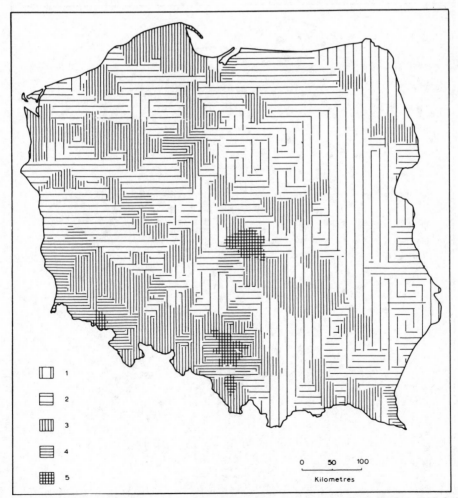

Figure 22.2 Index of industrialization: industrial workers per thousand population, by county in 1949. 1, 0-15; 2, 16-45; 3, 46-105; 4, 106-225; 5, over 225

have been greater or where the 'multiplier' effect of large-scale projects on the local economy has been planned to lead to the growth of new urban and industrial nodes.[9] In highly industrialized counties, by comparison, industry has also been enlarged because of close links with other factories in the same area, because of the desire to restrict the movement of bulky fuels or materials between source and consumer, or because of the existence of skilled labour in the area.[10] However, old industrial premises have occasionally been demolished and operations transferred to new premises in less industrialized counties.[11] Thus, the government has planned the future distribution of industry in terms of population and resource, rather than euclidean, space.

Although it has been government policy (which, in this study, is measured by the changes in industrial employment in each county), which has provided the stimulus for changes in the distribution of industry, area differences in the inherited distribution of industry and population and areal contrasts of population growth have also affected the pattern of industrialization between 1949 and 1965. The general characteristics of these factors and of the distribution of industrial growth will now be described.

The Changing Distribution of Industry: General Pattern

The distribution of industry, expressed by the indices of industrialization, at the beginning of the period under study is portrayed in Figure 22.2. The important elements of the map, in the context of government policy, are the very small number of counties with high and medium values, and the very large number with low values, an indication of the low level of industrialization

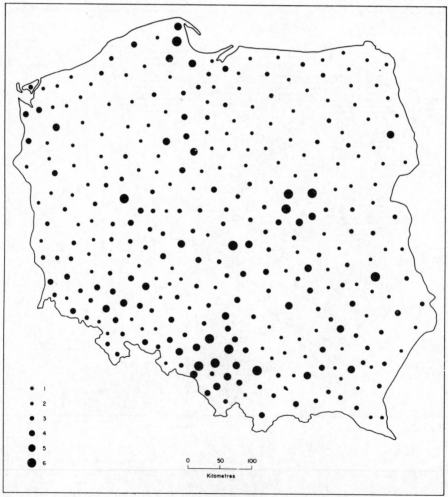

Figure 22.3 Changes in the number of industrial workers between 1949 and 1965, by county: 1, Decline 2-6, Increase: 2, 1-1999; 3, 2000-5999; 4, 6000-13,999; 5, 14,000-29,999; 6, more than 29,999

of the country as a whole. The extreme range of values should also be noted. Fewer than one in twenty of the population worked in industry in 63 per cent of the counties, and fewer than one in a hundred in 18 per cent. At the other extreme, the economies of several counties where industry employed more than one in four of the population were also too specific. Thirdly, counties with high values were largely concentrated in peripheral locations in the south and south-west; and few industrialized counties, which could be developed as growth points, existed in the north and east.

The impact of industrial growth between 1949 and 1965 was extremely widespread (Figure 22.3). The number of workers increased in all except two counties, but the size of increase appears to have depended largely upon the already-existing degree of urban and industrial development. Many of the counties which include large

towns and cities, such as the industrial region of Upper Silesia, the Łódź and Warsaw areas, the Gdansk-Gdynia conurbation, and the few counties in the east where an infrastructure existed, such as Bialystok, Kielce, Lublin and Tarnów, experienced very large increases in the number of industrial jobs. Other counties with similar growth occur in the south-east, but in the Lower Silesian Industrial Region increases were small. Comparison of Figures 22.2 and 22.3 shows that, at the other extreme, the large areas with very low indices in the eastern half of the country only experienced small increases. Thus, government plans to diminish the regional inequalities of economic development appear to have been largely frustrated.

However, the distribution of absolute increases in employment in Figure 22.3 is less significant, in the context of government policy, than the areal variations

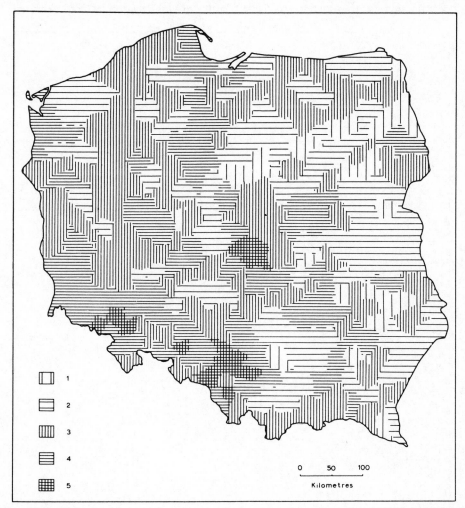

Figure 22.4 Index of industrialization: industrial workers per thousand population, by county in 1965: 1, 0-15; 2, 16-45; 3, 46-105; 4, 106-225; 5, over 225

in the growth of the index of industrialization. Comparisons of Figures 22.2 and 22.4 show that, as the result of the widespread creation of new jobs, high and medium indices were more widely distributed by 1965, and that the area of low values had been substantially reduced. At the same time the indices of high-value areas had not greatly increased, despite the large absolute increases in employment. These impressions are confirmed when the distributions of index values in the two years are generalized into linear and cubic trend surfaces.[12] Both pairs of surfaces show that the whole country experienced increases in index values, and the changes in the dip and strike of the surfaces indicate that significant reductions had been achieved in the contrasts between one part of the country and another. In the case of the linear surface (Figures 22.5A and 22.5B), the angle of dip from south-west to north-east had been reduced, thus indicating that greater progress was made

in industrializing counties in the rural north and east than among those with higher indices in the south and west. The strike of the surface had also changed slightly, apparently in response to the considerable development of new industry in the south and south-east. The cubic surface (Figures 22.5C and 22.5D), which for 1949 reveals a trough of low values in central western Poland between higher indices to north and south, and a uniformly low-value area throughout the east of the country, suggests that the chief areas of the growth of the index were in the central south, central north and extreme north-west, and that the smallest increases occurred in the extreme south-west and south-east. The north-east continued to be an area of very low indices. Thus, the changing pattern of industrialization coincides more nearly with government policy than the distribution of new jobs suggests, but it under-emphasizes the scale of job-creation which occurred in the most

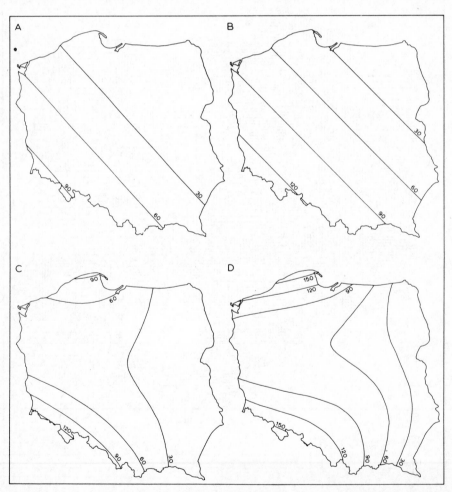

Figure 22.5 Index of industrialization: generalized distributions. A, Linear surface 1949; B, Linear surface 1965; C, Cubic surface 1949; D, Cubic surface 1965. Percentage fit; A, 23-27; B, 22-06; C, 34.07; D, 31.6

industrialized counties between 1949 and 1965.

Figure 22.3 also creates a false impression of increasing concentration of Polish industry in a few counties. Despite the large growth in employment among the major industrial counties, the thirty-eight with indices in excess of 105 in 1949, which had accounted for 56 per cent of the total workforce, claimed only 42 per cent in 1965. The Lorenz Curve (Figure 22.6) shows how this pattern of change was reflected in population, rather than euclidean, space. The y-axis represents the aggregate of industrial indices for the 318 counties, rather than the absolute numbers of workers, and thus the change in the curve between 1949 and 1965 indicates that opportunities for industrial employment were enlarged in the many counties with little industry, and that the concentration of such opportunities in a few counties and the necessity for labour to move to these counties were weakened.

Although Figures 22.4, 22.5 and 22.6 portray a widening distribution of industry, they conceal a marked change in the regional emphasis of industrial development between 1949 and 1965. The extent of this change is revealed by the fact that no correlation existed between the growth of employment in counties in the two sub-periods 1949-60 and 1960-65. This probably reflects not only the inability of a poor country to develop new sources of employment in all rural counties simultaneously and the consequent concentration of development in a restricted number at any one time, but also the attempt to meet the varying regional incidence of demands for new jobs caused by regional contrasts in population growth.

Slow population growth was widespread among rural counties in the east and centre of the country, but this was a reflection of emigration rather than low rates of natural increase. Emigration was the symptom of the urgent need for non-agricultural employment and of the paucity of city amenities and amusements in these areas in 1949. Large increases in population, which were typical of the urban areas and the Northern and Western Territories, were of more complex origin. Immigration swelled the population in both cases, but in the towns the rate of natural increase remained below that for rural areas, while high birth rates among those who had settled in the Northern and Western Territories after the war resulted in an increased demand for new jobs in the early 1960s.[13] Such large increases depressed the index of industrialization, with the result that, for every new job required in many of the eastern counties to offset population growth and maintain the existing level of the index, three or four were needed in the areas of rapid growth.

Thus, the distribution of both new industry and of population growth varied during the period. Some indication has already been given of the general relationship between the two and the consequent changes in the pattern of industrialization, so that it is now possible to turn to the detailed analysis of the areal association of these phenomena and to a preliminary description of the method of analysis employed.

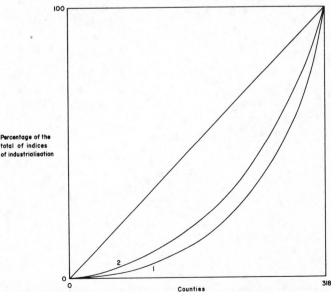

Figure 22.6 Distribution of industrial employment in 1949 and 1965, expressed by the Index of industrialization for each county (the diagonal represents a state of equal Index values for all counties): 1, Distribution in 1949; 2, Distribution in 1965

Method of Analysis

In seeking a typology of areas of industrial change, nine variables were employed:

Index of industrialization for each county for 1949, 1960 and 1965 (variables 1, 2 and 3)

Percentage change in the number of industrial workers in each county for the periods 1949-60, 1949-65 and 1960-65 (variables 4, 5 and 6)

Percentage change in the population of each county for the periods 1950-60, 1950-65, 1960-65 (variables 7, 8 and 9)

The data were subjected to factor analysis, and the factor scores were assigned to each county. The counties were then grouped, using an improved form of mode analysis, *dense space*, which D.C.D. Pocock and D. Wishart have shown to be more discriminating than the minimum-variance centroid and group-average

methods.[14] Before a cluster of counties was recognized, a minimum of four counties with similar scores, as defined by the *enclosure ratio*, was required. With the use of this K-value, the existence of four distinct clusters of counties in nine-dimensional space was revealed at the *basic* level of classification (clusters, 3, 4, 7 and 8). Each cluster was characterized by a considerable degree of internal homogeneity for all nine variables; the cluster variances of the variables were, in almost all instances, less than 0.3 per cent of the total population variances. However, because the data were positively skewed and because small groups of very high and very low values existed, several small clusters of countries with well-pronounced characteristics, but with relatively high intra-cluster variance, remained unclassified. Their existence was revealed only at later stages of the classification when the clusters first obtained (Figure 22.8A) had been

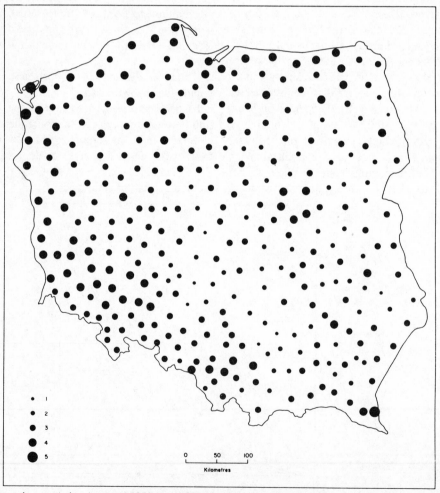

Figure 22.7 Changes in population between 1950 and 1965 by county: 1, Decline of 1 per cent – increase of 2 per cent. 2-5 Increase: 2, 3-12 per cent; 3, 13-40 per cent; 4, 41-108 per cent; 5, more than 108 per cent.

absorbed into one dominant group, and much of the detail had been lost. The scatter diagram of the first three principal components (accounting for 81.4 per cent of the variance) in Figure 22.9 indicates the problem; the loose clustering of small numbers of exceptional values of peripheral location, and the dominance of the larger, tightly knit clusters of central and low values.

In order to preserve the detail of differences between the clusters with intermediate and those with exceptional values, the 148 counties which the first classification had failed to include at the *basic* level were reclassified, using the same technique and the same K-value. The result was that the later stages of the first analysis (Figure 22.8) were reproduced by the second, without the intermediate agglomeration of the clusters. The *coefficient threshold* which produced the second classification was therefore larger than that for the first, and the less compact clusters in Figure 22.9 (clusters 1, 2, 4, 5, 9 and 10) were thus revealed as loose groupings of counties with like characteristics.

Even after this second stage, sixteen counties remained unclassified at the *basic* level. Several were characterized by such exceptional values that it has not been possible to show them in their correct locations in Figure 22.9. They were analysed individually.

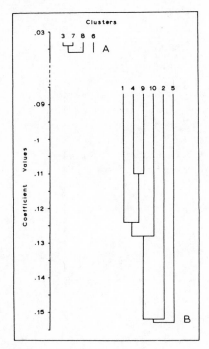

Figure 22.8 Cluster identification and fusion produced by: A, the first stage of classification; B, classification of the 148 remaining counties

The Changing Distribution of Industry: A Typology of Industrialization

Cluster analysis produced a ten-region division of the country, leaving sixteen counties unclassified. The relationship of the clusters to each other and to the unclassified counties is shown in Figure 22.9, where the position of each county is plotted against the first three principal components.

Table 22.1 shows the four highest correlations between the first three principal components and the nine primary variables. It shows that the components were not closely connected with any one variable, but tended to be associated with one or two groups of variables, such as those expressing population growth (7 to 9) or those for the indices of industrialization (1 to 3). Thus, component 1 is associated with the indices of industrialization, and counties with high scores for this component are therefore characterized by high indices for 1949, 1960 and 1965. Counties with high scores for component 2 are characterized by large increases in population and/or employment, but only during the 1950s, and counties with low scores by small increases. Component 3 strongly reflects changes in employment and the level of industrialization in 1960 and 1965. Thus in Figure 22.9, counties with high industrialization indices and low population and industrial growth (in percentage terms), which have high values for component 1 but low scores for component 2, and counties with low industrialization indices and substantial growth, which have low scores for component 1 and high values for component 2, are at opposite ends of the diagram. The characteristics of each cluster will now be described, beginning with those having the lowest indices of industrialization in 1949 (Table 22.2).

Extreme dependence upon agriculture, amounting to overdependence and concealed unemployment on farms, was characteristic of counties in **Clusters 1, 2 and 3**. Those with the lowest indices in 1949 were characterized by the largest percentage increases in employment, and reflected the intention of the government to spread non-agricultural employment more evenly over the country, but the changing locations of growth suggest the scale of the task set by this policy. Table 22.2 shows that, after substantial efforts had been made in the 1950s in cluster 1, the emphasis was transferred to counties in cluser 2 during the early 1960s. The achievement of very high rates of growth throughout the period in all counties appears to have been beyond the country's resources. Yet change in population indicates that an even larger investment was required in these

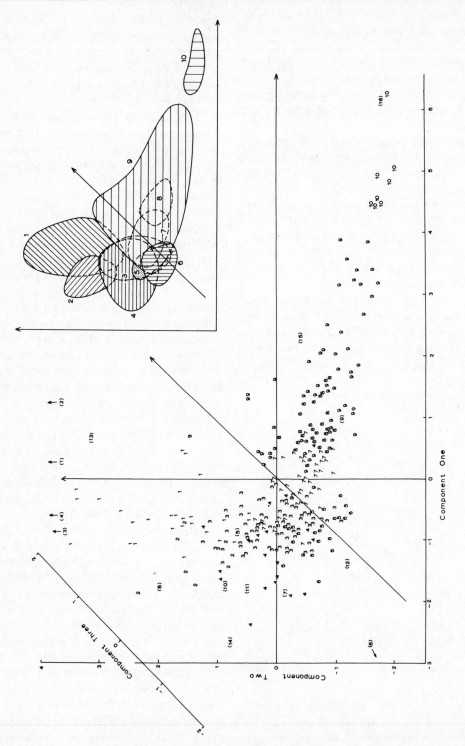

Figure 22.9 Scatter diagram of the first three principal components. Each county is represented by its cluster number (see Table 22.2). Figures in parentheses refer to the unclassified counties shown in Figure 22.10E. Inset, the generalized distribution of clusters

Table 22.1 Correlations between principal components and primary variables

Principal component	Variable	Correlation	Var.	Cor.	Var.	Cor.	Var.	Cor.	Percentage of variance
1	1	0.469	2	0.457	3	0.445	8	0.291	40.1
2	8	0.507	7	0.495	5	0.415	4	0.402	22.8
3	4	0.514	5	0.510	3	0.364	2	0.348	18.5

Table 22.2 Characteristics of the clusters of counties (at the basic level of classification)*

Cluster	1	2	3	4	5	6	7	8	9	10	All Poland
Number of constituent counties	27	8	80	20	10	16	44	30	59	8	318
Index of industrialization 1949	8	9	15	24	24	39	42	75	109†	258	75
Index 1965	42	39	34	48	30	47	75	127	164	262	119
Increase in industrial employment 1949-1965 (1949 = 100)	669	574	299	337	189	191	240	220	256	128	203
– of which 1949-1960 (1949 = 100)	518	236	232	236	233	170	193	178	203	119	169
– of which 1960-1965 (1960 = 100)	132†	246†	128	147	85	113	124	124	123	108	120
Increase in population 1950-1965 (1950 = 100)	114	115	114	141	126	143	124	126	146	125	126

* The 16 counties which could not be classified at the *basic* level are included under All Poland.
† Clusters with *F*-values in excess of 0.3 (a random distribution would give an *F*-value of 1).

areas. Despite the continuing pattern of greater fertility in villages than in towns and the rural character of the clusters, they were distinguished from the others by their small increases in population. Considerable though the increase in industrial employment was, many people moved away to more industrialized parts of the country, especially to the larger towns. Thus the traditional solution to rural population pressure in these areas was perpetuated largely because they formed a compact and very large group of rural counties in eastern and central Poland (Figure 22.10A) which contained few major industrial and urban nodes in which new growth could be fostered. Four of the unclassified counties (numbered one to four in Figures 22.9 and 22.10E) exemplify the attempt to build up new nodes. At the *basic* level of classification they were excluded from cluster 1, not because their indices were not extremely low in 1949, but on account of the exceptionally large growth of employment in them and the very rapid rise of their indices of industrialization.

The growth of industry in clusters 1 and 2 brought the indices of both into line with those of most other rural areas by 1965, and the combined impact of industrialization at home and migration, on a scale never previously possible within the country's own frontiers,

to similar employment elsewhere, was revealed in the falling numbers of farm workers and of the total farm population. Nevertheless, the economy of many counties in the three clusters remains primarily agricultural, and scope for further development of the non-agricultural sectors exists. The density of farm population continues to be higher than in areas with similar physical environments but with greater opportunities for industrial employment, and the industrialization indices of sixteen of the 115 counties in the clusters were still below fifteen. It may be that such counties, possessing few natural resources and little urban settlement, but located close to counties with rapidly growing industries, may remain almost entirely agricultural.

In contrast to these clusters, several different situations are incorporated in the small group of counties in **Cluster 4** (Figure 22.10B). Substantial increases in employment throughout the period and some of the highest rates of population growth are a reflection of the policies of industrial growth in rural areas and the consequent inflow of workers to some counties, but also of the dispersal of factories and workers to peripheral areas of the Upper Silesian Industrial Region in others, and the final stages of resettlement of some of the former German lands in a third group.

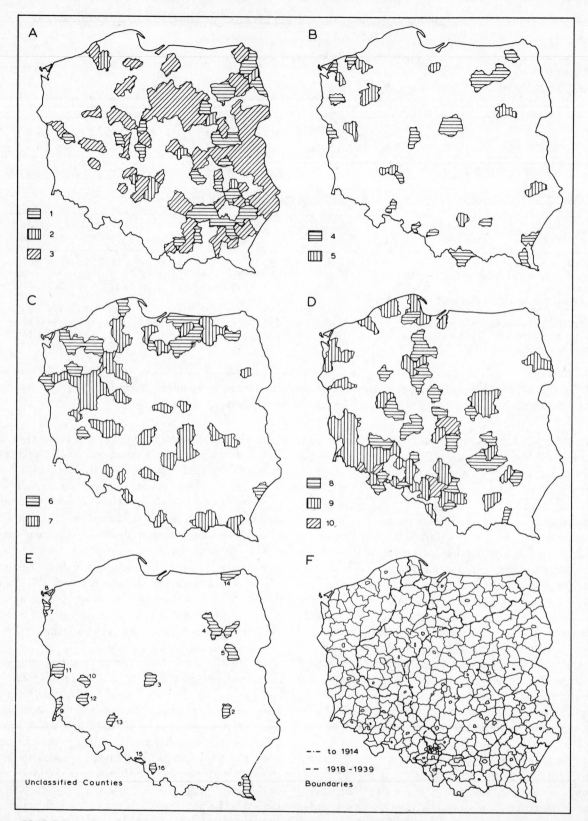

Figure 22.10 Distribution of clusters: A, 1-3; B, 4-5; C, 6-7; D, 8-10; E, unclassified counties; F, county boundaries and location of international frontiers before 1914 and before 1939. The Northern and Western Territories are those areas lying to the north and west of the Polish frontier of 1939

Cluster 5 (Figure 22.10B) is distinguished by the fall in employment in the 1960s after earlier growth, and one of the lowest increases in the index of industrialization. This pattern is difficult to explain, for little has been published about the consequences of changing policy emphasis and few exact admissions have been made of mistakes in settlement and industrial location within the Northern and Western Territories by the Poles. It may be noted that falling employment was accompanied by very small increases in population after 1960, which suggests that emigration to other parts of the country may have been occurring.

Clusters 6 and 7 (Figure 22.10C) are complementary. Both had small indices in 1949, but were not entirely rural. After that date they experienced contrasting patterns of change. Cluster 6 is located almost entirely within the pre-war German lands and, although the growth of population was well above the national average, the small growth of employment and of the index of industrialization suggests that these counties were not faced by a rural population surplus. Cluster 7, in contrast, is dominated by counties in central Poland within the pre-war Polish boundary and areas which, although they lay within Germany until 1945, contained a large Polish element in the population. These counties did not experience total resettlement after the war, and the density of the farm population may have remained at a higher level than the government considered necessary, because the considerable increase in employment and in the index of industrialization seems to reflect a need for alternative sources of employment. However, they may also reflect the relative ease with which industrial expansion could occur in an area with some tradition of factory work, raw materials, and a relatively well-developed infrastructure upon which new industry and settlement could be grafted. In this context, it should be noted that the cluster contains a majority of counties in areas which were under German control until at least 1918 (Figure 22.10F), and when the distributions of clusters 6 and 7 are compared with those of 1, 2 and 3 some positive correlation appears to exist between German settlement or political control in the recent past and an urban-industrial tradition. By 1965, cluster 7 had come to occupy a position between the rural clusters 1 to 6 and the relatively highly industrialized clusters 8 to 10.

However, it is **Cluster 8** (Figure 22.10D) which represents the point of balance, both areally and statistically, among the counties, although significantly, in the context of government policy, the point lies far

from the median of the total of counties. Although characterized by values for all variables which are close to the average for the whole county, the seven clusters with lower average indices of industrialization than cluster 8 account for 205 counties, while those with higher indices include only sixty-seven. The areal distribution of the cluster is also striking, avoiding both the predominantly rural north-east and also most of the re-settled territories, many of which had higher index values, and thus occupying a central triangle of counties with its base in the south and its apex on the Baltic coast at Gdańsk. Together with cluster 9, it experienced the largest rise in industrialization, and this was probably connected with the fact that many of the counties contained towns of medium size in 1949, with populations of between thirty and one hundred thousand, such as Kielce, Piotrków, Torun and Włocławek, in which substantial potential for growth existed before urban congestion and shortage of transport and other services could be expected to occur on a scale which would raise social costs and thus reduce the yield from any investment. However, the growing role of industry was probably also a reflection of the need to draw people away from farms in central as well as eastern Poland.

Even higher levels of urban and industrial development characterized the areas which were re-settled after the war. If cluster 3 is most representative of areas of uninterrupted Polish settlement, much of Lower Silesia and the areas around the Baltic ports appear within **Cluster 9**, with relatively high indices in 1949 and a substantial rise thereafter. But Cluster 9 also includes 'outliers' to the east, especially the Warsaw area and the eastern margins of the Upper Silesian Industrial Region, where very many new jobs were created as industrial growth was dispersed from the core-areas of those regions, and the larger towns of the east and centre, such as Białystok, Bydgoszcz and Lublin. Although index growth in these areas was similar to that in cluster 8, the size of the absolute increase in employment and the high level of population growth are characteristic only of cluster 9. Half the new jobs were located in the fifty-nine counties in the cluster, and many must have been taken by immigrants to these areas from more rural counties.

Table 22.2 shows that, with the exception of the low-index clusters 1 to 3, the size of increases in the index of industrialization roughly follows the pattern of rising index values among the clusters in 1949, but that cluster 9 appears to represent a threshold beyond which this trend ceases; for the highest value and the smallest increase in the index occur together in **Cluster 10**. This cluster contained the highly, and probably excessively, industrialized counties of central and eastern Upper Silesia, the Łódź area and parts of Lower Silesia, for which a policy of restriction of the growth of industry and population, and the dispersal of both to peripheral areas and beyond, has been adopted. However, the small percentage rise in employment conceals a large absolute increase and underestimates the strength of the agglomerative factors in decisions on industrial location which exist even under a communist government, for between 1949 and 1965 about 10 per cent of the new jobs in industry were located in these few counties.

In addition to the ten clusters, *sixteen counties proved to be unclassifiable* at the *basic* level because of exceptional values for some variables or a unique mixture of patterns of change. The counties with very low indices in 1949 which were selected for major industrial projects have already been mentioned, and counties 5 to 14 (Figures 22.9 and 22.10E) were in territories acquired from Germany in 1945 or from the U.S.S.R., in which resettlement had not been completed by 1949. All except 10, 11 and 14 were included in cluster 9 at the complete level of classification, but were characterized by very high values for population growth. Counties 15 and 16 possessed the characteristics of clusters 9 and 10 respectively, and Figure 9 shows that their values were only slightly dissimilar from those of the counties which were included in those clusters at the basic level.

Conclusion

Although cluster analysis distinguished several patterns which were diagnostic of at least four counties, no correspondingly sharp boundaries appeared on the map between the clusters. Rather, a few core-areas were revealed, such as the east of the country in cluster 3 or Silesia in cluster 9, and even these included and were broken by counties belonging to other clusters, while many counties in these clusters were physically separate from the core-area. Furthermore, every cluster does not possess a readily discernible core on the map, and some appear to occupy areas between the larger and areally more compact clusters or to be found in association with one or more other clusters. Central Poland seems to be characterized by a confused and varied situation of this type.

This pattern provokes several thoughts. At the level of the particular, it throws doubts upon several hypotheses concerning the causes of the distribution of

economic development in Poland. The suggestion that industry shows a strong connection with areas of former German control, and a complementary weak connection with areas of Polish control before 1945 or of Russian and Austrian control before 1914 appears to be less accurate than the suggestion that these contrasts were associated with areas of German and Polish *settlement.* Secondly, the nineteenth-century frontiers which crossed the present area of Poland do not appear to have produced linear areas of economic backwardness which are easily recognizable in the post-war period. The distribution of soil quality and population density before 1939, which are possible indicators of farm incomes and market potential, might account for, or reflect more fully than political factors, the variations in the degree of industrialization, especially in non-coalfield areas.

At a more general level, the pattern of clusters in Figure 22.10 suggests that the technique of dividing counties 'horizontally' according to their values for a chosen range of variables may not be appropriate. In Figure 22.10, most clusters are represented in every part of the country, suggesting that, in a planned socialist economy, with economic balance between and within the country's regions, counties with different characteristics may exist in a fairly regular numerical and spatial relationship with each other in a hierarchical, 'vertical' arrangement. The poor percentage fit for the trend surfaces indicates that there is substantial scope for the residuals to show strong regional patterns beneath the overall, national picture, and the division of the country into this type of region might throw light upon the apparent shortage of order within the distribution of the clusters. Alternatively, it is possible to see such regional variations as the legacy of the former, free-market economy.

If well-developed regional patterns exist, the county may be too large a unit to reflect them accurately. Each county contains a variety of patterns (accentuated by the inclusion of towns within the counties) and, if these form a continuum along any line drawn from city centre to city centre which passes through intermediate suburban and rural zones, after the pattern which has been recognized in capitalist economies,[15] some smaller unit will yield a more accurate picture of this variety than the county. However, the use of the *gromada* would fail to reflect the importance of long-distance commuting in post-war Polish industrialization, for workers often cross several *gromady* between residence and workplace. The county is also unsatisfactory because differences of shape and size, the different location of county towns within counties, and the uneven distribution of transport services and of road and rail networks result in differing degrees of accessibility to towns among rural areas. Thus, to assign county towns to the surrounding counties and to divide those that are contiguous to two counties, is too artificial and must introduce further distortions into the data. Only careful analysis of the pattern of journeys to work at the scale of the *gromada*, and the publication of information at this administrative level, will enable an accurate picture to be built up of the distance over which urban industry influences surrounding areas. Moreover, more data, including a breakdown by type of occupation and sex and age-structure of the population, would permit more detailed assessments to be made of any areal contrasts in the character of the economy in inter-urban areas.

The apparent lack of order in Figure 22.10 might also be reduced through an examination of the higher levels of the clustering hierarchy, where some fusion of clusters has occurred. Such an examination would reveal the pattern of linkages and would show whether a smaller number of more broadly based clusters would lead to any greater compactness of the core-areas. However, this approach is limited for two separate cluster analyses are involved, and it is only possible to examine the linkages within each dendrogram. Those in the first classification (Figure 22.8A) show that, at the second level of the hierarchy, clusters 3 and 7 are linked, and that cluster 8 is added to them at the third level. The junction of this enlarged cluster with cluster 6 leads to the second dendrogram (Figure 22.8B) where, because of the high level which has been reached in the hierarchy, clusters with very different characteristics are fused until only clusters 2 and 5, which Table 22.2 shows to possess very distinctive patterns of industrial growth between 1960 and 1965, remain.

If applied to Figure 22.10, the fusion of clusters 3, 7 and 8 would produce a widespread group of 154 counties representing, in three dimensions, a plateau-like surface of considerable undulation below which the smaller groups of unindustrialized counties would appear as deep depressions and above which those of highly industrialized areas would form isolated peaks. Although this further degree of generalization does not increase the compactness of core-areas in any way which suggests that a small number of large-scale, homogeneous regions exists, it may indicate the distribution of industry and the pattern of industrialization towards which Poland is moving.

A broad view of the successes and failures of the policies of the Polish government reveals that the economy of almost all counties was broadened during the period under study to the point where at least 10 per cent of the working population was employed in industry and mining, and the pattern of contrasting levels of industrialization between areas with similar natural resources, which had been inherited from the capitalist economy, had been much weakened. As a result, the natural increase of population in rural areas was offset by the growth of industrial employment, and the density of agricultural population on the land fell, but the agglomerative forces affecting industrial location decisions have proved strong. With the achievement of a 20 per cent employment level in industry in many counties, a balanced economy both for the nation and for each county probably requires that further enlargement of the role of industry there should be eschewed, even where this would be the cheapest method of expanding output, and that development should be concentrated in those areas which continue to be characterized by little industry, high densities of population, and emigration. Thus, perhaps, two 'levels' of industrialization are developing in communist Poland, one formed by a plateau of medium values, which is broadly representative of rural areas, but which is being invaded by another higher 'level' as the present major urban-industrial regions grow outward through the dispersal of industry, and as new growth-points are established. The variance within each 'level' will be small and the only substantial contrast in the degree of industrialization will be that between the two 'levels'.

Acknowledgements

The author acknowledges the assistance given to him by Professor A.J. Cole, Miss W.E. Maddren and Mr D. Wishart of the Computing Laboratory in the University of St Andrews in the processing of the data, to Mr Wishart for reading and commenting on those sections of the paper dealing with cluster analysis, and to the University of St Andrews for a grant towards the cost of the illustrations.

Notes

1 A. Wróbel and S.M. Zawadzki, 'Location policy and the regional efficiency of investments', in J.C. Fisher (ed.) *City and regional planning in Poland* (Ithaca, 1966), 433

2 A. Kukliński, 'The interregional differentiation of Poland's national economy', *Geogr. Polonica* 7

(1965), 49-56; S.E. Brown and C.E. Trott, 'Grouping tendencies in an economic regionalization of Poland', *Ann. Ass. Am. Geogr.* 58 (1968), 327-42; S. Leszczycki, 'Zmiany rozmieszczenia przemyslu w Polsce po drugiej wojnie swiatowej', *Acta Univ. Carol. Geogr.* 1-2 (1966), 25-34.

3 Poland, Gtówny Urzad Statystyczny, *Rozwój Gospodarczy Powiatow w Latach 1950-1965* (Warszawa, 1967).

4 M. Dobrowolska, 'Przemiany struktury spoleczno-gospodarczej wsi malopolskiej, *Przegl. geogr.* 31/1 (1959), 3-30; S. Mankowska, 'Dojazdy do pracy jako problem strefy podmiejskiej', *Przegl. geogr.* 31/1 (1959), 33-46; T. Lijewski, *Dojazdy do Pracy w Polsce* (Warszawa, 1967).

5 A. Wróbel and S.M. Zawadzki, op. cit., 437.

6 The data were processed on one of the University of St Andrews computers (IBM 1620 II) using a program by Mr D. Wishart (D. Wishart, 'Fortran II programs for 8 methods of cluster analysis (CLUSTAN I), *Comput Contr.,* State Geologic Survey, Kansas: in press). Copies of the program may be obtained from Mr Wishart or from the Editor, *Comput. Contr.,* on request.

7 H. Köhler, *Economic integration in the Soviet Bloc* (New York, 1965), 80, 135.

8 A.H. Dawson, 'The industrial geography of woollen textile manufacturing in Poland' (unpubl. Ph.D. thesis, Univ. of London, 1966), 358-88; W. Kawalec, 'Zaloźenia ustrojowe i praktyczne wnioski z deglomeracji Warszawy i innych osrodków miejskich', *Biul. K.P.Z.K. (PAN)* 38 (Warszawa, 1966), 29-54.

9 W. Kawalec, *Problemy rozmieszczenia Przemystu w Polsce Ludowej* (Warszawa, 1965); T. Mrzygeod, *Polityka rozmieszczenia Przemystu w Polsce 1946-1980* (Warszawa, 1962).

10 W. Kawalec, 'Problematyka rozmieszczenia zakladów przemyslowych w planie na lata 1961-5'. *Nowe Drogi* 14/8 (1960), 32-41.

11 W. Kawalec (1966), op. cit.

12 The trend surfaces were fitted by one of the University of St Andrews' computers, using a program by Professor A.J. Cole.

13 B. Ziotek, 'Rozwój demograficzny Ziem Zachodnich', in W. Kawalec (ed.) *Ziem Zachodnich w Dwudziestolecie Polski Ludowej i jego Perspektymy* (Poznan, 1964), 11-42.

14 D.C.D. Pocock and D. Wishart, 'Methods of deriving multi-factor uniform regions', *Trans. Inst. Br. Geogr.* 47 (1969), 73-98. In the computation of the clusters Pocock and Wishart chose both the density level and the critical threshold distance, but for this study modifications to the program led to the computer distinguishing all levels of clusters at a given density — in this case $K = 4$. Thus, it is possible to examine the clusters at any or every level. In this paper, the most detailed division of the counties into clusters, suggested by Wishart (1969) as *that lowest level of grouping which is taxonomically significant,* was adopted for the examination of the pattern of industrialization between 1949 and 1965 (D. Wishart, 'A numerical classification method for deriving natural classes', *Nature, Lond.* 221 (1969), 97-8).

15 D.J. Bogue, *The structure of the metropolitan community: a study of dominance and subdominance* (Ann Arbor, 1949), 47-58.

Reprinted from *Transactions,* 50, 1970, Institute of British Geographers, London, with permission.

23 Industrial Location and Development Policy: The Nigerian Case

by O. Aboyade

University of Ibadan

I Introduction

The last two decades have witnessed an increasing interest in industrial location studies well beyond the problem of transport network in a partial equilibrium framework. As analytical techniques become more sophisticated, attention turns more and more to general equilibrium implications of spatial distribution of industrial activities.[1] On the policy level, a motive force behind these analytical discourses was provided by an increasing realization of the need for regional balance in the process of national economic development. Moreover, efficiency in production and distribution within appropriate time sequences now constitutes the objective of economic planning in most developing countries. A necessary corollary of that preoccupation, indeed an inevitable prerequisite, is the problem of how to achieve optimum spatial distribution of industrial projects in the economy. Properly designed and executed, industrial location policy can provide the development planner with a powerful tool for achieving a good measure of socio-economic welfare combined with a rapid rate of economic growth. Like many instruments of economic policy, however, industrial location may be necessary but is not sufficient. It can also be a bad master as well as a good servant.

In the development strategy of most economies of the world, private benefit-cost analysis has given way to that of social benefit-cost. Industrial location decisions cannot be left to entrepreneurial freedom of action. The industrial decision-making process was so beset by imperfect knowledge about the full linkage effects of each individual investment project that by the inter-war years, the advanced industrial countries were already taking steps to remedy locational defects in their industrial structure. In Britain, for example, the realization that the great congested industrial conurbations involved substantial economic and social wastes coupled with the desire to stem the tide of rural depopulation, led to legislative measures in Parliament as early as 1934. In that year, the *Special Areas (Development and Improvement) Act* was passed to initiate a series of policy instruments to achieve regional industrial diversification.[2] There is little doubt that in spite of some qualifications and reservations, these measures — especially those taken in the post-war period — accounted in part for some of the successes achieved by post-war Europe with respect to industrial growth, income distribution and regional development.[3]

With the vantage point of historical experience, the developing countries are even less ready to accept the traditional view that locational efficiency is best achieved by industries seeking their most 'natural' homes. Even the so-called rooted, tied or swarming industries can be defended as logical only up to a point; and their 'natural' locations are not necessarily compatible with the modern view of dynamic general equilibrium. In any case, one cardinal strategy of development planning in such countries today is that purely economic valuation should be seen in the wider context of social welfare considerations. So that even if one judged existing or potential location decisions as rational from the purely economic standpoint, there could still be justification for further intervention to alter the apparently sound location pattern. A good industrial location policy should therefore, in an underdeveloped economy, extend beyond its traditional boundaries of descriptive geography, transport cost, external economies and the like — no matter how dynamic in their formulation — to take account of vital social and political consequences; especially in these days of growing supranational economic communities. It is the judicious balance between economic and non-economic considerations that should provide the test for any location policy. Applying this test to the Nigerian case, we shall see from the succeeding paragraphs that the country cannot claim a respectable measure of success. Whatever the stated principles, Nigeria's industrial policy in practice has hitherto been more of a bad master than a good servant.

2 Growth of Industries

Manufacturing on any intensive and sustained scale in Nigeria is a post-1945 phenomenon. Up to the second World-War, economic expansion depended almost completely on agricultural production, the spread of commerce, the extension of a transport-communication net-work and the gradual construction of public utilities in the main cities. To the metropolitan countries, Nigeria for many centuries was seen only as a 'traders' frontier'. Until the last two decades, the main industrial activities were in mining (especially of coal and tin), electricity and mechanical workshops. The few processing activities that existed were only in respect of modest cotton-ginning and rice-hulling plants.

But both the length and intensity of the second World War meant a great strain on shipping space and import availability. The collapse of the Far East during the war meant a diversion to West Africa of supply source for vital vegetable oils, and hence an intensification of effort to design and install suitable plants for oil extraction on a larger scale than hitherto. The increased wartime demand for timber products stimulated the establishment of saw-mills on more serious industrial lines. Whether for import substitution or export promotion or both, the end of the war saw Nigeria with a series of young light manufacturing activities like the canning of fruit; the making of preserves; the bottling of drinks; the tanning of hides; the making of rope, textiles, soap and margarine; and the repair of vehicles. The post-war boom (fostered by prosperous agricultural export, continued import shortage, expanding internal trade, a carry-over of substantial military expenditure by the Allies and a rapidly extending cash frontier within Nigeria) encouraged demand for the new manufactures.

At the achievement of political independence, there were only about 150 plants of medium- and large-scale size in the industrial sector.[4] The bulk of these, some fifty-five per cent, were in fact established only in the last five years before independence. The growth of industries in Nigeria had been exponential in pace. Of all the medium- and large-scale plants in existence in Nigeria by 1965, again fifty-five per cent of their number were established only in the five years following independence. Only about five per cent of the number in existence that year were in fact in operation before the end of the second World War.[5] And in the nine years from 1946 to 1955, only fifteen per cent of the total number of plants in existence by 1965 were established. This contrasts sharply with the corresponding figures of twenty-five per cent in the five years from 1956 to 1960 and fifty-five per cent for the five years from 1961 to 1965.

Another remarkable feature of Nigeria's industrial growth in the last two decades has been the shift in orientation. Whereas by 1938 virtually all industrial plants of any significant size were rooted to local raw materials (the notable partial exceptions being the cigarette plant in Ibadan and a couple of soft drink bottling plants in Lagos), by 1965 the position had been almost completely reversed. In that year, less than thirty per cent of the total number of plants can be regarded as rooted to local raw materials. The orientation had changed to the need to follow the market for consumption of manufactured goods. This reversal was indicative of the fact that post-war industrial development in Nigeria was a movement from export promotion of intermediate products (sawn timber, sheet rubber and kapok cleaning) to import substitution of manufactured consumer goods. Of all industrial plants established between 1961 and 1965, about eighty per cent of their number could be traced to import-substitution activities of a direct consumption nature.

It is also necessary to recall that as the industrial process becomes cumulative, the linkage effects (backward and forward) of existing industries provide stimulus for a new kind of investment catering not directly for household consumers but indirectly through other industries. Before the end of 1965, proposals for more plants producing intermediate products were already in evidence in such industries as cork products, glass, starch and cocoa butter. The foundation for some modest degree of capital-goods manufacturing was also being laid in such activities as asbestos, cement, metal doors and windows, fabricated transport equipment and steel structures. A steel mill (or a set of steel mills) was also already being actively considered. Of total current value added in manufacturing, the proportion relating to the output of capital goods rose from eight per cent in 1957 to fifteen per cent in 1963 and about twenty-three in 1966.

In terms of growth of output, manufacturing witnessed a phenomenal increase in the fifteen years from 1950, growing at an impressive average rate of about seventeen per cent per annum. At constant prices, the output from manufacturing and public utilities had increased by almost ten times in the decade before the achievement of independence. And although the share of industrial output was still only an estimated five per cent of the gross domestic product by 1965, that share had grown from something like 0.5 per cent in 1950 – both figures based on constant-price valuation of national income and its components. This reflects the significant contribution of the industrial sector in the process of structural transformation and growth which the Nigerian economy experienced in the post-war era. On a product-by-product basis, the most outstanding growth of output within the industrial sector took place in the manufacture of food, drink and tobacco, textiles, rubber and wood products, plastics, building materials and metal fabrication.

The bulk of investment for the new and expanding industries was being increasingly provided by foreign private firms. Apart from petroleum development and refining, the inflow of foreign private capital to Nigeria was heavily orientated towards manufacturing from 1960 onwards. Even the reinvestment policy of existing firms reflected the same shift of emphasis. The older trading companies were visibly moving away from commerce into industrial production both as a reaction to the changing competitive structure of the import-export trade and in the race to protect established import markets behind the new tariff walls as well as to keep their initiative and leadership in tapping the increasingly sophisticated expenditure pattern from the rising real incomes of the domestic economy. Reinforcing these two movements was the intensification of the formation of joint industrial ventures, especially as between overseas technical partners (or management agents) and regional governmental authorities (often the public corporations). And although this system was abused through contract kick-backs, nepotism and financial mismanagement, there was little doubt that it contributed enormously to the industrial boom and investment optimism of the post-independence era. The general point remains, however, that while public policy created a favourable investment climate the success story of Nigeria's industrial expansion depended more on foreign private enterprise and management.

3 The Changing Industrial Landscape

The economic consequences of industrial growth are to be seen not only in terms of increased domestic output and increased employment. They also have a locational dimension in terms of the geographical distribution of plants and of their impact on differential regional development. Attention has been drawn above to the fact that within the last decade, the broad emphasis of Nigeria's industrial structure had shifted from raw-material, export-promotion orientation to that of the domestic market for import substitution. Within this generalization, there are some significant differences of detail which are relevant to any consideration of location pattern.

One point of modification is that the simple classification system between market and raw-material orient-

ations is not adequate to explain the location pattern of a number of industries that satisfy both criteria. A flour-milling plant may, for example, be rationally located at a port to utilize imported wheat, and the port may historically have developed into a large centre of urban concentration generating a plethora of bakery plants as outlet for the mill's flour. Some branches of the building materials industry (sand, gravel and stones) have locations which can be defended on either or both grounds. Or the earlier plants of a particular industry may have been determined by one or the other locational influences, which through a dynamic historical process have become completely irrelevant technologically for the later plants. Those simpler factors of an earlier period often become submerged in the complexity of structural linkages, external economics and inertia of a great industrial conurbation. Beyond a certain threshold, an industrial area may develop inner forces of its own which are sufficiently strong to pull a variety of plants to itself for reasons which are not uniformly obvious. Already, it would appear that the Greater Lagos area (i.e. Metropolitan Lagos and its sub-urban environs) was, relative to other areas of the country, showing such tendencies by about 1965.

Another point to note is that even within the simple location classification system where a particular factor had decided its general location, it may not always be obvious that the actual point of location was necessarily the most logical. There could be more than one favourable point of location which may or may not have been considered in the process of decision-making. Of a number of competing centres for a given plant, the final choice may bear little relationship to their relative merits and yet may be justified within the general nomenclature of raw-material or market orientation. Examples of such a case in the Nigerian context would include canning, bags and sacks, some cement plants and some oil-extracting mills. This point may be particularly important in cases of plants over which public authorities have an effective say and in which decision-making may be guided by powerful non-economic considerations.

It is easy to see, therefore, that a full and valid explanation of the changing industrial landscape in Nigeria over the last two decades cannot rest merely on whether the location of plants was guided by considerations of raw material or those of market. But before examining the rationale behind the observed location pattern, we must first analyse the general industrial landscape and assess as far as possible what significant changes have taken place in the pattern over our period of analysis. In the rest of this section, we shall concentrate on this factual picture, beginning with the overall regional distribution of industrial plants. As the previous regions were in fact politically and administratively large and economically uneven, and as new states have in any case been created — with wide implications for the strategy of national industrial development — we shall move at a later stage to a more stratified measure of location zones.

No matter what measure of spatial concentration is used, there is little doubt that the greatest concentration of manufacturing industries lies in the south-west tip of the country – i.e. around Lagos and the old Colony Province. One measure of concentration in common use is the location quotient which attempts to relate the different degrees of specialization of one area to another with respect to one kind of economic activity, using employment or output data as indicator of relative size.[6] From the official Industrial Surveys of 1962 and 1963, and taking the old political regions as geographical units, the following basic distribution pattern emerges from manufacturing industries as whole.

Table 23.1 Regional Pattern of Manufacturing Industries Percentage Distribution of Employment and Net Output, 1962-63

	Employment Indicator		Net Output Indicator	
	1962	1963	1962	1963
Lagos	26.4	22.5	29.3	24.3
West	15.1	18.6	18.3	31.0
Mid-West	15.2	17.0	13.0	8.6
East	19.0	19.6	17.1	16.5
North	24.3	24.3	22.3	19.6
Total	100.0	100.0	100.0	100.0

Source: Federal Office of Statistics, *Industrial Survey, Nigeria,* 1962 and 1963.

When we bear in mind that the political regions varied enormously in size and that the smaller regions were in the South, then the great disparity in industrial distribution is further highlighted. Relative either to its surface area or its population density, industrial activities would appear superficially to be more concentrated in the South, and particularly disproportionate in the Lagos district. This disproportionate concentration is, however, less when we move from the simple regional distribution of industries to the more meaningful measure of

industrial location quotient. Because of the fragility of the basic data, we have analysed the employment statistics for the period 1958 to 1962 to achieve some measure of stability in the quotient values (Table 23.2).

Table 23.2 Regional Pattern of Manufacturing Industries Location Quotient by Employment Indicator, 1958-62

Lagos	1.4
West (incl. Mid-West)	1.3
East	0.8
North	0.8

The dominance of the south-west part of the country (as represented by Lagos and the old West) in manufacturing activities is still evident from the table. But since the location quotient is also influenced by the regional distribution of employment generally, it can be inferred that: (a) regional differences in manufacturing concentration are a reflection of regional differences in overall employment opportunity, and (b) on the basis of the relative territorial size of the old regions, industrial activities would appear more evenly spread within the context of overall employment distribution. In other words, the North had about the same degree of industrial concentration it was 'entitled' to, considering its total employment base *vis-a-vis* the East. This picture would not, of course, hold under the present structure of twelve states which has replaced the four old regions and whereby the North has been split in six; given the narrow concentration of the 'Northern' industries in virtually only two of the states.

If we move away from the indicators of employment and output to the crude (but, in its own way, interesting) measure of sheer number of plants of the medium- and large-size categories, we can gain yet another impression of regional differences in industrial concentration. For the picture in Table 23.3 we have used the data of the stock of manufacturing plants in existence in the country as at 1965. To underpin the industrial importance of the Greater Lagos area (which used to be part of the old Western Region but is now included in the Lagos State), we have disaggregated the data accordingly.

We can say from this rough indication that, in general, about one-third of Nigeria's total manufacturing plants was located in the industrial belt of Lagos stretching from Apapa to Ikeja. The rest of the old Western Region (now Western State) can be said to account for just one-tenth of the total — slightly more than the Mid-West which had about one-twelfth. The

Table 23.3 Regional Pattern of the Number of Medium-
and Large-Scale Industrial Plants
Percentage Distribution by Locational Factors, as of
1965

	Market-Oriented	Raw-material Oriented	Total
Lagos	24.1	9.3	19.5
Greater Lagos	17.5	0.8	12.3
West	9.3	15.3	11.2
Mid-West	3.1	21.2	8.8
East	23.4	15.2	20.7
North	22.6	38.2	27.5
Total	100.0	100.0	100.0

Source: Alan Sokolski: *The Establishment of Manufacturing in Nigeria*, date in Appendix, pp. 287-343.

Eastern Region's share was approximately one-fifth (that is about double that of the Western Region outside Greater Lagos) and that of the Northern Region a little more than one-quarter.

If we make allowance for regional differences in the size distribution of plants, the situation is not much different; although there are some interesting marginal variations in the picture we have described above. The latest edition of the *Industrial Directory*[7] lists industrial plants all over the country employing at least ten people. Approximately two-thirds of the total plant population so listed in 1967 had less than 100 employees each; and only ten per cent of the plants had at least 200 employees. As among the regions however, Lagos, West and North had a percentage share below the national level of total number of plants with less than 100 employees, and both the Mid-West and East had a corresponding percentage share above the national level. In other words, there was a greater proportion of small-size plants in the Mid-West and East in their total plants population. The North had the least relative share of small-sized plants followed by the old West (i.e. including Colony Province); while the East had the highest relative share of small-sized plants followed by the Mid-West, Lagos had a share of small-sized plants closest to the national average. This regional pattern of size-distribution of plants broadly reflects differences in the composition of industrial activity in the different regions. In the North, the influence of the textile plants (which typically have relatively large size of employees) in the region's industrial structure is reflected in the lower ratio of small-sized plants below the national average. Conversely for the East, where the leading

industries are vegetable and animal oils and fats, printed products and bakeries, all of which are characterized by small-sized plants. It is also true to say that, in general, differences in regional size-distribution are negatively related to differences in regional density of the number of plants. The East which has the highest ratio of the total number of industrial plants in the country also has the lowest typical plant size; and conversely for the North.

In terms of Sokolski's classification between plants which are market-oriented and those which are oriented towards raw materials, it is also clear that the bulk of the number of medium- and large-sized plants in Lagos were oriented towards the market.[8] Some eighty-five per cent can be so classified. For the Greater Lagos area, the proportion is indeed much higher – almost 100 per cent. There, only one major plant can be said not to be clearly oriented towards the market; that is the Vegetable Oil plant.[9] And even then, it is export-market oriented. For the rest of the Western Region, the position is a little more balanced between the two types of plant, although the Ibadan zone itself had a higher proportion of its plants dictated more by market considerations. All these are in sharp contrast to the situation in the Mid-West where the bulk of the major plants were located there for reasons of raw-material availability. In the case of Benin City, as well as of Sapele, there was only one plant which could conceivably be regarded (and even that only partially) as being dictated not primarily by raw-material consideration. Natural factors were also strong in particular parts of the East (Enugu) and North (Zaria, Jos), but market inducements were very much in evidence in the location pattern of plants in Onitsha, Aba, Port-Harcourt, Kano and Kaduna.

Nigeria's industrial location pattern is so well-defined, that once we move out of Lagos and the old Colony Province, most of the remaining plants are located in one or the other of a dozen towns – Ibadan, Abeokuta, Benin, Sapele, Onitsha, Aba, Port-Harcourt, Kano, Kaduna, Zaria and Jos. Among them, these twelve towns account for about half of total manufacturing activities. It follows that outside Lagos proper, Greater Lagos and those twelve towns, the rest of the sprawling Nigerian landscape is only marked by an occasional industrial plant accounting for at most twenty per cent of the country's industrial activity.

Another way of indicating the structure of locational concentration is to take an industry-by-industry approach, summing up the plus or minus deviation of its regional percentage (using employment or output indicator) from the corresponding regional percentage of all manufacturing industries as a whole. Using this measure – the co-efficient of localization[10] it is clear from the 1962 and 1963 Industrial Survey that the most localized industries[11] are textiles, tanning, rubber processing, cement, saw-milling and oil-milling. A number of processing industries are in fact almost completely localized within one region or the other – tin smelting, sugar refining, cotton ginning, petroleum refining, margarine, spirit distilling, glass manufacture, toys, towels, surgical products, sewing machine assembly, perfumes and cosmetics, cork products and ordnance. On the other hand, some industries are well scattered with plants (usually associated with relatively smaller size and more dispersed ownership) all over the country. Such low-concentrated industries[12] include food products (especially bakeries), soft drinks bottling, furniture, printing, some metal fabrication, singlets and knitted goods, tire retreading, rice hulling and meat abattoirs.

It is important, however, to note that this categorization is not necessarily valid for all the period since the second world war. No doubt, some industries which had earlier concentrated in one or the other part of the country have moved outwards as the balance of locational factors changed, sometimes in response to inducement and pressure from public policy. Others have tended to increase their concentration ratio as production techniques changed to the advantage of large size or in order to tap external economies of existing industrial centres. Moreover, since the two alternative measures of locational concentration (by reference to employment or net output) do not always yield the same results, the differences are in some cases significant enough for marginal cases to qualify for different locational categories even within the same period. But after allowing for these kinds of qualification, the broad picture described in the preceeding paragraphs can be defended as having general validity.

4 Logic of Industrial Location

The different forces which determine the location of a particular plant or set of plants have received attention in the literature, especially since the classic work of Alfred Weber early in this century.[13] Much articulation has taken place in the last fifty years as the general tools of economic analysis have become more sophisticated.[14] A rough-and-ready system of classifying the different forces determining the industrial location pattern is the conventional one based primarily on 'orientation' in terms of (a) raw materials, (b) labour, (c) power and (d)

market. Our discussion has been conducted so far largely in terms of this approach, chiefly because the nature of industrial data on Nigeria does not allow for a more refined classification system.[15] In this section, we shall try to extend our classification system a little in order to distinguish among geographical, technological, economic (in terms of factor and product prices) and institutional (social, cultural and political) influences on the formulation and execution of economic policy.

A greater proportion of Nigeria's industrial plants in the early stages was undoubtedly located for reasons of relative geographical advantage. The cotton-ginning plants established by the British Cotton Growing Association were located in the cotton-growing belt to facilitate the propagation of cotton production for export of cotton lint to the textile plants of Britain. Such also was the locating of plants for hulling rice, extracting palm oil, processing rubber or sawing timber. Plants located at the ports can no doubt be ascribed to the combination of geographical, technological and economic considerations. As most of the pre-Independence industries were both foreign financed and foreign-trade oriented, it is easy to see why the Lagos and Port Harcourt areas offered a natural vantage point for the location of the greater proportion of the country's industry plants.[16] Similarly for the expanding rubber and timber processing industries of the Sapele-Warri zone. Among them, the various ports and their immediate hinterlands now account for about seventy per cent of total industrial activity in the country in terms of capital investment, output or employment.

Once an industrial centre is firmly established, its growth process becomes cumulative. With increased urban concentration around it, incentives for establishing further secondary and ancillary industries are provided. The initial reason for locating the earlier plants in the centre may become submerged in, or indeed irrelevant to, the new complex of decision motives and locational pull associated with large industrial conurbations. Sometimes, the original activities may not even be of an industrial nature: they may be associated with entrepot commerce or governmental administration. The Kaduna-Zaria-Kano zone provides a fair illustration of such development. Historically a great centre of traditional commerce, the zone grew into a strong pool of urban population concentration and a focal point for the process of political modernization and administrative control. With the added advantage of being surrounded by large areas of rising export-oriented agricultural incomes, it grew into a centre of industrial concentration for both internal and external markets. The same process of development can be attributed to such growing industrial centres as Ibadan and Onitsha. Lately, Benin City and Asaba have also started showing traces of a similar tendency. The point must be made, however, that in some of these cases of commercial-administrative-industrial growth sequence, a full explanation of their development over the last decade must take into account the possible impact of public policy on location decisions.

Although the details of specific factors vary from case to case, there seems to be an underlying structural unity in the growth of the great industrial zones of Nigeria (the Lagos and Greater Lagos zone, the Port Harcourt-Aba zone and the Kaduna-Zaria-Kano zone). They all have characteristics which are often identified in location studies with 'swarming', 'linked' and 'rooted' industries. Analytically of course, once industrial growth becomes cumulative, it is difficult if not impossible to distinguish plants of the three different typologies. But the Nigerian case is not yet too complex to present a fair evaluation of the respective forces at play.

Swarming industries are generally highly localized, but without necessary reference to the availability of extractive materials or the presence of consumers. Some of the port industries – soap, cosmetics, pharmaceuticals and chemical products – as well as those plants which although have some room to manoeuvre in terms of alternative locations nevertheless move towards specific parts of the country in response to locational incentives (for example, industrial estates with generous public utility and repair facilities), will fall in this category. Part of the phenomenal growth of Ikeja can be explained by the existence of an attractive industrial estate set up close to the industrial congestion from a serious land bottleneck in Lagos. So can some of the medium-sized plants established in the 1960's around Port Harcourt and Kano. Swarming also arises from the presence of real and potential external economies, such as in the latter stages of textiles, cosmetics and toiletries manufacture in the Kaduna-Kano industrial district. A specific example of a swarming industry is probably provided by the establishment in 1965 of the glass plant in the Port Harcourt area (the Trans-Amadi industrial estate) to take advantage of available low-cost power from gas being generated by the oil industry. Although the port provides a cheap source for receiving essential material inputs from abroad (such as soda ash) and the surrounding area provides a source of another raw material (glass sands), there is little doubt that the most crucial factors

in the location decision were the presence of cheap power and the existence of a growing industrial market for the products of the plant – glass containers, flat glass and glass mosaic.

Linked industries are those associated with forward or backward linkages, through the attraction of low processing costs and suppliers' market. The three great industrial centres in Nigeria have started to yeild some interesting examples of such plants. The textile industry's most significant recent development has been the vertical integration of spinning, weaving and finishing processes in the same or in contiguous establishments. On a more modest scale, so too is the rise of the industry producing paper products with paper converting plants linked with timber and wood processing plants; and likewise the rise of leather goods production. It is significant that, with one or two exceptions which depended on quota-determined imported baft, practically all plants for printing and finishing textiles recently established have been sited at or near existing centres of spinning and weaving. Short of policy intervention of a more political nature, linked industries are located for technological and economic reasons.

The rooted industries are, by their nature, even more determined by geographical and economic necessities. They are rooted because they are based firmly on localised extraction or, sometimes, on specific market outlet. Plants in the timber, rubber and ore-processing industries, as well as oil crushing, petroleum refining, industrial gases, cement and boat building are of this nature. So also are some plants in the food, drink and tobacco trades. Most rooted industries engage in processing which involves considerable loss of weight through combustion or waste, with a consequent great pressure to save on inherent high transport cost. Depending on the differential weight lost and on packing and distribution costs, the processing plants become either rooted to the source of primary raw material (as in timber) or rooted to the market (as in beverages). Some rooted industries also tend to generate other linked or swarming plants, as in the case of some rubber products which may follow the rubber sheet and crepe rubber plants already rooted to the source of raw rubber latex.

While from the various examples given all the three great industrial zones of Nigeria exhibited these three typologies of locational factors, it does not by any means suggest that the different types cannot be found outside the great centres of industrial concentration. A plant may be rooted to a raw material or linked to another plant in a part of the country geographically distant from any of the great areas of concentration. Dispersed industries can also have one or more of these locational typologies, although the dispersed industries are found both within and outside the great industrial zones. Vegetable oil extraction is rooted to the areas of vegetable oil production, which are of course spread all over the country (groundnuts in the Northern plains and palm-produce in the Southern forests); and so hundreds of oil-seed mills are dispersed in different parts of the country. Similarly cotton-ginning plants are distributed over the North, rice-hulling plants in the South, and food-processing plants throughout the country. Most agro-industries are dispersed. Bread-making is rooted to urban residential consumers, but there are small-plant bakeries throughout the country catering for different concentrations of population. Dispersal is also found in a number of rooted or linked industries providing building materials of a local nature, especially stone quarries, sand and gravel, saw-mills and furniture plants.

A special kind of dispersed location is that provided by the foot-loose industries, in the sense that they have no visible locational uniqueness. They are not specifically oriented towards any particular decisive factor, but enjoy a great freedom of choice of location almost anywhere in the nomenclature of urban population distribution. Most service industries like laundry and dry-cleaning, repairing trades, blacksmithing and kindred activities belong to this group. On a slightly higher level are such industries as printing and publishing, toy manufacture, small-scale abattoirs and clothing. It is clear that because of their general flexibility and adaptability, dispersed and foot-loose industries are much easier for policy manipulation. Of all the hosts of factors which determine their observed location pattern, it would be relatively more difficult to isolate the economic from the non-economic. It follows, therefore, that what may appear superficially as a logical consequence of the combination of geographical, technological and economic considerations, may owe as much to institutional and other 'non-ration' influences.

5 Locational Decision-Making Process

The problem of isolating the purely economic from other considerations in the actual location pattern of our empirical observation will be more tractable if we distinguish among different types of industrial ownership and control. In his study of foreign private industrial investors, Hakam's analysis[17] shows that locational decision-making by that group had mostly to do with economic considerations (in terms of product market and availability of productive factors); and hence the preponderance of plants owned by the group in the three great industrial zones. Even where political elements were present, these were seen more in terms of the specific economic policies pursued by the respective public authorities to attract foreign direct investment. Whatever the difference in the locational motivations by the different firms (product market, availability of factors, external economies, transport facilities, public utilities, ancillary services, potential room for expansion, etc.), one cannot but be impressed by the cold rational calculations of the major industrialists in the private sector when considering the location of their plants. On balance, their observed decisions would seem to be consistent with private benefit-cost considerations or the simple logic of profitability.[18]

However, in most developing countries today, the strategy of economic development is directed at designing a framework of public policy which substitutes social benefit-cost considerations for private ones in all spheres of investment decision-making. It is therefore not surprising that since the late 1950's (with the gradual achievement of self-rule and a reformulation of economic policies), location decisions have been restructured in areas where the public authorities have an effective voice — mostly in plant owned as a joint venture of public and foreign private partnerships or owned entirely by a public corporation or public agency. It is not difficult to see why decisions about plant location based on objective social benefit-cost calculations could be superior and justified when at variance with those based on private benefit-cost. Location decisions are only a part of an overall set of investment decision-making processes and should therefore be seen in a more dynamic general equilibrium context, which is often alien or unattractive to private investors.[19] But the main danger is that, given the political character and administrative machinery of a country like Nigeria, the substance of developmental strategy is likely to be missed by the rulers for the shadow of narrow self-interest. Social benefit-cost analysis is often only vaguely understood, badly applied and readily claimed as a cloak for more dishonest or incompetent decisions.[20]

A few of these cases of mal-location decisions inspired or influenced by the public authorities warrant discussion. Seen as an *ex-ante* decision-making process, there is little doubt that the initial decision to locate the Nigerian Textile Mill's plant at Ikeja was influenced more by political considerations — to forestall all attempts in the late 1950's by the Federal Government to extend the boundaries of the capital territory on grounds of industrial need.[21] Strong elements of regional political rivalry can also be found in the siting of an integrated textile plant in Aba, as well as in the policy of a ten per cent discriminatory internal duty by the Northern Nigeria Marketing Board on all cotton bought by the other Regions (although this last case could be partially explained by possible revenue loss from altern- ative export duty). Many industrial plants in the country suffer enough from irregular supply of electrical power, water, transport and other public utilities, not to add the problem of irregular and artificially high-priced raw materials. Assumptions which are made in some cases about the smooth and adequate supply of raw materials are not justified by later experience. Notable examples of substantial excess capacities arising from this cause are many in Western Nigeria — the oil extracting plant in Apoje, the canning plant in Ibadan, the shoe factory in Ogbomosho · and the bags and sacks plant in Badagry. Perhaps if enough attention had been paid to all vital locational factors at the pre-planning stage and if economic considerations had been given freer and greater weight in the decision-making process, this kind of problem could have been minimized or even possibly eliminated.

Fallacies of composition are a common source of error in locational decision-making in the country's public sector. Because one essential raw material has been discovered in a particular place, then irrespective of all transport costs for all other inputs and for the finished products, that particular location may be defended as a 'natural' site for the industry! And if arguments are raised as to the inadequacy of the 'economic' justification — that the discovery of the raw material may be a necessary but not a sufficient basis for locational decision — then the policy-makers counter back by the need to diversify industrial activity and then hide behind nebulous claims of social benefit-cost advantages. The case of the Kalambaina (Sokoto) cement plant is a good case in point. Recently, even under the military regime in Western Nigeria, a textile plant has also been decided for Ado Ekita on similar grounds. Perhaps the case of the ordnance plant in Kaduna on so-called 'strategic grounds' also qualifies as a fair example.

It is, however, important to emphasize that most of the plants caught in wrong locational decisions are not just bad propositions in terms only of location. They are invariably also bad potential propositions in terms of general investment viability. They are usually of the turn-key project type, financed by short-term credit provided by those foreign suppliers more anxious to sell their machinery and equipment. With no stake in the profitability of the plant, it obviously is no concern of theirs where in space the plant is situated; and they are always willing to oblige with professional-looking statistics to justify any location for which they sense the policy makers have a predisposition. Much elegant feasibility case study can often be constructed on the most slender foundation of locational virtue for minds ready to rationalize a political or personal advantage. Even where joint-venture agreements are signed as earnest proof of the sincerity of the foreign partners, the costs data are often so loaded that the shrewd foreign partners, could not possibly lose. So suffering no risk, they could afford to be generous, accept the political susceptibilities of the participating public authorities, agree to whatever location is desired, retain much-valued political goodwill and ensure their own high financial returns into the bargain. No doubt, corrupt politicians and naïve administrators are ready victims of the foreign private financial do-gooders roaming industrial pro- motion offices of the developing countries as economic carpet-baggers. In many cases, defective locational decisions only worsen an already bad candidate of an investment project.

Perhaps the most classic case of locational conflict arising from political considerations is the iron and steel mill that never was. Several reports have been written on the project with the feasibility of alternative locations and alternative productive capacities. The three altern- ative sites mentioned as early as 1958 were Enugu, Lokoja and Onitsha in the technical reports of Mr Renken and Dr Bones; and the National Economic Council was already under pressure from that year to undertake a policy review of the project with a view to determining, as a matter of urgency, the most economic- ally favourable location of the plant. The various regional lobbies went to work; and by 1961 the alternative locations between the East and North already had powerful backers in both the National Economic Council and the joint Planning Committee. The compet- ing plant programmes submitted by suppliers such as Westinghouse, Demang, Ferrostaal-Mecco Consortium, International General Electric and Kaiser were knocked out as unsatisfactory by the lobby whose regional fortune was to be threatened. The Sub-Committee on Iron and Steel at the official level soon became little more than a platform for regional sentiments over a matter of the greatest national economic importance.

Soon the technical consultants joined the movement and played the game according to their estimation of the balance of regional political power in Lagos, the same consultant sometimes changing sides. Some reports complained of the low ferrous and high phosphorous contents of Enugu coal. Others rejected the quality of coal at Orukpa (in the North) but would not dismiss the quality of the near-by iron ore at Agbaja. Not to be outdone, the West which had hitherto been out of the picture promptly announced a technical report which swore to the existence of iron ore deposits with a seventy per cent ferrous content at Ikare and suggested that a *prima facie* case had been demonstrated in its favour, especially in the light of potential power supply from the Kainji Dam. The Mid-West also weighed in late with claims for Ukpilla limestone and Asaba lignite. For good measure the Economic Commission for Africa, taking a West African picture of the matter, unwittingly threw a spanner in the wheel of the location battle by suggesting Port Harcourt as a reasonable site.

With the famous Nigerian ingenuity for compromise through avoidance of the main issue, by the beginning of 1964 policy thinking was already moving towards the establishment of two iron and steel mills instead of one. Already, the case for even one was marginal enough for the conventional blast furnace technique.[22] Two plants in different locations are only conceivable with the more unconventional direct reduction process designed to cope with smaller size steel markets combined with low quality and high costs of raw material — and this technique was at best still technically questionable and commerically suspect in the Nigerian case. For the same level of output, splitting the industry between two sites would cost an estimated additional sum of £2.3 million in capital investment and the profit rate (after allowing for all the direct and indirect subsidies) would fall from 2.5 per cent to 0.17 per cent. At the sixteenth meeting of the National Economic Council in May 1964, and with the Council fully conscious of the implications for prospective viability, it was nevertheless agreed to have two plants, one at Idah (North) and one at Onitsha (East). The decision was defended primarily on the ground that it would foster 'lasting national unity'. In the same spirit of political bargaining, it was also agreed to start investigations into the possibility of a third plant at Ikare 'or any other part of the West'!

Had it been that the risk capital was being provided by the Nigerian public authorities, that decision of the National Economic Council would have become opera-

tional soon afterwards; with the great probability of the resulting plants swelling the ranks of white-elephant schemes resplendent in the country's public sector. As it happened, the proposed company to operate the two plants — the United Nigerian Iron and Steel Company — was to be a joint venture with a Consortium of American, German and British steel interests (Koppers, Westinghouse, Demang, Didier-Werke, Ferrostaal, and Wellman Smith Owens). External financial aid was also being sought through the United States Agency for International Development. To all these external interests, it just did not make sense to split a marginal steel mill of £50 million investment between two distant sites which are not necessarily complementary in their locational nomenclature. The production process that was to be used (the Strategic Udy) under the dual-site arrangement was also known to have encountered serious difficulties in trial production runs in Venezuela; and the next new alternative technique (the Elkem Process) was expected to start on a commerical scale in Yugoslavia not until the end of 1965. Consequently, the Council's decision remained only a paper compromise of the conflicts of industrial location. The country still (in 1968) has no iron and steel mill and is not yet in immediate sight of having one — in one sense, an expensive victim of political forces in the process of locational decision-making. But in retrospect, this is probably a blessing in disguise. It has given the country another valuable chance for thorough technical study and proper economic planning for a viable iron and steel complex, especially in the context of a possible West African Economic Community.

6 Instrument of Location Policy

Our discussion in the last section is not intended to portray a general ineffectiveness of public policy or to suggest that the impact of governmental intervention was inherently negative or unwholesome to rational industrial growth. Government's share of industrial investment has been a minor proportion of the total in any case. And it has not always been the case that its locational decision-making process was against the expectation of economic logic. In total, the cases of mal-judgment were few and largely a phenomenon of the period since 1962. But they did reflect a general trend of a growing political bias in the location of governmental activities as a whole (agricultural schemes, industrial projects, public utilities, welfare amenities and various positions of patronage), a bias which characterized the peculiar form of parliamentary democracy in post-colonial Nigeria. More specifically, they reflected the absence of a definite public policy on industrial location for the economy as a whole.

In the arsenal of government instruments for stimulating industrial growth, locational programme only belongs to the class of incentives of very limited importance called 'sundry assistance'.[23] The most crucial instrument on which government has long relied is the set of fiscal concessions known in official circles as 'industrial incentives'.[24] They consist mostly of import duty relief, income tax relief for plants declared as pioneer industries and high initial capital allowance. Location policy as a means of achieving a higher level, and a rationally-distributed pattern, of industrial activity was not only marginal in overall importance, but incoherently formulated and haphazardly applied. What in fact so far constitutes location policy in Nigeria is to be inferred more from the general action of Government in the practical process of administering the broad industrial incentive measures, rather than in any well-articulated set of official statements, publications or documents. The main exception to this broad conclusion is to be found in the establishment of industrial estates to encourage ordered industrial development in particular localities and to offer competitive site advantage against areas under rival public authorities. But since the Regional governments have in fact been more active in the establishment and operation of industrial estates, it is not surprising that to the limited extent to which the estates have made contribution, the Regions have had more influence on the resulting industrial location pattern than the Federal government itself.

Industrial development, within the federal structure of distribution of power and responsibility, has been a concurrent subject in Nigeria. But in terms of power for direct territorial assignment, the Federal government was limited in practice to the very small area of Lagos capital city. This was why it has had to depend more on general legislative and fiscal measures as policy incentive for industrial development, and probably why there has been little co-ordinated programme for industrial location on a national level. Even at the Federal level, the actual implementation of these broad incentive measures with respect to industrial location decision-making depended, as we have seen, on the balance of political bargaining by the regional pressure groups in the federal government. It was of course not every project that generated the same locational controversy as the iron and steel mill which we considered in the last section. Often, the conflicts were reflected in more subtle forms in the administrative machine; and in any case such industries sponsored by the Federal government which can generate locational rivalries among the Regions have been few and far between.

At the federal level, therefore, the location policy was little more than a general process of persuasion addressed to foreign private investors to invest in Nigeria. To the extent that this persuasion had any regional distribution dimension, it was probably conducted on a more personal and more informal level. The active competitive inducement for particular private plants to be located in alternative areas of the country was more of an activity pursued at the level of regional government. However, there were grumblings that federal authorities sometimes used their administrative influence to divert foreign investments to politically favourite areas. But it would appear on balance that overt effort of the Federal government with regard to active encouragement for a specific location was in fact by the early 1960's already showing signs of becoming not only neutral but indeed negative, in the sense that firms were being driven by sheer desperation to locate outside the immediate capital territory to relieve a growing industrial congestion – especially at Apapa. For example, the administrative machine was making it increasingly difficult to get approval for industrial land within the jurisdiction of Lagos. Sometimes the loss was not just to Lagos but to the country as a whole. There were two good separate cases of intending foreign private investors who waited in vain for about two years to secure suitable industrial sites in Lagos, and then left the country in utter repulsion for the country's bureaucratic machine. There were many other cases of investors who had to pay more than once for their sites, a situation which derives from a defective legal process for assigning ownership and use of landed property. Although there are few official statements of industrial location policy by the Federal government, there is little doubt that the balance of thinking and practice is in favour of the maximum possible dispersal of industrial activity, whether as a reflection of regional political pressure or as a reaction against overcrowding in the federal territory.

This undertone of inter-regional dispersal can be detected in the administration of the general industrial incentive scheme. Although, as Asiodu argues, the policy measures are not sufficiently discriminatory and selective,[25] they have probably had the effect of encouraging the location of some plants in areas which would have been otherwise considered as submarginal.

With the combination of 'pioneer' status, import duty relief, tax holiday (including offsetting accumulated losses against future profits) and accelerated depreciation allowance, it was indeed theoretically possible for an investor to move to an apparently unattractive area of the country. He has very little to lose at least in the first years of his operation if he could cover his current running cost; and he may even have very much to gain by way of lower wage rate, cheap rent, extensive land and goodwill of the local community. It may well be that it was precisely because the administration of the measures was so full of loopholes that a financially-smart investor may be able to turn an ostensibly disadvantaged location to a commericaly attractive one in the end, by exploiting the loopholes to the fullest during the initial years of his operation. Now, there is currently a rethinking in official circles (as Asiodu's article clearly indicates) to restructure the administration of these incentive measures towards greater selectivity and less generosity. But unless there is an explicit locational criterion built into the new policy structure, a mere functionally-determined discriminatory incentive administration will not necessarily achieve a different industrial spatial distribution.

A more direct and more active industrial location policy is to be found more at the level of regional government in the Nigerian case. And the most potent instrument of incentive employed by the regions has been the establishment of industrial estates, designed to encourage the location of industries in their respective regions.[26] In the West, the Mushin-Ikeja estate, with about 3,000 acres, was placed sufficiently near the edge of the region to tap potential industrial entrants into the Lagos area as well as attract existing firms which could only expand by avoiding the growing congestion of inner Lagos. The North has slightly over 2,000 acres of industrial layout just outside Kano; and the East has about double that size in its Trans-Amadi estate. In a dozen or so more towns all over the country – Ibadan, Sapele, Kaduna, Gusau, Zaria, Jos, Ilorin, Umuahia, Aba, Onitsha, to mention a few – there are also smaller layouts either under construction or still at the planning stage, designed not just as part of the urban renewal process but as centres of attraction for existing and potential industries of the small and medium-scale types.[27] Like similar projects elsewhere in the world, these industrial estates (or industrial parks) are characterized by their modernizing amenities – good access road, rail siding, electricity, telecommunication facility, water supply, sanitation disposal system, mechnical repair workshop, ancillary services for banking and finance, and invariably a set of contiguous housing plots for workers and executives. They are designed not only to minimize the perennial and expensive problem of industrial land acquisition, but also to reduce the cost of developmental infrastructure to individual investors and especially to the foreign private investors.[28]

Since the main industrial zones in Nigeria are so well-defined, since they somehow correspond to the old base of political power, and since the major industrial estates are themselves set contiguous to the existing major industrial zones, then it can be inferred that the estates are designed more for inter-regional competition in industrial location than for the dispersal of industries within particular regions. To the extent that an increasing number of smaller estates were being developed by the regional authorities outside the main zone of industrial concentration, these were geared more to town planning and urban renewal programmes. These smaller estates in the secondary towns and cities are designed to cater more for the small-scale indigenous private enterprises, to encourage them to move out from their typical traditional areas of activity to the more expansive and modernizing atmosphere of the estates. However, in some cases where the regional government had pursued a deliberate policy of spatial diversification of medium- and large-scale industries, it has not often been necessary to invoke the instrument of industrial estates. Notable examples of less than optimal location in this connection would be the fibre sack industry in Badagry, the integrated cement industry in Sokoto, the shoe plant in Owerri and the ordnance factory in Kaduna.

In the development programme of the West regional government, the policy of industrial diversification within the region was only an implicit objective. The written stated objective of establishing industrial estates was unambiguous: '... to facilitate the process of industrialization by relieving industrialists of part of the heavy capital expenditure on getting their business to a start'.[29] Implied diversification can, however, be inferred from a provision of over £3 million to develop about 1,800 additional acres of industrial estates (that is, additional to the initial acreage at Ikeja-Mushin) in nine centres all over the region. But to the extent that some of these centres already had a fair crop of small-scale industries, the original intention of the estates was probably not designed to give the centres competive advantage in attracting industrial activities; although this potential tool of locational policy crept into political thinking as its administrative possibilities were becoming evident. In the last five years, the government has been pursuing a simultaneous policy of greater industrial concentration at the Ikeja-Mushin area and of greater dispersal in the rest of the region. The concentrated area in general tends to have more of the medium- and large-scale plants, whilst the dispersed areas are in general characterized by small- and medium-scale plants.[30]

From the point of view of the West regional government (though not necessarily from the viewpoint of the industries themselves), effort was concentrated on the Ikeja-Mushin estate for a decade (1955-65) of active industrial promotion for reasons which included a large ingredient of political strategy – i.e. to forestall the expansionist policy of the rival Federal government in Lagos to extend the area of the capital territory. But the more the estate attracted industries to itself and the more it developed as an integral part of the Lagos metropolitan economic zone, the greater the incentive for the Federal government to effect its expansionist policy and wrestle the administrative control of Greater Lagos. This temptation became increasingly manifest in succeeding urban renewal proposals by various international agencies and technical experts. They all tended to support the view that it would make for better economic and administrative logic to have common public utility, urban service, uniform tariff, housing programme, transport and communication network, and welfare amenities in a zone which was really structurally a single entity but only artificially divided by a political power-play. The political risk of such a proposal was of course too great for the kind of civilian government which for long ruled in Lagos. It was left to the second military government (for reasons that are too complex for this paper), to effect the necessary political change through the creation of a Lagos State which encompassed and went beyond the Greater Lagos area itself. Thus, from the West regional government's point of view – but only from its point of view – its political strategy of encouraging an industrial concentration in the Mushin-Ikeja estate has backfired. By the middle of 1967, the rest of the old region was left with only a handful of worthwhile industrial projects; the Warri-Sapele zone having been lost since 1963, with the creation of the Mid-West region.

Whatever the motivation of the private investors – and it is important to recall our earlier conclusion that the bulk of Nigeria's industrial manufacturing investment was provided by foreign private investors – it is clear that political considerations played an important role in the design and execution of industrial policy in the country. The political factor discussed above in the case of the Western region was probably an unusual one. But it does serve in its own way to illustrate the inevitable ambivalence of location policy to be expected from the peculiar form of parliamentary democracy practised in a socially heterogeneous and economically underdeveloped country. The location policy must not only recognize the fact of industrial life (that the foreign private investors who make the major industrial decisions are governed by the simple logic of private profitability), but also be socially relevant (that every small community wants an industry in its own area and has been politically educated to expect one in exchange for electoral support). Official policy statements therefore tend to laud the virtue of industrial diversification and the administration of industrial policy tend to exert pressure on investors to disperse their activities. But the results do not seem to match either the policy statement or its prosecution. And where the political pressure is so great that some measure of dispersal is operationally feasible, these are either of minimal quantitative importance or they consist largely of white-elephant plants owned by public agencies.

Perhaps the experience of what used to be the North regional government[34] typifies this policy ambivalence in industrial location. In its development plan, the conflict seems to be evident in the very policy statement: 'Industrial areas with full services, similar to those in Kano, Zaria, Kaduna and Jos, will be established. In choosing these, a balance will be struck between the desire of industrial managements to go where the fullest services already exist and the desire of Government to pursue a policy of dispersing industry to areas so far without it. Appropriate concessions will be considered for special areas.'[32] The major instrument of diversification policy has been the establishment of industrial areas all over the region – Kaduna, Kano, Zaria, Sokoto, Jos, Gusau, Jebba, Ilorin, Gombe, Bauchi, Yola, Nguru, Makurdi and Maiduguri – in varying sizes of from sixty to 600 acres. It may well be that the existence of these locational infrastructures within the region facilitated the prosecution of the undeclared war of inter-regional competition for the potential foreign investors coming to the country. They would no doubt have complemented the political wire-pulling in Lagos (an exercise in which the Northern group had more than a head-start) and provided a backing for its promotional effort of the propaganda type (through the publication, for example, of such well-documented brochures as *The Industrial*

Potentialities of Northern Nigeria). But by and large, these industrial areas appear to have been designed more for stimulating intra-regional dispersal of manufacturing activities.

In reality, however, the positive effect of these industrial areas on the actual location pattern was not much in evidence. For one thing, the government itself freely admitted that it could not and would not compel investors to erect their factories in particular areas, with or without an industrial estate. The significance of this point can be seen in the following published statement: 'Any attempt by Government to influence the choice of site is always firmly refused and if pressure is brought to bear the industrialist is disinclined to proceed with his proposal although advice is invariably appreciated. This attitude is understandable, but as far as Northern Nigeria is concerned the outcome has been large concentrations of industry at Kaduna and Kano, which are well served by public utilities and have a convenient distribution network with potentially large local markets.'[33] For another thing, not having an estate in a particular location is not necessarily too serious a disadvantage for an industry that has other good reasons for going there. The Government was clearly always willing to acquire local land for such an industry for sublease at very low rent. The industrial estates, in retrospect, have been neither a necessary nor a sufficient prerequisite for effectively influencing locational decision-making. Regardless of the established industrial areas elsewhere, industrial plants in the Northern region, as indeed in other parts of the country, still gravitated towards their 'natural' or logical zone of locational attraction (i.e. the Kano-Zaria-Kaduna belt).

It is, therefore, easy to see why the most successful industrial estates are in general those located within or contiguous to already established zones of industrial concentration – the Apapa-Iganmu estate in Lagos,[34] the Ikeja-Mushin estate in Greater Lagos, the Kano, Zaria, Kaduna and Jos estates in the North's industrial centres, and the Trans-Amadi estate just off Port Harcourt. These estates only helped to reinforce an already strong incentive to locate within the main industrial zones, by making land acquisition easy and cheap and by offering attractive facilities for future expansion. They attracted industries which were in themselves basically profitable and the cumulative effect of whose success served as a pull for other complementary or ancillary services within the same area. Contiguously placed to the main industrial zones, these estates provided an essential service of breaking an important investment bottleneck – the perennial problem of land acquisition in the old centres of industrial concentration. That the estates are far from being the main cause of industrial attraction (except in a marginal sense within the context of inter-regional locational competition for plants with more than one degree of locational freedom), is evident in the emptiness of most of the other estates established all over the country outside the main industrial zones.

No doubt, a failure on the part of the policy-makers to distinguish carefully among different investment motivations and among different types of industrial estate has led to the proliferation of the establishment of industrial estates or industrial parks all over the country. They must have had the mistaken belief that those estates would promote an otherwise non-existent set of industries. Most of these estates outside the main industrial zones appear indeed to have been established too long before there was demand for them. The truth is that Nigeria's so-called industrial zones are themselves relatively young centres of industrial concentration with still enormous capacity to attract more industries. With the establishment of contiguous industrial estates around them to take care of future growth, these industrial zones are very far from reaching a permissible maximum level of spatial concentration. Industrialists have little or no incentive to move elsewhere, especially where these other areas offer little locational advantage with respect either to factor inputs or product markets.

It is clear that there is a dichotomy between the motivations of those industrialists who take most of the location decisions and the policy makers who pursue industrial diversification through the establishment of industrial estates. The latter group, apart from the general objective of promoting overall industrial expansion through continuous improvement in the investment climate, appears to be guided by the desire to achieve socio-political equity as among different districts and the need to contain the growing concentration of urban unemployment. Not only are the industrial estates attractive to the local population – at least in the initial stages – as proof of the earnest desire of government to promote their 'development and welfare', they are also expected to help reverse the process of labour migration to the main industrial zones and capital cities. Neither of these two objectives are important or even relevant to the location decisions of those who actually invest in the industrial sector, the bulk of whom as we have seen consist of foreign private businessmen dedicated to the active pursuit of the highest possible profit in the shortest possible time.

The results are a continuing concentration of industries in the main zones, a sprawling set of empty industrial estates in the rest of the country, a growing economic frustration by a politically disenchanted population and the intensification of an unemployment distribution pattern that was fast becoming a source of national embarrassment. Missing the policy wood for the trees, the industrial location effort of the Nigerian public authorities has provided another testimony of a development strategy that is fundamentally defective.

7 Towards a New Policy Synthesis

The Nigerian experience thus illustrates the futility of a partial approach to the problem of industrial location. A particularly evident lesson is the fact that mere governmental exhortations and mere creation of industrial estates do not by themselves promote industrial growth or achieve effective spatial industrial diversification. A move towards a more positive policy must therefore start from a recognition of certain simple propositions. First, industrial location is only a part of the wider problem of the location of economic activities and of the general problem of area or regional development. Second, locational issues are themselves only part of the bigger question of development strategy. A redefinition of location policy must therefore be seen in the wider context of general economic planning. Third, there is a basic locational conflict between the profitability requirement of the foreign private enterprises who in fact provide the bulk of industrial investment, the diversification pursuit of the policy maker wanting to maximize some vague notion of economic welfare and the high expectation of local communities all over any developing country for industrialization to take place in their respective areas. The task of a new policy synthesis is to evolve a locational strategy that would take a simultaneous account of all these factors.

Perhaps one should start with the simple assertion that, since natural resources are never evenly spread over any national economy, there will always be a differential spread of industrial activity in space. This is important, not only for the technical task of ascertaining the optimum industrial distribution pattern consistent with an unequal distribution of resources across space and over time, but also for the politics of local popular demand for industrial development. There would always be some areas of a country with very little or no industrial activity and with very little or no industrial potential.

Given such limitation, the policy reformer can approach the problem of industrial location in a development context by one of two approaches. He can take a project-by-project feasibility approach and ask which area or areas, in a dynamic context of changing factors mix, are relatively best suited for what projects and at what point in time. Alternatively, he can take a given area with ascertained and well-defined resources and then, on the basis of given information on prevailing technology, relative costs of input, transport network and prices of output determine what activities the area is most suited to engage in over a feasible future. Pushed to their logical conclusion, the two approaches are in fact ultimately complementary and not competitive. At a dynamic level of analysis, the two can only represent two different starting positions of the same objective; given the structural interdependence of different industrial projects and of different centres of economic activity within a national economy.

The second approach would seem more appropriate to the Nigerian kind of situation, with its new broadly-based federal structure, development potential and planning possibilities. The large increase in the number of component states both poses many problems of public administration as well as offers new opportunities for an effective planning arrangement that would blend local initiative with central control. With respect to the spatial dispersion of industrial activity, the first step is to reform and expand the physical survey and statistical organization of the country, raise its conception and status to that of a National Bureau of Census and gear its operation to the needs of planned economic development, particularly at the states' level. For a rational industrial policy, there is a crying need for extensive and detailed maps of resource distribution for each district administrative unit. One of the main tasks of the new Bureau of Census (with a different staffing size and structure) should be the determination of development potential of each district as redefined for purposes of national planning. A combination of cartographical, inventory, statistical and other techniques should yield valuable data on both the human and environmental factors that define the locational characteristics of each area.[35] Such data would help not only local leaders to accept the different developmental challenge of their areas but considerably enhance the level of rational decision-making at both state and national levels with respect to projects location. Using whatever investment criteria he deems appropriate for his overall development strategy, the economic planner would be in a much better position to confront the locational determinants of any set of projects with the locational characteristics of the competing areas of attraction.

The objection might be raised that this prescription is too idealized for a country the size and poverty of Nigeria; that it would require much manpower and financial resources which are simply not yet there; that it would take several generations before such an exercise could be accomplished; and that what is really needed is a simple rule of thumb to correct excessive policy defects. Why use a sledge-hammer to crack a nut, especially when the sledge-hammer is not there in the first instance? The simplest rule of thumb of course is to plead for the elimination of political and arbitrary administrative pressures on locational decision-making and to let pure economic considerations (in a wide but disciplined sense) have full sway. If this were to happen, then on the basis of our existing knowledge of resource distribution and pattern of industrial activities, we can predict that at least over the next decade most new plants will be located within or near the present industrial zones in the country.[36] It is yet too early in the history of Nigeria's industrial development for these broad zones to be faced by a serious threat of overconcentration. The minimum requirement for a reformed location policy is to ensure that each and all projects are fully, honestly, objectively and carefully costed[37] and that all non-economic considerations in any final decision are minimized, clearly stated and openly administered. If the recent modest beginning at policy redefination by the national meeting of Permanent Secretaries and officials dealing with the country's industrial development is an indication of greater expectations, then there is some consolation that Nigeria is now learning from her past mistakes in this field.

Acknowledgement

The author would like to acknowledge gratefully the valuable comments on earlier drafts of this article made by many colleagues, and especially the generous assistance of Mr Philip Asiodu, Dr Arch Calloway and Professor Akin Mabogunje.

Notes

1 A good illustration of this is provided by L. Lefeber: *Allocation in Space – Production, Transport and Industrial Location* (North-Holland Publishing Co., Amsterdam, 1958), Vol. XIV in the series 'Contributions to Economic Analysis'. A discussion of the analytical development of this field of study is contained in Chapter 1 of the book.

2 The enabling legislations included the *Special Areas Act,* 1937; the *Distribution of Industries Act*, 1945 and 1950; the *New Towns Act*, 1946 and the *Town and Country Planning Act*, 1947.

3 A general assessment of the efficacy of locational policy in post-war Britain is contained in J. Sykes: 'Some results of Distribution of Industry Policy', *Manchester School of Social and Economic Studies*, January 1955. A more quantitative treatment in defence of regional diversification is provided in R.J. Nicholson: 'The Regional Location of Industry', *Economic Journal*, September 1956.

4 For this purpose, plants employing not less than twenty-five direct labour fall into these categories. The basic information for the period up to 1965 was derived primarily from the raw data contained in the Appendix to Alan Sokolski: *The Establishment of Manufacturing in Nigeria* (Frederick A. Praeger, New York, 1965), pp. 287-343.

5 Although coal- and tin-mining activities were also in existence and were sizeable in output and employment, they could not be properly regarded as industrial in the manufacturing sense of the term.

6 Specifically, using employment indicator as illustration, the location quotient is a ratio of two ratios. The first ratio, the numerator, relates the industrial employment in any given Region to the total employment in that Region. The second ratio, the denominator, relates the industrial employment in the country as a whole to the total employment in the country.

7 Federal Ministry of Industries: *Industrial Directory*, fourth edition, 1967 (Federal Ministry of Information, Lagos, 1968).

8 This classification system should really be regarded as a first approximation to a fuller and more valid analysis. As Lefeber (op. cit., p. 110) has argued, conventional concepts 'such as supply orientation or market orientation may be either too broad or too narrow.'

9 This was as at 1965. Soon after, two large plants were under construction to process cocoa beans for export, one of them coming into actual production by 1967.

10 The actual computation of the coefficient consists of three basic steps: (*a*) subtracting for each region its percentage share of total employment or output for any given industry from its percentage share of total manufacturing employment or output for the

country; (b) adding all positive differences, or all negative differences; and (c) dividing the sum of the positive or negative differences by 100. The limits to the value of the coefficient are 0 and 1.

11 High localization here is taken as those industries having *a minimum* coefficient of localization of 0.6 with respect to either employment or output spatial distribution.

12 In this case, we take as low localization those industries with a *maximum* of 0.4 coefficient of localization with respect to either employment or output spatial distribution.

13 Alfred Weber: *Theory of the Location of Industries*, translated by Carl J. Fredrich (University of Chicago Press), 1929.

14 A good exposition of these developments is contained in L. Lefeber, op. cit., Chap. 4, pp. 2-8.

15 One such system, which has empirical application in other case studies, especially in the advanced industrial countries, is that by L.N. Moses in his article 'Location and the Theory of Production', *Quarterly Journal of Economics*, vol. 75, no. 2, May 1958, pp. 259-272. He summed up the different determinants of industrial location into five groups: namely (a) transportation rates on inputs and final products, (b) geographic location of inputs and product markets, (c) supply schedule of production factors or inputs, (d) production functions or input-output ratios (technology) and (e) demand functions for products.

16 One recent estimate has put the proportion of all foreign-owned industrial investment in these two port areas as fifty-seven per cent. See A.N. Hakam: 'The Motivation to Invest and the Locational Pattern of Foreign Private Industrial Investment in Nigeria', *Nigerian Journal of Economic and Social Studies*, vol. 8, no. 1, March 1966, pp. 49-65, at p. 59.

17 A.N. Hakam, op. cit., pp. 56-60.

18 Indigenous private industrial firms have not been considered, not only because of their relative unimportance in modern manufacturing processes but also because they are mostly small-scale and of the dispersed and foot-loose varieties.

19 A theoretical scheme for such an approach is provided by Louis Lefeber, op. cit. His system was not only designed to determine an optimal transport network solution but more importantly to provide a solution for the optimal spatial distribution of investment projects. In his scheme, 'the locations of production do not necessarily have to coincide with the sources of inputs or with the locations of markets. Resources can be hauled to the location from any source and goods can be dispatched to any market. Any number of goods can be produced in any one single location.' (pp. 9-10).

20 It is of course an extremely difficult exercise to translate the theoretically attractive propositions of optimal spatial distribution into empirical measurement (see Lefeber, op. cit., pp. 133-134). But various approximating approaches are being tried even in economies not usually associated with general equilibrium planning. Some interesting empirical case-studies for Puerto Rico are contained in Walter Isard, Eugene W. Schooler and Thomas Vietorisz: *Industrial Complex Analysis and Regional Development* (The Technology Press of the Massachusetts Institute of Technology and John Wiley & Sons, Inc. New York, 1959).

21 See R.A. Akinola: 'Factors Affecting the Location of a Textile Industry – The Example of the Ikeja Mill', *Nigerian Journal of Economic and Social Studies*, vol. 7, no. 3, Nov. 1965, pp. 245-256. However, Dr Akinola has tried to show that the subsequent performance of the plant in exploiting the facilities of the Lagos industrial-commercial zone, will tend to suggest that its location may be considered as economically rational, *ex-post*.

22 Practically all proposals for the mill by technical consultants based their viability case on the assumption of a twenty per cent protective tariff, interest-free equity funds and other government subsidies.

23 See P.C. Adsiodu: 'Industrial Policy and Incentives in Nigeria', *Nigerian Journal of Economic and Social Studies*, vol. 9, no. 2, July 1967, pp. 161-174, especially pp. 162-167.

24 Even public policy as a whole for industrial stimulation, Asiodu argues, was not as important in explaining Nigeria's industrial development in the last two decades as the size of the country's market in terms both of population and expanding income. (Ibid.)

25 P.C. Asiodu, op. cit.

26 The Federal government is of course also involved in some form of industrial layout as Apapa and Yaba. But these are of a different order of importance and effectiveness in terms of competitive inter-governmental locational incentives. See an evaluation of one of these sites in Sayre P. Schatz: 'Aiding Nigerian Business: 'The Yaba Industrial Estate', *Nigerian Journal of Economic and Social Studies*, vol. 6, no. 2, July 1964, pp. 199-217. It is clear anyway that

inadequate industrial land has been a persistent location problem in Lagos – a problem which is well beyond the capacity of those two layouts.

27 A brief description of the different estates is contained in an official article 'Industrial Estates,' *Nigerian Trade Journal*, vol. 13, no. 3, July/ September 1965, published by the Federal Ministry of Information, Lagos.

28 In some parts of the world (for example, India and Pakistan), some industrial parks for small-scale industries even go much further by constructing highly-subsidized standard unit factory shells for tenant-purchase and providing them with a variety of management service in engineering, organization, marketing, accounting, finance and labour training. Except the Yaba case, most of Nigeria's industrial estates are of the leased type and not such continuous-managed type.

29 Federation of Nigeria, *National Development Plan 1962-68* (Federal Ministry of Economic Development, Lagos, 1962), chap. 9, section IV, p. 308. See also the *First Progress Report on the Western Nigeria Plan*, Western Nigeria Official Document No. 2 of 1964 (Ministry of Economic Planning and Community Development, Ibadan, 1964), Chap 3, section B, p. 23.

30 See Leslie Green and Vincent Milone: *Physical Planning in Western Nigeria* (Ministry of Lands and Housing, Western State of Nigeria, Ibadan, December 1967), pp. 86-91.

31 Under the new military dispensation, the old North was broken up into six States in the major political reform of May 1967.

32 *National Development Plan, 1962-68*, op. cit., Chap. 7, section V, pp. 140-141. A similar statement, unequivocally expressed, is also to be found in the Ministry of Trade and Industry's pamphlet, *The Distribution of Industry in Northern Nigeria* (Kaduna, 1965), pp. 12-15 and pp. 24-25.

33 *The Distribution of Industry in Northern Nigeria*, op. cit., p. 15.

34 The exception to the Lagos case (which in a way proves the rule) is that of the Yaba estate which, in spite of very high subsidies and great rental bargains, has been ineffectual in stimulating the growth of small-scale industries for which it was intended. The Yaba example does indeed illustrate the fact that the mere provision of an industrial area at subsidized cost to industrial tenants cannot by itself convert an essentially unprofitable set of projects to one of profitability, or transform a fundamentally defective set of managerial personnel into successful entrepreneurs. See Sayre P. Schatz: 'Aiding Nigerian Business: The Yaba Industrial Estate', op. cit.

35 The technical conception of the old Niger Delta Development Board is illustrative of this approach. But rather than be the exception, the message here is that this approach should now be the rule throughout the country.

36 Even the so-called 'foot-loose' industries are exhibiting a market tendency in Nigeria to move towards the main industrial zones. See, for example, Leslie Green and Vincent Milone, op. cit., pp. 89-91 and especially Table 28.

37 The exhaustive analysis of Walter Isard, Eugene W. Schooler and Thomas Victorisz in their case study of Refinery-Petrochemical-Synthetic Fibre complexes in Puerto Rico, op. cit., is illustrative of the statistical rigour required in linking location to development.

Reprinted from *The Nigerian Journal of Economic and Social Studies*, Vol. 10 (3), November, 1968, Nigerian Economic Society, Ibadan, with permission.

24 The Spatial System and Planning Strategies in Developing Countries

by M. L. Logan

Monash University, Melbourne

In Developing countries interest is growing in the way geographical space can be organized to increase national rates of economic growth and to ensure that the benefits of growth are passed on to the greatest number of people. The close historical association of economic development with spatial change in the economically advanced countries suggests that in developing nations both aims can be achieved by planning the allocation of investment in space as well as in economic sectors.[1] The need for spatial planning, in particular, is great in ex-colonial nations whose spatial structures remain oriented to a colonial economic system and therefore are not necessarily geared to rapid economic growth or nation building. Indeed, many of the difficulties of extending linkages among economic activities in a nation and among ethnic groups closely identified by area can be related directly to colonialism, which left countries not only economically backward but with a spatial system not conducive to the mobilization of resources for internal, as distinct from overseas, markets. Moreover, the highly centralized spatial structure and the dual economy associated with colonialism in some countries have contributed to marked variations in regional wealth and in standards of living. Since political independence these trends have, if anything, been accentuated by striving for a rapid rate of economic growth through industrialization. Evidence suggests that it is entirely possible for national economic growth, as measured by surrogates such as increases in gross domestic product, in per capita income, and in industrial production, to generate greater regional imbalance in the nation;[2] in other words, the drive toward a high rate of growth based on industrialization may lead to a movement of the most productive resources to specific areas of concentrated development.

At this point policy conflicts may emerge. If locational efficiency is used as the sole criterion for investment, regional imbalance will almost certainly increase. This may lead to pressure to disperse the benefits of growth evenly throughout the nation, which, in turn, could slow the rate of national growth. But a high rate of economic growth and the internal demand it generates are obviously critical for regional economic development. There are ways of trying to circumvent this policy conflict by concentrating solely on public investment: for example, in a federal political system the central government may allocate revenue back to the states according to some formula based on population size. But even here, by ignoring the revenue-generating capacity of the states in this reallocation, the center is probably retarding the national rate of economic growth. Alternatively, the central government may concentrate on nonprofit welfare investments (for instance, schools and hospitals) and distribute these as equitably as possible on the basis of certain standards. Once again, this would almost certainly mean a disbursement of public money away from the areas where it is being generated to more backward areas; such a policy might also have little effect on private investment, which remains the major growth sector in most developing nations.

Neither of these policies of striving for locational efficiency or regional equity confronts the fundamental problem of how to rearrange the spatial system to increase productivity per capita. In this context, it is useful to distinguish between two purposes to which spatial planning can be directed. One aims to disperse the nongenerative concomitants of economic growth (hospitals, schools, banks, piped water supplies, post offices, and so on) in as equitable and efficient a manner as possible; another tries to mobilize the productive capacities of all regions by linking them in both a structural and an organizational sense to the mainstream of the national economy. The first, which is simply an allocative problem, is oriented toward regional welfare considerations; the second, which attempts to bring a structural transformation by fostering activities in which a region has a comparative advantage, is directed toward productivity.

Structural transformation implies breaking down the spatial, economic, and institutional barriers that limit a society's capacity for growth. It may demand new technology, better use of existing technology, or simply innovativeness that enables a producer to organize his production differently when incentives are provided. It is true that limited growth may occur in a system simply by a horizontal expansion, but long-term growth is impossible without a change in the system's structure. In developing countries this structural change will mean a new spatial organization of the economy and possibly of the sociocultural pattern.

My purpose here is to explore the issues concerned in using the spatial system as an instrument in the structural transformation of ex-colonial developing countries. The key components in the spatial system are the urban centers, the transportation network that links them, and the organization structure that propels demand and other incentives through the system. To elaborate on these concepts specific reference is made to Nigeria, which in its colonial background, in its current poverty and rich resources, and in its recent tendency toward national disintegration serves to illustrate the problems that are associated with spatial organization in the developing nations.

Spatial Organization in Nigeria

Many current developmental problems arose from the colonial system itself, which in West Africa was geared to economic exploitation rather than to political control. In Nigeria the present transportation network, the urban system, and the organizational control mechanism are related directly to British colonial policy. The institutional basis of British policy was a few large trading companies that handled the collection and dispatch of all goods produced for export and the importation and distribution of manufactured consumer goods. The largest of these was the United Africa Company, formed in 1929 through a merger of the Niger Company and the African and Eastern Trading Corporation: by the 1940's it accounted for more than 40 per cent of the export and import trade of Nigeria.[3] The companies enjoyed enormous privileges (until 1939 Nigeria did not tax their incomes), and though their investment was relatively small, they played a dominant role in the spatial organization of the country. For one thing, they provided the organizational control necessary to incorporate millions of small-scale subsistence farmers into commercial agriculture, and these farmers at present account for about 60 per cent of Nigeria's Gross Domestic Product and for about 70 per cent of total Nigerian exports.

Small-scale peasant export farming, as distinct from plantation farming, was the second component in the colonial system in Nigeria. The British consistently refused to alienate land to Europeans; as a result, plantations and European rural settlement, so widespread in Southeast Asia and East Africa, were never established in Nigeria. As Helleiner comments, 'rather than acquiring the ownership of the means of production, as he [the foreigner] did elsewhere in his exploitation of mineral resources or establishment of plantations, he contented himself (or was forced to be content) with purchasing the output of the existing producers.'[4] Increased agricultural production occurred by bringing more land into production and by using more labor rather than by applying capital (technical innovation). In its surplus of good quality land Nigeria differs from Southeast Asia, where increased productivity has been achieved through the application of either more capital in the commercial sector or more labor in the subsistence sector.

The British policy of working within the existing economic system but of organizing it in a different way (which was similar to their policy of indirect political rule) meant that a 'dual economy' did not evolve in Nigeria. The spatial system, on the other hand, was created deliberately to facilitate the organizational control that was the real basis of British economic policy. The British-created spatial organization, which operated through a corridor-type transportation system, was superimposed on an indigenous pattern characterized by substantial trade and a relatively high degree of urbanization. Although it is doubtful if a national urban system existed in Nigeria – or, indeed, if one was created by colonialism – the impact of the British certainly had spectacular effects on urban places and rural areas.[5]

Large increases in agricultural productivity were achieved through the new colonial spatial organization, and a number of distinct regional economies quickly emerged, each based on its comparative advantages for the production of cocoa, oil palms, groundnuts, and cotton. Towns on the new transportation lines that linked the agricultural areas to the ports grew rapidly, and those not so favorably sited experienced relative, if not absolute, decline. Improved transportation technology, then, had both favorable[6] and unfavorable effects. The developmental impulses propelled along the transportation system by the British trading firms created a dynamic situation in which labor moved to the new export crop areas and to the towns that served them. These elements – the export-agriculture areas, the growing towns closely associated with the new agricultural areas, and the food-production areas linked to the towns – constituted what Friedmann has referred to as the core areas of the space economy.[7] But the rest of the nation remained isolated and experienced the back-wash effects of development, including a loss of productive human resources, a movement of people out of the indigenous settlements to the growing towns, and even deindustrialization.

Immediately after World War II, government-controlled marketing boards were established for cocoa, groundnuts, oil-palm produce, and cotton. Their initial purpose was to stabilize prices paid to farmers in a fluctuating world market, but later they took on the role of agricultural tax collection and investment bodies — that is, they became vehicles for mobilizing savings for public investment. Helleiner estimates that up to 1962 the development organizations operating with marketing-board funds had invested £40 million, or about 10 per cent of all investment by Nigerian governmental and public corporations between 1949 and 1962.[8] Funds were initially invested in agriculture, but later they were diverted to big and growing urban areas, consolidating the new spatial pattern established by the colonial regime. Since political independence the marketing boards have done little in the way of structural transformation of the rural areas; they have provided few incentives to farmers to innovate and have continued to operate through the colonial system's spatial structure. Their spatial organization is similar to that used by the large merchant houses when they handled the agricultural export trade.

If the movement of subsistence farmers into export agriculture represented the first major development thrust in Nigeria, the second was the growth of secondary industry from about 1958 on. In 1958 secondary industry contributed only 4 per cent of the Gross Domestic Product (at current factor cost); by 1963 the proportion had increased to 5.6 per cent, and by 1967 to 8.4 per cent.[9] Moreover, the current National Development Plan, which emphasizes intermediate and capital-goods production, will have to rely heavily on industrial growth if the 6.6 per cent overall annual growth rate is to be achieved during a period when the value of agricultural production is not expected to maintain its previous rate of increase.

Despite the substantial growth of secondary industry in Nigeria, it is questionable in view of the ownership and type of industry whether the growth has had any substantial generative effect. Most of the productive capacity in industry is controlled by the same firms that at an earlier date organized the export of agricultural products and the import of manufactured goods. With

political independence, tariff protection, and growing awareness of the potential size of the Nigerian market, these firms now manufacture locally goods that were formerly imported; they continue to use the organizational structure already in effect. Kilby has argued that this type of import substitution has developed not only because growing demand created a market threshold but also because of a need in a 'market threatening' environment to protect one's 'stake in the market.'[10] With tariff protection, an importer in an underdeveloped country can shift from a highly competitive environment to an oligopolistic market environment simply by meeting the cost of investment. This procedure has been followed by some overseas manufacturers and by entrenched merchant firms.

Although manufacturing in Nigeria has led to some import replacement, it has not brought any restructuring of the space economy; rather it has consolidated the organizational and spatial structures originally imposed by the old merchant firms and the marketing boards. Managerial and production units are strongly localized in the port cities of Lagos and Port Harcourt, in Kaduna in the north, and in wholesale distribution outlets strategically scattered throughout the nation. So far manufacturing has not brought any real economic independence to Nigeria, but inasmuch as it increases the dominance of a few cities, it may have transferred the metropolis-satellite relationship from an international to an intranational scale. The current Nigerian development plan, which views manufacturing as the agent for a structural transformation of the economy, shows little awareness of the developmental problems associated with increasing primacy in the urban system. The development plan refers only to locational efficiency, which means that industry will continue to locate in the few large urban centers and that the structural transformation which results from secondary industry will be highly localized, at least in the short run. Aboyade[11] has hinted at the kinds of structural changes that he hopes will occur in the hinterlands of the cities: improved farming technology; increased agricultural production, especially in food crops; out-migration of farmers; and rising rural incomes — changes that reduce differences in living standards between urban and rural areas. At any particular point in time it is difficult to assess the strength of these deviation-reducing processes relative to the deviation-amplifying processes that also exist between a city and its hinterland. However, regional-planning policies must be directed as closely as possible to both these processes, which sometimes counteract each other yet occur simultaneously and affect both regional and national rates of economic growth.

The Spatial Component of Growth

It is apparent from the Nigerian experience that the economic development achieved to date has been within the spatial and organizational structures imposed by colonialism. These structural limitations have permitted the growth of regional economics which, through their orientation to external, as distinct from internal, markets, fostered regional self-containment rather than national integration. Imbalance in regional economic development and the lack of spatial integration can both be traced, therefore, to a spatial organization that did not allow free movement of production factors (labor, capital, entrepreneurs, information) throughout the nation. Friedmann[12] has drawn attention to the interplay between economic and spatial processes and, as did Taaffe, Morrill, and Gould,[13] has emphasized the key role played by the transportation and urban systems in the spread of development. In fact this sort of worldwide systemic approach to the study of ex-colonial developing nations provides valuable insights into the kinds of developmental problems they currently face and into the planning strategy they might adopt. As Frank[14] correctly observes, it can be misleading to study any part of an economic system in isolation and to ignore the metropolis-satellite relationships that exist at both national and international levels.

The developmental impact of a spatial structure results primarily from the way in which it is used, that is, from the commodities, people, capital, and innovations propelled along the spatial structure by the organizational system of which it is only a part. It is doubtful whether the limited technical innovations that were introduced under the colonial system did more than organize more thoroughly the dependency on the colonial power, and there is strong evidence to show that the capital flow has always been to the disadvantage of the developing country. At the same time, colonialism in Nigeria created regional differences; certain regions have been more responsive to the demand generated by the economic growth of the colonial power, and in this respect these regions generated more income for the persons directly concerned in the production of goods to meet this demand.

In Nigeria, and in West Africa generally, the additional income was gained not through any major technological innovations but rather through farmers working longer hours on their existing farms and on new land. The farmers' additional income was spent on consumer items — imported foods, textiles, furniture — and not on technological or organizational innovations that would generate indigenous economic growth.

Although some of the material possessions associated with regional economic development might have been diffused along the spatial framework, there was little that actually generated growth, that increased productivity, or that laid the basis for future growth. In other words, no structural transformation occurred. But the close correlation between the distribution of the goods and the area of most direct European influence has probably led to confusion: some students have described the so-called 'modernization' of parts of Africa in terms of the distribution of modern goods and welfare investments.[15] If, however, modernization is conceptualized as the introduction and spread of innovations in organization[16] that relate directly to productive processes, the areal dimension of 'modernization' may not correlate highly with the distribution of modern goods. Frank's warning is pertinent in this context: 'The diffusion which follows in the train of new roads, buses, transistor radios, etc., is not increasing the economic development of the recipient regions. Often it has helped sink them into even deeper and more hopeless underdevelopment.'[17]

The achievement of political independence in the developing nations has brought a striving for more economic independence, usually through industrialization policies that, when superimposed on a colonial spatial structure and not carefully planned, increase regional differences in economic development. As Nigeria demonstrates, under colonialism a concentrating trend was apparent as strategically located urban centers pushed ahead because of the bulking and distribution services they provided for agricultural producers. The advent of modern industry will undoubtedly increase the dominance of the large cities. The decentralizing effect of high urban wages is not felt in developing countries because of the rapid rate of population migration to the cities. If big-city dominance occurs without an improvement in methods of diffusion and without the deliberate building of strong urban-rural structural relationships, there will be a contraction rather than a dispersion of development as national economic growth proceeds.

Over time, as cities grow, the demand for foodstuffs will increase; the type of organization called forth to meet this demand may be the most important lever for generating economic development in the agricultural areas. But a substantial time lag is likely before the city has this generative effect on its hinterland, and even then, its effect will depend on the responsiveness of farmers to new demand patterns and on the efficiency of the organizational system. Until this generative effect occurs, the city could have some adverse 'draining-off' effects (backwash effects), or, at best, would simply provide various consumer items that do not generate economic development. This conclusion is not dissimilar to that reached by Williamson,[18] who, on another scale, showed that regional inequalities in developing nations may actually increase with industrialization up to a point when agglomeration diseconomies lead to a dispersion of industry and more regional equality.

The Planning Response

The conclusion that may be drawn from the Nigerian experience is that certain parts of a developing country are more responsive than others to new demands, but given the locational characteristics of the economic activities that are called forth to meet changes in demand, the growth areas contract over time rather than diffuse. This evolving pattern is geared to the spatial structure, especially to its urban and transportation components, but an equally significant element is the organization and control of space. The last is the key variable that distinguishes 'generative' from 'nongenerative' urban places and transportation lines. The solutions to developmental problems, therefore, do not lie in enlarging the spatial structure but in improving the organization that propels commodities, information, and production factors through the existing spatial structure. However, it is not always easy to separate process, organization, and structure. Process gives rise to structure but is itself conditioned by the existing structure. Thus a neocolonial economy can function efficiently in a colonial spatial structure. Similarly, the organizational and institutional control exercised over the location of economic activities both affects, and is affected by, the spatial structure. This means that solutions to the problems of regional imbalance and the diffusion of development must be sought on a number of fronts: regional development may be restrained by imperfections in organization and not just in the spatial structure.[19]

In the context of developing areas, the term 'regional economic development' means essentially a steady increase in output per capita achieved through a mobilization of resources and the use of resources in a more productive manner. This mobilization is facilitated by changes in demand and by new methods of organization

and production. Technological innovations may play a role, but in the early stages of development increased productivity is more likely to be achieved by a change in the attitude of producers, leading to the use of new combinations of production factors. Examples in the rural sector include the use of hired labor and the acquisition of more land for the production of crops in strong demand. Callaway[20] has documented other instances of indigenous response to economic incentives in urban activities. The important point is that regional economic development is based on a form of growth from below and does not generate any conflict between policies of locational efficiency and regional equity. All that is required is the involvement of people in the growth process by the establishment of organizational linkages.

It is difficult to assess the role of the urban hierarchy in stimulating growth from below, but the forging of strong links between a large city and its rural hinterland will encourage farmers to bypass towns at lower levels for the delivery of their produce. On the other hand, for the purchase of consumer goods and services of all kinds a well-articulated urban hierarchy might be necessary for a farming community. Once again, then, a distinction should be drawn between what is needed to generate increased productivity and what is needed to acquire the material possessions of economic development. This is not to deny that in particular situations where organizational linkages are weak the establishment of low-order centers may facilitate both production and consumption.

Spatial and organizational problems exist at the national scale where interregional (interurban) linkages are most important and at the intraregional (city-hinterland) scale. The difference in scale emphasizes the two kinds of economic development problems, that of building a spatial system conducive to overall economic growth, where intercity interaction is essential, and that of incorporating isolated rural inhabitants in the development process, where linkages are provided between regional capitals and farming areas. These problems are complementary. Aggregate demand in the nation must be high enough to stimulate regional economic development, and unless the incomes of farmers, who make up a large part of the total population, are rising, demand for manufactured goods and for urban services is limited. Therefore a need exists for a holistic approach to planning a spatial and organizational system that will foster national economic growth and will also provide the 'inducement mechanisms,' which Hirschman[21] argues are necessary 'to enlist for development purposes resources that are hidden, scattered or badly utilized.' Although short-run disequilibria will exist, the long-run effect of this policy is to maximize both regional and national growth rates.

In seeking to implement this developmental approach, the points of leverage are the urban and transportation components of the spatial system and the organizational arrangement that propels the inducements to change through the system. Thus one of the most widely discussed paradigms for regional development policy is that of using the coincidence of urbanization and industrialization in space as a tool for achieving a high national growth rate and an areal spread of development. The city is seen as the agent for the introduction of new ideas, for the development of innovations, and for social change generally, or, as Hoselitz[22] put it some twenty years ago, 'They [the cities in underdeveloped societies] exhibit a spirit different from the countryside. They are the main force and the chief locus for the introduction of new ideas and new ways of doing things. One must look, therefore, to the cities as the crucial places in under-developed societies in which the adaptation to new ways, new technologies, new consumption and production patterns and new social institutions are achieved.' More recently, there has been an upsurge of interest in 'growth poles' or 'growth centers,' especially in the European literature.[23] Friedmann,[24] although he makes few references to this literature, bases his ideas for regional development to a large extent on urban growth and on the establishment of a national system of urban centers. It is usually assumed that the growth of regional cities depends on interaction in the urban system and that city-rural diffusion proceeds through the urban hierarchy by a neighborhood effect.

A closer examination of these ideas reveals some unanswered questions. It is true, of course, that industrial and tertiary activities tend to cluster and thereby generate external economies of scale and greater innovative capacity, which in turn induce more growth. Few would disagree with the proposition that it is in the interest of a developing nation, seeking to rid itself of a neocolonial dependency on foreign powers for the disposal of its crops and for the import of its manufactured goods, to foster secondary industries. But another central issue for a backward country is the mechanism whereby the growth generated in the city is diffused outward. Tornqvist[25] argues that 'spread effects appear to be greater the higher the level of economic develop-

ment of a country . . . probably because of improved communications . . . and a higher level of education and stronger forces for the removal of obstacles to the operation of these spread effects.' This generally conforms with the findings of Pedersen[26] on Chile, in which he concluded that 'the stronger the distance decay, the closer will diffusion follow physical distance.' It follows that underdeveloped countries, which have the greatest distance-decay effects, will have the most concentrated distribution of economic development.

Regional planning policies that might be derived from this observation would aim not only at urban development but at the improvement of transportation, communication, and organizational linkages between the urban centers and the rural areas or, alternatively, at creating a spread of towns of particular sizes to foster the articulation of the developmental impulses generated in the largest center. Growth-pole protagonists would argue that investment in infrastructural linkages is inherent in the growth-pole concept; that is, once self-generating urban growth is under way, extensions will automatically be made in intraregional transportation networks because of the needs of the city. But it does not necessarily follow that investment in regional transportation will also increase productivity in the rural area.

Indeed, Myrdal and Hirschman[27] have both emphasized the polarization and backwash effects of concentrated development, arguing that the movement of production factors, especially the selective nature of labor migration, will benefit the city and will therefore increase regional imbalance, at least in the short run. This hypothesis is supported by the fact that the city is likely to be most exploitive of the resources in its hinterland while it is growing, and as it grows it attracts resources from a wider and wider area. But as urban wages rise the city becomes less attractive to economic activities, which may then locate in smaller towns. On the other hand, it can be argued that the industrial city-hinterland relationship is similar to a colonial situation, in that structural weaknesses are generated which may keep the hinterland in a permanent state of backwardness. Hirschman's 'trickling down' will occur because of purchases made by the city, but these can produce an exploitive rather than a developmental relationship[28].

Approaching this problem from another viewpoint, Friedmann[29] has advanced reasons why spatial equilibrium between his 'core' and 'periphery' will not automatically be achieved; namely, the failure by entrepreneurs to perceive peripheral investment opportunities, the greater export demand for the goods produced at the center than at the periphery, the concentration of innovative spirit in urban areas, and so on. But if rural development is conceptualized as simply an improvement in living standards, this could be achieved by a rise in agricultural incomes, which would not require any of the urban-industrial investment he emphasizes. The combined effect of a migration of population out of the rural areas and a rise in the demand for food should increase rural incomes; that little equalization has in fact been achieved is attributed to poorly developed structural relationships between the city and its hinterland.

On the other hand, interaction of all kinds within the urban system is quite strong, especially in developing countries, where both private and public investments are centralized. The transportation and communication networks and the organizational structure of administrative institutions and large-scale firms facilitate interurban interaction, with the result that wealth generated in one urban place will move more easily to other urban centers than to rural areas. Moreover, movement of wealth up the hierarchy toward the largest centers is more likely than movement down the hierarchy, because of the location of head offices of most national manufacturing and retail firms; this 'upward influence' may disappear into the economy in general, reducing the possibilities of intraregional diffusion and increasing regional imbalance. It can only be concluded that the relevance of growth-pole planning policies to developing nations is reduced by the weak structural relationships between the urban system and the rural sector.

Structural Transformation

The developmental planning strategies relevant to developing countries such as Nigeria can now be presented a little more clearly. The structural relationships between urban centers are stronger than those between large urban-industrial nodes and their rural areas, a situation in which backwash effects are dominant. Two complementary planning strategies can be directed to this problem: the allocation of resources to build up a number of second-tier cities carefully selected on the basis of their growth potential and their location in the nation; and the extension and consolidation of organizational links between these cities and their hinterlands. The second policy requires much more than simply extending transportation linkages, which may lead to a more widespread diffusion of backwash effects. Organization implies the transmittal of developmental impulses

and of incentives to which farmers can respond by increasing their productivity; it is the major element in promoting the structural transformation that is the aim of planning policies in developing countries. Moreover, for a policy of regional urbanization to be successful, structures must be established to give more regional independence to economic activities. There is a need to retain at least some of the wealth that is generated in the region, not by the region turning in on itself but by encouraging more local ownership and control of productive enterprises, especially those oriented to agricultural activities. This means that the region must achieve a form of economic independence from the metropolis in the same way that the nation as a whole had to achieve economic independence from the colonial power. In Nigeria the new twelve-state structure provides an obvious framework for the selection of urban centers to be developed by investment in infrastructure, so that they will become more attractive to private investors.

Justification for these strategies lies in the argument that regional centers will disperse development more rapidly than will a policy of directing or encouraging investment in only a few centers and in transportation lines linking them to all parts of the nation, which represents little more than a form of neocolonialism. But in the long run the success of any development policy depends on how effectively economic growth can be diffused from the city to the rural areas. This is a form of diffusion not widely studied, though Berry[30] has argued from his Indian experience that a well-articulated urban hierarchy is essential. Others have emphasized the responsiveness of farmers when they are presented with a packet of incentives — markets, credit facilities, rural roads, extension services, and verification trials for crops — which are made available in a large number of closely spaced rural settlements. Both may be important, but they are solutions in terms of spatial structure rather than of process or organization.

Brown,[31] however, does distinguish between two types of diffusion processes — a relocation type and an expansionary type based on what he calls an 'associative transfer.' The second type includes information about different methods of farm organization, the uses to which credit can be put, the kinds of fertilizer suitable in certain areas, and market conditions; that is, information that can generate economic development in the rural sector. If in fact the source of this information is in the urban system, the effectiveness of its transfer depends on the propulsive and regional strength of the city and on the organizational structure that links it to its hinterland.

It is essential for a number of reasons that the city selected as the regional growth center be relatively large. In the first place, because of the inelastic demand for low-order goods, a small center stands to gain little from rising incomes, for the increased spending will move to larger cities. A large center will minimize leakage and will also provide the external economies that are essential for the self-sustaining growth of secondary and tertiary activities. There are certain difficulties here: if external economies are highly localized, they will give the city a decided cost advantage that will have a deindustrializing effect on smaller urban places within its hinterland. But a policy of building up a second tier of cities will offset the incipient primacy always present in urban systems in underdeveloped economies. Furthermore, the development of rural areas is fundamentally dependent on the sustained strength of demand for agricultural products, which in the first instance must come from large urban areas.

The effectiveness of the organizational structures is probably the most critical variable in the whole development process. There are some lessons to be learned from colonialism, which was an economic success as much because of the strength and efficiency of the organization it imposed at the national scale as because of the spatial system it established. In the period of growing economic independence new forms of indigenous organization are emerging, especially at the local scale. Probably the greatest need in regional planning in developing countries is temporarily to divert attention away from spatial structure to a systematic study of these organizational systems that bind together people and economic activities.

Notes

1 T. Hermansen: Spatial Organisation and Economic Development: The Scope and Task of Spatial Planning (United Nations Research Institute for Social Development, Geneva, 1969: duplicated).

2 William Alonso: Urban and Regional Imbalances in Economic Development, *Econ. Development and Cultural Change*, Vol. 17, 1968-1969, pp. 1-14.

3 Michael Crowder: West Africa under Colonial Rule (London and Evanston, Ill., 1968).

4 Gerald K. Helleiner: Peasant Agriculture, Government, and Economic Growth in Nigeria (Homewood, Ill., 1966), p. 3.

5 Akin L. Mabogunje: Urbanization in Nigeria – A Constraint on Economic Development, *Econ. Development and Cultural Change*, Vol. 13,

6 Allan McPhee: The Economic Revolution in British West Africa (London, 1926), p. 104.

7 John Friedmann: Regional Economic Policy for Developing Areas, *Papers and Proc. Regional Sci. Assn.*, Vol. 11, 1963, pp. 41-61.

8 Gerald K. Helleiner: A Wide Ranging Development Institution. The Northern Nigerian Development Corporation, 1949-1962. *Nigerian Journ. of Econ. and Social Studies*, Vol. 6, 1964, pp. 239-257. See also *idem*: The Eastern Nigerian Development Corporation, *ibid.*, pp. 98-123.

9 'Second National Development Plan 1970-74' (Nigeria, Federal Ministry of Information, Lagos, 1970), p. 137.

10 Peter Kilby: Industrialization in an Open Economy: Nigeria, 1945-1966 (Cambridge, Eng., 1969), pp. 58-59.

11 O. Aboyade: Industrial Location and Development Policy: The Nigerian Case, *Nigerian Journ. of Econ. and Social Studies*, Vol. 10, 1968, pp. 275-302.

12 Friedmann, *op. cit.* [see note 7 above]

13 Edward J. Taaffe, Richard L. Morrill, and Peter R. Gould: Transport Expansion in Underdeveloped Countries: A Comparative Analysis, *Geogr. Rev.*, Vol. 53, 1963, pp. 503-529.

14 Andre Gunder Frank: Latin America: Underdevelopment or Revolution (New York and London, 1970).

15 See, for example, the discussion in Thomas H. Eighmy: Modernization in a Regional Context: Proto-Theory and Practice in Western Nigeria (unpublished Ph.D. dissertation, Department of Geography, Pennsylvania State University, University Park, 1969).

16 I am grateful to Professor A.L. Mabogunje for valuable discussions on organizational systems.

17 *Op. cit.* [see note 14 above], pp. 65-66.

18 Jeffrey G. Williamson: Regional Inequality and the Process of National Development: A Description of the Patterns, *Econ. Development and Cultural Change*, Vol. 13, No. 4. Part 2, 1964-1965, pp. 5 and 44.

19 See the argument in Brian J.L. Berry: Relationships between Regional Economic Development and the Urban System: The Case of Chile, *Tijdschr. voor Econ. en Soc. Geogr.*, Vol. 60, 1969, pp. 283-307; reference on pp. 287-290.

20 Archibald Callaway: Unemployment among African School Leavers, *Journ. of Modern African Studies*, Vol. 1, 1963, pp. 351-369.

21 Albert O. Hirschman: The Strategy of Economic

Development (New Haven, 1968), pp. 190-195.

22 B.F. Hoselitz: Sociological Aspects of Economic Growth (New York and Toronto, 1960), p. 163.

23 For a review of growth-pole literature, see D.F. Darwent: Growth Poles and Growth Centers in Regional Planning, *Environment and Planning*, Vol. 1, 1969, pp. 5-32.

24 John Friedmann: Regional Development Policy: A Case Study of Venezuela (Cambridge, Mass., and London, 1966), pp. 28-37.

25 Gunnar Tornqvist: Contact Systems and Regional Development (Lund, Sweden, 1970).

26 Poul Ove Pedersen: Innovation Diffusion within and between National Urban Systems, *Geogr. Analysis*, Vol. 2, 1970, pp. 203-254: reference on p. 224.

27 Gunnar Myrdal: Economic Theory and Underdeveloped Regions (London, 1957): Hirschman, *op. cit.* [see note 21 above], p. 187.

28 Hirschman, *op. cit.* [see note 21 above], p. 189.

29 Friedmann, Regional Development Policy [see note 24 above], pp. 13-17.

30 See, for example, Brian J.L. Berry: Policy Implications of an Urban Location Model for the Kanpur Region, *in* Regional Perspective of Industrial and Urban Growth: The Case of Kanpur (edited by P.B. Desai, I.M. Grossack, and K.N. Sharma [Bombay, 1969]), pp. 203-219; reference on p. 203.

31 Lawrence A. Brown: Diffusion Processes and Location, *Regional Sci. Research Institute, Bibliogr. Ser. No. 4* (Philadelphia, 1968), pp. 2-6.

25 Regional Development: Problems and Lines of Advance in Europe

by Myles Wright

University of Liverpool

In the past decade almost every country in Europe has adopted in part a regional approach to national investment and development problems. Belief has grown that the new approach promises something of value, and the organizations to enquire into or promote regional developments in Western European countries are now very numerous.

A number of summaries of regional development problems and policies in Europe are available and are listed at the end of this article. These show that the broad objectives are the same in every country, and so are many of the approaches to solutions of particular problems. The basic aim of all regional policies has been and is to promote the fullest development of the country's total resources by suitable guidance of investment, region by region, over a period of years. The phrase 'balanced development' is often used: this implies a need and duty on the part of central governments to correct disparities in living conditions and opportunities and employment that now exist between one region and another.

These disparities are the main reason why regional policies have come into existence. That acute shortage of labour in one region should co-exist with unemployment in another is felt to be wasteful as well as unjust. Governments are unwilling to wait until 'market forces' correct these inequities, and have indeed grave doubts whether they ever would or could. In addition, the new mobility arising from the increased use of motor vehicles is changing most local problems into regional problems, while at the same time the huge cost of modern physical investments – motor roads, power stations, housing estates and the like – makes it essential that their location and relationships should be the subject of skilful forethought and decision. The proper scale for such guidance today is clearly regional.

On the other hand, Governments in Europe still have doubts about the validity and proper extent of a regional approach to national development problems: on how much guidance or aid should be given to less favoured districts, and about new administrative machinery that may be needed. There is a good deal of evidence that the central governments of most countries hoped, to begin with, that Ministerial declarations of intention to help less developed regions, backed by some simple system of grants to new factories established therein, would do all that was needed. These hopes have not been fulfilled.

Three Kinds of Problem Region

In terms of national development and regional 'imbalance' there are in all countries two, and in most three, quite different kinds of region. These are:

1 Poorly developed rural regions, having relatively primitive living conditions and few opportunities for employment, which are losing population.

2 Urban-regions that contain a large proportion of the country's total population, are still growing, and increasingly reveal national and local disadvantages of over-growth.

3 Urban industrial regions that are in decline or are growing much more slowly than the more prosperous industrial regions.

The E.F.T.A.[1] and P.E.P.[2] publications state that the characteristics of problem regions are the same in all countries. Those of types 1 and 3 are unemployment, outward migration of the young, low incomes, poor services and often apathetic local administrations who feel that the whole problem is too much for them. The introduction of the most modern techniques in agriculture, forestry and fishing may lead to a further decline of population in rural regions, despite a rise of average income; and modern growth industries established in such regions have tended to become 'islands', drawing staff from, and transmitting dividends to more prosperous regions.

Remedies for the stagnation in older industrial regions are no easier to find. The main assets of such regions are under-employed labour, a long industrial tradition and existing transport networks. On the other hand, craft divisions may have become somewhat rigid during economic depression, and low standards of housing and services and much derelict land may discourage new immigrant enterprises. Unresilient industrial regions of this kind exist in Germany, France and

Britain. They are of special importance in the formulation of British regional policies. Their populations could not possibly be moved elsewhere, they contain fixed assets of great value for many years to come, and they are obvious candidates for choice as 'counter-attractions' to London and Birmingham by reason of their transport networks, status as regional capitals and labour reserves. Above all, they provide the most challenging test for theories of 'balanced' regional development: how much aid the country can or must give to less favoured regions; the proportions in which such aid should be divided between direct provision of new industrial employment and general improvement of 'infrastructure'; and whether new administrative machinery is needed for the effective guidance of regional development.

The drawbacks and potential dangers of overgrowth within one or a very few urban regions have been a cause of disquiet for many years; first in France in relation to Paris, but for more than 30 years in Britain and smaller countries. This is a world-wide phenomenon, irrespective of the country's economic circumstances or technological advance. Usually it is the capital city that has grown excessively. Easy access to central government and to capital for new ventures, a large market for talent, labour and produce, and cross-fertilization between new processes, are obvious causes of metropolitan growth. One might also add that, since Roman times, it has proved expedient for central governments to shield the populations of their capitals from the worst of current economic stresses.

In the last decade however a new urgency has come into discussions of how to slow down the growth of Europe's largest cities. The cause of this has been the demand for much more urban space which has been generated by rising prosperity and the huge space demands of motor vehicles. European governments now fully realize that there comes a point where the economic advantages of a concentration of population and activities begins to be demonstrably off-set by difficulties of movement, and by deterioration of other aspects of social and physical environment. They have also been clearly warned that the inevitable and rapid increase in the use of motor vehicles may soon raise these disadvantages to a dangerous level. It seems certain that central governments' appreciation of the threat to metropolitan regions has added impetus to regional development studies and acceptance of the idea of developing centres of 'counter-attraction'.

The existence of problem regions of these three kinds in western European countries, coupled with much increased demands for space for urban purposes, may thus be regarded as the common origin of regional studies and policies. Ideas of social justice impelled governments to try to aid backward regions; the labour reserves in such regions provided a second incentive; and the motor vehicle threat to overgrown, and particularly metropolitan, regions clinched the matter.

Governments have however been cautious in adopting ideas of a regional approach to the solution of national economic and development problems. The transformation in the last decade of at least major local problems into regional ones, has pushed governments to the half-way house of a central appraisal of regional problems, but progress has been cautious. Certainly British Governments (of both political parties) have disliked the implications of the change; the main reason being their unwillingness to upset any further a long-established and recently somewhat shaky local government structure. This attitude is understandable, though not necessarily wise on a long view. The detached observer may be convinced that the effective guidance of regional development – in a co-ordinated pattern of costly investments in particular projects at chosen places – will soon be found incompatible with a local government system which makes a sharp distinction between town and countryside, and often takes a parochial view of development. Yet suitable machinery for the guidance of region-wide physical development has not been the subject of much serious study, and certainly is not agreed. Holland has probably made the most progress in this difficult field. But measures of guidance of physical development that are essential in a country whose survival, and in part creation, has depended on them, are not necessarily suitable for application elsewhere.

Approaches to Solutions

The publications listed disclose some agreement among European countries on how best to try to solve the problems of the three kinds of region. There should be a long term programme extending over 20 to 40 years. Help for less developed regions should be of a 'pump-priming' type and not a charitable dole. Aid should be concentrated on the places and projects that offer the best chance of economic success, in the hope that prosperity will spread outwards from the chosen points in concentric ripples. Larger centres, including some in older industrial regions, should be deliberately developed as counter-attractions to over-developed metropolitan regions. Some 'relief of pressure' is essential for over-grown regions in terms of land, but (in a way not clearly seen as yet) this relief should be provided in a manner that will not halt the renovation and development of regions of counter-attraction. One or more of these ideas may be emphasized or left unmentioned in a particular country according to its special circumstances or polit-ical pressures, but so far as there is a European consensus of opinion on the strategy and tactics of regional development, it seems to be along these lines.

In carrying out these aims all governments have moved cautiously. In particular, they have been unwill-ing to make changes in the relationships and responsibil-ities of central departments and local government. Before making such changes they have tried to test the validity of 'regionalism', and of regional development policies, by means of special agencies. The number of special agencies, funds or committees now wholly or partly concerned in the furtherance of regional policies in Europe is very large, and their methods of operation appear almost infinitely diverse. Moreover, it is almost impossible for a foreigner to judge the results of an agency's work, even though this work is described in plain terms in his own language: for the results will depend on the influence of the agency's work on other authorities or attitudes of mind in the country con-cerned, and of these he has no knowledge of the convincing kind that only comes from experience.

Two tentative conclusions however do emerge from study of European regional policies so far. The first is that a considerable fog overlies the boundary between the economic and physical components of regional development, and that the latter have received so far very little attention. The economic and social aspects are summarized lucidly, both as regards problems, altern-ative remedial policies and the general lines along which these might be implemented. But when description of implementation approaches the boundary of topo-graphy, land use, and physical relationships of the various works – which it rarely does – then the fog begins to gather. There is the suggestion that these things are second stage processes: and this is quite true. There is also however, some implication that the location and relationship of needed physical works within a region may be left for 'local' decision: and this is surely untrue. The renovation or further development of a region will demand – if maximum benefit and economy are to be achieved – that major physical works should be co-ordinated for the region as a whole, both in location and in accordance with a regional programme and budget over a period of years. Effective machinery to secure this co-ordination is certain to be needed.

The second conclusion that emerges from a study of European regional policies is that actions taken so far are' broadly divisible into four groups, each of which is worth brief description. These groups may be called employment aids; declarations of policy; regional econ-omic studies; and studies of physical feasibility. Des-cription is confined to actions taken in Britain, but readers of the publications listed at the end of this article will probably agree that actions in Britain have been paralleled broadly, and sometimes almost exactly, by those of other countries.

Employment Aids

By the phrase 'employment aids' is meant the whole range of legislation and grants which was and is intended to encourage the provision of additional employment in particular areas. In Britain the Special Areas Act of 1934 may be said to have established these aids as part of a continuing policy.

The seeming merit of these aids is that they go straight to the heart of the matter. Given more employ-ment and so more money in circulation, it was hoped that backward regions would soon catch up with the rest; and there need be no interference with the normal working of local government. At one time (1960), the desire for simplicity in giving such aid -- or desire to escape political lobbying – led to legislation that a district with more than a certain percentage of unem-ployment should automatically qualify for aid. It thus became possible for small and widely dispersed districts to slide in and out of eligibility for aid over quite short periods of time and rendered a long-term policy extre-mely difficult to put into effect.

Up to 1939 comparatively little was achieved in Britain by employment aids. Since 1945, a great deal of new employment has been created in less favoured regions wholly or partly by means of such aids. Yet this success has been accompanied by growing doubts whether concentration on the provision of new indus-trial employment could halt the continuing (though diminished) migration to the Midlands and South East. The steady increase of office and service employment, as opposed to manufacturing, increased these doubts, which were not greatly diminished by the removal from London to the provinces of portions of Government departments concerned with routine work. By 1955 it was being argued that the 467 factories and large extensions provided on Merseyside in the previous decade were, many of them, placed in districts from which, on valid social grounds, there should be a sizeable removal of population. In some cases it could be demonstrated that the policy of the Board of Trade was directly opposed to that of the Ministry of Housing and Local Government, which was responsible for town and regional planning.

From 1955 onwards two views on regional policies gained ground in Britain. The first was that the less-favoured industrial regions should each be examined as a whole, so that major aspects of its economic and social life and its potentialities could be seen in relation to one another. This view thus advocated a return to studies begun in the period 1943-1950 and later abandoned. The second view flowed from the first. It was that the whole physical environment of certain northern urban regions should be upgraded and, if need be, renewed, so as to enable them to act as counter-attractions to London and Birmingham.

These views were slow to gain Government support, but they may be said to have ended belief that employment aids alone could correct Britain's regional imbalance.

In 1963, the National Economic Development Council stated that underemployed labour in northern regions should be regarded as a national resource, and not merely a social burden. This had been preceded (1960-63) by a considerable change in Government opinion towards much more positive and broadly based regional policies. The first steps to give effect to the change of view were the setting up of inter-Departmental study groups or special committees. Their aim was mainly to examine the inter-Departmental aspects of demands for land and projects for development in the largest urban regions. A change towards a co-ordinated programme for renovation or extension of such a region would plainly affect the policies, local programmes and relationships of five or more Ministries, and it was these matters which the study groups set out to examine, against a somewhat fragmentary background knowledge of regional circumstances and trends.

It seems fair to say that by 1963 the British Government (then Conservative) had concluded that a much broader and more vigorous approach was needed to correct regional imbalances, but that they were not agreed on the forms, scale and co-ordination of the remedial measures that would prove practicable. In this situation of agreement on broad objectives and reasonable doubts over means, the Government decided to

arouse and test public support by declarations of policy.

Policy Declarations

The first two of what are here called policy declarations were published in the autumn of 1963. Both Central Scotland[5] and The North East[6] were described as programmes for growth and development, and were accompanied by diagrammatic maps, showing main roads, new towns and areas of intended growth. The documents were short and carefully written. They expressed determination to act, sketched a programme of co-ordinated actions and promised Government support. On the other hand, they avoided discussion of new administrative machinery that might be needed to ensure effective guidance of the location, relationship and timing of the various widely spaced and costly proposals. The omissions were noted at the time, and may at the time have been prudent. For new machinery would almost inevitably affect local government structure and powers, and these were and still are under examination by a Local Government Commission – the second since 1945. There was good reason for not adding to the Commission's already extremely difficult task by speculations about possible new administrative needs that lay outside the Commission's term of reference.

The brevity, simplicity of aim and perhaps the impact of the first two reports were all diminished in their three successors. The South East[7] report has been criticised as declaring a policy of defeatism by accepting the need to provide for a large increase of population within 60-70 miles of London, though it made plain that most of the increase forecast would arise from natural increase rather than by immigration.

The two most recent reports, for the North West[8] and West Midlands[9] are included under 'declarations of policy' more because that is what they were expected to be than for their contents. They have suffered by being ordered by the Conservative Government and published by its successor, which has ideas of its own on how the foundation for regional policies should be prepared. The groups of civil servants – from various Departments – who produced the reports were therefore probably left without firm policy directives during crucial months. As a result, the North West and West Midland reports are long, and mainly descriptive of what is. Both contain cautious indications of new centres of growth. In the West Midlands, new centres are advocated mainly to avoid the evils of expansion closely around Birmingham. In the North West, the reason given for proposing new centres of growth is partly the difficulty of finding places near the older cities that would be attractive to new enterprises or as places to live.

It may be held that only one recommendation is common to all five 'declarations of policy' reports in Britain – Central Scotland, North East, South East, North West and West Midlands. This is that 'growth' should be spread over a considerable area around big cities, based on a much expanded framework of communications, employments and places of residence. In view of the growth of motor traffic and enormous cost of providing for it in older and densely developed cities, this recommendation may be seen as recognition of the inevitable for all urban regions. But it is a recommendation that raises two separate problems. In the South East and West Midlands the new growth points are intended as a relief of intolerable pressures, present and to come, within existing built-up areas. But their designation carries the threat that it will not lead to a thinning out of people and employments from nearby big cities but rather to the attraction of immigrants from other parts of the country.

In the North, the problem is different and perhaps smaller, but one to which it is equally difficult to find the right answer. The danger there is that new growth points, on pleasant sites 30 miles from older and somewhat grimy cities, may attract too much capital, brains and youthful energy, and so leave the older central cities in an even worse state, economically and physically, than they are now.

Declarations of policy do however seem a simple means of promotion of regional growth, though their effectiveness may depend on the firmness with which they are supported, and specially on their being restricted to a few chosen areas. Development and renovation have in fact taken place on a large scale in Central Scotland and the North East in recent years. Much of it must have been in preparation long before 1963 and so would have taken place in any event. Yet the increase of optimism and self-confidence in both regions in the last two or three years has been marked. There are therefore grounds for holding that policy declarations by central Government, backed by a reasonable increase in Exchequer grants, are potentially powerful instruments towards correction of regional disparities. But they are instruments that are readily blunted. There cannot be growth everywhere, and managements and investors know it well. A succession of policy declarations – especially long ones – which suggest growth areas in many different parts of a country, will inevitably lessen confidence in the central Government's will or capacity to correct regional disparities that have been obvious for 30 years. In this connection, Chapter 4 of *Depopulation in Mid-Wales*[10] seems relevant.

Regional Economic Studies

The phrase 'regional economic studies' is used to cover a wide range of enquiries that are intended to enable central government to compare the social and economic circumstances and prospects of different regions. Their aim is to enable government to decide the best practicable long-term 'balance' between the various regions, and the forms and scale of investment needed to achieve it. Such studies should desirably be inclusive, covering all regions, and be completed within a relatively short period. If enquiries are confined to regions where action is allegedly most urgent, the government will not have the means to make an informed comparison between prosperous and backward areas, and will be liable to be assailed by a variety of pressure groups whose arguments will be difficult to refute. It is also becoming much more widely held that these regional reviews should be repeated at suitable intervals. Major weaknesses of past studies of this kind have been, first, that their findings and recommendations were regarded as of permanent value, requiring no later review, and, secondly, that too little attention was paid to the machinery needed to implement the recommendations. The publications referred to in this article suggest that governments in Western Europe have now come to regard regional development as a continuing process of readjustments and renewals over a period of 40 years, and subject to review on the basis of a new survey every five or seven years.

This attitude is broadly that of the 1964 British Labour Government, who have set up regional economic planning boards and councils covering a large part of England. Each region has an executive board of civil servants and an advisory council drawn from industry and universities. It is expected that a report will be prepared and published for each region during the next two years. It may be that the reports published in July for the North West[8] and West Midlands[9] foreshadow the form of the coming regional economic reports; or the former may be seen as a bridge between the earlier Policy Declarations (with which they have been grouped in this article) and future reports of the regional economic boards, who may adopt a new approach to the same group of problems.

The general European acceptance of the need for a regional balancing process is emphasized by what has happened in Britain's near neighbour, the Republic of Ireland, whose 1961 population was 2,800,000. A variety of employment aids have been offered in Ireland since 1952 – in addition to tariffs since the 1930s – and a number of them have been intended to help districts that were losing population most heavily. In the past year, the Republic has accepted the need for a broader approach, and the country has been divided into nine regions and a series of comparative studies of resources and development prospects have been put in hand. It is intended to entrust these studies to private consultants and three firms have already been appointed.

The recent Irish approach to regional problems is of interest for two reasons.

The studies begun this year may be regarded as a combination of the broad economic enquiries described above, and the 'feasibility studies' that are briefly examined later in this article. The small size of the Irish regions (with a population range from 923,000 to 87,000) is a sensible explanation of this combined approach. All economic programmes must eventually be expressed in physical terms, and in a small region investment possibilities are so closely tied up with topography, communications, the relationship of settlements, and infrastructure generally, that economic, social and physical circumstances are most suitably considered together.

The second aspect of the Irish approach to regional problems that is of special interest is the quite strong political pressure for growing prosperity to be widely diffused, and that some special consideration should be shown to the more remote districts. This impulse to help historic and often very beautiful districts and to re-invigorate traditional ways of life commands sympathy in all countries. It is evident in Scandinavian and Scottish and Welsh regional policies, and in the help given to Southern Italy. It is, however, an attitude which the central Government of each of the countries concerned has to try to reconcile with compelling duties and modern economic facts: their responsibility for economic growth in the country as a whole; the fact that growth is most rapid in a few highly populated centres: that aid for less favoured regions is most economically rewarding if concentrated in a few most promising centres; and the plenitude of evidence that most of the traditional rural livelihoods – agriculture, fishing, forestry – would be probably most economically rewarding (in the narrow sense) if they were changed into capital intensive rather than labour intensive enterprises of large size. That none of the countries concerned has much enthusiasm for the changes of the latter kind has some economic justification. Modernization would not only greatly change ways of life which many would wish to retain, they would almost inevitably call for change in the appearance of large districts whose present beauty and ancient landscape and settlement forms are a great and growing tourist attraction. There seems no answer to this problem save in slow and cautious changes carried out with skills that are scarce and expensive.

Another view of British regional needs should be mentioned here as an introduction to the fourth and last method of approach to the solution of regional problems.

This view is difficult to summarize, but seems mainly to arise from anxiety over timing and machinery. Physical planners – with a background in the landusing professions and skills – have seen that regional development must mainly take place through a series of building and civil engineering projects at particular places, arranged in a programme and subject to a budget. These men are aware that pre-war and post-war 'regional plans' foundered because they were just a series of aspirations in pictorial form. There was no programme and no machinery for execution. Moreover, these earlier plans lacked the essential base of economic studies of the resources and strength and failings of the region, and considered suggestions for a mutually supporting series of remedies and new investments.

This essential economic base is now being supplied. It is however felt by some physical planners that the new regional boards and councils are examining regions that are far too large to be of practical assistance in guiding regional redevelopment – at least for some years. Although the broad national comparisons that will emerge from study of the English regions will be of value in determining strategy for 40 years ahead, they will be of little immediate use in the places where action is most needed. To summarize the second view somewhat crudely, it is that the places where regional guidance is most needed in Britain are in the six or eight urbanized regions which are obvious candidates for choice as counter-attractions to London and Birmingham. It is argued that a concentration of effort upon these regional capitals presents the greatest opportunity to establish real counter-attractions, and centres from which, by outward spread of prosperity, regional unbalance may be permanently redressed. It is further held that the shortage of time available to prepare for mounting motor traffic, the land shortage, administrative sub-division and other local problems in these urban regions, confirms the demand for a concentration of effort. The relatively small size of the urban regions concerned would enable economic and physical problems to be considered together, and firm recommendations made for a programme of action and the machinery needed to carry it out.

This alternative view has been over-simplified in this summary. There does however appear to be some real difference of opinion concerning the best use of economic manpower in Britain for the solution of regional problems in the next few years. At one extreme, there is the need for a long-term strategic view, dealing in broad comparisons. At the other, there is a demand for economists to help solve immediate and extremely complex problems in a few very important areas: problems of the comparative value of investment in communications, infrastructure generally, new employ-ments, redevelopment, and regional programmes and budgets. Until recently economists have been uneasy colleagues in this more limited field. Their training, like that of many geographers and sociologists, has been concentrated upon accurate description of what is – or was; and appeals for help to determine what should be, in a particular locality and within ten years, have been received with something like alarm. Yet few questions could be more important than where Britain places works which Dr P.A. Stone has estimated to cost about £100,000 millions before the year 2004, and occupy 1½ million acres of additional land.

British Governments of the past five years have been aware of the opinion just described. It was indeed obvious that the land use and development problems of the larger urban regions were growing more and more complex, and could not be solved by a planning system under which each local authority in an urban region prepared its own independent plan. A radius of 10 miles from the centre of Manchester embraces in whole or part the territories of nine such planning authorities, who are by no means agreed on the best future pattern of development for their region. The need for unbiased examination of the problems of land use in urban regions of this kind led to investigations that are here called feasibility studies.

Feasibility Studies
Feasibility studies, as now being undertaken in Britain, are in part an extension of the housing needs and land availability studies begun by the Ministry of Housing and Local Government's own staff about five years ago, and in part an extension of the New Towns' procedure of preparing an outline plan for the rapid growth of a new settlement. They comprise a co-ordinated study of the economic, social and physical possibilities of a limited area with the aim of achieving specific objectives within a limited period of years. The objective may be a large extension of an existing town (Peterborough, Ipswich, Runcorn); the creation of virtually new towns (Skel-mersdale, Mid-Wales); or the renovation and further development of an older industrial region which also contains progressive chemical industries (Teesside). The area and objectives vary greatly in size and complexity, but all these studies are alike in two respects. They have all been commissioned by central government, and they will result in proposals for physical developments of great size, together with a suggested programme and some estimate of costs.

These larger feasibility studies have special interest in that they will require joint consideration of the economic, social, physical and administrative aspects of urban regional development on a larger scale, and probably more realistically, than has taken place in Britain hitherto. Up to now, regional economic studies, actual construction projects (such as the building of a new town) and questions of changes in local government boundaries and powers, have been examined or carried out by separate bodies and on greatly differing scales. A decision to proceed with the renovation of further development of Portsmouth-Southampton or Teesside would however require an integrated solution to be found for problems in all three fields, in relation to a particular area and within a few years. Such solutions will be essential if urban regional development is to be effectively guided, and the manifest difficulty of achiev-ing them suggests strongly that some new administrative machinery will be necessary. The huge cost of motor-ways, new housing schemes and other major units of investment, coupled with scarcity of resources, will require – as has been stated earlier – that the location and timing of each new investment should be the best that is practicable from the point of view of the region as a whole. It is very unlikely that the necessary firmness of control could be achieved by the existing system of relationships between Government and local authorities.

The Major Problems
Regional problems and approaches to their solution in Western Europe may thus be summarized as follows:

The regions that are causing most concern are of three kinds: 'underdeveloped' (mostly rural); 'over-developed', usually including the capital city; and declining or unresilient industrial regions, some of which contain much derelict land or are otherwise unattractive in physical environment and general living conditions.

The solutions to these problems that have been or are being tried are very numerous but fall broadly into four groups: employment aids; declarations of policy; regional economic studies on a national and comparative basis; and feasibility studies of how to carry out, in physical terms, desirable changes in selected areas where action is most urgently needed.

Two further generalisations seem valid. All governments have been reluctant to disturb the existing pattern of central and local government responsibilities and relations. They have therefore examined regional problems by means of special committees or agencies, in the hope that the problems could be solved by a limited number of special aids or projects, combined with improvements in liaison between central and local government authorities. This general approach — extremely diverse in its detailed forms — has had some successes, but has brought no conviction that it offers more than a temporary solution for problems that continue to grow.

The second generalisation follows from the first. No vigorous examination seems to have been made of interrelated economic, physical and administrative problems that would have to be solved in order to guide a programme of regional development over an extended period, and of how this could be done. It is easy to see why this examination has not been made. Men and women with the necessary skills are few and busy; such a study might miss some of the biggest difficulties until it was related to a particular region; and if it were so related there would be much opposition to its being put in hand on the grounds, *inter alia*, of the damage it might do to the work and recommendations of the Local Government Commission.

It may be that in Britain the nearest politically acceptable substitute for such a study would be an impartial examination of the proposals in the Teesside feasibility study in relation to the future local government structure proposed for the same area.

Future Lines of Action

In trying to foresee future lines of action towards solving regional problems, it is useful to begin by noting the most powerful and seemingly permanent forces making for regional changes. Two of these seem dominant and are interconnected. The first is the normal human desire for a better job, a better home, schools and hospitals and more opportunity for popular forms of leisure activity. The second force is the demand for more space in and around almost every kind of building and — above all — much more space for moving and storing motor vehicles. The first attracts, as it always has attracted, young people from isolated communities towards big cities. The second diminishes, and is now doing so at an accelerating rate, the advantages of living in a big city and produces a counterflow outwards.

These are very obvious facts. The two forces have been at work in Europe for several centuries and probably since cities existed and migration became reasonably safe. But until the last 30 or 40 years they have been at work at a leisurely pace. It is their rapidly increasing strength and rate of operation that has been underestimated by Governments.

A publication from Sweden[11] has usefully summarized recent data on the two forces. In all countries, irrespective of their economic structure, the largest cities have grown fastest. Mobility of employees in search of jobs has grown greatly, and is not confined to movement from less to more favoured areas, and in broad terms this mobility is regarded as economically beneficial. As average income rises each individual, family and firm, demands more space, and to this personal or industrial demand there has been added in the last 20 years the huge land demands of motor vehicles. Demand for space in an urban region grows more than proportionately to the increase of population.

In Sweden the land area per head in urbanized districts is growing by 3.25 per cent per year. This is the same rate of growth as that of the gross national product and almost the same as the annual increase in goods carried by road (3.8 per cent). In the U.S.A. the land area per head in urbanized areas now exceeds a quarter of an acre and is expected to rise to half an acre by 1980. Figures are given for the increase in floorspace per user for most types of building. These figures, and the fact that every country in Europe expects a continuing increase in motor traffic, have obvious implications for those who frame regional policies.

One of these is that for those who have or soon will have the use of a motor car, most economic and social activities have become regional in scale: since the area within reach in an hour's journey — given favourable conditions — is about 50 times what it was half a century ago. A second implication is that the advantages of living and working in a low density area are substantial for those who travel to work by car. For example, 62 per cent of those who travel by road to Bishops Stortford (population 20,000) and Maidenhead (40,000) between 7 and 10 a.m. travel by car; for Watford (76,000) the percentage is 48; for Leeds, (309,000) 27. Third, the advantages of living in big cities of the normal densely developed kind are growing less, and will inevitably continue to do so. The twofold demand for extra space within each building and for the movement and storage of vehicles, cannot be fulfilled. The difficulty of providing for the movement of people and goods at reasonable speed and cost is now the major anxiety in big cities. It has led to a ban in Greater Paris on new buildings likely to increase employment and to the recent ban on new office buildings in Central London. In Britain, proposals have been made for restricting traffic on urban roads by imposing a charge on vehicles, and it is probable that some such restriction will have to be introduced.

Low density development on new land is far less costly than redevelopment of existing cities, less disturbing and far quicker. It follows that demand for more urban space will be supplied, in the main, by large new developments at low density. The key question for regional policy makers in all countries is where the extra land should best be provided. The answer should try to meet the needs of 40 years ahead so far as these can be foreseen: it must also have regard to the present location of employments, the need to keep the country as a whole prosperous and to the limited resources available for new developments.

The physical solution is to enlarge the framework of every urban region, so as to relieve damaging pressures and facilitate movement, while seeking to divert to new or old centres in less favoured regions an appreciable proportion of new growth. As a general aim, this is what European governments are trying to do, but there is little agreement on methods, timing or administrative machinery. Moreover, there are grounds for the same complaints as were made by those in high command in the Allied forces in World War II: that they could rarely obtain a clear statement of the resources that would be made available for a given operation, and that too little attention was given to the machinery needed to carry out a complex plan.

There is some agreement on methods for the carrying out of regional development policies in under-developed and usually rural areas; and the physical problems are relatively simple. These areas have the assets of plenty of land and usually of a reserve of labour. As a bus service, or a car of some kind, comes within the reach of most families, some disadvantages of isolation can be removed at a relatively cheap cost. A larger school, churches, clinic and perhaps tourist camping grounds or hotels could be concentrated at 'key' villages, where piped water and electricity and domestic sewerage also become practicable.

The next order of magnitude of 'growth centre' is the rural regional centre to which many countries are paying attention. This is seen as a single larger town, or a group of smaller ones close together, which would become a focus for the communities within 25 or 30 miles. In general, such a centre is seen as the smallest unit to which substantial centre government aid would be given. Roads, electricity and sewerage would be provided, and economic hopes pinned to a slow growth of rurally based enterprises: forest products and fish and dairy processing, veterinary and agricultural service stations, technical training, and regional craft centres. In addition, it is hoped that the probable huge future demand for tourist holiday accommodation will provide rural regional centres with opportunities for profitable development and a substantial summer income. This particularly applies to centres near the sea or other large water areas, as these are specially attractive to the modern holiday maker. There are doubts whether it would be desirable to try to establish in such rural centres branches of modern industry that are not closely tied to local resources. The availability of labour may not be a great enough advantage to off-set the drawbacks of a lack of a local network of sub-contractors and industrial linkages, and difficulty in attracting able managers. Industrial development may also discourage tourist and holiday development and some of the older people who often retire to centres of this kind. The general approach to the establishment of rural regional centres is supported by the settlement hierarchy studies from Christaller onwards.

In physical terms, the growth of rural centres will depend for its progress on the right kind of plan, which need not be elaborate, and on implementation that manages to avoid the ill effects of local authority rivalries.

Enlargement of the framework of larger urban regions and choice of growth centres in or near them are problems of an entirely different order of magnitude: equally great, though different, for 'unresilient' and 'overdeveloped' regions.

The key factor, already stated, is that the growth of motor traffic is markedly reducing the overall advantages of big cities for living and working. The best position now for the go-ahead family and firm is a position near but not in a big city — where the twofold advantages of regional concentration and local spaciousness may be enjoyed. The physical solution, diagrammatically, is to bring into existence a grid of communications (mainly roads) which will link new and old settlements in the region in mutual support and spread the traffic load. This grid or network pattern has developed on a large scale, largely unplanned, in the United States, and exists in Europe in more rudimentary forms.

It is clear that if it were possible to plan and guide the development of such a new pattern of communications and settlements, the advantages would be very great. In broad terms this is what European governments would like to do, but the process is slow and fumbling, mainly from doubts as to the extent of guidance that will prove practicable — politically, financially and administratively.

The present position in Britain is probably as complex as any in Europe. The biggest urban regions contain about half the country's population, a high proportion of economic activities and very costly traffic networks, mostly radial. Two of these (London and Birmingham) are overloaded, and threaten severe congestion and general deterioration of environment. The most obvious solution is to try to spread future growth and development more equally between 8 or 10 existing urbanized regions. Indeed, this may be called the only solution, since mass migration would create impossible conditions both at the receiving and exporting ends. It is the solution adopted — again in very broad terms — by the Government.

A decision to implement it more forcefully would cause acute controversy over two major questions that have long been obvious.

To what extent will it prove practicable to repress further development in the South East and West Midlands and divert new enterprises elsewhere? Judged by Government action so far the answer seems to be: not very much. It has been held, rightly, that there must be some relief of intolerable pressure on urban space in the South East and West Midlands. The easiest way to relieve pressure on London is to make more use of medium-sized towns within 60 to 100 miles, which could take a large increase of population without serious deterioration in their present traffic and living conditions. This is being done, but apart from the movement of some Government departments (to Worthing, Basingstoke, Southend, Hastings, etc.) it is doubtful how much relief of pressure in London will be achieved by these means. It is probable that London and its peripheral towns will both continue to grow and to continue to attract population from elsewhere. The suggestion of growth areas in an arc 30 miles to the west and north of Birmingham may have similar results. These may either attract enterprises from Birmingham (and thus contribute to relief of pressure in Birmingham but do nothing for less favoured regions), or new enterprises from other parts of the country which are anxious to gain a foothold near Birmingham. The effect of 'relief of pressure' decisions near London and Birmingham on potential areas of counter-attraction should receive study and may demand some hard decisions, as does the extra aid for development in these other regions that would be economically practicable.

The second major problem concerns the scale of the new regional framework of communications and settlements that is needed to spread the traffic load, and to provide a large part of 1½ million acres of extra urban land likely to be needed during the next 40 years. These frameworks should be no larger than will provide for easy movement and good living and working conditions for an expanded population, for they will be very costly. The danger is that a wealthy region with easy topographical conditions will treat itself to a super-grid that will add to its attractive power. A super-grid of this type — approximately 100 miles square — is already emerging in the South East, fortified by expansion proposals from Southampton round to Ipswich, and even Peterborough, and may fill in rapidly. Its attractive power is likely to become very great.

In the North of England and in Scotland a grid on the same — or at least a large — scale may be suggested by difficult topography, derelict land and unattractive living conditions in major cities, but the difficulties of creating it and the diffused prosperity needed to justify it, would seem enormous. It would appear preferable in the North to concentrate aid on a few chosen areas, and to hope for an outward spread of prosperity concentrically. The Northern grids, to begin with, should therefore be no larger than is likely to be needed for 20 years ahead, though they might well be open-ended. The 15 mile radius from Liverpool, suggested by proposals for Skelmersdale, Runcorn and Warrington, appears about right for Merseyside. It promises mutual support rather than rivalry between old cities and new settlements: and mutual support of towns and enterprises on the basis of an expanded but not too large grid would seem the best recipe for renovation and development of unresilient urban regions. The scale of the desirable framework for expanded urban regions would therefore be a rewarding field for study.

It is possible to suggest some certain conclusions concerning the future development of the urban regions of Europe. These conclusions are very general and mainly concern physical arrangement.

1 Each country will try to spread growth over a number of urban regions and to slow down the rate of growth in present dominant regions.

2 It will be essential to provide for a considerable expansion at low density to take place in urban regions in order to relieve the pressure on space in large cities. A redevelopment plan for a large city that is not integrated with a plan for the surrounding region is likely to be of little practical value and may prove harmful by advocating solutions that can never be fulfilled.

3 The need for a great increase in urban space will require an enlarged framework of communications, of a grid type rather than radial. The framework would encourage 'loosening up' by bringing into existence new places for residence and work, which would be linked with one another as well as with older cities and towns.

4 The size of the enlarged framework chosen for a particular region will be of great importance. The balance of arguments suggest that it should be as small as is consistent with easy movement by road and reasonably quiet living and working conditions. This would be more economical and encourage cross-linkages which make an important contribution to growth. Provision could be made for later expansion of the framework. All countries favour concentration of aid upon relatively few urban regions.

5 New administrative machinery will be needed to choose the urban regions of growth, prepare the framework and guide their fabrication. The investments required will be so costly that their location, relationship and timing will require guidance for the whole urban region. In general, the new machinery will be concerned with the translation of economic plans for the region into physical plans for particular projects at particular places.

Notes

1 European Free Trade Association. *Regional Development Policies in Efta.* Geneva, 1965.

2 Political and Economic Planning. *Regional Development in the European Economic Community.* Prepared by B.C. Robertson, Published by P.E.P. and Allen and Unwin, London, 1962.

3 *Au Foras Forbartha Teoranta. Regional Planning Conference Dublin 1965.* J.V. Curtin: Regional Problems and Possibilities in Ireland. Pierre Viot: Economic Planning and Physical Planning in France. U.N. Economic Commission for Europe: Regional Physical Planning and its relation to Economic Planning.

4 Republic of Ireland. *Second Programme for Economic Expansion.* Stationery Office, Dublin. Pr. 7239, 1963 and 7670, 1964.

5 Scottish Development Department, *Central Scotland: a programme for development and growth.* Cmd. 2188, H.M.S.O. Edinburgh, 1963.

6 Secretary of State for Industry, Trade and Regional Development. *The North East. A programme for regional development and growth.* Cmnd. 2206 H.M.S.O. London, 1963.

7 Ministry of Housing and Local Government. *The South East Study, 1961-1981.* H.M.S.O. London 1964.

8 Department of Economic Affairs. *The North West a regional study.* H.M.S.O. London 1965.

9 Department of Economic Affairs. *The West Midlands a regional study.* H.M.S.O. London 1965.

10 Minister of Housing and Local Government and Minister of Welsh Affairs. *De-Population in Mid-Wales.* H.M.S.O. London 1964.

11 International Conference of the International Federation for Housing and Planning. *Growing space needs in the urbanized region,* Orebro, Sweden, 1965.

12 Robert Grieve. *Regional Planning.* Town Planning Inst. Journal. June 1965.

13 Myles Wright. *The Dublin Region: Preliminary Report.* Stationery Office, Dublin, 1965.

Reprinted from *Town Planning Review*, vol. 36 (3), 1965, Liverpool University Press, Liverpool, with permission.

26 The Movement of Manufacturing Industry

by A. Beacham and W. T. Osborn

University of Liverpool

In September 1968 the Board of Trade published a report by R.S. Howard on the Movement of Manufacturing Industry in the United Kingdom 1945-65.[1] It analyses the movement taking place between fifty designated areas (or from abroad to one of the fifty areas) in terms of the number of establishments moving (and still in operation in 1966) and in terms of the employment they were giving *ca.* November 1966.

The purpose of this note is to review and interpret the findings with particular reference to the effectiveness of Government policies designed to promote movement from the congested areas of the South-East and West Midlands to the Development Areas.[2] But it is not easy to disentangle such policies from others affecting location of industry. It was also Government policy to relieve congestion by the establishment of new towns in the vicinity of congested areas and this needs to be borne in mind when considering any implied criticism of the effectiveness of development area incentives. It was nevertheless an overriding objective of Government to 'direct' industrial establishments by Industrial Development Certificate control, or to bribe them by various subsidies, to move into the Development Areas which had surplus labour resources.

There were 3014 'moves' (defined later) employing (in 1966) 870,000 persons between 1945 and 1965, i.e. rather more than 5 per cent of all establishments employing more than ten persons were moved and just under 10 per cent of all persons employed in manufacturing were employed in these moves. The moves were also analysed in terms of movement between economic planning regions which in effect eliminated those moves between designated areas which were within the same region (intra-regional). The inter-regional moves were 1779 with an employment total of 574,600.

A move is defined as the opening in a new location of a new manufacturing establishment (employing more than ten persons at some time during the period) which in some sense could be said to have originated in another area. A firm (or enterprise, depending on which was reckoned to take decisions in location matters) made a move if it opened an establishment in another area where it had not previously operated an establishment in the same industry, i.e. minimum list heading (M.L.H.)[3] Moves included the transfer of an establishment which was closed in another area or establishment of a branch where an additional establishment was opened. The origin of a transfer was clearly the area where the establishment closed. The origin of a branch was the area where the manufacturing headquarters of the firm was located or, if this was in doubt, the area in which the firm's largest manufacturing unit was located.[4] The origin of a branch move was not necessarily in the same area as the board room where the decision was taken.

It is usual to show changes in the regional location of manufacturing industry by changes in the employed population in different areas. The Howard Report charts only one influence on this, i.e. 'moves' as defined above.[5] It excludes growth in the size of establishments already in the area prior to 1945, employment in new establishments set up by firms whose manufacturing headquarters are in the area, employment in new establishments set up by firms mainly located outside the area which had similar establishments in the area prior to 1945, employment in new establishments set up by firms whose manufacturing headquarters are in the area, employment in new establishments set up by firms mainly located outside the area which had similar establishments in the area prior to 1945, and employment by entirely new firms setting up in the region. All of these might have been affected by incentives and in some cases might represent decisions by firms with establishments in development areas and non-development areas to concentrate more of their production in the former. To this extent any conclusion reached on the effect of incentives and direct controls on moves is not a valid conclusion on the influence of incentives on directing a higher proportion of total industrial employment towards development areas. Moreover, it has to be remembered that incentives may have affected the total volume of industrial employment by making possible projects which otherwise would not have been undertaken.

Nevertheless, it was an important part of the justification for development area incentives that it would provide new jobs in these places by encouraging moves (in the Howard Report sense) from congested areas to the peripheral areas. So it is not without interest to try to discover to what extent they have succeeded in doing this.

We have no means of knowing what would have happened in the absence of incentives. Urban renewal would have caused some displacement of firms from big towns in development areas and elsewhere. It is not likely, however, in view of the availability of labour and premises that much industry displaced from large towns in the Development Areas would have been lost to these regions. At the same time some of the displacements and new growth in congested areas would have been attracted by these advantages of the Development Areas though no doubt most firms would prefer to move as short a distance as possible. In other words there might have been some bias towards Development Areas in the absence of incentives and I.D.C. controls.

The evidence in favour of the proposition that these incentives and controls had a pronounced effect in promoting moves to development areas is quite impressive.[6] If we define as net movement the employment generated by moves into regions minus the employment 'lost' by outward movement we have the following picture.

Table 26.1

Region	Net inter-regional movement (1945-1965) as % of employees in manufacturing (mid-1966) in the region
Northern Ireland*	21.3
Scotland*	12.1
Wales*	26.1
Northern*	18.5
North-West†	5.6
South-West†	6.4
Yorkshire & Humberside	- 1.3
East Midlands	- 0.7
West Midlands‡	- 6.7
East Anglia	3.2
South-East‡	- 7.3

Derived from Table 1, Howard Report, p. 9.

* Regions approximately coterminous with Development Areas in 1966.

† Regions partially scheduled as Development Areas in 1966.

‡ 'Congested' areas.

Of inter-regional moves, the South-East and West Midlands contributed most of the outward movement and the Development Areas were the main recipients. The South-East and West Midlands by outward moves to other regions contributed over 300,000 'jobs' out of a total of 575,000 involved in all inter-regional moves. In other words the congested areas contributed 53 per cent of all outward inter-regional moves. But is this so surprising since these areas also had 43 per cent of the total employees in manufacturing industry and were generally suffering from acute labour shortages?

Also we need to remember that we are considering only inter-regional moves. Out of 870,000 persons involved in moves between the fifty designated areas 295,000 moved within a region, i.e. about one-third of all moves in terms of employment were short distance moves, i.e. were intra-regional.[7] For the Greater London area, where congestion might seem likely to restrict short distance movement, as much as 60 per cent of the 329,000 employees in outward moves went to other parts of the South-East and East Anglia.

So whilst it is true to say that movement of manufacturing industry gave the Development Areas a valuable shot in the arm there is another side to the medal. In fact, according to the Howard Report, peripheral areas (roughly equivalent to Development Areas) attracted only 35 per cent of the employment 'exported' by the Greater London area and 51 per cent of that exported by the West Midlands conurbation.

So we are left wondering a little about how effective incentives and I.D.C. control actually was. Some light may be thrown on this by comparing the actual number of moves (and employment moved) with several alternative estimates of the 'random' pattern of moves which might have been expected in the absence of any policy providing incentives to move.

Data concerning the total number of establishments (and employment) in the various regions would provide evidence of those regions from which large (or small) numbers of *originating* moves might be expected – or perhaps evidence of the attractiveness of large concentrations of industry as destinations. But data from the Census of Production for 1954 (the latest available in the required detail and close to the mid-point of the Howard period) are only available on the old regional definitions, and so the number of regions must be reduced in order to provide reasonable consistency of area definitions in the following way:

Region No.	Old Title	New Title
1	London & South-East, Eastern and Southern	South-East and East Anglia
2	South-Western	South-Western
3	Midland	West Midland
4	North Midland, East & West Ridings	Yorkshire & Humberside, East Midland
5	North-Western	North-Western
6	Northern	Northern
7	Scotland	Scotland
8	Wales	Wales
9	Northern Ireland	Northern Ireland

This reduces the number of origins and destinations of movement, by comparison with Appendix B of the Howard Report but makes possible their comparison with census data. It is, however, also necessary to omit from Appendix B those moves that are styled 'G.B. unallocated' and moves from 'abroad', as there can be no evidence about the total numbers of establishments (or volume of employment) in these categories. This reduces the total number of establishments that moved between 'regions' to 1310, and the employment involved to 431 thousand; i.e. to 2.3 per cent of all establishments, and 5.8 per cent of all employment in 1954.

Table 26.2 shows (a) the Census of Production data of total numbers of establishments (in manufacturing industry and employing more than ten persons) for 1954, classified by regions: (b) the expected number, if 2.3 per cent of all establishments had moved from each region (except Northern Ireland[8]); (c) the actual number of moves originating in these regions: and (d) the ratio between actual and expected numbers.

Table 26.3 shows the same regional classification of census data and moves, but relating to the volume of employment involved, the actual moves here comprising 5.8 per cent of the total employment. In both cases, the actual pattern is very significantly different from the assumption that the origin of moves is dependent on total numbers (or employment) in the regions in 1954. The value of χ^2 is twenty-times the value of the 5 per cent point for Table 26.1 and twelve-times the 5 per cent point for Table 26.3. Clearly the chief differences which affect χ^2 are the much larger number of moves (and employment) originating in Region 1 (South-East) than is expected, and the much smaller number (and employment) originating in Region 7 (Scotland). Employment moving from Region 5 (North-Western) is also less than the number of employees there would imply.

Tables 26.2 and 26.3 thus clearly imply that movement originating in a region cannot be adequately explained by the relative size of the region in terms of either number of establishments or volume of employment. This leaves open the possibility that such originating moves may be governed by the Government incentives offered, or the controls imposed to prevent congestion. But it also leaves open the possibility of a host of other factors that determine the decision to 'move' from one region to another, e.g. relative rates of growth.

Turning to the other side, it is perhaps more difficult to postulate any convincing hypothesis about the factors that determine the pattern of regional *destinations* for those moves, in the absence of incentives. To assume that the attraction of different regions depends on their size would seem unreasonable in view of what has been said already, and a χ^2 test confirms this, the result being very highly significant. The possibility that regional destination might be associated inversely with size also gives an exceedingly high χ^2-value, and in any case it would not seem reasonable to suppose that firms would be more attracted to smaller areas.

Two alternative hypotheses were tested. In both cases, the *actual* moves originating from each regions are spread over all *other* regions, and then compared with the actual pattern of moves. In the first case it was assumed that destinations were proportional to the average rate of unemployment in each region over the 20 years 1946-1965. The pattern of actual moves is still very significantly different from that given by this hypothesis, but the most striking discrepancies (in terms of their contribution to the value of χ^1) are the moves from Region 1 to Region 9 which is much less, and from 4 to 6 which is much larger than the unemployment picture would suggest. (This applies both to numbers of moves as well as volume of employment.) Regions 1 to 2

Table 26.2 Originating establishment moves compared with total numbers

Region	(a) Number of manufacturing establishments with more than 10 employees, 1954.	(b) Number of moves expected (2.3 per cent of number of establishments)	(c) Actual number of moves originating	(c) as percentage of (b)
1	18,035	422	645	153
2	2,384	56	38	68
3	6,712	157	215	137
4	11,105	260	200	77
5	8,930	209	151	72
6	2,129	50	17	34
7	5,100	119	28	24
8	1,574	37	16	43
G.B.	55,969	1,310	1,310	100
9	1,241	—	—	—
U.K.	57,210			

Table 26.3 Volume of employment, in establishments of Table 26.1

Region	(a) 1954 Employment	(b) Expected employment moves (5.8 per cent of Col. 1) (thousands)	(c) Employment given by actual moves originating (thousands)	(c) as percentage of (b)
1	2,114,640	122.3	218.5	179
2	299,581	17.3	11.0	64
3	1,026,091	59.3	92.6	156
4	1,335,155	77.2	62.0	80
5	1,314,760	76.0	28.2	37
6	391,279	22.6	5.2	23
7	706,611	40.9	4.9	12
8	264,185	15.3	8.5	56
G.B.	7,452,302	431.0	431.0	100
9	179,067	—	—	—
U.K.	7,631,369			

also make a large contribution (the actual flow being larger than expected) and for 3 to 9 the flow is less than expected for numbers of establishments. In terms of employment, moves from 1 to 5 and from 3 to 5 are higher than expected.

In the second case the rather unlikely hypothesis that random flows would be governed inversely by the distance between regions was tested. For this, the distances were measured for a key town in each region and the actual number of moves from each region was allocated to destinations in inverse proportion to the distances between the key towns. The actual pattern of destinations was still significantly different from the pattern expected on this hypothesis. Here the extreme discrepancies were in the flows from Regions 1 to 3 (the actual flow being low compared with the expected flow) and 1 to 8 (high), and from Regions 4 to 6 (high) – all of these applying both to establishments and employment. In addition, for establishments, the flow from 1 to 6 (high) and to 7 (high) was markedly at odds with the hypothesis. None of these comparisons provides a hypothesis that adequately explains the actual pattern of interregional moves and the possibility must therefore be left open that the controls and incentives operated by the Government may have been a major influence on the movements which actually took place.

One way of testing this more fully is to relate the moves over time to changes in incentives affected and to changes in the demand for labour. The demand for labour can be measured by differences between vacancies notified and registered unemployment. Variation in inducements is almost impossible to measure. They are not fully measured in terms of cash expenditures and in any case we only have such figures for recent years. For much of the period the actual content of the 'bribe' was separately negotiated with firms proposing to move. Moreover, there seems to be general agreement that the amount of incentives has not been very influential in producing a decision to move though this may have changed in recent years when these inducements have been considerably stepped up. Cameron and Clark (1966), for example, state that 81 per cent of the employment provided by moves in their sample was in respect of firms who wished to develop in, or near, their existing locations after evaluation of the relative advantages and disadvantages of moving to other areas. The general picture was that refusal of an I.D.C. made a long-distance move inevitable. This sparked off negotiations with the Board of Trade with a view to obtaining the best cash, or cash equivalent, inducement they could get. The authors conclude that without Government I.D.C. policy, movement would have been exceptionally limited (Cameron and Clark, 1966, p. 80). This turns us back to a consideration of I.D.C's as the main Government 'inducement' to move. Figures for refusal of I.D.C.'s are available only since 1960 (Board of Trade Journal, 1968) and probably tell us very little about the toughness of I.D.C. policy since many applications were not proceeded with after an approach to the Board of Trade indicated that a Certificate would be refused. The best available indication of changes in I.D.C. policy over the period is probably the I.D.C. approvals for the South-East Region as a percentage of approvals for Great Britain.[9]

The only data on moves over time is contained in Appendix A of the Howard Report. This sets out, year by year, the number of moves (and employment involved) for the United Kingdom as a whole and for moves into (a) the South-East and East Anglia regions and (b) the peripheral areas. These data are plotted in Figures 26.1 and 26.2 which show quite clearly the different characteristics of moves in the periods 1945-1951, 1952-1959 and 1960-1965. In particular it shows the marked upsurge of moves into the South-East and East Anglia (and decline in moves into the peripheral areas) during the middle period when Government incentives to move into peripheral areas were reduced and I.D.C.'s were fairly easily obtainable even for new development in the South-East and Midlands (McCrone, 1969). This tends to confirm evidence that Government policies have been effective in controlling the direction of moves.

The data in Appendix A is subject to two important limitations which are carefully stated in the Howard Report (p. 12). First, the number of moves which actually took place in the early part of the period is probably understated since it is likely that many such moves did not survive until 1966. Secondly, employment in more recent moves has probably been understated because such moves have not had sufficient time to work up to their full potential.

In spite of all the limitations inherent in the data a number of regression equations were calculated using moves to peripheral areas (by number and employment) as the dependent variable (X^1 by number of moves X_4 by employment). The likely explanatory (independent) variables were:

1 Movement to the South-East and East Anglia region as a complementary variable inversely related to movement into the peripheral areas (X_2 by number of moves, X_5 by employment).

2 The issue of I.D.C.'s in the South-East Region as a percentage of Great Britain approvals (X_3).

3 The demand for labour measured by the difference between vacancies notified and registered unemployment for the South-East Region (X_6) and for Great Britain as a whole (X_7).[10]

Of a dozen equations seeking to explain number of moves, or employment involved in moves into peripheral areas only three showed R^2 values above 0.3. These were as follows:

1 $X_1 = 152.3 - 4.067X_3 + 0.121X_6$ $R^2 = 0.684$
           (0.794)   (0.090)   (1949-65)

2 $X_1 = 179.3 - 5.021X_3 + 0.028X_7$ $R^2 = 0.887$
           (0.023)   (0.023)   (1954-65)

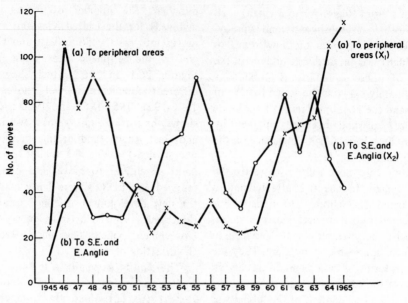

Figure 26.1 Number of moves

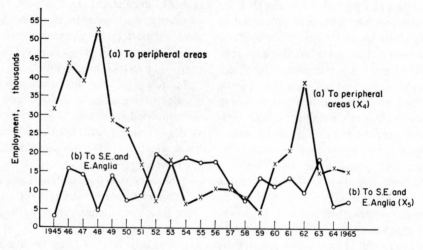

Figure 26.2 Employment in moves

$$3 \quad X_1 = 43.5 + 0.847X_6 - 0.251X_7 \quad R^2 = 0.511$$
$$(0.264) \quad (0.086) \quad (1954\text{-}65)$$

The association of movement into the peripheral areas with a measure of the relative ease with which I.D.C.'s were granted in the South-East is not particularly surprising or interesting, since it is to some extent 'built in'. The correlation of movement into the peripheral areas with the pressure of demand is perhaps of greater interest but is less statistically significant.

Figure 26.3 shows swings in the demand for labour in the South-East and West Midlands following closely in step with the demand for the country as a whole after 1954. These are plotted against I.D.C. approvals for the South-East and West Midlands as a proportion of approvals for Great Britain. Broadly speaking, as the excess demand for labour fell after 1957 the proportion of approvals for the South-East and Midlands has dropped and, of course, movement into the peripheral areas has increased.

The general conclusions would appear to be:

1 The effect of Government policies in promoting industrial movement to peripheral areas has been limited. A surprising number of firms appear to have coped

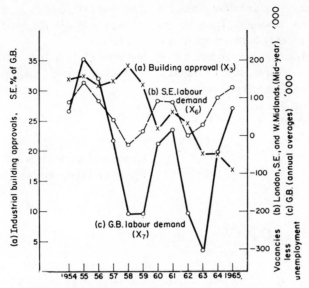

Figure 26.3 Demand for labour and building approvals

with their expansion and displacement problems without making long distance moves from low unemployment to high unemployment regions.

2 Where inter-regional movement has taken place it does appear to have been significantly affected by Government policy to channel it towards the peripheral areas. Inter-regional movement has not been random and neither the distance involved nor relative long-term rates of unemployment appear to have been factors influencing the direction of movement between individual regions.

3 An important part of the justification for regional policies has been the argument that they permit the operation of the economy at higher levels of aggregate demand with less inflationary pressure. As the excess demand for labour rose one would, therefore, expect more active Government policies to divert industry towards the peripheral areas, though policies are likely to lag behind events.

There is no very clear evidence that this has motivated Government policy. During the 1950s and particularly up to 1958 unemployment rates were low but movement into the peripheral areas slackened. No doubt the Government were responding to the lower unemployment rates in the peripheral areas rather than the increased labour shortages in the South-East and West Midlands. On the other hand, over the period as a whole some part of movement to the peripheral areas seems to be explained by increased pressure of demand for labour in the South-East.

Notes

1 H.M.S.O. 1968. Referred to in this paper as the Howard Report.

2 Those areas as defined in 1968 are roughly equivalent to the peripheral areas of the Howard Report.

3 If a firm had opened an establishment since 1945 which had already qualified as a move and then opened another of like kind in the same area the latter did not qualify as a move but its employment was added to that of the move.

4 It follows that when we talk of moves originating in an area it does not follow that the area has been deprived of anything. The origin of a completely new establishment is rather hypothetical. There might never have been any question of its location at headquarters.

5 Assuming that the Board of Trade succeeded in tracking down all moves. The Report comments that it is not always easy to trace new establishments setting up in existing premises.

6 It is very frequently claimed that firms are not influenced in their location decisions by Government inducements. The Board of Trade are now making a systematic study of the motivation of industrial movement.

7 About 40 per cent of all moves (in numbers of establishments) were intra-regional.

8 No case was recorded of a move originating in Northern Ireland.

9 In calculating these figures certain adjustments have

had to be made for changes in definition, regional boundaries and industrial coverage. There is no evidence of a systematic time lag between approvals, starts, and completions. Approvals for the South-East Region were taken because of limitation of the data in Appendix A of the Howard Report (see below).

10 Mid-year figures used in the absence of annual averages for vacancies by region.

References

Board of Trade Journal, 23 August 1968, p. 551.

Cameron G.C. and Clark B.D. (1966) *Industrial Movement and the Regional Problem*, Oliver and Boyd, London.

McCrone G. (1969) *Regional Policy in Britain*, p. 115, Allen & Unwin, London.

Reprinted from *Regional Studies*, Vol. 4(3), 1970, Pergamon Press, Oxford, with permission.

27 The Movement of Manufacturing Industry– Comments

by D. E. Keeble
University of Cambridge

In their interesting analysis of the Howard Report's data (Howard, 1968) on postwar industrial movement in the United Kingdom, A. Beacham and W.T. Osborn raise the important question of the explanation for spatial variations in volume of inter-regional industrial migration, whether measured by numbers of firms or employment created. Having discussed possible reasons for variations recorded by the Report in volume of out-migration from 'origin' regions, the authors suggest that 'it is perhaps more difficult to postulate any convincing hypothesis about the factors that determine the pattern of regional *destinations* for those moves, in the absence of incentives': and they in fact test only two such hypotheses, one of which relates variations in movement to the pattern of average regional unemployment rates in destination regions, while the other postulates that migration to a given region declines linearly with distance from a given origin region. On the basis of the χ^2 test, the authors conclude that 'none of these comparisons provides a hypothesis that adequately explains the actual pattern of inter-regional moves'.

The authors' statements, analysis and findings noted above demand comment for several reasons. One is because the initial quotation appears to betray lack of acquaintance with the considerable existing volume of industrial migration literature based on detailed firm-by-firm surveys. The findings of these 'micro-level' studies, such as those by Loasby (1961, 1967), Cameron and Clark (1966) and the present author (Keeble 1965, 1968) provide an obvious source of hypotheses for an analysis at a more aggregate level. Unlike Beacham and Osborn's analysis, which provides no logical reason for selecting the two hypotheses listed above, recent quite independent work by the present author on the same sort of problem has been deliberately designed to test at the 'macro-level' logical hypotheses derived directly from these detailed 'micro-level' studies.

However, much more important comments concern Beacham and Osborn's analysis and findings: for the present author's own work indicates that although focussing, presumably intuitively, on valid explanatory variables, the authors' analytic design contains two major flaws, which are probably largely responsible for the inconclusive results achieved. The first is the measurement of unemployment in terms of its percentage *rate*, rather than absolute volume. Clearly, firms considering inter-regional movement and seeking assurance of available labour supplies, will be influenced far more by the actual numbers of unemployed workers available in particular areas than by mere percentage rates, which in the case of areas with both large and small work forces can be a very misleading guide to labour availability (Davies, 1967). The second is the failure to realize that, if operative, the two explanatory variables of labour availability and distance decay must be considered simultaneously, not separately, if their influence upon the pattern of industrial movement is to be adequately tested. The latter point is of course the fundamental basis for all gravity model analysis, which has been extensively, and on the whole successfully, used in recent years by geographers, regional scientists and planners in studying many different types of spatial interaction.

Brief discussion of the present author's own analysis and findings, to be published in full elsewhere (Keeble, forthcoming), may help to clarify these points. In aim, this analysis differs from that of Beacham and Osborn only in seeking to explain variations in migration to the six peripheral regions distinguished in the Howard Report (N. Ireland, Scotland, Wales, Northern, Merseyside, and Devon and Cornwall), rather than to all regions; while it is also more selective in examining only migration flows from the South-East region and the West Midlands Conurbation. Selection of these two areas firms from which have provided no less than 205,000 jobs, or 57 per cent of all peripheral area 'migrant' employment (excluding that provided by foreign firms setting up for the first time in this country), is justified by their dominance as origins in movement to the periphery. Further detail was provided by carrying out separate analyses for the G.L.C. area in particular, as well as for the South-East region (including the G.L.C. area) in general.

Examination of the 'micro-level' survey literature

focused attention on four main location factors, which are singled out in various studies as important determinants of peripheral migration. These are government influence and inducements, labour availability, distance from the firm's original location, and access to regional (and to some extent national) markets (see, for example, Keeble, 1968, pp. 30-35; Cameron and Clark, 1966, pp. 162-66). Since government influence may be regarded as indiscriminating spatially between the peripheral areas selected, all of which are Development Areas and have benefited from government action for a reasonable period of time, this factor was excluded from the analysis. Consideration of the remaining factors immediately suggested the use of some sort of gravity model formulation, such as

$$M_{ij} = \frac{A_j}{d_{ij}^b}$$

where M_{ij} is the volume of industrial movement (in this case measured by employment created) between origin area i and peripheral area j, A_j is a measure of the attractiveness to mobile industry of area j, and d_{ij} is the distance between the two areas, raised to some exponent b. Since movement from each origin area (e.g. the West Midlands Conurbation) was analysed separately with the aim simply of predicting differences in movement to different destination regions, it was unnecessary to include a mass value for the origin area, of the kind common in simple gravity models.

Given that micro-level studies have invariably stressed the dominant influence of labour availability in peripheral migration, it was decided to test two alternative simple gravity models constructed around this factor. The first (A_1/d) measured attractiveness solely in terms of the total unemployed labour force in the destination region. For simplicity, this was defined as the size of this labour force in a single year (1954) roughly midway during the Howard Report's study period (1945-65). The second (A_2/d) measured attractiveness by the total unemployed labour force in 1954 weighted by the region's average 'economic potential' index. The latter index, values for which were taken from Clark's study (1966), provides an interesting measure of an area's relative proximity to regional and national markets. Because of the small size of the sample investigated (six areas), parametric correlation techniques could not be used. Comparison of the predicted gravity model indexes and actual migrant employment for the set of six peripheral regions was therefore carried out by less powerful but statistically more valid rank correlation

methods (Spearman's r_S).

The results clearly indicate the importance of using a gravity model formulation which measures labour availability in absolute, rather than percentage, terms, and which handles simultaneously the positive influence of labour availability and the negative influence of distance decay. As in Beacham and Osborn's study, initial separate correlation of unemployment totals and distance with actual migration employment totals for the six peripheral areas yielded totally insignificant correlation coefficients. However, simultaneous evaluation (A_1/d), in a gravity model whose distance exponent was varied to determine the best possible fit with the observed data, produced surprisingly good results. For movement from the South-East as a whole, rank correlation coefficients of 0.943 and 1.000 (both significant at the 0.01 level) were achieved with distance exponents of 2 and 2.5 (see Fig. 27.1). For migration from the West Midlands Conurbation, a distance exponent of 1.5 (see Fig. 27.2) yielded an r_S value of 0.929 (significant at the 0.05 level). Only with movement from Greater London did r_S values fail to achieve an 0.05 significance level, although an r_S value of 0.814 was calculated ($b = 2.5$). Not surprisingly, given the success of the initial model, the (A_2/d) model failed to achieve higher maximum correlation coefficients: but weighting by accessibility to markets did nonetheless yield r_S values higher than or equal to the (A_1/d) model for a given

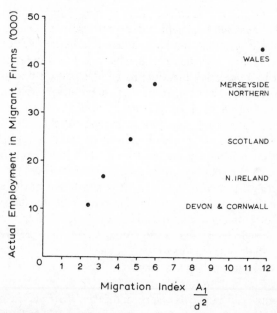

Figure 27.1 Manufacturing movement from South-East England: gravity model predictions and actual migration

regions, while relative proximity to regional and national markets appears also to have exerted some influence upon the migration pattern.

References

Cameron G.C. and Clarke B.D. (1966) *Industrial Movement and the Regional Problem*, Oliver & Boyd, Edinburgh.

Clark C. (1966) Industrial location and economic potential, *Lloyds Bank Rev.* 82, 1-17.

Davies G. (1967) Regional unemployment, labour availability and redeployment, *Oxf. Econ. Papers,* **19**, 59-74.

Keeble D.E. (1965) Industrial migration from North-West London, 1940-1964, *Urban Studies* 2, 15-32.

Keeble, D.E. (1968) Industrial decentralization and the metropolis: The North-West London case, *Trans. Inst. Brit. Geogr.* **44**, 1-54.

Keeble D.E. Employment mobility in Britain, Ch. III in *Spatial Policy Problems of the British Economy* (Edited by M. Chisholm and G. Manners), 1973 Cambridge University Press, Cambridge.

Loasby B. (1961) The experience of West Midlands industrial dispersal projects, *Tn Ctry Plann.* **29**, 309-313.

Loasby B.J. (1967) Making location policy work, *Lloyds Bank Rev.* **83**, 34-47.

Reprinted from *Regional Studies*, vol. 4 (3), 1970, Pergamon Press, Oxford, with permission.

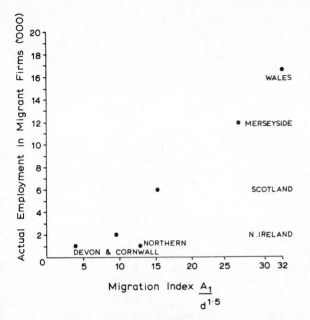

Figure 27.2 Manufacturing movement from the West Midlands Conurbation: gravity model predictions and actual migration

distance exponent in nine out of eleven applications. These results therefore strongly support at an aggregate level the findings of micro-level migration studies noted above. Contrary to the conclusions of the Beacham and Osborn study, spatial variations in migration to the peripheral regions can be largely explained by variations in labour availability and distance from major origin

Index